Research Anthology on Strategies for Using Social Media as a Service and Tool in Business

Information Resources Management Association
USA

Volume IV

IGI Global
PUBLISHER of TIMELY KNOWLEDGE

Published in the United States of America by
IGI Global
Business Science Reference (an imprint of IGI Global)
701 E. Chocolate Avenue
Hershey PA, USA 17033
Tel: 717-533-8845
Fax: 717-533-8661
E-mail: cust@igi-global.com
Web site: http://www.igi-global.com

Library of Congress Cataloging-in-Publication Data

Names: Information Resources Management Association, editor.
Title: Research anthology on strategies for using social media as a service
    and tool in business / Information Resources Management Association,
    editor.
Description: Hershey, PA : Business Science Reference, [2021] | Includes
    bibliographical references and index. | Summary: "This book of
    contributed chapters provides updated information on how businesses are
    strategically using social media and explores the role of social media
    in keeping businesses competitive in the global economy by discussing
    how social tools work, what services businesses are utilizing, both the
    benefits and challenges to how social media is changing the modern
    business atmosphere,"-- Provided by publisher.
Identifiers: LCCN 2021016024 (print) | LCCN 2021016025 (ebook) | ISBN
    9781799890201 (hardcover) | ISBN 9781799890218 (ebook)
Subjects: LCSH: Social media--Economic aspects. | Marketing. | Branding
    (Marketing) | Customer relations. | Customer services--Technological
    innovations.
Classification: LCC HM742 .R4678 2021 (print) | LCC HM742 (ebook) | DDC
    302.23/1--dc23
LC record available at https://lccn.loc.gov/2021016024
LC ebook record available at https://lccn.loc.gov/2021016025

British Cataloguing in Publication Data
A Cataloguing in Publication record for this book is available from the British Library.

For electronic access to this publication, please contact: eresources@igi-global.com.

List of Contributors

Table of Contents

    Muhammad Aslam Jarwar, Department of Computer Sciences, Quaid-i-Azam University,
        Islamabad, Pakistan & Department of Information and Communications Engineering,
        Hankuk University of Foreign Studies (HUFS), Seoul, South Korea
    Rabeeh Ayaz Abbasi, Faculty of Computing and Information Technology, King Abdulaziz
        University, Jeddah, Saudi Arabia & Department of Computer Sciences, Quaid-i-Azam
        University, Islamabad, Pakistan
    Mubashar Mushtaq, Department of Computer Science, Forman Christian College (A
        Chartered University), Lahore, Pakistan & Department of Computer Sciences, Quaid-i-
        Azam University, Islamabad, Pakistan
    Onaiza Maqbool, Department of Computer Sciences, Quaid-i-Azam University, Islamabad,
        Pakistan
    Naif R. Aljohani, Faculty of Computing and Information Technology, King Abdulaziz
        University, Jeddah, Saudi Arabia
    Ali Daud, Faculty of Computing and Information Technology, King Abdulaziz University,
        Jeddah, Saudi Arabia & Department of Computer Science and Software Engineering,
        International Islamic University, Islamabad, Pakistan
    Jalal S. Alowibdi, Faculty of Computing and Information Technology, University of Jeddah,
        Jeddah, Saudi Arabia
    J.R. Cano, Department of Computer Science, University of Jaén, Jaén, Spain
    S. García, Department of Computer Science and Artificial Intelligence, University of
        Granada, Granada, Spain
    Ilyoung Chong, Department of Information and Communications Engineering, Hankuk
        University of Foreign Studies (HUFS), Seoul, South Korea

Section 3
Tools and Technologies

    Gopal Krishna, Aryabhatt Knowledge University, India

    Marcello Chedid, University of Aveiro, Portugal
    Leonor Teixeira, University of Aveiro, Portugal

    Ned Kock, Department of International Business and Technology Studies, Texas A&M
        International University, Laredo, TX, USA

Volume II

Section 4
Utilization and Applications

Volume III

Section 5
Organizational and Social Implications

Volume IV

Section 6
Managerial Impact

Section 7
Critical Issues and Challenges

Preface

Since its conception, social media has become an integral part in how society communicates. As with the development of any other important piece of communication, business and industry must adapt to utilize this tool to reach its vast audiences to survive. Moreover, social media can be applied for internal processes for organizations and should be considered by human resources managers. Through this transition, it is essential for businesses to be aware of how to best utilize these tools and services in order to best promote themselves within the social sphere. The *Research Anthology on Strategies for Using Social Media as a Service and Tool in Business* provides these strategies for businesses to grow under this new era of communication.

Staying informed of the most up-to-date research trends and findings is of the utmost importance. That is why IGI Global is pleased to offer this four-volume reference collection of reprinted IGI Global book chapters and journal articles that have been handpicked by senior editorial staff. This collection will shed light on critical issues related to the trends, techniques, and uses of various applications by providing both broad and detailed perspectives on cutting-edge theories and developments. This collection is designed to act as a single reference source on conceptual, methodological, technical, and managerial issues, as well as to provide insight into emerging trends and future opportunities within the field.

The *Research Anthology on Strategies for Using Social Media as a Service and Tool in Business* is organized into seven distinct sections that provide comprehensive coverage of important topics. The sections are:

1. Fundamental Concepts and Theories;
2. Development and Design Methodologies;
3. Tools and Technologies;
4. Utilization and Applications;
5. Organizational and Social Implications;
6. Managerial Impact; and
7. Critical Issues and Challenges.

The following paragraphs provide a summary of what to expect from this invaluable reference tool.

Section 1, "Fundamental Concepts and Theories," serves as a foundation for this extensive reference tool by addressing crucial theories essential to understanding the concepts of social media in multidisciplinary settings. Opening this reference book is the chapter "The Role of Social Media in Public Involvement: Pushing for Sustainability in International Planning and Development" by Prof. Tooran Alizadeh of University of Sydney, Australia and Profs. Reza Farid and Laura Willems of Griffith

University, Australia. This chapter explores social media's potential to enhance public involvement to pursue sustainable practices on an international scale across planning and development projects. This first section ends with the chapter "Social Media and Social Identity in the Millennial Generation" by Prof. Guida Helal of American University of Beirut, Lebanon and Prof. Wilson Ozuem of University of Cumbria, UK, which focuses on theoretical implications and managerial implications. The concluding section offers some significant roles that social media and social identity may play in keeping up with the design and development of marketing communications programs.

Section 2, "Development and Design Methodologies," presents in-depth coverage of the design and development of social media strategy for its use in different applications. This section starts with the chapter "An Absorptive Capacity Perspective of Organizational Learning Through Social Media: Evidence From the Ghanaian Fashion Industry" by Profs. Richard Boateng, Edna Owusu-Bempah, and Eric Ansong from University of Ghana, Ghana, which examines the role social media has played on brand perceptions in the fashion apparel and accessories industry from a social identity theory perspective. This section ends with the chapter "CommuniMents: A Framework for Detecting Community Based Sentiments for Events" by Prof. Muhammad Aslam Jarwar of Quaid-i-Azam University, Pakistan & Hankuk University of Foreign Studies (HUFS), South Korea; Prof. Rabeeh Ayaz Abbasi of King Abdulaziz University, Saudi Arabia & Quaid-i-Azam University, Islamabad, Pakistan; Prof. Mubashar Mushtaq of Forman Christian College (A Chartered University), Pakistan & Quaid-i-Azam University, Pakistan; Prof. Onaiza Maqbool of Quaid-i-Azam University, Pakistan; Prof. Naif R. Aljohani of King Abdulaziz University, Saudi Arabia; Prof. Ali Daud of King Abdulaziz University, Saudi Arabia & International Islamic University, Pakistan; Prof. Jalal S. Alowibdi of University of Jeddah, Saudi Arabia; Prof. J.R. Cano of University of Jaén, Spain; Prof. S. García of University of Granada, Spain; and Prof. Ilyoung Chong of Hankuk University of Foreign Studies (HUFS), South Korea, which proposes a framework CommuniMents that enables us to identify the members of a community and measure the sentiments of the community for a particular event. CommuniMents uses automated snowball sampling to identify the members of a community, then fetches their published contents (specifically tweets), pre-processes the contents, and measures the sentiments of the community.

Section 3, "Tools and Technologies," explores the various tools and technologies used in the implementation of social media for various uses. This section begins with the chapter "Social Networking Data Analysis Tools and Services" by Prof. Gopal Krishna of Aryabhatt Knowledge University, India, which explains the methods and tools used for the analysis of the huge amount of data produced by social networks. This section ends with the chapter "Social Media as a Tool to Understand Behaviour on the Railways" by Prof. David Golightly of University of Nottingham, UK and Prof. Robert J. Houghton of Griffith University, Australia, which highlights important factors such as the broad range of issues covered by social media (not just disruption), the idiosyncrasies of individual train operators that need to be taken into account within social media analysis, and the time critical nature of information during disruption.

Section 4, "Utilization and Applications," describes how social media is used and applied in diverse industries for various technologies and applications. The opening chapter in this section, "Adoption of Web 2.0 Marketing: An Exploratory Study About the Nigerian SMEs," by Prof. Maryam Lawan Gwadabet of IT and Business School, Blue Sapphire E-Solutions ltd, Kano, Nigeria, explores the value which Web 2.0 marketing adds to the Nigerian SME's. The final chapter in this section, "An Evaluation of Toronto's Destination Image Through Tourist Generated Content on Twitter," by Profs. Hillary Clarke and Ahmed Hassanien of Edinburgh Napier University, Edinburgh, UK, evaluates the cognitive, affective, and conative components of destination image from the perception of tourists on social media.

Section 5, "Organizational and Social Implications," includes chapters discussing the impact of social media on society and shows the ways in which social media is used in different industries and how this impacts business. The first chapter, "An Empirical Evaluation of Adoption and Diffusion of New ICTs for Knowledge Sharing in IT Organizations," by Profs. Srinivasan Vaidyanathan and Sudarsanam S. Kidambi of VIT Business School, VIT University, Chennai, India, describes how knowledge is one of the most important assets in organizations which should be carefully managed and is continuously generated throughout an organization. The last chapter, "Fast-Fashion Meets Social Networking Users: Implications for International Marketing Strategy," by Prof. Tehreem Cheema of Clark University, USA, contributes to the existing literature on the influence of digital marketing on fast fashion, and it provides a number of pertinent marketing recommendations in regard to the practice of apparel retailers.

Section 6, "Managerial Impact," presents the uses of social media in industry and management practices. Starting this section is "Management and Marketing Practices of Social Media Firms" by Prof. Abdulaziz Alshubaily of University of Liverpool, Jeddah, Saudi Arabia, which examines the key variances in application and strategy between different social media management strategies and its effective marketing. Ending this section is "Tweeting About Business and Society: A Case Study of an Indian Woman CEO" by Profs. P. Vigneswara Ilavarasan, Ashish Kumar Rathore, and Nikhil Tuli of Indian Institute of Technology Delhi, India, which examines the social media content posted by a woman Indian chief executive officer (CEO) on Twitter.

Section 7, "Critical Issues and Challenges," highlights areas in which social media provides challenges for the industries utilizing it. Opening this final section is the chapter "E-Reputation in Web Entrepreneurship" by Profs. Sylvaine Castellano and Vincent Dutot of Paris School of Business, France, which gives to web-entrepreneurs the key elements in order to manage their e-reputation efficiently by presenting what e-reputation is, what its main components are, how to measure it, and what tools exist. The final chapter, "Ethical Dilemmas Associated With Social Network Advertisements," by Prof. Alan D. Smith of Robert Morris University, USA and Prof. Onyebuchi Felix Offodile of Kent State University, USA, explains the three hypotheses dealt with the interplay of online social networking, advertising effectiveness, gender and age trends, and remaining the interplay with positive comments of the use of the "like" function and its impacts on consumer behavior, as derived from the review of relevant operations literature and from applying the basic tenants of uses and gratification theory.

Although the primary organization of the contents in this multi-volume work is based on its seven sections, offering a progression of coverage of the important concepts, methodologies, technologies, applications, social issues, and emerging trends, the reader can also identify specific contents by utilizing the extensive indexing system listed at the end of each volume. As a comprehensive collection of research on the latest findings related to social media, the *Research Anthology on Strategies for Using Social Media as a Service and Tool in Business* provides researchers, instructors, social media managers, IT consultants, business managers, students, executives, practitioners, industry professionals, social media analysts, and all audiences with a complete understanding of the applications and impacts of social media. Given the vast number of issues concerning usage, failure, success, strategies, and applications of social media in modern industry, the *Research Anthology on Strategies for Using Social Media as a Service and Tool in Business* encompasses the most pertinent research on the applications, impacts, uses, and development of social media as a tool in business.

Chapter 68

This Thing of Social Media!
Is Purchasing Through Its Clout Habit or Sheer Influence?

Akwesi Assensoh-Kodua

(iD) https://orcid.org/0000-0002-1669-6044

Durban University of Technology, South Africa

ABSTRACT

Studies on online purchases abound, but are rarely on social media or social networking service (SNS) to highlight its influence on participants with regards to online purchases. This paper dares to do this. The SNS, although it was envisaged to be a platform for socialisation, has transmuted into a business model that is actually impacting on sales volume of organisations. Predictably, it could be said that the sustainability of this new business phenomenon depends on the continuance patronage of the SNS participants. This study investigated the dynamics impacting on SNS participant to find out whether what makes them purchase through it depends on habit or sheer influence. The study embarked on an online data collection process and performed a structural equation modelling (SEM) with the aid of a partial least square (PLS) program known as PLS-SEM.

1. INTRODUCTION

The third (3) paragraph of the online Oxford English Dictionary (OED) describes a "thing" as a matter with which one is concerned in action, speech, or thought: an affair, a business, a concern, a subject, and these days, in *plural as* affairs, matters, or circumstances (www.oed.com). It cited an example as public thing or thing public. True to the above definition, social media could therefore, be said to have become a "Thing" for business these days, deriving support from the LoyaltyOne study that, positive social media interaction can, and does lead to a significant and sustained increase in transaction volume from participating customers (Everett & Sullivan 2012).

DOI: 10.4018/978-1-7998-9020-1.ch068

Many other studies have also depicted prominence impacts of social media on consumer purchasing behaviour (Goh et al., 2013; Rapp et al., 2013), giving the impression that this thing of social media is a "silver bullet" that automatically leads to business when used for that intention. Nevertheless, after some period of its existence (of which it has now transmogrified to include social networking services (SNSs), researchers still battle to establish how doing business on this platform differ from traditional website, popularly known as ecommerce. Studies are yet to establish the difference between the socio-psychological dynamics that underpin the modalities of social media and that of the traditional website. Researchers are still wondering whether social media and their networks are able to influence business (Everett & Sullivan, 2012), and if so, are these dynamics different from what pertains in the traditional ecommerce platforms?

The objectives of this study is therefore meant to show that (1) social media is really able to lead to actual business, and that (2) purchasing through the clout of social media is mainly due to influence on the platform than being habitual. These are intended to help SNSs and their vendors take full advantage of the platform in these times of global pandemic, dubbed COVID-19 and beyond..

Business models of SNS which are integral parts of social media abounds with majority of them primarily focusing on the general issues surrounding online trading, the architecture of business, trends of SNS and identification of key users of SNS (Trainor et al., 2014; Shiau & Luo, 2013). This notwithstanding, to the best of this study's knowledge, no study has proven that SNS really translates into business and that purchasing through "this thing of social media" is due to sheer influence more than habit. From the extensive review of literature, no study has done this through the arms of social norm, satisfaction, trust and habit to demonstrate their influence on the phenomenon under consideration. These constructs are popular sociopsychological concepts, commonly used to investigate online purchasing behaviour. Nevertheless, social media and for that matter SNS is a novel business model, whereby, if care is not taken, could be treated as "just another online platform". This study argues to differ by showing that SNS is fundamentally different from the traditional website (Maamar et al., 2011; Assensoh-Kodua, 2015).

Sections 2 presents background information about SNSs followed by extension of theories to the SNS environment in 3 and discussion of methods used in 4. Section 5 is data analysis and results, and 5.4 is testing the role of habit where this study really kicks in to prove that habit plays no role of online purchasing through SNS, but instead, influence is the main reasons why participants buy through their SNS. The paper ends with a discussion of the two scenarios, limitations and then conclusion after making some recommendations.

2. BACKGROUND INFORMATION

Social media is a virtual community where users create public profiles, build social collaborations, interact with friends and meet people based on shared interests (Kuss & Griffiths, 2011; Clark, Algoe, & Green, 2018) either in the user's blogs or communities of networks. Thus, social networks are websites that link millions of users all over the world with same interests, ideas, beliefs and hobbies within the social media, making the two terms to be used interchangeably. The Blogs, YouTube, MySpace, Facebook, LinkedIn and Twitter are examples of SNSs that are popular amongst all levels of consumers of social media (Sin et al., 2012). The level of patronage of social networks compared to traditional websites made industry leaders to argue in favour of SNS usage (Trainor et al., 2014; White et al., 2016).

Historically, SNSs are not meant for business purposes, but to establish and maintain relationships with people from different locations. Recently however, SNSs have attracted business professionals to the extent that LinkedIn and Twitter could be pointed out to be among the SNSs with intriguing business models for their participants. For instance, LinkedIn, considered the business world's version of Facebook (Murphy et al., 2014; Wu et al., 2014), drove a high number of users to the MAZDA 6 site and delivered some of the highest key performance indicator ratings of all lifestyle on the plan (Qualman, 2011).

The scope of Twitter network is twofold: business transactions and entertainment. The platform is used for electioneering campaigns, educational training and building public relationships, of which the 2008 and 2020 US Presidential campaigns are typical examples. Twitter service is a content oriented SNS website because a participant's network is determined by the underlying social relationships, created by being followed or becoming a 'follower'. By following or being followed, those wielding the power of effect are able to influence friends purchasing decisions, thus giving them self-confidence and trust of their own sites, and this is similar to generating continuance behaviour (Assensoh-Kodua, 2015). Suffice this by noting that, Twitter boasts a growth rate of posting exceeding 1300 percent in the recent past (Seeking, 2009).

Records have shown that SNS are used to generate business in the Czech Republic, Romania and Turkey (Kirakosyan & Danaita, 2014), hence, altering and redefining how companies and their customers communicate. Survey of some 399 randomly selected European and US companies suggested that 88.2% of them have started taking on social network initiatives and almost 50% have completely incorporated SNS into their business strategies (Karahanna, Xu, & Zhang, 2015). Consumers use SNS to socialise with buddies, view videos and pictures and locate brands and companies, and more than 50% of online shoppers socialise with retailers using SNS. More than 93% of business-to-business marketers use more than one type of social network to socialise with their clients (HoldenBache, 2011) these days. The use of SNS drastically affect business performance through the value created from client interactions and customer engagement, as companies look to forge stronger links with their clients in a competitive market (Trainor et al., 2014; White et al., 2016). A sales expert had mentioned that, salespeople pursuing leads using social media end up with sales between $30,000 and $250,000 (Francis, 2014), with the biggest sales coming from Twitter to find opportunities and LinkedIn to find the names of the true buyers in organisations. Monty (2014), head of social media function of Ford Company, proved in a closing keynote address at the Vision Critical's 2014 summit that, a well-managed SNS platform could be used to generate actual business by sharing the below snapshots of Figures 1 and 3:

True to the above, many more scenarios have surfaced on the web to show that, indeed, social media is being stormed by the business world, as shown in figure 2.

3. EXTENSION OF THEORIES TO THE SOCIAL NETWORKING SERVICE

A host of theories such as the expectation-confirmation theory (ECT) (Bhattacherjee, 2001; Zielke, 2017) and the theory of planned behaviour (TPB) (Ajzen, 1991) have been used extensively in the fields of online marketing and information systems to foster understanding of consumer behaviour and post continuance intentions. This theory shares compatible underlying assumptions and address substantially similar phenomena of determining behavioural intentions. For example, the social norm (SN) of the TPB origin is used as a proxy to determine continuance intention of IS such as SNS, since usage behaviour is sometimes influenced by the social settings (Bhattacherjee, 2001). When a user is pressured to conform to the usage or SN of his/her referent others, coupled with satisfactory reasons (from the ECT) intentions to continue using could be measured. In this manner, Martínez-López et al. (2015) in addition to TPB and ECT, added trust to gather their model, while Liang et al. (2014) added habit to the two for their work. Yun and Lee (2015) added trust to TPB and Bai et al. (2014) added habit to this same theory of TPB for their work. While the following (Limayem et al., 2007) moderated ECT with habit to build a new model, Chiu et al. (2012) displayed that selected constructs from the two theories, together with trust and habit could lead to a new model.

In brief, when theories explain common phenomenon, authors are allowed to use them together. They can capitalise strongly on existing knowledge, allowing them to elaborate phenomena in greater depth (Bonardi & Okhuysen, 2011). Nevertheless, none of the aforementioned papers did their study on social media, in addition to showing that, online purchasing habit is not a match for influence exerted by social media for purchases through this medium. -

The original theories of ECT and TPB are not capstones of facts that do not permit alterations or improvements. For instance, talking about the TPB, research has proven that the original model based on the theory of reasoned action (TRA) and its constructs were not sufficient to explain all the variance in intentions and behaviour predictions (Snippe, Peters, & Kok, 2019). TRA is aimed at explaining behavioural intention and actual behavior (similar to ECT), which in turn is influenced by subjective norm and attitude (Masrek, & Samadi, 2017). To improve on the criticisms of TRA, TPB was born to account for both the reasoning and the needed resources critical to perform a task (Ajzen & Madden, 1986). Following these new discoveries, researchers have been called upon to embrace other constructs to improve the predictive capabilities of models (Baker & White, 2010) to advance knowledge.

Regarding the ECT, Bhattacherjee and Bafar (2011) revisited the proposed IT continuance intention model by the former in 2001, and critically reviewed the ECT which was originally based on Oliver`s (1991) model. Of the reviewed model, satisfaction was still considered very central in determining IT continuance intention and usage.

Figure 1. A snapshot of Twitter follower testimony (Chrislovett@fordtwitter)

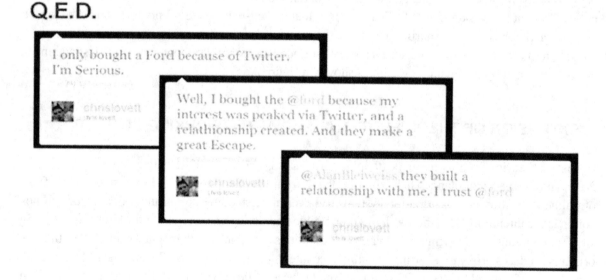

Figure 2. A snapshot of combined images on google n.d. (https://www.searchenginejournal.com/social-proof-ecommerce/304801)

5 Ways to Improve Customer Loyalty With ...
socialmediaexaminer.com

social media marketing | marketing ...
searchenginepeople.com

Social Media Website Theme...
template.net

How Social Media Can Move Your Business
forbes.com

Figure 3. A snapshot of a Twitter follower who decided to buy (Collinkromke.com/ford-twitter)

@KayserFord
Kayser Ford Inc.

@collin_k Hi Collin, Can we provide any information for you on the 2011 Explorer? 2011 North America's Truck of the Year!

20 Jun via web   Unfavorite   Undo Ret

9:34 AM Jun 20th
Mentioned in this Tweet

@CollinKromke
Collin Kromke

@KayserFord It pays to listen on Twitter. I'm buying from @mikerobards at @uptownmotors in Milwaukee. He responded Friday, not 3 days later.

20 Jun via Seesmic for BlackBerry   Unfavorite   Reply   Delete   Buffer

Thus, this study used theory bases from the ECT and TPB plus literature from trust and habit, as explained below to investigate this new phenomenon. The reasoning behind this is based on the various influences these theories exert on behaviour more than habit.

3.1 Influence of Expectation-Confirmation Theory

The ECT is one of the leading theories normally used in continuance intention studies. The objective of the theory is to find consumer satisfaction and repeat behaviour for transactions. The basic logic of the ECT is as follows (Bhattacherjee, 2001; Brown et al., 2012; Zielke, 2017). Firstly, a consumer forms expectation of the goods and services. The consumer shapes the senses about his/her transaction behaviour after a time of use. Secondly, the consumer calculates his/her perceived deed, which is compared to initial expectation and decides the measure to which the expectation was met. Consequently, the consumer accumulates satisfaction decision based on the degree of validation and expectation on which that validation was built. At the end, the consumer forms the repeat purchase or continuance intention behaviour on the degree of satisfaction. Notice need be served here that, all the constructs in ECT other than expectation are repurchasing factors (Limayem et al., 2007) and the evaluation is found in the actual experiences of consumers with an online vendor of which SNS is no exception. However, since the expectation or the expected benefits of social media is no doubt self-evidence to the participant hence the level of patronage we see today, this current study wants to evaluate satisfaction level with regards to purchases on "this thing of social media". Many authors have made substantial contributions in using ECT to study user satisfaction and continuance behaviour (Bhattacherjee, 2001; Bhattacherjee & Premkumar, 2004) and have come out with varied answers. Probably this is what has caused Bhattacherjee and Bafar (2011) to revisit the original ECT (2001) and call for new direction in IT continuance studies upon which this study has found solace for H1-H3. Thus making use of the influence of consumer satisfaction from the above theory to predict intention of the SNS participants, this study hypothesis that:

H1: Participants' satisfaction with SNS will positively influence their continuance intention to use SNS as a medium for business transactions.

H2. Participants' satisfaction with SNS will positively influence them to use SNS as a medium for business transactions.

H3: Participants' satisfaction with SNS will positively influence their trust in SNS as a medium for business transactions.

In as much as this study agrees with Limayem et al. (2007) above, the influence of trust in a particular SNS is equally an important factor that online vendors should consider when building relationships with consumers. Following this line of conviction, this study adopts perceived trust from the socio-cognitive trust theory (TST), to explain the continuance intention of the participants using the SNS for business transaction.

3.2 Influence of Trust

Trust is one of the greatest assets in building lasting and engaging relationships for companies to engage and secure customers continuously for ongoing, real-time feedback and insight. Companies that need a deeper understanding of their customers through this trust have not relented in their effort to register their presence on the SNS platforms because it is a very significant determinant of SNS loyalty. While trust is found on personal correlations and back-to-back interactions between consumer and vendor, it will affect the confidence of consumers in the vendor's performance in the future. It can grow the positive feeling of consumers to repeat visits to the website to create business opportunity. The SNS platform has become one of the best tools to build meaningful relationships with customers online based on trust because of its social nature.

The sociocognitive trust theory (TST) defines trust as a notion that is appraised by agents, in terms of cognitive ingredients (Castelfranchi & Falcone, 2010). TST treats the cognitive trust as a relational factor between a trustor (trust giver) and a trustee (trust receiver). This relationship can be established in a given environment or context and most importantly, about a defined activity or task to be fulfilled such as those on SNSs. Individuals choose whom they will trust based on their own 'good reasons' (Wang, Qiu, Kim, & Benbasat, 2016). Accordingly, the choice to trust and the search for 'good reasons' suggest a process by which one determines that an individual, group of people or organisation is trustworthy (Wang et al., 2016). Creating trust on SNS makes participants comfortable when sharing personal information, making purchases, creating relationships and acting on advice given which is behavioural and essential to the widespread adoption of electronic commerce (McCann & Barlow, 2015). Thus, the investigation of trustworthiness of technology and the examination of the extent to which consumers place their trust in online vendors is given some attention in the recent past. The result has shown that trust is a critical factor for SNS providers and vendors to create within their site in order to turn their participants into customers. Consequently, the following hypotheses are stated:

H4: Perceived trust in SNS will positively influence continuance intention of users to use SNS as a medium for business transactions.

H5: Perceived trust in SNS will positively influence participants to use SNS as a medium for business transactions.

3.3 Social Norm From The Theory of Planned Behaviour

The TPB discusses how attitude, social norm and perceived behavioural control (PBC) influences continuous behavioural decision-making. Of these, social norm has received the least attention (Masrek, & Samadi, 2017), thus, this study takes it on.

3.3.1 Influence of Social Norms

Social norms refer to an individual's perception of whether people who are important to him/her, think that a behaviour in question should or should not be performed (that is the opening up to SNS for influence and continuous engagement for purchases) (Ajzen & Fishbein, 1980). They are the functions of how a participant of SNS with a mind for purchases, referent others' view (respected relatives, friends or colleagues), regarding the behaviour and how the participant is pressured to comply with those beliefs.

Zych, Ttofi, and Farrington (2019) found that the processes of peer pressure and the desire to be accepted by peers can urge bystanders to join in bullying on SNS. Moreover, Pozzoli Gini and Thornberg, (2016) revealed that positive peer pressure for intervention positively predicted defending behaviour in SNS. Peer influence can arise in settings where social norms and observed peer behaviour pressure the individual toward expected choices (Bettinger Fox, Loeb, & Taylor, 2015). It could occur in group sites such as SNS, with a growing number of literature documenting how peers affect performance, friendships and college student's behaviour and attitudes (Bettinger et al., 2015; Wu et al., 2014). Again, it is noted that, Internet business models through strategies of web 2.0 such as SNS are subjected to peer pressure (Marchisotti, Joia, & Carvalho, 2019). The current study draws on the above analysis by testing the extent to which friends influence themselves through the medium of social norm to continue using SNS as a source for purchases. The following hypothesis is therefore proposed:

H6: Social norm will positively influence participants to use SNS as a medium for business transactions.

3.4 Influence of Continuance Intention

If it is possible to use intentions of culprits to predetermine their possible behaviour for judgement at the court of law, then it is possible to use intentions of SNS participants to predict their SNS continuous behaviour and usage.

Bhattacherjee (2001) and Hsu, Yu and Wu (2014) define IS continuance intention in the ECT as an individual's intention to continue using an IS. The definition becomes more pertinent for SNS because such a Web 2.0 application typically has some intrinsic benefits that could only be realised in the long term. For instance, the issue of trust in SNS can only be generated because of familiarity and the continuance visit to a particular SNS. The retention of social media participants will ensure SNS sustainability because participants are in constant search to find the SNS platform that better serves their personal and social needs. They may be inclined to switch or at least become members of multiple platforms when such new ones prove better than the current one. Given SNS successful acceptance rate and popularity, retention and continuity of the users are crucial to ensure sustainability. Enforcing participation in Web 2.0 systems will contribute greatly to the continued existence of SNS. This is an area worthy of pursuit because of the business value of SNS as a tool of both leisure and convenience, a way of communication and a new business venture (Marchisotti et al., 2019; Wu et al., 2014). Figure 4 shows the research model of this study based on the hypotheses stated from H1 to H6.

3.5 Habit

Habit continues to be a controversial issue as to why people perform certain acts.

Bhattacherjee and Barfar (2011) have suggested an investigation of information systems (IS) continuance, after adding habit to the extended ECT model of IS to highlight post acceptance continuance issues, and usage of IT research has suggested that a lot of continued IT usage is influence by habit (Limayem & Cheung, 2011). In their efforts to explain habit, De Guinea and Markus (2009) elucidated that, habit is a well learned action, the beginning of which it might be intentional, but as time goes on, it becomes replicated since it was learned without conscious intent, when initiated by environmental cues in a firm context.

Given the enormous patronage of social media, it could be said that, it usage has become habitual among certain participants, who ceases to be guided by conscious planning but instead, do so when triggered by certain environmental cues (such as, socialisation and/or business needs) in a non-thinking or automatic method. This has contributed to the high levels of usage that we witness today, to the extents that, some participants have even become addicted. The practice of logging on to social media to get news update or read from ones` community of network has become habitual stress releasing phenomenon whereby we all take to this platform to release tension, when we need a break from normal work activities. In so doing, we are caught up in the trap of following others and this sometimes lead us into purchases.

The suggestions of habitual factors to be added to studies, to improve the predictive capability of models mean that researchers believe there are hidden gaps that scholars need to address. Consequently, this study adds habit to realise a unified research model that determines whether purchasing through "this thing of social media" is habit or sheer influence. Based on the ECT that is widely used in the consumer behaviour literature to study consumer post-purchase behaviour, Bhattacherjee's (2001) sought to explain an IS user's intention to continue using an IS (SNS), and moderates the relationship by the degree to which the behaviour in question has become habitual. The study only suspected habit to exert an effect on the relationship between SN, US, and trust on one hand, and SNS continuance intention for business on the other. When the predictive power of the conceptual base model changes from the original results with the habit variable, then habit has effect, otherwise the outcome is sheer influence.

Figure 4. Proposed SNS continuance intention index (SNSCII)

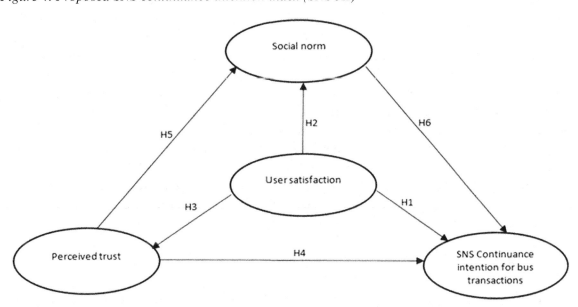

4. RESEARCH METHODS

On the basis of the above evidences, the Partial Least Square (PLS)-for Structural Equation Modelling (SEM), known as PLS-SEM has been settled on as a good analytical program to decipher between habit and sheer influence, as being the motive behind purchasing through the clout of this thing of social media. The PLS-SEM is appropriate for studies of exploratory or an extension of an existing structural theory (Hair, Ringle, & Sarstedt, 2011; p. 144) similar to the current one.

4.1 Measurement Model

The measures (or items) of this research model is based on a 5point Likert Scale ranging from 1 (strongly disagree) to 5 (strongly agree). The operational variables were reliably taken from pre-validated studies, sourced from various authors such as: social norm (SN) from (Venkatesh & Davis, 2000; Teo & Lee, 2010). User satisfaction (US) from (Oliver, 1981; Bhattacherjee, 2001; Devaraj et al., 2002). Perceived trust (PT) were adopted from (Gefen et al., 2003; Hassanein & Head, 2007) and items for continuance intention (CI) from (Bhattacherjee, 2001; Devaraj et al., 2002). Consistent with the extant studies of technology continuance, the variables were measured as exemplified in table 1.

4.2 Data Collection Procedure and Participants

The empirical data for this study were collected through the world wide web (WWW) data collection system called the "SurveyMonkey'. This system has been widely used by numerous researchers to administer online surveys (Custin & Barkacs 2010; Lambeth, 2013). This webbased surveys were used in this study to take advantage over traditional paper based methods (Bhattacherjee, 2001). The data collection process lasted for about six months between 2013 and 2014 during which the web link of SurveyMonkey was posted to participants who are members of the LinkedIn and Tweeter networks and this yielded 317 responses of which 17 were rejected because of missing information. The study participants were SNS clients who ever purchased because of the influence of their various platforms from the LinkedIn and Twitter and who constituted the database used by the SurveyMonkey. The system allowed the researcher to monitor respondents through the internet protocol (IP) address accompanying all responses and ensuring respondents were within the targeted group. Even though only respondents who are able to access the Internet were able to participate in this survey, this bias is exactly what was desired for this study as people who purchase through the influence of SNS were expected to have access to the internet. Although the survey accommodated participants of other SNS, the emphasis was on Twitter and LinkedIn because of their growing popularity of business models (Assensoh-Kodua, 2015).

4.2.1 Descriptive Statistics of Respondent Characteristics

A summary of the descriptive statistics of respondents who participated in this study sets out as follows: 300 valid responses received, 55% were females, implying females are more business oriented on SNS platforms than their male counterparts are. Reasonable percentages (83.33%) of respondents were Twitter or LinkedIn users. The statistics show that 16.77% of the respondents use SNSs, which differ from Twitter and LinkedIn for business transactions. Forty percent fall within the 26 to 35 age group, which is also the working class that spend between 13 hrs per week on SNSs. Twenty-five percent were within the range of 18 to 25 years, 18% within the 36 to 45 age group, 9% within 46 to 55 age group, 4% between 56 to 65 and another 4% above 66 age group. The information provided by the respondents on their SNS usage behaviour revealed that they were experienced SNS users. A sizable number of respondents (29%) indicated the use of both Twitter and LinkedIn for business transactions, while 28% have used SNSs between 21 and 50 times. Respondents residing in Europe (22%) constituted the majority of SNS users for business transactions.

5. DATA ANALYSIS AND RESULTS

The objective of the present study, as hinted before is to show that the dynamics affecting online SNS consumers to purchase through the power of this medium are sheer influence and not habit.

5.1 Tests of Measurement Model

The partial least squared structural equation modelling (PLS-SEM) was applied to assess the reliability and validity of the measures for this study due to (1) its goal of predicting key target constructs or identifying key 'driver' constructs, and (2) this research being exploratory or an extension of an existing structural theory (Hair et al. 2011; p. 144).

The confirmatory factor analysis (CFA) tested for reliability and validity, wherein, each item was modelled in a reflective way to their resultant latent constructs. Reliability is the extent to which factors measured with a multiple item scale reflect the true scores on the factors relative to the error (Nitzl, 2016), and validity tells whether a measuring instrument measures what it was supposed to measure (Raykov, 2011). Cronbach`s alpha was applied to test the reliability of the questionnaire. Based on table 1, where all the variable`s Cronbach alpha values are greater than 0.70, confirmation of the measurement items being reliable is made.

The strength of a measurement model is demonstrated through the measures of convergent and discriminant validity (Hair et al., 2010). Convergent validity measures the agreement between measures of the same construct assessed by different methods. Discriminant validity refers to the distinctiveness of different constructs of a model (Bagozzi & Yi, 2012). The study assessed convergent validity using the average variance extracted (AVE), composite reliability (CR), Cronbach alpha and factor loadings (Henseler et al., 2009; Hair et al., 2010). These are expected to meet the following minimum criteria: AVE=0.5, CR=0.7, Cronbach alpha=0.7 and factor loadings=0.7. Collectively, the results from the above criteria, together with the test of reliabilities shown in table 1, suggest that the indicators accounts for a large portion of the variance of the corresponding latent construct and, thus, provide support for the convergent validity of the measures (Skoumpopoulou, Wong, Ng, & Lo, 2018).

AVE is a measure of the total amount of variance attributed to a construct in relationship to the amount of variance attributed to the measurement error (Henseler et al., 2009; Bagozzi & Yi, 2012). For satisfactory discriminant validity, the square root of the AVE from the construct should be greater than the variance shared between the construct and other constructs in the model. Table 2 shows the correlation matrix, with correlations among the construct and the square root of AVE on the diagonal, proving strong evidence of discriminant validity (Henseler et al., 2009; Bagozzi & Yi, 2012).

The square roots of the AVEs shown on the diagonal exceed the inter factor correlations, which is an indication of acceptable discriminate validity. This paper therefore concludes that measurement scales have sufficient validity and demonstrate high reliability.

A collinearity test was also performed to determine if there was repetition problem among the latent variables. Relying on the variance inflation factors (VIFs), this test calculates each latent variable in relation to all other latent variables (Kock, 2010). The full collinearity test results display VIF values less than the threshold of 5 (Hair et al., 2010). The highest VIF value was 2.012 for the US factor as shown in Table 3. This means that collinearity can be ruled out as a significant source of bias, thus trusting this model to be free from data measurement problems (Kock, 2010).

Table 1. Standardised loadings and reliability test

	Items	Standardised loadings	Comp. reliability	AVE	α
Social norm (SN)			0.936	0.746	0.915
It is expected that people like me use SNS for my business transactions	SN1	0.854			
The nature of my life and work influences me to use SNS for my business needs	SN2	0.905			
People who influence my behaviour think that I use SNS for my business needs	SN3	0.865			
People I look up to as mentors expect me to use SNS for my business transactions	SN4	0.865			
People important to me motivate that I should use SNS for my business transactions	SN5	0.859			
User satisfaction (US)			0.943	0.806	0.920
I am satisfied with the use of my SNS for business transactions	US1	0.877			
I am pleased with the use of my SNS for business transactions	US2	0.922			
I am content with the use of my SNS for business transactions	US3	0.926			
I am delighted with the use of my SNS for business transactions	US4	0.865			
Perceived trust (PT)			0.919	0.739	0.882
I feel safe in my business transactions with my SNS	PT1	0.839			
I believe my SNS can protect my privacy	PT2	0.897			
I select SNS which I believe are honest	PT3	0.889			
I feel that my SNS is trustworthy	PT4	0.811			
Continuance intention (CI)			0.930	0.816	0.886
I intend to continue sharing knowledge about SNS with others	CI1	0.904			
In future, I would not hesitate to use SNS for business transactions	CI2	0.942			
In future, I will consider SNS for business transactions as my first choice	CI3	0.862			
Habit (HB)			0.911	0.719	0.869
I have positive perception about using SNS for business transactions	HB4	0.805			
Generally speaking, I use SNS for business purposes unconsciously / Using SNS for business transactions anytime, anywhere appeals to me	HB5 / HB6	0.882 / 0.888			
I would like to encourage others to use SNS for business transactions	HB7	0.814			

Cronbach's alpha (α)

Table 2. Correlation amongst measures and squared root of AVE

Factor	SN	US	PT	CI
SN	**0.864**			
US	0.608	**0.898**		
PT	0.564	0.588	**0.860**	
CI	0.555	0.531	0.565	**0.903**

Table 3. Latent variable coefficient showing collinearity results

	SN	US	PT	CI CI
R^2	0.441		0.450	0.453
Adjusted R^2	0.437		0.448	0.448
Comp. reliab.	0.936	0.943	0.919	0.930
Cronbach`s alpha	0.915	0.920	0.882	0.886
Ave. var. extrac.	0.746	0.806	0.739	0.816
Full Collin. VIF	1.947	2.012	2.002	1.750
Q^2	0.445		0.444	0.450

5.2 Structural Model

As a rule of thumb, the PLS-SEM allows for the assessment of the structural relationship of the hypothesized causal paths after confirming reliability and validity of measurement models.

The variance denoted by Rsquared (R^2) of each dependent variable is an indication of how well the model fits the data. It is the amount of variance in a dependent variable that is explained by the dependent variables. The global goodnessoffit (GoF) criterion for path modelling was suggested to account for the model performance at both measurement and structural terms (Kock, 2010), the aim of which is to find the overall predictive power of a model. Each of the hypotheses (H1 to H6) corresponds to a path on the structural model to be tested, and the (R^2) results and path coefficients indicate the model fit or effectiveness (Nitzl, 2016). The overall fit, explanatory power of the structural model and relative strengths of the individual causal path were examined and shown in Figure 5.

The path coefficient between social norm and SNS continuance intention is worth noting ($ß = 0.36$) at the significance level of $p<0.01$ as shown in Figure 5. This result supports hypothesis H6. While Philander and Zhong, (2016) noted that satisfaction ratings are determined in part by measurement artifacts or personal characteristics of survey customers, hence caution needs to be exercised when interpreting or using them in decision making, this study seems to be supporting these assertions. By this statement, the authors meant that satisfaction ratings are tinted with so many biases, it is over rated and it no longer serves any good purpose. This study is proving what these authors said long ago, as this US construct tend to be the only one which was not significant in the current study.-As expected, all hypothesised paths in the structural model were significant other than this satisfaction (US) ($ß = 0.058$, $p=0.155$). Thus H1 is not supported. Table 4 (rounded to 3 significant levels) shows the summary of the result of hypothesis testing in which it can be seen that with a significance level of $p<0.001$, hypotheses H2, H3, H4, H5 and H6 are supported.

5.3 Model Fitness

The overall fit of the research model was assessed using six measures of the average path coefficient (APC), the average R^2 (ARS), average block inflation factor (AVIF), the goodness of fits (GoF), average adjusted R^2 (AARS) and R^2 contribution ratio (RSCR). Each of the model fit metrics is discussed according to Kock (2010). Based on the result of model fit depicted in Table 5, the studys' model has a good fit. The values of APC and ARS are significant at a 5% level, while AVIF is still lower than 5. This concludes that a good fit exists between the model and the data (Kock, 2010).

Figure 5. Empirical result of testing the social networking service continuance intention model

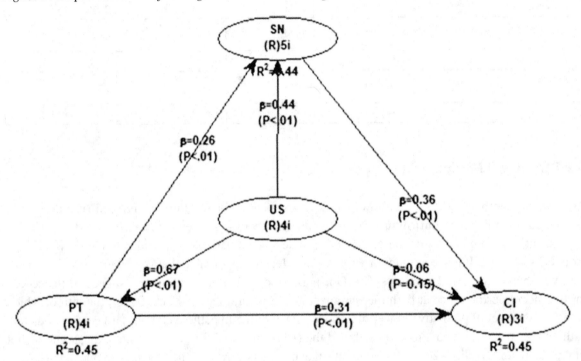

Table 4. Summary of the result of hypothesis testing

Effect	Cause	Est (β)	SE	P-value	Result
CI	US	0.058	0.057	0.155 ns	H1 unsupported
PT	US	0.671	0.052	<0.001***	H2 supported
SN	US	0.441	0.054	<0.001***	H3 supported
CI	PT	0.314	0.055	<0.001***	H4 supported
SN	PT	0.261	0.055	<0.001***	H5 supported
CI	SN	0.357	0.054	<0.001***	H6 supported

Note: Est (Estimate), SE (standard error), ns (not significant), *p<0.05, **p<0.01, ***p<0.001 (twotailed ttests). SNScontinuance intention (SNSCI), User satisfaction (US), Perceived trust (PT), Social norm (SN), Perceived behavioural control (PBC)

5.4 Testing the Role of Habit

Prior research in IT usage indicates that habit determines much of IT continued usage (Bhattacherjee & Barfar, 2011), and researchers (Limayem et al., 2007; Bhattacherjee & Barfar, 2011; Limayem & Cheung, 2011; Shiau & Luo, 2013) have investigated habit in numerous ways to uncover the hidden truth of its effect on both dependent and independent variables. This study, in a bit to show it effect on the phenomenon being studied, imposed habit onto the base model. This was directly linked to the dependent variable of SNS continuance intention for business, as displayed in figure 6.

Per Demir, and Kutlu (2016), a theory is confirmed if the interaction effect of other determinants, that is the path coefficient (β) is significant and independent of the magnitude of the path coefficients of other determinants. This study did not hypothesise on the direction of this (habit), therefore, a two-sided test of significance is applied. As can be seen from figure 6, the explained variant ($R^2 = 45$) of the experiment was still the same as figure 5 ($R^2 = 45$), when there was no habit. Thus, habit had no effect nor made any contribution on the SNS continuance intention for business transaction. Rather, it reduced the predictive powers of the exogenous construct on the endogenous construct of SN®CI from $\beta = 0.36$ to $\beta = 0.34$, US®CI from $\beta = 0.06$ to $\beta = 0.04$, and PT®CI from $\beta = 0.31$ to $\beta = 0.29$. This confirms (Limayem et al, 2007; Hsu et al., 2014) prove that habit limits the predictive power of intentions. In short, the above scenario shows that, purchasing through the clout of social media is due to influence from this medium and not habit. Table 6 shows the summary results.

Table 5. Model fit and quality indices

Fit index	Model	Model's p-value	Recommendation
Average path coefficient (APC)	0.350	<0.001	Good if P<0.05
Average R-squared (ARS)	0.448	<0.001	Good if P<0.05
Average block VIF (AVIF)	2.779		Acceptable if <= 5, Ideally <= 3.3
Goodness of Fit (GoF)	0.586		Small >= 0.1, Medium >= 0.25, Large >= 0.36
Average adjusted R^2 (AARS)	0.444	<0.001	Good if P<0.05
R^2 contribution ratio (RSCR)	1.000		Acceptable if >= 0.9, Ideally = 1

Figure 6. Results of habit effect

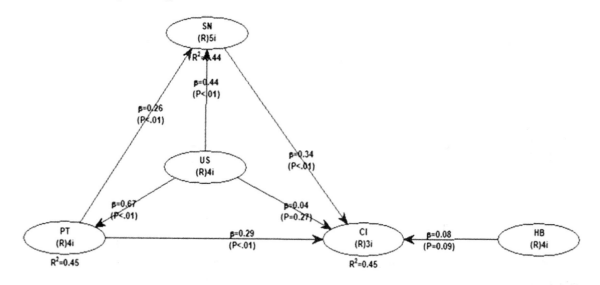

Table 6. Summary of the result of habit testing

Effect	Cause	Estimate (β)	SE	P-value
CI	US	0.036	0.057	0.266[ns]
PT	US	0.671	0.052	<0.001***
SN	US	0.441	0.054	<0.001***
CI	PT	0.298	0.055	<0.001***
SN	PT	0.261	0.055	<0.001***
CI	SN	0.336	0.055	0.001***
CI	HB	0.077	0.057	0.089[ns]

SE (standard error), ns (not significant), *p<0.05, **p<0.01, ***p<0.001 (twotailed ttests)

Note: the values in this table have been rounded to 2 decimal places on the experimented model

To control any mediating effect that habit might have caused on the model (Fig 6), and show the unidimensionality of the various constructs, another round of model testing was performed individually, whereby, each variable was directly modelled on the endogenous construct. This was to demonstrate the true effect of habit, and not because it was used as mediating variable in the base model. Thus, the results below:

Figure 7. Individual models on endogenous construct

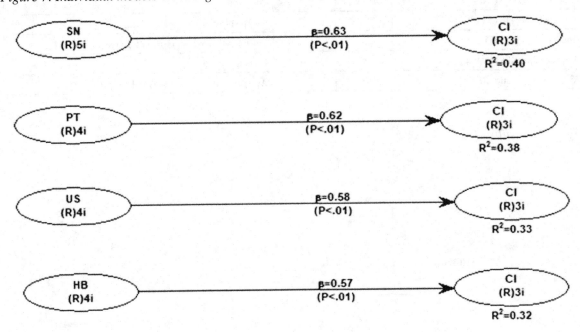

From Figure 7, it is crystal clear that the relationships between SN→CI ($\beta = 63$, $R^2 = 0.40$) is the most influencing factor, followed by PT→CI ($\beta = 62$, $R^2 = 0.38$), US→CI ($\beta = 58$, $R^2 = 0.33$) and then HB→CI ($\beta = 57$, $R^2 = 0.32$). The impact of habit is the least. There seems to exists a reciprocal relationship between satisfaction and habit. Future research should incorporate this view into the research model and design.

6. DISCUSSION OF RESULTS

6.1 Implications for Theory and Practice

The result of this study clearly highlights the contribution to Information Systems research (and in particular online transactions and SNS). This generally has practical implications for both individuals and organisations desiring to create a customer base through SNSs.

This study has once again underscored the importance of trust in building a long-term relationship with would-be customers in SNSs. It is said that individuals develop trust gradually over time based on positive outcomes from repeated behaviour (Akrout, Diallo, Akrout, & Chandon, 2016), and this is what this study has proven. As participants engaged in a long-term social exchange with SNS vendors, they develop trust for these vendors which become "a brain habit in long-term relationships." When this trust was qualified with habits of individual participants to investigate whether purchasing through the influence of this platform is really based on trust or habit, the outcome saw a "no show" from habit to prove that trust is still the influencing factor why participants purchase after visiting their SNSs. This is explained from the point of view of "How habit limits the predictive power of intentions", by Limayem et al. (2007) that, if individuals are habitual performers of a particular behaviour (say, purchasing through the power of SNS), the predictive power of intention is weakened (as we have seen between PT and CI in this study). Thus, the more a behaviour is performed out of habit, the less cognitive planning is involved.

Theoretically, this means that the practice of purchasing a product or service through the influence of SNS is based on trust of both the SNS sites and the sociodynamics interactions between vendors on these sites and their participants. The reason being that, as the initial trust is built among one`s community of networks for a long period, it enters the subconscious minds of these friends as brands until a point in time when participants become so much trusting that their purchase decisions are based only on trust and nothing more. The mere mention of the SNS vendor or the company in question generates "intention to purchase" without participants thinking about whether to buy or not.

Practically, this explains why certain brands and products command higher prices than others do, though they may perform the same function and give the same satisfaction. The investment in building such trust among participants now yields dividends in the form of high prices. The study advice that SNS vendors do everything possible to guide against this attitude of participants because it can cause their organisations great fortunes if taken for granted. As SNS vendors reach this level of trust, they should be more frequent on the network to service the relationship than ever before for continuance clientele loyalty. As an example, when SNS vendors think of composing their blog and related information, they should include recommendations based on particular (regular) participants' interests (as well as their immediate social needs) instead of considering general and static behaviours of the service composition (Maamar et al., 2011).

Social Norm says people perform a behaviour to please others (friends, colleagues, relatives, etc.) and this is exactly what this study has discovered. The sociodynamics of SNS have the capability to create addiction among participants, and there are a lot of studies that have proven this fact (Karaiskos et al., 2010; Kuss & Griffiths, 2011) just to list a few. The real habits of people are sometimes hidden just to create acceptance among their social settings until such a time that they are able to break loose from these recoiling predispositions to manifest their actual habits.

The effect of habit on SN–CI saw a negative value. In other words, the joining of social groupings limits the real habit of the individual so as to accept the norm of the groups and flow with the group.

This creates acceptance by the referent others as the individual is seen as a team player. After the imposition of habits on the model, the strength of the SN reduced. This means that, participants in a particular social group accepts the practice of purchasing (through the influence of SNSs) to please their referent others. But when they have the option to show their real intentions, they might not purchase or reduce the influence that their social settings impose on them. This underscores the real effect or importance of the concept of social norm.

Practically, such agenda is achieved through promotional strategies as the "bandwagon" effect or group purchases. This will imbue in members who still have not formed the habit of allowing themselves to be influenced to purchase on their own, except in the company of friends the practice of purchasing. They might do so for acceptance until they become addicted to the act. In this regard, the social based connection among the group members and the SNS vendor should stress on the interaction that occur between group members, a regular visit to the vendor`s site and product or services enquiry. Rewards packages could be given to high volume visitors who induce or introduce others to visit and purchase vendor`s products (online or physical store).

E-satisfaction has an impact on e-loyalty (i.e. continuous behaviour), however, the outcome of the user satisfaction in the base model was not surprising because satisfaction measures are likely to be positively biased (Philander & Zhong, 2016). Establishing the relationship between satisfaction and repurchase behaviour has been intangible for many firms (Mittal & Kamakura 2001). This stems from the unfinished business surrounding the satisfaction element and since this study is meant to contribute practically to the body of knowledge, it calls for further studies to resolve any controversy. Satisfaction measurement and research design studies share the following common biases: "virtually all self-reports of customer satisfaction process are distribution, in which a majority of the responses indicate that customers are satisfied and the distribution itself is negatively skewed" (Langan, & Harris, 2019). Moreover, the modal response to a satisfaction question, is typically the most positive response allowed. This study takes these criticisms seriously because it is noted by other researchers (e.g. Oliver, 1981; Ali, Zhou, Hussain, Nair, & Ragavan, 2016). Some (Ladeira, Santini, Sampaio, Perin, & Araújo, 2016) have even tried to develop a scale that would produce a more normal distribution just for this construct.

As hinted earlier on (research design section) the satisfaction measurement items used in this study were borrowed from prior research studies and therefore cannot be exonerated from these biases. This could explain the result seen in this paper, as explained by Hossain and Zhou (2018), that the relationship between satisfaction and continuous behaviour seems almost intuitive. This intuitive appeal notwithstanding, the strength of the relationship between satisfaction and continuous behaviour, has been found to differ significantly under different conditions, depending on the competitive organisation of the industry. This notwithstanding, satisfaction leads to continuous behaviour (Zielke, 2017), and true loyalty can only be achieved when other factors, such as an embedded social network, are present. True to this statement, this study, being a social networking research expected satisfaction to positively connect to SNS continuous intention but this was not to be. It is therefore no surprise to find out that, some studies have even labelled satisfaction measurement as a 'trap' and argued for curtailing it measurement efforts long ago (Reichheld, 1996), while others termed it as "too good to be true" (Tanner & Stacy, 1985; p.148). The big question then is "how can participants continue enjoying SNS on social media if they are not satisfied with it?" This is why this paper is calling for more research regarding the satisfaction construct.

While none of the above explanations and criticism can be summarily dismissed, this research does not intend to add injury to an already controversial issue, until further research is undertaken to set the records straight. To this end, readers are referred to Assensoh-Kodua, (2019) expository analysis on similar study incorporating satisfaction construct. Hopefully a new sense of direction could be attained.

7. LIMITATIONS

The study is supposed to point out limitations for future consideration. The conceptual model of this paper seems to be the first of its kind used to investigate SNS purchasing behaviour as the author found no similar studies to compare with the current model. This therefore denies us the opportunity to do any critical analysis for the research community. The paper therefore invites studies in this direction to come up with more competitive models.

Generalising the results to other types of online purchases (popularly known as ecommerce) should be done with care. This is because ecommerce and SNS have different characteristics and sociodynamics. One challenge of social networking integration into business model is that, it may not be easy to quantify its impact for action. Although many providers use social networking as something that encourages border crossing, providers do not have any measure of whether their brand message, delivered through a social network, propagates across the route to reach end consumers. Associate operations as well as the message's greatest effects on brand are also difficult to quantify. Again, many SNS businesses are saddled with messages that are inconsistent, ambiguous policies, and dearth of a defined social network strategy.

8. CONCLUSION

This study is one of the few that has responded to the call for researchers to show the effect of habit in order to give an alternative result of an investigation. In doing so, the study has used habit as a controlled variable to examine it explicit effect on SNS continuous intention for business, and has discovered that habit makes no contribution to this phenomenon, but rather has negative effect on trust, social norm and satisfaction in predicting SNS continuous intention. It became clear from this study that, the recent move by organisations to establish their presents in the social networks to take advantage of the teeming followers of these platforms for business, do indeed pay off. Nevertheless, they should not forget that, this phenomenon of purchasing from SNS is not based on purchasing habit of participant but instead, the sheer influence of their representatives on the network.

Consequently, it is recommended that, before joining a social network to do business, organisations must first train their SNS representative on interaction strategies. They should spend time to investigate the purchasing behaviour of their would-be clients and how easy they could be influenced to purchase, and then connect with those who belong to a social setting. This is because, these class of participants listen to their peers for decision making. The precious time organisations spend in interacting with SNS participants should be geared towards building a community of online social network instead of trying to do business with them from the onset. This means, the particular social network that is intended to be used for business should have a component in the profile of their followers that captures their online purchasing behaviour, and this should give a hint to the organisation as to who they should spend time socialising with. This also creates room for future study. Organisations should add such potentials to their panel of networks when requested, in the case of LinkedIn for instance. They should accept request from participants to add them to the company`s online community, and follow participants, in the case of Twitter. Social media can be a smart selling platform only if ones` clients and prospective clients are made to feel part of any kind of network that wields the power of influence, otherwise it could be a titanic waste of time and resources if organisations just connect with participants, and hope they could automatically build a habit of online purchasing into them, that will make them strike any significant business deals. They can influence participant to purchase through SN, and influence them to trust through PT, but cannot influence them to be satisfied when they are not satisfied.

REFERENCES

Ajzen, I. (1991). The theory of planned behavior. *Organizational Behavior and Human Decision Processes*, *50*(2), 179211. doi:10.1016/0749-5978(91)90020-T

Ajzen, I., & Fishbein, M. (1980). *Understanding attitudes and predicting social behavior*. Prentice Hall.

Ajzen, I., & Madden, T. J. (1986). Prediction of goaldirected behavior: Attitudes, intentions, and perceived behavioral control. *Journal of Experimental Social Psychology*, *22*(5), 453474. doi:10.1016/0022-1031(86)90045-4

Akrout, H., Diallo, M. F., Akrout, W., & Chandon, J. L. (2016). Affective trust in buyer-seller relationships: A two-dimensional scale. *Journal of Business and Industrial Marketing*, *31*(2), 260–273. doi:10.1108/JBIM-11-2014-0223

Ali, F., Zhou, Y., Hussain, K., Nair, P. K., & Ragavan, N. A. (2016). Does higher education service quality effect student satisfaction, image and loyalty? A study of international students in Malaysian public universities. *Quality Assurance in Education*, *24*(1), 70–94. doi:10.1108/QAE-02-2014-0008

Assensoh-Kodua, A. (2019). This thing of social media! Going business or socialisation? Solving the great dilemma. *Foresight*.

Assensoh-Kodua, A. (2015). *Determinants of Online Social Networks for Successful Business*. Available at: http//www.amazon.fr/Livresanglais

Bagozzi, R. P., & Yi, Y. (2012). Specification, evaluation and interpretation of structural equation models. *Journal of the Academy of Marketing Science*, *40*(1), 834. doi:10.100711747-011-0278-x

Bai, L., Tang, J., Yang, Y., & Gong, S. (2014). Hygienic food handling intention. An application of the Theory of Planned Behavior in the Chinese cultural context. *Food Control*, *42*, 172–180. doi:10.1016/j.foodcont.2014.02.008

Baker, R. K., & White, K. M. (2010). Predicting adolescents' use of social networking sites from an extended theory of planned behavior perspective. *Computers in Human Behavior*, *26*(6), 15911597. doi:10.1016/j.chb.2010.06.006

Bettinger, E., Fox, L., Loeb, S., & Taylor, E. (2015). *Changing Distributions: How Online College Classes Alter Student and Professor Performance*. CEPA Working Paper No. 15-10. Stanford Center for Education Policy Analysis.

Bhattacherjee, A., & Barfar, A. (2011). Information technology continuance research: Current state and future directions. *Asia Pacific Journal of Information Systems, 21*(2), 118.

Bhattacherjee, A. (2001). Understanding information systems continuance: An expectationconfirmation model. *Management Information Systems Quarterly, 25*(3), 351370. doi:10.2307/3250921

Bhattacherjee, A., & Premkuma, R. G. (2004). Understanding changes in belief and attitude toward information technology usage: A theoretical model and longitudinal test. *Management Information Systems Quarterly, 28*(2), 229254. doi:10.2307/25148634

Bhattacherjee, A., Perols, J., & Sanford, C. (2008). Information technology continuance: A theoretical extension and empirical test. *Journal of Computer Information Systems, 49*(1), 1726. doi:10.1080/088 74417.2008.11645302

Bonardi, J. P., & Okhuysen, G. (2011). The challenges of theory building through the combination of lenses. *Academy of Management Review*, 6–12.

Brown, S. A., Venkatesh, H. V., & Goya, L. S. (2012). Expectation confirmation in technology use. *Information Systems Research, 23*(2), 474–487. doi:10.1287/isre.1110.0357

Castelfranchi, C., & Falcon, E. R. (2010). *Trust theory: a sociocognitive and computational model. Wiley Series in Agent Technology*. John Wiley and Sons Ltd., doi:10.1002/9780470519851

Chin, W. W. (1998). The partial least squares approach to structural equation modelling. In *Modern methods for business research*. Lawrence Erlbaum.

Chiu, C. M., Hsu, M. H., Lai, H., & Chang, C. M. (2012). Re-examining the influence of trust on online repeat purchase intention: The moderating role of habit and its antecedents. *Decision Support Systems, 53*(4), 835–845. doi:10.1016/j.dss.2012.05.021

Clark, J. L., Algoe, S. B., & Green, M. C. (2018). Social network sites and well-being: The role of social connection. *Current Directions in Psychological Science, 27*(1), 32–37. doi:10.1177/0963721417730833

Cohen, J. (1988). *Statistical power analysis for the behavioural sciences*. Lawrence Erlbaum.

Constanza, B., & Lynda, A. (2012). Risk, trust, and consumer online purchasing behavior: A Chilean perspective. *International Marketing Review, 29*(3), 253–275. doi:10.1108/02651331211229750

Custin, R., & Barkacs, L., (2010). Developing sustainable learning communities through blogging. *Journal of Instructional Pedagogies*, (4), 18. .

Davis, F. D. (1989). Perceived usefulness, perceived ease of use, and user acceptance of information technology. *Management Information Systems Quarterly, 13*(3), 319340. doi:10.2307/249008

De Guinea, A. O., & Markus, M. L. (2009). Why break the habit of a lifetime? Rethinking the roles of intention, habit, and emotion in continuing information technology use. *Management Information Systems Quarterly, 33*(3), 433–444. doi:10.2307/20650303

Demir, Y., & Kutlu, M. (2016). The Relationship between loneliness and depression: Mediation role of Internet addiction. *Educational Process: International Journal*.

Devaraj, S., Fan, M., & Kohli, R. (2002). Antecedents of B2C channel satisfaction and preference: Validating ecommerce metrics. *Information Systems Research*, *13*(3), 316333. doi:10.1287/isre.13.3.316.77

Everett, N. & Sullivan, J., (2012). *The social media payoff: Establishing the Missing Link Between Social Media and ROI*. Available at Payoff_from_LoyaltyOne.pdf

Feige, T. (2013). Social Media Marketing-Analysis of Online presence of Slovak banks. *Journal of Systems Integration*, *4*(3), 20.

Francis, C. (2014). *How to use social media to make sales*. Available from http://www. forbes.com/sites/jacquelynsmith/2014/01/10/

Gardner, B. (2015). A review and analysis of the use of 'habit'in understanding, predicting and influencing health-related behaviour. [PubMed]. *Health Psychology Review*, *9*(3), 277–295. doi:10.1080/17437199.2013.876238

Gefen, D., Karahanna, E., & Straub, D. W. (2003). Trust and TAM in online shopping: An integrated model. *Management Information Systems Quarterly*, *27*(1), 5190. doi:10.2307/30036519

Goh, K., Heng, C., & Lin, Z. (2013). Social media brand community and consumer behavior: Quantifying the relative impact of userand marketergenerated content. *Information Systems Research*, *24*(1), 88–107. doi:10.1287/isre.1120.0469

Gopi, M., & Ramayah, T. (2007). Applicability of theory of planned behavior in predicting intention to trade online: Some evidence from a developing country. *International Journal of Emerging Markets*, *2*(4), 348360. doi:10.1108/17468800710824509

Hair, J. F., Ringle, C. M., & Sarstedt, M. (2011). PLS-SEM: Indeed a Silver Bullet. *Journal of Marketing Theory and Practice*, *19*(2), 139–151. doi:10.2753/MTP1069-6679190202

Hair, J. F., William, C. B., Barry, J. B., & Rolph, E. A. (2010). *Multivariate Data Analysis*. Academic Press.

Hassanein, K., & Head, M. (2007). Manipulating perceived social presence through the web interface and its impact on attitude towards online shopping. *International Journal of Human-Computer Studies*, *65*(8), 689708. doi:10.1016/j.ijhcs.2006.11.018

Holden-Bache, A. (2011, Apr. 18). Study: 93% of B2B marketers use social media marketing. *B to B Magazine*.

Henseler, J., Ringle, C., & Sinkovics, R. (2009). The use of partial least squares path modeling in international marketing. *Advances in International Marketing*, *8*(20), 277–319. doi:10.1108/S1474-7979(2009)0000020014

Hsu, C. L., Yu, C. C., & Wu, C. C. (2014). Exploring the continuance intention of social networking websites: An empirical research. *Information Systems and e-Business Management*, *12*(2), 139163. doi:10.100710257-013-0214-3

Hossain, M. S., & Zhou, X. (2018). Impact of m-payments on purchase intention and customer satisfaction: Perceived flow as mediator. *International Journal of Science and Business*, *2*(3), 503–517.

Karahanna, E., Xu, S. X., & Zhang, N. (2015). Psychological ownership motivation and use of social media. *Journal of Marketing Theory and Practice, 23*(2), 185–207.

Karaiskos, D., Tzavellas, E., & Balta, G. (2010). P02232Social network addiction: A new clinical disorder? *European Psychiatry,* 25–855.

Kirakosyan, K., & Danaita, D. (2014). Communication Management in Electronic Banking. Better Communication for Better Relationship. *Procedia: Social and Behavioral Sciences, 124,* 361370. doi:10.1016/j.sbspro.2014.02.497

Kock, N. (2010). Using WarpPLS in ecollaboration studies: An overview of five main analysis steps. *International Journal of e-Collaboration, 6*(4), 111. doi:10.4018/jec.2010100101

Kuss, D. J., & Griffiths, M. D. (2011). Online social networking and addictiona review of the psychological literature. [PubMed]. *International Journal of Environmental Research and Public Health, 8*(9), 35283552. doi:10.3390/ijerph8093528

Kwak, H., Lee, C., Park, H., & Moon, S. (2010). What is Twitter, a social network or a news media. In *Proceedings of the 19th International Conference on World Wide Web.* ACM. doi:10.1145/1772690.1772751

Ladeira, W. J., Santini, F. D. O., Sampaio, C. H., Perin, M. G., & Araújo, C. F. (2016). A meta-analysis of satisfaction in the banking sector. *International Journal of Bank Marketing, 34*(6), 798–820. doi:10.1108/IJBM-10-2015-0166

Lambeth, J. M. (2008). *Research foci for career and technical education: Findings from a national Delphi study.* Texas A&M University.

Liang, C. Y., Tao, F. J., Gu, D. X., Ding, B., & Wang, R. L. (2014). It Usage Behavior of Medical Personnel: an Empirical Study Based on the Theory of planned Behavior. *PACIS,* (212).

Limayem, M., & Cheung, C. M. K. (2011). Predicting the continued use of Internetbased learning technologies: The role of habit. *Behaviour & Information Technology, 30*(1), 9199. doi:10.1080/0144 929X.2010.490956

Limayem, M., Hirt, S., & Cheung, C. (2007). How habit limits the predictive power of intentions: The case of IS continuance. *Management Information Systems Quarterly, 31,* 705–737. doi:10.2307/25148817

Maamar, Z., Haci, D. H., & Huhns, M. N. (2011). Why web services need social networks. *IEEE Internet Computing, 15,* 009094.

Marchisotti, G. G., Joia, L. A., & Carvalho, R. B. D. (2019). The social representation of Cloud Computing according to Brazilian information technology professionals. *Revista de Administração de Empresas, 59*(1), 16–28. doi:10.15900034-759020190103

Martínez-López, F. J., Esteban-Millat, I., Cabal, C. C., & Gengler, C. (2015). Psychological factors explaining consumer adoption of an e-vendor's recommender. *Industrial Management & Data Systems, 115*(2), 284–310. doi:10.1108/IMDS-10-2014-0306

Masrek, M. N., & Samadi, I. (2017). Determinants of mobile learning adoption in higher education setting. *Asian Journal of Scientific Research, 10*(2), 60–69. doi:10.3923/ajsr.2017.60.69

Mayer, J. H., Davis, F. D., & Schoorman, R. C. (1995). An integrative model of organizational trust. *Academy of Management Review, 20*(3), 709–734. doi:10.5465/amr.1995.9508080335

McCann, M., & Barlow, A. (2015). Use and measurement of social media for SMEs. *Journal of Small Business and Enterprise Development, 22*(2), 273–287. doi:10.1108/JSBED-08-2012-0096

Meiseberg, B., & Dant, R. P. (2015). A cross-national comparison of the role of habit in linkages between customer satisfaction and firm reputation and their effects on firm- level outcomes in franchising. In *Interfirm networks* (pp. 99–124). Springer., doi:10.1007/978-3-319-10184-2_6

Monty, S. (2014). *Has social media lost its way?* www.visioncritical .com/resources/UTMcampaign

Murphy, J, Hill, C.A., & Dean, E., (2014). Social Media, Sociality, and Survey Research. Social Media. *Sociality, and Survey Research*, 133. .

Nitzl, C. (2016). The use of partial least squares structural equation modelling (PLS-SEM) in management accounting research: Directions for future theory development. *Journal of Accounting Literature, 37*, 19–35. doi:10.1016/j.acclit.2016.09.003

OED. (n.d.). *Oxford English Dictionary, the definitive record of the English language.* Available at: https://www.oed.com/view/Entry/200786/eid18542815

Oliver, R. L. (1981). Measurement and evaluation of satisfaction processes in retail settings. *Journal of Retailing, 57*(3), 2548. https://psycnet.apa.org/record/1984-10995-001

Oliver, R. L. (1999). Whence customer loyalty. Journal of Marketing, 63(4_suppl1), 33–44. doi:10.1177/00222429990634s105

Research, O. T. X. (2008). *Impact of social media on purchasing behavior.* Retrieved 20120410 from http://174.133.170.120/files/DEIStudy Engaging Consumers Online Summary.pdf

Paul, T. J., & Jacob, J. (2017). Information system continuance usage: Moderating role of habit. *International Journal of Business Information Systems, 26*(2), 166–184. doi:10.1504/IJBIS.2017.086328

Philander, K., & Zhong, Y. (2016). Twitter sentiment analysis: Capturing sentiment from integrated resort tweets. *International Journal of Hospitality Management, 55*, 16–24. doi:10.1016/j.ijhm.2016.02.001

Pozzoli, G., Gini, G., & Thornberg, R. (2016). Bullying and defending behavior: The role of explicit and implicit moral cognition. [PubMed]. *Journal of School Psychology, 59*, 67–81. doi:10.1016/j.jsp.2016.09.005

Qualman, E. (2011). *100 million on LinkedIninfographic by country.* Available at http://www.socialnomics.netlinkedin/hits/100millionbreakdownby countrygraphic

Rapp, A., Beitelspacher, L. S., Grewal, D., & Hughes, D. E. (2013). Understanding socialmedia effects across seller, retailer, and consumer interactions. *Journal of the Academy of Marketing Science, 41*(5), 547–566. doi:10.100711747-013-0326-9

Raykov, T. (2011). Evaluation of convergent and discriminant validity with multitrait– multimethod correlations. [PubMed]. *British Journal of Mathematical & Statistical Psychology, 64*(1), 3852. doi:10.1348/000711009X478616

Reichheld, F. (1996). *The loyalty effect: The hidden force behind growth, profits, and lasting value.* Harvard business school Press.

Seeking, A. (2009). *Twitter posts meteoric 1,384% YoY growth.* Available from: http:// seekingalpha. com/article/127580twitterpostsmeteoricyoygrowth

Shiau, W., & Luo, M. M. (2013). Continuance intention of blog users: The impact of perceived enjoyment, habit, user involvement and blogging time. *Behaviour & Information Technology*, *32*(6), 570–583. doi:10.1080/0144929X.2012.671851

Sin, S., Nor, K. M., & AlAgaga, A. M. (2012). Factors Affecting Malaysian young consumers' online purchase intention in social media websites. *Procedia: Social and Behavioral Sciences*, *40*, 326333. doi:10.1016/j.sbspro.2012.03.195

Skoumpopoulou, D., Wong, A., Ng, P., & Lo, M. (2018). Factors that affect the acceptance of new technologies in the workplace: A cross case analysis between two universities. *International Journal of Education and Development Using ICT*, *14*(3).

Snippe, M. H., Peters, G. J., & Kok, G. (2019). *The Operationalization of Self-Identity in Reasoned Action Models: A systematic review of self-identity operationalizations in three decades of research.* Academic Press.

Tanner, B. A., & Stacy, W. Jr. (1985). A validity scale for the Sharp consumer satisfaction scales. [PubMed]. *Evaluation and Program Planning*, *8*(2), 147153. doi:10.1016/0149-7189(85)90009-6

Teo, T., & Lee, C. B. (2010). Explaining the intention to use technology among student teachers: An application of the theory of planned behavior (TPB). *Campus-Wide Information Systems*, *27*(2), 6067. doi:10.1108/10650741011033035

Trainor, K. J., Andzulis, J., Rapp, A., & Agnihotri, R. (2014). Social media technology usage and customer relationship performance: A capabilities-based examination of social CRM. *Journal of Business Research*, *67*(6), 1201–1208. doi:10.1016/j.jbusres.2013.05.002

Yun, S., & Lee, J. (2015). Advancing societal readiness toward renewable energy system adoption with a socio-technical perspective. *Technological Forecasting and Social Change*, *95*, 170–181. doi:10.1016/j. techfore.2015.01.016

Venkatesh, V., & Davis, F. D. (2000). A theoretical extension of the technology acceptance model: Fthis longitudinal field studies. *Management Science*, *46*(2), 186204. doi:10.1287/mnsc.46.2.186.11926

Wang, W., Qiu, L., Kim, D., & Benbasat, I. (2016). Effects of rational and social appeals of online recommendation agents on cognition-and affect-based trust. *Decision Support Systems*, *86*, 48–60. doi:10.1016/j.dss.2016.03.007

White, K., Kenly, A., & Poston, B. (2016). *Social Media and Product Innovation Early Adopters Reaping Benefits amidst Challenge and Uncertainty.* Academic Press.

Wu, Y. L., Tao, Y. H., Li, C. P., Wang, S. Y., & Chiu, C. Y. (2014). User-switching behavior in social network sites: A model perspective with drill-down analyses. *Computers in Human Behavior*, *33*, 92–103. doi:10.1016/j.chb.2013.12.030

Zielke, S. (2017). The impact of price-related incidents on store loyalty. In *The Customer is NOT Always Right? Marketing Orientations in a Dynamic Business World* (pp. 121–124). Springer., doi:10.1007/978-3-319-50008-9_31

Zych, I., Ttofi, M. M., & Farrington, D. P. (2019). Empathy and callous–unemotional traits in different bullying roles: A systematic review and meta-analysis. [PubMed]. *Trauma, Violence & Abuse, 20*(1), 3–21. doi:10.1177/1524838016683456

This research was previously published in the International Journal of Social Media and Online Communities (IJSMOC), 11(2); pages 35-57, copyright year 2019 by IGI Publishing (an imprint of IGI Global).

Chapter 69

An Evaluation of the Effects of Social Media on Client:
Advertising Agency Relationships in the UK

Kristina Krasimirova Dimitrova
Birmingham City University, Birmingham, UK

Steve MacKay
Birmingham City University, Birmingham, UK

ABSTRACT

High level of informality in the relationship between brand managers and advertising account representatives has been described as factor affecting positive work dynamic and long – term success. Although means of informal communications such as emails are still used, social networks have been gaining increasing popularity in the business landscape. This paper examines the effects of social media on client – agency relationships with focus on Facebook as an example of personal network. The methodology combines primary and secondary research. The paper reviews literature on client – agency relationships and social media, which provide the foundation for primary research. The paper concludes that connecting on Facebook with a client or agency representative is a way of showing the relationship has moved beyond strictly a working one. However, connecting with a work contact on Facebook should not be done in order to make the work relationship stronger. The study offers recommendations for practitioners and direction for future research.

INTRODUCTION

The Internet has been transforming all areas of everyday life and the business environment for years. Over the last decade social networking sites have drastically changed the way people communicate and do business. Almost every employee today has some kind of online presence on social media sites and although these platforms vary based on function and use, it is true to say that social media is increasingly blurring the lines between personal and professional relationships.

DOI: 10.4018/978-1-7998-9020-1.ch069

Bearing in mind the nature of the marketing and communications industry, the client – agency relationship is a highly complex one. The importance of a good relationship between brand and agency account managers for a successful project outcome cannot be questioned. In "The Implications of the Internet on the Advertising Agency-Client Relationship" Durkin & Lawlor (2001) found that a high level of informality in the personal relationship of a client representative and agency executive was often described as a factor affecting long-term success.

Although the study mentioned above states phone calls as the most common means of informal communication, it is worth noting that the paper is not recent and has not taken into account the evolution of the Internet and the recent shift in technology which has resulted in the rise of social networking sites and changed the way people communicate today.

Since 2003, social networking sites have been gaining increasing popularity in the cultural and business landscape. Although some academic literature on how organisations can use social networking sites for businesses and recruitment purposes exist, there is little research on whether or not client representatives should be connected with advertising agency executives on personal social media sites such as Facebook, and if so, how such interaction affects their working relationship.

The aim of this paper is to address this and explore the connection between the two topics. This paper focuses on Facebook as an example of personal social networking site and examines if and how connections between clients and agencies influence their working relationship.

The Literature Review looks at academic literature on the two topics. The Methodology part states the types of research undertaken and the reasons they are considered appropriate. The most relevant insights from the primary research are discussed in the Findings section, while key results are analysed in the Conclusions section. The paper concludes with Recommendations for Practitioners, Direction for Future Research and possible research topics that stemmed from the main findings.

Research Objectives

This paper pursues the following objectives:

- To outline the nature of client – agency relationships within the advertising industry;
- To assess the different ways in which clients and advertising agencies maintain working relationships; investigate ways of communication between them;
- To critically review the academic literature available on the topics of client-agency relationships and social media (with focus on Facebook);
- To evaluate the effects of social networks on client – agency relationships and the way in which online connections between these brand and account managers influence the working relationship;
- To make recommendations for practitioners in the industry and further academic research based on the findings.

LITERATURE REVIEW

Types of Agencies

An advertising agency is a service business dedicated to creating, planning and handling advertising for its clients. Within the advertising industry sector, two broad categories can be identified – specialist and full service. Specialist agencies focus on specific sectors (for example print, direct mail) whereas full service agencies include all of the services offered by specialist agencies and combine them into one package for their clients (Keynote, 2012).

The Client – Agency Relationship

Further literature suggests that a good relationship between the client and the agency depends on co-operation behaviour between both parties and smooth-working relations for mutual benefit (Ellis & Johnson, 1993; Waller, 2004). A study carried out by Levin, E. & Lobo, A. (2011) identified four key themes as to why clients use agencies, which are: special knowledge and creative ideas; working with people not internally linked with the client's brand and image; experience through working with other products and brands; and in order for the client's staff to focus on core business activities rather than specialised services that can be outsourced.

Although it is true to say that for a successful client-agency relationship every team member is important (for example designers, developers, planners), it should be noted that the people who lead these teams are mostly kept responsible for ensuring the good working relationship. These people are the agency account executives/managers/directors and the brand managers. As Haytko (2004) says, "the interorganisational relationship remains steadfastly in the hands of a few boundary-spanning account management personnel, primarily between the agency account executive and the client brand manager."

Factors Influencing Successful Relationship

Academic literature and a number of studies have been published on the importance of client – agency relationships, approaches for maintaining working relationships and factors influencing successful, long – term relationships. They have identified that "an effective advertising agency – client relationship is driven by both personal and structural factors; personal, referring to the interpersonal dynamics between agency executive and client representative such as advice, trust, empathy and structural, including the range of agency services being offered (media options and expertise, creativity within these media, value for money, results). Thus, the agency's goal is to add value in both personal and structural contexts." (Meenaghan, T. & B. Patton, 1995)

Murray, R. (2009) summarises four factors that have an influence on the success of the client-agency relationship. These factors are:

- **Work Product:** Creative strategy, execution, media planning and media buying, research, marketing strategy;
- **Work Pattern:** Authority structure, approval process, deadlines and timing, productivity of meetings, quality of communication;
- **Organisational Factors:** Corporate policy, organisation structure, organisation politics;

- **Personnel and Relationship Factors:** Competence, experience, rapport/comfort, energy levels, trust/respect, control patterns, personnel turnover.

In "The Implications of the Internet on the Advertising Agency-Client Relationship" (2001), Durkin & Lawlor found that a high level of informality in the personal relationship between client representative and agency executive was often described as a factor affecting long-term success. These factors are also important for developing trust and commitment.

To examine the commitment from the client's perspective, Cater and Zabkar (2009) conducted a study consisting of three components: calculative, affective and normative commitment. They tested the relationships between three dimensions of commitment and social bonds, trust and satisfaction in the context of professional business service providers and their clients. The results of the model they developed showed that affective commitment is the only one of the three components that significantly influences customer loyalty. They note that affective commitment means "that firms want to stay in the relationship because they like their partner, enjoy the partnership and feel a sense of loyalty and belongingness." Based on this finding, this paper examined whether connection between agency and brand managers on Facebook have an effect on the affective commitment and whether it can be a factor that increases the trust between the representatives.

Relationship Management between Client and Agency Representatives

Waller (2004) notes that advertising agencies place a great deal of effort on obtaining and maintaining a positive client-agency relationship. Thus, relationship management in client-agency relationships is vital for the success or failure of those relationships.

Waller (2004) mentions that the study of relationship development and maintenance observes two areas – the factors that may cause satisfaction/dissatisfaction by the client with how the agency is taking care of its business, and whether the advertising agency executives and client representatives share the same attitudes towards particular topics.

This is also confirmed in a study on clients' expectations of their advertising agencies by Levin and Lobo (2011), who found that, some of the participants in the study discussed the client-agency relationship by making reference to marriages. If we interpret this further, it means that there needs to be "a match" between the client and the agency. Both need to have shared values and ethics and there needs to be a comfort factor between the organisations, as well as the individuals within them. Without such chemistry it is unlikely that such partnership will be successful or have a prolonged existence.

Importance of Interpersonal Factors in Client – Agency Relationships

Haytko (2004) notes that "the importance of the personal relationship for both advertiser and the agency is heightened by the fact that the interactions between key personnel (very specific human capital) in each firm drive the processes and outcomes that result from the interfirm relationship."

As the focus of this research is the effect of Facebook on client-agency relationships, it pays more attention to the personal factors affecting the working relationship.

The author also summarises Wackman's survey (1987), which found that relationship factors become increasingly important over time compared to more tangible performance measures.

Although it is not the single most important factor when choosing an agency, it is evidenced that developing personal relationship with the agency or client personnel increases the commitment and trust between both parties, which in turn results in a long-term relationship. Morgan, Robert M. et. al (1994) commitment-trust theory of relationship marketing also suggests that commitment and trust are the key factors in on-going exchange relationships.

However, it should be noted that a model developed by Cater and Zabkar (2009) which included three dimensions of commitment in the context of professional business service providers (affective, normative and calculative) revealed that trust and social bonds have no significant relations to either normative or calculative commitment while a relation of overall satisfaction with normative and calculative commitment is negative.

Social Media Networks and the New Ways of Communication between Clients and Agencies

Communication (especially between account executives and brand managers) is one of the most important factors for a successful client-agency relationship and one of the main factors for the termination of many relationships. While traditional ways of communication such as phone calls and emails are still relevant, over the last decade social networking sites that enhance communication at both personal and professional level have been growing to the point of explosive use. Platforms like LinkedIn, Facebook and Twitter have transformed the way people connect and communicate with one another. They have also made it very easy to find the right people to whom to communicate to.

"The introduction of social media in companies enables a new method of communication among colleagues and with customers. Although social media is on the top of the agenda for many companies to date, there seems to be very limited understanding of the usage of social media for work-purposes, information sharing, knowledge and relationship management." (Leftheriotis & Giannakos, 2013, p. 134)

Some of the most popular social networks include Facebook, Twitter and LinkedIn, differentiating from each other based on their functions and usage. For example, Twitter is a micro-blogging platform that makes connection and communication possible with all users in the network in an instant. It is also usually open to the public and anyone can have access to a user's Twitter profile. LinkedIn is mostly used as a professional social network where people can connect on a professional level. Facebook, on the other hand is used as a more personal social networking site, where users usually connect with people they know and share photos, videos and status updates on a more emotional level. Having said that, sometimes there is confusion about which social network is best suited or appropriate for a certain purpose.

Another movement that has had significant impact in the way people communicate with friends, families and colleagues is the proliferation of smartphones and the rise of mobile messaging. While mobile messaging (or instant messaging) was designed for consumers, it is increasingly used in the enterprise (TechTarget, 2016). Moreover, a survey conducted by market intelligence company IDC in 2014 showed that over the next 12 months, 14% of companies will use text messaging to communicate with colleagues and 19% will use it to generate direct sales (FierceMobileIT, 2014). This is noteworthy, mainly because of a key feature of mobile messaging: emoji. These are series of icons used to add nuance, personality and informality to digital communications. Like instant messaging, emoji were first designed for consumers, but the rise of mobile messaging in the enterprise is making them increasingly acceptable in business communications (see Figure 1).

Figure 1. Popular emoji

This shift of communication results in blurring the lines between personal and professional networks and personal and professional communications. As an article in *American Agent & Broker US* (2009) suggests "although not everyone is comfortable with using sites like Facebook to connect with professional contacts, it is wise to be prepared for these types of requests."

Facebook: Characteristics and Implications for Fostering Business Relationships

While there is some literature on the benefits and risks for companies using social media for work purposes (Fortino, 2010; Jussila, 2013; Langheinrich, 2010) there is little that focuses specifically on how the use of personal social networks like Facebook affect the interpersonal relationship between clients and service providers which in turn might affect the interfirm working relationship. Again, there is little literature on this topic which focuses specifically on client-agency relationship in the advertising industry.

Jussila et al. (2013) found that "there is a need for companies to support formal and informal learning related to social media use in especially B2B context and external social media use with customers and partners."

From the earliest days of social media, platforms were presented as tools for making connections, promoting human connectedness and community building (Dijck, 2013). Dijck (2013) states that for most users there is a distinct difference between one's professional persona, addressed mainly to colleagues and employers, and one's self-communication towards friends. However, Facebook and other social networking sites favour the idea of people having one transparent identity that they disclose online, releasing habitual behavioural data and personal information in the process of socialising. While initially platforms like Facebook were seen as places for personal self-expression, users have gradually come to understand the art of online self-presentation and the importance of social networking sites as tools for professional self-promotion.

Summary

Taking the literature on client-advertising agency relationships and combining it with the existing studies on social media networks and particularly Facebook, this paper investigates whether connections between advertising agency account executives and brand managers have an effect on the interpersonal relationship between them and if in turn this affects the working relationship. In an attempt to identify the effects of Facebook on the interpersonal and working relationship between clients and advertising agencies, a number of key themes from the literature review were tested in the primary research that was carried out. The key themes were:

- The most important factors for a successful client-agency relationship;
- The importance of interpersonal relationships between the agency and client representatives for the working relationships;
- The use of Facebook as a tool to connect with client/agency representatives;
- The effects of connecting with client/agency representatives on Facebook.

RESEARCH METHODOLOGY

Both primary and secondary research was required in order to identify the effects of social media within the client-agency relationships and to examine how connections on Facebook between account executives and brand managers affect the working relationship.

Secondary Research

In order to identify areas where primary research was needed, it was necessary to look at studies that have already been conducted. The secondary research examined for this project focused on literature on client-agency relationships and social media. More details can be found in the literature review chapter but to summarise, some of the main findings are:

- An effective client – advertising agency relationship is driven by both personal and structural factors;
- Key personnel in the client-agency relationship are the account executives and the client brand managers;
- A high level of informality in the relationship of client representative and agency executive was often described as a factor affecting long-term success. These factors are also important for developing trust and commitment;
- Affective commitment significantly influences loyalty;
- Developing personal relationship with the agency or client personnel increases the commitment and trust between both parties, which in turn results in a long-term relationship;
- Social networking is among one of the most significant business developments of the twenty first century and adds another dimension to the communication among colleagues and with clients;
- This shift in the means of communication results in blurring the lines between personal and professional networks and personal and professional communications;
- Keeping in contact with customers / clients is the second reason why employees use social media for work;
- While initially platforms like Facebook were seen as places for personal self-expression, users have gradually come to understand the art of online self-presentation and the importance of social networking sites as tools for professional self-promotion.

The main issue with the secondary research was that there was little literature combining both topics: client-agency relationships and social media. In addition, where there was some connection between the two, and specifically on the effect of Facebook for businesses, the studies focused on how Facebook affects the communications between businesses and their customers as opposed to how connections between agency and client representatives on Facebook affects the working relationship. Therefore, there was a requirement for further research that combines these topics in a specific way.

Primary Research

The type of primary research used for this paper was semi-structured in-depth interviews with both client side and agency members. The interviews took place in February, July and August 2014. The semi-structured interviews were considered appropriate for this study as "the interviewee is given the opportunity to talk freely about events, behaviour and beliefs in relation to the topic area." (Saunders et al., 2012) As the respondents were selected both from client and agency side, the semi – structured interviews covered a list of main themes but the questions varied from interview to interview.

This research method was used in order to let the respondents answer the questions freely and in an honest way. The collected data is qualitative data as it includes details and insights from the interviewees which are not possible to access with quantitative data. Semi-structured interviews were considered the most appropriate for the following reasons: focus groups were unsuitable because the participants had a lot of experience on the subject and a lot to contribute, therefore it was important to let them talk freely about the topic; surveys and questionnaires would not provide enough in-depth information required to understand the participants' views on the topic.

The purpose of the semi-structured interviews and the research strategy was not only to reveal and understand the "what" and the "how" but also to place more emphasis on exploring the "why". Semi-structured and in-depth interviews provide the opportunity to "probe" questions or build on the participants' responses, which adds significance and depth to the data obtained (Saunders et al., 2012).

Collection of Data

As mentioned above, the data was collected through in-depth semi-structured interviews which are particularly useful for exploratory studies like this one. Exploratory research is also said to be good "if you wish to clarify your understanding of a problem, such as if you an unsure of the precise nature of the problem." (Saunders et al., 2012)

The primary research can be described as an exploratory study as it has not yet been determined whether connections between account executives and brand managers on Facebook have effects on the working relationship and if so, whether these effects are positive or negative.

Selection of Participants

In order to understand the dynamics of the relationship and the effects of Facebook on the relationship participants from both client and agency side had be selected. It was felt that for the information to be credible the participants should have considerable experience with aspects of the relationship and be social media savvy. This included experience in different ways of managing the client – agency relationship, going through the different stages of the relationship as well as experience in using various social networks for professional and personal purposes.

It was felt that the best way of finding participants with this type of experience was to approach key personnel from both sides of the relationship – that is, account managers from agencies and brand managers. Overall around 30 potential candidates were approached directly. Eighteen of the approached individuals participated in the research. The interviewed respondents were nine agencies and nine client representatives.

The agency participants came from nine different marketing and advertising agencies, varying in size and based in either London or Birmingham, UK. The participants were either leading their division, held a senior position in the agency such as Head of Social or Account Director, or management position such as Digital Strategist or Account Manager and their responsibilities included regularly interacting with clients.

The respondents from the client side were based in London and Birmingham from companies ranging from automotive to fashion, retail, consumer electronics and property. The candidates held senior or managerial marketing and communication positions within their companies such as Communications Manager, Marketing Director, Chief Marketing Officer and Senior Communications Officer.

The Interview Process

Eight out of the total eighteen interviews were conducted during one to one meetings, while the other ten interviews were done over Skype as agreed by the participant and the researcher. The interviews lasted between 30 minutes to an hour. All interviews were recorded using a voice recorder and supported by note taking. The researcher had developed a question guide to follow to ensure that the main areas being researched were covered and in order to understand the opinions each of the interviewees had on particular areas of the topic.

The interview guide for agency and client respondents was slightly different as both operate in a different environment and their experience of the client – agency relationship differs. The questions covered the main areas of the research and the interviewer was free to ask further questions as the interviews were progressing. This helped the researcher to "be able to infer causal relationships between variables, understand the reasons for the decisions that your research participants have taken, or to understand the reasons for their attitudes and opinions" (Saunders et al., 2012).

Analysing the Data

After the interviews had been conducted it was found out that the responses from client and agency representatives were very similar at times, which is why the data was analysed and displayed by identifying themes, arguments and relationships that exist within the research results which are also related back to the objectives of the project.

Study Limitations

Certain limitations exist when conducting research using in-depth interviews that need to be taken into account. These limitations are:

- **Time Restraints:** Due to the nature of the research and the chosen method (semi-structured interviews) it was unclear how much time each of the interviews would last. Although all interviewees were very generous with their time, this factor put off some of the selected candidates, which resulted in them abandoning the interview and therefore participation in the research;

- **Generalisation of the Research:** Because of the scope of this study, it would not be possible to apply the results obtained through the research to all client – agency relationships as not enough research has been conducted to make assumptions about the effects of social media and specifically Facebook on client – agency relationships in general;

- **Reliability of the Research:** Saunders (2012) says that "the lack of standardisation in such interviews may lead to concerns about reliability" and that the reliability is concerned with whether "alternative researchers would reveal similar information". To the best knowledge of the researcher, similar project has not yet been investigated which can be both advantage and disadvantage: advantage as this is a new research area that could be the basis of further and more in-depth research into the topic; disadvantage as the researcher cannot rely on much academic literature about the chosen topic; this creates the need for the researcher to combine literature on the two main research areas (client – agency relationships and social media) and layer the findings in order to formulate new patterns and ideas which needed to be tested through the interviews.

FINDINGS

The main findings as a result of the primary research are discussed below as follows.

Factors for Successful Client: Agency Relationships

When respondents were asked to comment on the relationships they have with their clients or agencies, nearly all of them said they have good or positive relationships. When asked to elaborate on the question the respondents stressed on both personal and structural factors which reconfirm findings from the secondary research within the literature review. After describing the relationship as "good", one of the client representatives said that the agency "understands the business inside out which helps. They understand how we work and we understand how the agency works. It is hard for an agency to provide clients with good service that the company trusts if they do not fully understand the business". One of the agency respondents who is involved in doing a lot of real-time marketing on behalf of their clients said that the best type of relationships are the ones where "the client trusts you enough to let the agency implement the things they think are good without always having to sign off the work". All interviewees recognised the importance of creative ideas, execution and commercial awareness for the good relationship: "We find it very hard to work with designers who don't have business knowledge" said one of the client respondents, stressing on the fact that although creative execution is important, the strategic mindset of every member from the agency is crucial in order the work to be done without going back and forth. An agency respondent said that from experience some of the most important factors when clients select an agency include reputation and capability, level of service that the client expects to get, the quality of the people within the agency, the scale of ideas and creative approach.

The interviewees were then asked about the factors which they considered most important for a successful and long-term client – agency relationship. The main findings were:

- **Trust and Understanding:** These are fundamentally important factors for both client and agency representatives and it was found that the scale of trust between both depends on how much the agency understands the client's business, their objectives and how they work. One of the client representatives said: "In terms of these relationships, you want to be able to trust your agency" while another stated that "They are the branding police because they know us so well". From an agency perspective, it was found out that trust and understanding were also very important in order to get closer to the client, establish a durable relationship and help the client understand why the agency do what they do. It was said that "the best relationship is when you know your client's business inside out which enables you to come up with different solutions and excite them". "If a client trusts you to keep giving good advice and follow through with the things you said, the relationship will be strong. Likewise, if you trust the client to treat you well, perceive you as a trusted advisor and value the relationship, that will be a strong relationship", said one of the agency respondents. They also warned that in the marketing and advertising industry, as in life in general, it takes a lot of time to build up that trust but takes seconds to break it;
- **Partnership-like Relationships:** It was found that if there was good level of trust in the relationship, the client perceived the agency as a partner and an extension of their team, which was significantly important for the successful and long-term relationship between the two parties. One of the agency representatives advised that agencies should avoid having purely transactional relationship with their clients, especially if they aim for a long-term relationship. They shared that it is crucial to make clients feel comfortable sharing information about their business that could help the agency come up with new ideas and in order to do that, "they need to trust you and perceive you as a part of their team".

From the client's perspective, having an agency acting as their partner is fundamental: "We don't want to be just a bill to them and be seen as a way of growing their business. We want them to want to help our business and grow together". Another client representative stressed on the importance of the agency's willingness to collaborate and challenge the client, to be energetic, passionate and enthusiastic about the accounts they manage. They advised that for a successful long-term relationship, the agency should not be thinking simply about what they could sell the client but rather sell their ideas first and suggest solutions in a credible way – "Sell your ideas, not your product first. It is more powerful to offer ideas first." (Figure 2)

Figure 2. Factors for successful client – agency relationships

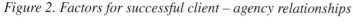

Importance of Personal Relationships between Client and Agency Personnel

Many of the interviewees mentioned the importance of good chemistry between the key people from the client and the agency for the success of the relationship (see Figure 3).

A client representative said that in many ways a good personal relationship with the account person from the agency is "everything". They linked that to the trust factor between the two: "It definitely increases the trust. There are many agencies that can do the exact same job but you need to trust them when they tell you they will do something or when they advise you against a certain idea that you have suggested because they know certain aspects of the market a lot better than we do". Interestingly, the same client respondent had recently changed their advertising agency. When asked to compare the two agencies he stated: "We now work with a smaller agency. We get better attention, more personal service, better response and ideas. They are also more accurate in terms of finance (billing and forecasting) because the clients they work with are the same size as us and they understand that. The team we work with also felt more "us" and in terms of these relationships this is really important. You can see many agencies which do the same thing but nine out of ten times you could pick an agency because there is better chemistry – you feel you could brief them in a more relaxed way and that type of closeness matters. The closer you are, the more honest and open you will be with each other."

Another client representative reconfirmed the above by saying that if they didn't get along with their agency, they would not trust them enough to treat them as a part of their team. However, they also noted that even if they worked with someone they would not be friends outside work, it is really important to have mutual respect in order to deliver good work.

From an agency point of view good chemistry is just as crucial for the success of the relationship. An agency respondent said that if the key people from the client and the agency don't get along, this is going to result in trust issues and make approval of the work more difficult. They recognised the effect a good personal relationship can have on the account. For example, if a client representative gets along really well with an account person in the agency, and if that account person leaves the agency and moves to another, it is possible that the client may go with them. However, they said that the above impacts more the day to day side of things and has less influence on the bigger strategic decisions which usually come from the client's CEOs who are not that involved in the day to day process.

Another agency interviewee said that good chemistry between key members from the client and the agency are paramount as "people buy from people". They said that good personal relationships with clients are at the forefront of everything their agency does: "You can present the best ideas but people would naturally respond to the people in the room."

Based on the answers of all interviewees it can be seen that good personal relationships undoubtedly helps improve the working relationship. Having a good personal relationship with the client or agency enables the depth of the relationship to happen on a higher level. When asked if they see a difference between working with a client or agency representative who they have a close personal relationship with as opposed to working with someone they are not very close to, most of the respondents agreed that this affects the working relationship in a positive way. However, they also noted that there should be a difference between business friendship and friendship outside of work and that a sense of professionalism should be maintained in most cases. Some of the comments were:

It is always good to set up a strong business relationship first and develop that into a business friendship once you feel comfortable enough. It is better for the business if you are working with a supplier that you feel comfortable socialising with and not have a strictly business relationship.

We work in a very pressured environment. Let's say you need something done quickly and you know two people who are able to do the job. If you have a good personal relationship with one of them you trust them more, so you are definitely more likely to call them first. It's a natural decision. Like calling a friend when you need a favour.

You have to know the boundaries. Business and pleasure can overlap at times but you have to be aware of that. If you have good personal relationship with someone this can help when you present a client your ideas about their business, they will naturally be more open. The process won't be very formal. When discussing business ideas while having a chat on a more personal level the client is less likely to be guarded, in terms of their budget or their comments, for example. It also helps spot potential issues that may have risen and deal with them in a more relaxed way.

Figure 3. Importance of good personal relationship for the working relationship

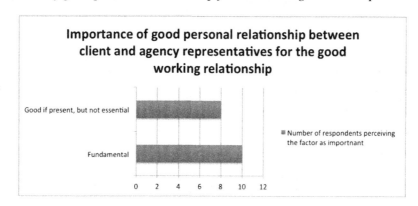

Usage of Social Media Platforms

In order to understand how these client – agency relationships translate online the interviewees were asked about the social media channel they use and what they use them for. The majority of the answers can be summarised as follows.

Facebook is used mainly for personal and social reasons, such as keeping in touch with friends and families. In some cases, Facebook was also used for business reasons such as monitoring competitor activity or finding new and engaging brand content. In almost all cases the interviewees had a client or agency representative they used to work with as a friend on Facebook. The content the respondents usually shared on Facebook included their hobbies, pictures, status updates and news articles.

LinkedIn was perceived as the obvious social media platform to connect with work contacts. All respondents said they did not have any problem connecting with people from work on LinkedIn as they saw it as the right medium to do that. This could be mainly because a user's profile on LinkedIn is usually quite static and displays career history.

Twitter was also mentioned as a preferred platform to connect with people on a more professional level, especially as this social media channel is usually open to the public so anyone can see what a person posts.

As the aim of this research is to concentrate specifically on Facebook and investigate if and what effects it could have on the client – agency relationship, questions followed around the respondents' usage and experience of Facebook, connected with their working relationship. To understand whether they differentiate their online persona on different social media platforms the respondents were asked whether they agree or disagree with the following statement:

You have one identity. The days of you having a different image for your work friends or co-workers and for the other people you know are probably coming to an end pretty quickly.

The answers varied widely which resulted in a mix of respondents agreeing and disagreeing with the statement. However, the interviewees recognised that social media platforms are blurring the lines between personal and professional relationships and that people as well as businesses and brands are still unsure how to make the best use of them.

One of the reasons for disagreeing with the statement was the comparison of how a person might act around family and friends as opposed to someone they meet for the first time in real life:

People have different identities online and they use different platform for their needs. Facebook is very much all about you as an individual – your name is verified, your date of birth, hometown and where you live are displayed. Twitter, on the other hand, is really open and democratic, which is great. It is a far more effective tool for building business relationships. Humans are very complicated characters and they need different channels in order to show their different sides.

People have different personas and react differently to other people. Just like you have a different relationship with your colleagues, family, friends, partner, you have different personas on different social media platforms. The persona is not any different, it is just the way of interaction that differs. On LinkedIn I am explicit about business because it is a more relevant platform to speak about that. On Facebook I share my hobbies and interests. There is a certain expectation of what you are going to see on each platform.

Interestingly, one of the reasons for agreeing with the statement was the fact that as people use various social media platforms it is becoming increasingly difficult to "hide" your real identity. This ties in with the response above and the fact that people do not have different identities online but rather use the different social media platforms to choose which side of their persona they show. Some of the responses in favour of the statement included:

When you post something on social media, you have to remember it is public, regardless of your profile settings. If you wouldn't say it to the world, don't post it on Facebook because it will come back and haunt you. Couple of years ago, people used to post things that portrayed them in a way they wanted to be seen from peers and family but as social media is becoming integrated in every aspect of our lives, it is harder to portray yourself any other way than the way you are.

My persona in and outside Facebook won't be any different, my tone is the same. It is difficult to maintain a very different tone on social media because inevitably you will have an overlap. Everything on the Internet and social media is so transparent and everyone is able to find you very easy, profile you and display adverts to you based one core persona that you really have.

The answers overlapped as both those agreeing and disagreeing with the statement mentioned authenticity on social media as a crucial factor:

I am who I am across all mediums but what I choose to share across them can be totally different. Not because I am a different person but because it depends on the audience that you have in each of those platforms. But if someone looks at my different profiles, authenticity can be sees across all of them.

A person has different identities throughout the day depending on their work, their company, their friends their environments. It's the same with social media as every environment requires a different persona and you create a persona to match these different environments.

To Friend or Not to Friend Client / Agency Representative on Facebook

Based on the respondents' opinions, they were then asked if they see any value in befriending a client or agency representative on Facebook and how they would react if they were to receive a friend request from someone that they work with (see Figure 4, Figure 5, and Figure 6). It is interesting that the majority of respondents would not initiate such action but would accept if a client or agency representative sends them a friend request. In the majority of the cases the interviewees said that they would accept a friend request only if the person initiating it has already become a friend outside of work and if both parties have established a good personal relationship as opposed to strictly business relationship. There has to be some form of a relationship and both parties have to have something in common before adding each other on Facebook. For example, adding someone could be more acceptable if both the client and agency representative have spoken offline about non-work-related things such as plans for the weekend, interests, hobbies or if they have attended a social event together. One of the respondents said: "If I am comfortable turning up to a client meeting in a T-shirt, I wouldn't mind adding them on Facebook." Usually agency representatives were more likely to accept a friend request if they were to receive one from a client, than the other way around. Both clients and agency representative could see the benefit of this action:

If I friend someone on Facebook it means that we are good enough friends which will improve the working relationship because we have that sort of connection.

It's not a bad thing - it helps you get to know the account manager on a personal level. It helps the relationship as long as your page doesn't display anything inappropriate that you don't want people you know on a professional level to see.

You get to learn more about the person behind the name which is really useful from a relationship point of view as you get closer to them, find out about their friends and family, what they have been doing over the weekend. You can have these conversations and even unlock new friends and relationships.

Figure 4. Number of respondents who would initiate befriending a client/agency representative on Facebook

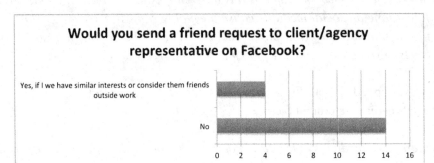

Figure 5. Number of respondents who would accept a friend request sent by a client/agency representative on Facebook

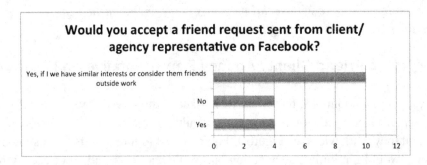

Figure 6. Number of respondents who see value in receiving more information about client/agency representatives as a result of being friends with them on Facebook

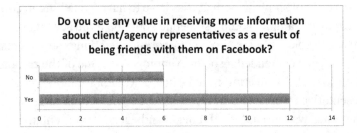

The main reasons for both client and agency representatives' choice not to add people they work with included the issue of their reputation being affected and the fact that if a person didn't know them directly things posted online could be misinterpret, which could potentially lead to work-related problems. Some of the interviewees noted that these judgements as to who you let in on Facebook should be firstly up to the person, their own views and that they should also consider their company culture and how this could be interpreted. Although interviewees realized the importance of being mindful about what they post on social media, some of the respondents also noted that in the marketing and advertising industry everyone appreciates that everything can be shared online – for example pictures from nights out or socials – and that people in this industry would not see it as a bad thing. However, this might affect people working in other industries.

Effects of Facebook on the Client: Agency Relationship

When asked about their opinion on the effect of Facebook on the quality of the interpersonal and working relationship between the client and the agency, the interviewees had mixed views. Some of them thought that it increases the trust and that this personal interaction can be very valuable. It is a way of saying "I work with you but you are also a friend outside of work", and communicates the closeness between the people in the relationship. According to some of the respondents, this can be quite helpful on a personal level and build a stronger working relationship by providing better interaction between the key people in the relationship. Others realised the potential of Facebook to impact positively the interpersonal relationship but did not necessarily think that it could have an effect on the working relationship as this platform is still considered very much a personal network rather than a place to build and manage relationships with people from work. If the personal connection is missing adding a client/agency representative on Facebook is usually seen as an intrusive action.

This was followed by a question asking the respondents whether they think receiving more information about the client or agency representative they work with via Facebook enables them to have a better relationship with them and translate that information into meaningful gestures. The answers were again split. Some of the respondents thought this might be beneficial for both client and agency representatives. For example, as agencies constantly try to keep clients happy, receiving personal information about them via Facebook such as getting engaged can be translated into a meaningful gesture which the client could appreciate. A client representative stated: "If I have crossed that line and added someone from the agency on Facebook I would usually expect it. I wouldn't dislike them if they didn't do anything about it but I would appreciate that they have taken the time to acknowledge something from my personal life. By letting someone in that area of your life you have to expect that."

You can learn about people's interest outside of work which can help you build that trusted relationship but you have to be careful and do that in an appropriate way.

An agency respondent shared that as a result of becoming friends with a client on Facebook they realised they shared the same music taste and this helped them bond on a personal level: "It helps build that personal relationship and to surprise the client. If you can connect on that level it definitely helps but there needs to a balance between wanting to get to know your client as much as possible and the level of professionalism."

However, some clients and agency representatives see this way of obtaining information as a "lazy way to manage client – agency relationships", a "shortcut for human interaction" and "a bit manipulative way of selling something" that could put clients off.

A client representative noted that this type of interaction could also benefit clients. For example if there is a deadline for a report approaching and the client expects it, if they see their account manager posting on Facebook something like "We just had a five hour working lunch" then they could really question the reason behind the delay of the work.

Summary

To summarise, some of the main findings are:

- Positive client – agency relationships depend on both structural and personal factors;
- Some of the most important factors for a successful long – term client – agency relationship are trust, understanding and to ability for the client to see the agency as an extension of their in-house team;
- Good personal relationship between client and agency representatives positively impacts the working relationship;
- Social media is blurring the lines between personal and professional relationships;
- Respondents were generally reluctant to connect with client or agency representatives on Facebook if they did not consider that person a friend offline;
- There is value in receiving more personal information about client or agency representatives via Facebook if this is done in an appropriate way;
- From a work perspective connecting on Facebook is usually more helpful for agencies but clients can also benefit from that;
- Connecting on Facebook is a way of showing that the two parties have established a good personal relationship outside of work but should not be seen as a way of making a working relationship stronger or more personal.

CONCLUSION

After reviewing the secondary and primary research, the following conclusions can be presented:

All respondents agreed that both personal and structural factors are important for successful client – agency relationships therefore agreeing with the theory developed by Meenaghan and Patton (1995).

All respondents agreed that trust and understanding are among the most important factors for successful long-term client – agency relationship. These factors were crucial to perceive the agency as a partner and "extended team" for the client, which reconfirmed the findings of Cater and Zabkar (2009) that affective commitment significantly influences customer loyalty and the commitment-trust theory of relationship marketing developed by Morgan et al. (1994).

10 out of 18 respondents strongly felt that good personal relationships are paramount for the good working relationship and that they affect the working process. Eight respondents felt that good working relationship can exist even if good personal bonds are not present because "the process is the same whether you get along or not" and also depends on the way the client likes to work: "some clients like to maintain a purely business relationship". One of the agency respondents stated that although good personal relationships are important for the day to day work interactions, they do not necessarily affect the more important strategic decisions which usually come from very senior client members. In addition, one of the client representatives stated that good working relationships can exist even if the two parties are not very close but rather have mutual respect for each other.

The main social media networks that were mentioned were Facebook, Twitter and LinkedIn. Although not all of the respondents were equally active on these networks, all of them had a profile on the three platforms. It was found that 17 out of 18 interviewees used each of these platforms differently and separated their personal and professional use of social networks, as found by Dijck (2013). It was generally found that the respondents used Facebook mainly for personal communications with friends and family, Twitter mainly as a business and micro-blogging tool but also sharing some sort of personal information, while LinkedIn was used primarily for connecting with business contacts, such as current and former clients or colleagues. One agency respondent said that they do not make a separation and "use everything for everything" because "my work is part of my life and my life is part of my work."

Interestingly then, although most of the respondents made a distinction in how they use Facebook, Twitter and LinkedIn, 8 out of 18 agreed that they have one transparent identity that they disclose online, releasing habitual behavioural data and personal information in the process of socialising. Even though they used the social networks in a different way and for different purposes, these inevitably overlapped and resulted in one core persona that they really have.

It was generally felt that both client and agency representatives are reluctant to connecting with people they work with on Facebook if they had not established a good personal relationship first and if they didn't consider the person a friend offline. The main reasons for that was the fact that they used Facebook mainly for personal reasons and because by letting a work contact who did not know them as a person well enough the respondents' posts on Facebook might be misinterpret which could result in damaging their reputation and credibility.

The value of having a work contact on Facebook and receiving more information about them was generally favoured from the respondents as 12 out of 18 respondents said it could potentially improve the working relationship and build the trust between the two contacts if they have a strong personal connection. Two agency respondents said they did not see any positives of adding clients on Facebook, other two agency respondents were unsure and two client respondents said that receiving information about a client on Facebook is a lazy way of managing the client – agency relationship and that they could potentially see that as someone who is using their personal information to sell them things.

Overall it was believed that connecting with a client or agency representative is a way of showing that the two sides have developed a strong personal relationship outside work but that they should not add each other on Facebook in order to make the relationship stronger.

RESEARCH RECOMMENDATIONS

Recommendations for Practitioners

For Facebook to work in favour of client and agency representatives, the following should be taken into account:

- Clients and agency representatives should establish good personal relationship offline before adding each other on Facebook;
- Receiving personal information about the client/agency representative could be beneficial if done in an appropriate manner, so both parties should know where the lines are between business, personal and too personal relationships;
- Both parties should be mindful as to not to get too caught in social media as way of managing their working relationships.

Direction for Future Research

Based on this research there are a number of areas that could test the findings on a greater scale:

- Further in-depth and more scalable research should be conducted into the impact of social media on client/agency relationships involving both junior and senior members of staff, as junior employees usually are more involved in the day to day relationship;
- Further research should be conducted on the frequency of usage of Facebook and the usage of social media for work-purposes, information sharing, knowledge and relationship management.

Closing Thoughts

The explosion of social networks in recent years has had a transformational effect on the ways we communicate with friends, families and colleagues. As the marketing industry is one where informality between clients and agencies is important, blurring the lines between personal and professional relationships as result of using social media platforms is even more apparent.

Although Facebook has been the most popular personal social network, in 2015 the company launched a new beta product, called Facebook at Work aimed at corporations. Facebook At Work is a collaboration tool that lets colleagues communicate through a web interface or a mobile app, instead of using email. It has the same look, apps and tools as Facebook but exists as a separate portal from Facebook. Even if users choose to link their personal Facebook profile to their Facebook at Work profile nothing they post on their company's social network will be shared on their personal Facebook. Reviews of the new product state that Facebook's popularity will be its unique selling point, making it easy for users to adapt to the service (Wall Street Journal, 2015). Another positive feature is that users will be able to create a profile for themselves with position description and areas of expertise, which could "shrink faceless enterprises" (Tech Crunch, 2015). The service has already signed a number of businesses as clients, including financial company RBS and beer brand Heineken (The Drum, 2016).

Currently the product is marketed as a social network purely within a company but it will be interesting to see if this evolves in the future. Facebook at Work could potentially enable users from different companies to add and communicate with each other, which might create a good balance between connecting on social networks while still keeping a level of professionalism.

REFERENCES

American Agent & Broker. (in press). Execs Say "No" to Facebook Friending.

Bennett, J., Owers, M., Pitt, M., & Tucker, M. (2009). Workplace Impact of Social Networking. *Property Management, 28*(3), 138–148. doi:10.1108/02637471011051282

Cater, B. & Zabkar, V. (2009). Antecedents and Consequences of Commitment in Marketing Research Services: The Client's Perspective. *Journal of Industrial Marketing Management,* (38), 785 – 797.

TechCrunch. (2015). How Facebook at Work Could Shrink Faceless Enterprises. Retrieved from http://techcrunch.com/2015/01/14/making-any-corporation-a-startup-again/

Dijck, J. (2013). You Have One Identity: Performing the Self on Facebook and LinkedIn. *Media Culture & Society, 35*(2), 199–215. doi:10.1177/0163443712468605

Durkin, M., & Lawlor, M. (2001). The Implications of the Internet on the Advertising Agency – Client Relationship. *Service Industries Journal*, *21*(2), 175–190. doi:10.1080/714005026

Ellis, R. S., & Johnson, L. W. (1993). Agency theory as a framework for advertising compensation decisions. *Journal of Advertising Research*, *33*(5), 76–80.

FierceMobileIT. (2014). IDC's Social Business Survey Shows Dramatic Change in Terms of How We Work, Commect with Employees, Customers, Partners and Suppliers. Retrieved from http://www.fiercemobileit.com/press-releases/idcs-2014-social-business-survey-shows-dramatic-change-terms-how-we-work-co

Fortino, A., & Nayak, A. (2010). An Architecture for Applying Social Networking to Business. *Proceedings of the Applications and Technology Conference (LISAT)*. 10.1109/LISAT.2010.5478285

Haytko, D. (2004). Firm-to-Firm and Interpersonal Relationships: Perspectives from Advertising Agency Account Managers. Academy of Marketing Science Journal, (32), 312 – 328.

Jussila, J. J., Kärkkäinen, H., & Aramo-Immonen, H. (2013). *Social Media Utilization in Business-to-Business Relationships of Technology Industry Firms.* Computers in Human Behaviour, (30), 606 – 613.

Kangas, P. (2007). "Ads by Google" and Other Social Media Business Models. *VTT Tiedotteita – Research Notes*, 2384, 59.

Keynote. (2012). Advertising Agencies Market Report. Retrieved from https://www.keynote.co.uk/market-intelligence/view/product/10556/advertising-agencies/chapter/4/strategic-overview?highlight=marketing%20agencies

Langheinrich, M., & Kanjoth, G. (2010). Social Networking and the Risk to Companies and Institutions. *Information Security Technical Report*, *15*(2), 51–56. doi:10.1016/j.istr.2010.09.001

Leftheriotis, I. & Giannakos, M. (2013). Using Social Media for Work: Losing Your Time or Improving Your Work? *Computers in Human Behaviour*, (31), 134 – 142.

Levin, E., & Lobo, A. (2011). *Clients' expectations of their advertising agencies: creativity and relationship management.* Hawthorn, Australia: Swinburne University of Technology, Swinburne Research Bank.

Meenaghan, T., & Patton, B. (1995). *Marketing Communications in Ireland.* Dublin: Oak tree Press.

Morgan, R. M., & Hunt, S. D. (1994). The Commitment-Trust Theory of Relationship Marketing. *Journal of Marketing*, *58*(3), 20–34. doi:10.2307/1252308

Murray, R. (2009). *An Evaluation of Client-Advertising Agency Relationships Within the UK.* Unpublished undergraduate dissertation, Birmingham City University, Birmingham, United Kingdom

Saunders, M.N... (2012). *Research Methods for Business Students.* Harlow: Pearson.

TechTarget. (2016). Mobile Messaging for the enterprise. Retrieved from http://searchmobilecomputing.techtarget.com/feature/Mobile-messaging-for-the-enterprise

The Drum. (2016). Facebook at Work Banks 100,000 RBS Users in Prep for 2016 Launch. Retrieved from http://www.thedrum.com/news/2015/10/26/facebook-work-banks-100000-rbs-users-prep-2016-launch

Wackman, & ... . (1986/1987). Developing an Advertising Agency – Client Relationship. *Journal of Advertising Research, 26*(6), 21–28.

Wall Street Journal. (2015). Facebook at Work Hits App Stores. Retrieved from http://blogs.wsj.com/digits/2015/01/14/facebook-at-work-hits-app-stores/

Waller, D. (2004). *Developing an account-management lifecycle for advertising agency-client relationships*. Sydney, Australia: University of Technology, School of Marketing.

West, D., & Paliwoda, S. (1995). Advertising Client-Agency Relationships. The Decision-Making Structure of Clients. *European Journal of Marketing, 30*(8), 22–38. doi:10.1108/03090569610130089

Wilson, M. (2010). *Advertising Services in Australia,* IBISWorld Industry Report.

This research was previously published in the International Journal of Online Marketing (IJOM), 7(2); pages 23-41, copyright year 2017 by IGI Publishing (an imprint of IGI Global).

Chapter 70
Analyzing the Impact of Social Network Sites and Social Applications on Buying Attitude in Developing Nations:
Consumers' Engagement Using Flourishing Digital Platforms

MD Sarwar-A Alam
University of Science and Technology Beijing, Beijing, China

Daoping Wang
University of Science and Technology Beijing, Beijing, China

Kalsoom Rafique
Zhongnan University of Economics & Law, Wuhan, China

ABSTRACT

This article investigates the relationships among social network sites (SNSs) and social apps (SAPs) on consumers' online purchase attitude (OPA) with moderating effect of gender (GND). Structural equation modeling using SPSS and supporting tools was employed to represent the correlations among adopted constructs. To this end, the questionnaires were distributed to online shoppers from September 2017 and November 2017. The findings revealed the positive relationships of SNSs, i.e., Facebook, LinkedIn, Twitter, YouTube, and Pinterest on consumers' OPA. Second, it is found that SAPs, i.e., Whatsapp, Facebook messenger, Wechat, Instagram, and Snapchat have positive relationships on consumers' OPA. In addition, it is found that GND did not moderate the relationships among SNSs, SAPs, and consumers' OPA. This study furnishes insights how strategic managers can utilize such social media tools in marketing communications to empower consumers' OPA in today's era. Aside, study provides future studies for academicians and professionals.

DOI: 10.4018/978-1-7998-9020-1.ch070

INTRODUCTION

The flourishing networks of information communication have transformed the ways of interaction for the organizations and customers due to the widespread acceptability and usability of an Internet. Internet has become a prime element for entire business activities where experts have examined the significance of the Internet in information systems (IS) and information communication technologies (ICT) related studies in unlike contexts, dimensions, and business operations (e.g., Venkatesh & Davis, 2000; Waheed & Jianhua, 2018; Venkatesh, Morris, Davis, & Davis, 2003; Tiago & Verassimo, 2014; Mathews, Bianchi, Perks, Healy, & Wickramasekera, 2016; Constantinides, 2004; Waheed & Yang, 2017). Besides, the individuals are also motivated to adopt Internet-based social platforms to exchange information, ideas, cultural values, and entertainment using SNSs and SAPs in the present digital era (Venkatesh & Bala, 2008; Venkatesh & Davis, 2000; Tiago & Verassimo, 2014; Hwang & Park, 2013). It is one of the prominent changes in individuals' interaction because social networks have shifted habitats and behaviour of the consumers (Tiago & Verassimo, 2014).

The acceptability of advanced communication networks allows several benefits to advertising companies such as provides quick and reliable information within minimum cost (Bayo-Moriones & Lera-Lopez, 2007; De Vries, Gensler, & Leeflang, 2012). Besides, consumers' behaviour has changed where they often prefer to acquire product information using disparate online platforms (El-Gohary, 2012; Tiago & Verassimo, 2014; Ozok & Wei, 2010). It is reported that 51% of the worlds' population is an Internet user and such numbers are rapidly increasing (InternetWorldStats, 2017). It is reported that nearly 55% of the worlds' population lives in the Asia region and 49% of Asians are Internet users (Maddox & Gong, 2005; InternetWorldStats, 2017).

In marketing perspective, such hip produces new opportunities for marketers to motivate the buying intention of such a huge consumer market using SNSs and SAPs (Tiago & Verassimo, 2014). Several SNSs and SAPs are operational though few got more popularity among Internet users, e.g., Facebook (FB), LinkedIn (LD), Twitter (TW), Youtube (YT), and Pinterest (PT) (Levy & Birkner, 2011; Michaelidou, Siamagka, & Christodoulides, 2011; Howard, Mangold, & Johnston, 2014). According to the report, worldwide FB users are 79.6%, LD .21%, TW 5.8%, YT 1.9, PT 9.1% (GlobalStatCounter, 2017). Likewise, several users are using SAPs on their m-devices, but some SAPs are highly acceptable, e.g., Whatsapp, Wechat, Facebook Messenger, Instagram, and Snapchat. It is noted that worldwide the users of the Facebook messenger (FBM) are 102.2 billion, Instagram (IG) 76 billion, Snapchat (SC) 51 billion, Whatsapp (WA) 17.4 billion, and Wechat users are 1 billion (Statista, 2017c). Wechat is one of more progressive Chinese mobile apps which are attaining the widespread attention of the individuals started its operation in 2011(Statista, 2017b). Wechat is a multifunctional app such as social, business, and commerce (Lien and Cao, 2014; Statista, 2017b).

Such an extensive usage of SNSs and SAPs furnishes a new paradigm for marketers in gaining the massive attention of the individuals across the nations, including developing country such as Bangladesh. Bangladesh. Bangladesh is a country of Bangal which is official recognized the People's Republic of Bangladesh with approximately 166 million of the population (World Meters, 2017). The trend to shop a product is moving from conventional to online buying. Most of the Internet users prefer to buy a product online due to ease of usefulness, availability of product variety, and ease of communications (Van der Heijden, Verhagen, & Creemers, 2003; Wong et al., 2014). Nevertheless, several security risks are associated with online shopping, still 1.6 billion consumers desire to purchase a product online across the world (Miyazaki & Fernandez, 2001; Koong et al., 2008; Gefen et al., 2003). Such an attitude represents modern proliferation and adoption of an Internet as a source of online shopping. Online consumers' buying is associated with an extent to which an individual buys a product or service using an Internet (Constantinides, 2004). Online purchase intention or attitude is defined as a condition to which consumers intends to buy or make a transaction online (Pavlou, 2003). There are distinct factors that may affect consumers' OPA, including e-service, e-store, privacy, payment systems, fraud threats, ease of use, and trust factors (Pavlou, 2003; Van der Heijden et al., 2003; Park & Jun, 2003).

Several researchers suggested that developing a productive marketing strategy is an essential for strategic management to well trigger consumers buying intention, but the selection of a weak promotional tool may influence intention negatively (Brengman et al., 2001; Tsai et al., 2016). However, researchers have been revealed a drastic contribution of emerging technologies in sustaining and fostering the relationships with different customers and consumers, e.g., e-marketing (Coviello et al., 2001), Internet, Intranet, and extranet marketing (El-Gohary, 2012), email marketing (Pavlov et al., 2008), mobile marketing (Aydin & Karamehmet, 2017; El-Gohary, 2012), digital marketing (Tiago & Verassimo, 2014), database marketing (Coviello et al., 2001), online marketing (Kiang et al., 2000; Zhu et al., 2011), network and transactional marketing (Coviello et al., 2001), social media, social apps, and social networks sites marketing (Park et al., 2015).

The research on social media is still on infancy stage that needs more scholarly attention, especially in developing countries (Okazaki & Taylor, 2013). According to the theories and models of technology adoption, acceptance, and usage, e.g., theory of planned behavior (TBP), theory of reasoned actions (TRA), and technology acceptance model (TAM), the influence of growing technologies concerning to acceptance might be determined in distinct perspectives and domains. Therefore, to contribute to the respective literature and fulfill the literature gap, this study attempts to reveal whether SNSs and SAPs are sources to drive consumers' OPA. It is worth mentioning that the current study is one of the pioneer studies on evolving technologies, while the first study exploring the empirical nexus of SNSs and SAPs on consumers' OPA together with moderating influences of the GND.

To this end, the first aim is to explore the relationship of SNSs on consumers' OPA. Second, the goal is to investigate the association of SAPs on consumers' OPA. Third, the objective is to reveal a moderating impact of GND between the relationship of SNSs and consumers' OPA. Fourth, the aim is to evaluate the moderating impact of GND between the relationship of SAPs and consumers' OPA. The outlines of the study are organized as follows. The review of the literature, research model, and formation of the hypotheses are presented to next. Subsequently, research methodologies, i.e., sampling procedures, statistically tools, and measures of constructs are explained. The results outcomes are accordingly laid down. The final section is based on hypotheses testing, discussion, managerial implications, shortcoming, and future directions.

THEORETICAL BACKGROUND AND HYPOTHESES FORMATION

Several researchers have focused on IS and ICT related studies to ensure the significance and relationships of unlike thriving technologies (Rondan-Cataluña, Arenas-Gaitán, & Ramírez-Correa, 2015). Most of the studies attempted to reveal the acceptability and utilization of information technology in diverse business activities since 1970s (Rondan-Cataluña et al., 2015). In the different span of period, various theories and models have been presented and tested by researchers across the nations to understand the behavioural intentions of the individuals (Rondan-Cataluña et al., 2015; Hew, Lee, Ooi, & Wei, 2015;

Venkatesh et al., 2003; Venkatesh et al., 2012). According to Rondan-Cataluña et al. (2015), such highly focused ICT and IS theories and models includes theory of planned behavior (TPB), theory of reasoned actions (TRA), technology acceptance model (TAM), innovation diffusion theory (IDT), diffusion of innovation (DOI), and unified theory of acceptance and use of technology (UTAUT). According to Hew et al. (2015) and Taylor and Todd (1995), such theories and models are concerned with two streams such as acceptability, usage, and adoption of the technology, while the second stream is concerned with distinct models in determining the individuals' intention.

Ajzen and Fishbein (1980) defined TRA as an individuals' behaviour related to behavioral intention (BI) influenced by norms and attitudes. Davis (1989) stated TAM as an individuals' system usage affected by BI in two distinct ways, i.e., usage attitude and perceived usefulness (PU) where such model adopted from TRA. TBP has developed by Ajzen (1991) adding an additional factor 'perceived behavioral control' into TRA. Concerning to the diffusion of technology, DOI is considered as a most appropriate model across the globe having five elements such as observability, trialability, complexity, compatibility, and relative advantages (Rogers, 1995; Yahya, Nadzar, Masrek, & Rahman, 2011). Venkatesh et al. (2003) proposed UTAUT model by combing eight renowned models related to BI in the use of information technologies. Venkatesh et al. (2003) introduced four elements of UTAUT model in which two more elements were added by Venkatesh et al. (2012) in UTAUT2 model. The UTAUT and UTAUT2 model are based on six determinants, i.e., facilitating conditions, social influence, effort expectancy, performance expectancy, motivation, and habits of individuals' BI (e.g., Venkatesh et al., 2012; Venkatesh et al., 2003)

Subsequently, diverse tools and techniques were proposed and tested in unlike marketing practices in order to assure the significance of numerous revolutionary tools of marketing communications. For example, Coviello et al. (2001) presented a model of contemporary marketing practices (CMP) consisted of five distinct factors such as database marketing, interaction marketing, e-marketing, network, and transactional marketing. El-Gohary (2012) extended work on e-marketing and proposed a comprehensive model of e-marketing in three distinct streams, i.e., B2C, B2B, and B2G. The e-marketing model of El-Gohary (2012) is also extracted from IDT and TAM models.

In consumers and marketing perspective, researchers autonomously worked on distinct IS and ICT related research to contribute in respective literature across the nations in unlike contexts and perspectives (e.g., Coviello et al., 2001; El-Gohary, 2012; Cantrell et al., 2017; Wymbs, 2011; Pavlov et al., 2008; Aydin & Karamehmet, 2017; Tiago & Verassimo, 2014; Kiang et al., 2000; Persaud & Azhar, 2012). However, as earlier stated that research on SNSs, SAPs, and consumers' online purchase intention is still unexplored and on the initial stage, particularly in developing countries. To fulfill such literature gap, this study reveals the linkages of SNSs and SAPs, towards consumers' OPA together with the moderating role of gender and education from B2C perspective (see Figure 1).

Social Network Sites (SNSs)

SNSs are online platforms that assist the organizations to interact and foster relationships with distinct individuals using unlike social sites, including Facebook, Cyworld, Twitter, LinkedIn, Twitter, Ryze, QQ, Orkut, Cyworld, Youtube, Flicker, and Tumblr, Hi5, MySpace, Pinterest, Friendster, Dodgeball, and Bebo (Ellison, 2007; Howard et al., 2014; Tiago & Verassimo, 2014; Hwang & Park, 2013; Michaelidou et al., 2011). SNSs are an affordable tool which facilitates the users with a wide range of access and visible information of other users (Ellison, 2007). SNSs facilitate to bring diverse people in a single platform to collaborate, share knowledge, cultural values, and create good relationships (Ellison, 2007). According to Howard et al. (2014), the scope of promotional campaigns using SNSs is higher than traditional tools because SNSs furnish two-way communication, while conventional tools often belong to one-way communications. There are hundreds of SNSs available; however, few SNSs have achieved more popularity over the past decades, e.g., Facebook, LinkedIn, Twitter, YouTube, and Tumblr even in developing countries (Ellison, 2007; GlobalStatCounter, 2017; Levy & Birkner, 2011). According to theory of planned behavior (TBP), it is immensely critical to understand the individuals' behaviour, intention, and belief concerning to adoption and usage of ICT (Ajzen, 1991). Additionally, Ellison (2007) suggested that research on SNSs is an emerging phenomenon consequently academicians and practitioners are conducting more work to validate the findings across the nations. Based on above discussion and significance of SNSs in marketing communications and due to the higher engagement with such platforms, we hypothesized the following relationship to empirically contribute to the respective literature.

H$_1$: SNSs are positively correlated to consumers' OPA.

Figure 1. Research Framework

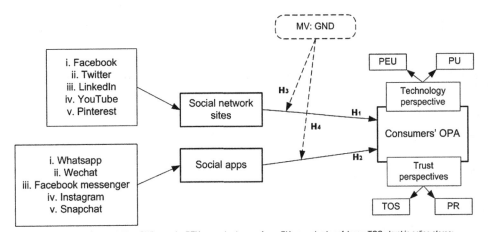

MV= moderating variables; GND= gender PEU= perceived ease of use; PU= perceived usefulness; TOS= trust in online stores; PR= perceived risk; OPI= online purchase attitude

Social Apps (SAPs)

SAPs also acknowledged as the mobile social networking applications (MSNAs) that consist of various apps, including Whatsapp, Wechat, Facebook Messenger, Instagram, Tumblr, Snapchat, and Pinterest (Logan, 2017; Thelwall et al., 2017). The trend and competition to adopt m-devices in distinct business practices have dynamically evolved in which developers have developed unlike mobile apps, including business apps, informational apps, assistance apps, entertainment apps, and social apps (Zhu et al., 2011; Logan, 2017). It is reported by Statista (2017a) that nearly 4.8 billion people are m-devices user across the world, while Zhu et al. (2011) argued that still, m-devices are getting a higher intention and popularity relatively than remainder communication devices. Furthermore, it is concluded that nowadays research on different aspects of social media has increased consequently experts are focusing to conduct more studies to understand insights of social media in distinct domains and context across the globe (Thelwall et al., 2017). Based on above discussion, the current concern is to empirically explore the impact of SAPs whether such apps influence on consumers' OPA. To this end, the following relationship is hypothesized based on a widespread acceptability and importance of SAPs in today's modern era.

H$_2$: SAPs are positively correlated to consumers' OPA.

Gender (GND) as a Moderator

The role of a moderator is critical that ensured an intensity of the relationships among variables (Garcia-Morales et al., 2006). GND is a factor that has been widely used in IS and ICT related work to disclose the effect of the males and female (Cho, 2011; Faqih & Jaradat, 2015). Dittmar et al. (2004) argued that usually male are more curious concerning to acceptance of technologies than females. Wong et al. (2014) and Venkatesh et al. (2003) argued that behaviour of the males and females is not same in adopting new technologies and shopping a product online. According to Yang (2005), GND effects on consumers' behaviour in purchasing a product/service online. However, the study of Waheed and Jianhua (2018) and Hew et al. (2015) revealed an insignificant effect of GND in ICTs studies in diverse dimensions and contexts. It is noteworthy to explore the effect of gender to contribute to the respective literature. Therefore, based on the above discussion, this study hypothesized the following relationship.

H$_3$: GND moderates between the relationship of SNSs and consumers' OPA.
H$_4$: GND moderates between the relationship of SAPs and consumers' OPA.

METHODOLOGIES

Study Sample and Procedures

The nature of the study is quantitative and data were gathered using questionnaires distribution to fifteen hundred online shoppers. Online shoppers were targeted because they can furnish better insights concerning to the present study. The consumers were targeted between September 2017 and November 2017 through personal visits and online techniques. All statements were culturally modified to avoid bias and clear understating of the respondents. The data collection is based on major cities of Bangladesh. Authors received back thirteen hundred questionnaires and after elimination of improper documents, eleven hundred were finally utilized for data analysis. Furthermore, questionnaires divided into two parts, i.e., demographic characteristics of the respondents and core questions regarding SNSs, SAPs, and consumers' OPA. In order to record the responses, five-point Likert scale employed inspired from the previous related studies. The scale ranged from strongly disagree to strongly agree where strongly disagree coded in SPSS as "1" strongly disagree "2" disagree, "3" neutral, "4" agree, and "5" strongly agree, respectively. Additionally, nominal and ordinal scales were used for demographic attributes. To treat the moderating variables, male is coded as "1" while females as "2," respectively.

Pilot Study

Data were collected from two major cities in order to conduct pre-testing using small sample size (n=50). Cronbach's alpha (CA) values were utilized to examine the reliability of major constructs and such techniques adopted from previous study Sung and Choi (2012). All values of CA are >0.7 as recommended criteria by Nunnally (1978). SNSs and SAPs employed as the independent variables (IV) while consumers' OPA as the dependent variable (DV). CA for SNSs stands at (α= .81), SAPs at (α = .80), and consumers' OPA at (α = .79). CA for each item of IV and DV were examined autonomously where all values are >.07 except one item of SNSs (Tumblr at α = .32) and one item of SAPs (Reddit at α = .28). Therefore, we deleted such items in the further collection of data because of poor CAs based on the current sample size.

Measures of Constructs

As earlier mentioned that SNSs and SAPs were adopted as IV, while consumers' OPA as a DV. Besides, GDR was used as the moderating variables to ensure the relationships intensity among SNSs, SAPs, and consumers' OPA. First, SNSs are measured using five top-ranked social sites, i.e., Facebook, LinkedIn, Twitter, YouTube, and Pinterest adopted from Howard et al. (2014) and Tiago and Verassimo (2014). Second, SAPs are measured using five renowned mobile apps, i.e., Whatsapp, Facebook messenger, Wechat, Instagram, and Snapchat, adopted from Lien and Cao (2014) and Logan (2017). Third, consumers' OPA are measured using two streams, i.e., technology aspect (TA1) and trust aspect (TA2) as already used Van der Heijden et al. (2003). TA1 further categorized into two perspectives, i.e., perceived ease of use (PEU) and perceived usefulness (PU), while TA2 is categorized into two perspectives, i.e., trust in online stores (TOS) and perceived risk (PR). All measurement constructs/items for consumers' OPA are adopted from Van der Heijden et al. (2003) (see Table 3).

Analysis Techniques

The statistical techniques were applied for data analysis using such as descriptive statistics (DS), Pearson's correlation (PC), discriminate validity (DVL), confirmatory factor analysis (CFA), and structural equation modeling (SEM). First, DS applied to obtain consumers' demographic profiles (see Table 1). Second, PC employed to ensure correlation/inter-correlation among constructs/items of SNSs, SAPs, and consumers' OPA. Third, DVL applied to determine the variations among study variables (see Table 2). Such variables might be examined using average extracted variance (AVEs) and associations between variables in which AVEs values should be higher than subsequent interrelationships values to assure DVL of variables (Deng et al., 2014; Leong et al., 2013). Fourth, CFA tool was used to explore the convergent validity (CV) and reliability (R) of the constructs (see Table 3). In such a scenario, CV is determined in two ways, i.e., FL and AVEs, while R is determined through CR. In order to ensure the CV the values of FL and AVEs should be higher than 0.5, while the values of CR should be higher than 0.7 (Kline, 2005; Fornell & Larcker, 1981; Nunnally, 1978). Finally, SEM employed to test all hypotheses of this study, as summarized in Table 4. SEM is used to treat the present variables where such technique have previously used by Burghy et al. (2012), Chang et al. (2009), and Hew et al. (2015). Additionally, the model fit indices for SEM were calculated that are best fitted as per the suggested criteria (see Table 5).

DATA ANALYSIS AND RESULTS

Demographic Profiles (DF)

Table 1 represents the DFs of target respondents based on seven unlike attributes, i.e., age, gender, marital status, education, since the SNSs user, and since using SAPs. The results indicate the higher ratio of male respondents (72%) relatively than female respondents (28%). The rest of DFs are illustrated as follows.

Table 1. Demographic profiles

Constructs/Items	Male		Female	
	Freq.	**%**	**Freq.**	**%**
Respondents' gender	800	72%	300	28%
Respondents' age in years				
16-20 year	100	12.5	050	16.7
21-24 year	140	17.5	080	26.7
25-29 year	450	56.3	120	40.0
>30 year	110	13.8	050	16.7
Respondents' marital status				
Single	600	75.0	250	83.3
Married	200	25.0	050	16.7
Respondents' education				
Undergraduate level	100	12.5	50	16.7
Graduate level	500	62.5	130	43.3
Post-graduate level	150	18.8	60	20.0
Other level*	050	6.30	60	20.0
Respondents using SNSs from (years)				
2-4 year	150	18.8	050	16.7
5-7 year	540	67.5	150	50.0
8-10 year	070	8.80	060	20.0
>11 year	040	5.00	040	13.3
Respondents using SAPs from (years)				
2-4 year	130	16.3	060	20.0
5-7 year	510	63.8	120	40.0
8-10 year	060	7.50	050	16.7
>11 year	100	12.5	070	23.3

*professional diploma holder/any other courses

Pearson's Correlations (PC)

PC was applied to reveal inter-association among each item and decisional criteria for PC is adapted from Taylor (1990). Taylor (1990) argued that values of PCs stand between -1 to +1 where higher positive values represent a higher positive association, while lower/negative values indicate lower or negative relationships as shown in Table 2.

Table 2. Pearson's correlations

	OPA	SNS	SAP	PEU	PU	TOS	PR
OPA	1.000						
SNS	0.429	1.000					
SAP	0.570	0.457	1.000				
PEU	0.645	0.349	0.598	1.000			
PU	0.632	0.267	0.408	0.428	1.000		
TOS	0.833	0.312	0.388	0.294	0.349	1.000	
PR	0.689	0.296	0.253	0.199	0.255	0.486	1.000

OPA = online purchase attitude; SNS= social network sites; SAP= social apps;; PEU= perceived ease of use; PU= perceived usefulness; TOS= trust in online stores; PR= perceived risks

Discriminate Validity (DVL)

Table 3 indicates the values of DVL which are calculated using square roots of AVEs and correlation between subsequent variables as recommended by Deng et al. (2014).

Table 3. Discriminate Validity

	PEU	PR	PU	SAP	SNSs	TOS
PEU	0.796*					
PR	0.200	0.769*				
PU	0.442	0.263**	0.718*			
SAP	0.610	0.256**	0.416**	0.832*		
SNSs	0.360	0.311**	0.274**	0.462**	0.796*	
TOS	0.313	0.509**	0.359**	0.378**	0.272**	0.838*

*Square roots of AVEs of particular constructs; ***Inter-correlation of the constructs; SNS= social network sites; SAP= social apps; PEU= perceived ease of use; PU= perceived usefulness; TOS= trust in online stores; PR= perceived risks

Confirmatory Factor Analysis (CFA)

Table 4 based on the values of means, SD, CR, FL, and AVEs. While the criteria discussed in the earlier section and results indicated the values of CR, FL, and AVEs are best fitted as per recommendations (e.g., Kline, 2005; Fornell & Larcker, 1981).

SEM and Fishers' Transformational Analysis Techniques

SEM and Fishers' transformational analysis tool employed to test hypotheses as summarized in Table 5. First, while calculating the major paths for the proposed relationships using SEM, few model fit indices were also evaluated through NFI, SRMR, and X^2/df Indices where output values are best fitted as per recommendations (see Table 5). Second, Fishers analysis techniques (FT) was used to explore the impact if GND among SNSs, SAPs, and OPA where initially regression values were converted to FT 'z' and afterward results assured such 'z' values for GND are less than critical values which is '1.96' and affirmed insignificant of GND among SNSs, SAPs, and OPA (Baron & Kenny, 1986), as summarized in Table 5.

Table 4. Confirmatory factor analysis

Constructs	Items	Mean	SD	Factor Loadings	Composite Reliability	AVEs
SNSs**	FB	3.811	1.003	0.614	.737	.634
	LD	3.884	1.018	0.632		
	TW	3.826	0.969	0.564		
	YT	3.833	0.965	0.581		
	PT	3.716	1.134	0.604		
SAPs**	WA	3.699	1.114	0.650	.754	.693
	FBM	3.864	1.063	0.651		
	WC	3.817	1.025	0.565		
	IG	3.868	0.926	0.588		
	SC	3.999	0.919	0.625		
TA1: PEU*	PEU1	4.017	0.963	0.503	.801	.550
	PEU2	3.884	0.949	0.738		
	PEU3	3.935	0.978	0.734		
	PEU4	3.946	0.970	0.677		
	PEU5	3.913	0.972	0.675		
PU*	PU1	3.795	0.976	0.694	.761	.516
	PU2	3.699	1.117	0.695		
	PU3	3.849	1.030	0.763		
TA2: TOS*	TOS2	3.553	1.475	0.706	.798	.703
	TOS3	3.524	1.074	0.630		
	TOS4	3.608	1.099	0.637		
	TOS5	3.738	1.051	0.709		
	TOS6	3.591	1.107	0.608		
	TOS7	3.578	1.219	0.556		
PR*	PR1	3.452	1.190	0.733	.799	.592
	PR2	3.697	1.031	0.734		
	PR3	3.472	1.149	0.721		
	PR4	3.648	1.002	0.634		

Note. TOS1 item of TOS was removed because of factor loadings <.5; *constructs/items of OPA; OPA= online purchase attitude; **IV while OPI is DV; SD= standard deviation; AVEs= average extracted variance

Table 5. Summary for SEM and Fishers' analysis

Paths (Proposed)	SEM**	Fisher***	Decision
H₁: SNSs--------> OPA	0.221*	--	Supported
H₂: SAPs--------> OPA	0.474*	--	Supported
H₃: GND--------> SNSs and OPA	--	0.073****	Unsupported
H₄: GND--------> SAPs and OPA	--	0.084****	Unsupported

Model fit indices: $X^2/df = \leq 3.0$; NFI= >0.9; SRMR= <0.08; Current indices: $X^2/df = 2.792$; NFI= >0.973; SRMR= 0.075; *Sig. $p < 0.01$, **,*** explained in earlier sections, ****Fishers' outcomes

Interrelationships and Hypotheses Testing

Table 5 and Figure 2 summarized that SNSs has a positive correlation with consumers' OPA together with the appropriate loadings of each predictor of SNSs such as FB, LD, TW, YT, and PT, respectively. Similarly, SAPs has positive relationships toward OPA along with appropriate loadings of each predictor, i.e., WA, FBM, WC, IG, and SC, respectively. Moreover, each construct/item of OPA is examined with the appropriate loadings, i.e., TA1, TA2, PEU, PU, PEU1, PEU2, PEU3, PEU4, PEU5, PU1, PU2, PU3, TA2, TOS, PR1, PR2, PR3, PR4, TOS1, TOS2, TOS3, TOS4, TOS5, TOS6, and TOS7, respectively (see Figure 2). Finally, results affirmed a non-significant effect of GND among the relationships of SNSs, SAPs, and consumers' OPA. Hence, results revealed an insignificant moderating effect of GND where our results are consistent with previous studies in which experts suggested an insignificant effect of GND in ICTs related studies (e.g., Hew et al., 2015; Waheed & Jianhua, 2018).

Figure 2. Measurement Model for latent variables/Paths relationships

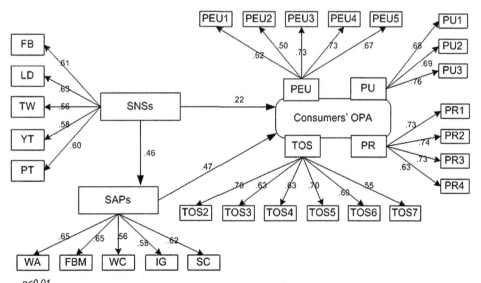

$p < 0.01$

SNS= social network sites; SAP= social apps; PEU= perceived ease of use; PU= perceived usefulness; TOS= trust in online stores; PR= perceived risks; OPA= online purchase attitude; TOS1 was removed because of lower factor loading <.5; prepared by author with loadings of each latent variable

Furthermore, all proposed relationships were tested using SEM and Fishers' approach as follows. It was proposed in hypothesis one that SNSs are positively correlated with OPA. The findings affirmed a significant correlation between SNSs, i.e., FB, LD, TW, YT, and PT and consumers' OPA at (β=0.221) consequently hypothesis one is supported (H_1). Second, it was assumed that SAPs, i.e., WA, FBM, WC, IG, and SC are positively correlated to OPA. The results revealed positive relationships between SAPs and OPA at (β=0.474). Based on significant results, hypothesis two is supported (H_2). It was proposed in hypothesis three that GND moderates between the relationship of SNSs and OPA. In contrast, the results revealed an insignificant effect of GND between the relationship of SNSs and OPA at (0.073). Hence, hypothesis three is not supported (H_3) because of the non-significant association. Hypothesis four is proposed that GND moderates the association between SAPs and OPA. However, the result indicated an insignificant relationship of GND between SAPs and OPA at (0.084). Therefore, hypothesis four is not supported (H_4) because of non-significant relationships (see Table 5).

DISCUSSION AND MANAGERIAL IMPLICATIONS

Technology has brought revolutionary transformation in consumers' behaviour where such inclination encourages the organizations to employ advanced methods of marketing communication in today's modern age. Nowadays, an extensive number of Internet users have attached to distinct social media platforms, including SNSs and SAPs to interact with each other. Such hip motivates businesses to convey a message using such online tools and tactics to foster the relationships with diverse consumers (De Vries et al., 2012). Therefore, most of the companies are creating the accounts on social media platforms, including Twitter, Facebook, and remainder online blogs (Okazaki & Taylor, 2013). The usage of social media in advertising perspective is still in its infancy stage and more research is needed to reveal further antecedents and consequences (Okazaki & Taylor, 2013; Ellison, 2007). Concerning to consumers' online behavior, diverse factors may influence during online shopping such as e-store contents, ease of use, ease of usefulness, privacy systems, perceived risk, fraud issues, trust factors, and some demographic factors (Van der Heijden et al., 2003; Park & Jun, 2003; Venkatesh et al., 2003; Faqih & Jaradat, 2015; Koong et al., 2008). However, the current findings suggested a positive influence of SNSs and SAs towards consumers' OPA without applicability of GDR. The findings of our research are associated with previous studies in which researchers have concluded the positive impact of social media, including distinct SNSs and SAPs in marketing perspective across the nations (e.g., Okazaki & Taylor, 2013; Ellison, 2007; Howard et al., 2014; Hwang & Park, 2013; Logan, 2017; De Vries et al., 2012).

Theoretical and Managerial Implications

The present study contributes to respective literature by investigating relationships among few renowned SNSs, i.e., Facebook (FB), LinkedIn (LD), Twitter (TW), Youtube (YT), and Pinterest (PT) as well as by investigating the correlations among SAPs, i.e., Whatsapp (WA), Facebook messenger (FBM), Wechat (WC), Instagram (IG), and Snapchat (SC) on consumers' OPA from the context of developing country. This study yields insights towards existing literature by evaluating the insignificant effect of GND to empirically contribute in the literature of ICTs and IS.

- In managerial standpoint, the marketers are suggested to embrace SNSs and SAPs together with sub-determinants in order to seize consumers' OPA in today's digital era where an extensive number of users are attached with social media. As reported in earlier sections that nearly 51% worlds' population is using an Internet. Such expansion encourages the marketers to approach those consumers to reinforce their buying intention using FB, LD, TW, YT, PT, WA, FBM, WC, IG, and SC in marketing communications.

- The marketers are further encouraged to adopt entire SNSs and SAPs' platforms or may adopt few selected social sites and social apps by considering financial resources. While FB, TW, WA, FB are some of the top-ranked tools having a large number of users across the world. Besides, this study revealed the significance of each SNSs and SAPs that can be utilized to drive consumers' OPA. Despite, marketers are advised to focus all the methods in order to disseminate product information in a widespread manner.

- The marketers are encouraged to identify distinct internal or external factor during the selection of SNSs and SAPs. For example, the current study affirmed that GDR did not moderate the relationships among the relationships of SNSs, SAPs, and OPA. Therefore, marketers may formulate particular promotional strategic without applicability of GND. However, some other factors, including behavioral factors, demographic factors, and societal factors might be considered before implementing a particular advertising strategy.

- The advertisers are suggested to avoid an excess of information sharing using such tools in marketing communications because researchers argued that such attitude may direct consumers' intention toward the negative direction and usually influences negatively (Schooley et al., 2016).

- Marketers must encourage the consumers with such information which may reduce their thinking related to online threats, risks, and fraud by ensuring secured payment systems together with the provision of post-purchase services.

- Finally, advertising companies are suggested to identify the most dynamic and effective promotional methods by understanding the dominated scenario in particular market where SNSs and SAPs are ascertained useful tools in triggering OPA in the present digital age.

Limitation and Future Research

This study is limited to a single country consequently a study might be expanded toward other nations to validate the findings. The sample size of this study is limited to eleven hundred online shoppers with Bangladesh, while a future study can be acknowledged with a large sample size to validate the results on a larger scale. Moreover, the sample size limits the generalizability where a future work might be conducted to other nations for its widespread generalization. This study is conducted from a B2C perspective; however, longitudinal studies could be carried from B2B within the current region and across the globe to ensure the significance of distinct SNSs and SAPs, especially within underdeveloped nations. This study can be considered a starting point where the impact of each SNSs and SAPs together with other social media tools can autonomously be considered particularly within developing countries where still a little literature is available. This study examined the influence of single moderating variables which is GND, therefore, this study suggested to remainder researchers to consider additional moderating factors, i.e., education, culture, and other environment-related factors in similar studies across the globe. As several researchers claimed that research on social media is still needed consequently academicians and practitioners may conduct more work to comprehend antecedents and consequences of distinct social media on consumers' behavior within unlike contexts and dimensions.

ACKNOWLEDGMENT

We are enormously thankful to my professors who helped me in accomplishing this research article together with friends and colleagues who helped me a lot in data collection and polishing this article.

REFERENCES

Abu-Shanab, E. A. (2011). Education level as a technology adoption moderator. In *2011 3rd International Conference on Computer Research and Development (ICCRD)* (pp. 324-328). IEEE.

Ajzen, I. (1991). The theory of planned behavior. *Organizational Behavior and Human Decision Processes*, *50*(2), 179–211. doi:10.1016/0749-5978(91)90020-T

Ajzen, I. & Fishbein, M. (1980). Understanding attitudes and predicting social behaviour.

Al-Gahtani, S. S., Hubona, G. S., & Wang, J. (2007). Information technology (IT) in Saudi Arabia: Culture and the acceptance and use of IT. *Information & Management*, *44*(8), 681–691. doi:10.1016/j.im.2007.09.002

Aydin, G., & Karamehmet, B. (2017). A comparative study on attitudes towards SMS advertising and mobile application advertising. *International Journal of Mobile Communications*, *15*(5), 514–536. doi:10.1504/IJMC.2017.086366

Baron, R. M., & Kenny, D. A. (1986). The moderator-mediator variable distinction in social psychological research: Conceptual, strategic, and statistical considerations. *Journal of Personality and Social Psychology*, *51*(6), 1173–1182. doi:10.1037/0022-3514.51.6.1173 PMID:3806354

Bayo-Moriones, A., & Lera-Lopez, F. (2007). A firm-level analysis of determinants of ICT adoption in Spain. *Technovation*, *27*(6), 352–366. doi:10.1016/j.technovation.2007.01.003

Brengman, M., Geuens, M., & Pelsmacker, P. D. (2001). The impact of consumer characteristics and campaign related factors on brand confusion in print advertising. *Journal of Marketing Communications*, *7*(4), 231–243. doi:10.1080/13527260127415

Burghy, C. A., Stodola, D. E., Ruttle, P. L., Molloy, E. K., Armstrong, J. M., Oler, J. A., ... Essex, M. J. (2012). Developmental pathways to amygdala-prefrontal function and internalizing symptoms in adolescence. *Nature Neuroscience*, *15*(12), 1736–1741. doi:10.1038/nn.3257 PMID:23143517

Cantrell, J., Ganz, O., Emelle, B., Moore, R., Rath, J., Hair, E. C., & Vallone, D. (2017). Mobile marketing: An emerging strategy to promote electronic nicotine delivery systems. *Tobacco Control*, *26*(e2), e1–e3.

Chang, H. H., Wang, Y.-H., & Yang, W.-Y. (2009). The impact of e-service quality, customer satisfaction and loyalty on e-marketing: Moderating effect of perceived value. *Total Quality Management*, *20*(4), 423–443. doi:10.1080/14783360902781923

Cho, Y. C. (2011). Measuring customer attitudes toward single vs. hybrid retail formats: Impact of gender and brand name familiarity. *Journal of Applied Business Research*, *23*(4). doi:10.19030/jabr.v23i4.1382

Constantinides, E. (2004). Influencing the online consumer's behavior: The Web experience. *Internet Research*, *14*(2), 111–126. doi:10.1108/10662240410530835

Coviello, N., Milley, R., & Marcolin, B. (2001). Understanding IT-enabled interactivity in contemporary marketing. *Journal of Interactive Marketing*, *15*(4), 18–33. doi:10.1002/dir.1020

Davis, F. D. (1989). Perceived usefulness, perceived ease of use, and user acceptance of information technology. *Management Information Systems Quarterly*, *13*(3), 319–340. doi:10.2307/249008

De Vries, L., Gensler, S., & Leeflang, P. S. (2012). Popularity of brand posts on brand fan pages: An investigation of the effects of social media marketing. *Journal of Interactive Marketing*, *26*(2), 83–91. doi:10.1016/j.intmar.2012.01.003

Deng, Z., Mo, X., & Liu, S. (2014). Comparison of the middle-aged and older users' adoption of mobile health services in China. *International Journal of Medical Informatics*, *83*(3), 210–224. doi:10.1016/j.ijmedinf.2013.12.002 PMID:24388129

Dittmar, H., Long, K., & Meek, R. (2004). Buying on the Internet: Gender differences in on-line and conventional buying motivations. *Sex Roles*, *50*(5-6), 423–444. doi:10.1023/B:SERS.0000018896.35251.c7

El-Gohary, H. (2012). Factors affecting E-Marketing adoption and implementation in tourism firms: An empirical investigation of Egyptian small tourism organisations. *Tourism Management*, *33*(5), 1256–1269. doi:10.1016/j.tourman.2011.10.013

Ellison, N. B. (2007). Social network sites: Definition, history, and scholarship. *Journal of Computer-Mediated Communication*, *13*(1), 210–230. doi:10.1111/j.1083-6101.2007.00393.x

Faqih, K. M., & Jaradat, M.-I. R. M. (2015). Assessing the moderating effect of gender differences and individualism-collectivism at individual-level on the adoption of mobile commerce technology: TAM3 perspective. *Journal of Retailing and Consumer Services*, *22*, 37–52. doi:10.1016/j.jretconser.2014.09.006

Fornell, C., & Larcker, D. F. (1981). Structural equation models with unobservable variables and measurement error: Algebra and statistics. *JMR, Journal of Marketing Research*, *18*(3), 382–388. doi:10.2307/3150980

Garcia-Morales, V. J., Llorens-Montes, F. J., & Verdú-Jover, A. J. (2006). Antecedents and consequences of organizational innovation and organizational learning in entrepreneurship. *Industrial Management & Data Systems*, *106*(1), 21–42. doi:10.1108/02635570610642940

Gefen, D., Karahanna, E., & Straub, D. W. (2003). Trust and TAM in online shopping: An integrated model. *Management Information Systems Quarterly*, *27*(1), 51–90. doi:10.2307/30036519

Hew, J.-J., Lee, V.-H., Ooi, K.-B., & Wei, J. (2015). What catalyses mobile apps usage intention: An empirical analysis. *Industrial Management & Data Systems*, *115*(7), 1269–1291. doi:10.1108/IMDS-01-2015-0028

Howard, D., Mangold, W. G., & Johnston, T. (2014). Managing your social campaign strategy using Facebook, Twitter, Instagram, YouTube & Pinterest: An interview with Dana Howard, social media marketing manager. *Business Horizons*, 5(57), 657–665. doi:10.1016/j.bushor.2014.05.001

Hwang, Y., & Park, N. (2013). Digital divide in social networking sites. *International Journal of Mobile Communications*, 11(5), 446–464. doi:10.1504/IJMC.2013.056955

InternetWorldStats. (2017). Retrieved from http://www.internetworldstats.com/stats.htm

Kiang, M. Y., Raghu, T., & Shang, K. H.-M. (2000). Marketing on the Internet—who can benefit from an online marketing approach? *Decision Support Systems*, 27(4), 383–393. doi:10.1016/S0167-9236(99)00062-7

Kline, R. (2005) 'Principles and practice of structural equation modeling. 2nd The Guilford Press', New York.

Koong, K. S., Liu, L. C., Bai, S., & Wei, J. (2008). Occurrences of internet fraud in the USA. *International Journal of Services and Standards*, 4(1), 33–53. doi:10.1504/IJSS.2008.016083

Leong, L.-Y., Hew, T.-S., Tan, G. W.-H., & Ooi, K.-B. (2013). Predicting the determinants of the NFC-enabled mobile credit card acceptance: A neural networks approach. *Expert Systems with Applications*, 40(14), 5604–5620. doi:10.1016/j.eswa.2013.04.018

Levy, P., & Birkner, C. (2011). Digital marketing 2011: What you need to know. *Marketing News*, 45(3), 10–14.

Li, Q., Yang, D., & Chen, X. (2014). Predicting determinants and moderating factors of mobile phone data flow service adoption. In *2014 Seventh International Joint Conference on Computational Sciences and Optimization (CSO)* (pp. 390-394). IEEE.

Lien, C. H., & Cao, Y. (2014). 'Examining WeChat users' motivations, trust, attitudes, and positive word-of-mouth: Evidence from China'. *Computers in Human Behavior*, 41, 104–111. doi:10.1016/j.chb.2014.08.013

Logan, K. (2017). Attitudes towards in-app advertising: A uses and gratifications perspective. *International Journal of Mobile Communications*, 15(1), 26–48. doi:10.1504/IJMC.2017.080575

Mathews, S., Bianchi, C., Perks, K. J., Healy, M., & Wickramasekera, R. (2016). Internet marketing capabilities and international market growth. *International Business Review*, 25(4), 820–830. doi:10.1016/j.ibusrev.2015.10.007

Michaelidou, N., Siamagka, N. T., & Christodoulides, G. (2011). Usage, barriers and measurement of social media marketing: An exploratory investigation of small and medium B2B brands. *Industrial Marketing Management*, 40(7), 1153–1159. doi:10.1016/j.indmarman.2011.09.009

Miyazaki, A. D., & Fernandez, A. (2001). Consumer perceptions of privacy and security risks for online shopping. *The Journal of Consumer Affairs*, 35(1), 27–44. doi:10.1111/j.1745-6606.2001.tb00101.x

Nunnally, J. (1978). *Psychometric methods*. New York: McGraw-Hill.

Okazaki, S., & Taylor, C. R. (2013). Social media and international advertising: Theoretical challenges and future directions. *International Marketing Review, 30*(1), 56–71. doi:10.1108/02651331311298573

Ozok, A. A., & Wei, J. (2010). An empirical comparison of consumer usability preferences in online shopping using stationary and mobile devices: Results from a college student population. *Electronic Commerce Research, 10*(2), 111–137. doi:10.100710660-010-9048-y

Park, C., Jun, J., & Lee, T. (2015). Consumer characteristics and the use of social networking sites: A comparison between Korea and the US. *International Marketing Review, 32*(3/4), 414–437. doi:10.1108/IMR-09-2013-0213

Park, C., & Jun, J.-K. (2003). A cross-cultural comparison of Internet buying behavior: Effects of Internet usage, perceived risks, and innovativeness. *International Marketing Review, 20*(5), 534–553. doi:10.1108/02651330310498771

Pavlou, P. A. (2003). Consumer acceptance of electronic commerce: Integrating trust and risk with the technology acceptance model. *International Journal of Electronic Commerce, 7*(3), 101–134. doi:10.1080/10864415.2003.11044275

Pavlov, O. V., Melville, N., & Plice, R. K. (2008). Toward a sustainable email marketing infrastructure. *Journal of Business Research, 61*(11), 1191–1199. doi:10.1016/j.jbusres.2007.11.010

Persaud, A., & Azhar, I. (2012). Innovative mobile marketing via smartphones: Are consumers ready? *Marketing Intelligence & Planning, 30*(4), 418–443. doi:10.1108/02634501211231883

Rogers, E. M. (1995). *'Diffusion of Innovations: modifications of a model for telecommunications', Die Diffusion von Innovationen in der Telekommunikation* (pp. 25–38). Springer. doi:10.1007/978-3-642-79868-9_2

Rondan-Cataluña, F. J., Arenas-Gaitán, J., & Ramírez-Correa, P. E. (2015). A comparison of the different versions of popular technology acceptance models: A non-linear perspective. *Kybernetes, 44*(5), 788–805. doi:10.1108/K-09-2014-0184

Schooley, B., Walczak, S., Hikmet, N., & Patel, N. (2016). Impacts of mobile tablet computing on provider productivity, communications, and the process of care. *International Journal of Medical Informatics, 88*, 62–70. doi:10.1016/j.ijmedinf.2016.01.010 PMID:26878764

Shin, D.-H. (2009). Towards an understanding of the consumer acceptance of mobile wallet. *Computers in Human Behavior, 25*(6), 1343–1354. doi:10.1016/j.chb.2009.06.001

Statista. (2017a). Forecast of mobile phone users worldwide. Retrieved from www.statista.com/statistics/274774/forecast-of-mobile-phone-users-worldwide/

Statista. (2017b). Number of active wechat messenger accounts. Retrieved from www.statista.com/statistics/255778/number-of-active-wechat-messenger-accounts/

Statista. (2017c). Most popular US social networking apps ranked by audience. Retrieved from www.statista.com/statistics/248074/most-popular-us-social-networking-apps-ranked-by-audience/

Taylor, R. (1990). Interpretation of the correlation coefficient: A basic review. *Journal of Diagnostic Medical Sonography*, 6(1), 35–39. doi:10.1177/875647939000600106

Taylor, S., & Todd, P. A. (1995). Understanding information technology usage: A test of competing models. *Information Systems Research*, 6(2), 144–176. doi:10.1287/isre.6.2.144

Thelwall, M., Thelwall, M., Vis, F., & Vis, F. (2017). Gender and image sharing on Facebook, Twitter, Instagram, Snapchat and WhatsApp in the UK: Hobbying alone or filtering for friends? *Aslib Journal of Information Management*, 69(6), 702–720. doi:10.1108/AJIM-04-2017-0098

Tiago, M. T. P. M. B., & Verassimo, J. M. C. (2014). Digital marketing and social media: Why bother? *Business Horizons*, 57(6), 703–708. doi:10.1016/j.bushor.2014.07.002

Tsai, C.-W., Shen, P.-D., Chiang, Y.-C. & Hsu, P.-F. (2016). Online Advertising and Promotion: Modern Technologies for Marketing.

Tseng, S.-C., & Hung, S.-W. (2013). A framework identifying the gaps between customers' expectations and their perceptions in green products. *Journal of Cleaner Production*, 59, 174–184. doi:10.1016/j.jclepro.2013.06.050

Van der Heijden, H., Verhagen, T., & Creemers, M. (2003). Understanding online purchase intentions: Contributions from technology and trust perspectives. *European Journal of Information Systems*, 12(1), 41–48. doi:10.1057/palgrave.ejis.3000445

Venkatesh, V., & Bala, H. (2008). Technology acceptance model 3 and a research agenda on interventions. *Decision Sciences*, 39(2), 273–315. doi:10.1111/j.1540-5915.2008.00192.x

Venkatesh, V., & Davis, F. D. (2000). A theoretical extension of the technology acceptance model: Four longitudinal field studies. *Management Science*, 46(2), 186–204. doi:10.1287/mnsc.46.2.186.11926

Venkatesh, V., Morris, M. G., Davis, G. B., & Davis, F. D. (2003). User acceptance of information technology: Toward a unified view. *Management Information Systems Quarterly*, 27(3), 425–478. doi:10.2307/30036540

Venkatesh, V., Thong, J. Y. & Xu, X. (2012). Consumer acceptance and use of information technology: extending the unified theory of acceptance and use of technology.

Waheed, A., & Jianhua, Y. (2018). Achieving consumers' attention through emerging technologies: The linkage between e-marketing and consumers' exploratory buying behavior tendencies. *Baltic Journal of Management*, 13(2), 209–235. doi:10.1108/BJM-04-2017-0126

Waheed, A., & Yang, J. (2017). The effect of mobile marketing and email marketing on exploratory information seeking (EIS) behavior of the consumers: Communication through wireless technologies. *International Journal of Enterprise Information Systems*, 13(4), 76–89. doi:10.4018/IJEIS.2017100105

Wong, C.-H., Wei-Han Tan, G., Loke, S.-P., & Ooi, K.-B. (2014). Mobile TV: A new form of entertainment? *Industrial Management & Data Systems*, 114(7), 1050–1067. doi:10.1108/IMDS-05-2014-0146

World Meters. (2017). Bangladesh Population. Retrieved from http://www.worldometers.info/world-population/bangladesh-population/

Wymbs, C. (2011). Digital marketing: The time for a new "academic major" has arrived. *Journal of Marketing Education*, *33*(1), 93–106. doi:10.1177/0273475310392544

Yahya, M., Nadzar, F., Masrek, N., & Rahman, B. A. (2011). Determinants of UTAUT in measuring user acceptance of e-syariah portal in syariah courts in Malaysia. In *2nd International Research Symposium in Service Management*, Yogyakarta, Indonesia.

Yang, K. C. (2005). Exploring factors affecting the adoption of mobile commerce in Singapore. *Telematics and Informatics*, *22*(3), 257–277. doi:10.1016/j.tele.2004.11.003

Zhu, X., Yang, J., Wu, X., & Wei, J. (2011). Online promotion and marketing of mobile communication devices: An empirical study. *International Journal of Mobile Communications*, *10*(1), 21–40. doi:10.1504/IJMC.2012.044521

This research was previously published in the International Journal of Enterprise Information Systems (IJEIS), 14(4); pages 108-123, copyright year 2018 by IGI Publishing (an imprint of IGI Global).

Chapter 71
Improving Customer Relationship Management Through Social Listening:
A Case Study of an American Academic Library

Margaret C. Stewart
University of North Florida, USA

Maria Atilano
University of North Florida, USA

Christa L. Arnold
University of North Florida, USA

ABSTRACT

In the dynamic world of social media strategy, developing an effective approach to customer relationship management (CRM) online is challenging. With best practices for CRM on social media still being uncovered, the value of social listening is becoming recognizable in contemporary social CRM. This chapter presents a case study that shares the actions, insights, and experiences of using social media for CRM at the academic library at a mid-size American university located in northeast Florida. Using specific examples of how social media is used to engage in social listening and to enhance CRM, the social listening practices and social media strategy of this library are highlighted in relation to how they influence and potentially improve CRM. By examining the practices of this individual institution's library, a better understanding of how academic libraries engage with customers using social media as a CRM platform comes to light. In addition, ideas for future research on the intersection of social listening, CRM, and social media strategy are discussed.

DOI: 10.4018/978-1-7998-9020-1.ch071

INTRODUCTION

Social media is changing the relationship between organizations and customers. As a result, social media platforms present unique opportunities for customer relationship management (CRM) and are becoming increasingly popular channels to deliver CRM. The dynamic nature of social media makes it difficult to establish guidelines and best practices for social media CRM. In this book chapter, an original case study presents how an American academic library uses social media for CRM practices, and emphasizes the role of social listening with the library's social media strategy. The Thomas G. Carpenter Library at the University of North Florida (UNF) in Jacksonville initiated its social media presence in 2009, and is committed to strategically developing an effective social media strategy to best engage with all university stakeholders. This book chapter presents a detailed case study examining the library's use of social media focusing on how social listening strategically contributes to CRM. This case study discusses the findings in consideration to two overarching questions: (1) How does an American academic library utilize social listening toward CRM strategy? (2) How does an American academic library engage in CRM using social media? Upon addressing these questions given the practices and social media of the UNF academic library, opportunities and suggestions for future research regarding social listening as a social media CRM strategy are posed.

REVIEW OF LITERATURE

Social Media's Role in Academic Libraries

According to a recent study published by Pew Research Center, 74% of individuals who have utilized a library or bookmobile in the past year are social media users (Rainie, 2016). On a daily basis, half a billion tweets emerge on Twitter and a good portion of these include interactions between businesses and customers. Not surprisingly, online customer interactions grew 70% between 2013 and 2014 (Coen, 2016). For these reasons, understanding the role of social media within the realm of academic libraries is increasingly important, especially as social media continue to evolve.

In 2005, when social media was still in its infancy, the term "Library 2.0" was coined by Michael Casey, author of the blog LibraryCrunch. By linking libraries to the technology-driven Web 2.0, web based tools such as social media effectively give "library users a participatory role in the services libraries offer and the way they are used" (Casey, 2010). While the number of users on social media continues to grow, libraries now have a presence on Facebook, Twitter and other websites in order to easily reach their constituents online (Palmer, 2014). According to a survey completed by the American Library Association in 2016, 86% of libraries in the United States use social media to interact with customers (Yu, 2016). Academic libraries in particular have developed a strong social media presence in order to reach students, most of whom are traditional students in the 18-22 age range and fervent users of social media. A survey of 104 undergraduate students completed by Florida State University found that students found social media posts regarding building operations, study support services, and library events to be beneficial to their academic success (Stvilia & Gibradze, 2016). In order to reach customers and communicate the worth of library resources, academic libraries have adopted social media as a cost-effective way to connect with users and promote library value (Gaha & Hall, 2015).

Through their online presence, academic librarians can move away from the physical service desk and literacy instruction models and engage directly with their students (Palmer, 2014). Nonphysical methods of outreach and instruction became necessary as academic libraries saw growing trends of lighter foot traffic and fewer requests for research assistance. As Gaha and Hall (2015) point out, with the ubiquitous presence of Google and other online search engines, "libraries are no longer the first stop for information" for tech savvy students (p. 49). Most libraries therefore use social media for outreach and networking, with the aim of advocacy and establishing community connections (Harrison, 2017). Library promotion has become vitally important due to a disconnect between what services a library offers and what its users perceive it offers (Thomsett-Scott, 2014). The online presence allows libraries to broadcast announcements and promote resources, although this often leads to a mirror of what is already displayed on the organization's website (Young & Rossmann, 2015).

According to King (2015) libraries share content that is centered around the library itself: "what's happening at the library, what will happen, and what recently happened" (p. 10). Libraries of all types (academic, public, school, special, etc.) are prevalent on both Facebook and Twitter, if only because of the sheer number of users already there (Thomsett-Scott, 2014). Similar to other customer-geared organizations, libraries use Twitter for time-sensitive notices and information about current events, whereas Facebook is used for static linking and community building (Palmer 2014). Potter (2015) comments that librarians should take advantage of informal social media tools such as Twitter because "you can boost your reputation, you can reach new audiences, you can engage existing customers and you can really show some personality" (p. 167).

Defining Social Listening

The concept of social listening emerges from the intersection of listening and communication studies and social media strategy. From an academic standpoint, Stewart and Arnold (2016) define social listening as an active process of attending to, observing, interpreting, and responding to a variety of stimuli through mediated, electronic, and social channels. Industry literature defines social listening as,

Social listening is the process of tracking conversations around specific phrases, words or brands, and then leveraging them to discover opportunities or create content for those audiences. It's more than watching @mentions and comments pour in via your social profiles, mobile apps or blogs. If you're only paying attention to notifications, you're missing a huge group of people that are talking about you, your brand and your product. (Jackson, 2017, p.1).

Another definition from practical literature qualifies social listening as, "The actionable element of social media listening is what differentiates it from social media monitoring, which also, like the name implies, involves monitoring social media," (Newberry, 2017, p.1). Newberry (2017) goes on to the active nature of social listening in saying, "Social media monitoring, though, is more about compiling data - it's gathering information about what's already happened rather than looking forward to determine future actions," (Newberry, 2017, p.1). Social listening emerges in how we communicate and listen to others using social media and related mobile and communication technologies, and the ways this process influences our interpersonal engagement.

The Digital Shift in Messages: Broadcasting to Conversations

Social listening marks a shift in equity among organizations and consumers online, where listening to consumers becomes more valuable than broadcasting to them.

This is a true reflection of the new media culture that is arriving, and demonstrates the power of social presence and its influence on customer relationship marketing and management. Social listening arrives as a response to listening during an era of technological determinism, and utilizing information discovered online in new and creative ways. (Stewart, 2017, p.1).

With this in mind, organizations should emphasize relationship-building as a cornerstone of their social media strategy.

Customers report dissatisfaction in the failure by companies to listen to their needs, and indicate the failure to listen as one of their top three overall customer service complaints. Social listening provides important insights into the customers' expectations and their level of satisfaction with how you are answering to them (Newberry, 2017). Social interactions happen constantly, so the ongoing challenge is to channel them, capture them, integrate them, and turn them into beneficial and actionable insights for CRM (De Clerck, 2011). Social listening highlights opportunities for consumer outreach and to engage in conversations that are already happening about a brand, both positive and negative. From customers singing praises, to customer service requests, or to potential consumers seeking recommendations for a product or service in your industry, social listening affords organizations the chance to quickly attend to and respond to these critical conversations (Newberry, 2017).

Social Listening in a Mediated Society

Our human increase in connectivity brought about by social media and mobile technologies appear to alter the way in which we attend to stimuli; therefore, impacting how we listen and respond to messages. The presence of social media and availability of mobile technologies contribute to the construction of social listening, which is becoming more recognizable in an increasingly mediated society. Social listening appears to have clear implications among organizations and interpersonal relationships, so it may be an important consideration to the best practices of social CRM.

Aaron Everson, co-founder and president of Shoutlet, explains that social listening is the ability to monitor activity on social networks, whether that be by setting up keywords to track, focusing on a specific hashtag or brand handles, or using listening as a channel for customer service, and describes its importance in the information it yields to inspires organizations with actionable insights that are based on fan behavior (Wagner, 2014). Dougherty (2015) acknowledges that customer service may be the least desirable aspect of social listening, yet social care, or customer service on social media, is the primary reason that many social users engage with organizations on social media. Listening to social media interactions fundamentally changes the relationship between organizations, brands, and consumers because it fosters a rich environment for peer recommendations which play a significant role in purchasing decisions.

Social listening invokes a more dynamic process of online attention and suggests it is an embedded part of social engagement, reflecting the fact that everyone moves between the states of disclosing and listening online as forms of interpersonal participation (Crawford, 2009). Customers today are interested in knowing what other existing customers are saying about an organization and this interaction adds a new dimension to how organizations interact with their customers in turn. Social listening comes into play because of its immediacy of rich information and its global scope, making it a powerful research tool capable of contributing to actionable insights (Genpact, 2012).

Building Customer Relationships

Brunner (2008) shares a curious revelation in that the terms of listening, trust, and communication are simultaneously discussed within the context of establishing the meaning of both good and bad business/ organizational relationships. Accordingly, "participants seemed unable to describe a good relationship without using the terms of listening, trust, and communication…Participants were hard pressed to describe a bad relationship without relying on the terms of listening, trust, and communication" (p. 78).

Although Brunner's previous study did not occur in the context of social media or online communication, the findings are relevant at present when considered with regard to the ways that social media augment the relationship building process. Specifically, the previous findings which feature listening at the forefront of business relationships preempt the notion of social listening and the prevalence of social media as an organizational tool. Nonetheless, the study recognizes the importance of an organizational relationship-building, while also acknowledging that listening is a critical component of that process. Brunner (2008) notes shortcomings due to the realization that while listening is a crucial relational behavior, it is not widely recognized in the literature which examines the building and maintenance of organizational relationships.

Customer relationships are built more on trust than distribution of information, and relationships are reciprocal. How to best use social CRM starts by recognizing the emergence of the two-way communication process, rather than where CRM has traditionally been, as a one-way messaging process. By listening and responding rather than broadcasting and pitching, organizations have a new opportunity to identify with their consumers and meet them where they are. These are among the reasons that social media is of keen interest to CRM. With 2/3 of American consumers using social media, the power is increasingly in the customers' hands. This change in landscape represents a 180-degree conversion in CRM practices, emphasizing relationship management, promoting a balance of trust among an organization and its customers, and sponsoring relationship equilibrium (McKee, 2012).

Social Customer Relationship Management (CRM)

As an inherently interactive space, social media foster an environment of open exchange comprised of multi-way communication processes, and as a result, social media must now be viewed as both a customer speaking platform and a customer listening platform (Alton, 2015). Social customer relationship management, or social CRM, exceeds beyond traditional outbound marketing today, and the new expectation is that social media will augment individualized, timely and shareable customer service (Chitwood, 2014). According to Templeman (2017), social listening contributes to CRM based on its influences to consumer engagement. For instance, it allows organizations to both create an effective engagement strategy and evaluate and adjust with agile readiness.

An imperative benefit of social listening is the opportunity it provides to respond and engage; thus, to be efficient with time and consistent with response among consumers, it is important to design an engagement strategy that comprises a variety find of comments, ranging from responses to complaints to praises, as well as relevant, value added conversation starters. The use of response rubrics can assist to organize message and platform content and aids the timeliness and efficiency of the strategy, and especially helps and organization to maintain voice and persona across multiple social media strategists or CRM professionals (National Institute for Social Media, 2017; Templin, 2017).

Additional results imply that social media may contribute more towards effective CRM than marketing (DeVivo, 2014). J.D. Power and Associates's Social Media Benchmark study found that 67% of consumers have used a company's social media page for service, compared to only 33% for social marketing (Chitwood, 2014). Further, J.D. Power and Associates found that 43% of branded social media engagement by consumers ages 18-29 was related to customer service, compared with 23% that was centered on marketing (DeVivo, 2014). Social media allow organizations the opportunity to tackle service problems in innovative and revolutionary ways and offers proactive customer service. Social Listening now affords the luxury of seeking out customers' problems, anticipate customer issues, and prepare responses before questions are even asked. Organizations can analyze sentiment to proactively address negative sentiment, turning public complaints into shareable solutions (Chitwood, 2014).

Among the reasons that social CRM is booming in a climate in the contemporary online social sphere where users value instant communication. Customers have come to expect this as the new norm in a culture where one in four social media users think that organizations should reply messages online within the hour. Customers also expect quality content, seeking a balance between marketing strategies and value added content. Above all, organizations need to present a genuine and authentic voice and persona and remain engaging. These techniques help to assure customers that they are interacting with real people of the organization and not faceless companies (Coen, 2016).

The Need for Social CRM

When it comes to evaluating social media strategy and CRM effectiveness, organizations must consider the necessity to make adjustments over time, especially as new platforms, features, and technologies emerge. From a communication standpoint, it is important to recognize that not every response on social media will be viewed universally or favorably. Keeping track of individual interactions and their outcomes allows for a better understanding to emerge which can influence your social media and social CRM strategies, and how you develop individual responses to consumer comments and content (Jauman, 2017; Templeman, 2017).

Traditional marketing tools including surveys, focus groups, and stratified random sampling can be costly, are time-consuming, and only reach small segments of a given audience. These methods also may focus on things that are of importance to the company but not to customers. In direct contrast, the spontaneous flood of ideas, information, and opinions available on social media can be integrated with traditional approaches and ultimately provide CRM professionals and related decision-making stakeholders with valuable, current, and real-time insights (Genpact, 2012). Organizations need to be mindful towards their commitment to proactively supporting customers using social media; doing social CRM partially, such as having slow response times and ignoring large volumes of inquiries, makes customers feel increasingly frustrated and decreasingly valued than if no social support presence exists (Chitwood, 2014).

A survey conducted by Oracle reports that 31% of social media users interact with organizations to access customer service representatives, and 43% interact for the purpose of receiving a direct response to a problem or question (Dougherty, 2015). The National Institute for Social Media (2017) remind us of the rich value of customer data to improve customer service; the more we know about our community and individual consumers, the better we are able to respond to their needs through social media strategy, social CRM, and products and services (Jauman, 2017).

Challenges and Solutions in Social Listening

Sunley (2015) recognizes the challenge that companies face because they are aware that they need to listen to their customers online, but have difficulty doing so effectively because customers use multiple social channels to engage with the organization. Social listening is suggested as the solution to this dilemma, because it allows for tracking and analysis of customer complaints online in a manner that will reveal which channels customers are using most to ask for support, as well as what the main topics of customer complaints are, and what is the overall sentiment towards organization CRM (Sunley, 2015). The National Institute for Social Media encourages social media strategists to consider what platforms customers use and how familiar you are with those platforms as a crucial component to identify relevant information to best reach and relationship-build with stakeholders (Jauman, 2017).

Social listening allows organizations to be more responsive to consumers in several ways, including: (1) actively engage consumer by leading conversation, (2) discover social influencers, and (3) improve products and services through social research (Hanratty, 2016). Hyken (2017) echoes the values of social listening to support the customer experience by creating brand ambassadors, as well as growing for customer retention and increasing customer spending. Stewart (2017) suggests asking a few questions when social listening to remain audience-centered:

(1) In what ways do I engage in social listening with members of my network?", (2) "What kind of information might be helpful to gather about my audience(s) using social media?", (3) and, "How might my brand or organization utilize online information to better engage with my audience(s)? (Stewart, 2017, p.1).

Case Study Questions

The existing research presented in the review of literature reveals the obvious trend toward social CRM and invites the opportunity to continue examining cases to develop best practices and effective strategies. The present study explores two inductive inquiries using an applied case study procedure: (1) How does an American academic library utilize social listening toward CRM strategy? (2) How does an American academic library engage in CRM using social media?

CASE STUDY

History

The University of North Florida's Thomas G. Carpenter Library in Jacksonville, Florida serves approximately 15,000 students, 1,700 employees including faculty, and many thousands of members of the community. For most academic libraries, the constituents that they serve are known as "users" or "patrons," if not by their affiliation with the university. The Carpenter Library's social media presence began July 2009, when its Twitter account was first established. The Carpenter Library's Facebook page was created in December 2009. In its early days, two different staff members were responsible for creating and posting content to Twitter and Facebook. Both accounts at first relied on largely text-based posts and tweets, and very little communication or planning was involved. By September 2010, the library's

Facebook page reached 200 fans. For the next four years, the success of the Carpenter Library's social media presence was based off how many followers/fans/likes each account received.

The Carpenter Library's approach to social media has been through three major stages. The first, infant stage included mostly original content, with very little interaction or set schedule. The second, teenager stage centered around the concept of share and share-alike: half original content, half shared. The third, early adult stage, which is still in effect, is focused on social listening, shared content, and less original content than ever.

The first version of the Carpenter Library's social media plan closely followed that of the University of North Florida, which was implemented in July 2010. The University asked that all campus departments and organizations who used social media to predominantly display a set of "Osprey Rules" regarding user conduct. As a result, the following missive was placed in the About section of the Carpenter Library's Facebook page:

Osprey Rules: We encourage you to leave comments, photos, videos and links. We will review all comments and will remove any that are inappropriate, offensive or contain insults.

The library's Twitter account shared exclusively original content - no retweets - until 2012, when management of all social media accounts was given to a sole staff member. Posted information on both Facebook and Twitter focused mainly on updates about the library's services, resources and events. This one-sided approach to social media meant that the library's accounts had very few followers, and little interactions or response from users. In Fall 2012, when the Carpenter Library's Twitter account began following numerous UNF departments, clubs, organizations, and prominent individuals, the library's follower count tripled in less than a month: from 33 to just over 100.

Figure 1. Examples of tweets from the @unflibrary account in Fall 2010. Links, no media, and a repeated #fb hashtag.

In the first iteration of the Carpenter Library's social media plan, the library outlined which customer groups were being targeted: primarily students, followed by faculty/staff, members of the community, and others. These groups were chosen based on statistics of who were currently following the library's social media accounts, and who were most likely to follow and interact us based on data at the time. Three fundamental goals were established in the plan:

1.   Build awareness of our organization and the services we offer
2.   Provide a variety of information and media – links to guides, images, videos – on a regular basis
3.   Simply and effectively use tools to connect with a diverse community, including students, staff, and the community at large

Second to these goals, the main responsibility of the library's social media presence was dedicated to original content creation strategies: daily posts about new library services, upcoming events, databases, and more. A consistent posting schedule was developed in order to ensure regular content added to Twitter and Facebook. Library staff were tasked with posting original content at least once a day from Monday thru Friday on both Facebook and Twitter. Some days were centered around themes such as Throwback Thursday, Tech Tuesday, and Whiteboard Wednesday. This initial social media plan also included the stipulation that library accounts share or retweet content from related accounts at least once a day. Shared content included posts, tweets, updates, and links from on local and campus offices, organizations, and clubs. Content was also regularly shared from the official University of North Florida accounts on both Twitter and Facebook.

Once the first social media plan was initiated, it became clear that focusing almost solely on writing and posting original content was not accomplishing the first stated goal; awareness of the library and its offered services was not being built among the library's social media followers. In order to reach this important goal more effectively, social listening and engagement on social media were written into the second iteration of the plan. Staff were asked to watch for opportunities to reply to or connect with library customers on Facebook and Twitter. In the third iteration, not only was the importance of social listening included, but as a priority it was placed above original content creation. In this version, staff were now tasked with seeking out opportunities to reply to, connect with, and encourage library customers to reach out to the library - whether for academic uses or lighthearted conversations - on social media.

The most current version of the Carpenter Library's social media plan, finalized in September 2017, is a continuance of the third, fully-realized stage. The three fundamental goals have expanded to cover new and evolving target audiences as well as new modes of communication. Listening is now not only a call to action, but a goal in and of itself. There are also eight overall social media strategies listed across all primary social media accounts, in support of the three fundamental goals:

1.   Increase awareness of our organization and the services, events, spaces, and resources we offer in support of academic and professional success
2.   Listen to, communicate with, and engage online users in order to foster norms of reciprocity and trust while also building a sense of community
3.   Simply and effectively use tools and media to connect with our constituents, including students, faculty, staff, and the community at large

Social Listening Strategy

The Thomas G. Carpenter Library practices social listening on three main websites: Twitter, Facebook and Instagram. Facebook's permissions, locked-down accounts, and wary users often make it difficult to "listen" from a public page. Listening via Facebook therefore becomes a waiting game, in which social media administrators simply wait for a notification that a user "mentioned" their organization or "checked in" to their location. Twitter accounts, on the other hand, are largely public, making it easy to track what customers have to say. Twitter's use of hashtags and its ability to be linked to other social media accounts (Facebook, Instagram, FourSquare, etc.) allow for additional listening opportunities.

The majority of the Carpenter Library's social listening on Twitter is accomplished by following established hashtags and keywords being used by customers. Rather than establish their own library hashtag as others have done, social media staff began following ones that were already established by students and other University departments. Popular tags include #SWOOPlife and #loveUNF which are used by Public Relations and the Admissions Office, as well as #universityofnorthflorida which is used less frequently because of its length. Less frequently-used hashtags include #SWOOP, #UNF, and others. Keywords that are followed include different iterations of "Thomas G. Carpenter Library," "UNF Library," and "TommyG" - a nickname coined by students and embraced by library outreach and marketing staff.

With the addition of social listening to the Carpenter Library social media plans, original content has become less of a focus. The benefits of utilizing a mixture of shared and original content are numerous. First, due to the small number of dedicated staff, less time is spent deciding who would write and post what content when and where. More flexibility with content and posting schedules allows for staff to fine-tune messages highlighting library services and resources. By reducing the number of original content posts to both Facebook and Twitter from three times a day, Monday-Friday, to one or two times a day, more time was freed up to share content from other accounts as well as respond to and follow potential customers.

The main drawback of engaging in social listening is that it requires constant surveillance. Customers often take to social media to vent or complain to their peers about certain aspects of a business or service. In order for social listening to have the highest impact, staff must be vigilant in finding, recognizing, and responding to these comments in a timely manner. For the Carpenter Library, this means having someone on call during normal business hours to watch for alerts and notifications on Facebook and Twitter. This model has helped address concerns from students who were both commenting to the library directly or just merely mentioning our name. For example, in November 2013 a student tweeted "Guy at the front desk is being SUPER RUDE. I pay for this, I don't want someone treating me like that #unf." In less than 15 minutes, a staff member from the Carpenter Library responded to the tweet and forwarded the message to library administration.

Staff at the Carpenter Library practice active listening by using a variety of tools, including Feedly, HootSuite and TweetDeck. Feedly is used to track posts to Instagram by following certain keywords and locations as RSS links. Because the University's online student magazine, the Spinnaker, also sporadically mentions the library, Feedly is also used to track posts and news updates to the Spinnaker website. HootSuite was used previously by staff to not only track hashtags, keywords, and locations, but also to schedule posts to Twitter and Facebook in advance. Due to the restriction on multiple accounts, HootSuite was not suitable for several staff members' use. Newer tools Sprout and TagBoard have been invaluable for listening on Twitter and Facebook, but also on websites such as Instagram where the library currently does not have a social media presence.

Figure 2. Student thanks Carpenter Library staff for addressing her concern via Twitter.

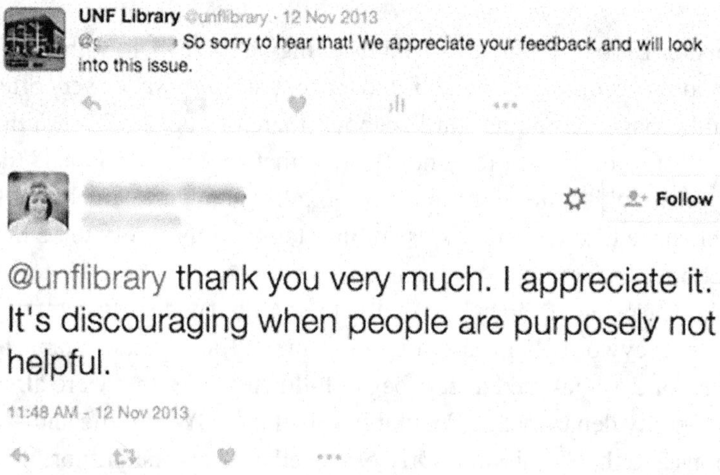

The Carpenter Library's entire social listening activities on Twitter is accomplished via TweetDeck. An application that was developed independently but is now owned by Twitter, TweetDeck is highly customizable and easy to use. Not only does the app allow you to follow numerous hashtags and keywords, but it also allows for composing and replying to tweets as well as scheduling of future tweets. Tweets tend to scroll by fast, so another benefit of using a tool like TweetDeck is that the social media manager can keep track of past interactions and alerts. Desktop notifications can be turned on so that staff need not keep their browser window pointed in the website's direction. In short, TweetDeck is an ecosystem built upon listening, following, and conversation.

While the Carpenter Library does not have an Instagram account, social listening via this platform is possible by tracking hashtags and geotags. Instagram allows users to tag their location, making it easy for organizations to keep track of whenever a customer tags their place of business. The Carpenter Library is often seen as the topic of photos and videos posted by students who "check in" while studying or attending library events. While the library cannot like or comment on Instagram posts as its own entity, library staff who have personal Instagram accounts are encouraged to reply on behalf of the organization. Most of these informal exchanges are light-hearted acknowledgements when students post particularly interesting photos of library spaces, events, or services.

Instagram has the added benefit of showing a visual representation of ways that academic libraries can highlight or improve its physical resources, services, programs, materials, and more. Students, faculty, staff, and visitors often share photos of their favorite study spots in the library, selfies with their friends, or snapshots from library events. During finals week, the #universityofnorthflorida hashtag is full of photos from the Carpenter Library's PAWS Your Stress event, where students have the opportunity to meet and cuddle with service dogs in training from the local chapter of Canine Companions for Independence (CCI). This event regularly attracts 300-400 students each semester, many of whom celebrate their opportunity to pet a dog in the library via their personal social media accounts. As one student posted on Instagram in December 2016, "Puppies make nervous break downs in the lib so much more enjoyable."

Listening for Positive Conversations

Academic libraries want to know that their numerous spaces, services and resources are appreciated by their target user groups. Feedback is gauged by surveys, focus groups, anecdotal evidence, and more. A major benefit of social listening is that while customers may not wish to share their thoughts in a formal survey or during a focus group meeting, they may feel differently about sharing their comments online. The Carpenter Library began practicing social listening as a way to collect informal, unsolicited quotes from students about what they liked or found notable about the library's spaces and resources. One of the first comments to be recorded and sent to the Library Dean as a social media "win" was about the library's collection of art: "Currently studying @unflibrary but got distracted.. #painting of downtown Jacksonville, amazing."

Figure 3. A tweet and photo from a thankful student before Midterms, Fall 2015.

Comments that tagged or mentioned the library were rare, but appeared often enough for staff to keep track. Library staff are encouraged to acknowledge these comments, whether they are positive or negative, to connect with customers on their own chosen platform. For example, when one student tweeted he was having a "Busy night of studying with Tommy G. @unflibrary #Finalsweek #Libraryofchampions,"

library staff not only liked his tweet but replied "Best of luck on finals!" The student then replied to say "Thanks!" and promptly followed the Library's Twitter account. Staff are also encouraged to interact with students in a less formal way in an effort to interject an element of fun. One student tweeted an exasperated gif with the comment "I just tried to use my debit card to get into the @unflibrary instead of my UNF ID....I'm done with today". Rather than moving onto a more academic interaction, library staff responded by jokingly thanking the student for their "accidental donation" to the library. The student responded with a friendly "lol" and immediately liked and shared the library's tweet.

Figure 4. An example of how the Carpenter Library welcomes new students to UNF. This tweet received 613 impressions and 68 engagements - an engagement rate of 11.1%.

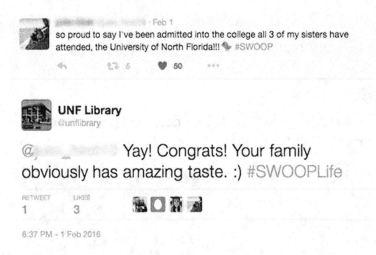

Once library staff began listening for any mention of "University of North Florida," it became clear that numerous incoming students enjoyed posting photos of their college acceptance letters. In 2014, Carpenter Library began following the example set by UNF's Admissions Office by replying to these tweets and posts to congratulate new students and welcome them to the University. These replies cause a surge of engagements for the library's accounts, including replies, likes/favorites and follows. Even a simple reply of "Woohoo! Congrats and welcome to the #SWOOPlife!" prove a successful use of time and effort. Athletes who commit to the University are particularly open to sharing their new affiliation on social media, so library staff are especially encouraged to search for and respond to these messages.

Beginning in 2012, the University of North Florida began a Twitter and Instagram contest in which students, faculty and staff can share why they #loveUNF over the course of one week. Library staff began tracking the hashtag and its usage, and made note of the numerous times that the Carpenter Library was mentioned, either directly or indirectly. By liking, sharing, and replying to any positive mention of the University and the Library during the #loveUNF contest, library staff have successfully increased their reach and their position in the University-wide conversation on social media.

Listening for Negative Conversations

In Fall 2014, the Carpenter Library's building was undergoing extensive construction on its first and second floors in order to complete a new Library Commons. The week before finals, the University scheduled for the library to also undergo exterior power washing, a lengthy and noisy process. In order to gauge overall comments and complaints from students during this time, the social media team decided to actively listen and then document any mentions of "UNF" "Library" and/or disturbances. Once documented, these comments were promptly and kindly responded to on the same platform that students made them: Twitter and Facebook. The spreadsheet was then sent to Library Administration to alert them not only of student concerns, but also how the library addressed them.

Table 1. Template used for social media documentation during renovation and power washing in late November, early December 2014.

Social Media Comments

Date	Comment	Reply (from Library account)	Facebook or Twitter	Link
11/20/2014	@unflibrary right before exams? This timing is terrible	"FYI there will be no construction during finals week. We're trying to get in as much work as we can, as quickly as possible!"	Twitter	Link
11/24/2014	UNF, you couldn't have picked a better time to renovate the library. 🏛	"Sorry for the inconvenience. We're trying our best to make the Library a better place with as little disruption as possible.	Twitter	Link
12/2/2014	I do not understand why UNF thought it would be a good idea to fix the shelves in the library the last week of classes. #distractions	Sorry for the distraction! We're trying to get the shelves cleared as fast as possible to make way for our new Library Commons :)	Twitter	Link
12/2/2014	UNF logic: oh yeah it's the end of the semester. That means finals. Ya know what's a good idea? Let's redo the library & pressure wash it. 😐	Sorry for the disruption! We're doing our best to make the Library a better place as quickly and quietly as possible.	Twitter	Link
12/2/2014	So happy UNF waited until finals week to do library renovations :)	Sorry for the timing! The ... will be a long process, not just the week before finals. Things will improve soon!	Twitter	Link
12/2/2014	UNF: "lets renovate the library the week before finals" Couldn't wait till winter break?	I'm afraid it couldn't - that's when the major construction starts in the Library. New paint, new carpet, new furniture, and more!	Twitter	Link
12/3/2014	So glad UNF decided finals week was the best week to renovate the library	Sorry for the inconvenience! We're working as hard as we can to finish things up before finals week starts, promise.	Twitter	Link
12/4/2014	Yes let's pressure wash the library windowed the last few days before finals while students are trying to study good thinking UNF	So sorry for the inconvenience. We hope they'll be done soon!	Twitter	Link

In Fall 2016, the Carpenter Library's social listening practices were put to the test when a damage control situation arose on Facebook. When the University's Student Union page posted a finals week meme from an unaffiliated academic library, many students assumed that the Carpenter Library was involved. The meme included crying emojis on an unbranded poster stating "For the courtesy of those studying around you, please relocate to the hallway if you wish to sob audibly." The Student Union employee who posted the meme tagged the library's Facebook page on the post, which quickly went viral.

Several hundred reactions (like, laughter, and anger) ensued, as well as dozens of comments from students. While most commenters appreciated the intended humor, many decried the Carpenter Library for making light of finals week stress and frustration by placing such a poster in its building; one individual even noted on the original post that they made an official complaint to the University President. Less than 24 hours after the post was originally made, library staff who monitor social media noted the evolving tone and reactions. They went into crisis mode by documenting the incident to library administration, contacting the Student Union, and directly replying to concerned students who had commented on the post or shared their disappointment on social media. The post was quickly deleted, and library staff were heralded for their quick reaction time. It is important to note that without the open lines of social media communication, and the established listening channels, the Carpenter Library likely would not have been aware of this post or its implications until it was too late. At a time in which many university students and employees are already stressed, the Carpenter Library was able to lessen negative opinions solely by listening.

Outcomes

Since the implementation of social listening, the Carpenter Library's social media presence has exponentially evolved to focus more on the needs of users, and less on original content creation. The fundamental goal of the social media plan is to create opportunities for communication and connections with customers. As a result of these implementations, user engagement has increased on both Facebook and Twitter, and more meaningful interactions have taken place between staff and customers. The Carpenter Library's Twitter account, for example, receives an average of 15,000 impressions per month, or an average of 350 per day. Library staff and administration have seen firsthand the numerous types of unsolicited feedback the library receives on social media, both positive and negative. New strategies have been put in place to address the feedback that must be attended to, such as customer complaints and concerns. These interactions have led to a more approachable, reliable and customer-friendly face for the library. Other organizations on campus have remarked on not only the informativeness of the Carpenter Library's Facebook and Twitter accounts, but also how friendly, funny, and helpful they are. In the future, library staff will continue to listen to, communicate with, and engage their online customers in order to foster norms of reciprocity and trust, while also building a sense of community.

DISCUSSION

For the past seven years, the Thomas G. Carpenter Library has devoted personnel, time, and other resources towards establishing and improving their social media strategy, which contributes to the library's CRM initiatives. The chapter set forth to summarize existing literature from a convergence of academic, trade, popular publications across the areas of social media strategy, social listening, CRM, and library management. In doing so, we identified an opportunity to share examples from the UNF library's social media strategy to demonstrate the relationship among social listening, social CRM, and consumer engagement online. By describing these actionable items, this article captures a snapshot of the library's successful efforts towards social listening and social media strategy at this moment in time. By sharing these practices with other CRM practitioners, social media strategists, academic researchers, library professionals in academic libraries, and other interested parties, the goal is to inspire ideas and considerations for developments and strategies to potentially implement. As this case study draws to a close, this information is considered within the context of the overarching case study research questions and best practices at present.

Case Study Implications

The first research question asks about how an American academic library, such as UNF, uses social listening to improve CRM. Based on the details revealed in this case study, this particular library engages in social listening on Twitter more frequently than the other social media platforms. The ability to search using established UNF hashtags, as well as hashtags that are library specific, afforded the library staff the insight to critical conversations laden in both positive and negative sentiments. For instance, the ability to be made aware of, and respond to, a student's dissatisfaction with rude customer service afforded the staff the opportunity to engage with the student and, by acknowledging the concern, repair the student's experience and build some goodwill.

The ability to enact social listening on platforms such as Twitter gives brands an upper hand to respond even when the customers do not tweet directly at the organization or tag them. By actively listening to identify tweets mentioning the organization's name to listening through the use of relevant keywords, staff members are able to discover and respond to tweets that may have otherwise been ignored. As such, social listening on social media can enhance proactive in providing customer care (Wagner, 2014). In the case of the disappointed student who allegedly received "super rude" treatment from library staff, this complaint was discovered through the process of listening to the #UNF hashtag. Summers (2015) recognizes that many social media users do tend to forget to add the @ sign on Twitter to tweet directly at an organization, or simply prefer to talk *about* the organization or brand rather than talking *to* them.

The strategies employed by the UNF library mirror two of the best practices revealed by Newberry (2017): (1) Identifying where the community exists (not simply what they say), and (2) examine what the social data is saying and take action accordingly. Stewart and Arnold (2017) emphasize active participation within their definition of social listening, and this is reinforced within trade literature. For instance, "Remember, if you're not taking action, you're just engaged in social monitoring, not social listening. Social listening is not just about tracking metrics, but about gleaning real insights into what your customers and potential customers want from you, and how you can better address those needs," (Newberry, 2017, p.3). These types of revelations from the professional sector invite seemingly limitless opportunities for social CRM research as social media continuous to evolve.

Social listening allows for the instant identification of both positive and negative feedback, and this capability for CRM provides the opportunity to show appreciation for positive comments or to find and respond to disappointed customers, which can turn potentially negative experiences into positive ones (Summers, 2015). This was clearly demonstrated in the way that the UNF library handled the construction complaints online. Rather than not responding or seeking to dismiss the concerns, the library responded in a way that was transparent and encouraging. For each complaint, the response was met with a positive or advantageous outcome of the temporary disturbance at the library, and focused on the benefits for students. By responding in a manner that played up the positive outcomes, reframing of the unsavory present experience into a favorable outcome for the *future* once the construction was finished may have influenced to student perception and reduced dissatisfaction. On the positive side, learning of students' appreciation for study spaces and resources, and the compliments to the library's art collection provide the library staff with valuable insights on the areas of the organization that are satisfying the customers.

According to these findings, an organization that is committed to using social media for CRM should be integrating social listening into the overall social media strategy, as it is critical to learn what customers are saying as an in order to determine the most effective social media and CRM strategy that best serves the individual organization and the particular customer base that they serve (Social Bakers, 2012).

The second research question asks about how an American academic library engages in CRM using social media, and this case study showcases many ways in which this is achieved. In addition to using social listening to drive CRM strategy and response, the goals set forth by the Carpenter library with regard to social media demonstrate CRM engagement by building awareness of services, providing information to customers, and using social media tools to connect with the customer community. Among the findings, the volume of interactions speaks to the engagement capacity of the library, drawing in an average of 350 impressions per day on Twitter alone. One example highlighted that showcases the CRM engagement involves replying to tweets about student experience, such as wishing students luck on final exams. In addition, the interactions with accepted students by extending congratulations to them also increased engagement on social media. The staff and administration at the Carpenter Library have benefitted greatly by using customer feedback to develop innovative means to interact with students, particularly when it comes to customer complaints and concerns. Their attention to these interactions have resulted in improved CRM on social media, which is leading to a continuously more approachable, customer-friendly, and dependable customer experience with the library.

Limitations

There are several limitations to the present study that are worthy of acknowledgment, and invite opportunities for the development of future research. To begin, the present study is limited in that it only examines the practices of a single academic library. A more comprehensive picture of how social media and social listening impact the CRM practices of other academic libraries might be gleaned by comparing and contrasting the functions of multiple and diverse institutions. Further, by using scales and measures for existing CRM practices, and developing new measures for social CRM, this area of study invite qualitative investigation that may provide more generalizable results regarding the practices among academic institutions and their libraries, their social media strategies, and their approaches to social CRM.

Another limitation to note is that these findings are restricted to a specific period of time in time. While they can serve as a benchmark for where social media CRM practices are at present and a springboard for where social CRM can grow; however, the unpredictable nature of social media challenges the ability for researchers to firmly establish best practices for lengthy periods of time. Nonetheless, as social media evolves, it is important to continue capturing the actions of CRM within this realm in order to inspire ideas and foster creativity.

Next Steps for Research

Generally speaking, moving on from the present study future research is encouraged to not only compare this institution's process with other libraries, but to also potentially relate these strategies and practices to other types of organizations as well. This can be achieved through future case studies, or by using social media metrics to evaluate which practices are most effective and yield the best CRM results. While the changing climate of social media will always be dynamic variable, the possibility exists that over time a firm set of best practices for social CRM, for academic library and beyond, may be more clearly established.

More specifically, these researchers plan to pursue this line of inquiry further by exploring more deeply the role of social listening in the context of the university library's social media strategy. We intend to examine some more recent examples where social media interactions both contributed to and were the agent of a threat to brand reputation. Existing research shows the value of social listening for crisis response (Stewart & Wilson, 2016); thus, analyzing these examples of reputational threats on social media and the associated CRM responses contributes towards the emerging findings of social CRM research, social listening research, and crisis communication research.

CONCLUSION

In conclusion, this case study explored the use of social listening to improve CRM and social media strategy at the academic library of a single American institution of higher education. By examining how UNF's Carpenter library uses social media to engage with and listen to customers, a better understanding of how social media strategy, consumer engagement, and social listening impact CRM are realized. The techniques and strategies used by this library may be implemented and evaluated within the social media strategy and the social CRM of other libraries and organizations, as they have proven to be successful in this case. The opportunity to reflect on these practices through the analysis of this original case study validates the importance of continually developing the long-term social media strategy of the Carpenter library and its associated approaches to social CRM. Over time, and as social media continues its innovation, social listening and CRM should continue to be evaluated and modified driven by technological changes and consumer needs. As new strategies, techniques, and best practices emerge, they need to be assessed in kind for how they may improve, or detract, from effective social CRM and overall social media strategy.

REFERENCES

Alton, L. (2015). How to use social media as a customer listening platform. *The Huffington Post.* Retrieved from: http://www.huffingtonpost.com/larry-alton/how-to-use-social-media-as-a- customer-listening-platform_b_7572148.html

Bizzle, B. (2015). *Start a revolution: Stop acting like a library.* Chicago: American Library Association.

Brunner, B. R. (2008). Listening, communication & trust: Practitioners' perspectives of business/organizational relationships. *International Journal of Listening, 22*(1), 73–82. doi:10.1080/10904010701808482

Burkhardt, A. (2010). Social media: A guide for college and university libraries. *College & Research Libraries News, 71*(1), 10–24. doi:10.5860/crln.71.1.8302

Casey, M. E., & Savastinuk, L. C. (2010). Library 2.0. *Library Journal.* Retrieved from: http://lj.libraryjournal.com/2010/05/technology/library-2-0/#_

Chitwood, L. (2014). 5 strategies behind awesome customer service on social media. *The Next Web*. Retrieved from: http://thenextweb.com/socialmedia/2014/07/21/5-strategies-behind-awesome-customer-service-social-media/#gref

Coen, B. (2016). Using social media for customer relationship management. *Social Media Today*. Retrieved from: http://www.socialmediatoday.com/social-business/using-social-media-customer-relationship-management#sthash.HrNGUQZM.dpuf

Crawford, K. (2009). Following you: Disciplines of listening in social media. *Continuum (Perth)*, *23*(4), 525–535. doi:10.1080/10304310903003270

De Clerk, J. (2016). Social CRM: social and communities in CRM and marketing. *i-SCOOP*. Retrieved from: http://www.i-scoop.eu/social-crm-social-communities-crm-marketing/

DeVivo, M. (2014). 4 Steps to implementing a social CRM strategy. *Social Media Examiner*. Retrieved from: http://www.socialmediaexaminer.com/4-steps-social-crm-strategy/

Dougherty, J. (2015). 3 things to know about social listening (that no one tells you). *CISION*. Retrieved from: http://www.cision.com/us/2015/05/3-things-to-know-about-social-listening-that-no-one-tells-you/

Gaha, U., & Hall, S. (2015). Sustainable use of social media in libraries. *Codex, 3*(2), 47-67.

Genpact. (2012). *Social listening: Turning conversation into actionable insights* (white paper). Retrieved From: http://www.genpact.com/insight/social-listening-turning-conversation-into-actionable-insights

Hanratty, N. (2016). Five ways companies can use social listening to be more responsive. *Forbes*. Retrieved on September 16, 2017 from https://www.forbes.com/sites/forbescommunicationscouncil/2016/12/01/five-ways-companies-can-use-social-listening-to-be-more-responsive/#2bd9b5f864c8

Harrison, A., Burress, R., Velasquez, S., & Schreiner, L. (2017). Social media use in academic libraries: A phenomenological study. *Journal of Academic Librarianship*, *43*(3), 248–256. doi:10.1016/j.acalib.2017.02.014

Huwe, T. K. (2016). Listening our way to E-awareness. *Computers in Libraries*, *36*(1), 17–18.

Hyken, S. (2017). *Six Ways Listening Improves The Customer Experience*. Retrieved on September 16, 2017 from https://www.forbes.com/sites/shephyken/2017/04/29/six-ways-listening-improves-the-customer-experience/#7369d2b672da

Jackson, D. (2017). *What is social listening & why is it important?* Retrieved on September 16, 2017 from https://sproutsocial.com/insights/social-listening/

Jauman, A. (2017). *Comprehensive field guide for social media strategists*. The National Institute for Social Media.

King, D. L. (2012). *Face2Face: Using Facebook, Twitter, and other social media tools to create great customer connections*. Medford, NJ: Information Today, Inc.

King, D. L. (2015). How to connect with and communicate with customers. *Library Technology Reports*, *51*(1), 16–21.

King, D. L. (2015). Landscape of social media for libraries. *Library Technology Reports, 51*(1), 10–15.

King, D. L. (2015). Why use social media? *Library Technology Reports, 51*(1), 6–9.

McKee, S. (2012). How social media is changing CRM. *Bloomberg*. Retrieved from: http://www.bloomberg.com/bw/articles/2012-06-08/how-social-media-is-changing-crm

Mon, L. M. (2015). *Social media and library services*. Chapel Hill, NC: Morgan & Claypool Publishers.

Newberry, C. (2017). Social listening: What it is, why you should care, and how to do. *Hootsuite*. Retrieved on September 16, 2017 from https://blog.hootsuite.com/social-listening-business/

Palmer, S. (2014). Characterizing university library use of social media: A case study of Twitter and Facebook from Australia. *Journal of Academic Librarianship, 40*(6), 611–619. doi:10.1016/j.acalib.2014.08.007

Rainie, L. (2016). Libraries and learning. *Pew Research Center*. Retrieved from: http://www.pewinternet.org/2016/04/07/library-users-and-learning/

Ramsey, E., & Vecchione, A. (2014). Engaging library users through a social media strategy. *Journal of Library Innovation, 5*(2), 71–82.

Social Bakers. (2012). *7 reasons why social listening is important* (white paper). Retrieved from: https://cdn.socialbakers.com/www/archive/storage/www/7-reasons.pdf

Steiner, S. K. (2012). *Strategic planning for social media in libraries*. Chicago: ALA TechSource.

Stewart, M. C. (2017). Social listening: Recognizing the ways that we listen online. *NISM*. Retrieved on July 21, 2017 from: https://nismonline.org/social-listening-recognizing-the-ways-that-we-listen-online/

Stewart, M. C., & Arnold, C. L. (2016). Defining social listening: Recognizing an emerging dimension of listening. *International Journal of Listening*, 1–16. doi:10.1080/10904018.2017.1330656

Stewart, M. C., & Wilson, B. G. (2015). The dynamic role of social media during Hurricane #Sandy: An introduction of the STREMII model to weather the storm of the crisis lifecycle. *Computers in Human Behavior, 54*, 639–646. doi:10.1016/j.chb.2015.07.009

Stvilia, B., & Gibradze, L. (2017). Examining undergraduate students' priorities for academic library services and social media communication. *Journal of Academic Librarianship, 43*(3), 257–262. doi:10.1016/j.acalib.2017.02.013

Summers, Z. (2015). 8 ways to use social listening for your business. *Social Media Examiner*. Retrieved from: http://www.socialmediaexaminer.com/8-ways-to-use-social-listening-for-your-business/

Sunley, R. (2015). Four tips to improve customer service using social listening. *MarketingProfs*. Retrieved from: http://www.marketingprofs.com/opinions/2015/28001/four-tips-to-improve-customer-service-using-social-listening#ixzz3zni0xdAO

Templeman, M. (2017). *Social-Listening: 5 Ways To Really Engage With Your Social Media Audience*. Retrieved on September 19, 2017 from: https://www.forbes.com/sites/miketempleman/2017/01/26/how-to-really-engage-with-your-social-media-audience/3/#2755a88f49f7

Thomsett-Scott, B. (2014). *Marketing with social media: A LITA guide*. Chicago: ALA TechSource.

Valenza, J. K. (2014). *Social media curation*. Chicago, IL: ALA TechSource.

Wagner, V. (2014). Hear, hear: The rise of social listening. *CRM Buyer*. Retrieved from: http://www.crmbuyer.com/story/81409.html

Xinyu, Y. (2016). What is Your Effort? *Mississippi Libraries*, *79*(4), 96–99.

Young, S. W. H., & Rossmann, D. (2015). Building library community through social media. *Information Technology and Libraries*, *34*(1), 20–37. doi:10.6017/ital.v34i1.5625

Zohoorian-Fooladi, N., & Abrizah, A. (2014). Personifying academic librarians' social media presence. *Malaysian Journal of Library and Information Science*, *19*(3), 13–26.

This research was previously published in Diverse Methods in Customer Relationship Marketing and Management; pages 202-222, copyright year 2018 by Business Science Reference (an imprint of IGI Global).

Chapter 72
Charging Fandom in the Digital Age:
The Rise of Social Media

Shuojia Guo
College of Staten Island, USA

ABSTRACT

In the digital age, the proliferation of fan-generated content on social media platforms is making the fan culture transitioning from the "static" online consumption to "dynamic" interaction. This is not only a result of the advancement of Information and Communication Technologies (ICTs), but also a cultural phenomenon driving by participatory fandom in cyberspace. The rise of social media has dramatically altered the dynamics of fan practices and spectatorship hence increased vocality and visibility within the fan community as well as the formation and facilitation of fan roles. In this chapter, we will explore why social media have such a profound impact upon fandom. In particular, what is new with these fan communities that social media has done so much to enable. Why there is a blurring in the lines between fandom producers and consumers in the participatory fandom. Given the new forms of cultural production, how fan culture enabled by social media is more powerful than it was ever before.

INTRODUCTION

One debate persists in mass communication research centers on the question, that is, "Is the audience active or passive" (Biocca, 1988)? In other words, is audience capable of making their own meaning out of media content or they are just helpless victims of mass media productions? Critical theorists who focus on how culture is produced and consumed, especially the economic and social implications of the process, have also raised questions about the nature of the audience. What we often forgot to realize beyond the dichotomy of active or passive consumers of popular culture, however, was the fact that they are contained within the sometimes loose, sometimes strict borders of fandom.

To some extent, we are all fans of something. Rather than a marginal subcultural phenomenon once populated by "fanatics", the status of fandom and fan culture are far more pervasive than it was in the

DOI: 10.4018/978-1-7998-9020-1.ch072

past. Focusing on the triviality of what some accused fandom, Gray, Sandvoss and Harrington (2007) questioned about the relevance of fan scholarship and wrote:

How can a focus on pleasure and entertainment be justified at the end of what will enter history books as a century of violence, driven by rapid social, cultural, economic and technological change, and with the twenty-first century set to follow the same trajectory? What contribution can the study of fandom make to a world faced with war, ethnic conflicts, widening inequality, political and religious violence, and irreversible climate change, among other disasters? -Fandom: Identities and Communities in a Mediated World

Those are important questions to fan scholars and cultural researchers. The answer, ultimately, is a simple one: *because it matters to those who are fans*. While critics ask questions about our world and ourselves, fandom offers us a venue into that questioning. What studying fandom can give us is a deeper understanding about the way in which people relate to others as well as the way they read the mediated texts that make up the world. Fandom studies offer insights into the relationships between fandom phenomenon and the overarching social and cultural transformations in the world.

Overall, there has been three distinct "waves" of pervasive fandom studies since the 1980s. The first wave that automatically considered as a "worthy cause" focused on taking what was sometimes viewed as a derogatory practice and status and turning it into a positive one, celebrating it as the resistant movement of the disempowered. The second wave followed a more sociological optic that explored how fan hierarchies mirrored those in the larger social and cultural world. The third wave of studies now emerges to examine fandom as "part of the fabric of our everyday lives" in order to capture "fundamental insights into modern life".

Fandom is becoming an integral part of our modern life, and it directly or indirectly affects global patterns of consumption, communication, identification and creation. The importance of fandom has reached an apex in cultural currency with the proliferation of social media and the expanding scope of the culture industry. Social media has positively affected fandom by allowing the interaction between fans as well as with producers, and aspects of fan culture to increase. As noted by the authors,

As we have moved from an era of broadcasting to one of narrowcasting, a process fueled by deregulation of media markets and reflected in the rise of new media technologies, the fan as a specialized yet dedicated consumer has become a centerpiece of media industries' marketing strategies... Rather than ridiculed, fan audiences are now wooed and championed by cultural industries, at least as long as their activities do not divert from principles of capitalist exchange an recognize industries' legal ownership of the object of fandom. -Fandom: Identities and Communities in a Mediated World

So, we hope to contribute to the third wave of fandom studies by examining fandom through the lens of modernity reflected in the rise social media technologies. It is the power rebalance between conglomerates and audiences, the blurred lines between fans and nonfans, the altered dynamics between cultural producers and consumers we want to explore in this chapter.

BACKGROUND

It's hard to keep up with a single definition of the term "Fandom" as it has greatly evolved since the age of Internet. According to the Oxford English Dictionary, the first recorded use of the term "fandom" was in 1903, originally in reference to sports fans. Later in the twentieth century, the term was expanded to describe the collective fans of something such as a sport, hobby, book series, films, bands, or other forms of pop culture. Only devoted fans are included in a fandom, separating them from people who may casually enjoy the subject in question.

Members of a fandom are generally interested in all of the details of their object of interest. As a result, they tend to be extremely knowledgeable about their hobby. For example, a "Star Trek" fan may be able to list all of the actors in the series, know every Star Trek trivia to argue passionately that Picard was the better Captain; A Lady Gaga "Little Monster" fan would know every song in her albums with their interpretation of the underlying themes in her music. In the early days, fans usually connect with each other through things like conventions and fanzines. They may also organize games and conferences, or compose art related to their hobby. It is common to see fans compose music, make sculptures, or create tribute films and shorts to show their infectious enthusiasm. These pursuits also indicate how devoted and committed the fans could become.

With the advent of modern information and communication technology, particular the rise of online forums and social media, many fandoms have taken their interest online. Numerous websites are built and maintained by committed fans, where fandom members can gather information, participate in conversations, or post their original artwork and writing to community forums. These sites have made it much easier for members of a fandom to connect, even if they never meet in the real world. Thus, fandom has taken on an evolved definition that has been supported by historic trends. It refers to the community that fans built on the basis of shared interest and passion. According to Jenkins (2006), fandom was regarded as a subculture characterized by microcosms, communities, and domains that surrounds hobbies, genres, fashions or persons etc. Fandom members are active consumers of their fandom object and they partake in a variety of fan practices. In a broader sense, fandom refers to the interconnected social networks of individual fandoms, many of which are often named in "pun-tastic ways" after the subject of admiration. Within certain subdomains fandoms take on different contexts. For example, a fanfiction fandom may refer to canon, the original work or text from where inspiration for fanfiction was drawn; fanart fandom often implies "photo manipulation", not traditional art, as the dominant form of art. What draws all fandoms together is the act of participating in "fannish" activities, such as participation on message boards, "livejournal" communities, conventions, events etc.

Fan Identification

Why are some people fans? How and why individuals choose their object of admiration among a set of alternatives? Why are some fans more loyal than others, and what takes them to go from casual to fanatical? The answer to these questions is linked with the concept of fan identification.

Fan identification refers to the psychological connection that individuals have with the object of fandom. It has also been defined as the level of personal commitment and emotional involvement a fan has with the subject. With its roots in social identity theory, Fan identification is a result of potential psychological, sociological factors that manifested in fans' activity levels. According to social identity theory, individuals have both a personal identity and a social identity (Tajfel & Turner, 1986). Whereas the personal identity consists of a wide variety of attributes, such as abilities and interests, the social identity is made up of significant group categories. In other words, the theory posits that when a person claims to be a member of a group, he or she observes "a oneness with or belongingness to the organization, where the individual defines him or herself in terms of the organization(s) of which he or she is a member "(Mael & Ashforth, 1992, p. 104). Individuals are more likely to become identified with an organization when it represents the attributes they assign to their own self- concepts.

Fandom plays an important role in fans' self-concepts. Fans construct identities based on the object of their fandom, the shared identity with the group they are a part of, and through their interaction with others in this group (Pearson, 2007). In the process of constructing identities around the object of fandom, fans choose to associate themselves with certain texts or characters that they feel are reflective of their own personalities, fashioning them into mirrors. For instance, fans choose to engage with certain shows or quote particular characters as a means of exploring their own identity in relation to them. As one joins fan communities, he or she is also able to form a collective group identity with other fans who share the same obsession. This shared identity that fandom facilitates is constructed around both the object of fandom and those who builds up the fandom space.

Motivation of Fan Practice

A greater identification might result in an individual's stronger willingness to participate and engage in fannish activities. Under the same theoretical framework, here we discuss the psychological and sociological factors that motivate fans to participate in voluntary fan practice.

Psychological Benefits

First, "fans are motivated by epistemaphilia - not simply a pleasure in knowing but a pleasure in exchanging knowledge" (Baym, 2000). Fans feel needed when the products of their fannish activities are shared by a large number of people. Kollock (1999) argues that when contributors realize that they have effects on the community, they become more willing to continue the voluntary work. The sense of mission and fulfilment make fans fulfills their sense of being needed. Second, the display of competency is another motivation for voluntary participating practices, which is always closely associated with self-esteem and self-confident enhancement. In the context of fandom, the relationship between fans and their fandom objects to some extent should be understood as fans "self-reflective reading and narcissistic pleasures". Fans are in fact fascinated by the imaginary extensions of themselves. Through transforming self-recognition to consistent and intense emotional investments to the fandom objects, fans realize the release of emotional desires and obtain gratification from the collective experience with fan community members (Lei, 2012).

Sociological Benefits

There are two types of connections among individuals, namely "explicit connection" (individuals are linked based on well-defined relationship) and "implicit connection" (individuals are linked based on loosely defined affinities or similarities) (Smith & Giraud-Carrier, 2010). The connections among fan community members are more likely to be implicit ones, which are based on shared interests and hobbies. Finding and staying with like-minded people make fans feel secure and help them build strong ties with each other. The sharing of fan-generated content opens up conversations between fans, which may evolve into the building of social ties. Moreover, there is an increase of the interaction and connection between fans when the Internet mediated environment came into being. The rise of social media makes it easier for fans to approach other fans, to carry out discussion and share fan labors across time and space, and to bond together. It is also common for online fans to go offline and become friends in the real world.

In addition, knowledge of fandom objects and the level of participation in fan community allow a fan to earn status within fandom and sometimes gain prestigious privileges to access fandom object or related products. For instance, "esoteric knowledge and resources" are open to participating members who always contribute to the community (Okabe, 2012). Also, more experienced members are authorized to amass knowledge and provide guidance to the less experienced ones. Thus, to achieve a higher status in fan community and win other fans' respects may also be key motivations for participating fandom activities.

FAN COMMUNITY AND PRACTICE IN THE DIGITAL AGE

Fans join groups related to fandom works to establish an identity that exists in relation to these groups and the object that they admire and discuss. In the digital age, it seems obvious that they congregate on social media as a common method for creating a space wherein they can consume, create, and share their love or criticism for a specific work. This congregation of fans at a precedent connectivity and speed than ever before is not only because of the convenience of instaneous connecting and sharing on social media, but also the fundamental concept that overlaps between fan community and social media. According to Noyes (1995), the constructs of community are ideologically and emotionally represented by both its social imaginary and its empirical reality, which two work together in a dialectic fashion constantly reinforcing each other. The network structure on social media offers a cyber-surrogate for the empirical world of day-to-day networks that described by Noyes; while aspects of knowledge and communion create the social imaginary of the community, building a shared sense of the ideological base of communal identity within the group. Kaplan and Haenlein (2010) also commented on social media as "a group of Internet-based applications that build on the ideological and technological foundations of Web 2.0, and that allow the creation and exchange of user generated content".

With the easy access on social media to connect with and contribute to online fandoms, how can someone be considered as a fan and what does becoming a fan entail in the digital age? Li et al. (2007) has studied users of social media and divided them into six categories based on their level of participation, which are: Creators, Critics, Collectors, Joiners, Spectators and Inactives. The Creators are people on the highest step of the "participation ladder" who make art, videos, write blog posts and fan fiction etc. Below them are the Critics, who rate and comment on the work of the Creators. Collectors use RSS feeds and tags to create bookmarks and structure online content made by others, while the only defining feature of Joiners is the usage of social networking sites, such as Facebook or Twitter. Spectators are the passive audience of other groups' work that they read blogs and listen to podcasts, and Inactives do not participate in any form of activities on social media. Bringing Fiskean paradigm of fan productivity into the digital age, Larsen and Zubernis (2012) made similar observation with Li et al. and proposed three kinds of skills required in fan practice, labeled as Technical, Interpretive, and Analytic. Fans who practice analytic and interpretive skills are often Creators in the fandom, while fans who only use their technical skills are merely consumers of the fan culture and can be compared to Spectators and Joiners.

In the pre-web 2.0 era, fan practice such as the creation of fan fiction, fan art, filk songs and fanvids often appeared to demarcate fan communities and identities because nonfan audiences would be far less likely to engage in these practices on analytic levels (Hills, 2013). However, with the rise of social media and participatory culture becoming the trend, fan practice on different analytic levels have become so common and the boundaries of fan productivities have been blurred. As noted by Crawford (2012), "there will inevitably be a great deal of crossover between forms of audience productivity". For example, some fan-created texts can "follow the stylistic and genre conventions of the original fan object", and also "take the conversational form of everyday life talk, providing a commentary and evaluation of the fan object as forms of paratext" (Sandvoss 2011). Some fan videos or fanvids distributed on social media also seem to combine the commentary of enunciative productivity with emulation and re-editing characteristic of textual productivity (Hills, 2013). As suggested by Jensen, there is no sharp distinction between fans and nonfans nowadays as the boundary of fandom has changed due to the changing media landscape.

The online fandom relationship also provides an interesting paradox in that it has become more complex, yet simpler. For example, before social media, the only kind of contact that could be established between the fans and their favorite singer was a real, tangible relationship, predicated on person- to-person communication. Today, however, a music icon like Lady Gaga connects with millions of fans via Twitter every day. This, of course, enhances the overall relationship between fans and celebrities in some ways, but it also creates the potential for diluted connections, to an extent, making such interactions less significant.

SOCIAL MEDIA AND ITS IMPACT ON FANDOM

The rise of social media has radically altered the existing dynamics of fans' social identity development and relationship between the creator and the consumer in fandom. The increasing consumption of social media content as a way of developing and demonstrating users' social engagement maps out an interesting evolution of the participatory culture. In this section, I will discuss how social media enable the fandom culture to become more powerful than it ever was before.

Promotion of Fandom Culture into Mainstream

Fans, who are also consumers of mass culture, were once perceived as obsessed and passive audiences that indiscriminatingly admire and adulate the products or people manufactured by cultural industries (Grossberg, 1992). Jenkins (1992) argues that fans were victims manipulated by mass culture and seduced by mass media into the most obsessive and slavish forms of cultural consumption. The theory of compensation is also applied to the sociological analysis of fandom. Milgram (1977) argues that fans sometime go to extremes in their feelings, beliefs and actions in order to protect their fragile self-esteem.

In the early days, fans were generally viewed fairly negatively in popular culture. Fandom was studied as "emblematic of pathological zeal" rather than a normal and everyday cultural phenomenon. As pointed out by Gwenllian-Jones (2003), these negative ideas of fandom arose in part because the "modes of consumption" used by fans are considered excessive then when compared to those used by "ordinary" person. For instance, fans often use fanfiction and fan art to build readings that distant from the intended meaning of the text and the "general hegemonic position" in society. In the pre Web 2.0 era, these resistant readings and fan "hostility" could be ignored or even face derision of the mainstream because fandom was largely decentralised and limited in mass without much cooperation, which inhibited the collective bargaining power of individuals. In the days before computer mediated communication, fandom communities were centered around face to face or written communication through mails and organized around fan clubs and conventions.

However, in the post era of internet-based communication, fans are able to overcome geographical limitations to gather together over a wide variety of topics and interests, and engage in a much broader spectrum of activities including writing blogs and reviews, editing wikis, posting comments on portals, blogs, forums, and sharing photos and playlists etc. As a result, fans make conscious and selective choices when they are given media texts, actively appropriate popular cultural content with new and original meanings, and make use of the self-empowerment to make meanings of their social experiences and identities from the semiotic resources of the cultural commodity described by Fiske (1989). Fans are redefined as active participators instead of passive sufferers, and fandom culture is viewed more positively as a participatory culture towards mainstream as noticed by Jenkins.

...sites like YouTube, Flickr, Second Life, and Wikipedia have made visible a set of cultural practices and logics that had been taking root within fandom over the past hundred-plus years, expanding their cultural influence by broadening and diversifying participation. In many ways, these practices have been encoded into the business models shaping so-called Web 2.0 companies, which have in turn made them far more mainstream, have increased their visibility, and have incorporated them into commercial production and marketing practices. The result has been a blurring between the grassroots practices I call participatory culture and the commercial practices being called Web 2.0. -Fandom, Participatory Culture and Web 2.0

Through the promotion of participatory culture social media has magnified and evolved fandom practices that existed pre web 2.0 into mainstream cultural practices. Social media has altered the dynamics between creator and consumer into something more transparent and two-way, shifting the balance of power to give the fans more control over the content of the media they consume and the way they consume it. Moreover, although the highly participatory nature of fandom remains and has become more prevalent in mainstream culture, the nature of the term "fans" and its expectations has ultimately changed by the increasingly media saturated culture driven by social media. While fandom originally required deep adoration of the source material, it appears that being a modern fan in the post-internet can be much relaxed, described by Jenkins as the "dilution of old fandom". In her book "Fan Fictions and Fan Communities in the Age of the Internet", Stein (2015) writes in complex and compelling ways about the "mainstreaming" of fandom within a networked culture and spotlights a new generation that "have made fan practices more socially acceptable by action, word, and image, if not name". As aforementioned, the distinction between fans and nonfans has been blurred and online fan communities gain the potential to produce "unified centers of resistant to influence the global industries of cultural production".

Facilitation of Fandom Communication

When engaging with people, individuals typically look for certain commonalities. Before the advent of Internet and its subsequent adoption within fandom, being a fan was largely a proposition that required participants to largely engage in physical encounters. Fandoms used to be transmitted via a personal, often individual level when geographical boundaries present obstacles for face-to-face communication.

Later conventions, newsletters and fanzines were employed to help reduce the need for face-to-face interactions but time and space constraints still posed as challenge to construct a thriving community.

The advent of Internet and rise of social media dramatically broadens the scope of fan communities and promotes communicative exchanges within because it enables immediate reaction, communication, discussion and reappropriation, all of which contribute to the thriving of current fandom culture on immediacy and participatory. The development of social media platforms makes fans feel easier and more urgent to connect with each other, of which Przybylski et al. (2013) terms the motivation as "Fear of Missing Out", a form of social anxiety developed at the thought of being left out of the discussion in online community. While some fans are content to use social media simply as a tool for acquiring information, others thrive more on the potential for socialization and interpersonal communication.

On some levels, no fandom has ever reached the heights portrayed in The Beatles: Eight Days a Week, at least not in public. But the rise of the likes of Twitter and Facebook has had an interesting impact on fans. Not only is fandom now more transparent than ever before, that community vibe is no longer contained to a two-hour concert — it transfers to the internet, 24/7 (or eight days a week). - "The Beatles: Eight Days A Week": Exploring The Psychology Behind Fandom And Social Media

When looking at the usage of social media sites, a predominant activity consists of engaging with fandoms. Tumblr, in particular, has become "fandom central" where entire Tumblrs are devoted to the support of a particular fandom. Even the structure of Facebook supports this shift towards fandoms, encouraging the participation of fandom activity with the use of two sidebars, while one sidebar constantly suggests pages to like or groups to join. The presence of those social network media fandoms encourages fans, through implicit incentives, to participate and contribute to their own fandom-related content, which in turn inspires the creativity and ingenuity among fandom members.

Fans can also relish in their fandom with other fans without fear of judgment by being anonymous. This is a positive development because not only does it provide a platform to allow fans to find other people to interact with, but it also creates a space for them to express their fanaticism creatively anonymously. In general, fans show general benevolence to other fans and form very strong relationships with these whom they have interacted with (Baym, 2011). Because this online relationship is based of common ground, it is also easier for this relationship to translate into friendship in the physical world.

Social media not only facilitate interaction between fans, it also made the interaction between fans and artists became possible. This increased interaction has allowed fans to feel more interconnected with the artists thus letting the fan be able to connect more personally with the celebrity, which cause a positive change in fan culture because fans now can add the personality of the celebrity as another dimension to their adoration and the increased interaction allows the icon to mobilize their fan bases better and more effectively. Research on new media has explored the ways celebrities use social media to heighten a sense of intimacy and offer greater possibilities for interaction. Marwick and boyd (2011) argue that, with Twitter in particular, "The fan's ability to engage in discussion with a famous person de-pathologizes the parasocial and recontextualizes it within a medium that the follower may use to talk to real-life acquaintances". Thus, they suggest that, by giving fans the impression that they are communicating with celebrities through a familiar and personal medium, Twitter "creates a new expectation of intimacy" between fans and celebrities. Although online relationships and conversations between celebrities and fans remain mediated, fans increasingly experience them as real and authentic, reinforcing their feelings of truly knowing celebrities. Celebrities' reciprocity gives the illusion of two-way communication, which deepens fan-celebrity relationships in ways not possible through traditional media forms. For instance, Lady Gaga's unprecedented use of social media has directly impacted her relationships with fans have built and has heightened fans' identification.

At last, social media also makes it easy for fan groups to coalesce into subgroups online – there are specific mailing lists or web boards or newsgroups for discussing fandom contents, which helps fans conduct further communications and develop in-group identities and norms in communities; Moreover, the inbuilt mechanism of likes, retweets, shares and upvotes etc. enabled by social media platforms significantly promotes participatory culture and a sense of community. If being part of a fandom is about a sense of community, social media enables the biggest communities as there can be.

Empowerment of Fans to be Promoters

The theory of the "New Organization" in the 1990s states that information and communications technologies allow businesses to "restructure their business model and adapt to the world where information is an increasingly prevalent commodity", in part by becoming less hierarchical and more entrepreneurial, and by being more networked and fragmented. Milner was considered as one of the first to apply this model to explain the free "labor" performed by fans for their favorite media texts and the mileage that media producers are increasingly getting from utilizing fan production. The increased vocality and visibility of the online fandom through social media has captured the attention of the corporate media producers. As Kerrigan (2010) discusses, media corporations are eager to employ, or perhaps exploit, online fan communities that are eager to discuss anything related to their favorite media topics. Essentially companies view fan discussions as a form of free advertising.

Online fans used to be obscure pockets of fringe activity with amazing potential. Now that potential has been fully realized in that fans are gaining tremendous power and influence with the help of social media which enables them to create a lot of things like videos, artwork, or game mods they couldn't easily make or share anywhere near before. We see this in effect when a film trailer is released to You-Tube. The fans will dutifully share it across their social media pages, and indulge in making gifs, memes and parodies all of which add to the discussion and therefore promotion of the content. With the rise of social media, there has been a shift from the traditional top down advertising approach to the bottom up method as the focus is no longer audience reach but audience engagement (Hanna et al. 2011). It has been suggested that audience activity occurs when fans move from the role of consumer to that of producer (McKee, 2004). The powerless has become powerful when they "mimic and extend the craft traditionally reserved for producers of the original text".

The increased desire of audience engagement can also be noticed in the fabric of the content itself, within the case of reality television. Early reality shows such as American Idol were built around the emergent technology of SMS and gain large fan base because of their strong desire to participate in the shows. An evolution of this idea now takes effects in a wider application through the usage of Twitter and the "hashtag". The "hashtag" once was used to help with resurrection of search and live viewing, as media has undergone a temporal and decentralized transformation due to the ease of audience access. Now "hashtag" is also used as a promotional device in that it gains maximum exposure in 'trending' if used by a sufficient large number of people. It is also interesting to think that the "hashtag" which started out as reactionary statements from fans was adopted as a preplanned "textual marker" of discussion by media producers (Highfield, et al. 2013).

Because of the promotional role that can be exploited from fandom, companies are motived to build "brandoms": "the pseudo-fan culture engineered by brand managers eager to cultivate consumer labor and loyalty while preempting the possibility of resistance that participatory fan culture promises" (Guschwan, 2012). With the advent of online social networking, the activities of "burgeoning online brand communities have piqued the interest of modern brand managers who are keenly interested in measuring and monetizing the brand-building 'labor' of these communities"(Arvidsson, 2005). Companies invest significant resources in building communities that support their brands. Thus, one can argue that as social media helps build and maintain fan communities, while, on the other hand, it exposes them to the new exploitation or "brandomization."

BUILDING "BRANDOM" ON SOCIAL MEDIA

Word of mouth marketing and brand advocacy are considered marketing gold. According the latest Nielson report, more than 80% global respondents say they completely or somewhat trust the recommendations of friends and family, and two-thirds (66%) say they trust recommendations of other consumer opinions posted online. Marketers know that peer-to-peer recommendations now worth much more credibility with consumers than brand generated content. Therefore recent efforts at understanding brand value have shifted the focus to the social communication of brands among consumers from the traditional flow of information from marketer to consumers. Arvidsson (2005) believed the value of a brand, "builds only in part on the qualities of products; to a great extent it is also based on values, commitments and forms of communities sustained by consumers". Muniz and O'Guinn (2001) defined "Brand Communities" as groups of avid consumers that "assemble, of their own accord, to discuss, critique and celebrate particular brands".

"Brand Community" has become a term used to encompass a brand's customers, fans and advocates. In the age of social media, a successful brand community is the holy grail of customer engagement. At their pinnacle, customers, prospects and partners come together organically to share their knowledge of and passion for a brand or product, resulting in a band of advocates that can be far more powerful and influential than any corporate marketing activity. The branding literature often discusses prototypical brand communities such as Harley-Davidson riders, Subaru drivers, Apple Computer enthusiasts, or Starbucks customers. It's relatively easy to identify brand fans of high profile brands, however not every brand need be a big name to have a brand fandom. By definition, affinity for a brand is personal: the consumers of local or regional brands may be every bit as passionate about their brands. Essentially, the two defining characteristics of a brand community are:

1. **Exclusivity:** How private or public is the access granted to members/prospects within the community.
2. **Depth of Involvement:** What is the scope of the collaboration being asked or commitment being required for consumers to engage in a public experience of the brand.

The benefits of having a highly engaged brand fan base, including:

- Increase the time consumers spend enjoying a brand;
- Articulate the brand message in a way that customers can transmit to new prospects;

- Provide an interactive communication and research channel that tracks members' interests over time;
- Support ongoing promotions, e.g., for new products, and events;
- Reduce advertising and promotions costs with programs that build upon each another.

Besides the short-term engagements, brand community also has the long-term benefit of shaping the evolution of the brand itself, strengthening the relationship, and building consumer trust and loyalty.

So how should marketers leverage social media to build highly engaged fan base for brands?

Choose the Right Platform

When thinking about creating highly engaged brand fandoms, we need to keep in mind the demographics and interests of our target audience as the first criteria before choosing the platforms to develop social communities. Fans have different incentives to engage in different social media platforms, therefore there is no one platform better than the other to dictate success. For example, Instagram and Pinterest are the most commonly used tools for fashion fandom, but companies like Free People, Juicy Couture and Rebecca Minkoff also use other platforms like Snapchat to provide a more exclusive interaction with the brand. By using Snapchat to give fans sneak peeks at new collections these brands are sharing exclusive content with their most highly committed fans before anyone else, making the content even more elite and ephemeral.

Set the Tone Right

Fandom can be potentially a brand's strongest ally in social media. To build such a deep level of advocacy, brands have to demonstrate their values by engaging their communities with the appropriate tone of voice. While communicating with fans, brand should speak like them, think like them, and act like them. Brands should provide a genuine interaction with fans online, and post content appeal to the target audience. Most of all, what brands should do is to focus on the quality of the content that shared online. Every piece of the content should be created, as a conversation starter, to initiate topic and discussion, all of which consist the fundamental parts of the story the brand is going to tell to its community. This facilitates an authentic opportunity to share brand messages with fans through creative dialogue.

Encourage Fans to Create Content

The success of a community isn't just about what can be offered to participants, it also requires its members to make a personal investment in participation. The best way to get members to invest in your community is simply to encourage them and ensure that they are aware of all the different ways they can get involved- liking a piece of content, submitting a comment, or attending an event etc, and remind them to engage on a regular basis. And a rewards system is a common characteristic of successful brand communities. Whatever the format is – no matter a gamification of the community membership with badges and symbols or simply a tweet saying thanks for participation-the recognition of the contribution by members is essential.

Fashion brands are known to be forward thinkers when it comes to brand communities. Black Milk, an Australian fashion brand specializing in shiny printed lycra, has a rabid fan base and leverage thousands of Sharkie selfies and create specific hashtags for every product they had on social media. Black Milk's fans are called "Sharkies" because of how quickly and ferociously they devoured (or as the fandom says, "nommed") the company's products. To some extent, the company's success can be attributed to its ability to make design choices and marketing initiatives from listening to what their customers have said in "extremely active Facebook groups". The brand encourages customers to be not just fans, but Black Milk models. The depth of brand advocacy for Black Milk can be seen in the way community members create their own art, songs and photography for the label. By inviting customers to participate in the story telling and play a big role in shaping the evolution of the brand culture, the brand successfully integrates social media fandom into its marketing strategy and e-commerce platform.

Figure 1. Professing my Sharkie pride. The Birds In Paradise dress seemed like an apt choice during this perfect holiday.
http://www.beautifulcuriosities.co.uk/2014/09/black-milk-sharkiecon-in-mallorca.html#.WEdI47R7WfQ

Build Emotional Connection

Building a sense of belonging is important for achieving fan identification, and it can as simple as welcoming new members to your community. LinkedIn, for example, allows brand to send a welcome message to new group members via email, which is a great opportunity to establish a more personal connection with them. If your brand is more high-end, you could even send out a welcome pack with branded goodies - this is something B2C brands do with bloggers all the time. A common symbol system, which can be achieved by developing a consistent calendar of content, events and features, is often used to reinforce members' association with the community. While it might take time to develop your community's own cultural symbols, something as simple as consistent branding icons across all touchpoints for your community can help fulfill this requirement. Building emotional connections within your community requires regular communication, quality interactions, and shared experiences for a long term. A dedicated community manager who can spend the time interacting with community members across channels is an invaluable asset.

Monitor Fans' Engagement With Brand

Finding the places where people are talking about your brand on the web is paramount to the success of your business. The monitor of fans' discussions will help you identify holes within your marketing and give you a better idea as to how your audience is responding to your brand messages. You can gain a wealth of information that can guide your marketing strategies.

Unfiltered feedback from online chatter will allow you to better understand how your audience engages with your product or service. By tracking the mention and discussion of your brand, brands can identify the key drivers of member conversations, new and interesting ways in which people are interacting with your product and service, and any influential individuals could be incredibly helpful when defining your community strategy. This information can help shape future marketing campaigns, and also highlight unseen product deficiencies or areas for improvement. You can even discover hidden or secondary benefits of your product you were previously unaware of.

CONCLUSION

The fandom world is ever changing and developing. The movement of fandoms from physically based, often geographically limited groups to disparate, worldwide cyber-communities has provided the group with limitless access for building complex, online communities constructed of both social imaginary and empirical reality filling of culturally significant contents. The rise of social media has a profound impact on this progression of fandoms, empowering and disempowering, blurring the lines between producers and consumers, altering the dynamics between creators and consumers, creating symbiotic relationships between powerful corporations and individual fans, and giving rise to new forms of cultural production and consumption...

Fans, who were initially viewed as passive consumers of cultural products, are taking the roles of active producers in the digital age, using their knowledge and specialties for interpreting, remixing and recreating the original media products in their own ways driven by psychological and sociological needs. The increasing consumption and production of social media content as a way of expressing admiration of and engaging with fandom and its objects has promoted participatory culture and magnified and evolved fan practices that existed pre web 2.0 into mainstream cultural practices. Fans are gaining tremendous power and influence with the help of social media which enables them to create and share a lot of things like videos, artwork, or game mods and interact with other fans and even celebrities they couldn't easily do anywhere near before, which in turn changes the role of "fans" and its expectations hold by mainstreams. The increased vocality and visibility of the online fandom through social media has also captured the attention of the corporate media producers, who are motivated to employ and exploit online fan communities or even build their own "brandoms". As technology moves forward, we will likely continue to see the dissolution of boundaries and borders that had once prevented fandom communities from creating new meaningful cultural products.

REFERENCES

Arvidsson, A. (2005). Brands: A critical perspective. *Journal of Consumer Culture*, 5(2), 235–258. doi:10.1177/1469540505053093

Baym, N. K. (2011). The Swedish Model: Balancing Markets and Gifts in the Music Industry. *Popular Communication*, 9(1), 22–38. doi:10.1080/15405702.2011.536680

Biocca, F. (1988). Opposing Conceptions of the Audience: The Active and Passive Hemispheres of Mass Communication Theory. *Communication Yearbook*, *11*, 51–80.

Bury, R., Deller, R., Greenwood, A., & Jones, B. (2013). From Usenet to Tumblr: The changing role of social media. *Participations – Journal of Audience and Reception Studies, 10*(1), 299-318.

Crawford, G. (2012). *Video Gamers*. London: Routledge.

Derisz, R. (2016). *"The Beatles: Eight Days A Week": Exploring The Psychology Behind Fandom And Social Media*. Retrieved from https://moviepilot.com/posts/4102990

Fiske, J. (1989). *Understanding Popular Culture*. London, UK: Routledge.

Gray, J., Sandvoss, C., & Harrington, C. L. (Eds.). (2007). *Fandom: Identities and Communities in a Mediated World*. New York, NY: New York University Press.

Grossberg, L. (1992). Is there a fan in the house? The affective sensibility of the fandom. In L. Lewis (Ed.), *The Adoring Audience: Fan Culture and Popular Media*. London, UK: Routledge.

Guschwan, M. (2012). Fandom, Brandom and the Limits in Participatory Culture. *Journal of Consumer Culture*, *12*(1), 19–40. doi:10.1177/1469540512438154

Gwenllian-Jones, S. (2003). Web Wars: Resistance, Online Fandom and Studio Censorship. In Quality Popular Television (pp. 163-180). London, UK: BFI Publishing.

Hanna, R., Rohm, A., & Crittenden, V. L. (2011). Were all connected: The power of the social media ecosystem. *Business Horizons*, *54*(3), 265–273. doi:10.1016/j.bushor.2011.01.007

Highfield, T., Harrington, S., & Bruns, A. (2013). Twitter as a technology for audiencing and fandom: The #Eurovision phenomenon. *Information Communication and Society*, *16*(3), 315–339. doi:10.1080/1369118X.2012.756053

Hills, M. (2013). Fiske's "textual productivity" and digital fandom: Web 2.0 democratization versus fan distinction? *Journal of Audience and Reception Studies*, *10*(1), 130–153.

Jenkins, H. (1992). *Textual Poachers*. New York: Routledge.

Jenkins, H. (2006). *Fans, Bloggers, and Gamers: Exploring Participatory Culture*. New York, NY: New York University Press.

Jenkins, H. (2010). *Fandom, Participatory Culture, and Web 2.0*. Retrieved from http://henryjenkins.org/2010/01/fandom_participatory_culture_a.html

Kaplan, A. M., & Haenlein, M. (2010). Users of the world, unite! The challenges and opportunities of Social Media. *Business Horizons*, *53*(1), 59–68. doi:10.1016/j.bushor.2009.09.003

Kerrigan, F. (2010). *Film Marketing*. Oxford, UK: Routledge.

Kollock, P. (1999). The Economies of Online Cooperation: Gifts and Public Goods in Cyberspace. In Communities in Cyberspace (pp. 220-239). London, UK: Routledge.

Lei, W. (2012). *Online Fandom and International Communication*. Beijing, China: Communication University of China Press.

Li, C., Bernoff, J., Fiorentino, R., & Glass, S. (2007). Social Technographics: Mapping Participation. In *Activities Forms The Foundation Of a Social Strategy*. Forrester Research.

Mael, F., & Ashforth, B. E. (1992). Alumni and their alma mater: A partial test of the reformulated model of organizational identification. *Journal of Organizational Behavior*, *13*(2), 103–123. doi:10.1002/job.4030130202

Marwick, A., & Boyd, D. (2011). To See and Be Seen: Celebrity Practice on Twitter. *Convergence (London)*, *17*(2), 139–158. doi:10.1177/1354856510394539

McKee, A. (2004). How to tell the difference between production and consumption: A case study in Doctor Who fandom. In Cult Television (pp. 167-185). Minneapolis, MN: University of Minnesota Press.

Milgram, S. (1977). The Social Meaning of Fanaticism. *Et Cetera*, *34*(1), 58–61.

Muniz, A. M. Jr, & OGuinn, T. C. (2001). Brand Community. *The Journal of Consumer Research*, *27*(4), 412–432. doi:10.1086/319618

Noyes, D. (1995). Group. *Journal of American Folklore*, *108*(430), 449–478. doi:10.2307/541656

Okabe, D. (2012). Cosplay, Learning, and Cultural Practice. In Fandom Unbound: Otaku Culture in a Connected World (pp. 225-248). New Haven, CT: Yale University Press.

Pearson, R. (2007). Bachies, Bardies, Trekkies and Sherlockians. In Fandom: Identities and Communities in a Mediated World (pp. 98-109). New York, NY: New York University Press.

Przybylski, A. K., Murayama, K., DeHaan, C. R., & Gladwell, V. (2013). Motivational, emotional, and behavioral correlates of fear of missing out. *Computers in Human Behavior*, *29*(4), 1841–1848. doi:10.1016/j.chb.2013.02.014

Sandvoss, C. (2011). Fans Online: Affective Media Consumption and Production in the Age of Convergence. In Online Territories: Globalization, Mediated Practice and Social Space (pp. 49-74). New York, NY: Peter Lang.

Smith, M., & Giraud-Carrier, C. (2010). Bonding vs. Bridging Social Capital: A Case Study in Twitter. In *Proceedings of IEEE Second International Conference on Social Computing* (pp. 385-392). Minneapolis, MN: IEEE.

Stein, L. E. (2015). *Millennial Fandom: Television Audiences in the Transmedia Age*. Iowa City, IA: University of Iowa Press.

Taijfel, H., & Turner, J. C. (1986). Social identity theory of intergroup behavior. In W. Austin & S. Worchel (Eds.), *Psychology of Intergroup Relations* (2nd ed.; pp. 33–47). Chicago, IL: Nelson-Hall.

Zubernis, L., & Larsen, K. (2012). *Fandom At The Crossroads: Celebration, Shame and Fan/Producer Relationship*. Newcastle Upon Tyne, UK: Cambridge Scholars Publishing.

KEY TERMS AND DEFINITIONS

Brandom: A notion developed by Guschwan, "Brandom" references the activities of corporate institutions towards fans, such as measuring, monetizing and exploiting the brand building labor of fans/consumers and the community that they have constructed.

Fan Culture: Fan culture is formed around specific cultural texts and the nature of these texts is what distinguishes fans from nonfans. According to Henry Jenkins, fan culture is a culture produced by fans and amateurs for circulation through an underground economy and that draws much of its content from the commercial culture.

Fan Identification: Fan identification refers to the psychological connection that individuals have with the object of fandom. It has also been defined as the level of personal commitment and emotional involvement a fan has with the subject.

Fan Practice: Fan practice refers to the productive activities engaged in by fans, primarily those of various media properties or musical groups. These activities can include creation and editing of written works (fanfiction), visual or computer-assisted art (fanart), videos (fanvids, fanedit) or costuming and collecting etc.

Mainstream: Mainstream is the dominant trend in opinion, fashion, or the arts. Mainstream culture is the culture that is held by or seems the most "normal" to a large amount of people that live in a society. It includes all popular culture and media culture, typically disseminated by mass media. It is to be distinguished from subcultures and countercultures, and at the opposite extreme are cult followings and fringe theories.

Participatory Culture: A culture that challenges the consumer culture, wherein individuals do not act merely consumers but also participate in cultural commodities as contributors or producers, that enables people to work collaboratively. It is emerging as the culture absorbs and responds to the explosion of new media technologies that make it possible for average consumers to archive, annotate, appropriate, and recirculate media content in powerful new ways.

Social Media: Social media is the collective of computer-mediated communication channels dedicated to community-based input, interaction, content creating and sharing, and collaboration. Websites and applications dedicated to forums, microblogging, social networking, social bookmarking, social curation, and wikis are among the different types of social media.

This research was previously published in Exploring the Rise of Fandom in Contemporary Consumer Culture; pages 147-162, copyright year 2018 by Business Science Reference (an imprint of IGI Global).

Chapter 73
Studying Celebrity Engagement on Social Media:
An Indian Experience

Tripti Dhote
Symbiosis Institute of Telecom Management, India

ABSTRACT

Leveraging a celebrity for instant recognition and visibility or building significant brand credibility and driving sales has been a long-established recipe for success over the years. Engaging a reputed face for brand promotion has ever been an exorbitant investment. Digital or social media as a communication platform has not only driven brands to create a desired recall without the burden of unreasonable spends, but has also strengthened and empowered celebrity engagement like never before by throwing a versatile array of options for individual branding and visibility. This chapter aims to explore and analyse the engagement of celebrity on different social media platforms like Facebook and Instagram, Twitter etc. with special reference to Bollywood. It delves into understanding the engagement patterns; aspects of celebrity evoked; brand impact; media celebrity brand fit, and intended target audience whether it leads to action or Influences perceptions.

INTRODUCTION

It's quite a known fact that celebrity endorsement has a huge market in India. It is one of the most popular approaches for communicating a brand or product to the consumers. Experts claim that almost 45% of commercials in India are endorsed by a celebrity. Roughly 10% of communication budgets are being used to pay for endorsers. Using celebrities facilitates recall of the message as well as the brand name which the celebrity is endorsing (Agrawal & Kamakura, 1995). According to this research; when a celebrity is paired with a brand, the image of the celebrity helps in shaping the image of the brand in the minds of the consumers.

DOI: 10.4018/978-1-7998-9020-1.ch073

Though endorsement deals in India have extended to an array of celebrity from sports, fashion, music, yet *Bollywood* or Hindi Cinema in particular continues to be the most admired place where celebrities enjoy maximum brand endorsements with admirable valuations ranging from 2.5 crore to as high as 10 crore per day depending upon their box office standing.

The simple logic behind this is that celluloid celebs in India have always been heavily aspirational as they are believed to have a God-like eminence. An element of curiosity and allure associated with *Bollywood* celebs in particular has been influence enough in setting an adrenalin rush, euphoria and triggering a frenzy of sorts for getting a glimpse into their lives.

Being a public figure, celebrities are individual brands in themselves. Audience perceive an image about them based on their attributes, appearances, personality, disposition, behaviour and lifestyle as displayed on the public platform. Precisely, it is the external interface which is the crux of any celebrity's brand image in the mind-space of their admirers manifesting into an impressionable outcome as viewers, audiences and even consumers. The recall value for a celebrity endorsed brand, the ability to reach out better and of course to bring a brand into a consumers' consideration set have all made celebrity endorsement an easy route for consumer connect. It is this Public acknowledgement of a celebrity that has been consistently leveraged across platforms for communicating a brand (McCracken, 1989) over the years.

Purchasing a brand endorsed by a favourite celebrity has therefore been a long-preferred strategy for generating a "me-too effect" among the target group. Hence whenever any celebrity is picked up for endorsement their ability to bring about an effective rub-off with the endorsed brand in terms of characteristics and image remains a prime concern for impact. Precisely, the brand image must be essentially matched with the celebrity image for the endorsement to be more effective and impactful. This is an indication that hiring one of the most popular celebrities may not essentially be a spot- on strategy; it might boomerang if the endorsed brand's values, personality and attributes do not coincide with those of the endorser. There may also be a possibility of overriding of the brand under the fame and popularity of the celebrity. Tracking down the years it has been observed that the range of celebrity engagement with the media and the audience has shown variations and evolved from magazine photo shoots, interviews, appearances at events like live shows, supporting a social cause, canvassing for political parties to extensive endorsement contracts for a particular Brand or organization. Depending upon the type of engagement the celebrities can display either a low, medium, high, or transformational level of commitment (Huddart, 2005).

Apart from congruence with the brand media and audience, an important attribute for effect has been the extent of familiarity of the celebrity to the TG being addressed as well as the esteem value & the ability to differentiate, be in sync with the TG and yet stand out (Lalwani, 2006). There are several studies reflecting that whenever celebrities are roped in for brand endorsement a mix of attractiveness (Baker & Churchill, 1977) and credibility (Sternthal, & Dholakia, 1978) has always been vital, the entire plan being translating these abilities to the products through marcom activities (Langmeyer & Walker 1991a, 1991b; Mc Cracken, 1989; Walker et al. 1992).

A suitable match between the celebrity's personality and product's attributes has the ability to trigger consumer senses more positively leading to favourable Brand perceptions. (Michael 1989 & Ohanin, 1991). Consumers tend to establish a linkage between celebrity lifestyle and that of the brand which prompts them to opt for particular brand disregards of its price, availability or any other factor. Various industry researches have also endorsed the findings that celebrities do create brand differentiation. Another major conclusion that can be drawn is that Celebrity Endorsement significantly impacts Brand Image.

SOCIAL MEDIA, THE COMPULSIVE INFLUENCER

Contemporary marketers and brands look at social media for customer engagement. They endeavour to do this by creating a distinctive personality and expression for their brand and then tying this up in the form of conversations with the overall communication. The evolution of platforms like *Facebook* and *Twitter* and the emergence of new alternatives like *Instagram* have driven the concept of shared information, content and a one on one conversation.

Traditional above the line (ATL) mass media and even below the line (BTL) tools of communication though extremely popular deliberately seemed to maintain a distance between the audience and the celebrity. In a sense, there has always been a larger than life feel, an aura and an enigma around a celebrity through these platforms making them aspirational as earlier observed. They were like demi Gods, not easily accessible, limiting the scope of interactivity. It was a very uni-dimensional connect with the TG either in the form of an onscreen character or a Brand advocacy, social responsibility or at times an on stage appearance.

But on the brighter side the extent of exclusivity was always at a peak. It was this exclusivity quotient which was being commercially leveraged by brands. However, over the year's equations have changed and a celebrity's pattern of engagement and involvement have undergone quite a remarkable transition. The rise and dominance of new age platforms, social media in particular, has transformed the role and extent of engagement.

The social media or digital platform has very effectively brought in a rare marriage of Realism authenticity and emotional connect with commerce enhancing word-of-mouth and purchase likelihood.

In fact, the business and communication landscape have altered and organizations seem to, either readily or unwillingly, acknowledge this change. With evolving forms of communication, collaboration, consumption, and innovation, new realms of interactivity for companies and stakeholders have shaped up (Kaul & Chaudhari, 2015).

The steady progression of social media has facilitated a direct communication between a celebrity and the user (Stever & Lawson, 2013). This could be attributed to the reach and moreover to the high involvement level and consciousness of todays' techno savvy, well informed and information hungry consumers and viewers. This is particularly rampant among the younger lot, where tracing their pet celebrity on *Twitter, Facebook* and *Instagram* (Chia & Poo, 2009) has become an extremely easy task.

Social media today is a compulsive influencer. Being on social media as a brand or as an individual calls for driving conversations with a user Focus. Hence, content becomes a crucial factor for impact on these platforms. With multiplicity of platforms, increased time spend on mobile devices and depleting attention span of consumers which experts believe is around 8% influential celebrity engagement is imperative. Multiplicity has made visibility a significant factor for survival endurance and sustainability.

The cool new generation has moved beyond flipping the pages of glossy magazines, Page 3 headlines, ramp walks, because for them influence is now synonymous with *Facebook Twitter* and *Instagram*. Hence while Social media has made a celebrity more approachable enhancing noticeability it has also created daunting challenges from them. Celebrities are now seen as more diversified more human and sensitive to their public expression.

They are seen as fully conscious of the fact that their engagement can fuel tremendous branding opportunities, coupled with the fact that they exert great power as critics and influencers for the Target Audience. As influencers they have the ability to build a relationship with their audience, as they enjoy a greater level of reliability and trustworthiness which brands would seek for themselves (Sen, 2014).

Therefore, celebrities on social media are able to convey the Brand message and proposition in a very convincing and engaging manner than any other common opinion maker.

It is this influence that is primarily also leveraged for pushing social causes in India. Endorsed by a celebrity, the cause becomes more visible and hence the outcome is always better.

CELEBRITY ON SOCIAL MEDIA: THE BRAND PERSPECTIVE

Also from the Brand's perspective more engagement and knowledge from a credible source translates into better recall and informed purchases hence brands too are extremely eager to facilitate and become a part of online conversations of digitally savvy consumers. Therefore leveraging a celebrity with a robust Fan following as a part of the social media strategy is an investment worth spending and makes great business sense.

With the advent of smartphones, social media has become a major channel of communication or engagement platform with the consumers. A survey says that at least an average smartphone user checks his smartphone 150 times a day. It is evident that the celebrities as well as brands should interact with those audiences frequently to create a favorable brand impact. To create a brand impact the following engagements are advised to be done.

Engagement Patterns

Celebrities or brands has range of engagement options with various social media channels such as *Twitter*, *Facebook*, *Instagram*, snap chat, etc. in which the engagement can be in the form of sporadic postings, unexpected tweets, a peak into their private lives, current trends, videos and posts on major events such as birthday, new year, etc. Celebrities or brands can choose either engaging in social media via individual channels or a common social media management tools such as sproutsocial.com

Media, Celebrity and Brand Fit

In the current media scenario dominated by social and digital it is extremely vital that the online presence, image and attributes of the celebrity must have a rub off not just with a brands' communication strategy but also with the chosen digital media platform. For instance, a cricketing Legend like Sachin Tendulkar is known for his credibility, he has a universal appeal hence it is imperious for a brand manager to check his online presence and activeness in the social media especially if the brand's communication strategy demands it. On the contrary, a celebrity like Ranveer Singh has a charming personality and is very popular among college goers; the Brands that he promotes like *Adidas, Vivo Phones Vogue* are also relevant to this TG. He is seen quite often on *Instagram* and *Facebook*, which is highly popular in this age group promoting these brands and hence finds a media -brand fit. Ranveer Singh with an admirable youth fan following hugely promotes relevant brands like *Vogue* and *Adidas*, on platforms like *Facebook* and *Instagram*, youth Fashion Icon and actor Sonam Kapoor energetically Tweets about almost all the Brands that she endorses like, *L'Oreal, Vogue* and *Kaysons NZ*.

Studies reveal that *Instagram* is not a very popular medium for brand promotion especially among movie stars In India, out of top 20 merely 5 leverage it for brand promotion. Unlike Brands celebrities today are well versed with the fact that their shelf life and popularity is extremely short lived. Hence, they are very conscious while opting for the right channel on social media so as to create maximum impact on their individual rating as well as on the endorsed brands in the quickest possible time.

Intended Target Audience

Apart from analyzing the media or channel well before designing the communication strategy, it is also equally important to analyze the demographics of the social media in which the promotion has been planned. In the current context, social and digital media is not only being leveraged by celebrity as a platform to keep their supporters informed and posted on their recent happenings but it has also become a major media for individual brand building and ROI for their professional initiatives. So while on one hand they can come out of the celebrity garb, be-friend the audience, share personal opinions sentiments and expressions on wide areas from food, culture and travel integrating content as per the social platform chosen, on the other hand they can continue to wield their impact and power in the form of tweets, hash tags, *Facebook* postings and *Instagram* Pics building their own image and creating buzz for their initiatives.

One thing is clear that the DNA of social media is different from that of traditional mass media since it has a very high susceptibility to go Viral. The communication is direct and the feedback and response is immediate. It thus brings in more responsibility to the celebrity.

Further given the context that celebrities are considered as Human Brands (Thomas, 2006) and aspirational they are apparently more cautious of guarding their brand image, as they not only bear their own image at stake but also the image of all the brands endorsed by them in the eyes of the consumers. As observed by (Miciak & Shanklin, 1994) unethical or unusual behaviour by endorsers in public domain tarnishes the image not only of the endorsers but also creates problems for the endorsement. Once an association has been established between brand and celebrity, negative information about a celebrity results in bad image in the minds of the consumers.

Though audience celebrity connects continues to rule the roost on the flip side being under incessant public glare and scrutiny almost 24x7, too much of engagement on social media can only threaten the celebrity exclusivity quotient eroding the curiosity levels. And hence the moment a celebrity falls short of delivering a return on investment (ROI) brands can also dissociate from them and discard them

Moreover, if the celebrity gets mired in some sort of controversy the Brand's equity takes a definite beating resulting in the contract termination with such celebrities. There have been quite a few instances of relations souring up between brands and celebrity due to controversies leading to contract dissolution, notable being Boxer Mike Tyson, Indian cricketers MS Dhoni, or *Bollywood* superstars Salman khan (*Coke*) and Aamir Khan (*Snap deal*).

Literature observes that consumers may construct their self-identity and present themselves to others through their brand choices based on the congruency between brand-user associations and self-image associations (Escalas & Bettman, 2005). Therefore, based on the rub off, there can be a connect, or a disconnect with celebrity endorsement, in case consumers find a relevance with their own need & life in some way. It's essentially due to the aspect of "Self enhancement" (Escalas & Bettman, 2003). This again is a clear indication that with through the line communication the focus is more on the engagement with the celebrity.

Table 1. Celebrity, brands, controversy and social media

Celebrity	Brand Endorsement and Outcome	Content and Controversy	Month and Year
Aamir Khan	1. Incredible India -- 7 year contract ended. 2. Snapdeal – One year campaign deal terminated. Actor replaced with a new campaign.	Comment on growing Intolerance In India & Political beef consumption related controversy that became viral on social media.	Jan & Feb 2016
Cricketer M.S. Dhoni	1. Resigns as Brand Ambassador of real estate Brand Amprapali 2. Brand PepsiCo- Drops Dhoni. Replaced by younger more socially active celebs like cricketer Virat Kohli and actor Ranbir Kapoor	Public Fury on *Twitter* over the quality and integrity of the builder forcing the celebrity to step down Waning fame and decreasing popularity on social media.	April 2016 August 2016
Salman Khan	1. Brand Coke- Terminates 4 Year deal with Thums up Actor replaced by younger socially savvy actor Ranveer Singh	Sensitive Remarks about Rape on *Twitter* for Film Promotion. Opposing Government and coming in support of Paki actors	Oct 2016

Source: Adapted from Economic Times, E Paper. Oct 21, 2016

CELEBRITY ENGAGEMENT ON SOCIAL MEDIA: AN AUDIENCE PERSPECTIVE

In order to understand the celebrity engagement pattern, it is first important to have a grasp on the target audience and what is their perspective and expectation about this engagement on social media. As part of the analysis, an online questionnaire was prepared to analyse the responses on different aspects of celebrity endorsed brands. This questionnaire was administered to total of 127 respondents which included people from different age groups and profession.

The survey was based on the following research questions:

1.   Age group of the respondents

Out of total 127 respondents, the maximum respondent was from age group of 25-30 and lowest were above 35. Age group 25-30 & 31-35 were mostly working professionals, age group 20-24 were post graduate students.

Figure 1. Age group of respondents

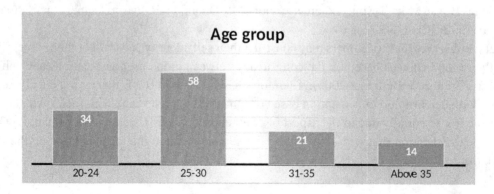

2.   Which Preferred Personality do you follow on social media?

48 respondents out of 127 followed film-stars, while 31 out of 127 respondents followed sportspersons. As per the analysis, age group of 25-30 mostly followed film-stars and sportsperson.

Figure 2. Preferred personality on social media

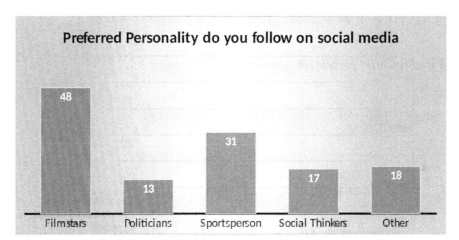

3.   Which Social Media Platform do you prefer to engage with them?

As per the analysis, people usually follow *Twitter* the most for engaging with their social figures followed by *Facebook*. The respondents in the 25-30 age groups in particular were influenced by lifestyle of the celebrity and other aspects like various events and happenings, brands endorsed, social responsibility initiatives, comments on issues etc also made an impact.

Figure 3. Preferred social media platforms

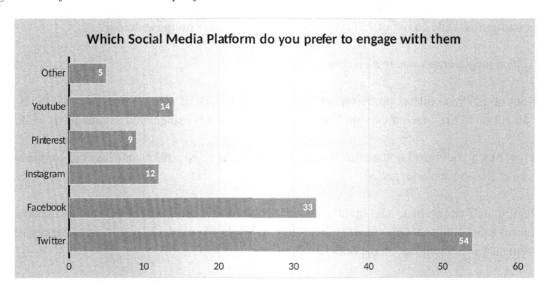

4.   What is your preferred celebrity content on Social media?

Interacting with their favourite celeb brings in a sense of belonging and hence, celebrity engagement and interactivity is the most preferred followed by lifestyle and happenings. The most potential age group that engages with a celebrity was found to be 25-30 yrs. essentially because they may have just embarked on a corporate career and are on the growth path. Their exposure to the internet and social media is also an important reason. The other age group that actively engage with a celebrity on social media was found to be the youngsters in the 20-24 years age group, predominantly PG students.

Figure 4. Preferred celebrity content on social media

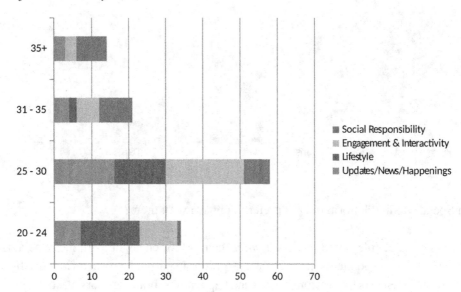

5.   Do you associate with the brands endorsed by your favourite celebrity ?

2 out of 127 respondents said that they would like to engage with the brands endorsed by their favourite social figures while 45 out of 127 respondents don't engage with those brands.

6.   Which media drives you to a celebrity endorsed Brand?

54 out of 127 respondents prefer online platforms such as social media to engage with the brands while 46 out of 127 respondents would like to engage with brands using television media as well.

7.   How much your brand association would get affected, if celebs make controversial comments on any of the above platforms?

59 out of 127 respondents said that the association they have with the brands is most impacted by any controversial comments provided by social figure. While 44 out of 127 respondents suggested that endorsement has least impact on the brand association.

Figure 5. Endorsement influence on preferred celebrity

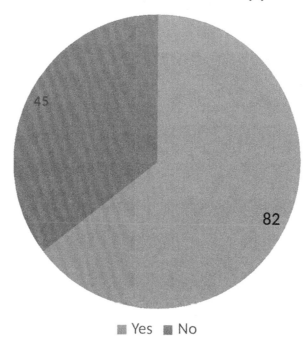

Figure 6. Media influence for celebrity endorsed brand

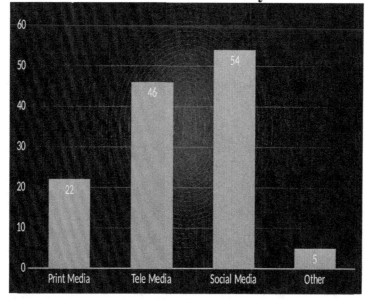

Figure 7. influence of celebrities' controversial comment

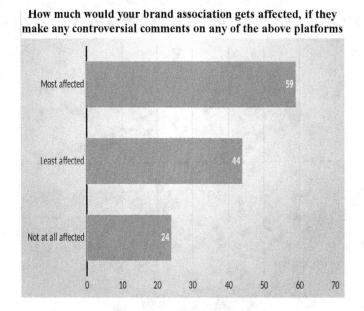

8.   What would be your reaction towards the brand based on above controversies?

43 out of 127 respondents said that they will un-follow social figure and spread a negative word of mouth about him/her. 22 out of 127 respondents said that they will un-follow the Brand and spread a negative word of mouth about it. 28 out of 127 respondents said that they will un-follow both the social figure & the brand and also spread a bad word about them. While 34 out of 127 respondents said that they will do nothing about it.

Figure 8. Reaction towards controversy-laden brands

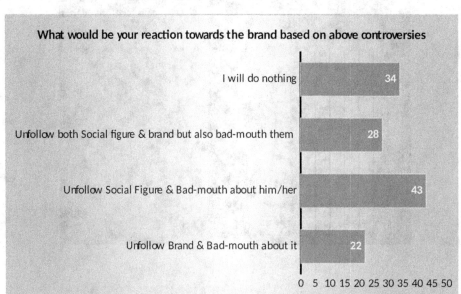

9.   After a while (period), would you be willing to associate yourself with the same?

56 out of 127 respondents said that they will associate with the brand again after certain period of time while 23 out of 127 respondents said they will associate with both brands and social figure after a period of time. 31 out of 127 respondents said that they will not associate either with the brand or the social figure.

Figure 9. Time period for re-association with brand and social figure

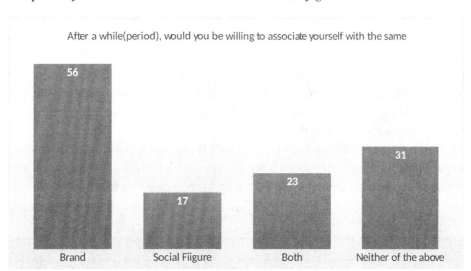

From the audience perspective, it was realized that demographics in the range of 25-30 are the most active participants in following a particular brand and its associated celebrity which also happens to be Film stars mainly (Figure 1 and Figure 2). This particular set of followers prefers engaging with the celebrities over social media platforms mainly *Twitter* and *Facebook* (Figure 3). However, such social media platforms act as enablers for brand association as well, apart from the conventional TV media platform (Figure 4 and Figure 5). We have also found that, respondents are very much affected by any controversial act or statement made by such celebrities on public forum, which in turn affects their association towards the brands endorsed by them (Figure 6). As a step further, our survey results also unveiled the possible instantaneous negative reactions towards both the brand and the associated celebrity (Figure 7). The results showed their instant disconnect with such brands, however over a period of time, the respondents are willing to reconnect with these brands irrespective of such events in past (Figure 8). The survey also revealed that the dissociation of the respondents from the celebrity was comparatively higher than the brand endorsed by him/her. Thus celebrity endorsement plays a crucial role in consumer's attitude towards a brand.

CELEBRITY, SOCIAL MEDIA AND CONTENT ANALYSIS

Celebrities today are more than conscious of the fact that social media is much more trustworthy than traditional media and has the definite ability to alter as well as build their public image. Film personalities in particular generously use the platform for pitching their movies; discuss their characters, and share their lifestyle with doting admirers. They also talk actively about their Brands and leverage the platform for projecting their philanthropic side, to develop a certain image. This facilitates a dual benefit for their endorsements and for their movies.

So while on one hand celebs are seen liberally using the social platform to create an online identity resonating with their on -screen image, the rising attractiveness of the medium on the other hand has stimulated companies to actively track the movement of celebrities and brands on social platforms like *Facebook* and *Twitter* thus giving way to an entirely new pecking order among *Bollywood*'s biggest brands.

To explore and analyse the engagement pattern of *Bollywood* celebrity in particular on different social media platforms, content analysis was the tool chosen. *Facebook* and *Twitter* were the platforms selected for analysis based on audience survey. Also based on observation of content in case of some celebrities *Instagram* was also sparingly considered.

A four month time frame from May 2016 to August 2016 was tracked for the content of eight celebrities which included six film stars, two sportspersons. The major factor considered for content analysis was Engagement and activity in the specified month and presence on *Twitter* and *Facebook*.

Table 2. Key areas of focus for content analysis

Understanding Engagement Patterns	Social Media Platforms Selected by the Celebrity. Involvement of the Celebrity: Controversy, Publicity, Brand Endorsement, Interaction With Fans, Celebration etc. a General Check on the Typical Patterns of Engagement, Language Used etc
Aspects of Celebrity Evoked	Personality, Social responsibility, humour, Intelligence, Brand endorsement, etc.
Brand and Other Impacts	What is the impact on Brands he/ she is endorsing, Impact on Individual, and impact on professional offering (his movies, shows, etc.) due to this engagement on social media.
Media Celebrity Brand Fit	What is the engagement on Twitter, what is the role on Facebook, is it different on Twitter, etc.
Intended Target Audience	Is it specifically intended for a particular target audience? Is it intended to influence some action or certain perceptions and commonalities drawn?

Key Areas of Focus for Content Analysis

It was observed that in the month spanning the study period namely May 2016 – August 2016 veteran actor Mr. Amitabh Bachchan apart from maintaining a regular blog was found to be the most prolific and consistent on *Facebook* and *Twitter*. Despite a frenetic timeline and schedule, the actor who always refers to his social media followers as his extended family was seen engaging and interacting with his fans every day across the four month span sometimes updating them on his personal life, glimpses of his grand- daughter through pictures, sharing memories about his past blockbuster movies while giving updates on his day to day professional activities like the progress on his upcoming releases, opinions on relevant issues like Olympics visits on various platforms generously coupled with relevant pictures.

The month of August saw him very active on social responsibility talking about his contribution in Hon'ble Prime Minister's *Swachch Bharat Abhiyan* (Cleanliness Drive). The actor was rarely engaged in brand endorsement during the study period. His social media presence is targeted at a very general population which includes his admirers across almost all age group. He extends his fan connect through his popular blog.

One unique aspect observed about the veterans' engagement patterns was his ability to maintain his relevance quotient and resonance with his followers. The content published by the legend was always based on well informed facts and the language used quite lucid and endearing.

While Mr. Bachchan comes across as a very humble, responsible and competent personality motivating his fans, another mainstream popular actor with a huge Fan Base Ranveer Singh was found to be high on brand endorsement aggressively sharing videos of his brands on *Twitter*, engaging with his brands actively on *Instagram* as well. The actor was found to be dominating on *Twitter* across the study period. Connecting with his fans through friendly chats, generously sharing pictures of his own fan moments, captivating shooting locations and rendezvous, celebration of one of his achievement as *Times* most desirable actor of 2015, gratitude tweets to his fans or compliments and greeting for his contemporaries and even appreciating the NBA legend Le'Bron James who had won his 3rd NBA championship clearly brought about his intention of enhancing visibility salience and retaining his Brand Image. The basic aspect of his personality that consciously came across platforms was his Energy vivaciousness and excitement. The approach and language used appeared cool and casual. On the social responsibility front the actor in tune with his image was tracked creating awareness on the need for sex education in India by sharing videos and tweeting about it. The typical target audience that the actor aimed at was essentially young and enthusiastic generation next that were hooked on to his movies. The chosen platforms by the actor seemed to be in perfect sync with his personality.

By observing all his posts on, it could be realized that yet another reigning actor of *Bollywood* Shah Rukh Khan in *Facebook, Twitter, Instagram,* was very interactive with his fans, personally acknowledging those who appreciated his work and appeared keen to keep them informed about his work on a regular basis. He was seen endorsing brands by posting launch videos etc but was observed to be more focussed towards personal branding. As a part of this he was seen acknowledging one of his fans for a presenting him with a sketch by tweeting a picture with her. The star never seemed to miss out on any opportunity to extend his warm greetings to public in general. Like on the occasion of the Independence Day on August 15, he made a video to greet fellow Indians. He also made it a point to effectively brand an upcoming movie of his by posting regular pics with the cast and crew and talking about it on both *Twitter* and *Facebook*. His social responsibility angle was also showcased during the period however what made him stand apart was his ability to frankly express his point of view and also respond to negative tweets and criticism with a sense of humour. The actor was observed making a conscious effort of tracking significant happenings around him and reacting to them.

This can be exemplified by his proud tweets revelling the victory of Olympic medallists P V Sindhu and Sakshi Malik. Conclusively the actor's social media expressions were observed to be full of wit and friendly connect. More female stars Deepika Padukone, Priyanka Chopra and Sonam Kapoor were the most active during the mentioned time frame of study. Both Priyanka and Deepika made their *Hollywood* debut in 2015 and hence as expected their tweets and posts on FB were mostly dominated by experience sharing, videos and regular updates on their international initiatives with Pictures and happenings. While Deepika in her FB posts and tweets focussed more on her professional side endorsing her brands in a bid to create a me-too feeling among her global fans and also uploading teasers of her international debut. She was also seen to be more comfortable posting pictures on *Instagram* and *Facebook* rather than tweeting her heart out. Fan interaction direct connect, arousing curiosity for her hollywood venture and enhancing her Global Brand image seemed to be on her agenda. The converstaion was mostly professionally oriented with very less personal touch to it.The actor made a concious effort to reflect a reticent no-nonsense competent personality.

Ex Miss World Priyanka Chopra on the other hand appeared much more happening versatile and diverse effectively engaging in retweeting, taking criticism in her stride, witty remarks, tweeting about her domestic and global brands innovatively, promoting her debut Marathi movie Ventilator and registering her social concern through posts about children's education. During this study, she was tracked garnering publicity by tweeting about her lookalike Navpreet Banga on Social networking sites which went viral and kept her in the news. The doppelganger issue was trending after her tweets. The common pattern observed in Priyanka's engagement in social media was her self-endorsement in various National and International magazines. Her approach throughout was observed to be very cool and easy going and hence the personality that emerged out of her social media content was essentially an excited spirit happy go lucky types.

Another Popular Indian mainstream actor, Sonam Kapoor who is also highly admired for her fashion sense and style was seen springing surprises at her fans on social media. Basking in the glory of a successful movie, She was found to be extremely active on both FB and *Twitter* platforms throughout the four months specified, but was seen more closely connected with her fans on *Twitter*. The typical pattern observed on her *Twitter* handle was fan engagement enthusiastically responding to their queries as well as tweets. The commonality on both the platforms was that she was actively engaged in brand endorsements for all her brands like *Oppo, Colgate, LO real, Kalyan Jwellers* aimed at triggering sales, hitting out at the young target market especially females. Other activities included talking about her shows, movies, award functions. and regularly posting all her daily updates. Promotion of family initiatives like father Anil Kapoor's TV series "24" and brother Harshvardhan's debut movie "Mirzya has also been a part of her engagementthat brought out a different shade of her personality.

Parelely to enhance her Brand value and image she also launched an app of her own and made announcements during this period to engage with fans directly on a platform and stay connected to them.

On the social responsibility front the actor was tracked spreading awareness about health of malnourished kids as well as child marriage through her close involvement with an NGO. Sonam Kapoor comes across as an extremely savvy, socially concious and sophisticated personality. This reflected in the choice of her language and brand endorsement.

In order to understand the differences in engagement patterns and also draw out commonalities two sports celebrity namely young cricketing sensation Virat Kohli, captain Indian cricket team and Sania Nehwal Badminton champion were tracked. One unique thing observed about these celebs was their extreme engagement with Brands. Virat came across as a very cheerful exciting personality. His way of representing endorsed brands reflected not just his social interaction but also his character of brand intelligence. He tweeted about his amazing experience after taking a ride in the new Audi R8 V10+ that had a two-pronged strategy where he endorsed the Brand and also able to connect with his followers by updating them about his passion for stylish cars. His support and appreciation for Olympic achievers was also effectively brought out through his tweets. He connected with his fans through his Brands on *Twitter* and unlike *Bollywood* celebrities, brands too leveraged Virat's Star power to reach out to their target audience.

Ahead of an upcoming match the cricketer was also seen engaging with his fans by sharing childhood experiences and posting selfies with his fans on *Facebook* Saina Nehwal Badminton champ due to Olympics season was also captured actively endorsing Brands. The special feature of all her endorsements was being a motivational social message through all the brands. The brand- celebrity fit was perfect generating a strong association with the sport. Unlike Virat Saina's personality came across as more responsible and sincere than cheerful and exciting. Her other engagements though not very prolific reflected her passion for varied sports like tennis which was evident when she tweeted cheers for Roger Federer during his Wimbledon 2016 performance, she also retweeted a couple of posts. What was missing was a close connect with her followers.

Content Connect and Nuances

Celebrities prefer to remain connected with their fans and admirers at all times for visibility and salience. Based on the study of celebrity content it was observed that a celebrity in India typically can assume following roles on social media:

- **Opinion Leaders:** Influencing opinions on different contemporary issues and creating a huge following on social platforms. Politicians and spokespersons are prominently inclined towards this and so were Film stars. *Twitter* is one medium which was found to be potential for celebrity opinion leaders.
- **Achievers and Anchors:** Celebrities highlight their achievements to gain maximum leverage and social media attention with their unique accomplishments in personal and professional lives. *Facebook* seems to be the perfect platform for boasting about achievements to create the right imagery and positioning in the minds of their followers.
- **Brand Ambassadors:** The popularity of a celebrity in India is measured not just by their glamour and professional laurels but also by the number and type of brands that they endorse. Because brands are where the entire quick buck comes from. Hence, celebrities were tracked generously using platforms like *Facebook*, *Twitter* and even *Instagram* to post videos and talk innovatively about the Brands they endorse. A two- pronged strategy, this not creates a recall and association for the endorsed brand but also multiplies the revenue and increases customer base both for the brand and the celebrity.
- **Social Cause Champions:** This was very extensive. It brings to the fore the human side of their personality as a responsible citizen. Almost every celebrity wants to enhance his or her Brand Image and create a special place of respect in the minds of their followers on social media. This is also their way of contributing to the society and influencing followers to wholeheartedly support significant social causes. Therefore, supporting social causes was found to an easy and potential route to facilitate a fast and effective word of mouth.
- **Social Media Buddies:** Presence on *Twitter* and *Facebook* was very evident due to the high engagement quotient and interactivity for encouraging follower intimacy and direct connect by shedding the larger than life image and thus making visibility of initiatives and brands a cake walk.

CONCLUSION

Unlike a decade ago when celebs were inaccessible and called the shots while their fans were all the time awestruck by their star power, *Bollywood* celebrities of contemporary times are found to be more approachable hence highly interactive on social media with content beyond brands. Social media to an extent has wiped off the exclusivity factor of traditional media. Sports personalities covered had more affiliation towards brands building their own personality through them. They were comparatively observed to be less engaging on the personal front, especially contemporary sports celebs. Some of them who had wrapped up their career were found to be more general in conversation ranging from wit to current awareness. Neither much of Brand savvy behaviour observed nor consciousness about the association and brand fit.

The study reflected that enhancing individual salience, visibility and a direct connect with their admirers was a major reason why celebs are hooked on to social media. *Bollywood* celebrities appeared to be more conscious of the larger than life image by virtue of the glamour in their profession. They seemed equally alert to the cluttered competitive scenario in their domain and hence visibly displayed every possible attempt to shed the screen persona and depict nuances and vivid shades of their real self, endorsing the fact that "I am one like you". The aim was essentially to reach out to their fans and establish a personal individual connect, not just to keep them updated but also to strike a resonance for leveraging their initiatives and even brands. The engagement pattern mostly appeared to rely on the career stage in which the celebrity was. Hence, in case of veterans, actors in the maturity stage the engagement pattern was broad based, inclined towards social consciousness and less on brands aimed at building and defending their existing image. The younger crop of actors seemed conscious of their image, personality and also their Brands and media fit. Actors like Shah Rukh Khan and Salman Khan who had surpassed growth moving towards maturity stage in their career were aggressive on creating a visibility to retain their star status. Sports personalities on the other hand were found to be more on the motivational side which also reflected in the brands that they talked about. The language and presentation, however, clearly differed with the kind of sport hence while a cricketing celeb was slightly more aggressive engaging and interactive other sports like Badminton were found to be more sober and subtle.

REFERENCES

Agrawal, J., & Kamakura, W. A. (1995). The economic worth of celebrity endorsers: An event study analysis. *Journal of Marketing*, *59*(3), 56–62. doi:10.2307/1252119

Baker, M., & Churchill, G. Jr. (1977). The impact of physically attractive models on advertising evaluations. *JMR, Journal of Marketing Research*, *14*(4), 538–555. doi:10.2307/3151194

Chia, S., & Poo, Y. (2009). Media, celebrities, and fans: An examination of adolescents' media usage and involvement with entertainment celebrities. *Journalism & Mass Communication Quarterly*, *86*(1), 23–44. doi:10.1177/107769900908600103

Huddart, S. (2005). *Do We Need Another Hero? Understanding Celebrities. Roles in Advancing Social Causes. Mimeo*. Montreal: McGill University.

Lalwani, R. (2006). Impact of Celebrity Endorsement on Brands. *International Journal of Scientific & Engineering Research*, *5*(12).

Langmeyer, L., & Walker, M. (1991). *A first step to identify the meaning in celebrity endorsers*. MN: ACR North American Advances.

McCracken, G. (1989). Who is the celebrity endorser? Cultural foundations of the endorsement process. *The Journal of Consumer Research*, *16*(3), 310–321. doi:10.1086/209217

Michael, A. (1989). Celebrity and non-celebrity advertising in a two-sided context. *Journal of Advertising Research*, *6*(7), 34–42.

Miciak, A., & Shanklin, W. (1994). Choosing celebrity endorsers. *Marketing Management*, *3*(3), 50.

Ohanian, R. (1991). The impact of celebrity spokespersons' perceived image on consumers' intention to purchase. *Journal of Advertising Research*, *19*(3), 39–52. doi:10.1080/00913367.1990.10673191

Sen, S. (2014). Social Media: The New influencer. Retrieved August 8, 2017, from http://www.afaqs. com/news/story/42048_Social-Media-The-New-Influence

Sternthal, B., Phillips, L. W., & Dholakia, R. (1978). The persuasive effect of scarce credibility: A situational analysis. *Public Opinion Quarterly*, *42*(3), 285–314. doi:10.1086/268454 PMID:10297222

Stever, G., & Lawson, K. (2013). *Twitter* as a way for celebrities to communicate with fans: Implications for the study of parasocial interaction. *North American Journal of Psychology*, *15*(2), 339.

Thomson, M. (2006). Human brands: Investigating antecedents to consumers' strong attachments to celebrities. *Journal of Marketing*, *70*(3), 104–119. doi:10.1509/jmkg.70.3.104

Walker, M., Langmeyer, L., & Langmeyer, D. (1992). Celebrity endorsers: Do you get what you pay for? *Journal of Consumer Marketing*, *9*(2), 69–76. doi:10.1108/07363769210037033

Chapter 74
Influence of Social Media Analytics on Online Food Delivery Systems

Ravindra Kumar Singh

https://orcid.org/0000-0003-1142-1954

Department of Computer Science and Engineering, Dr. B. R. Ambedkar National Institute of Technology, Jalandhar, India

Harsh Kumar Verma

Department of Computer Science and Engineering, Dr. B. R. Ambedkar National Institute of Technology, Jalandhar, India

ABSTRACT

Online food delivery applications have gained significant attention in the metropolitan cities by diminishing the burden of traveling and waiting time by offering online food delivery options for various dishes from many such restaurants. Users enjoy these services and share their experiences and opinions on social media platforms that impact the trust of customers and change their purchasing habits. This drastic revolution of user activities is an opportunity for targeted social marketing. This research is based on Twitter's data and aimed to identify the influence of social media in food delivery e-commerce businesses including decision making, marketing strategy, consumer behavior analysis, and improving brand reputation. In this article, the authors proposed an Apache Spark-based social media analytics framework to process the tweets in real time to identify the influences of generated insights on e-commerce decision making. The experimental analysis highlighted the exponentially grown influence of social media in food delivery e-commerce portals in past years.

DOI: 10.4018/978-1-7998-9020-1.ch074

1. INTRODUCTION

E-commerce platforms are serving various goods and services in almost every corner of the country within a reasonable time at very competitive prices. These e-commerce businesses have obtained a very positive response from the consumers and are still improving. A successful demonstration can be seen in the online food delivery platforms (Gupta et al., 2016), here the time taken from ordering, to the food preparation, to its doorstep delivery is improving at an unbelievable pace. Despite stretching the delivery services, with the ever-improving technology and analytics, it will definitely improve. Nowadays these food delivery applications are one of the most popular applications in metropolitan cities and serving as hunger saviors, they are attracting millennials, young students, and professionals (Rathore et al., 2018). These businesses have invested a lot of capital in advertisements, discounts, and offers, to promote themselves, increase the market share, and improve their reach among masses. One of the key exciting features on these services is that consumers can order various dishes from many such restaurants and enjoy the food at their comfortable place without investing extra time to visit the place and wait for the order to be prepared. Additionally, they have enough freedom to explore menu for an eternity before placing an order without any curb to quench the hunger anytime (Nagpal et al., 2020). Few added attractions like quick order, excessive discounts, no limitation on order value, and acceptance of numerous payment options including credit card, debit card, net banking, digital wallets, and cash on delivery are cherry on top in its acceptance. As usual, these applications are competing with each other in terms of process, discount offers, delivery, food quality, a wider range of vendors, and customer service points of view.

The various social media platforms have become an important channel in collaboration and sharing opinions, thoughts, and experiences (Jansen et al., 2009). The internet revolution has brought a lot of changes in people's life via social media, it's very common nowadays to share the eating and check-in events of various restaurants on social media. These kinds of posts along with its sentiments are very useful for food delivery services (Yeo et al., 2017). These posts are accessible to other people in the network and it engages users to share more and more and build a platform to know more about the products and services of various e-commerce platforms. This social impact can be observed in all the business segments, but e-commerce business has its profound effect and it helps companies to know better about their customers and their products to make appropriate business decisions and act accordingly (Hong et al., 2016). At the same time, it helps users to know about the quality of particular goods and services, its post-sale customer services, and the reputation of the e-commerce portals by the experiences and opinions shared by other users, which ultimately boosts the trust and intention to buy in the customers. So, e-commerce businesses have jumped into online advertisement and promotion of their products and services for maintaining a good social profile to represent themselves on various social media platforms (Vernier et al., 2018).

This research is mainly focused to identify the influence of social media and its analytics on food delivery applications and comparing the customer service and marketing strategy of four most popular food delivery applications namely, Zomato, Swiggy, Ubereats, and Foodpanda. The highlights of this research are mentioned as follows.

- This research proposes an effective framework for social media analytics that is capable of handling high-velocity data streams, distributed data processing, and task scheduling. It ensures the high availability of the system.
- It highlights the influence of social media analytics on online food delivery systems.

- Sentiment analysis is the base of this research, so this research went through multi-directional sentiment analysis to gain the polarity of opinions in multi-directional space rather just on an overall basis.
- It highlights the sentiment and brand reputation of four most popular online food delivery applications namely, Zomato, Swiggy, Ubereats, and Foodpanda in India.
- It highlights the brand reputation of online food delivery applications and demonstrates the decision-making processes for task prioritization.

The rest of the article is arranged as follows. Section 2 provides a brief overview of related work in social media influence in e-commerce. Section 3 presents an overview of the research design and methodology. Section 4 discusses the proposed framework and details of its various components. Section 5 focuses on the experimental setup for the research. In Section 6, the analysis of the results of this research is illustrated. Section 7 concludes the research and also presents recommendations for further work.

2. BACKGROUND

The influence of social media has radically transformed the perception and purchasing habits. That's why there is cut-throat competition among various online food delivery services, all of them are exclusively investing in social media on advertisements, brand reputation, and remitting post-order services on social media channels. The key factor to evaluate the effectiveness of their advertising and to know the customer satisfaction in social media sentiment analysis. It's used as a tool for a decade to understand the trends and to be competitive in the business. A study concluded that social media can be utilized to obtain the sentiment of a brand and provides a mechanism to deal with negative sentiments posts by interaction with users on the portal (Schweidel & Moe, 2014). Another research concludes that Twitter can be the most effective medium to engage with customers, even a low involvement product can earn huge followers and spread the content with the multiplication effect of retweets and quoted tweets (Soboleva et al., 2015). The recent evolution of Twitter tactics like hashtags has proven a positive effect on spreading content even having low follower supports. Different companies may adopt different marketing strategies to be successful. Lots of research papers were referred to in baselining of this research, these are organized in various categories as follows.

2.1 Sentiment Analysis on Twitter Data

Twitter's data has gained enough popularity in the sentiment analysis world because it comprises opinions, feelings, sentiments, user reviews, current trends, user's liking, and disliking information. Apart from that Twitter has provided its free public application programming interface to collect data based on custom keywords for a specific timeline, language and many more filtering criteria for the research purpose that makes these posts are very crucial in sentiment analysis. (Jain et al., 2017) presented a machine learning with a natural language processing capable framework to detect the emotions in the reviews and the user's post to achieve better accuracy on sentiment analysis. This study was based on an e-commerce portal to improve the quality of service based on sentiment analysis. Social media even helps in forecasting various events like election results before the declaration of the actual results, (Jain et al., 2017) presented a novel intelligent prediction technique to predict election results based on voter sentiment by using dynamic keywords and topic modeling on social media data. Similarly, there are many such use cases of sentiment analysis that are influencing business decisions.

2.2 Twitter Analytics in Online Food Delivery Services

With the augmented importance of various analytics in the product and services industry, it became essential to be competent in online food delivery applications as well. A study by (Kedah et al., 2015) concluded that efficient delivery, reliable customer service, food quality and trust in the service provided on payment options are the key success factors that lead to loyalty in an online food ordering service. Similarly (Jain et al., 2016) proposed a queuing based model for take-away restaurants to solve the long waiting queues issues, the proposed model is capable to accept the order in-person as well as from call and online and based on simulation it is very effective in predicting the time to receive the order, that is the most crucial part in this business.

Online food delivery business models rely on urban transportation to serve the requests and avoid the user's burden of traveling to restaurants (Yeo et al., 2017). Users generally share the service experience of online food delivery applications on the social media, so by exploiting user-generated contents, (Correa et al., 2019) proposed the impact of traffic conditions on key performance indicators of online food delivery services by using Google Maps API and web scraping techniques to retrieve customer's ratings and restaurant's location. Subsequently (Luo et al., 2020) proposed a machine learning model that takes delivery locations and food orders of various customers as input and suggests delivery men and suitable routes to optimized the delivery.

Apart from that few research were more focused on comparing the service quality and popularity of various online food delivery services, in this sequence (Rathore et al., 2018) analyzed survey reports to identify the factors influencing ordering food online and to capture the user's preferences on online food ordering services in India. The study revealed that youngsters, especially students are the most poised user class in online food ordering services and most fascinated by fast-food orders. The most influential factors are the price and discounts, convenience and user-friendly interface, on-time delivery. In this study, Zomato, Ubereats, Swiggy, and Foodpanda and few other services were included. This research concluded Zomato and Ubereats, as more popular than other alternatives. Subsequently (Das, J., 2018) discussed the consumer's perception, influencing factors, needs, overall satisfaction towards various online food ordering and delivery services in Pune (India), and their positioning among them. This study was based on survey responses of online food delivery application users and restaurants and concluded that Zomato has gained popularity because of their better, on-time delivery and attractive discounts. Subsequently (Nagpal et al., 2020) analyzed Zomato, Swiggy, and Foodpanda and highlighted the sentiment of users based on tweet processing and analysis using the Big Data Analysis Tool.

The way online food delivery services are operating in the competitive mode, food safety checks became difficult to ensure. The food industry is based on the consumer's trust in food, food chain supply, and food technologies used to process it. (Galvez et al., 2018) proposed a blockchain technology-based system where manipulation of records would be impossible once entered into the system to ensure transparency, authenticity in the food supply chain, It would solve the traceability issues as well in the food supply chain. Later (Macready et al., 2020) concluded that the user's confidence is majorly determined by the user's beliefs on the trustworthiness of the food and food supply chain.

2.3 Social Media Analytics Using Apache Spark

The increasing amount of social media data is the biggest challenge nowadays in the researcher's world to effectively process data promptly to avoid any business impacts. So Big Data ecosystem tool Apache Spark has gained the most attention to solving these kinds of issues. In such a study, (Baltas et al., 2017) presented a machine learning and natural language processing based sentiment analysis approach implemented on Apache Spark. This framework is utilizing the machine learning library (MLlib) of Apache Spark for analysis and prediction tasks and concluded the framework is very scalable and efficient in processing. Similarly (Maragatham et al., 2018) presented a novel framework using Apache Spark as a processing engine and Elasticsearch Kibana as a visualization tool for sentiment analysis and finding trending hashtags from Twitter Data. They are using Stanford natural language processing library coreNLP using Spark to make the framework capable of effectively handling the huge amount of data in a distributed and parallel computing environment. Another approach discussed by (Elzayady et al., 2018) demonstrates the implementation of 4 nodes Spark cluster to do the scalability analysis and finally concluded that adding additional nodes in the cluster is boosting the performance. The proposed framework was to process tweets stream on distributed mode and by applying MLlib library of Apache Spark to do the sentiment analysis on it and concluded that Naïve Bayes performed well as compared to Logistic Regression and Decision tree classification algorithms on their research on sentiment analysis. (Mohapatra et al., 2019) presented an Apache Spark based real-time cryptocurrency price prediction platform based on sentiment analysis on tweets. Apache Spark is a proven better-suited framework in this research due to its persistent and fault-tolerant nature of real-time data processing. Similarly (Ly et al., 2020) used Apache park based sentiment analysis framework to predict the stock price based on the price movement of an IPO and concluded 9.6% better prediction with this framework.

3. RESEARCH DESIGN AND METHODOLOGY

There are lots of insights accumulated in social media posts, which can be uncovered using social media analytics and utilized to improve the effectiveness of the applications, products, and services. The exponentially growing popularity of social media and online food delivery applications has created a space for analyzing the influence or impact of social media data on online food delivery applications. The proposed research is targeted for doing this analysis which has the following research design.

3.1 Research Objective

This research is aimed to identify the influence of social media analytics on online food delivery applications.

3.2 Research Questions

By using social media analytics on online food delivery applications, this research is targeted to answer the following research questions.

- How to represent the brand reputation of any business using social media data?
- How to represent the polarity of online users towards any business using social media data?
- How social media data can contribute to the business decision-making process?

3.3 Scope of the Research

The scope of this research is limited as follows.

- Twitter posts, formally known as tweets would be considered as social media data.
- The analysis will be done for the duration of 2 months, from Jan 2020 to Feb 2020.
- This research will be conducted in English texts only.
- The geographical scope of this research is India only.
- This analysis is designed for online food delivery applications only and the following four online food delivery applications are considered for this research.
  - Zomato
  - Swiggy
  - Ubereats
  - Foodpanda

3.4 Research Challenges

The major challenges of this research are mentioned as follows.

- Twitter has become a very popular platform and generates a huge number of posts on a daily basis. Hence, its analysis in real-time becomes a very crucial and a very challenging task.
- Gaining high efficiency on the analytics task is an addon challenge in the research.

3.5 Research Method

This research is based on Twitter data analytics against the tweets of online food delivery applications, in this regard following methods and techniques were used in this research.

- All the tweets are collected using Twitter's free API by considering the scope of this research.
- Currently, processing and analysis of huge number of tweets coming into the system in real-time is a very challenging task. To address this problem, we propose an Apache Spark-based tweets processing framework to effectively process and analyze collected Twitter posts. This framework is described in the section 4 in great detail.
- All the data cleaning and processing of tweets are done through the proposed framework.
- In this research, word-cloud of the posts is utilized to represent the brand reputation of online food delivery applications.
- This study utilizes four most popular supervised machine learning algorithms and benchmarked their performance to choose the best algorithm to gain high efficiency on the analytics task.
- This research will conduct the sentiment analysis on various aspects of online food delivery applications to obtain the user's polarity on these aspects.

- This research is utilizing the outcome of these sentiment analyses for the decision-making processes and prioritizes the action items by having a weightage system provided by the business management team.
- All the experimental setup details are provided in section 5 in detailed manner.

3.6 Research Novelty and Contribution

The novelty and contribution of this research are highlighted as follows.

- In this research, an Apache Spark based social media data processing framework with better fault-tolerance and horizontally scalable architecture to effectively process the social media posts, is proposed.
- The sentiments of user's posts on various aspects for Zomato, Swiggy, Ubereats, and Foodpanda on Twitter are presented.
- The decision-making process for online food delivery applications along with their brand reputation on Twitter is demonstrated.
- The Spark MLlib library for machine learning tasks is utilized. Additionally, the following supervised machine learning algorithms are benchmarked.
  - Logistic Regression (LR)
  - Random Forest Classifier (RF)
  - GBT Classifier (GBT)
  - Multilayer Perceptron Classifier (MLPC)

4. PROPOSED FRAMEWORK

This research proposes an Apache Spark based social media data processing framework with better fault-tolerance and horizontally scalable architecture to effectively process and analyzes high-velocity tweets (Maragatham et al., 2018). Tweet's stream is getting captured using Apache Flume and sinks it in the Spark cluster by utilizing the power of Apache Kafka to handle the high-speed data flow (Kumar et al., 2018). Later, Apache Spark is utilized to process and analyze these tweets stream using Spark Streaming API, Spark SQL, and Spark ML to draw useful insights. This framework is equipped with Apache Zookeeper for high availability (Kumar et al., 2018) and Apache Oozie for scheduling these tasks to run on any specified time or condition (Bandi et al., 2018). The novelty of this framework is as follows.

- Most of the studies (Al-Saqqa et al., 2018; Baltas et al., 2017; Elzayady et al., 2018) don't explain the implementation part of the framework whereas this research is highlighting the implementation part and also describes its various components and use cases.
- Integration of Apache Oozie in this framework for task scheduling is an add-on for automated operations of the tasks with minimal human interventions.
- This Apache Spark based framework is utilizing Apache Zookeeper to ensure high availability of the system.
- Using Apache Spark SQL and Apache Spark ML is improving the performance of the framework.

A well-organized illustration for the architectural overview of the proposed framework is given as follows in Figure 1. The building blocks of the proposed framework are described as follows.

4.1 Twitter API

Twitter API requires consumer key, consumer secret, access token, and access token secret in order to fetch the tweets. This application can be generated freely on https://apps.twitter.com/, there are many tutorials and blogs available to assist in creating Twitter applications and generating required keys. Twitter has restricted the streaming APIs in fetching tweets by limiting the number of tweets in a given time frame.

4.2 Tweet Collector

Tweet Collector is a module/script that is utilizing Twitter streaming API to collect tweets matching certain trends or keywords. Tweepy is a module for python users to stream tweets based on, they require the Consumer key, Consumer secret, Access token, and Access token secret to interact with Twitter API and fetch the tweets matching certain trends or keywords in JSON data. These tweets may be limited by countries and languages as well.

4.3 Apache Kafka

Apache Kafka is a queue and distributed publish-subscribe messaging system for handling high volume message passing from one end-point to another. Kafka stores the messages in a logical boundary called as Topic, Kafka is simply a collection of topics split into one or more partitions and provides both pub-sub and queue-based messaging system in a fast, reliable, stable, persisted, fault-tolerance and zero downtime manner (Kumar et al., 2018). It is capable to deal with high throughput sources like streaming, log aggregators, etc., and persist the messages on the disk in distributed, partitioned, and replicated manner within the cluster to ensure zero data loss. It is easily scalable without any downtime. In this framework, we are utilizing Apache Kafka as a Channel in Flume to sink streamed tweets into HDFS.

4.4 Apache Flume

Apache Flume is a highly reliable, distributed, fault-tolerant, horizontally scalable, manageable and configurable service or data ingestion mechanism for collecting aggregating and transporting large amounts of streaming data such as social media data streams, events log, etc. from various sources at very high speed that is difficult to manage on the traditional way to a centralized data store as HDFS, HBase, etc. on run time and provides a steady flow of data between them(Kumar et al., 2018). In this framework, it rescues us in storing the stream tweets collected from Tweet Collector in JSON format on Spark Cluster. It is configured with the Kafka channel for high through systems.

4.5 Apache Spark

Apache Spark is a fast, robust, and effective unified analytics engine for processing big data and machine learning. It is an in-memory high-speed cluster computing technology that is based on Hadoop MapReduce and extends its capabilities for solving interactive queries and stream processing too along with batch processing (Elzayady et al., 2018). In this framework, Spark is used to process the stream of tweets at lightning speed.

4.5.1 Apache Spark Streaming

It is an extension of the core Spark API that enables scalable, high-throughput, fault-tolerant stream processing of live data streams. It accepts and processes the stream data using complex algorithms expressed with high-level functions like map, reduce, join, etc. and finally, push it to some file-systems, databases, or live dashboards(Kumar et al., 2018). In this framework, it is used to process live tweets pushed by Apache Flume.

Figure 1. Proposed framework to capture and analyze tweets with scheduling capabilities

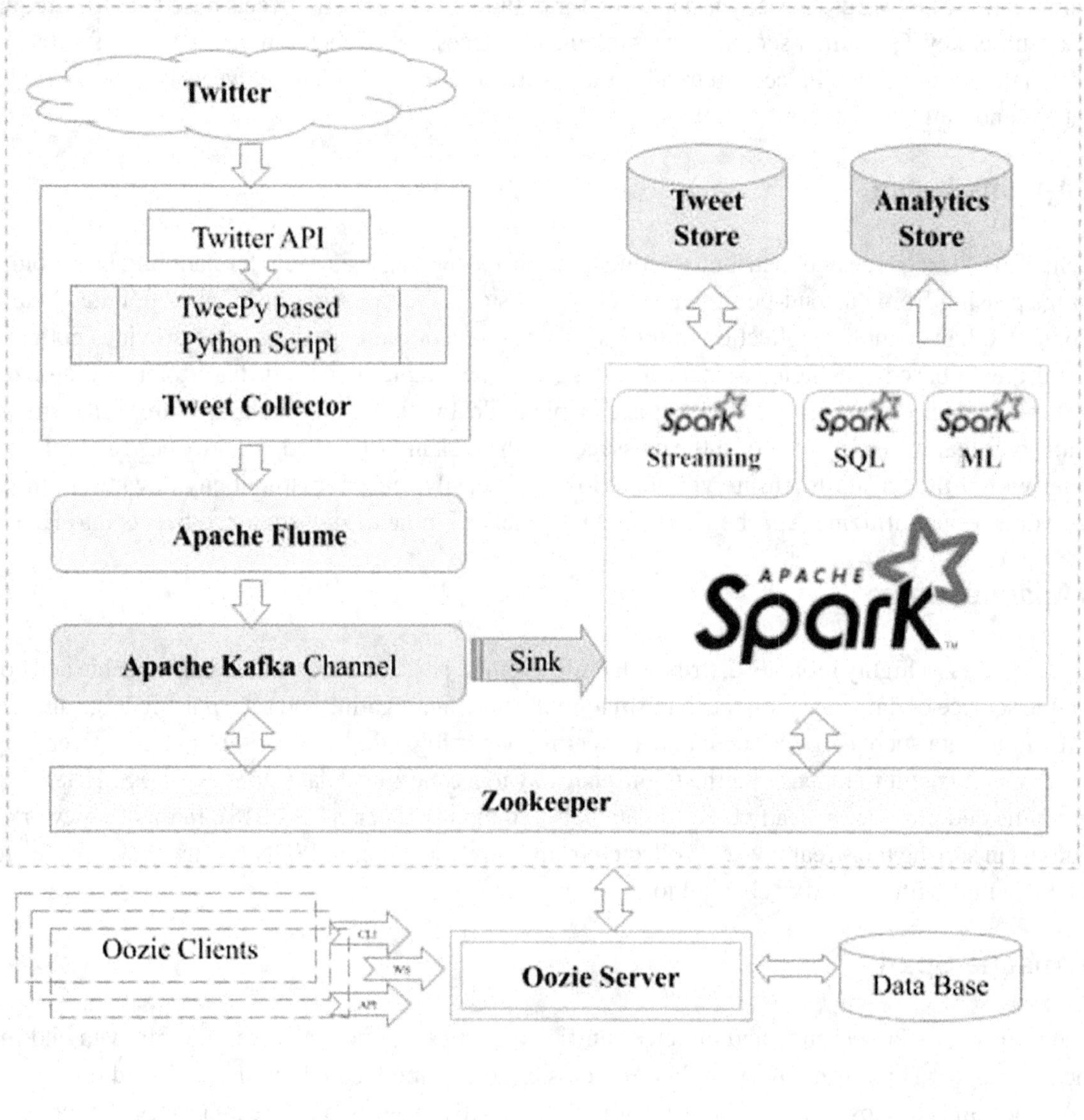

4.5.2 Apache Spark SQL

Apache Spark SQL is a module of Apache Spark's to work with structured data, it enables us to query structured data inside Spark programs either using SQL or DataFrames(Kumar et al., 2018). In this framework, Spark SQL is utilized to process semi-structured tweets into a structured form that is suitable for analysis with Spark ML.

4.5.3 Apache Spark ML

It is an Apache Spark's library for machine learning algorithms including classification, regression, clustering, dimensionality reduction, etc(Kumar et al., 2018). It is very scalable and using distributed computing engines is to distribute the calculations to the spark cluster to speed up the learning phase and allows us to create better models. In this framework, Spark ML is used for analytics on the collected tweets.

4.6 Apache Zookeeper

Apache Zookeeper is an open-source mechanism to ensure high availability in running Hadoop based architectures and avoid the single point of failures due to failure of the master node, it monitors the state of the current master node along with a list of standby master nodes(Kumar et al., 2018). Zookeeper provides a mechanism for leader election and if the current master dies, it elects another standby instance as a master and updates the state of the older master before failure in the new master before resuming the scheduling. In this framework, Apache Zookeeper is used to provide high availability to Kafka and Spark clusters.

4.7 Apache Oozie

Apache Oozie is an open-source scheduler to manage and execute Hadoop jobs on specified schedules in a distributed environment. It allows combining multiple complex jobs to be run in a sequential and parallel order to achieve a bigger task in a well-planned manner(Bandi et al., 2018). Oozie is tightly integrated with the Hadoop stack and supports all kinds of Hadoop jobs including Spark, Pig, Hive, Sqoop, Java, Shell scripts and it is also leveraging the existing Hadoop machinery for load balancing, fail-over, etc. to effectively manage the jobs. Oozie detects and notifies the completion of tasks through callback and polling. Here in this framework, Apache Oozie is responsible for managing and executing the Oozie Coordinator Jobs to run the analysis block on Apache Pig and Apache Hive at defined intervals.

5. EXPERIMENTAL SETTING

This section will provide detailed information about the tweet collection strategies, data preprocessing methods, selection of machine learning algorithms, and their evaluation parameters along with the system configuration to setup this framework.

5.1 System Configuration

All the benchmarking and result calculation of this research were done on a 4 node cluster of 8GB RAM, 4 Core, Ubuntu 18.04 Linux operating system AWS servers installed with Python 3.6, MongoDB 3.6.3, Spark 2.3.4, Apache Flume 1.6.0, Apache Kafka 2.2.0, Apache Zookeeper 3.5.6 and Apache Oozie5.1.0 on the cluster.

5.2 Data Set

This research has considered 4 applications Zomato, Swiggy, Ubereats, and Foodpanda for the analysis purpose and it is based on Indian tweets of the English language only for the duration of 2 months from Jan 2020 to Feb 2020, so the topics, hashtags, events, and users were considered accordingly, these keywords mentioned as follows in Table 1.

Table 1. Keywords for tweets collection

Application Name	Keywords
Zomato	ZomatoIN, zomatocare, ZomatoGold, Zomato
Swiggy	swiggy, swiggy_in, WeAreSwiggy, SwiggyCares
Ubereats	ubereats, uber eats
Foodpanda	FoodPanda, Food Panda, foodpandaIndia, FoodPandaPROMO

The tweet collections against these keywords were done through Flume using the Tweepy library of python using Twitter free API and data was sunk directly in the Spark cluster. Collected tweets stats are given in Table 2.

Table 2. Statistics of experimental data

Application Name	Number of Posts	Number of Users	Number of Posts from Application	Number of Posts from Users
Zomato	106987	36129	14591	92396
Swiggy	88219	32113	7487	80732
Ubereats	65070	34523	3363	61707
Foodpanda	8916	4276	2613	6303

In these collected datasets, we tagged the sentiments for 1k tweets in each category with 50% positive sentiment and 50% negative sentiment for training purposes. So collectively we created the training dataset of 4 k tweets for the model training and its performance evaluation.

5.3 Preprocessing Methods

In this research, we are preprocessing the tweets to make it more effective in analytics (Singh et al., 2020). The list of preprocessing techniques applied in this research are as follows.

- Handling Special Characters
- Non-English Word Elimination
- Slang Word Removal
- Emoji to Words
- Hashtags to Words
- Handling Para Languages
- Stop Words Removals
- Apply Word Stemming
- Tense Identification
- POS Tagging
- Handling Para Languages

5.4 Selection of Machine Learning Algorithms

The aim of the proposed research is to perform sentiment analysis on tweets using supervised machine learning algorithms. In this research, we are utilizing the Spark ML modules for the analytics purpose and doing the benchmarking on the following 4 machine learning algorithms based on their working principle and effectiveness (Singh et al., 2020; Kumar et al., 2019; Faker et al., 2019; JayaLakshmi et al., 2018) on the classification problems.

5.4.1 Logistic Regression (LR)

Logistic regression (LR) is one of the popular methods to predict a categorical response, it is a generalized case of linear regression models to predict the probability of the outcomes (Al-Saqqa et al., 2018). It utilizes a logistic function to measure the relationship between the input feature vector and the instance class. It can be used to predict a binary outcome by using binomial logistic regression, or multiclass outcome by using multinomial logistic regression (Elzayady et al., 2018).

5.4.2 Random Forest Classifier (RF)

Random forests are a popular family of regression and classification methods due to its easy to use and flexibility (Kumar et al., 2019). It is a bagging based ensemble method that combines a set of Decision Trees to obtain a higher accuracy and stability prediction. Random Forest Classifier (RF) is a supervised learning algorithm, it relies on the Decision Tree algorithm to build trees. It uses one or more combinations of features at every node to expand a tree (Faker et al., 2019). In this method, a higher number of trees ensures better efficiency of classification because each tree casts one vote to classify the input vector. Furthermore, the ability to operate within distributed and parallel computing offers the advantage of scalability and adaptability to high volume and variety datasets (Kozik et al., 2018).

5.4.3 GBT Classifier (GBT)

Gradient Boosting Tree (GBT) is a popular classification and regression method using boosting ensembles of decision trees. An ensemble method is nothing but a set of predictions that are integrated to obtain the final prediction. Ensembling is used to minimize bias, noise, and variance factors and to improve the stability and accuracy of the machine learning algorithms. GBT is a supervised machine learning method and based on weak learners (Faker et al., 2019). A weak learner means a shallow tree starts with the shallow tree to build a predictor, followed by calculating the error of expectations and passing the errors to the next tree as a target. The next tree adopts the new prediction model according to the data of the previous tree model (Kozik et al., 2018). The error is calculated for the new predictive model and passed to the next tree and so forth.

5.4.4 Multilayer Perceptron Classifier (MLPC)

Multilayer Perceptron Classifier (MLPC) is a classification based on the feed-forward artificial neural network (ANN), it contains multiple layers of nodes resulting in deep learning where each layer is inter-connected to the next layer to form a network (JayaLakshmi et al., 2018). An MLPC consists of an input layer, an output layer, and one or more hidden layers. Nodes of the input layer are connected with the feature vector, whereas nodes of the hidden layer are using a sigmoid function as the activation function and nodes of the output layer use the softmax activation function (Ain et al., 2017). MLPC algorithms are utilizing a supervised learning technique known as backpropagation for training. It's multiple-layered architecture and non-linear activation functions distinguish MLPC from a linear perceptron and it can distinguish the data that is not linearly separable. It is useful in various research due to its ability to solve problems stochastically, which often allows approximate solutions for notably complex problems like fitness approximation, speech recognition, image recognition, and machine translation software.

5.5 Evaluation Parameters

Sentiment analysis is a classification task and the results of the predicting model can be arranged in the following classes.

- True Positive (TP): The outcome of the correctly predicted positive class.
- True Negative (TN): The outcome of the correctly predicted negative class.
- False Positive (FP): The outcome of the incorrectly predicted positive class.
- False Negative (FN): The outcome of the incorrectly predicted negative class.

Classification algorithms can be evaluated through various evaluation metrics. In this research, the following evaluation parameters are utilized to gaze the performance for the analytics (Singh et al., 2020).

5.5.1 Accuracy

The accuracy is the ratio of correctly classified samples versus the total number of samples. It lies between 0 to 1, where 0 and 1 respectively represent the worst and the best value. A high accuracy describes that model classified substantially most of the results correctly. It can be computed using equation (1).

$$Accuracy = \frac{TP + TN}{TP + FP + TN + FN}$$ (1)

5.5.2 Precision

The precision is the ratio of the number of predicted true positives by model versus the total number of predicted positives by model. It lies between 0 to 1, where 0 and 1 respectively represent the worst and the best value. A high precision describes that model classified substantially more relevant results than irrelevant ones. It can be computed using equation (2).

$$Precision = \frac{TP}{TP + FP}$$ (2)

5.5.3 Recall

The recall is the ratio of the number of predicted true positives by model versus the total number of actual positive. It lies between 0 to 1, where 0 and 1 respectively represent the worst and the best value. A high recall describes that model correctly classified most of the relevant results. It can be computed using equation (3).

$$Recall = \frac{TP}{TP + FN}$$ (3)

5.5.4 F1 Score

The F1 score is the harmonic mean of precision and recall. It lies between 0 to 1, where 0 and 1 respectively represent the worst and the best value. A high F1 score describes that model has perfect precision and recall. It can be computed using equation (4).

$$F1Score = \frac{2 \times Precision \times Recall}{Precision + Recall}$$ (4)

6. RESULTS AND DISCUSSIONS

This section provides the statistical output of this research, it includes the accuracy measurement of the implemented machine learning models using the proposed framework along with the use-case basis experiments of this research. These experiments are word-cloud implementation, sentiment analysis, and decision-making processes.

6.1 Machine Learning Model's Accuracy Measure

In this research, we are using the Spark ML library for the machine learning tasks and we identified 4 supervised machine learning algorithms to perform the sentiment analysis on our training data. In this section, we are measuring the effectiveness of these 4 supervised machine learning models.

We have prepared a tweets training dataset of 4k with 50% positive and 50% negative tweets. In this analysis, we are using 10 fold cross-validation method, in which each model was trained on 3600 tweets and validated against 400 tweets. The result of accuracy measurement of the proposed framework is given in Table 3 along with its graphical representation in Figure 2.

Table 3. Effectiveness measurements of machine learning algorithms on various datasets

Data Set	Logistic Regression (LR)				Random Forest Classifier (RF)				GBT Classifier (GBTs)				Multilayer Perceptron Classifier (MLPC)			
	Accuracy	Precision	Recall	F1	Accuracy	Precision	Recall	F1	Accuracy	Precision	Recall	F1	Accuracy	Precision	Recall	F1
Zomato	0.82	0.82	0.82	0.82	0.85	0.83	**0.85**	0.84	0.84	**0.88**	0.82	0.85	**0.85**	0.87	0.83	**0.85**
Swiggy	0.82	0.82	0.83	0.82	0.84	0.83	**0.85**	0.84	0.85	0.88	0.82	0.85	**0.86**	**0.88**	0.84	**0.86**
Ubereats	0.83	0.83	0.82	0.83	0.84	0.84	**0.85**	0.84	0.82	0.84	0.81	0.83	**0.86**	**0.87**	0.85	**0.86**
Foodpanda	0.82	0.83	0.82	0.82	0.84	0.83	**0.84**	0.84	0.83	0.83	0.82	0.83	**0.86**	**0.89**	0.83	**0.86**

Figure 2. (a) to (d) are displaying the benchmarking of LR, RF, GBT and MLPC on various data sets

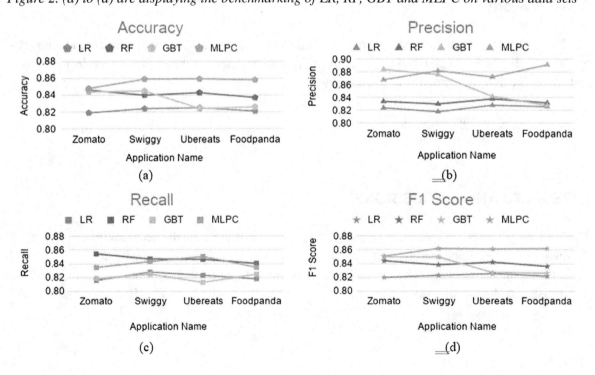

In this benchmarking, Multilayer Perceptron Classifier performed well on Accuracy, Precision, and F1 score scale on the other side Random Forest Classifier secured well in Recall base analysis. So after overall analysis, we considered Multilayer Perceptron Classifier best with 86% accuracy, 89% precision, 83% recall, and 86% F1 score on Foodpanda's dataset. So going forward in this research, we would utilize a Multilayer Perceptron Classifier for the analytics related tasks.

6.2 Use Cases of the Research

In this section, we would solve various use cases associated with our research questions.

6.2.1 Word-Cloud Analysis for Brand Reputation Analysis

Word-clouds are the easiest way to understand the brand reputation of any business. So, we processed the content of all collected tweets of each dataset using our framework, prepared the word frequency by removing the stop-words and generated the word-cloud to represent the summary of the conversations on these applications on social media. Word-cloud of Zomato, Swiggy, Usereats, and Foodpanda is given in Figure 3.

Figure 3. (a) to (d) are displaying the word-cloud of Zomato, Swiggy, Ubereats, and Foodpanda in the sequence

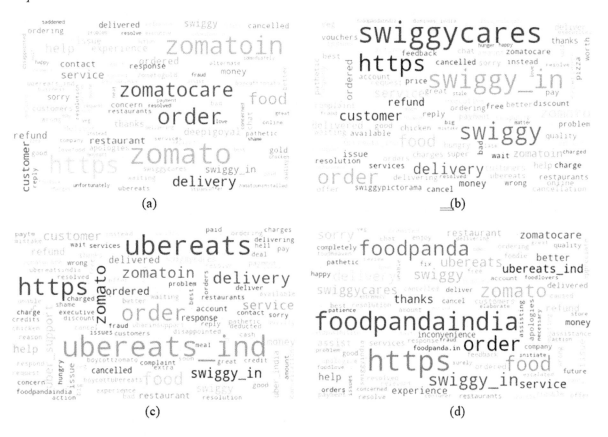

In these experiments, we can easily determine that Zomato and Swiggy are playing well but Ubereats and Foodpanda related posts have often mention Zomato and Swiggy, which is somehow reflecting that customers are comparing these applications with Zomato and Swiggy.

So, we can conclude that the brand reputation of Zomato and Swiggy is high where Ubereats and Foodpanda are still struggling in this regard.

6.2.2 Sentiment Analysis

In this research, we conducted a sentiment analysis using Multilayer Perceptron Classifier (MLPC) on below 5 parameters to understand the polarity of user's on various services offered by these online food delivery applications.

1. Overall sentiments
2. Delivery related sentiments
3. Food quality related sentiments
4. Discount and Offer related sentiments
5. After issue resolution sentiments

We collected 200 tweets per parameter per application and used a Multilayer Perceptron Classifier (MLPC) to tag the sentiment of these posts in 3 states: Neutral, Positive, and Negative. Based on this tagging, we calculated the polarity of users by using equation (5).

$$Polarity = \frac{Number of Positive Sentiment}{Number of Positive Sentiment + Number of Negative Sentiment} \tag{5}$$

The number of neutral sentiments was ignored while calculating the polarity because it's not adding any value in the polarity analysis neither or any business decisions. These polarities can be considered as a matrix for understanding the impact of sentiments analysis on any data set.

Sentiments tagging and polarity analysis was conducted for all 5 parameters and results are illustrated in Table 4 and Figure 4.

Table 4. Sentiment analysis on tweets

Application Name	Overall				Delivery				Food Quality				Discount				After Issue Resolution			
	Neutral	Positive	Negative	Polarity	Neutral	Positive	Negative	Polarity	Neutral	Positive	Negative	Polarity	Neutral	Positive	Negative	Polarity	Neutral	Positive	Negative	Polarity
Zomato	96	59	45	56.73	73	79	48	62.20	71	80	49	62.02	43	98	59	62.42	56	113	31	78.47
Swiggy	105	52	43	54.74	81	76	43	63.87	71	82	47	63.57	57	87	56	60.84	47	119	34	77.78
Ubereats	108	50	42	54.35	90	59	51	53.64	62	84	54	60.87	66	83	51	61.94	73	97	30	76.38
Foodpanda	87	49	64	43.36	77	59	64	47.97	78	71	51	58.20	84	53	63	45.69	86	76	38	66.67

Figure 4. (a) to (e) are displaying overall sentiments, delivery related sentiments, food quality related sentiments, discount and offer related sentiments and sentiments on posts after issue resolution in a sequence

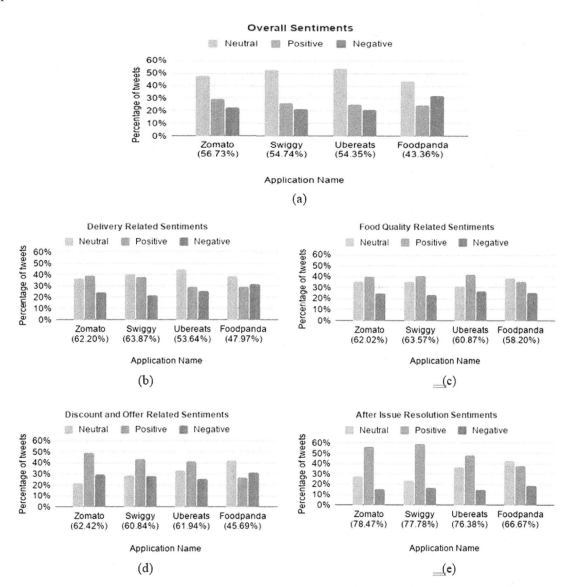

By analyzing the polarity outcome, it's observed that Zomato is leading with 56.73% in overall sentiment analysis followed by Swiggy at 54.74%. In delivery related sentiments Swiggy is leading with 63.87% followed by Zomato at 62.20%, similarly, Swiggy is leading with 63.57% in food quality related sentiment followed by Zomato at 62.02%. In discount and offer related sentiments, Zomato is leading with 62.42% followed by Ubereats at 61.94%, Swiggy is in 3rd place in this analysis. Sentiments on posts after the issue resolution, Zomato is again leading with 78.47% followed by Swiggy 77.78%.

This analysis clearly represents that Zomato is the market leader by offering better discounts and customer services. Swiggy is good in terms of delivery timing and food quality and securing second place in the market.

6.2.3 Decision-Making Process

In this research, the decision-making process is based on the polarities of online food delivery applications on the following parameters and their weightage in decision making.

1. Delivery related
2. Food quality related
3. Discount and Offer related
4. Issue resolution

This overall task can be majorly divided into 3 steps, mentioned as follows.

6.2.3.1 Decision-Making Parameter's Weightage

It is the weightage of paraments involved in the decision-making process, to better gauge the effectiveness of these paraments on the business, these weightage would be provided by the stakeholders of the business, can be different for various online food delivery applications, but in this research, we are taking a dummy weightage for the analysis, it would be same for all the application in this research. Weightage of these parameters are given in Table 5.

Table 5. Decision-making parameters and their weightage

Parameter	Weightage
Delivery related sentiments	0.2
Food quality related sentiments	0.3
Discount and Offer related sentiments	0.4
After issue resolution sentiments	0.1

6.2.3.2 Decision-Making Parameter's Polarity

The polarities of various online food delivery applications based on the decision making parameters would be calculated as per the section 6.2.2 by using equation (5), it is represented as follows in Table 6.

6.2.3.3 Decision-Making Parameter's Prioritization

The decision-making process in this research is a two-step process, mentioned as follows.

Table 6. Application wise satisfaction % of decision-making parameters

Parameters	Zomato	Swiggy	Ubereats	Foodpanda
Delivery related sentiments	62.20%	63.87%	53.64%	47.97%
Food quality related sentiments	62.02%	63.57%	60.87%	58.20%
Discount and Offer related sentiments	62.42%	60.84%	61.94%	45.69%
After issue resolution sentiments	78.47%	77.78%	76.38%	66.67%

6.2.3.4 Weighted Polarity Impact of Decision-Making Parameters

It is the polarity impact scaled at the level of the parameter's weightage. It is an intermediate stage of the decision-making process. It can be achieved by multiplying the weightage of the parameter with the polarity of the parameter as mentioned in the equation (6).

$$Weighted\ Polarity\ Impact = Parameter\ Weightage \times Parameter's\ Polarity \tag{6}$$

Weighted polarity impact of all these parameter-application pairs is calculated using equation (6) and mentioned in Table 7.

Table 7. Application wise weighted polarity impact of decision-making parameters

Applications	Zomato	Swiggy	Ubereats	Foodpanda
Delivery related sentiments	12.44%	12.77%	10.73%	9.59%
Food quality related sentiments	18.61%	19.07%	18.26%	17.46%
Discount and Offer related sentiments	24.97%	24.34%	24.78%	18.28%
After issue resolution sentiments	7.85%	7.78%	7.64%	6.67%

6.2.3.5 Decision-Making Parameter's Selection Score

In this section, decision-making parameters are getting scored in the range of 0 to 1, where 1 signifies the most important parameter and 0 signifies the least important parameter. In this research, all the alternative parameters are also ranked with the same strategy to facilitate a base to compare the selection scores of these parameters. The parameter selection score can be calculated by equation (7).

$$ParameterSelectionScore = 1 - \frac{WeightedPolarityImpactofApplication}{Max\left(WeightedPolarityImpactofalltheApplications\right)} \tag{7}$$

The parameter selection score of all parameter-application pair is calculated by equation (7) and given as follows in Table 8.

These parameter's selection score is the outcome of the decision-making process, by analyzing these values, it can be concluded that Zomato and Ubereats should focus to improve the delivery related services whereas Swiggy and Foodpanda should focus on discount and offers.

Table 8. Application wise decision-making parameter's selection score

Applications	Zomato	Swiggy	Ubereats	Foodpanda
Delivery related sentiments	**0.03 *[Rank 1]**	0.00 *[Rank 3]	**0.16 *[Rank 1]**	0.25 *[Rank 2]
Food quality related sentiments	0.02 *[Rank 2]	0.00 *[Rank 4]	0.04 *[Rank 2]	0.08 *[Rank 4]
Discount and Offer related sentiments	0.00 *[Rank 3]	**0.03 *[Rank 1]**	0.01 *[Rank 4]	**0.27 *[Rank 1]**
After issue resolution sentiments	0.00 *[Rank 4]	0.01 *[Rank 2]	0.03 *[Rank 3]	0.15 *[Rank 3]

6.3 Result Discussions

This research is aimed to identify the influence of social media analytics on online food delivery applications and to represent the brand reputation and user's polarity on these applications offerings along with the contribution of this research on decision-making processes. Apart from that real-time high velocity and high efficiency in the analysis were the key challenges.

In this research, we proposed a high speed horizontally scalable Apache Spark based social media data processing framework to overcome the challenge in real-time high-velocity social media processing, and by using Spark MLlib implemented machine learning algorithms of various working principle including the ANN deep learning models and their bench-marking ensures high efficiency in the analytics processes.

Apart from that, we conducted 3 experiments for describing the relevance of social media analytics with the research problem and to answer, how this research contributed to solving the research problems using social media analytics. The first experiment mentioned in section 6.2.1 is representing the brand reputation of online food delivery applications with the help of word-cloud those were generated on the word frequencies of users tweets regarding these applications. Similarly, the second experiment mentioned in section 6.2.2 is calculating and displaying the polarity of online users on the various offering of the services. This experiment was done on the basis of 5 paraments for each online food delivery application and concluded the findings. The third experiment of this research is a hybrid business-decision making process which utilizes the user's opinions and scales it on the stockholder's weightage and ranks various alternatives, its mentioned in section 6.2.3 and allow stakeholders to choose an option by analyzing its alternative's score.

The cumulative outcome of this research is indicating the influence of social media analytics on online food delivery applications and providing the appropriate answer to all research questions and research challenges.

7. CONCLUSION AND FUTURE WORK

Twitter is one of the best platforms for Social media interactions and gaining more traction with the ever-growing popularity of online food delivery services in urban areas to share feedback, opinion, and experience related to these applications. This research is aimed to identify the influence of social media analytics on online food delivery systems, by analyzing their user's opinions and brand reputation on social media. Additionally, this research unhitches the association of social media analytics with decision-making processes. Due to the abundant amount of tweets, it became a complex task to collect, process, and analyze these tweets effectively so, this research proposed an Apache Spark based efficient social media framework to accomplish it efficiently. In a bench-marking on sentiment analysis, this framework achieved 86% accuracy, 89% precision, 83% recall, and 86% F1 score by using Multilayer Perceptron Classifier (MLPC) built-in Spark MLlib. This framework was tested on Twitter data against the four most popular online food delivery applications, Zomato, Swiggy, Ubereats, and Foodpanda in India for the accumulation of the brand reputation and performing sentiment analysis. The experimental results have concluded that Zomato is leading in overall sentiment, discounts and offers sentiment and post-issue-resolution sentiments, whereas Swiggy is leading in delivery and food quality related sentiments. The outcome of the brand reputation is also favoring Zomato and Swiggy. Furthermore, this research has demonstrated a decision-making process by using the user's polarity and business stakeholder's weight-age on specific parameters and exhibited the essence of social media analytics with decision-making processes. Concluding all these findings, the influence of social media analytics has been ascertained on online food delivery applications and also exhibited its various use cases to be competitive in the market.

This research is about the collection and processing of tweets and drawing the analytics using Spark ML libraries. It can be partially used for data processing till feature forming and these features can be modeled with any machine learning algorithms out of the Spark processing ecosystem. This framework can be used for processing other data streams like logs, purchase records, etc. along with introducing ensembling methods to obtain better analytics performance (Troussas et al., 2016).

REFERENCES

Ain, Q. T., Ali, M., Riaz, A., Noureen, A., Kamran, M., Hayat, B., & Rehman, A. (2017). Sentiment Analysis Using Deep Learning Techniques: A Review. *International Journal of Advanced Computer Science and Applications*, 8(6), 424–433.

Al-Saqqa, S., Al-Naymat, G., & Awajan, A. (2018). A Large-Scale Sentiment Data Classification for Online Reviews Under Apache Spark. *Procedia Computer Science*, *141*, 183–189. doi:10.1016/j.procs.2018.10.166

Baltas, A., Kanavos, A., & Tsakalidis, A. (2017). An Apache Spark Implementation for Sentiment Analysis on Twitter Data. Algorithmic Aspects of Cloud Computing: Second International Workshop, ALGOCLOUD, Aarhus, Denmark. 10.1007/978-3-319-57045-7_2

Bandi, R., & Anitha, G. (2018). Machine learning based Oozie Workflow for Hive Query Schedule mechanism. In *2018 International Conference on Smart Systems and Inventive Technology (ICSSIT)*. IEEE. 10.1109/ICSSIT.2018.8748711

Correa, J. C., Garzón, W., Brooker, P., Sakarkar, G., Carranza, S. A., Yunado, L., & Rincón, A. (2019). Evaluation of collaborative consumption of food delivery services through web mining techniques. *Journal of Retailing and Consumer Services, Elsevier*, *46*, 45–50. doi:10.1016/j.jretconser.2018.05.002

Das, J. (2018). Consumer Perception Towards 'Online Food Ordering And Delivery Services': An Empirical Study. *Journal of Management*, 5(5), 155–163.

Elzayady, H., Badran, K. M., & Salama, G. I. (2018). Sentiment Analysis on Twitter Data using Apache Spark Framework. *13th International Conference on Computer Engineering and Systems*. 10.1109/ICCES.2018.8639195

Faker, O., & Dogdu, E. (2019). Intrusion Detection Using Big Data and Deep Learning Techniques. In *Proceedings of the 2019 ACM Southeast Conference*. Association for Computing Machinery. 10.1145/3299815.3314439

Galvez, J. F., Mejuto, J. C., & Simal-Gandara, J. (2018). Future challenges on the use of blockchain for food traceability analysis. *TrAC Trends in Analytical Chemistry, Elsevier, 107*, 222–232. doi:10.1016/j.trac.2018.08.011

Gupta, T., & Paul, K. (2016). Consumer attitude towards quick service restaurants: A study across select quick service restaurants in Gurgaon. *Indian Journal of Applied Research, 6*(3), 639–641.

Hong, L., Li, Y., & Wang, S. (2016). Improvement of online food delivery service based on consumers' negative comments. *Canadian Social Science, 12*(5), 84–88.

Jain, P., & Ali, R. (2016). A case study of take away restaurant using simulation modelling approach. *Journal of Service Science Research, Springer, 8*(2), 207–221. doi:10.100712927-016-0011-x

Jain, V. K., & Kumar, S. (2017). *Predictive Analysis of Emotions for Improving Customer Services. Applying Predictive Analytics Within the Service Sector*. IGI Global.

Jain, V. K., & Kumar, S. (2017). Towards Prediction of Election Outcomes Using Social Media. *International Journal of Intelligent Systems and Applications, 9*(12), 20–28. doi:10.5815/ijisa.2017.12.03

Jansen, B. J., Zhang, M., Sobel, K., & Chowdury, A. (2009). Twitter Power: Tweets as Electronic Word of Mouth. *Journal of the American Society for Information Science and Technology, 60*(11), 2169–2188. doi:10.1002/asi.21149

JayaLakshmi, A. N. M., & Kishore, K. V. K. (2018). Performance evaluation of DNN with other machine learning techniques in a cluster using Apache Spark and MLlib. *Journal of King Saud University - Computer and Information Sciences*.

Kedah, Z., Ismail, Y., Ahasanul, A., & Ahmed, S. (2015). Key Success Factors of Online Food Ordering Services: An Empirical Study. *Malaysian Management Review, 50*.

Kozik, R., Pawlicki, M., & Choraś, M. (2018). *Cost-Sensitive Distributed Machine Learning for NetFlow-Based Botnet Activity Detection*. Wiley.

Kumar, S., & Goel, E. (2018). Changing the world of Autonomous Vehicles using Cloud and Big Data. In *2018 Second International Conference on Inventive Communication and Computational Technologies*. IEEE. 10.1109/ICICCT.2018.8473347

Kumar, S., Koolwal, V., & Mohbey, K. K. (2019). Sentiment analysis of electronics product tweets using big data framework. *Jordanian Journal of Computers and Information Technology, 5*(1).

Luo, H., Liufu, M., & Li, D. (2020). *Intelligent Online Food Delivery System: A Dynamic Model to Generate Delivery Strategy and Tip Advice*. arXiv:2002.01713 [stat.AP]

Ly, T. H., & Nguyen, K. (2020). Do Words Matter: Predicting IPO Performance from Prospectus Sentiment. In *2020 IEEE 14th International Conference on Semantic Computing*. IEEE.

Macready, A. L., Hieke, S., Klimczuk-Kochańska, M., Szumiał, S., Vranken, L., & Grunert, K. G. (2020). *Consumer trust in the food value chain and its impact on consumer confidence: A model for assessing consumer trust and evidence from a 5-country study in Europe. In Food Policy* (Vol. 92). Elsevier.

Maragatham, G. (2018). Twitter Sentiment Analysis and Visualization Using Apache Spark and Elasticsearch. *IACSIT International Journal of Engineering and Technology, 7*(3.12), 314–321. doi:10.14419/ijet.v7i3.12.16049

Mohapatra, S., Ahmed, N., & Alencar, P. (2019). *KryptoOracle: A Real-Time Cryptocurrency Price Prediction Platform Using Twitter Sentiments. IEEE International Conference on Big Data*, Los Angeles, CA. 10.1109/BigData47090.2019.9006554

Nagpal, M., Kansal, K., Chopra, A., Gautam, N., & Jain, V. K. (2020). *Effective Approach for Sentiment Analysis of Food Delivery Apps. Soft Computing: Theories and Applications. In Advances in Intelligent Systems and Computing* (Vol. 1053). Springer.

Rathore, S. S., & Chaudhary, M. (2018). Consumer's Perception on Online Food Ordering. *International Journal of Management & Business Studies, 8*(4).

Schweidel, D. A., & Moe, W. W. (2014). Listening in on social media: A joint model of sentiment and venue format choice. *JMR, Journal of Marketing Research, 51*(4), 387–402. doi:10.1509/jmr.12.0424

Singh, R. K., & Verma, H. K. (2020). Effective Parallel Processing Social Media Analytics Framework. *Journal of King Saud University - Computer and Information Sciences.*

Soboleva, A., Burton, S., & Khan, A. (2015). *Marketing with Twitter: Challenges and Opportunities. In Maximizing Commerce and Marketing Strategies through Micro-Blogging*. IGI Global.

Troussas, C., Krouska, A., & Virvou, M. (2016). Evaluation of ensemble-based sentiment classifiers for Twitter data. *2016 7th International Conference on Information, Intelligence, Systems & Applications*, 1-6.

Vernier, M., Farinosi, M., & Foresti, G. L. (2018). *Twitter Data Mining for Situational Awareness. Encyclopedia of Information Science and Technology* (4th ed.). IGI Global.

Yeo, V. C. S., Goh, S. K., & Rezaei, S. (2017). Consumer experiences, attitude and behavioral intention toward online food delivery (OFD) services. *Journal of Retailing and Consumer Services, Elsevier, 35*, 150–162. doi:10.1016/j.jretconser.2016.12.013

This research was previously published in the International Journal of Information System Modeling and Design (IJISMD), 11(3); pages 1-21, copyright year 2020 by IGI Publishing (an imprint of IGI Global).

Chapter 75

The Impact of Rumors on Social Media Sites in Behavior of Purchasing Food Products in the Egyptian Market

Ali Ahmed Abdelkader

Faculty of Commerce, Kafrelsheikh University, Kafrelsheikh, Egypt

Hossam El Din Fathy Mohamed

International Academy of Engineering and Media Sciences, Giza, Egypt

ABSTRACT

The purpose of this article is to detect the impact of rumors on social media on the purchasing behavior of food products. The descriptive approach on four rumors related to food products were identified in the Egyptian market. A sample of 387 participants were selected from consumers who use Facebook in Egypt. The primary data was collected via an E-Questioner method. The results indicated that there is a significant relationship between the rumors on social media, and purchasing behavior of food products. There is also a significant difference between the products and the impact of rumors. These results assure the importance of social media and its impact on a customer's decision to purchase food products. This article not only explains the importance of rumors on social media in the food sector but also enhances the understanding of the influence of social media on consumer's behavior. It also provides some insights for facing the rumors. Organizations are advised to adopt social media in their business.

INTRODUCTION

It is well-known that SM indicates to a collection of online services that support social interactions among users and allow them to create, find, share and evaluate the online information. It is "a set of Internet-based applications which is created on the ideological and technological foundations of Web 2.0, and that permit the innovation and exchange of customer created Content" (Kaplan and Haenlein, 2010, p.

DOI: 10.4018/978-1-7998-9020-1.ch075

61). SMhas changed users from passive content readers into content publishers, thereby making their role more significant. SM take many platforms such as Instagram, Facebook, MySpace, and YouTube, Twitter and many others of those networks that go up dramatically.

Most of these individuals use products or services like the ones you sell. Heads-up business people are learning how to leakage SM tools to encourage the online population to talk positively about their Products) Safko, 2010). It's true that SM platforms excel in the level of effectiveness in the transfer of information and events, but no wonder if we say that SM have negative effects, it is a good environment for the growth of rumors, because of the simplicity of production and dissemination of information in a short time, which led to the spread of rumor via SM networks, with the inability to control and difficulty of monitoring content attached by individuals on these sites. It has been observed in recent times, the spread of rumors through SN and their rapid circulation among members of society, which led to change the purpose of rumor, and the way it spread in society, because of the difference of nature and the features of SM platforms (Zubiaga, 2015).

The objective of the publication of the rumor varies based on the objectives of their promoters and their ideas, the objective of publishing rumor may be related to the type of rumor. In some cases, the purpose is commercial, seek to increase the demand for a certain product as a marketing technique, or to confuse a competing company by distorting the facts, or a faked story that has no basis in reality or contains a small part of the truth. Therefore, rumors are a major source of crises for commercial organizations. (Roux-Dufort 1993) (Coombs, 2002) (Zubiaga, 2015) (Chen 2016). Crisis can, and often does begin with rumors. In fact, a crisis can indeed be a rumor. A rumor can be defined as "information passed by word of mouth and SM with no verification of fact and no credible source" (Fearn-Banks, 2007, p. 81).

One of the most important features of SM is the ability to quickly reach large numbers of web browsers and consumers through these sites, and to identify the needs and desires of existing or potential customers, prompting many companies to develop content on SM, to benefit from Marketing opportunities offered by SM. The great use of SM is an opportunity to promote rumors about organizations and their products. Hence, affect the purchasing decisions of consumers, Therefore, the promotion of rumors leads to the loss of many consumers, and thus the decline in sales, and the loss of competitiveness of organizations.

Food companies and fast-food restaurants became an integral part of our society, far from the rumors; the researchers have noticed many rumors related to food on SM. Four rumors related to food products were identified in the Egyptian market for the present study, as follows:

- The employ of rotten meat which is not suitable for human use in many famous restaurants such as Umm Hassan, and Kentucky Fried Chicken (KFC). As well as the use of (donkey meat) in the meal industry provided by these restaurants and spread in many districts in the Egyptian governorates;
- The video shows damaged and unsuitable tomatoes in the factory (Heinz Egypt). The video shows that these tomatoes are used in making sauce and ketchup;
- The video contains fruit (Guava) damaged which is unsuitable for use in the factory (company Betty). The video shows that the guava is used in the juice industry;
- Many of the videos that explain the health damage that occurs to humans as a result of eating noodles prepared by the company (Indomie).

Both Heinz Egypt and Betty Company have been quick to react with these rumors. Both companies have published short films (videos) explain the manufacturing process of these companies, additionally, publishing some documents that confirm the quality and safety of their products. On the other hand, the approach of dealing with restaurants varied with rumors, some of them responded to and dealt with this rumor (such as an Umm Hassan restaurant), and some of them ignored the handling of these rumors and that was the trend of most restaurants. (Indomie) also ignored the rumors (at least in the Egyptian market).

Thus, it is difficult to affirm to what extent rumors in social network sites affect the consumer behavior of purchasing food products and to what extent to restaurants and food companies are influenced by such rumors. Therefore, it can be discussed that the current research problem is reflected in the measurement of the impact of food rumors on SM sites in influencing consumer behavior and determining the extent to which organizations and their products, and certain restaurants, were influenced by such rumors.

This problem raises a number of questions that need through the examination and analysis providing clear and accurate answers, as follows:

- What is the impact of rumors on the purchase of food products from markets and restaurants?
- What is the level of consumer trust in the quality of food products?
- What restaurants and food products are most influenced by rumors?
- Is there a difference in the effect of rumor, depending on the type of food product or the type of restaurant?

So, the purpose of this research is to investigate the impact of rumors in SM of purchase of consumers. Thus, the study is done from the consumer standpoint. It is a response to the need to recognize the impact of SM (Zeng et al., 2009) and a need to understand the rumors in SM and their reaction to purchase of consumers (Yang et al., 2016). The existing literature has largely examined SM with a focus on identifying what generally motivate consumers (Taylor et al., 2011), rather than exploring how rumors affect the purchase of consumers. We attempt to remedy this gap by providing an extended understanding of the consumer response to rumors on SM, especially; we investigate a level of the trust in food products based on consumer behavioral responses following exposure to rumors on SM.

Our primary research objective is to explore whether consumers exist and differ on the basis of their level of trust in food products, and purchasing food products from markets and restaurants, following exposure to rumors on SM, which can help with the practical knowledge of the effect of rumors on social sites (SN) on the behavior of purchase of food products, which can affect companies and restaurants. It is also important to draw the attention of organizations on the role of social network sites (SNS) in influencing their customers. Moreover, it is significant to point out the negative impact of rumors that affect the image of the organization, and therefore its sales and profits. A secondary research objective is to determine the restaurants and food products that are more affected by rumors, as well the effectiveness of SM.

For the rumors in these sites seem to be an effective tool for consumers' purchasing. Consequently, learning more about the rumors may reveal new insights. Ignoring this aspect, companies will be greatly affected those that wonder whether they are worth it and those that refuse to deal with such rumors, and helping the management of companies and restaurants to build a strategy to confront rumors on these sites. The Egyptian market can benefit from this study in improving their ability to deal with rumors in general; they also help them to support their competitiveness in the food products market. Several studies indicate the impact of SN on the marketing activity of organizations, especially in customer relationship management and effect on their purchasing behavior, and as a marketing communication tool, as well as crisis management.

Many studies proposed that social networking has an influence the image, and the brand of organizations. Many studies indicated that there is a difference in the impact of SN on behavior. The results of previous studies differed in determining the influence of rumors on SN on behavior. This research comes in the framework of complementary study to the previous studies, in order to study the impact of rumors on SM sites in behavior of purchasing food products in the Egyptian market, which differ in the following: most previous studies have focused on the study of the influence of SN in general, and did not focus on the spread of rumors via SN and the impact on business organizations. They did not examine the influence of rumors on SN on purchasing behavior, particularly in the field of food products. Moreover, previous studies focused on the influence of rumors on the marketing activities of organizations, but did not focus on examining the influence of rumors on different types of products.

THEORETICAL FRAMEWORK AND DEVELOPMENT OF RESEARCH HYPOTHESES

Purchasing Behaviors and Social Media

Given the unprecedented reach of SM, firms are increasingly relying on it as a channel for marketing communication. Many commercial organizations have benefited from social networking in marketing, because of their impact on customers. In the Kumar study, (2016) which aimed to explore the influence of firm-generated content (FGC) in SM on three basic customer metrics: spending, cross-buying, and customer profitability. The results confirmed that after the authors account for the influences of TV advertising and e-mail marketing, FGC has a positive and significant effect on customers' behavior. In Bashir's study, (2017), which examined the use of SM in a new product development processes.

It is relying on an in-depth study of multinational corporations everywhere in the fast-moving consuming goods sector. The results supposed that SM can be gazed as an informal source for earning the perception of customers' preferences, competitors' activities, market trends and product feedback. It ascertains that the use of SM platforms as a source for providing information for new product projects does not constitute a formal part of Multinational Corporation's new product development process. Organizations that depend on traditional form also used SN in its work. In the Chua study, (2013), the key objective of this study is to explore the extent to which the usage of SM can support customer knowledge management (CKM) in organizations based on a traditional bricks-and-mortar business model.

The lessons collected from the case study suppose that SM is not a tool only to online businesses. It must be a possibility game-changer in supporting CKM efforts even for traditional businesses. Many companies in different sizes (small-medium-large) used marketing through SN to influence consumer behavior and increase the impact of the brand.

Godey's study (2016) explored these relationships by analyzing pioneering brands in the luxury sector (Burberry, Dior, Gucci, Hermès, and Louis Vuitton). The study demonstrated the links between SM marketing efforts and their outcomes (price premium, brand preference, and loyalty). The study assessed brands' SM marketing efforts as a holistic term that incorporates five features (entertainment, interaction, trendiness, customization, and word of mouth). Additionally, this study contributed that it finds that SM have a significant positive impact on brand equity and on the two main dimensions of brand equity: brand awareness and brand image. SM has revolutionized the ways of communication in sharing information and interests. The rapid growth of SM and SNS, especially, in improving countries like Egypt is providing marketers a new avenue to contact customers.

As it is known that SM is trending so much these days for a variety of reasons for which one of it is purchase decision. With regard to purchasing decision process, the consumer goes through five stages, in the first Problem or need recognition, Information search, Evaluation of the alternatives, Making Purchase decision, and in the Last purchase evaluate, SM plays a critical in all stage of the consumer purchasing decision (Gupta, 2016). Customers have been showed up to a different window of information and varieties of products; many great deals of choices and options available in the marketplace push their purchase decision. However, the decision making is different among individuals and also influenced by internal consumer behavior and external factors (Nguyen 2014).

The purchase decision depends primarily on information available to the consumer or the buyer, the type and size of this information depend on the methods of communication systems, upon which the set of society take into consideration their culture and customs, where the individual's purchasing behavior is influenced by through contacts and relations with others.

When the consumer creates the real purchase decision, it takes many risks, the risk is that the consumer usually does not have the expertise or knowledge of every part of the goods purchased and their components, and there are risks of fear on the body and health. A number of rumors related to marketing have appeared on SN (With its 4P'S), which led to financial losses for some companies, Marketing rumor is information related to the marketing performance of the organizations, which are usually tender and incorrect, and easily believable by the consumers. Some reasons for marketing rumors including, negative consumer attitudes toward organizations. Some companies do unethical practices to destroy their competitors through rumors.

The companies themselves, which create the environment for the emergence of such rumors, as to choose a brand name for its product, which raises doubts, or does not follow market reactions. There is no doubt that these rumors have harmful effects. It is sometimes devastating for companies that are exposed to it, especially the studies in this field have reached the attitude of consumers in general to believe these rumors) KRÓL, 2017; Lee, 2010). Given the results of previous studies, we can formulate the first main hypothesis as follows:

H1: There is no real difference between consumers in being influenced by rumors, according to their demographic characteristics (gender, education).

SN also plays a role in influencing the purchase decision; the Song study (2016) examined whether SM may influence on a customer's purchasing decision during the pre-purchase phase of service consumption. The results confirmed that the benefits of SM do have a positive relation with customers purchase decision, and in Gupta study (2016) which analyzed the behavior of the people: how their purchase decision is influenced by SM. The results showed that as SM generate both positive and negative comments, so it affects the decision making.

Instant communications via SM platforms have enabled consumers to build publish and share content, data and information regarding brands and products. Thus, the Sheth study, (2017) explored the effects of information sharing, peer pressure, entertainment and emotional connection in a SM setting on the user's attitude toward a brand current in SM, thereby influencing their purchase intentions from the brand. Ouoba's study (2011) focused on the online social interactions existing between companies in the food and beverage industry and their audience and attempts to investigate the effectiveness of Facebook and

Twitter. The results showed that SM used to collect information and follow companies in the food and beverage industry, Facebook ranked first before other internet resources.

The Mikalef study (2013) also elucidated how specific aspects of SM websites foster user intention to browse products and the effect that this has in shaping purchasing. SN also influences the brand. Hutter's, et al. study (2013) pointed out how SM activities, specially the Facebook page of a car manufacturer, and user interactions with these brand related activities affect the perception of brands and ultimately influence consumers purchase decision.

Their findings demonstrate that engagement with a Facebook fan page has positive effects on consumers' brand awareness, and purchase intention, and showed that SM activities actually indeed affect the purchase decision-making process. Moreover, The Schivinski study (2016), analyzed 60 brands across three different industries, the results showed that user-created SM communication had a positive impact on both brand attitude and equity. Additionally, purchase intention influenced positively by both brand equity and brand attitude.

Accordingly, the second main hypothesis can be formulated as follows:

H2: Rumors on SN have an effect on consumer purchasing.

Rumors

A rumor can be defined as "distorted, overstated, irrational and inauthentic information" (Miller 1992), which is a commonly-held view in practice (Donovan 2007; Fine et al. 2005). It can also be defined as a message that is presently unconfirmed by a message receiver.

This can include rumors later proven to be true and rumors later verified to be false (Liu 2014). Moreover, Vosoughi (2015) defined a rumor as an unverified assertion that starts from one or more sources and spreads over time in a network. A rumor in its new form is the news, subject or issue that is being circulated through the Internet, SN or mobile phones; it differs from the traditional rumor in terms of content and construction, as expressed in writing and text, image, sound, animation, and video.

In this paper, we adopt the definition of a rumor as" News which is published on SNS without confirmation of authenticity, it is mysterious and important, false information is added or exaggerates in the narrative, to influence consumers and attract their attention". Rumors can spread fast through SN.

Traditionally, this occurs by word of mouth, but with the appearance of the internet and its possibilities, new methods of rumor propagation are available. People write an email, use instant messengers or publish their thoughts in a blog. Many factors influence the dissemination of rumors (Kostka, 2008). Rumors on SN take a somewhat different form from the traditional rumor.

The characteristics of SM rumors are the quick spread of information, no editors, anonymity, the domination of emotions, and fragmented information (Zhang, 2015). Rumors spread through communication, as part of the news or information exchanged, digital communication rely on the usage of computers and the internet has emerged as one of its most recent forms which are social networking, which changed the way people communicate with each other.

Spreading of rumors through SN simulate the spread of rumors in its traditional form. However, the difference lies in the structural nature of these large networks (Bloch, 2014). The usage of web sites is influenced by the trust in these sites (Abdelkader, 2015). The prevalence of rumor depends on two basic conditions: First, the significance of the topic that revolves around the rumor for the listener or reader or viewer.

Second, the ambiguity of the situation to the audience; due to of the lack of news or lack of confidence or not formulated clearly or the inability to be understood by the people. As we move through SN, we find many unknown news sources, most of them are categorized as rumors, which may cause countless problems, and rumors can be divided across SN in terms of publishing goals into two parts (Liu 2014): rumors on purpose: they are rumors that their publishers are fully aware that this news is baseless.

They usually have a specific goal of publishing Rumors, either purely commercial purpose, seeking to increase the demand for a certain product by using rumors as an innovative marketing technique or to confuse a competitor by distorting the facts. (Oh, 2010 and Kwon, 2013). Unintended rumors: this type spreads spontaneously and unintentionally, either due to the rush to publish the news without verifying the original sources or by distorting the speech issued by the original source as a result of bad quoting which affects the meaning (Kwon, 2013).

The third main hypothesis can be formulated as follows:

H3: Rumors of SN have a significantly different effect among types of food product companies.

SM provides both opportunities and challenges to companies in crisis situations. In ZHU study (2017), employing a case study approach, the study explored how McDonald's and KFC used SM to deal with their 2012 crises in China. The study finds that McDonald's emerged stronger after the crisis because of their effective crisis management. KFC, in contrast, needed over a year to recover. The several types of rumors spread on the Internet have shown their possibility danger to business, particularly on the business of consumable products. Internets rumors can be readily accessed by consumers through via different channels and impact on their purchase behavior.

The Yang study (2016) the researchers has discussed the contents, formation, and transmission of rumors. Accordingly, the study purpose is to explore consequences of different methods of spreading internet rumors on college students' beliefs regarding internet rumors and their influence purchase intention. These studies suggest that several media sources of rumors will not affect consumer's belief related to internet rumor, or affect their purchase intention. In the Aditya study (2014) the researcher investigated why companies are not always successful in combating damaging rumors about their brands. Findings confirmed that a well-crafted denial statement that provides sufficient evidence against the rumor is only successful in curbing transmission intention when a well-known brand is involved in the rumor. However, well-known brands also serve as common grounds for conversation amongst consumers.

As such, they are more prone to being victims of rumors as they are more probable to be talked about. In this way, brand familiarity act as accountability, instead of being an advantage for well-known brands in the context of rumors. Features of the rumors via SN rapid deployment, and the inability to control what is published on these sites and authenticity. The KR?L study (2017) analyzed that the rumor source detection on three Twitter accounts of different sizes. The study described an empirical investigation of finding the position of the rumor-teller, calculating the length of the propagation path. The results confirmed that we are not able to detach the initial rumors users from the most effective spreaders in the small networks. In addition, Lee's study) 2010) has confirmed that the use of videos and multimedia add more credibility in the judgment of the content without linking to the source of news. Finally, SNs have many advantages and disadvantages, which affect commercial organizations as well as consumers.

The Alexander study (2014) reviewed the actual and possibility use of SM in emergency, catastrophe and crisis situations. Appreciation of the positive side of SM is balanced by their possibility for negative improvements, such as sharing rumors, undermining the authority and promoting terrorist acts. This leads to an inspection of the ethics of SM usage in crisis states. At the same time, they must be attention the ethical warnings and assure that SM are not abused or misapplied when crises and emergencies occur.

The fourth main hypothesis can be formulated as follows:

H4: Rumors of SN have a significantly different effect on restaurants.

RESEARCH POPULATION

This research is a descriptive research, which uses two kinds of data. Secondary data - for a theoretical overview and secondary data were collected from several websites and research papers that dealt with the topics related to the problem of research. Data were got from the food industry companies and restaurants in Egypt. Primary data - The needed primary data to achieve the research objectives were collected via the E-Questioner method using Google, models to apply the questionnaire via the internet and was filled by different people.

To answer our research questions and test our hypotheses, a link to an online questionnaire was applied through a post on Facebook. After purification of missing values, 387 cases remained for further analysis. Of the respondents, 57 percent were male and 43 percent female. Of the respondents, 40 per cent were aged between 18 and 25 and 53 per cent were aged between 25 and 45. Only 14 percent of the respondents were over 45.

In terms of marital status, 49 percent of respondents were single, 50 per cent were married and 1 percent were widowed or divorced. In order to measure the effect of rumors on SM in behavior of purchasing food products, the society of this research consists of users of SN, and where there are many SN, the researchers chose the site Facebook, which is one of the most used sites in Egypt, the set of Facebook users in Egypt is more than 33 million, which constitute 37% of the population. (Salem, 2017).

The study required that participants be selected among Facebook users using judgment sample. Thus, the sampling unit is the individual user of the SN (Facebook). The sample size in a society with more than 500 thousand items is 384, and the sample size of the sample is (384) Single. (Ryan, 2012). The E-Questioner questionnaire was followed to a sample of (387) which have Facebook accounts (users)) via the Internet using Google Forms.

Measures

The study included two types of variables, the first type is related to rumors on SN (independent variable), the second type relates to purchasing behavior (the dependent variable) The questions and items used were set up and refined based on literature and measured on a five-point Likert-scale. Rumors were measured using 2 adapted items (Aditya, 2014, Bloch, 2014, Fine et al. 2005; Kostka, 2008), while purchase of food products was captured by three items.

The impact of restaurants was measured through three items (Nguyen, 2014, Ouoba, 2011, Song, 2016, Gupta, 2016, Hutter 2013). Finally, some closed questions have been given to measure the demographics of the sample. After collecting the survey data, all the data collected from the surveyor were reviewed, (387) form that was collected electronically through the Internet.

In a later step, the variables entered into the computer using the SPSS.23rd package to be ready for analysis. The following statistical methods and tests were used for analysis, simple linear regression analysis of the relationship to demonstrate the relationship between rumors and purchasing food products, one-way ANOVA to determine the source of the difference between the product comparisons, the Scheffe's test of the Post Hoc in the SPSS program.as well as the correlation coefficient to identify the difference in the extent of the effect of the rumor on the restaurants, t-test, and F-test were used to test the research hypotheses (Aaker et al., 2014, Malhotra, 2011).

Results

The following is an analysis of the study data and discussion of the results and hypothesis testing, through the presentation of the results of the descriptive study, and the tests of hypotheses, as follows.

The Descriptive Results of the Study: Consumer's Preference to Buy Food From Restaurants

As shown in Table 1, 62.8 percent of the respondents preferred to eat or buy from restaurants sometimes, while 22.5 percent of the sample did not prefer to eat or buy food from restaurants. A few came with a small preference to eat and buy food from restaurants by 14.7 percent. Consequently, the results revealed that around 87.5% of consumers can buy and eat through restaurants.

Table 1. Consumer's preference to buy food from restaurants

The Extent of Preference	Frequency	Percent
Yes	57	14.7
Sometimes	243	62.8
No	87	22.5
Total	387	100.0

Influence of Consumers With Rumors on Social Media Sites

The results of the Influence of consumers with rumors on SM sites appear in Table 2 and shows that an effect somewhat with rumors through social networking for consumers (Somehow affected) at 36.4 per cent. While 30.2 percent of the sample was strongly affected, came the affected rumor on consumers by 22.5 percent, while the percentage of non-impact together was 10.9 per cent. Thus, it is in the results, that about 52.7 percent of consumers affected rumors on their behavior.

Consumer Trust in Restaurants and Food Products

As shown in Table 3 the Egyptian consumer trust in restaurants and food products with which he deals is medium, with (somewhat trust) 47.3 percent, while the confidence rate, in general, was 30.2 percent of the sample and came at a lower rate affected the rumor to consumers by 37.2 percent, while the percentage of distrust together was 15.6per cent. Thus, the results show that, about half the size of the sample of consumer trust in the food in restaurants or food products.

Table 2. Influence of consumers with rumors on social media sites

The Effect	Frequency	Percent
Strongly not affect	3	0.8
Not affect	39	10.1
Somehow affected	141	36.4
Affect	87	22.5
Strongly affect	117	30.2
Total	387	100

Table 3. Consumer trust in restaurants and food products

Extent of Confidence	Frequency	Percent
Strongly Distrust	6	1.6
Distrust	54	14.0
Somewhat Trust	183	47.3
Trust	123	31.8
Strongly Trust	21	5.4
Total	387	100.0

Favorite Restaurants to Consumers

Table 4 shows that restaurant franchises ranked first among Egyptian restaurants were amounted to 53 percent in the sample of the study, McDonald's ranked first in the sample, followed by Pizza Hut. KFC ranked third, and the percentages for other restaurants was low.

Restaurants Affected by Rumors

The results of the affected restaurants with rumors appear in Table 5 and show that KFC came in the first restaurants which were affected by rumors at 25 per cent, followed by one of the Egyptian restaurants (Umm Hassan) by 19 percent, In the third rank came McDonald's by 13 percent, and the affected percentages for other restaurants was low.

Table 4. Favorite restaurants to consumers*

The Restaurant	Frequency	Percent
McDonald's	144	0.20
Pizza Hut	135	0.19
KFC	108	0.15
Mo'men	69	0.10
Sobhy kaper	66	0.09
Om Hassan	39	0.05
El Berens	30	0.04
Zizo	24	0.03
Various Syrian Restaurants	18	0.03
Other	84	0.12
Total	717	100

* Can choose more than one replacement

Table 5. Most restaurants affected by consumer rumors*

Restaurant	Frequency	Percent
KFC	159	0.26
Om Hassan	120	0.20
McDonald's	84	0.14
Mo'men	60	0.10
El Berens	54	0.09
Zizo	42	0.07
Other	33	0.05
Sobhy kaper	30	0.05
Pizza Hut	21	0.03
Various Syrian Restaurants	12	0.02
Total	615	100

* Can choose more than one replacement

The Impact of Rumors on Food Products

Table 6 shows that the convergence of the impact of rumors on different products Except for Indomie, which was more affected by rumors than other companies Where about 67 percent of the sample, who stopped completely from the purchase of the product. While the other companies came close to the degree of non-impact, or consumer choice alternative product.

Table 6. Level and degree of impact of rumors on products

The Influence	Heinz Egypt		Indomie		Betty	
	Frequency	Percent	Frequency	Percent	Frequency	Percent
X1	165	42.6	258	66.7	117	30.2
X2	105	27.2	39	10.1	165	42.6
X3	117	30.2	90	23.2	105	27.1
Total	387	100.0	387	100.0	387	100.0

TEST THE RESEARCH HYPOTHESES

Results of Testing the First Hypothesis

Results of Testing the First Hypothesis: An independent samples t-test used to compare the means between gender, the results referred that there is no statistically significant difference (p = .436). In other words, there is no difference between male and female who are influenced by rumors. To determine the difference between consumers in being influenced by rumors, the one- way ANOVA test was used in this analysis. The results indicate that is no statistically significant difference (F = 1.752, p = 0.20). Based on the above, in relation to the second hypothesis testing, which provides "There is no significant difference between consumers in being influenced by rumors according to their demographic characteristics (gender, education)", the results of the tests show that there is no significant difference in accordance with the t-test and F-test.

Results of the Second Hypothesis Testing

Testing: To determine the type and degree of relationship between rumor and purchasing behavior, the simple linear regression analysis method was used in this analysis (Aaker et al., 2014; Malhotra, 2011). The researchers applied the method of simple linear regression analysis on the relationship between the rumor as an independent variable and the purchasing behavior of a dependent variable, the type, and strength of this relationship can be explained as shown Table 7.

Table 7. Simple linear regression analysis

R	R2	t	Sig.
0.446	0.198	19.611	.000

Type and Strength of Relationship

There is a positive correlation between the variables. The correlation between the selected variables was tested with the impact of rumor in SM on purchase behavior of consumers at the .01 level of significance. Using T-test, this relationship has strength of about 44 percent, according to the correlation coefficient R in the regression analysis model. In addition, these dimensions have the ability to explain variance up to about (19 percent) according to the R Square parameter in the regression analysis model.

This means that the independent variable (rumor) interprets (19 per cent) of the changes in the behavior of the dependent variable (purchasing behavior). That is, 19 percent of the change in purchasing behavior is due to rumors. Thus, in the view of the researchers there is a weak effect of rumors on purchasing behavior, which may be due to the economic conditions in Egypt, low income, and higher prices of the products, which makes the goal of purchasing behavior of the consumer is to obtain food products regardless of their quality or impact on human health.

Based on the above, in relation to the first hypothesis test, which Provides "Rumors on SN has an effect on consumer purchasing" the results of the test used show that there is a significant difference at the level 0.1 in accordance with the t-test, these findings are consistent with a Song study (2016), and Schivinski study (2016). On the other hand, these results are not consistent with results that appeared in the Yang study (2016).

Results of the Third Hypothesis Testing

To determine the difference in the impact of rumors depending on the type of food product, the one-way ANOVA was used in this analysis, as shown in Table 8.

Table 8. ANOVA

	Sum of Squares	df	Mean Squares	F	Sig.
Between Groups	11.721	3	3.909	6.143	.001
Within Groups	325.783	512	.636		
Total	337.510	515			

Note from Table 8, the analysis of the one-way ANOVA, that the value of P.value (.001) is less than the normal level (1%), which means that there is a difference between the products in the degree of their impact on rumors. To determine the source of the difference between the products, the Post Hoc Test method of the SPSS program was used to determine the source of the difference, based on the results of Scheffe's test for multiple comparisons, as shown in Table 9.

It is clear from Table 9 that there's a significant difference between the restaurants with Indomie, the value of P.value (.004), as well as between Heinz Egypt and Indomie. The value of P.value (.000), and finally between Betty and Indomie where the value of P.value (.000), while, the difference between other food products was insignificant where the value of P.value was greater than 1%.

Table 9. Multiple comparisons (Scheffe)

	Mean Difference	Sig.
Restaurants with Heinz Egypt	-.02326	.815
Restaurants with Betty	-.11628	.242
Heinz Egypt with Betty	-.09302	.349
Heinz Egypt with Indomie	-.31008*	.002
Restaurants with Indomie	-.28682*	.004
Betty with Indomie	-.40310*	.000

* The mean difference is significant at the 0.05 level.

Based on the above, in relation to the third hypothesis testing, which Provides "Rumors of SN have a significantly different effect among types of food product companies", the results of the test used show that there is a significant difference at the 0.1 level in accordance with the F-test. Thus, in the view of the researchers, maybe the reason due to the fast reply to rumors of both Heinz Egypt and Betty, As well as the few restaurants such as the restaurant (Umm Hassan), while the company (Indomie) Egypt ignored reply to rumors these rumors.

Results of Testing the Fourth Hypothesis

To identify the difference in the impact of rumors depending on the type of food product, the Coefficient of contingency test was used in this analysis (Aaker et al., 2014; Malhotra, 2011). To determine to what extent there is a difference between restaurants in the degree of their impact on rumors. That the value of P.value (< 0.001) and the Coefficient of contingency value is (0.32), which means that there is a difference between the restaurants in the degree of their impact on rumors.

Based on the above, in relation to the fourth hypothesis testing, which provides "Rumors of SN have a significantly different effect on the restaurants", the results of the test used show that there is a significant difference 0.1 in accordance with the Coefficient of contingency test. As explained in Table 10 it is clear in accordance with the attitudes of simple in this study that the KFC restaurant was one of the most affected restaurants by rumors, while McDonald's and Pizza Hut of were one of the least affected restaurants by rumors. These findings are consistent with ZHU study (2017) that was applied in China.

It is also noted through the results that the most famous restaurants are the most affected by the rumors. That KFC came in the first restaurants where affected by rumors at 27.9 per cent, followed by (Umm Hassan) Restaurant with 21.1 per cent, while the less famous restaurants were the fewer restaurants affected by rumors, except for Pizza Hut Restaurant. These findings are consistent with Aditya's study (2014), as the more fame of the brand increased the degree of impact of rumors.

Table 10. Impact of rumors on restaurants*

Restaurant	X1		X2		Total	
	Frequency	Percent	Frequency	Percent	Frequency	Percent
Pizza Hut	135	22	21	3.68	156	13.2
KFC	108	17.6	159	27.9	267	22.5
McDonald's	144	23.4	84	14.7	228	19.2
Om Hassan	39	6.34	120	21.1	159	13.4
Mo'men	69	11.2	60	10.5	129	10.9
El Berens	30	4.88	54	9.47	84	7.09
Sobhy kaper	66	10.7	30	5.26	96	8.1
Zizo	24	3.9	42	7.37	66	5.57
Total	615	100	570	100	1185	100

*Restaurants with a frequency of less than 20 were excluded.

RECOMMENDATIONS

- The need for companies to use SM networks in their work and focus their efforts on increasing the effectiveness of their content on these networks, and create a business unit responsible for monitoring and developing and updating their content on SN, and follow up on customer feedback on content, which contributes to rapid response;

- Posted periodically on SN (monthly or bi-monthly bulletins), about the activities of the organization, for customers to be familiar with all services provided by the organization;

- Increase awareness among marketer and organizations' management in general, the subject of rumors that can be risky to their organizations, and what can cause marketing crises, and how to deal with rumors and the methods of analysis and response, through training courses in the management of marketing crises in general and rumors in particular, or by encouraging them to access the references, researches and studies in this field;

- Establishment of a specialized unit to communicate with customers on SM, as part of its work, the analysis of the rumors and response, to include that specializes in marketing, especially in the management of marketing crises;

- Prevention of rumors via the use of many methods, including marketing intelligence, marketing research, measuring the attitude and satisfaction of customers. In addition, to following closely with SM, the immediate reaction to the news published about the organization;

- Organizations should not consider rumors as a threat, but rather only as an opportunity that can be exploited through conversion to the benefit of the organization, by exploiting what is published, in improving some of the misconceptions about the organization, and trying to improve its image, and publishing positive messages about the company. If it is achieved well, there will be a positive impact for the organization;

- The government must make a rumor-fighting unit which follows state Information service administratively, which can be contacted or accessed on its website to inquire about the rumors being promoted, thus eliminating the rumor before it spreads further;

- The need to improve new laws to confront electronic crimes in different forms and types, given the limitations of the existing legislation, which includes among these crimes dissemination of rumors should be addressed.

LIMITATIONS AND FUTURE RESEARCH

Some limitations regarding the research should be addressed. First, our focus in one type of SM, Facebook, and further research should attempt to understand other SM applications that exist - Twitter, Instagram, and YouTube. Second, we examine only Rumors in SM in our research design. There is myriad potential factor which could exist on social network sites, could impact on consumer behavior.

The study is geographically constrained in terms of both its sample and relevance. We thus encourage similar research to be carried out in different locations. In-depth study of cases of commercial organizations that were exposed to rumors, and that led to marketing problems, and how organizations dealt with rumors should be discussed. The marketing activities of the organizations on other SN, Twitter, Instagram, and YouTube should be evaluated. The study on the services sectors, such as the impact of rumors on the telecommunications sector or health services should be applied.

REFERENCES

Aaker, D. A., Kumar, V., & Day, G. S. (2014). *Marketing Research* (10th ed.). New York John, Wiley and Son Inc.

Abdelkader, A. (2015). Integrating Smartphone Talking Applications, Trust, Switching Cost and Customer Switching Behaviour in the Mobile Phone Market: The Case of Egypt. *International Journal of Customer Relationship Marketing and Management*, 6(1), 17–34. doi:10.4018/ijcrmm.2015010102

Aditya, S. (2014). Role of brand familiarity in combatting rumors. *Journal of Marketing Development and Competitiveness*, 8(3), 120–129.

Alexander, D. E. (2014). Social media in disaster risk reduction and crisis management. *Science and Engineering Ethics*, 20(3), 717–733. doi:10.100711948-013-9502-z PMID:24306994

Bashir, N., Papamichail, K. N., & Malik, K. (2017). Use of social media applications for supporting new product development processes in multinational corporations. *Technological Forecasting and Social Change*, 120, 176–183. doi:10.1016/j.techfore.2017.02.028

Bloch, F., Demange, G., & Kranton, R. (2014). Rumors and social networks (working papers N 2014-15). PSE.

Chen, G. (2016). New challenges from popular politics: NGOs, commercial organizations, social media, and civic society. In The Politics of Disaster Management in China (pp. 93-108). Palgrave Macmillan US.

Chua, A. Y., & Banerjee, S. (2013). Customer knowledge management via social media: The case of Starbucks. *Journal of Knowledge Management*, 17(2), 237–249. doi:10.1108/13673271311315196

Coombs, W. T., & Holladay, S. J. (2002). Helping crisis managers protect reputational assets: Initial tests of the situational crisis communication theory. *Management Communication Quarterly, 16*(2), 165–186. doi:10.1177/089331802237233

Donovan, P. (2007). How idle is idle talk? One hundred years of rumor research. *Diogenes, 54*(1), 59–82. doi:10.1177/0392192107073434

Fearn-Banks, K. (2007). *Crisis communication – a casebook approach.* New Jersey: Lawrence Erlbaum Associates.

Fine, G., Campion-Vincent, V., & Heath, C. (2005). *Rumor Mills: The social impact of rumor and legend.* New Brunswick, NJ: Transaction Publishers.

Godey, B., Manthiou, A., Pederzoli, D., Rokka, J., Aiello, G., Donvito, R., & Singh, R. (2016). Social media marketing efforts of luxury brands: Influence on brand equity and consumer behavior. *Journal of Business Research, 69*(12), 5833–5841. doi:10.1016/j.jbusres.2016.04.181

Gupta, V. (2016). Impact of social media on purchase decision making of customers. *International Journal on Global Business Management & Research, 5*(2), 73.

Hutter, K., Hautz, J., Dennhardt, S., & Füller, J. (2013). The impact of user interactions in social media on brand awareness and purchase intention: The case of MINI on Facebook. *Journal of Product and Brand Management, 22*(5/6), 342–351. doi:10.1108/JPBM-05-2013-0299

Kaplan, A. M., & Haenlein, M. (2010). Users of the world, unite! The challenges and opportunities of social media. *Business Horizons, 53*(1), 59–68. doi:10.1016/j.bushor.2009.09.003

Karpf, D. (2012). Social science research methods in Internet time. *Information Communication and Society, 15*(5), 639–661. doi:10.1080/1369118X.2012.665468

Kostka, J., Oswald, Y. A., & Wattenhofer, R. (2008, June). Word of mouth: Rumor dissemination in social networks. In International Colloquium on Structural Information and Communication Complexity (pp. 185-196). Springer Berlin Heidelberg.

Król, D., & Wiśniewska, K. (2017, April). on rumor source detection and Its experimental verification on twitter. In *Proceedings of the Asian Conference on Intelligent Information and Database Systems* (pp. 110-119). Springer. 10.1007/978-3-319-54472-4_11

Kumar, A., Bezawada, R., Rishika, R., Janakiraman, R., & Kannan, P. K. (2016). From social to sale: The effects of firm-generated content in social media on customer behavior. *Journal of Marketing, 80*(1), 7–25. doi:10.1509/jm.14.0249

Kwon, S., Cha, M., Jung, K., Chen, W., & Wang, Y. (2013, December). Prominent features of rumor propagation in online social media. In *Proceedings of the 2013 IEEE 13th International Conference on data mining (ICDM)* (pp. 1103-1108). IEEE.

Lee, H., Park, S. A., Lee, Y., & Cameron, G. T. (2010). Assessment of motion media on believability and credibility: An exploratory study. *Public Relations Review, 36*(3), 310–312. doi:10.1016/j.pubrev.2010.04.003

Liu, F., Burton-Jones, A., & Xu, D. (2014). Rumors on Social media in disasters: Extending Transmission to Retransmission. In PACIS (p. 49).

Malhotra, N. K. (2011). *Basic marketing research* (4th ed.). New Jersey: Prentice Hall.

Mikalef, P., Giannakos, M., & Pateli, A. (2013). Shopping and word-of-mouth intentions on social media. *Journal of Theoretical and Applied Electronic Commerce Research*, 8(1), 17–34. doi:10.4067/S0718-18762013000100003

Miller, D. E. (1992). "Snakes in the greens" and rumor in the innercity. *The Social Science Journal*, 29(4), 381–393. doi:10.1016/0362-3319(92)90002-Y

Nguyen, T. H., & Gizaw, A. (2014). Factors that influence consumer purchasing decisions of private Label food products. School of Business, Society and Engineering. Retrieved from http://www.Diva-portal.Org/smash/get/diva2

Oh, O., Kwon, K. H., & Rao, H. R. (2010, August). An exploration of social media in extreme events: rumor theory and twitter during the Haiti earthquake 2010. In ICIS (p. 231).

Ouoba, S. E. M. (2011). Investigating the effectiveness of social media Sites in shaping the opinion of the audience of companies in the food and beverage industry: facebook and twitter [Doctoral dissertation]. Hawaii Pacific University.

Tamlyn, R. (2012). Internet Inquiry: Conversations about method. doi:10.1080/1369118X.2011.586435

Roux-Dufort, C., & Pauchant, T. C. (1993). Rumors and crises: A case study in the banking industry. *Industrial & Environmental Crisis Quarterly*, 7(3), 231–251. doi:10.1177/108602669300700305

Safko, L. (2010). *The social media bible: tactics, tools, and strategies for business success*. John Wiley & Sons.

Salem, F. (2017). Social media and the Internet of Things towards Data-Driven Policymaking in the Arab World: Potential, Limits and Concerns. Retrieved from http://www.mbrsg.ae/getattachment/05534635-16f6-497a-b4a3-d06f061bda0b/Arab-Social-Media-Report-2017

Schivinski, B., & Dabrowski, D. (2016). The effect of social media communication on consumer perceptions of brands. *Journal of Marketing Communications*, 22(2), 189–214. doi:10.1080/13527266.2013.871323

Sheth, S., & Kim, J. (2017). Social media marketing: The Effect of Information Sharing, Entertainment, Emotional Connection and Peer Pressure on the Attitude and Purchase Intentions. *GSTF Journal on Business Review*, 5(1).

Song, S., & Yoo, M. (2016). The role of social media during the pre-purchasing stage. *Journal of Hospitality and Tourism Technology*, 7(1), 84–99. doi:10.1108/JHTT-11-2014-0067

Taylor, D. G., Lewin, J. E., & Strutton, D. (2011). Friends, fans, and followers: Do ads work on social networks. *Journal of Advertising Research*.

Vosoughi, S. (2015). Automatic detection and verification of rumors on Twitter [Doctoral dissertation]. Massachusetts Institute of Technology.

Yang, H. L., & Wu, W. P. (2016). The Effects of Consumers' Belief regarding Internet Rumors on Purchases Intention from Different Spreading Channels, International Journal of Information Systems *Management Research & Development*, 6(1).

Zeng, F., Huang, L., & Dou, W. (2009). Social factors in user perceptions and responses to advertising in online social networking communities. *Journal of Interactive Advertising*, *10*(1), 1–13. doi:10.1080 /15252019.2009.10722159

Zhang, Q., Zhang, S., Dong, J., Xiong, J., & Cheng, X. (2015, October). Automatic detection of rumor on social network. In *Proceedings of the National CCF Conference on Natural Language Processing and Chinese Computing* (pp. 113-122). Springer International Publishing. 10.1007/978-3-319-25207-0_10

Zhu, L., Anagondahalli, D., & Zhang, A. (2017). Social media and culture in crisis communication: McDonald's and KFC crises management in China. Public Relations Review. doi:10.1016/j.pubrev.2017.03.006

Zubiaga, A., Liakata, M., Procter, R., Bontcheva, K., & Tolmie, P. (2015). Towards detecting rumors in social media. arXiv:1504.04712

This research was previously published in the International Journal of Customer Relationship Marketing and Management (IJCRMM), 9(1); pages 19-35, copyright year 2018 by IGI Publishing (an imprint of IGI Global).

Chapter 76
Spanish Museum Policies Through Social Media to Enhance Communication With the Stakeholders

Juana Alonso-Cañadas
University of Almería, Spain

Federico Galán-Valdivieso
 https://orcid.org/0000-0001-9632-2941
University of Almeria, Spain

Laura Saraite-Sariene
University of Almeria, Spain

Maria del Carmen Caba-Pérez
University of Almeria, Spain

ABSTRACT

The main aim of this chapter is to describe the current status of participation and commitment of stakeholders in museums and cultural institutions through social networks. The study and analysis were developed following a quantitative methodology to calculate an index of online engagement through direct observation of data from the social network Facebook. Results show low levels of engagement, being most of interactions carried out through "like" and "share" actions, with few comments. It has been also detected that science museums lead in popularity, thematic museums are more prone to comments, and virality stands out in monuments. Likewise, the publication of posts containing audio-visual content are more frequent, and its publication is usually carried out during the week and in the morning.

DOI: 10.4018/978-1-7998-9020-1.ch076

INTRODUCTION

The irruption of Web 2.0 has led to the general development of social media, and of social networks, in particular. Their levels of popularity have made them present in any area of life at a social, political, business and cultural level. The communication strategy in social networks is based on the fundamental principle of content generation, especially if the generation is carried out by the user (Consumer Generated Media, CGM) (Viñaras & Cabezuelo, 2012). In this context, users become active agents in the communication process, with "engagement" as a concept of increasing importance.

According to the dialogical theory, the achievement of a true commitment by organizations on the part of their stakeholders has different benefits, mainly the establishment of open and two-way relationships with stakeholders that helps to effectively improve the organization performance (Kent & Taylor, 2002). A growing interest aroused in researchers about social networks has caused the previous literature to be expanded with research aimed at studying online engagement in different areas (Sobaci, 2016). Thus, works have been developed in the field of public government (Bonsón, Royo & Ratkai, 2014), politics (Vergeer, 2015) or in economic sectors such as tourism (Gálvez-Rodríguez, Saraite, Alonso-Cañadas & Caba-Pérez, 2017).

Regarding the cultural sphere, and specifically the museum field, the emergence of the Internet and Web 2.0 technologies have improved the access to information about museums and collections they offer (Tasich, 2014). Traditional image-based and text-based formats have given way to digital formats which, together with the fast expansion of new information technologies, have provided the opportunity for these cultural institutions to expand their audiences (Badell, 2015).

The constant increase in the use of social media by citizens has forced museums to change their way of communicating, from an official website to foster their presence in different social platforms like Facebook, YouTube or Twitter (Rio Castro, 2011; Badell, 2015). Thus, museums have integrated the potential offered by social media in their communication strategy (Martínez-Sanz, 2012; Claes & Detlell, 2014; López, Margapoti, Maragliano & Bove, 2010), to gain access to a greater audience at a lower cost, and to improve engagement with their stakeholders (Solis, 2007; Fletcher & Lee, 2012).

In the cultural sphere, one of the goals of social media is to promote art by increasing audience participation (Suzic, Karlíček & Stříteský, 2016). In this sense, social media provide added value to museums, going from being a physical space to a virtual one, in which the participatory communication capacity is multiplied, hence achieving wider spaces and more open museums (Diaz & Capriotii, 2015). This is the origin of what is known as "museum 2.0" (Srinivasan, Boast, Furner & Becvar, 2009), that is, a museum whose objective is to bring the visitors experience beyond the physical space, to form a space for creation, discussion and negotiation between centres, curators, artists and visitors (Simon, 2010).

The current communicative potential of social media in the museum field has not yet sufficiently exploited, since it is mainly used as a marketing and information dissemination tool (López et al., 2010; Langa, 2014). Several authors note that, in general, the publications made are limited to disseminate information about future events, promotions and various announcements, without generating and promoting a true bidirectional interaction between user and organization (Kidd, 2011; Fletcher & Lee, 2012; Langa, 2014).

Undoubtedly, few museums use social media to engage in dialogue with users (Fletcher & Lee, 2012), something that different stakeholders expect to obtain when approaching the social media environment (Chung, Marcketti & Fiore, 2014; Baker, 2017). This situation is confirmed at the Spanish level, where the majority of cultural entities maintain a way of relating to their users in social networks very similar to the one they had in the analog era (Gómez-Vilchez, 2010).

Among the different platforms, Facebook is the most popular social network, not only among Internet users, but also among different organizations due to its potential to interact (Chung et al. 2014; Suzic et al., 2016) and its ability to stimulate communication with different audiences (Vinarás & Cabezuelo, 2012). In the museum field, Facebook has also been adopted in a massive way, being the most used social platform (Gronemann, Kristiansen & Drotner, 2015; Koo, 2015). However, the mere creation of Facebook pages does not automatically generate visibility or participation (Waters, Burnett, Lamm & Lucas, 2009), so it is necessary to make real use of the interactive potential of this social network.

Given the above and also knowing that Facebook is the network with the largest presence of Spanish museums (Gómez-Vilchez, 2010), the main aim of this study is to determine, through the direct observation of the main Spanish museums and cultural entities fan-pages, the level of stakeholder participation and commitment. With this, it is intended to advance in the knowledge of online engagement in the cultural context, in addition to showing some of the main characteristics posts emission policies carried out by museums. This work is divided into eight sections. After the introduction, second to fourth sections are devoted to the state of the art and previous literature. In the sixth section the sample and the study methodology are described, seventh presents the main results, and in eighth the main conclusions are presented.

BACKGROUND

The evolution from Web 1.0 to 2.0 technology has allowed the development of social media, which are defined as digital platforms that facilitate the exchange of information, the generation of content by the user and the collaboration between them (Elefant, 2011), among which social networking platforms stand out. Social networking can be defined as a web-based service that allows people to create a public (or semi-public) profile within a system, generate a list of other users with whom to share a connection, as well as to see and contact users from their contact list (and even with other users outside their contacts but belonging to the system) (Mcfarland & Ployhart, 2015).

The high penetration of social networks in society has allowed them to be perfectly integrated in any field, such as economic, social, political and cultural. Its appearance has substantially changed the way in which society is confronted with its decision-making processes regarding consumption, both of products and of services. They have eliminated the monopoly of information by reducing their access and increasing the number of sources. In addition, it is common for the information circulating in social networks to reach the filtered audience and recommended by trusted people, which gives it greater value and truth than the classic models of unidirectional information dissemination (Peña, 2014).

Undoubtedly, social networks provide an environment where users can publish their views, experiences and recommendations for purchase and consumption, without forgetting that they are designed to allow such information to be available to other users (Flanagin & Metzger, 2013; 'Connor, 2008). This eases the virtual interaction, information sharing, as well as diversity of opinions, all together resulting in a greater knowledge about all kinds of goods, services and brands (Filieri & McLeary, 2014). In summary, social networks are mainly focused on the generation of content and, especially, allow its generation by the user (CGM) (Viñaras & Cabezuelo, 2012).

The benefits of CGM help in two ways. From the purely consumerist point of view, CGM reduces the uncertainty inherent in the purchase process by allowing the consumer to obtain information about the different alternatives available (Fang, Zhu and Zhang, 2017; Kim, Wang, Maslowska and Malthouse, 2016; Liu & Park, 2015). From a social point of view, it implicitly leads users to belong to a community, which contributes to the achievement of social benefits, such as the satisfaction of helping others self-lessly, and the possibility of obtaining a certain reputation or status within from that community (Cheung & Lee, 2012; Hennig-Thurau, Gwinner, Walsh & Gremler, 2004).

In a context of active participation of users in social networks, the concept of engagement is particularly important. Under the principles of the theory of dialogical communication (Kent & Taylor, 1998), commitment is one of the key characteristics of an adequate dialogue, since both the organization and the users must be willing to have a dialogical relationship. If the organizations get a real commitment from their stakeholders, they could obtain benefits such as knowing in advance whether the stakeholders agree or not with certain issues, and using open and bidirectional relations with them to effectively improve the organization (Kent & Taylor, 2002). Therefore, organizations use social networks as a means both to consult their groups of interest and to be consulted by them, on matters that directly affect them both (Bonsón et al., 2014).

Precisely, and following dialogic theory, Bonsón & Ratkai (2013) affirm that online engagement through social networks is contained in three dimensions: popularity, commitment and virality. Each of these dimensions represent a type of interaction that would be associated with a lower or higher level of involvement with the information disclosed by the organization through its different postings. The "popularity" dimension measures the commitment of the users with the information published through the "Like" action. The "commitment" dimension reflects a more interactive user commitment, since it requires users to comment on the publications, which implies more time and effort than simply clicking "Like". And, finally, "virality" shows the extent to which users have an active participation in the information disclosed by the organization, since this action involves "sharing" a posting.

The concern on the part of researchers about online engagement is clear in previous literature, with different lines of research focusing on both public and private organizations. Since previous research about online engagement covers a wide range of research topics, the literature review presented below may not be exhaustive, this being a mere approximation to the state of the question.

Regarding the public sphere, the topics and areas of study on the use of social networks are diverse, highlighting those that deal with governments at the local level (Sobaci, 2016). In this area, some works such as Bonsón et al. (2014) study citizen engagement in the case of the Western European local governments. Likewise, Galvez-Rodriguez et al. (2016) perform an analysis on the use of social networking as a communication strategy to encourage citizen participation among local governments in the United States, Canada and Mexico. And Sáez-Martín, Alonso-Cañadas, Galán-Valdivieso & Caba-Pérez (2018) analyse the level of online engagement of citizens with the local governments of Paraguay and identify the social, political and economic factors that influence such participation.

The main conclusions of this line of research show that there is no clear evidence that citizens are using social networking for interactive participation with governments (Brainard & McNutt, 2010; Gil de Zúñiga, Jung & Valenzuela, 2012; Mergel, 2013a). Therefore, public administrators, in addition to promoting the use of social media by governments, must mobilize citizens to participate and engage in the public sphere, with the intention of collaborating in decisions or creating solutions for problems of the government (Mergel, 2013b; Zhen & Zheng, 2014). In this regard, authors such as Mergel (2013a) and Hofmann, Beverungen, Räckers, & Becker, 2013, argue that this situation is due to the unidirectional use made by government agencies of social networking.

Regarding the relationship between politics and social networks, literature has focused especially on electoral processes (Vergeer, 2015), showing a special interest in the communications made by political leaders (López-García, 2016). Likewise, the relationship between online and offline political engagement (Steinberg, 2015) has been studied and the behaviour of citizen engagement in different pre-election periods in countries such as the US has been analysed. (Carlisle & Patton, 2013), Norway (Larsson & Ihlen, 2015), Belgium (D'Heer & Verdegem, 2014), Italy (Ceron & d'Adda, 2015; Valeriani & Vaccari, 2015), Holland (Vergeer & Hermans, 2013) or Spain (Gámir, 2016; López-García, 2016).

Some of the main conclusions highlight that social media exert a powerful influence to reach and influence voters (Effin, Van Hillegersberg & Huibers, 2011) and that online participation leads to a significantly higher probability of voting (Rustad & Saebo, 2013, Steinberg, 2015, Valenzuela, Correa & Gil de Zuñiga, 2017). Likewise, Guillamón, Ríos, Gesuele & Metallo (2016) observes that right and left parties disseminate a similar amount of information online, while Sáez-Martín et al. (2015) do not find the political ideology in the application of dialogic principles in the context of social networks.

In the field of private companies, an extensive research has been carried out in different economic sectors. An outstanding example is the hotel sector, where some works such as the one by Phelan, Chen & Haney (2013) show that the clients of national hotels use Facebook to make positive comments. Other works highlight different aspects of users' opinions. For example, Pantano & Di Pietro (2013) identify a frequent use of social networks to transmit complaints to the company, and Aluri, Slevitch, & Larzelere (2015) conclude that travellers would experience higher levels of perceived social interaction when using hotel websites with integrated social media channels, compared to websites that do not have integrated social media channels. In Asian countries, lack of interaction between hotels and customers prevails (Chan & Guillet, 2011; Yu-Lun Hsu, 2012). And more recently Gálvez-Rodríguez et al. (2017) perform a study to analyse the use of social networks as a communication strategy for encouraging stakeholder engagement in hotels from Brazil, Russia and India.

Cultural institutions around the world are increasingly noticing that social networks would help to improve knowledge and dissemination of culture. In this field, social networks allow cultural institutions to interact with users, collect their comments, get to know them better and establish a lasting relationship (Peña, 2014). Despite the benefits, there is a gap between theory and empirical evidence extracted from the virtual reality in which cultural organizations move. Although there is literature on social networks and the museum environment (as will be carefully analysed below), and as far as our knowledge is concerned, there exists a lack of works specifically aimed at quantifying and analysing the level of online engagement of users with the museums.

FROM TRADITIONAL MUSEUMS TO MUSEUMS 2.0.

The International Council of Museums (ICOM), in the international context, defines the museum as a non-profit, permanent institution, at the service of society and its development, open to the public, which acquires, conserves, researches, communicates and exposes the material and immaterial heritage of humankind and its environment for the purposes of education, study and recreation. This definition gives the museum an ultimate goal: to socialize, that is, to make available to the public the knowledge that comes from heritage and collections, to provide educational, study or enjoyment material to the members of a community (Valdés, 1999).

In fulfilling its basic purpose, museums have been slowly but gradually incorporating information and communication technologies (ICT) into their daily processes (Celaya & Viñarás, 2006). Back in 1947, André Malraux in the essay "Le musée imaginaire", drew a museum as an institution open to society that was not limited to the space where it was located, but that its knowledge could surpass it. Undoubtedly, the emergence of the Internet has made it possible to eliminate the mandatory physical visit to access the knowledge contained in the museum, eliminating physical and time barriers (Quijano, 2012; Martinez-Sanz, 2012).

The evolution of museums has been conditioned not only by the application of ICT in the museum context, but also by the approval of new legal systems that promoted culture, as well as by the contribution of two schools of thought that advocated public participation. in the planning and evolution of the museum (the Museology Move) and which are positioned against a culture sheltered in museums, aspiring to turn them into spaces for debate, reflection and negotiation (the Critical Museology) (Martinez-Sanz, 2012; García, 2009; Santacana-Mestre & Hernández-Cardona, 2006).

The first applications of ICT in the museum context are circumscribed in the late 80s and early 90s of the 20th century. Basically, they consisted of computers in the halls of exhibition to let the visitor interact with them, thus limiting the interaction only to the visitor who physically went to the museum. At the same time, the first CD-roms appear (later replaced by digital format or DVD) and after that the first websites of museums emerged as a virtual access door to the museum that has the capacity to complement, magnify and revive the experience of the face-to-face visit, as well as being an effective knowledge transmission channel (Báscones & Carreras-Monfort, 2009). However, it is not until the beginning of the 21st century when the online museum dissociates itself from its physical organism by offering services and contents that complement the institution's global offer (Forteza, 2012).

Beyond what the emergence of the Internet has meant for museums, the real revolution has come from the development of social media, and specifically social networks, substantially expanding the capacity of participatory communication of museums, and creating larger spaces and more open museums (Losada-Díaz & Capiotti, 2015). In this sense, social networks have involved a paradigm shift in the prevailing institutional communication model based on unidirectionality. In this sense, a significant change takes place: enabling the recipient of the message to become an active part of the communication process, which implies important changes in the relationship between institutions and their publics, facilitating and improving the interaction between them (Capriotti, Carretón & Castillo, 2016).

In the exposed context of continuous technological innovation and renovation to which museums and society in general are exposed, it can now be stated without any doubt that the traditional museum has given way to the museum 2.0 (Srinivasan et al., 2009). Also known as "social museum", it is defined as one that aims to expand the experience of visitors beyond the physical space to become a platform for creation, debate and negotiation between the centre, curators, artists and visitors (Simón, 2010). Despite the consensus on the existence and virtues of the 2.0 museum, and focusing on Spain, even the museum spaces are in an embryonic phase of adoption of a new management model for their public, although there is a need for the museum to establish conversations with virtual visitors and participate actively in debates not generated by the organization itself (Claes & Detlell, 2014).

SOCIAL MEDIA USE TO IMPROVE STAKEHOLDER ENGAGEMENT IN SPANISH MUSEUMS

Museums and cultural entities (hereinafter museums) are organizations that depend on good relations with their stakeholders. In this sense, social media offer museums the opportunity to establish a constant and varied dialogue with all kinds of public, approach institutions in a different way and allow visitors to reach more people than traditional campaigns (Gómez- Vílchez, 2012).

Among the goals of social media in cultural institutions, several authors have highlighted marketing and education (Arends, Goldfarb, Merkl & Weingartner, 2009; Evans, 2010; Bocatius, 2011; Drotner & Schrøder, 2013). The same conclusions are offered by Koo (2015) who points out that social media in the field of museums has an impact on communication and also on learning. In this sense, the author adds that museums should work in collaboration with several experts in communication and information, designers and educators.

By communicating their activity, museums promote culture and stimulate the richness of the geographical area as well as the image (Garibaldi, 2015). In this context, social media offers a quick and easy way to communicate and promote cultural activity (Grönroos & Ravald 2011). In fact, museums now are no longer organizations that offer science, but organizations that communicate on the basis of science (Skola, 2012), contributing to give greater visibility to culture and art (Martínez-Sanz, 2012).

Nowadays, presence in social media has almost become a users' requirement. But it is not enough simply to have online presence, but also to analyse the implications of managing online users to improve communication and interaction through these platforms (Kaplan & Haenlein, 2010; Kidd, 2011; Filippini, Fantoni, Stein & Browman, 2012). In this sense, social media can help create audio-visual content for exhibitions, thus increasing the interest of users and giving greater visibility to all the activity offered by a museum (Sokolowicz, 2009). On the other hand, they can also contribute to broadening the audience of museums by attracting a younger audience (Baker, 2017), or meeting the need of those who use social media in search of cultural information (Richards, 2007; Macchiavelli, 2008).

One of the key features offered by social media is bidirectional communication, which is user-centred and allows quick content creation and exchange (Aghaei, Nematbakhsh & Farsani, 2012). The speed with which the communication process occurs increases the potential for two-way communication between museums and their audience. However, this requires effective management of the projects (Fletcher & Lee, 2012), because otherwise, users may quickly lose interest, thus lowering participation (Waters et al., 2009).

Despite the potential of social media to obtain a competitive advantage, involving, collaborating and involving the audience (Kidd, 2011), many museums solely use their online profile as an exclusive promotional tool (Lehman and Roach, 2011). This is definitely a mistake, especially in the current context of cultural sphere, where several organizations (not only cultural, but also entertainment and leisure-focused in general) operate (Suzic et al., 2016).

Concern regarding the role of social media in the cultural field has been evident in the research carried out so far, focusing primarily on two approaches: technology and audience (Gronemann et al, 2015). Studies focused on technology are carried out through surveys or content analysis to identify what types of social media applications are available, and how they are organized (Capriotti & Kuklinski 2012; Fletcher & Lee, 2012). In this sense, López et al. (2010) analysed the degree of visibility that museums offer on their official websites to web 2.0 tools, while Garibaldi (2015) studied if cultural institutions in Italy are able to maximize the usefulness of such tools.

On the other hand, museums are increasingly aware that they need to focus on improving audience engagement (Koo, 2015). In this line, research focuses on the relationship between the online presence of a cultural entity and the increase of visitors in the physical space (Loran, 2005; Griffiths & King, 2008), the need for interaction to sustain this relationship (Arends et al., 2011) or how communication in the museum sector has changed with the arrival of new technologies, allowing for an increase in the loyalty of users (Kelly, 2010; Wilson, 2011). In addition, Gronemann et al. (2015) study how audiences and museums favour the growth of each other, both in communicative and social terms. Other works show how museums seek to build relationships with key stakeholders to attract potential audiences and maintain the existing (Drotner & Schrøder, 2013; Runnel, Pruulmann-Vengerfeldt, Viires & Laak, 2013).

In this area of research, a set of studies focuses on exploring commitment through social networks. Spiliopoulou, Mahony, Routsis and Kamposiori (2014) analyse the way to use social platforms to improve engagement with British Museum users more effectively. Suzic et al. (2016), in their study on social media strategies in museums, assert that the frequency and characteristics of the published messages are correlated with the level of fans reactions. In the same line, Chung et al. (2014) state that museums should develop more specific strategies to improve their relationship with online visitors. In this regard, strategies aimed at content design could involve more users and thus improve online participation (Bernstein, 2008). In this way, museums could take advantage of the potential social networks users as active content creators, as opposed to users of mass communication (Gronemann et al., 2015). This differentiation is also reflected in the museographic studies (Thumim 2010; Drotner & Schrøder, 2013; Runnel et al., 2013; Lotina, 2014).

AIM OF THE STUDY

As shown in previous sections, museums are important in society in general, because as Valdés (1999) point out, this institution provide educational, study and enjoyment material to the members of a community. In addition, in the cultural field coexist museums with different specialties (painting, photography, visual arts, science, etc.). Therefore, the main aim of this study is to determine, through the direct observation of a set of museums fan-pages, the level of stakeholder´s engagement to answer the following research questions:

RQ1: What is the status of the stakeholder´s engagement with museums through social networks?
RQ2: Does the level of stakeholder´s engagement through social networks differ according to the specialty of museums?

These questions will be answered by performing a descriptive analysis to shows the level of online engagement reached by stakeholders with the museums. Also, a means test is carried out to verify the existence of differences between the level of online engagement reached by museums with one specialty or another.

METHODOLOGY

To achieve the goal above mentioned, an empirical methodology in two different stages is developed. In the first phase, the sample is selected, and the necessary data are collected through direct observation of the Facebook pages. The second phase involves processing the observed data applying a descriptive analysis to show the degree of online participation reached by the Spanish museums through their official Facebook pages, as well as the different practices performed regarding publications management.

Sample and Data Collection

To gather information about the largest number of Spanish museums possible, and for the greater diversity in terms of size and type of museum, TripAdvisor webpage has been consulted because of its extensive information on cultural activities. In fact, TripAdvisor is considered as one of the most popular sources of travel information on the web (O'Connor, 2010), being used in academic researches related to the tourist sector (Sigala, 2009; Duffy, 2015). Results initially yield 106 entities.

Facebook profiles were first searched through the official website of each entity, and if not found, the word "Facebook" was entered in Google search engine of the official website (Ellison & Hardey, 2014). Of the 106 initial museums, 82 of them have an official Facebook page, but those accounts that were not active during the analysed period had to be eliminated from the sample, finally totalling 76 entities.

Table 1. Main quantitative parameters used for Facebook pages

	Total Posts	Number of Fans	Number of Posts Liked	Total Likes	Number of Post Commented	Total Comments	Number of Posts Shared	Total Shares
Total	21.059	3.506.621	20.834	2.593.950	8.838	68.716	16.517	823.209
Mean	277	46.140	274	31.131	116	904	217	10.832

The activity of the accounts was analysed for 12 months, since it is considered an acceptable time space to examine information in social media (Mariani et al., 2016). Specifically, the study was conducted between January and December 2017. A total of 21,059 post were by the entities, and with respect to actions taken by stakeholders, 2,593,950 shares of "likes", 68,716 comments, and 823,209 "shares" were computed (see Table 1).

Analysis of Stakeholder's Engagement via Facebook

An engagement index (E*) is calculated to determine the level of stakeholder commitment in museums' fan pages (see Table 2). This index was initially created by Bonson and Ratkai (2013) to quantify the level of online engagement in the field of governments. However, it has been applied in other research areas such as the tourist sector, specifically in the hotel sector (Gálvez-Rodríguez et al., 2017). This measure consists of three dimensions: Popularity (P), Commitment (C) and Virality (V). Popularity is defined as the users' acceptance of an organization's messages posted on the Facebook page, Commitment focuses on greater involvement interacting with the messages, and Virality is defined as the diffusion and extension achieved by the organization's messages posted on its Facebook page (Bonsón et al., 2014).

Table 2. Metrics used to measure users' engagement with organization via Facebook

Name	Sign	Formula	Measures
Popularity	P1	Posts with likes/ total posts	Percentage of total posts liked
	P2	Total likes/total posts	Average number of likes per post
	P3	(P2/number of fans) * 1000	Popularity of messages among fans
Commitment	C1	Posts with comments/ total posts	Percentage of total posts that have been commented on
	C2	Total comments/ total posts	Average number of comments per post
	C3	(C2/number of fans) * 1000	Commitment of fans
Virality	V1	Posts with shares/ total posts	Percentage of the total posts that have been shared
	V2	Total shares/ total posts	Average number of shares per post
	V3	(V2/number of fans) * 1000	Virality of messages among fans
Engagement Index: $E^* = P3 + C3 + V3$			

Source: Bonsón and Ratkai (2013).

A descriptive analysis of the data is first carried out, intending to know the average level of engagement for all Spanish museums, paying special attention to the pre and post-vacation months in order to identify possible behavioural patterns in the level of engagement. Likewise, the main characteristics of the published posts are identified, which is an indication of the policy currently applied. To conclude, an engagement index analysis is carried out taking into account the typology of the museums. Data were treated with SPSS software.

RESULTS

Level of Stakeholders Engagement via Facebook

Table 3 shows the main results. As can be seen, the engagement index exhibits a mean value of 8.24, showing great dispersion in view of the standard deviation (11,48). Regarding its components, the dimension with a greater value is "Popularity" (5.91), followed by "Virality" (2,16) and "Commitment" (0.26). Results point out that stakeholders are more likely to interact within this social network through quick actions that require little effort and time, such as clicking on "like" or "share". It is also worth noting that the results for the three dimensions present high dispersion, mainly due to the presence of high values in the case of popularity and virality for some of the entities analysed

The time frame considered has made possible to monitor the level of engagement during different periods within the year (Table 4). We observe differences up to 60% in the level of engagement reached on a monthly basis, ranging from 0.15 in the case of April to 9.24 observed in October. Months with higher interaction levels are October (9.24), July (8.59), August (8.38), September (8.26) and January (7.99), that is, the holiday periods by excellence. Figures observed in October and January deserve special attention because although not being especially prone months for vacation, they are actually post-holiday periods. In this sense, during the days or weeks after the holidays, the stakeholders could be taking advantage to reflect their cultural experiences through social networks, increasing interactions with museums in those months.

Table 3. Average results of stakeholder engagement via Facebook (N=76)

	Engagement (E*)	Popularity (P3*)	Commitment (C3*)	Virality (V3*)
Mean	8,34	5,91	0,26	2,16
Median	4,21	3,17	0,08	0,86
Maximum	63,59	41,61	3,10	32,89
Minimum	0,31	0,25	0,00	0,05
SD	11,48	7,70	0,53	4,56

Table 4. Monthly average results of stakeholder engagement via Facebook (N=76)

Month	E*	P3	C3	V3	N° Post
January	7.99	6.18	0.19	1.69	1,449
February	0.15	0.11	0.00	0.03	1,729
March	5.00	6.89	0.33	5.00	2,034
April	7.98	6.11	0.22	1.63	1,694
May	6.92	5.19	0.12	1.61	2,027
June	6.95	4.92	0.26	1.76	1,853
July	8.59	6.21	0.18	2.21	1,633
August	8.38	5.90	0.18	2.30	1,331
September	8.26	6.22	0.33	1.71	1,619
October	9.24	7.19	0.21	1.83	1,842
November	7.97	5.94	0.24	1.80	1,955
December	6.94	5.00	0.32	1.62	1,893

Surprisingly, when focus is placed on the relationship between the number of post published and engagement, months with greater number of publications (March and May) are not the ones with better levels of engagement. Furthermore, and analyzing the different dimensions of the index, monthly breakdown shows once again that the "Popularity" component yields much higher levels of engagement than the dimensions "Virality" and "Commitment" in each of the months analyzed.

With respect to the main formatting and publication features of posts released during 2017, aspects related to the type of post, day of the week and time frame have been identified. These three aspects are important in active management of a social network, since both the format and the date and time of release could have an effect on the level of interaction and, therefore, on the level of commitment achieved.

Table 5. Main characteristics of format and publication of posts

Format	Number of Posts	Day of the Week	Number of Posts	Time Frame	Number of Posts
Picture	13,608	Monday	1,825	Morning (6 a.m. – 12 a.m.)	13,823
Video	1,876	Tuesday	3,060	Afternoon (12 a.m. – 6 p.m.)	6,237
Status	208	Wednesday	3,303	Evening (6 p.m. – 12 p.m)	876
Event	484	Thursday	3,578	Night (12 p.m. a – 6 a.m.)	123
Link	4,873	Friday	3,581		
Music	10	Saturday	3,605		
		Sunday	2,107		
Total	21,059	Total	21,059	Total	21,059

As observed in Table 5, 64% of the published posts incorporate an image or a photograph, and 23% publicize a link for the user. On the contrary, posts with musical content are the least frequent in the social networks of museums. Regarding the date of release, almost 73% are made during the week, being only 27% sent during the weekend. In this case, it is observed that the preferred days of the week for the publications of the posts, are Thursday, Friday and Saturday. Also, most posts (95.25%) are launched in what could be considered as working hours (between 6 a.m. and 6 p.m.). In the case of mornings, 65% of the posts are published, while in the afternoon is almost 30%.

Analysis of Engagement According to the Type of Museum

To carry out this part of the research, the sample has been classified into 6 categories (Table 6) in accordance with the main objective or its specialty. Specifically, they are grouped into: monuments, archaeology-focused institutions, art museums (dedicated to different pictorial genres), museums dedicated to the dissemination of science, and institutions dedicated to various topics related to the naval field, to flamenco culture or the promotion of viticulture, among others. The number of art museums stands out, representing 43.42% of the sample, representing the category of monuments and museums of different themes a relative importance of 19.73% and 14.47%, respectively. The rest of the groups (historical museums, those dedicated to science and archaeology) represent 22.36% of the sample.

As Table 6 shows, Facebook pages that receive the highest percentage of "likes" per publication (P1), with 99.26%, are those in the category of museums of different topics, followed by the museums of art and science, with 99.12% and 99.02%, respectively, which represents the almost entire visibility of the publications made. However, the category that receives the greatest number of "likes" per post (P2), 159.12, is the category of art museums, while historical museums exhibit the lowest values (21.77).

Although science museums have a low P2, they enjoy greater popularity when considering the number of fans. In fact, its popularity (P3) is higher (9.73) than that of the art museums (4.09).

The dimension "Commitment" presents a more homogeneous behaviuor: 48.61% of posts published by art museums receive a comment (C1), showing 4.14 comments per post on average. However, when taking into account the number of fans, the category monuments shows better figures with respect to the comments by fans (C3), with a value of 0.45. Similar results are obtained for "Virality", since 81.65% of publications are shared, and have an average of shares per post (V2) of 49.92. The best result regarding the virality of the publication is shown by Monuments, while the posts made by the archaeological museums are the least viral among their fans.

In summary, the category that encompasses museums of different topics offers the best results of Engagement (E*), but the group of science museums show greater popularity among their fans. It is against the results of commitment and virality, since it is in the monuments category where the greatest interaction by stakeholders is appreciated. To verify if the observed differences between categories are significant or not, Kruskal-Wallis test is applied, since the tests performed with respect to the normality of the data do not confirm this extent (Bonsón, Bednarova and Escobar-Rodríguez, 2014; Gálvez-Rodríguez, et al., 2017).

Kruskal-Wallis (K-W) test is a non-parametric technique commonly used to evaluate the significant differences in a continuous dependent variable by means of a categorical independent variable (with two or more groups), in cases where one-way ANOVA requirements are not met. The null hypothesis tested is that the samples (groups) come from identical populations, while the alternative hypothesis assumes that at least one group comes from a different population.

Table 6. Facebook pages aggregated data by type of museums

Type	Number of Institutions	Number of Post	Number of Likes	Number of Comments	Number of Shares	Number of Fans
Monuments	15	2.566	86.862	2.584	21.726	95.016
Archaeological Museums	4	1.684	126.326	3.434	41.218	78.858
Art Museums	33	10.683	2.200.135	56.586	700.464	2.992.268
Science Museums	5	884	36.359	971	7.314	173.603
History Museums	8	2.483	54.906	1.839	20.548	96.997
Museums of various topics	11	2.759	89.362	3.302	31.939	69.879
Total	76	21.059	2.593.950	68.716	823.209	3.506.621

Results of K-W test are shown in the final column of Table 7. Globally considered, p-value of total engagement scores is 0.011, less than the significance value of 0.05, which means that the null hypothesis is rejected. According to this test, there are also significant differences between P3 y V3 scores (p-values below 0.05), that is, in two out of three components of the engagement index. This means that the engagement of stakeholders with museums through their fan pages differs significantly from one type of museum to another.

Table 7. Popularity, Commitment and Virality metrics, average Engagement scores and results of Kruskal-Wallis test (by type of museum)

		Monuments	Archaeological Museums	Art Museums	Science Museums	History Museums	Museums of Various Topics	K-W Test (2-Tailed)
		Mean	Mean	Mean	Mean	Mean	Mean	p-value
Global Index Engagement E*		14,75	3,51	5,44	11,19	5,18	11,01	0,011*
Popularity	P1	97,22%	97,53%	99,12%	99,02%	98,44%	99,26%	0.199
	P2	28,08	55,09	159,12	29,66	21,77	29,43	0.105
	P3	9,51	2,61	4,09	9,73	4,07	7,27	0.015*
Commitment	C1	31,19%	35,47%	48,61%	31,07%	29,61%	37,60%	0.264
	C2	1,14	1,50	4,14	1,17	0,73	1,36	0.322
	C3	0,45	0,07	0,13	0,42	0,11	0,50	0.051
Virality	V1	66,78%	65,50%	81,65%	67,34%	70,99%	72,10%	0.132
	V2	12,79	18,04	49,92	5,73	8,39	11,38	0.328
	V3	4,79	0,82	1,22	1,04	1,00	3,25	0.038*

Significant at: p<0.05*

CONCLUSION

The benefits of social media as communication channels allow reaching a wider audience while increasing the participation of stakeholders in the organization (Distaso & McCorkindale, 2013). It is notorious the concern about how to improve this participation in order to obtain popularity and virality of the information published by the organizations, as well as to promote dialogue between the stakeholders and the organization (Bonsón & Ratkai, 2013).

In the context of the evolution of the traditional museums to the museums 2.0., they have integrated the potential offered by social media into their communication strategy (Martínez-Sanz, 2012; Claes & Detlell, 2014; López, et al., 2010). However, the communicative potential of social media in the field of museums has not yet been sufficiently exploited, since they are usually used more as an informative tool (López, et al., 2010) than as a bidirectional communication channel, capable of providing real opportunities for dialogue with the public in new and substantive conversations and learning experiences (Gómez-Vílchez, 2012).

In this scenario, this chapter aims to determine, through the direct observation of the fan pages of the main Spanish museums and cultural institutions, the level of participation and engagement of their stakeholders. With this goal in mind, an empirical methodology is used, performing a descriptive analysis of the information collected. Likewise, a classification of the museums is carried out in different categories, in order to identify possible differences between types of museums.

Answering the first research questions, results show that the average value of the index of engagement for the group of analysed institutions, in general, is low and presents high dispersion. Analysing the three dimensions that shape the engagement index, the dimension that yields the highest values is "Popularity", followed by "Virality" and "Commitment". This would indicate that stakeholders are willing to commit themselves through social networks to the affairs of museums, through actions that involve little effort, such as clicking to execute a "like" or a "share". However, when the interaction requires a somehow bigger effort, as it is to comment on the messages, the levels of engagement decrease.

These results are in line with those obtained by other research focused on other sectors, both public and private, as well as different geographical areas (Bonsón et al., 2014; Gálvez-Rodríguez, Haro-de-Rosario & Caba-Pérez, 2016; Haro-de-Rosario, Sáez-Martín, & Caba-Pérez, 2016; Sáez-Martín, Saraite-Sariene, López-Hernández & Caba -Pérez, 2016). In this way, it can be said that, in the field of museums and cultural entities, the level of engagement through Facebook is low, and that the use of "likes" predominates over "shares" and especially over "comments". By performing an analysis on the monthly behaviour of the index, it is observed that during the vacation periods the highest levels of engagement are reached.

Regarding the second research question, it can be concluded that there are significant differences between the groups, both in the level of total engagement as well as in terms of popularity and virality. Furthermore, the publication of posts during the week is notorious, although the greater number of them is released on Saturday and in the morning. Finally, the posts that include audio-visual content (photo and videos) stand out, as well as the publication of links that can be easily accessed by the different stakeholders.

With the results obtained in the context of Spanish museums and cultural institutions, the idea reflected in the previous literature, that stakeholders are mainly interested in showing their agreement or disagreement with the information published by local governments albeit in a fast and easy (Gálvez-Rodríguez et al., 2016), the unidirectional character of the dialogue predominates (Sáez-Martín et al., 2016), which means that these organizations do not take advantage of the potential of Facebook to improve the interaction organization-stakeholder (Haro-de-Rosario, Sáez-Martín & Gálvez-Rodríguez, 2017).

In the cultural field, this chapter aims to contribute to the lack of research focused on the geographical area of Spain. From an academic point of view, literature on the participation of stakeholders in organizations through social media is expanded. In addition, and in line with those observed at the international level, the results obtained can guide practitioners and organizations in the actions to be followed in order to manage social networks, so as to improve the participation of stakeholders in the organizations affairs.

In this sense, it would be convenient to expand the research in this area. In this way, different issues could be analysed in future works, such as, for instance, the evolution of stakeholder engagement in social networks over a longer time period to identify behavioural trends, and especially when these organizations are related to the tourist sector. More detailed studies could also be carried out focusing on how the content and format of the message issued by the cultural institutions can influence stakeholder engagement. Similarly, it would be interesting to analyse if stakeholders prefer to engage in cultural activities fostered by museums via other social networks, such as Twitter. Finally, it is worth mentioning the possibility of extrapolating these research proposals to the rest of European countries.

REFERENCES

Aghaei, S., Nematbakhsh, M. A., & Farsani, H. K. (2012). Evolution of the World Wide Web: From Web 1.0 to Web 4.0. *International Journal of Web & Semantic Technology*, *3*(1), 1–10. doi:10.5121/ijwest.2012.3101

Aluri, A., Slevitch, L., & Larzelere, R. (2015). The effectiveness of embedded social media on hotel websites and the importance of social interactions and return on engagement. *International Journal of Contemporary Hospitality Management, 27*(4), 670–689. doi:10.1108/IJCHM-09-2013-0415

Arends, M., Goldfarb, D., Merkl, D., & Weingartner, M. (2009). Interaction with Art Museums on the Web. *Proceedings of the IADIS Intl Conference WWW/Internet.*

Arends, M., Goldfarb, D., Merkl, D., & Weingartner, M. (2011). Museums on the Web: Interaction with Visitors. In Handbook of Research on Technologies and Cultural Heritage: Applications and Environments. Hershey, PA: IGI Global.

Badell, J. I. (2015). Museums and social media: Catalonia as a case study. *Museum Management and Curatorship, 30*(3), 244–263. doi:10.1080/09647775.2015.1042512

Baker, S. (2017). Identifying behaviors that generate positive interactions between science museums and people on Twitter. *Museum Management and Curatorship, 32*(2), 144–159. doi:10.1080/09647775.2016.1264882

Báscones, P., & Monfort, C. C. (2010). Unas breves consideraciones sobre los museos ante el reto digital. In *Crisis analógica, futuro digital: actas del IV Congreso Online del Observatorio para la Cibersociedad, celebrado del 12 al 29 de noviembre de 2009* (p. 237). Academic Press.

Bernstein, S. (2008). Where Do We Go from Here? Continuing with Web 2.0 at the Brooklyn Museum. In J. Trant & D. Bearman (Eds.), *Museums and the Web 2008: Proceedings* (pp. 37–47). Toronto: Archives & Museum Informatics.

Bocatius, B. (2011). *Education and Learning in Museums 2.0–German Museums and the Web 2.0. Kunstgeschichte.* Open Peer Reviewed Journal.

Bonsón, E., & Ratkai, M. (2013). A set of metrics to assess stakeholder engagement and social legitimacy on a corporate Facebook page. *Online Information Review, 37*(5), 787–803. doi:10.1108/OIR-03-2012-0054

Bonsón, E., Royo, S., & Ratkai, M. (2014). Facebook Practices in Western European Municipalities an Empirical Analysis of Activity and Citizens' Engagement. *Administration & Society.*

Brainard, L. A., & McNutt, J. G. (2010). Virtual government–citizen relations: Informational, transactional, or collaborative? *Administration & Society, 42*(7), 836–858. doi:10.1177/0095399710386308

Caballero-García, L. (2009). Análisis de la función social de los museos en la museología crítica. *VII Congreso de museos del vino de España.*

Capriotti, P., Carretón, C., & Castillo, A. (2016). Testing the level of interactivity of institutional websites: From museums 1.0 to museums 2.0. *International Journal of Information Management, 36*(1), 97–104. doi:10.1016/j.ijinfomgt.2015.10.003

Capriotti, P., & Kuklinski, H. P. (2012). Assessing Dialogic Communication through the Internet in Spanish Museums. *Public Relations Review, 38*(4), 619–626. doi:10.1016/j.pubrev.2012.05.005

Carlisle, J. E., & Patton, R. C. (2013). Is social media changing how we understand political engagement? An analysis of Facebook and the 2008 presidential election. *Political Research Quarterly*, *66*(4), 883–895. doi:10.1177/1065912913482758

Celaya, J., & Viñarás, M. (2006). *Las nuevas tecnologías web 2.0 en la promoción de museos y centros de arte [en línea]*. Madrid: Dosdoce.com/NV Asesores.

Ceron, A. & D'Adda, G. (2015). E-campaigning on Twitter: The effectiveness of distributive promises and negative campaign in the 2013 Italian election. *New Media & Society*.

Chan, N. L., & Guillet, B. D. (2011). Investigation of social media marketing: How does the hotel industry in Hong Kong perform in marketing on social media websites? *Journal of Travel & Tourism Marketing*, *28*(4), 345–368. doi:10.1080/10548408.2011.571571

Cheung, C. M., & Lee, M. K. (2012). What drives consumers to spread electronic word of mouth in online consumer-opinion platforms. *Decision Support Systems*, *53*(1), 218–225. doi:10.1016/j.dss.2012.01.015

Chung, T. L., Marcketti, S., & Fiore, A. M. (2014). Use of social networking services for marketing art museums. *Museum Management and Curatorship*, *29*(2), 188–205. doi:10.1080/09647775.2014.888822

Claes, F., & Deltell, L. (2014). Museos sociales. Perfiles museísticos en Twitter y Facebook 2012-2013. *El Profesional de la Información*, *23*(6), 594–602. doi:10.3145/epi.2014.nov.06

Claes, F., & Detlell, L. (2014). Museos sociales. Perfiles museísticos en Twitter y Facebook 2012-2013. *El Profesional de la Información*, *23*(6), 594–602. doi:10.3145/epi.2014.nov.06

D'Heer, E., & Verdegeer, P. (2014). Conversations about the elections on Twitter: Towards a structural understanding of Twitter's relation with the political and the media field. *European Journal of Communication*, *29*(6), 720–734. doi:10.1177/0267323114544866

DiStaso, M. W., & McCorkindale, T. (2013). A Benchmark Analysis of the Strategic Use of Social Media for Fortune's Most Admired U.S. Companies on Facebook, Twitter and YouTube. *The Public Relations Journal*, *7*(1), 1–33.

Drotner, K., & Schrøder, K. C. (2013). *The Connected Museum. Museum Communication and Social Media: The Connected Museum*. New York: Routledge.

Duffy, R. (2015). Nature-based tourism and neoliberalism: Concealing contradictions. *Tourism Geographies*, *17*(4), 529–543. doi:10.1080/14616688.2015.1053972

Effing, R., Van Hillegersberg, J., & Huibers, T. (2011). Social media and political participation: are Facebook, Twitter and YouTube democratizing our political systems? *Electronic Participation*, 25-35.

Elefant, C. (2011). The power of social media: Legal issues & best practices for utilities engaging social media. *Energy LJ*, *32*, 1.

Ellison, N., & Hardey, M. (2014). Social media and local government: Citizenship, consumption and democracy. *Local Government Studies*, *40*(1), 21–40. doi:10.1080/03003930.2013.799066

Evans, D. (2010). *Social Media Marketing: The Next Generation of Business Engagement*. Indianapolis, IN: John Wiley & Sons.

Fang, J., Zhao, Z., Wen, C., & Wang, R. (2017). Design and performance attributes driving mobile travel application engagement. *International Journal of Information Management*, *37*(4), 269–283. doi:10.1016/j.ijinfomgt.2017.03.003

Filieri, R., & McLeay, F. (2014). E-WOM and accommodation: An analysis of the factors that influence travelers' adoption of information from online reviews. *Journal of Travel Research*, *53*(1), 44–57. doi:10.1177/0047287513481274

Filippini Fantoni, S., Stein, R., & Bowman, G. (2012). Exploring the Relationship between Visitor Motivation and Engagement in Online Museum Audiences. Museums and the Web 2012 Conference, San Diego, CA.

Fletcher, A., & Lee, M. J. (2012). Current Social Media Uses and Evaluations in American Museums. *Museum Management and Curatorship*, *27*(5), 505–521. doi:10.1080/09647775.2012.738136

Forteza Oliver M. (2012). El papel de los museos en las redes sociales. *Revista de bibliotecolo-gía y ciencias de la información*, *48*, 31-40.

Gálvez-Rodríguez, M., Haro-de-Rosario, A., & Caba-Pérez, M. C. (2016). A Comparative View of Citizen Engagement in Social Media of Local Governments from North American Countries. In Handbook of Research on Citizen Engagement and Public Participation in the Era of New Media (pp.139-156). Academic Press.

Gálvez-Rodríguez, M., Saraite, L., Alonso-Cañadas, J., & del Carmen Caba-Pérez, M. (2017). Stakeholder Engagement via Social Media in the Hospitality Sector: The Evidence from BRIC Countries. In *Opportunities and Challenges for Tourism and Hospitality in the BRIC Nations* (pp. 15–30). IGI Global. doi:10.4018/978-1-5225-0708-6.ch002

Gámir, J. (2016). Blogs, Facebook y Twitter en las Elecciones Generales de 2011. Estudio cuantitativo del uso de la web 2.0 por parte de los cabezas de lista del PP y del PSOE. *Dígitos*, *2*, 101–120.

Garibaldi, R. (2015). The use of Web 2.0 tools by Italian contemporary art museums. *Museum Management and Curatorship*, *30*(3), 230–243. doi:10.1080/09647775.2015.1043329

Gil de Zúñiga, H., Jung, N., & Valenzuela, S. (2012). Social media use for news and individuals' social capital, civic engagement and political participation. *Journal of Computer-Mediated Communication*, *17*(3), 319–336. doi:10.1111/j.1083-6101.2012.01574.x

Gómez-Vílchez, M. S. (2010). *Estadística*. Museos&Redes 2010.

Gómez-Vílchez, S. (2012). Museos españoles y redes sociales. *Edita: Fundación Telefónica Patronato de Fundación Telefónica*, *90*, 79.

Griffiths, J. M., & King, D. W. (2008). *Interconnections: The IMLS National Study on the Use of Libraries, Museums and the Internet*. Institute of Museum and Library Services.

Gronemann, S. T., Kristiansen, E., & Drotner, K. (2015). Mediated co-construction of museums and audiences on Facebook. *Museum Management and Curatorship*, *30*(3), 174–190. doi:10.1080/09647775.2015.1042510

Grönroos, C., & Ravald, A. (2011). Service as Business Logic: Implications for Value Creation and Marketing. *Journal of Service Management*, 22(1), 5–22. doi:10.1108/09564231111106893

Guillamón, M. D., Ríos, A. M., Gesuele, B., & Metallo, C. (2016). Factors influencing social media use in local governments: The case of Italy and Spain. *Government Information Quarterly*, 33(3), 460–471. doi:10.1016/j.giq.2016.06.005

Haro-de-Rosario, A., Sáez-Martín, A., & Caba-Pérez, M. D. C. (2016a). Using social media to enhance citizen engagement with local government: Twitter or Facebook? *New Media & Society*, 1–21.

Haro-de-Rosario, A., Sáez-Martín, A., & Gálvez-Rodríguez, M. D. C. (2017). Facebook as a Dialogic Strategic Tool for European Local Governments. *Transylvanian Review of Administrative Sciences*, 13(50), 73–89. doi:10.24193/tras.2017.0005

Hennig-Thurau, T., Gwinner, K. P., Walsh, G., & Gremler, D. D. (2004). Electronic word-of-mouth via consumer-opinion platforms: What motivates consumers to articulate themselves on the Internet? *Journal of Interactive Marketing*, 18(1), 38–52. doi:10.1002/dir.10073

Hofmann, S., Beverungen, D., Räckers, M., & Becker, J. (2013). What makes local governments' online communications successful? Insights from a multimethod analysis of Facebook. *Government Information Quarterly*, 30(4), 387–396. doi:10.1016/j.giq.2013.05.013

Hsu, Y.-L. (2012). Facebook as international eMarketing strategy of Taiwan hotels. *International Journal of Hospitality Management*, 31(3), 972–980. doi:10.1016/j.ijhm.2011.11.005

Kaplan, A. M., & Haenlein, M. (2010). Users of the World, Unite! The Challenges and Opportunities of Social Media. *Business Horizons*, 53(1), 59–68. doi:10.1016/j.bushor.2009.09.003

Kaufman, J.E. (2009). Museums make deep cuts in face of global financial crisis. *The Art Newspaper*, 198.

Kelly, L. (2010). How Web 2.0 Is Changing the Nature of Museum Work. *Curator (New York, N.Y.)*, 53(4), 405–410. doi:10.1111/j.2151-6952.2010.00042.x

Kent, M. L., & Taylor, M. (1998). Building dialogic relationships through the World Wide Web. *Public Relations Review*, 24(3), 321–334. doi:10.1016/S0363-8111(99)80143-X

Kent, M. L., & Taylor, M. (2002). Toward a dialogic theory of public relations. *Public Relations Review*, 28(1), 21–37. doi:10.1016/S0363-8111(02)00108-X

Kidd, J. (2011). Enacting Engagement Online: Framing Social Media Use for the Museum. *Information Technology & People*, 24(1), 64–77. doi:10.1108/09593841111109422

Kim, S. J., Wang, R. J. H., Maslowska, E., & Malthouse, E. C. (2016). "Understanding a fury in your words": The effects of posting and viewing electronic negative word-of-mouth on purchase behaviors. *Computers in Human Behavior*, 54, 511–521. doi:10.1016/j.chb.2015.08.015

Koo, B. K. (2015). The Use and Impact of Social Media on the Work of Museum Professionals. *Journal of the Korea Entertainment Industry Association*, 9(1), 11. doi:10.21184/jkeia.2015.03.9.1.11

Langa, A. L. (2014). Does Twitter Help Museums Engage with Visitors? *iConference 2014 Proceedings*, 484 - 495. doi:10.9776/14130

Larsson, A., & Ihlen, Ø. (2015). Birds of a feather flock together? Party leaders on Twitter during the 2013 Norwegian elections. *European Journal of Communication, 30*(6), 666–681. doi:10.1177/0267323115595525

Lehman, K., & Roach, G. (2011). The Strategic Role of Electronic Marketing in the Australian Museum Sector. *Museum Management and Curatorship, 26*(3), 291–306. doi:10.1080/09647775.2011.585806

Liu, Z., & Park, S. (2015). What makes a useful online review? Implication for travel product websites. *Tourism Management, 47*, 140–151. doi:10.1016/j.tourman.2014.09.020

López, X., Margapoti, I., Maragliano, R., & Bove, G. (2010). The Presence of Web 2.0 Tools on Museum Websites: A Comparative Study between England, France, Spain, Italy, and the USA. *Museum Management and Curatorship, 25*(2), 235–249. doi:10.1080/09647771003737356

López-García, G. (2016). Nuevos'y 'viejos' liderazgos: La campaña de las elecciones generales españolas de 2015 en Twitter. *Communicatio Socialis, 29*(3), 149–167.

López-García, G. (2016). 'Nuevos'y'viejos' liderazgos: La campaña de las elecciones generales españolas de 2015 en Twitter. *Comunicación y Sociedad, 29*(3), 149. doi:10.15581/003.29.3.sp.149-167

Loran, M. (2005). L'ús dels webs per a afavorir l'accés i l'increment de públic als museus: experiències dels museus nacionals britànics. In *TIC i patrimoni". Digithum, 7.* UOC (Open University of Catalonia). Avalaible at http://www.raco.cat/index.php/Digit/article/view/18539/18381

Losada-Díaz, J. C., & Capriotti, P. (2015). La comunicación de los museos de arte en Facebook: Comparación entre las principales instituciones internacionales y españolas. *Palabra Clave (La Plata), 18*(3), 889–904.

Lotina, L. (2014). Reviewing Museum Participation in Online Channels in Latvia. *Museum Management and Curatorship, 29*(3), 280–292. doi:10.1080/09647775.2014.919167

Macchiavelli, A. (2008). Lo sviluppo del turismo dal dopoguerra ad oggi [Tourist Development from the Second Post-war]. In R. Garibaldi (Ed.), *Economia e gestione delle imprese turistiche* (pp. 33–65). Milan: Hoepli.

Mariani, M. M., Di Felice, M., & Mura, M. (2016). Facebook as a destination marketing tool: Evidence from Italian regional Destination Management Organizations. *Tourism Management, 54*, 321–343. doi:10.1016/j.tourman.2015.12.008

Martínez-Sanz, R. (2012). Estrategia comunicativa digital en el museo. *El Profesional de la Información, 21*(4), 391–395. doi:10.3145/epi.2012.jul.10

McFarland, L. A., & Ployhart, R. E. (2015). Social media: A contextual framework to guide research and practice. *The Journal of Applied Psychology, 100*(6), 1653–1677. doi:10.1037/a0039244 PMID:26052712

Mergel, I. (2013a). A framework for interpreting social media interactions in the public sector. *Government Information Quarterly, 30*(4), 327–334. doi:10.1016/j.giq.2013.05.015

Mergel, I. (2013b). Social media adoption and resulting tactics in the US federal government. *Government Information Quarterly, 30*(2), 123–130. doi:10.1016/j.giq.2012.12.004

Metzger, M. J., & Flanagin, A. J. (2013). Credibility and trust of information in online environments: The use of cognitive heuristics. *Journal of Pragmatics, 59*, 210–220. doi:10.1016/j.pragma.2013.07.012

O'Connor, P. (2008). User-generated content and travel: A case study on Tripadvisor.com. *Information and communication technologies in tourism 2008*, 47-58.

Quijano Pascual, M. (2012). La Revolución de los museos y las instituciones culturales. *Telos: cuadernos de comunicación e innovación, 90*, 55-60.

Peña Aznar, de la J. (2014). ¿Sirven para algo las redes sociales en el sector cultural? *Anuario A/CE de cultura digital*.

Phelan, K. V., Chen, H.-T., & Haney, M. (2013). "Like" and "Check-in": How hotels utilize Facebook as an effective marketing tool. *Journal of Hospitality and Tourism Technology, 4*(2), 134–154. doi:10.1108/JHTT-Jul-2012-0020

Richards, G. (2007). *Cultural Tourism: Global and Local Perspectives*. New York: The Haworth Hospitality Press.

Río Castro, J. N. (2011). Museos y redes sociales, más allá de la promoción. *Redmarkauima, 7*(3), 111–123.

Runnel, P., Pruulmann-Vengerfeldt, P., Viires, P., & Laak, M. (2013). *The Digital Turn: Users' Practices and Cultural Transformations*. New York: Peter Lang. doi:10.3726/978-3-653-02325-1

Rustad, E., & Sæbø, Ø. (2013, September). How, why and with whom do local politicians engage on facebook? In *International Conference on Electronic Participation* (pp. 69-79). Springer. 10.1007/978-3-642-40346-0_7

Sáez-Martín, A., Alonso-Cañadas, J., Galán-Valdivieso, F., & Caba-Pérez, C. (2018). Citizens' Engagement in Local Government in a New Political Scenario: Emergent vs. Traditional Parties. In *Sub-National Democracy and Politics Through Social Media* (pp. 107–128). Cham: Springer. doi:10.1007/978-3-319-73386-9_6

Sáez-Martín, A., Haro-de-Rosario, A., & Caba-Pérez, M. D. C. (2015). Using twitter for dialogic communication: Local government strategies in the European Union. *Local Government Studies, 41*(3), 421–444. doi:10.1080/03003930.2014.991866

Santacana Mestre, J., & Hernández Cardona, F. X. (2006). *Museología crítica*. Gijón: Trea.

Sigala, M. (2009). WEB 2.0, Social Marketing Strategies and Distribution Channels for Taylor, M., & Kent, M. L. (2014). Dialogic engagement: Clarifying foundational concepts. *Journal of Public Relations Research, 26*(5), 384–398.

Simon, N. (2010). *The Participatory Museum*. Santa Cruz, CA: Museum 2.0.

Skola, T. (2012). *La eternidad ya no vive aquí: un glosario de pecados museísticos*. Girona: Documenta Universitaria.

Sobaci, M. Z. (2016). Social media and local governments: An overview. In *Social Media and Local Governments* (pp. 3–21). Cham: Springer. doi:10.1007/978-3-319-17722-9_1

Sokolowicz, B. (2009). *Guerrilla Marketing: Museos 2.0*. In The 9th International Conference dedicated to Museum Professionals Communicating the Museum, Málaga, Spain.

Solnik, C. (2009). For museums, financial crisis is not a pretty picture. *Long Island Business News, 27*.

Spiliopoulou, A. Y., Mahony, S., Routsis, V., & Kamposiori, C. (2014). Cultural Institutions in the Digital Age: British Museum's Use of Facebook Insights. *Journal of Audience & Reception Studies, 11*(1), 286–303.

Srinivasan, R., Boast, R., Furner, J., & Becvar, K. (2009). Digital museums and diverse cultural knowledges: Moving past the traditional catalog. *The Information Society: An International Journal, 25*(4), 265–278. doi:10.1080/01972240903028714

Steinberg, A. (2015). Exploring Web 2.0 political engagement: Is new technology reducing the biases of political participation? *Electoral Studies, 39*, 102–116. doi:10.1016/j.electstud.2015.05.003

Suzić, B., Karlíček, M., & Střítecký, V. (2016). Social Media Engagement of Berlin and Prague Museums. *The Journal of Arts Management, Law, and Society, 46*(2), 73–87. doi:10.1080/10632921.2016.1154489

Tasich, T. (2014). *Estratègies de transformació dels museus en l'era digital* [Museum Transformation Strategies in the Digital Age]. CCCBLab Seminar, Barcelona, Spain.

Tasich, T., & Villaespesa, E. (2013). Meeting the Real User: Evaluating the Usability of Tate's Website. In N. Proctor & R. Cherry (Eds.), *Museums and the Web 2013*. Silver Spring, MD: Museums and the Web.

Thumim, N. (2010). Self-representation in Museums: Therapy or Democracy? *Critical Discourse Studies, 7*(4), 291–304. doi:10.1080/17405904.2010.511837

Valdés Sagüés, M. C. (1999). *La difusión cultural en el museo: servicios destinados al gran público*. Gijón, España: Trea.

Valenzuela, S., Correa, T., & Gil de Zúñiga, H. (2017). Ties, Likes, and Tweets: Using Strong and Weak Ties to Explain Differences in Protest Participation Across Facebook and Twitter Use. *Political Communication*, 1–18.

Valeriani, A., & Vaccari, C. (2016). Accidental exposure to politics on social media as online participation equalizer in Germany, Italy, and the United Kingdom. *New Media & Society, 18*(9), 1857-1874.

Vergeer, M. (2015). Twitter and political campaigning. *Sociology Compass, 9*(9), 745–760. doi:10.1111oc4.12294

Vergeer, M., & Hermans, L. (2013). Campaigning on Twitter: Microblogging and Online Social Networking as Campaign Tools in the 2010 General Elections in the Netherlands. *Journal of Computer-Mediated Communication, 18*(4), 399–419. doi:10.1111/jcc4.12023

Viñarás Abad, M., & Cabezuelo Lorenzo, F. (2012). *Claves para la participación y generación de contenido en las redes sociales: estudio de caso del Museo del Prado en Facebook*. Academic Press.

Waters, R. D., Burnett, E., Lamm, A., & Lucas, J. (2009). Engaging Stakeholders through Social Networking: How Nonprofit Organizations Are Using Facebook. *Public Relations Review*, *35*(2), 102–106. doi:10.1016/j.pubrev.2009.01.006

Wilson, R. J. (2011). Behind the Scenes of the Museum Website. *Museum Management and Curatorship*, *26*(4), 373–389. doi:10.1080/09647775.2011.603934

Zheng, L., & Zheng, T. (2014). Innovation through social media in the public sector: Information and interactions. *Government Information Quarterly*, *31*, 106–117. doi:10.1016/j.giq.2014.01.011

ADDITIONAL READING

Benito, D. C., & González, D. G. (2016). Museos y comunicación: Los nuevos medios como herramienta de diálogo y sociabilidad de la institución. El uso de Twitter por el museo del Prado, museo Thyssen-Bornemisza y museo Reina Sofía. *Fonseca. Journal of Communication*, *12*(12), 149–165.

Biedermann, B. (2017). 'Virtual museums' as digital collection complexes. A museological perspective using the example of Hans-Gross-Kriminalmuseum. *Museum Management and Curatorship*, *32*(3), 281–297. doi:10.1080/09647775.2017.1322916

Frieman, C. J., & Wilkin, N. (2016). "The Changing of the Guards"?: British Prehistoric Collections and Archaeology in the Museums of the Future. *Museum Worlds*, *4*(1), 33–50. doi:10.3167/armw.2016.040104

Holdgaard, N., & Klastrup, L. (2014). Between control and creativity: Challenging co-creation and social media use in a museum context. *Digital Creativity*, *25*(3), 190–202. doi:10.1080/14626268.2014.904364

Jareontananan, A. (2016). Museum Websites beyond the Digital Reproduction of Museums. *Transcommunication*, *3*(2), 293–306.

Padilla-Meléndez, A., & del Águila-Obra, A. R. (2013). Web and social media usage by museums: Online value creation. *International Journal of Information Management*, *33*(5), 892–898. doi:10.1016/j.ijinfomgt.2013.07.004

Parry, R. (2007). *Recoding the museum: Digital heritage and the technologies of change*. Routledge. doi:10.4324/9780203347485

Schweibenz, W. (2011). Museums and Web 2.0: Some thoughts about authority, communication, participation and trust. In Handbook of Research on Technologies and Cultural Heritage: Applications and Environments (pp. 1-15). IGI Global.

Solima, L. (2014). Digital resources and approaches adopted by user-centred museums: the growing impact of the Internet and social media. In Handbook of Research on Management of Cultural Products: E-Relationship Marketing and Accessibility Perspectives (pp. 181-199). IGI Global.

Wong, A. S. (2011). Ethical issues of social media in museums: A case study. *Museum Management and Curatorship*, *26*(2), 97–112. doi:10.1080/09647775.2011.566710

KEY TERMS AND DEFINITIONS

Cultural Entities: Organization whose existence depends on there being a culture.

Information and Communication Technologies (ICT): Networking components, applications, and systems that combined allow stakeholders and organizations to interact in the digital world.

Museum 2.0.: Evolution of the traditional museum supported by information and communication technologies.

Online Commitment: The interaction of messages generated within a social network like Facebook.

Online Engagement: Participation and commitment reached through social networks.

Online Popularity: The acceptance and support of a decision or action taken by an organization and that is communicated via social network.

Online Virality: The spread of information given through a social network, which occurs when the online community that receives that information decides to share the message with other users.

This research was previously published in the Handbook of Research on Examining Cultural Policies Through Digital Communication; pages 182-204, copyright year 2019 by Information Science Reference (an imprint of IGI Global).

Chapter 77

Fast–Fashion Meets Social Networking Users:
Implications for International Marketing Strategy

Tehreem Cheema
Clark University, USA

ABSTRACT

With the emergence of e-commerce, the fast fashion industry has experienced a revolution in terms of its management and how it is marketed. Rapid advancements in internet-related infrastructures and services have propelled explosive growth in what is considered to be one of the fastest growing industries in the global economy. The future of fast fashion is now being influenced by advanced technologies. The growing role of online social media and networks in marketing has important implications for how consumers, channels, and companies interface. Shoppers harness social media and user-generated content to make key purchase decisions. This chapter contributes to the existing literature on the influence of digital marketing on fast fashion, and it provides a number of pertinent marketing recommendations in regard to the practice of apparel retailers.

INTRODUCTION

Over the last 25 years, the fashion apparel industry has experienced significant change, which has given rise to the concept of 'throwaway' or 'fast-fashion'. The phrase "fast-fashion" refers to low-cost clothing collections that mimic current luxury fashion trends from runway catwalks to racks in record time (Brooks, 2015). The industry is characterized by high turnover of stock to ensure that shelves are replenished with new styles and fashions in response to real-time demand (Hansson, 2011). Fast fashion is the contemporary practice of designing and manufacturing clothing within a timely manner, at affordable prices, and targeted at mainstream consumers (Bhardwaj & Fairhurst, 2010; Agarwal & Aggrawal, 2012). Fast fashion retailing is a relatively new idea that has been driven by persistent consumer demand

DOI: 10.4018/978-1-7998-9020-1.ch077

for high fashion trends. Such trends have been translated into low-priced garments and accessories by mass-market retailers at low cost (Joy, Sherry, Venkatesh, Wang & Chan, 2012; Choi, 2014). The underlying aim of this chapter is to critically examine the effects of social networking users on fast-fashion.

The purpose of developing a new market for fast-fashion products is to serve the target audience of young adults who prefer cheap, but trendy clothes. The market segment is driven by cost-pressures, mainly due to repetitive purchases amongst lower-income target groups (Atwal, Bryson, & Von Gersdorff, 2010). The key ingredient of fast fashion is the ability to track consumer preferences quickly and help sate the demand for 'cheap luxury fashion' amongst young consumers in the industrialized world (Ertekin & Atik, 2015). Fast-fashion diffuses designs based on the traditional concept of *haute couture* with reasonably priced ready-to-wear pieces, which are important to fashion markets (Amatulli, Mileti, Speciale, & Guido, 2016). In doing so, it captures the essence of time and quickly adopts current trends in the market.

Global retailers have developed fast-fashion business models based on three main pillars: the price of the apparels and accessories, the process and speed of manufacturing, and the style-oriented nature and disposability of garments. Fast fashion companies, unlike conventional clothing retailers, take an *ad hoc* approach towards designing, manufacturing, and releasing new products rather than planning product lines every season (Barnes & Lea – Greenwood, 2010; Lago, Martínez-de-Albéniz, Moscoso, & Vall, 2016). Nonetheless, the fast fashion industry owes its worldwide success to its "out-of-the-box" thinking rationale, which deviates from traditional approaches.

From a product-driven perspective, the fast fashion model originated in Europe in the 1980s. What started off as a basis for a new manufacturing model also referred to as "quick response" later transitioned to a market-based model of "fast fashion" during the 1990s (Lowson, King, & Hunter, 1999; Christopher, Lowson, & Peck, 2004; Barnes & Lea - Greenwood, 2010). Since the turn of the 21st century, the fast fashion industry has occupied a very profitable position in the market. Leaders in the fast fashion industry expanded around Europe and infiltrated the U.S. in the 2000s. The shift from "planned production" to a quick response production system has enabled global fast fashion companies to immediately adapt to the latest trends and prepare inventory for the season in advance to meet consumer demand (Doyle, Moore, & Morgan, 2006; Barnes & Lea – Greenwood, 2010; Joey, 2011). With globalized operations and a focus on dominating emerging markets, the fast fashion industry has experienced a shift from local business to global business.

Moreover, fashion retailers have repositioned themselves in the market as trendsetters instead of trend followers by taking on leadership and innovation practices (Hemphill & Suk, 2009). With the advent of social media, the fast-fashion industry has been vigorously undertaking innovative marketing strategies which continue to influence consumer attitudes towards brands as well as creating brand equity (Kim & Ko, 2012; Godey, Manthiou, Pederzoli, Rokka, Aiello, Donvito, & Singh, 2015; Azemi and Ozuem, 2016). Advertising and promotional campaigns on social media platforms such as Instagram, Facebook, and YouTube, are increasingly influencing brand communications and brand building (Chae, Ko, & Han, 2014). These online marketing communication campaigns are identified by fast-fashion companies as business take-off tools that not only enhance brand-to-consumer relationships, but also amplify consumer-to-consumer communities (Kaplan & Haenlein, 2010). This creates an electronic word-of-mouth effect and thus facilitates viral marketing opportunities (Wolny & Mueller, 2013).

Social networking sites combined with user-experienced content facilitate an online interactive environment to exchange ideas and information among consumers (Kaplan & Haenlein, 2010; Chae et al., 2014; Ozuem, Patel, Howell & Lancaster, 2017). Through social media engagement, fast-fashion brands increase their profit-making capacity, and positively influence customer equity drivers and purchase intentions (Amoye, 2011; Kim & Ko, 2012). Social media marketing activities thus, enable fast-fashion retailers to gain a powerful insight into consumer perceptions (Kucukusta, Law, Besbes, & Legoherel, 2015; Ryan, 2016). This chapter draws attention to the fast-fashion sector as one of the most dominant and highly competitive industries worldwide. It examines H&M and ZARA as apparel market leaders and at the forefront of fast-fashion. It explores the role of strategic competences in obtaining a competitive advantage over rivals. In addition, the chapter illuminates some of the implications of social networking sites for fast fashion.

BACKGROUND

The concept of fast-fashion also known as 'quick-fashion' was first observed in Europe in fashion brands, ZARA and H&M, before emerging in the US and Asia (Hansson, 2011). In recent years, fashion has been recognized as a large market in Europe, especially in Sweden. Swedish fashion is known for its functionality, prestigious quality and fair prices (VisitSweden, 2011). Today H&M, one of Sweden's more affordable brands, has earned a global reputation for its bargain-priced and fashion-forward ethos. Based on its efforts to penetrate the global market, along with its noteworthy market strategies, H&M continues to dominate the fashion empire.

H&M is the pioneer of the 'fast-fashion industry': a concept used to describe new fashion trends easily found in stores within a short time period (Youell, 2013). The fast-fashion industry is an evolving market driven by consumer desires for innovation and affordability (Joy et al., 2012; Choi, 2014). The dynamic forces within the fashion apparel industry have pushed retailers to implement key strategies to sustain a profitable position in an increasingly global market (Bhardwaj & Fairhurst, 2010). There are several key elements to H&M's fast fashion process, and specifically, these are short production and distribution times, highly fashionable design, and affordable prices (Zhenxiang & Lijie, 2011; Regnér & Yildiz, 2014).

ZARA, an exemplar of fast fashion, and the world's biggest fashion brand belongs to publicly held Spanish parent company, Inditex (Regnér & Yildiz, 2014). As one of the largest distribution groups in the world, Inditex, operates in eighty-eight markets and owns some 6,683 stores globally (Zhenxiang & Lijie, 2011). The global apparel chain designs, manufactures, and sells apparel, footwear and accessories for men, women, and children. It primarily targets the youth market by offering everything from sophisticated through to casual wear (Regnér & Yildiz, 2014). Over the years, ZARA has successfully maintained a dynamic business that not only makes reasonably priced fashion available to consumers, but also drives accustomed consumers to frequently visit its stores (Lambert, 2014; Rosenblum, 2015).

GAP Inc. is a giant, fast-fashion American chain that offers an extensive range of casual apparel at moderate prices to the masses. Its garments, accessories, and personal care products are mainly targeted towards men, women, and children (Zhenxiang & Lijie, 2011). The company's brands include Banana Republic, Old Navy and Athleta (Regnér & Yildiz, 2014). Each brand caters to the needs of different market segments ranging from value-priced family attire to active women's sport apparel and footwear. With over 3,200 stores worldwide, the global chain operates through the following segments: direct sales, franchise stores, and online websites (Regnér & Yildiz, 2014; Vecchi, 2016). GAP Inc. is recognized for both manufacturing its own products and selling them in its own stores. To avoid unpredicted demand, the company adopts a merchandising strategy that enables it to manage high stock levels at all stages of the supply chain. Based on its internal design team and longer lead-times, the company has become resilient to external pressures and quicker at responding to current fashion trends (Zhenxiang & Lijie, 2011; Vecchi, 2016).

American apparel company, Forever 21 operates under the fast-fashion model. The business model is based on high profit margins, low prices, low quality, and high quantity. Forever 21 addresses consumer needs by offering current fashionable styles at a reasonable price and more accessible location (Zarley & Yan, 2013). With over 750 stores, Forever 21 is strategically located in brick-and-mortar spaces around the globe (Lambert, 2014; Huang, Lee, Kim, & Evans, 2015). Most of its products are manufactured in local markets specifically, Los Angeles. Although manufacturing costs are relatively higher compared to the costs borne by its competitors, Forever 21 reaps the benefits of greater flexibility (Comunale 2008; Zarley & Yan, 2013). This means that the fast-fashion company produces goods in moderate quantities that are completely sold to the market, and therefore prevent the occurrence of high costs associated with overstock merchandise. Forever 21 also takes advantage of sophisticated e-commerce and social networks, which allow it to compete against luxury brands (Lambert, 2014; Huang et al., 2015). Such a fast-fashion business model, thus seems to be a natural fit for Forever 21.

A relatively new, but vibrant player in the fast-fashion industry is the Japanese company UNIQLO. In 2002, UNIQLO entered and positioned itself in the Chinese market to deliver high quality products at a low price. UNIQLO switched its marketing strategies in 2006 (Zhenxiang & Lijie, 2011). Today, the retail chain operator is aggressively expanding worldwide. UNIQLO now specializes in in-house designed casual apparel for urban, middle-class men and women between the ages of 20 and 30 (Regnér & Yildiz, 2014). With more than 1,574 stores worldwide, UNIQLO undertakes a business model that comprises all stages of an organization – from design and manufacture to retail (Jang, Ko, Chun & Lee, 2012). It quickly responds to changing consumer trends by adjusting its production while minimizing operational costs (Caro & Martínez-de-Albéniz, 2015). UNIQLO, thus successfully differentiates itself from competitors by extending unique, high-quality products to consumers (Regnér & Yildiz, 2014; Caro & Martínez-de-Albéniz, 2015).

Contextualization and Theoretical Framework

The 'fast' part of the fast-fashion industry reflects the speed with which high-street market leaders 'translate' trends off the catwalks into garments on the shop floor (Brooks, 2015). Fast-fashion brands capitalize on their own interpretations of catwalk designs by creating replicas of the hottest runway trends and celebrity styles (Gabrielli, Baghi, & Codeluppi, 2013; Miller, 2013). Bauman (2005) identifies fast fashion as a postmodern phenomenon that exploits the market segment of young avid consumers by offering a constant stream of alluring products and of-the-moment designs. Market leaders in the fast-fashion industry, H&M and ZARA, have pioneered an approach to address the issue of rapidly changing market trends. While high fashion encompasses the traditional seasonal calendar of collections, fast-fashion, in contrast, navigates market volatility (Press, 2016).

The standard turnaround time from catwalk to consumer has been reduced from six months down to a matter of weeks by profitable companies including H&M and ZARA (Jacobs, 2006; Tokatli, 2008; Arrigo, 2010). This allows mainstream consumers to purchase current clothing styles at reasonable prices. The philosophy of designing and manufacturing apparel products in a time and cost-efficient manner is applied to other global retailers such as GAP, UNIQLO and Forever 21 (Jacobs, 2006; Arrigo, 2010).

Ritzer (2011: 1) notes that the term "McDonaldization" has become fashionable in describing the changes that capitalist economies are experiencing as they progress towards greater rationalization. The fast fashion framework is thus global and has given rise to the term "McFashion" which aptly describes the industry's ability to provide speedy gratification. The "Mcfashion" phenomenon is an analogy that refers to clothing lines that manufacture, package, and distribute the most updated fashion fads in a way that is comparable to the speed and convenience of fast food (Ritzer, 2011; Jefferies, Clark & Conroy, 2015).

In contrast, however, Fletcher (2008) uses the term "slow fashion" to refer to a philosophy of attentiveness. "Slow" in this context does not refer to time in the same way as the "fast" in fast fashion does. Instead slowness is associated with the approach that encourages the recognition of stakeholder needs and the impact of creating fashion on consumers, workers, and eco-systems (Fletcher, 2008; Zarley & Yan, 2013). Slow fashion is, thus a unified movement that comprises of all things "eco", "ethical", and "green" (Fletcher 2008; Fletcher 2010).

Since time is so important in the fashion industry and stock quickly goes 'out of fashion', stylists traditionally plan their collections well in advance, before their market launch (Hansson, 2011). In doing so, they run a high risk of failure due to the instability of demand and short clothing product lifestyles. However, fast fashion businesses do not spend as much time defining their clothing ranges (Barnes & Lea- Greenwood, 2010). Instead they wait for large fashion houses to release their collections and then design items that reflect current prevailing fashion trends (Lago et al., 2016). In a timescale of between four to six weeks, fast-fashion companies can take a new range of trendy items to the marketplace (Jacobs, 2006; Arrigo, 2010).

Today, global retailers such as H&M, UNIQLO, GAP, ZARA and Forever 21 pursue strategies that intensify the launch of spot collections in periods well in advance of seasonal requirements, thus motivating consumers to purchase products independent of seasonal needs (Ghemawat, Nueno, & Dailey, 2003; Sheridan, Moore, & Nobbs, 2006; Barnes & Lea- Greenwood, 2010). These companies are time-based competitive. This means that they take advantage by cutting down on time intervals from purchasing times, through manufacturing to marketing (Lago et al., 2016). More importantly, the short time lag between product design and market launch is what enables stores to present highly fashionable product offerings (Sheridan et al., 2006; Barnes & Lea – Greenwood, 2010; Lago et al., 2014).

Impact of Digital Marketing on Fast-Fashion

Over the last few years, there has been a steep rise in the use of digital marketing due to the accelerating levels of disposable income and the growing consumer propensity to utilize online services (Ryan, 2016; Bendoni, 2017). Market-oriented organizations that adopt digital marketing strategies drive their businesses to the crest. Fashion operators that fail to quickly embrace shifts in trends, on the other hand, risk losing significant ground, whereas those who respond to such shifts tend to thrive in the market (Zhenxiang & Lijie, 2011; Kim & Ko, 2012; Vecchi, 2016). Not only do successful fast fashion companies exist in brick-and-mortar spaces, but they have also established a strong internet presence. Through the alchemy of 'click and mortar' retailers – (traditional retailers offering a virtual marketplace) – fashion retailers renew and revitalize their brand identities (Hines & Bruce, 2007; Wu, 2014; Bahtar & Muda, 2016).

In addition to having an internet presence, it is imperative for fashion retailers to actively engage with shoppers and potential customers as brand apparel itself does not suffice (Ramaswamy & Ozcan, 2016). To thrive in today's rapidly changing digital environment, a fashion retailer must undertake more activity than a physical store and must work to integrate its services into the interactive facets of the virtual world

(Pride & Ferrell, 2014). This can be done through key aspects of digital marketing such as Social Media Marketing (SMM), mobile marketing, and User-Generated Content marketing (UGC) (Adesoga, 2016).

The transition of the fast fashion industry from traditional media into the digital world has been the core focus of marketing scholars and practitioners (Wertime & Fenwick, 2011; Ozuem et al., 2016). While some marketers perceive digital marketing as a branch stemming from traditional marketing, others argue that it is not a niche. Rather, it is acknowledged as part of the long-term future of marketing (Wertime & Fenwick, 2011; Ryan, 2016). Digital marketing is, thus the process whereby fashion companies engage with digital generation customers on their terms (Pride & Ferrell, 2014; Ryan, 2016). Digital marketing has not only increased consumer awareness and outreach, but it has also improved the ability of business to analyze buying behavior. Thus, fast-fashion retailers are able to identify the latest consumer trends and preferences (Ramaswamy & Ozcan, 2016; Ryan, 2016). The burgeoning ability of digital media to engage with customers has further helped apparel companies to build brand value and brand loyalty (Ozuem et al., 2015b; Ramaswamy & Ozcan, 2016).

Fast fashion retailers have benefited from the rise of digital technology and changing consumer purchasing behaviors. Financial market volatility has prompted businesses and consumers to engage in a global marketplace in which the time saving, distance-shrinking nature of the internet has improved business productivity and consumer connectivity (IBISWorld, 2017). Companies that use digital marketing as a gateway to global marketing reap two main benefits: cost-efficient savings and accessibility (Kim & Ko, 2012; Vecchi, 2016). In comparison to traditional distribution channels and communication tools such as media advertisement and magazines, the internet is a cheap source of marketing that offers an elusive competitive edge to companies (IBISWorld, 2017). Therefore, to compete in today's global marketplace, it is crucial for organizations to have digital savvy human resources and mediums (Pride & Ferrell, 2014; Ramaswamy & Ozcan, 2016). Companies such as H&M, ZARA, Forever 21, UNIQLO and GAP have proved themselves at the coalface of digital marketing.

Successful global market leaders plan e-commerce endeavors to gain a solid understanding of prospective clients (Pride & Ferrell, 2014; Ryan, 2016). To avoid the risk of falling out of fashion, retailers including H&M, GAP and ZARA adapt to fast-paced technological advances and changing consumer preferences. With ever-growing online market and digitalization, H&M continues to excel in its development phase. H&M constantly strengthens its market position through global innovation and change. This conscious effort is explained by Ozuem et al. (2015b) who argue that long-term success is dependent on loyal customers who are a reliable source of revenue. As part of a daily routine, new fashion items are introduced in global stores. For instance, key elements include changing display windows about every 10 to 14 days (H&M, 2016). By the end of three years, an entirely new interior design collection is launched and implemented in stores in key markets worldwide (H&M, 2013). H&M's constant product and service changes combined with its high-street locations ensure the company has a steady catchment of retained customers who are crucial to the success of its business loyalty model (Kim & Ko, 2012; Ozuem et al., 2015b).

In addition to the presence of 4,300 stores worldwide, H&M also offers online retail operations in key markets (H&M, 2016). In 1998, H&M experienced a dramatic change when it engaged in e-commerce practices and started selling products over the internet. However, internet shopping was, at this time, only available to Europeans (H&M, 2013). Only recently have H&M expanded their online market to the United States (H&M, 2013). Although H&M was slow to expand their online markets and portals, they are working towards improving their e-commerce and mobile application sales.

Upon visiting H&M's official website, it is evident that the fashion-giant is committed to its business concept, "Fashion and quality at the best price" (Regnér & Yildiz, 2014). H&M's webpage along with its existing corporate image positively influences customer perceptions through its effective web-based corporate sustainability communications. The website is clearly structured with visualized, objective and sustainability-specific content. For customer-centric company H&M, web marketing is geared towards educating customers to better meet their needs and develop long-lasting relationships. It has established a concrete place in online markets to boost sales by also offering special discounts and creating a market niche for hard-to-find products that are no longer produced.

Panteva (2012) notes that fashion companies must partake in the mobile environment to capture consumer attention, as traditional websites are no longer sufficient. Retailers that fail to establish a mobile presence face the threat of quickly being outperformed. With the upward trend in smartphone usage, consumers are taking advantage of on the go fashion purchases (Muslim, Rezaei, & Abolghasemi, 2014). One of the first fashion retailers to jump on the bot bandwagon was H&M. In doing so, it has employed marketing and technology innovation to drive sales. The company recently started reaching out to customers through chatbots on the mobile application Kik. It enquires about a few basic questions to determine the mobile owners style of clothes. Based on gender, outfit preferences from a few selected photos, and a short description, the mobile application displays a range of clothes along with their prices (H&M, 2016; Spencer, 2016).

Similarly, the ZARA App developed by the Inditex Group, enables fashion-lovers to scroll through new season must-haves, purchase inventories instantly, track orders and deliver customer support via the service team. In terms of mobile marketing, the ZARA mobile application acts as a pull force whereby it offers consumers shopping convenience (Spencer, 2012). The mobile application has a clear, simple layout, and features a barcode scanner for in-store use, which allows customers to obtain detailed information about the color, size, and availability of items (Spencer, 2012). Additionally, the ZARA App is a form of interactive marketing since it encourages direct consumer communication with the support team (Spencer, 2012). This not only facilitates customer opinion sharing, but it also responds to any queries they have in a time-efficient, and cost-effective manner (Arrigo, 2010; North, 2013).

Over the last decade, social media has become an effective marketing tool and has fundamentally changed the consumer decision-making process (Sheehan, 2010, Buzzetto-More, 2013; Pride & Ferrell, 2014). The emergence of social media as a compilation of online platforms and communication channels has not only created a new aspect of marketing, but has also created wider marketing prospects for organizations to build brand visibility and brand equity (Kim & Ko, 2012; Kucukusta et al., 2015). As a transparent and interactive form of public relations, social network platforms continue to modify digital communication in the fashion industry (Dorsey, 2012; Moran, 2012). The influx of social surfing in today's tech savvy environment has provided many opportunities for fashion marketers to create brand awareness amongst consumers (Godey et al., 2015; Ramaswamy & Ozcan, 2016). While tech savvy fashion businesses benefit from social media engagement, those who fail to capitalize on social media optimization services give leeway to their competitors (Kim & Ko, 2012; Vecchi, 2016).

The indispensable trend of social advertising in digital marketing is increasingly becoming popular in fast fashion (Wertime & Fenwick, 2011; Ryan, 2016; Bendoni, 2017). The fast fashion industry embraces social media to anticipate fashion trends and consumer behaviors (Pride & Ferrell, 2014; Ryan, 2016). Apparel businesses such as Forever 21, H&M, and ZARA have embraced social media to better understand their brand's target audience. Social media channels impact on marketing strategies employed by the fashion industry and, other facets of the company such as — legal, finance, R&D, operations, and customer service. Fashion industry professionals integrate social media networking to increase customer loyalty, raise brand awareness, create online communities and drive sales (Apparel Magazine, 2010; Pride & Ferrell, 2014). Nonetheless, the emerging phenomenon of social media has become a strategic business element for apparel companies.

Moreover, the fast-fashion online retailer, Forever 21 has been the focus of case studies that examine how online visual merchandising impacts consumer behavior (Wu, 2014). Forever 21 was cognizant of the e-commerce trend that was rapidly increasing at the turn of the 21st century. As one of the early adopters of social media and e-commerce, Forever 21 launched its online shopping platform before H&M and ZARA (Wu, 2014). Forever 21's official webpage appears to be very interactive, and this positively influences consumer buying behavior. The provision of customized information and the high level of interaction with Forever 21 officials makes consumers feel empowered and in control. In addition to the success of brick-and-mortar stores, Forever 21 has online stores that target the youth market (Comunale, 2008; Hendriksz, 2013; Wu, 2014). The market segment of college students who have greater internet access are more vulnerable to indulge in online shopping, particularly girls. Not only do young male and female adults consistently surf through social media websites, but they tend to also engage in electronic word-of-mouth communication (Wolny & Mueller, 2013; Bahtar & Muda; 2016).

As opposed to traditional marketing, social media is a powerful marketing tool that involves two-way communication (Eley & Tilley, 2009; Sheehan, 2010). Within the realm of the fashion blogosphere, fashion bloggers produce highly diverse blog content that incorporates different social group tastes and trends (Crane, 2000; Buzzetto-More, 2013; Strähle, & Grünewald, 2017). According to Bourne (2010) social media provides bloggers and designers with a fashion platform that has a global reach. Through blog monitoring, apparel companies analyze consumer sentiments by extracting valuable information from social media conversations and dialogues (Kucukusta et al., 2015). This also enables fashion retailers to gather social media market intelligence. Based on such intelligence, which they debut new products, or offer solutions to test how the consumer market responds. Blogs are identified as a tool to drive organic traffic to fashion websites (Gehi, 2006; Bourne, 2010; Pride & Ferrell, 2014). Thus, it has become vital for fashion retail brands to have a strong presence on social media sites.

With over 30 million Facebook fans, H&M attracts and engages with consumers through posting new updates about once or twice every day. While most of the posts focus on promoting new products, the Facebook page also provides links to other services such as a store locator and style guide (Wigmo & Wikström, 2010). H&M is also involved in promotional ideas such as photo competitions. H&M has four official twitter accounts, which are mainly used to promote special events and provide special updates (Wigmo & Wikström, 2010). More recently, H&M offered fans the chance to win tickets to Coachella after submitting photos using the hashtag #HMCoachella. Another noteworthy Twitter campaign involved a Q&A session with H&M's brand ambassador and famous footballer, David Beckham.

Ozuem et al. (2015a), note that collaboration is significant in achieving business prosperity. H&M has initiated partnerships with luxury designer fashion brands such as Karl Lagerfeld and Versace (H&M, 2013). Such collaborations between 'fast fashion' and designer fashion brands helps increase H&M's brand equity and brand image (Amoye, 2011; Ozuem et al., 2015a). It further generates retail innovation and boosts sales turnover for both the partners (Amoye, 2011). This creates marketing synergies through 'fast fashion co-branding' which produces a favorable situation for both brand names as it appeals to brand loyalists (Thackery, Neger, & Keller, 2012; Montecchi & Nobbs, 2017).

To increase its exposure to the global market, H&M has adapted a multi-channel promotion strategy including advertising, internet promotion, and sales promotion. H&M's partnership with designers and celebrities as a form of celebrity endorsement supports the company's brand image and product offering (Friedman, 2014; Ozuem et al., 2015a). Extensive collaboration with world-famous pop stars and designers has contributed towards increasing its brand equity value (Kumar & Shah, 2004; Kim & Ko, 2012; Kucukusta et al., 2015). For instance, in 2011, H&M worked with the renowned high fashion company Jimmy Choo, to create a line that ensured consumers they were purchasing high fashion items at affordable prices (H&M, 2013). Later that year, H&M worked with famous football star, David Beckham, to launch his new bodywear and promote his mens' underwear line (H&M, 2013). This past summer, they also collaborated with Beyoncé to come up with a bathing suit line (H&M, 2016). Working with famous celebrities and fashion icons is thus, a major component of H&M's marketing strategy that allows it to be unique, since fashion brands in the global popular culture have become ubiquitous (Cayla & Arnould, 2008; Ozuem et al., 2015a).

Another fast-fashion brand that indulges in collaborative marketing practices, to achieve what Kim and Ko (2012) describe as brand and consumer equity, is UNIQLO. It is popularly known for employing innovative designer collaborations to enhance its brand recognition. In 2009, UNIQLO introduced a variety of new products which featured Disney characters and in 2012 it partnered with an electronics retailer, Bic Camera, to open a store outlet which upon collaboration was named "BICQLO" (Reboux, 2014). To further attract consumer attention, UNIQLO has launched marketing campaigns by hiring celebrities such as Orlando Bloom, Charlize Theron and Japanese football players (Reboux, 2014).

Social media channels especially Pinterest and Instagram have been a boon for the fast fashion industry as fashion retailers heavily rely on the visual aspects of their products (Sheehan, 2010, Buzzetto-More, 2013; Pride & Ferrell, 2014). Global fashion brands such as ZARA, H&M, UNIQLO, and GAP have been capitalizing on the global appetite for apparel and are therefore implementing effective digital marketing tools including social networking, proprietary blogging, advertising and event planning (IBIS-World, 2017). Corporate blogs and microblogs introduced on behalf of fashion retailers are now firmly entering the social media network. These channels are designed to encourage collaborative dialogue and participation between fashion companies and consumers (Kaplan & Haenlein 2010; Logan 2010).

Fast-fashion retailer, Forever 21 has employed internet and social media tactics to market its brand on a global scale. Forever 21's website reveals its content marketing strategy that seems to have effectively placed their products in the minds of consumers. The webpage has an entirely separate segment, the Social Media Hub, dedicated to Forever 21's social media activities (Forever 21, 2017). It provides the latest updates on Forever 21 by creating a visual collection of their trending products. The brands primary mode of communication is Facebook (Lowry, 2016). Forever 21 updates their Facebook page daily to encourage customer engagement and create brand awareness. The webpage features its in-style trends as well as an interactive space for consumer feedback (Yu-Fan, 2011). Other social networking sites through which Forever 21 reaches out to its target audience include Twitter, Instagram and YouTube (Lowry, 2016). Nonetheless, Forever 21 leverages the power of social media platforms to showcase their brand initiatives and boost website traffic (Yu-Fan, 2011; Kucukusta et al., 2015).

More recently, marketers have viewed social media as a vigorous marketing tool that has been challenging the power of fast fashion companies. This means that consumers can now reshape the way that other people and shoppers view items in the fashion industry. User-generated content – an online medium of electronic word-of-mouth – is primarily used as a new product launch tool that offers brand building potential (Ozuem and Lancaster, 2014; Bahtar & Muda, 2016; Ramaswamy & Ozcan, 2016). Not only do user-generated content sites create new viewing patterns by empowering consumers, but they also develop more creative business opportunities (Cha, Kwak, Rodriguez, Ahn, & Moon, 2007; Bahtar &

Muda, 2016). Due to the deluge of user-created content on the internet, social influences greatly determine what consumers adopt and when they adopt it (Bakshy, Karrer, & Adamic, 2009).

Dennhardt (2014) describes user-generated content as a rich storytelling opportunity for marketers to share their brand story and experience. A study conducted by MacKinnon (2012) reveals that customers heavily rely on, and trust content generated by peer internet users. These usually range from videos and photos to product reviews and blogs (Fader & Winer, 2012). User-created content has significantly changed marketing strategies and tools for consumer communication, and has magnified the effect of consumer-to-consumer discussions in the virtual marketplace (Mangould & Faulds, 2009; Ozuem, Howell & Lancaster, 2008; Kaplan & Haenlein, 2010; Dennhardt, 2014).

According to Bahtar and Muda (2016) social network users are heavily influenced by the evolution of consumer feedback, also known as consumer-generated content. Fast-fashion companies have devoted resources to designing user-generated content and interactive forums (Kucukusta et al., 2015). In doing so, these companies take advantage of consumer contribution and feedback. Fast-fashion retailers depend on consumer-trusted peer networks to further amplify their consumer base (Dorsey, 2012; Kucukusta et al., 2015). Thus, this helps ensure that consumers acquire ample information about available products as well as create value for other stakeholders (Montecchi & Nobbs, 2017).

The fast-fashion industry recognizes user-generated content as an official marketing strategy (Kucukusta et al., 2015). In addition to enhancing customer relationships and purchase intentions, consumer-experienced content contribute significantly toward fashion brand's profits (Kim & Ko, 2012). Social media networks help retain old customers while attracting new cross-shoppers (Kucukusta et al., 2015; Montecchi & Nobbs, 2017; Stokinger and Ozuem, 2015). Nonetheless, social networking services place active consumers at the center of marketing strategies, which allow fast-fashion companies to enhance customer relationship management (CRM) and improve brand management (Thackery et al., 2012).

Global fast-fashion companies like H&M, ZARA, and UNIQLO have prompted user-generated content as a means to establish an emotional connection with consumers, which in turn, helps create a strong, resonant brand (Kim & Ko, 2012; Montecchi & Nobbs, 2017). The use of consumer-produced content enables ZARA fans to comment on the informative product in question (Gonzalez, 2017). Not only does this acknowledge and value consumer input, but also provides ZARA with valuable content that can be used to better target-market their audiences. In addition to sales maximization, user-generated content also creates brand advocacy and brand equity for ZARA (North, 2013).

Fashion retailer, H&M, has developed a social media campaign, HM Loves, in which user generated content plays a key role and utilizes the imparting influence of social media on H&M followers (Thackery, Neiger, & Keller, 2012). Tapping into the 'selfie' craze, H&M has also created consumer-generated content by asking their fans to post pictures of themselves to Instagram using hashtags corresponding to their state locations (North, 2013). Moreover, H&M has assigned influential bloggers and promoters as 'style ambassadors' in each state. Through prominent individuals, H&M has thus entered new markets and created brand recognition by actively engaging in a national user-generated content campaign (H&M Loves, 2017).

Japanese fast-fashion titan UNIQLO has also incorporated digital marketing strategies to effectively communicate with its audience and appeal to its consumers worldwide (Reboux, 2014). UNIQLO launched 'UNIQLOOKS', the brands own online social community (Vasquez, 2011; Zhao & Balagué, 2015). The social-centric application was designed to allow fans to showcase unique outfits that featured the brands products. Not only does this create a social platform where consumers can critique and comment on UNIQLO's clothing and styles, but also helps populate the brands global community (Zhao &

Balagué, 2015). Vasquez (2011) notes that UNIQLOOKS is not only focused on social media promotions and user-generated content, but in fact, it fosters brand engagement by allowing a global audience to determine which 'look of the week' is featured on their official Facebook page. Brand advocates who are given the opportunity to be both UNIQLO's models and stylists, thus contribute towards spreading brand 'Likes' and communicating positive brand images in a peer-to-peer manner across social networks (Zhao & Balagué, 2015).

In recent years, however, fast-fashion companies have been struggling in maintaining a balance in terms of control and in handling new generation, empowered consumers (Montecchi & Nobbs, 2017). Sheehan (2010) notes that the emergence of digital technologies in the fast-fashion market have shifted the balance of power from marketers to consumers. This means that consumers are equally involved in the multiple stages of design process. Not only do they participate in online consumer communities and social networks, but they also contribute to new product development by influencing marketing strategies and plans (Montecchi & Nobbs, 2017). Sheehan (2010) describes the shift in market power from producers to consumers as 'prosumerism'. This ideology is the basis of fast-fashion business models, which assume that with the advent of the internet and social networking sites, customers propagate product information to a multitude of potential consumers (Buzzetto-More, 2013; Strähle, & Grünewald, 2017).

Furthermore, the credibility and level of expertise of the unknown source have been brought into question (Bahtar & Muda, 2016). While user-produced content on social media facilitate consumers to mitigate their perceived risks of online purchases, it also creates the issue of over-reliance on customer opinions (Bahtar & Muda, 2016). Since product reviews can go either direction, there is a chance that potential consumers are misled and discouraged from buying items associated with negative feedback. Although fast-fashion companies acknowledge the importance of online social marketing, they still lack an adequate understanding of how to use social media effectively and what type of performance-based indicators they should be measuring (Hanna, Rohm, & Crittenden, 2011; Muslim et al., 2014).

Disposability and Sustainability

The phenomenon of fast-fashion has caused a shift in competitive advantage and has moved the focus from price to an emphasis on a quick response production system that encourages disposability (Fletcher, 2008; Barnes & Lea - Greenwood, 2010). The fast-fashion business model that aims to offer elite fashion at affordable prices, lures customers into purchasing fashion items more frequently due to the element of disposability. Sustainability is generally described as an activity that can be prolonged indefinitely without causing damage to the surrounding environment (Partridge, 2011) whereas sustainability within fast-fashion refers to the incorporation of eco-friendly measures in the production phase and the management of resource flow into the fashion industry. While sustainability is difficult to achieve in the fashion sector, Lejeune (2016) notes that sustainable fast-fashion is even more challenging for businesses to accomplish. This is precisely because the commercial drivers of fast-fashion companies are an inherent contradiction of mitigating adverse environmental impacts.

Gardetti and Torres (2012) focus on fast-fashion within the context of sustainability and deduce that the industry results in detrimental social and environmental effects. Southwell (2014), on the other hand, undertakes a unique approach in the interpretation of sustainability within fashion by offering a feminist perspective. After drawing on extensive literature review and observing fashion and sustainability social media networks, Southwell (2014) argues that the fashion industry is gender biased. This means that the fashion business has feminized environmental responsibility and as key players in the fashion industry, women are held responsible for directing consumption towards sustainability endeavors (Pentecost & Andrews, 2010; Southwell, 2014). Thus, within the corporate realm, female leaders experience pressures in the form of 'eco-stress'.

In contrast to Thorpe (2012), who contextualizes sustainable fashion in terms of consumer-driven business growth, Strauss and Fuad-Luke (2008) explore the fashion and sustainability discourse which places the onus of environmental deterioration on the advent of fast-fashion. Further critics note that the fast-fashion industry has contributed to the sustainability challenge today and in some instances, compromised Corporate Social Responsibility (CSR). Suppliers belonging to the fast-fashion supply chain have experienced time and cost related pressures (Perry & Towers, 2013). Fashion retailers have previously been accused of business malpractices such as violating labor laws and using sweatshops. However, to reap the benefits of a socially responsible behavior and obtain sustainable development, Arrigo (2013) proposes that fast-fashion companies should integrate corporate social management into their business decision-making process.

Companies such as H&M, for example, employ innovative marketing strategies by hiring fashion designers like Stella McCartney and Karl Lagerfeld to create limited, one-time collections (Amoye, 2011). Industry players typically have very short production times, which results in small clothing batches that generally sell out within days. The supply side of fast fashion brands including ZARA, GAP and H&M use shortened product life cycles to create a scarcity effect. Brondoni (2009) describes this as market-bubble management. This phenomenon describes situations in which consumers are prompted to impulse-buy transient product lines that will not be repeated. Through occasional shortages, companies build up a scarcity value for their products, which in turn drives consumer demand. Consumers thus feel more inclined to purchase products on the spot, as delays may result in sold out stock. By compressing production cycles these businesses have thus enabled shoppers not only to expand their wardrobes, but also to restore them rapidly.

The logic behind affordable prices is for clothes to possess a disposable characteristic. Hence, consumers buy more clothes more frequently. Fast fashion retailers themselves openly proffer the number of ten washes as a benchmark at which to dispose of items that may no longer retain their original value (Joy et al., 2012). A limited product life span can be attributed to poor-quality materials and manufacturing or the fact that certain articles may have gone out of fashion. By creating goods that are highly disposable in nature, fast fashion companies train consumers in ways that propagate continuous consumption and product replacements (Fletcher, 2008; Joy et al., 2012). The fashion industry – in common with the technology industry – recognizes planned obsolescence as a prime goal; fast-fashion simply raises the stakes (Brondoni, 2009; Abrahamson, 2011).

With fast fashion comes a repercussion. In recent years, sustainability, corporate social responsibility and ethical conduct have gained vast importance in the fashion industry (Emberley 1998; Moisander & Personen, 2002; Turker & Altuntas, 2014). Global companies have adopted an emerging green orientation (Bansal & Roth, 2000) and have acknowledged that while inexpensive, trend-sensitive fashion is profitable, it also raises concerns about ethical demeanor (Aspers & Skov, 2006; O'Keeffe, Ozuem and Lancaster, 2015). The elements of trust and long-lasting consumer relationships have therefore increasingly become important in marketing ethics (Srnka, 2004; Ozuem et al., 2015b; Ramaswamy & Ozcan, 2016).

Smit (2016) heavily criticizes the fast-fashion business model that provides a continuous flow of fashionable products at cheap prices and in doing so, places the commercial pressure onto suppliers and workers operating the supply chain. These pressures are exerted either directly or indirectly in the form of unpaid overtime work, illegal subcontracting and low wages (Turker & Altuntas, 2014; Smit, 2016).

Fletcher and Tham (2014) argue that if the fast-fashion industry wishes to commit to sustainability, it must first acknowledge two aspects of sustainability. These include defining a clear goal and in-depth understanding of the roots of unsustainability. Wu and Pagell (2011) note a positive correlation between environmental practices and financial outcomes and therefore, suggest that fast-fashion companies must embed sustainability measures into their decision-making process.

While fashion retailers innovate luxury products, the fast fashion system continues to outsize environmental effects regarding the use of water and chemicals and the emitting of greenhouse gases. The fast fashion industry further draws attention to ethical labor standards in product sourcing and manufacturing and the waste associated with disposing of unfashionable or worn-out garments (Turker & Altuntas, 2014). The inherent dissonance among fast fashion consumers suggests that most shoppers either overlook, or tolerate the social and environmental costs of fast fashion (McKinsey & Company, 2017). While some apparel companies have formed coalitions to avoid consumer backlashes, and to tackle environmental and social challenges together, other fast fashion businesses have started their own sustainability initiatives. Global brands such as H&M and Forever 21 have effectively counteracted some of the problems endemic to fast fashion and provide leadership on issues relating to sustainability. They have each partnered with I: Collect (I:CO) to assemble clothing and footwear for reuse and recycling (McKinsey & Company, 2017).

Fashion retailer, H&M, aims to provide consumers with fashionable, high-quality clothing at the best price possible. Its corporate vision entails: 'Fashion and quality at the best price'. The CEO Karl-Joan Persson stated that, "Our goal is for H&M to be at the forefront of sustainability. We work hard to always strengthen our customer offering. I think that adding sustainable value to our products is one of the keys to do so" (H&M, 2013). Thus, it is apparent that H&M's philosophical values as a diligent company, has allowed it to embrace sustainability strategies that are pertinent in gaining a strong competitive advantage. H&M uses corporate social responsibility as an asset to reinforce a relationship based on customer trust and loyalty (Kim & Ko, 2012; Ramaswamy & Ozcan, 2016). Instead of owning their own factories, H&M outsources its production overseas and purchases products from long-term partnered independent suppliers. Ozuem, Thomas and Lancaster (2015) note this shift in commercial transactions between customers and suppliers.

With increasing awareness via social media, customers expect companies to exhibit corporate transparency and ethical conduct (Pride & Ferrell, 2014; O'Keeffe et al., 2015). H&M has managed to do just this undertaking numerous initiatives to become sustainable. In 2004, H&M committed to the use of organic cotton in children's clothing. By 2010, it was ranked as the top user of organic cotton in the world (H&M, 2013). H&M's more recent collaboration with I:CO aims to save natural resources and cut waste by offering £5 discount vouchers to consumers who turn in their old clothes at any H&M store. This form of CSR means that H&M reflects what Srnka (2004) refers to as strong and ethical decision-making corporate leadership.

Customer and Supplier Relationships

Operating in a competitive fashion industry, H&M aims to improve loyalty orientation by prioritizing environmental factors such as its awareness of end-customers and adaptation to their changing needs (Ozuem et al., 2015b). An analysis at the product level offers key insight into the brand's target customers (Pride & Ferrell, 2014). H&M primarily targets style-conscious consumers while taking into consideration their age, religions, class background, culture and lifestyle (Zhenxiang & Lijie, 2011; Regnér &

Yildiz, 2014). Their target audience ranges from young college students to mature working and middle class women. H&M's target customers are identified as a group of fashionable and trendy consumers who view shopping as a social, pleasure-seeking activity and want to follow affordable market trends (H&M, 2013). The company employs a concentrated targeting strategy by offering lower priced clothing and accessories to its target market of up-to-date seasonal consumers. H&M offers two main seasons collections: spring and fall supported with a few sub-collections each season (H&M, 2016).

According to Ozuem et al. (2015b), customer loyalty is dictated by the company's ability to deliver their products and services in a reliable manner. In this case, H&M has been successful in its customer retention. As an all-encompassing brand, H&M caters for consumer needs by offering fashion apparel, cosmetics, accessories and shoes for women, men, teenagers and children (H&M, 2013). However, what Kumar & Shah (2004) define as attitudinal loyalty does not seem to fit with H&M's client base. Rather, H&M's customer base is characterized by behaviorally loyal customers, who are not emotionally attached to the organization (Zhenxiang & Lijie, 2011). As Mascarenhas, Kesavan, & Bernacchi (2006) note, their attachment is conditioned on situational triggers such as sale promotions and lower prices.

Global fast fashion retailers thrive on fast cycles. Central to these are rapid prototyping, a variety of small batch productions, transportation and delivery efficiency, and the availability of instant merchandise (Skov, 2002; Zhenxiang & Lijie, 2011). The fast-fashion sensation raises questions about traditional approaches to product sourcing and buying. Fast fashion further emphasizes the need for efficient supply chain management so that retailers can develop strategies which enable them to navigate the supply chain more closely and thus, source high quality products at competitive prices (Cachon & Swinney, 2011; Fletcher & Grose, 2012). Fast fashion international brands such as ZARA take advantage of current emerging trends by adopting sophisticated, vertically integrated supply chains (Thomachot & Student, 2008; Bhardwaj & Fairhurst, 2010). While ZARA previously manufactured the majority of its products with enhanced quality control in Europe, it now outsources at least 13 percent of its manufacturing to China and Turkey (Tokatli & Kizilgun, 2009).

As a pioneer of 'fast fashion' principles, ZARA has portrayed a shift in the culture of fashion from ready-to-wear to fast fashion. With an increased variety of fashion to offer, ZARA has skewed competitive advantage towards firms in industrialized countries, rather than away from them (Tokatli, 2008). Instead of investing huge resources into conducting stylist research, ZARA rapidly responds to new fashion trends (Barnes & Lea – Greenwood, 2010; MacCarthy & Jayarathne, 2010; Joey, 2011). Unlike its main competitors, ZARA produces part of its clothing directly, which allows the company to vary product assortment and control its entire supply chain (Zhenxiang & Lijie, 2011; Belk, 2014). Meanwhile, the remainder of production is outsourced to foreign companies that are located throughout Europe and Asia.

Market-oriented companies aside from ZARA include the Swedish firm H&M, and the American firm, GAP Inc. They significantly invest in innovation management, distribution and communication methods and have recently been the focus of case studies. ZARA and H&M are a global operating chain of single-brand stores that are unified upstream. These global giants take advantage of e-commerce in improving supply chain communication and enhancing service offering, while reducing costs (Zhenxiang & Lijie, 2011; Belk, 2014). The use of the Internet helps fashion companies to create competitive differentiation by curbing the costs associated with managing supplier relationships, purchasing and streamlining inventory and logistics (Tokatli, 2008; Barnes & Lea – Greenwood, 2010; Ryan, 2016).

While the fashion sector ranges from prestigious tailor-made articles known as 'haute couture' to mass markets, global companies such as ZARA, Forever 21, and H&M belong to the mass-market where they specialize in selling fashion items at accessible prices to a broader public (Amatulli et al., 2016).

These fashion retailers take on a combined approach that not only focuses on fashion, but also offers low costs to the audience. In spite of economic booms and recessions, their entry into the clothing sector has helped sustain global growth and consumption (Cillo & Verona, 2008). These global giants greatly focus on the distribution process of their products so as to control the distribution network and be closer to the end consumer. Of the many specialist fashion chains, H&M, ZARA, GAP, and UNIQLO in particular experience rapid stock turnaround and vertical integration of design through just-in-time production, fast delivery and sales (Tokatli, 2008; Zhenxiang & Lijie, 2011). They adopt vertical integration strategies to demonstrate how critical it is to own the sales network despite having manufacturing outsourced to external partners (Thomachot & Student, 2008; Bhardwaj & Fairhurst, 2010).

The fast fashion model is based on the combination of two production systems: quick response production capabilities and enhanced product design capabilities (Zhenxiang & Lijie, 2011). Large apparel retailers including ZARA and H&M have significantly promoted quick response times (Ghemawat et al., 2003; Hayes & Jones, 2006; MacCarthy & Jayarathne, 2010). Unlike traditional production systems, the fast fashion system successfully captures the latest consumer trends and exploits minimal production lead times (Barnes & Lea – Greenwood, 2010; Fletcher & Grose, 2012). Such enhanced design plays a role in mitigating strategic consumer behavior, i.e., the deliberate delay in purchasing items at the original price to obtain items during an end-of-season clearance (Cachon & Swinney, 2011; Joey, 2011). Instead, fast fashion encourages risk-averse consumer behavior by offering highly coveted products to ensure consumers are less willing to wait for a clearance sale and to possibly experience stock-out. Quick response, on the other hand, alleviates strategic behavior by opting a different mechanism. This is done by better matching supply with demand to reduce the chance of a clearance sale in the first place (Cachon & Swinney, 2011). Hence, the operation of both production systems in fast fashion results in greater profit increments.

In order to remain profitable and above its competitors, H&M has adopted a marketing strategy to differentiate itself and draw in a larger target audience. H&M adopts a cost leadership strategy that sets high barriers for competitors to enter the market. To ensure the best price for their consumers, H&M cuts out the middleman and purchases supplies in bulk (H&M, 2013). The company benefits from location-economies by outsourcing the labor-intensive production of its products to independent manufacturers overseas in countries like China, Bangladesh, and Turkey (H&M, 2013).

Fast Fashion in a Globalized World

Today H&M has a strong presence in diverse markets as its extensive product line is broadly categorized into clothes, self-branded cosmetics, accessories and footwear for women, teenagers, men, and children. H&M appeals across the entire consumer market and is a one-stop shop for any fashion needs. An analysis of the product offerings reveals that the top moving garments show huge diversity around age and trend preference (H&M, 2016). H&M offers a mix of styles: bodycon, occasion wear, skater dresses and casual jersey dresses (H&M, 2016).

In addition to the competitive top category, H&M also excels in its active wear. Under Ansoff's matrix model (Watts, Cope, & Hulme, 1998), H&M has employed a product development strategy to place new products into new markets. It further undertakes a diversification strategy to expand new products, such as sportswear, into new markets. For example, H&M has recently penetrated the Australian market, which until now had been dominated by premium priced active wear. The company has launched several pursuits – yoga, tennis, running and trekking – that seem to appeal to the overseas market (H&M, 2013).

Singh, Scriven, Clemente and Lomax (2012) emphasize the importance of establishing a steady and increasing volume of sales before stepping into brand extension. This methodology has been adopted by H&M in its approach to branch into independent brands with a different theme, attracting customers from each market segment. H&M's brand portfolio is comprised of six independent brands: H&M, COS, Monki, Weekday, Cheap Monday, and the newest addition, & Other Stories, along with home interiors at H&M Home (H&M, 2016).

The Collection of Style (COS) brand launched in 2007. This upmarket brand appeals to the high-end consumer by offering a combination of timelessness and distinctive trends. It opened the doors to both men and women core customers between the ages of 18 and 30 for a more mature audience (H&M, 2016). The more recent young fashion brands Monki, Weekday and Cheap Monday serve a fashion-savvy audience. The Monki stores focus on a more playful or creative individual. They provide innovative collections and an inspiring fashion experience characterized by colorful graphic designs (H&M, 2016). Weekday mostly engages in design collaborations with independent fashion labels (H&M, 2016). The Cheap Monday stores introduce street fashion and subcultures with a catwalk vibe, whereas H&M Home offers fashion-focused homewares (H&M, 2016). The latest addition is the luxury store concept '& Other Stories' which is successfully operating in 45 stores across the world.

H&M started its international expansion in 1964 by entering other Scandinavian markets – Norway and Denmark. By 1974, H&M was enlisted on the stock exchange market and had successfully expanded to most European countries. In 2000, H&M opened its first store in a foreign territory outside Europe, in Manhattan, New York (H&M, 2013). This was the foundation of the penetration of H&M into global markets around the world.

H&M strives for constant expansion, targeting 10-15% growth of both stores and online sales with continued profitability (H&M, 2016). In 2017, H&M plans to open approximately 430 new stores and expand into five new-markets – Iceland, Kazakhstan, Colombia, Vietnam and Georgia (H&M, 2016). This year it will also increase the number of its online markets to Hong Kong, Singapore, Macau, Malaysia, Taiwan, and Turkey. One of its newer additions, H&M Home will also expand by nearly 50 new departments (H&M, 2016).

With the rapid development of a global marketplace, adopting an ethnocentric approach towards branding has increasingly become an issue (Cayla & Arnould, 2008). For many years, H&M operated with an ethnocentric orientation within Sweden, making limited changes to products because of the similar cultures and styles followed in Scandinavian countries. Soon after, the company by-passed the polycentric approach and instead opted for a regiocentric orientation stage. This is reflected in H&M's successful expansion into the Western world due to its assimilation and accommodation of region-specific cultural norms (Kumar, 2014).

Drawing on a cohesive framework, Srnka (2004) describes the role of culture in the process of ethical decision-making and discusses how it developed within a multicultural marketing context. For international companies to succeed, including H&M, ZARA, and GAP, they need to be culturally aware, and act in clear conscious in terms of adapting to differing cultural norms (Kumar, 2014). Before penetrating a market, each company' s headquarters team conducts a macro- and microanalysis of the market environment (Srnka 2004; Gonzalez 2017).

As discussed by Matusitz (2010) the theory of 'glocalization' applies to fashion retailers H&M, ZARA, and GAP. They act as 'glocal' brands that operate globally, but act locally by particularizing their global products to specific local markets. In 2007, H&M applied its existing marketing strategies used in the global market to expand into China (H&M, 2013). H&M followed a strategy similar to the one it had previously employed for others in the international market to leverage economies of scale. The decision proved profitable, as the company's performance in the Chinese market was higher than speculated. Sales between 2007 and 2014 increased on a year-to-year basis (H&M, 2013). H&M successfully operated under a 'glocalized' marketing orientation by adjusting its strategies according to China's market-based needs (Matusitz, 2010). In doing so, H&M made significant changes to its icon style collaboration, social media promotion strategies and pricing.

Over the years, H&M, ZARA, and Forever 21 have implemented a reactive market approach whereby they opt for a direct sales network of flagship stores disseminated in major cities all over the global territory. After conducting detailed market research and an analysis of what Srnka (2004) describes as the micro and macro environment, these global competitors then decide which country to operate in. Having stores worldwide enables fashion retailers to collect ample information regarding the peculiar characteristics of the various types of consumers in different countries. Not only does this help H&M, Forever 21, and ZARA to practice a polycentric and geocentric marketing approach, but it also results in high customer retention (Hollensen 2007; Kumar 2014). Another means through which fast fashion companies manage to attract and retain customers on their premises is by defining its interior design layout. The development strategy of ZARA, H&M, and Forever 21 aims to create a shopping environment in which customers take their time to shop and this also increases the probability that they will make a purchase.

With a strong internet presence and a prolonged experience in e-tailing, Forever 21 prefers to connect with their consumers through the use of social media platforms, such as Facebook, Instagram and Twitter (Hendriksz, 2013). Forever 21 has been driving social traffic as well as sales by introducing campaigns that focus on consumer-generated content (Bahtar & Muda, 2016). In addition to social media and 'selfie' campaigns, Forever 21 has implemented a unique approach by launching a mobile-optimized site that features a shoppable gallery (Jaekel, 2015). This produces a conducive shopping experience for customers, enticing them to shop the looks showcased in the gallery. This social campaign not only increases sales revenue via social networks, but it also creates consumer equity and a strong bond between Forever 21 and consumers (Kim & Ko, 2012; Jaekel, 2015).

With the emergence of e-commerce, the fast fashion industry has experienced a revolution in terms of its management and traditional marketing. Rapid advancements in internet-related infrastructure and services have propelled an explosive growth in fast fashion; one of the fastest growing industries in the global economy (Wertime & Fenwick, 2011). The future of fast fashion is now influenced by advanced technologies. Digital marketing strategies are a key driver behind the performance of any fashion brand in emerging markets, as well as existing markets (Ryan, 2016; Bendoni, 2017). In recent years, the occurrence of globalization has led to market evolution and one of the leaps in marketing is digital marketing: an online marketing tool used to promote products and services in a fashion that will attract customers.

CONCLUSION

Fast fashion retailers are experiencing an ever-changing model due to the fad of fast-paced technological changes and consumer preferences. Digital marketing strategies including mobile commerce, social interactions and consumer-experienced content reshape the way fashion retailers operate in the global market (Ramaswamy & Ozcan, 2016; Montecchi & Nobbs, 2017). Fashion brands such as H&M, ZARA, and Forever 21 have joined the social media bandwagon and have incorporated social networks as a central part of their marketing strategies. Today social media empowers 'fashion conscious' consumers by disseminating valuable consumer information and thus, potent marketing power (Uzunoğlu & Kip, 2014).

The growing role of online social media and networks in marketing has important implications for how consumers, channels, and companies interact. Social media and user-generated content are used to help potential shoppers to make purchase decisions (Lloyd & Luk, 2010; Kim & Ko, 2012; Kucukusta et al., 2015). This study contributes to the existing literature on the impact of digital marketing on fast fashion, and it provides a number of pertinent marketing implications in regard to the practice of certain companies including H&M, ZARA, and Forever 21. Lessons from this chapter include ideas in relation to assisting fashion brands to engage with the target audience via digital marketing strategies and social media platforms to reinforce their brand positions. In conclusion, the expeditious integration of social media networks into digital marketing strategies has significantly facilitated the fast-fashion industry and its future marketing practices.

ACKNOWLEDGMENT

Special acknowledgment is given to Professor Wilson Ozuem for his consultation in the research process for this chapter.

REFERENCES

Abrahamson, E. (2011). The Iron Cage: Ugly, Cool and Unfashionable. *Organization Studies*, *32*(5), 615–629. doi:10.1177/0170840611405425

Adesoga, A. (2016). Examination of the Relevance of Traditional Promotional Strategy: A Descriptive Method. In J.G. Fowler & J. Weiser (Eds.), the Society for Marketing Advances (pp. 326-327). San Antonio, TX: Society for Marketing Advances.

Agarwal, S., & Aggrawal, A. (2012). A Critical Analysis of Impact of Pricing on Consumer Buying Behaviour in Apparel Retail Sector: A Study of Mumbai City. *International Journal of Multidisciplinary Educational Research*, *1*(1).

Apparel magazine. (2010). How Social media is revolutionizing the Apparel Industry-One message at a time. 2010. *Apparel magazine*, *52*(4), 1-6.

Amatulli, C., Mileti, A., Speciale, V., & Guido, G. (2016). The Relationship between Fast Fashion and Luxury Brands: An Exploratory Study in the UK Market. In Global Marketing Strategies for the Promotion of Luxury Goods (pp. 244–265). Hershey, PA: IGI Global. doi:10.4018/978-1-4666-9958-8.ch011

Amoye, E. (2011). Questionable Co-branding, Lessons in Luxury. Retrieved March 27, 2017, from http://lessonsinluxury.com/2011/11/23/focus-focus-focus-through-cobranding/

Arrigo, E. (2010). Innovation and market-driven management in fast fashion companies. *Symphonya: Emerging Issues in Management*, *2*, 67–85.

Arrigo, E. (2013). Corporate responsibility management in fast fashion companies: The Gap Inc. case. *Journal of Fashion Marketing and Management: An International Journal, 17*(2), 175–189. doi:10.1108/JFMM-10-2011-0074

Aspers, P., & Skov, L. (2006). Encounters in the Global Fashion Business. *Current Sociology, 54*, 745–763. doi:10.1177/0011392106066814

Atwal, G., Bryson, D., & von Gersdorff, J. (2010). *Luxury brands: Deluxurification is in Fashion As luxury labels continue to diversify into more affordable, mass-market lines, they run the risk of devaluing the whole brand . Admap*, 44–46.

Azemi, Y., & Ozuem, W. (2016). Online service failure and recovery strategy: The mediating role of social media. In Ozuem and Bowen (Eds.), Competitive social media marketing strategies (pp. 112-136). Hershey, PA: IGI Global.

Backhaus, K., Muhlfeld, K., & Van Doorn, J. (2001). Consumer Perspectives on Standardization in *International* Advertising: A Student Sample. *Journal of Advertising Research, 41*(5), 53–61. doi:10.2501/JAR-41-5-53-61

Bahtar, A. Z., & Muda, M. (2016). The Impact of User–Generated Content (UGC) on Product Reviews towards Online Purchasing–A Conceptual Framework. *Procedia Economics and Finance, 37*, 337–342. doi:10.1016/S2212-5671(16)30134-4

Bakshy, E., Karrer, B., & Adamic, L. A. (2009, July). Social influence and the diffusion of user- created content. In *Proceedings of the 10th ACM conference on Electronic commerce* (pp. 325-334). *ACM*. 10.1145/1566374.1566421

Bansal, P., & Roth, K. (2000). Why Companies Go Green: A Model of Ecological Responsiveness. *Academy of Management Journal, 43*(4), 717–736. doi:10.2307/1556363

Barnes, L., & Lea-Greenwood, G. (2010). Fast Fashion in the retail store environment. *International Journal of Retail & Distribution Management, 38*(10), 760–772. doi:10.1108/09590551011076533

Bauman, Z. (2005). *Liquid Life*. Cambridge: Polity Press.

Bendoni, W. K. (2017). *Social Media for Fashion Marketing: Storytelling in a Digital World*. Bloomsbury Publishing.

Belk, R. (2014). You are what you can access: Sharing and Collaborative Consumption Online. *Journal of Business Research, 67*(8), 1595–1600. doi:10.1016/j.jbusres.2013.10.001

Bhardwaj, V., & Fairhurst, A. (2010). Fast fashion: Response to changes in the fashion industry. *International Review of Retail, Distribution and Consumer Research, 20*(1), 165–173. doi:10.1080/09593960903498300

Bourne, L. (2010, September 07). Social media is fashion's newest muse. *Forbes*. Retrieved From http://www.forbes.com/2010/09/07/fashion-social-networking-customer-feedback-forbes-womastyle-designers.html

Brondoni, S. M. (2009). Market-driven management, competitive customer value and global network. *Symphonya: Emerging Issues in Management*. Retrieved from www.unimib.it/symphonya

Brooks, A. (2015). *Clothing Poverty: The Hidden World of Fast Fashion and Second-hand Clothes*. London: Zed Books Ltd.

Buzzetto-More, N. A. (2013). Social media and prosumerism. *Issues in Informing Science and Information Technology, 10*, 67–80.

Cachon, G. P. & Swinney R. (2011). The value of fast fashion: quick response, enhanced design, and strategic consumer behaviour. *Management Science, 57*(4), 778–95.

Caro, F., & Martínez-de-Albéniz, V. (2015). Fast fashion: business model overview and research opportunities. In *Narendra Agrawal and Stephen Smith (2015). Retail Supply Chain Management* (pp. 237–264). New York: Springer. doi:10.1007/978-1-4899-7562-1_9

Studies, C. H&M Loves. (2017). Breed Communications. Retrieved 24 March 2017, from http://www.breedcommunications.com/case-studies-hm-loves/

Cayla, J., & Arnould, E. (2008). A Cultural Approach to Branding in the Global Marketplace. *Journal of International Marketing, 16*(4), 86–112. doi:10.1509/jimk.16.4.86

Cha, M., Kwak, H., Rodriguez, P., Ahn, Y. Y., & Moon, S. (2007, October). I tube, you tube, everybody tubes: analyzing the world's largest user generated content video system. In *Proceedings of the 7th ACM SIGCOMM conference on Internet measurement* (pp. 1-14). ACM. 10.1145/1298306.1298309

Chae, H., Ko, E., & Han, J. (2014, July). Exploring Social Media Services of Global Fashion Brands: Does Customer Social Participation Have an Impact on Customer Equity? In *Proceedings of the 2014 Global Marketing Conference at Singapore* (pp. 1609-1612).

Choi, T. M. (2013). *Fast fashion systems: Theories and applications. 4 (2013)*. London: CRC Press.

Christopher, M., Lowson, R., & Peck, H. (2004). Creating agile supply chains in the fashion industry. *International Journal of Retail & Distribution Management, 32*(8), 367–376. doi:10.1108/09590550410546188

Cillo, P., & Verona, G. (2008). Search Styles in Styles Searching: Exploring Innovation Strategies in Fashion Firms. *Long Range Planning, 8*(1), 1–22.

Comunale, A. (2008). You are who you wear: A conceptual study of the fashion branding practices of H&M, forever 21, and urban outfitters. *Journal of the Re-Tail Image*.

Crane, D. (2000). *Fashion and its Social Agendas: Class, Gender and Identity in Clothing*. Chicago: University of Chicago Press. doi:10.7208/chicago/9780226924830.001.0001

Dennhardt, S. (2014). *User-generated content and its impact on Branding: How users and communities create and manage brands in social media*. Wiesbaden: Springer Fachmedien Wiesbaden. doi:10.1007/978-3-658-02350-8

Dorsey, P. (2012). Social media is not social CRM, but it can be with these five steps. *Marketing Profs Dot Com*. Retrieved 7/23/2012 from http://www.marketingprofs.com/articles/2012

Doyle, S., Moore, C., & Morgan, L. (2006). Supplier management in fast moving fashion retailing. *Journal of Fashion Marketing and Management, 10*(3), 272–281. doi:10.1108/13612020610679268

Eley, B., & Tilley, S. (2009). *Online Marketing Inside Out*. Melbourne: SitePoint.

Emberley, V. (1998). *Venus and Furs: The Cultural Politics of Fur*. London: I. B. Tauris & Co.

Ertekin, Z. O., & Atik, D. (2015). Sustainable markets: motivating factors, barriers, and remedies for mobilization of slow fashion. *Journal of Macromarketing*, *35*(1), 53–69. doi:10.1177/0276146714535932

Fader, P. S., & Winer, R. S. (2012). Introduction to the special issue on the emergence and impact of user-generated content. *Marketing Science*, *31*(3), 369–371. doi:10.1287/mksc.1120.0715

IBISWorld. (2017). Fast Fashion in Australia Market Research. Retrieved 18 March 2017, from https://www.ibisworld.com.au/industry-trends/specialised-market-research-reports/consumer-goods-services/fast-fashion.html

Fletcher, K. (2008). *Sustainable Fashion & Textiles: Design Journeys*. Oxford: Earthscan.

Fletcher, K. (2010). Slow fashion: An invitation for systems change. *Fashion Practice*, *2*(2), 259–265.

Fletcher, K., & Grose, L. (2012). *Fashion and sustainability: design for change*. London: Laurence King Publishing Ltd.

Fletcher, K., & Tham, M. (2014). *Routledge handbook of sustainability and fashion*. London: Routledge.

Forever 21. (2017). *Social Media. Forever 21 Newsroom*. Retrieved 9 April 2017, from http://newsroom.forever21.com/social-media

Friedman, V. (2010). Assessing the Alexander Wang/H&M collaboration. *Financial Times*. Retrieved March 27, 2017, from http://blogs.ft.com/material-world/2014/04/14/assessing-the-alexander-wanghm-collaboration/

Gabrielli, V., Baghi, I., & Codeluppi, V. (2013). Consumption practices of fast fashion products. *Journal of Fashion Marketing and Management*, *17*(2), 206–224. doi:10.1108/JFMM-10-2011-0076

Gamboa, A. M., & Gonçalves, H. M. (2014). Customer loyalty through social networks: Lessons from Zara on Facebook. *Business Horizons*, *57*(6), 709–717. doi:10.1016/j.bushor.2014.07.003

Gardetti, M. A., & Torres, A. L. (2012). A special issue on textiles, fashion and sustainability. *Journal of Corporate Citizenship*, 45.

Ghemawat, P., Nueno, J. L., & Dailey, M. (2003). *ZARA: Fast fashion* (Vol. 1). Boston, MA: Harvard Business School.

Giertz-Mårtenson, I. (2012). H&M–documenting the story of one of the worlds largest fashion retailers. *Business History*, *54*(1), 108–115. doi:10.1080/00076791.2011.617203

Godey, B., Manthiou, A., Pederzoli, D., Rokka, J., Aiello, G., Donvito, R., & Singh, R. (2015, June). Luxury brands social media marketing efforts: influence on brand equity and consumers' behavior. In *Proceedings of the 2015 Global Fashion Management Conference at Florence* (p. 68).

Hanna, R., Rohm, A., & Crittenden, V. L. (2011). Were all connected: The power of the social media ecosystem. *Business Horizons*, *54*(3), 265–273. doi:10.1016/j.bushor.2011.01.007

Hansson, M. (2011). What impact has a fast fashion strategy on fashion companies supply chain management?

Hayes, S. & Jones, N. (2006). Fast fashion: A financial snapshot. *Journal of Fashion Marketing and Management*, *10*(3), 282–300.

H&M group. (2013). Markets & Expansion. Retrieved February 22, 2017, from https://about.hm.com/en/about-us/markets-and-expansion.html

H&M group. (2016, November 30). Retrieved February 23, 2017, from https://about.hm.com/en/brands/stories.html

Hemphill, C. S., & Suk, J. (2009). Remix and cultural production. *Stanford Law Review*, *61*(5), 1227–1232.

Hendriksz, V. (2013). Clash of the Fashion Titans: H&M vs Forever 21. *Fashionunited.uk*. Retrieved 1 April 2017, from https://fashionunited.uk/v1/fashion/clash-of-the-fashion-titans-ham-vs-forever21/2013121712941

Hines, T., & Bruce, M. (2007). *Fashion marketing*. London: Routledge.

Hollensen, S. (2007). *Global marketing: A decision-oriented approach*. Harlow: Pearson education.

Huang, R., Lee, S. H., Kim, H., & Evans, L. (2015). The impact of brand experiences on brand resonance in multi-channel fashion retailing. *Journal of Research in Interactive Marketing*, *9*(2), 129–147. doi:10.1108/JRIM-06-2014-0042

Jacobs, D. (2006). The promise of demand chain management in fashion. *Journal of Fashion Marketing and Management*, *10*(1), 84–96. doi:10.1108/13612020610651141

Jang, J., Ko, E., Chun, E., & Lee, E. (2012). A study of a social content model for sustainable development in the fast fashion industry. *Journal of Global Fashion Marketing*, *3*(2), 61–70. doi:10.1080/20932685.2012.10593108

Jefferies, J., Clark, H., & Conroy, D. W. (2015). *The Handbook of Textile Culture*. New York: Bloomsbury Publishing.

Joey, L.W. (2011). *How Does Fast Fashion Influence the Consumer Shopping Behavior of Generation Y in Hong Kong*?

Joy, A., Sherry, J. F. Jr, Venkatesh, A., Wang, J., & Chan, R. (2012). Fast fashion, sustainability, and the ethical appeal of luxury brands. *Fashion Theory*, *16*(3), 273–295. doi:10.2752/175174112X13340749707123

Kaplan, A. M., & Haenlein, M. (2010). Users of the world, unite! The challenges and opportunities of Social Media. *Business Horizons*, *53*(1), 59–68. doi:10.1016/j.bushor.2009.09.003

Kim, A. J., & Ko, E. (2012). Do social media marketing activities enhance customer equity? An empirical study of luxury fashion brand. *Journal of Business Research*, *65*(10), 1480–1486. doi:10.1016/j.jbusres.2011.10.014

Kucukusta, D., Law, R., Besbes, A., & Legoherel, P. (2015). Re-Examining Perceived Usefulness and Ease of Use in Online Booking: The Case of Hong Kong Online Users. *International Journal of Contemporary Hospitality Management, 27*(2), 185–198. doi:10.1108/IJCHM-09-2013-0413

Kumar, V. (2014). Understanding Cultural Differences in Innovation: A Conceptual Framework and Future Research Directions. *Journal of International Marketing, 22*(3), 1–29. doi:10.1509/jim.14.0043

Kumar, V., & Shah, D. (2004). Building and sustaining profitable customer loyalty for 21st century. *Journal of Retailing, 80*(4), 317–330. doi:10.1016/j.jretai.2004.10.007

Lago, A., Martínez-de-Albéniz, V., Moscoso, P., & Vall, A. (2016). The role of quick response in accelerating sales of fashion goods. In *Analytical Modeling Research in Fashion Business* (pp. 51–78). Singapore: Springer. doi:10.1007/978-981-10-1014-9_4

Lambert, M. (2014). *The Lowest Cost at Any Price: The Impact of Fast Fashion on the Global Fashion Industry*. Lake Forest College.

Lejeune, T. (2016). Fast Fashion: Can It Be Sustainable? *The Ethical Fashion Source*. Retrieved 9 April 2017, from http://source.ethicalfashionforum.com/article/

Lloyd, A. E., & Luk, S. T. (2010). The devil wears Prada or Zara: A revelation into customer perceived value of luxury and mass fashion brands. *Journal of Global Fashion Marketing, 1*(3), 129–141. doi:10.1080/20932685.2010.10593065

Logan, R. K. (2010). *Understanding new media: extending Marshall McLuhan*. New York: Peter Lang.

Lowry, B. (2016). Meet Mario Moreno, Social Strategy Builder for Forever 21. *Curalate Visual Commerce Platform*. Retrieved 9 April 2017, from https://www.curalate.com/blog/mario-moreno-guess-forever-21/

Lowson, B., King, R., & Hunter, A. (1999). *Quick Response: Managing the supply chain to meet consumer demand*. New York: John Wiley & Sons.

MacCarthy, B. L., & Jayarathne, P. G. S. A. (2010). Fast fashion: achieving global quick response (GQR) in the internationally dispersed clothing industry. In *Innovative Quick Response Programs in Logistics and Supply Chain Management* (pp. 37–60). Berlin, Heidelberg: Springer. doi:10.1007/978-3-642-04313-0_3

MacKinnon, K. (2012). User Generated Content vs. Advertising: Do Consumers Trust the Word of Others Over Advertisers? *The Elon Journal of Undergraduate Research in Communications, 3*(1), 14–22.

Mascarenhas, O. A., Kesavan, R., & Bernacchi, M. (2006). Lasting customer loyalty: A total customer experience approach. *Journal of Consumer Marketing, 23*(7), 397–405. doi:10.1108/07363760610712939

Matusitz, J. (2010). Disneyland Paris: A Case Analysis Demonstrating How Glocalization Works. *Journal of Strategic Marketing, 18*(3), 223–237. doi:10.1080/09652540903537014

McDougall, D. (2007, October 28). Indian 'Slave' Children Found Making Low Cost Clothes Destined for Gap. *The Observer*.

McKinsey & Company. (2017). Style that's sustainable: A new fast-fashion formula. Retrieved 20 March 2017, from http://www.mckinsey.com/business-functions/

Miller, K. (2013). Hedonic customer responses to fast fashion and replicas. *Journal of Fashion Marketing and Management, 2*(17), 160–174. doi:10.1108/JFMM-10-2011-0072

Montecchi, M., & Nobbs, K. (2017). Let It Go: Consumer Empowerment and User-Generated Content–An Exploratory Study of Contemporary Fashion Marketing Practices in the Digital Age. In Advanced Fashion Technology and Operations Management (pp. 294-317). Hershey, PA: IGI Global.

North, P. (2013). The Best Examples of User Generated Content UGC in ecommerce. *Biggroup.co.uk*.

Ozuem, W., O'Keeffe, A., & Lancaster, G. (2015a). Leadership Marketing: An Exploratory Study. *Journal of Strategic Marketing, 23*(1), 1–25.

Ozuem, W., Howell, K. E., & Lancaster, G. (2008). Communicating in the new interactive marketspace. *European Journal of Marketing, 42*(9/10), 1059–1083. doi:10.1108/03090560810891145

Ozuem, W., & Lancaster, G. (2014). Recovery strategies in on-line service failure. In A. Ghorbani (Ed.), *Marketing in the cyber era: Strategies and emerging trends* (pp. 143–159). Hershey, PA: IGI Global. doi:10.4018/978-1-4666-4864-7.ch010

Ozuem, W., Patel, A., Howell, K. E., & Lancaster, G. (2017). An exploration of customers' response to online service recovery initiatives. *International Journal of Market Research, 59*(1), 97–116.

Ozuem, W., Thomas, T., & Lancaster, G. (2015b). The Influence of Customer Loyalty on Small Island Economies: An Empirical and Exploratory Study. *Journal of Strategic Marketing*.

Panteva, N. (2012). *Trends Outfitting the Fashion Retail Sector*.

Partridge, D. J. (2011). Activist Capitalism and Supply Chain Citizenship: Producing Ethical Regimes and Ready-to-Wear Clothes. *Current Anthropology, 52*(S3), S97–S111. doi:10.1086/657256

Pentecost, R., & Andrews, L. (2010). Fashion retailing and the bottom line: The effects of generational cohorts, gender, fashion fanship, attitudes and impulse buying on fashion expenditure. *Journal of Retailing and Consumer Services, 17*(1), 43–52. doi:10.1016/j.jretconser.2009.09.003

Perry, P., & Towers, N. (2013). Conceptual framework development: CSR implementation in fashion supply chains. *International Journal of Physical Distribution & Logistics Management, 43*(5-6), 478–501. doi:10.1108/IJPDLM-03-2012-0107

Press, C. (2016). *Wardrobe Crisis: How We Went from Sunday Best to Fast Fashion*. Black Inc.

Pride, W., & Ferrell, O. C. (2014). *Marketing* (16th ed.). Boston, MA: Cengage Learning.

Ramaswamy, V., & Ozcan, K. (2016). Brand value co-creation in a digitalized world: An integrative framework and research implications. *International Journal of Research in Marketing, 33*(1), 93–106. doi:10.1016/j.ijresmar.2015.07.001

Reboux, B. (2014). UNIQLO: A Stitch in Time. In *Case Studies in Asian Management* (pp. 87-102).

Regnér, P., & Yildiz, H. E. (2014). H&M in Fast Fashion: continued success? In *Johnson, Whittington, Scholes, & Regner* (pp. 574–582). Harlow: Pearson.

Ritzer, G. (2011). *The McDonaldization of Society* (6th ed.). Newbury Park, CA: Pine Forge Press.

Rosenblum, P. (2015). Fast Fashion Has Completely Disrupted Apparel Retail. *Forbes*. Retrieved March 30, 2017, from www.forbes.com/sites/paularosenblum/2015/05/21

Ryan, D. (2016). *Understanding digital marketing: marketing strategies for engaging the digital generation*. London: Kogan Page Publishers.

Sheridan, M., Moore, C., & Nobbs, K. (2006). Fast fashion requires fast marketing: The role of category management in fast fashion positioning. *Journal of Fashion Marketing and Management: An International Journal, 10*(3), 301–315. doi:10.1108/13612020610679286

Singh, J., Scriven, J., Clemente, M., Lomax, W., & Wright, M. (2012). New Brand Extensions: Patterns of Success and Failure. *Journal of Advertising Research, 52*(2), 234–242. doi:10.2501/JAR-52-2-234-242

Smit, C. (2016). *Fast Fashion & Social Sustainability: Challenges and Opportunities for Responsible Supply Chain Management* [Master's thesis].

Southwell, M. (2014). Fashion and Sustainability in the context of gender. In *Kate Fletcher and Mathilda Tham (2014). Routledge handbook of sustainability and fashion*. London: Routledge.

Spencer, A. (2012). Zara Launches Samsung-Exclusive App - Mobile Marketing. *Mobilemarketingmagazine.com*. Retrieved 24 March 2017, from http://mobilemarketingmagazine.com/zara-launches-samsung-exclusive-app/

Spencer, A. (2016). Top of the Bots: Who Can You Chat to in Facebook Messenger, Skype and Kik? - Mobile Marketing. *Mobilemarketingmagazine.com*. Retrieved 24 March 2017, from https://mobile-marketingmagazine.com/best-facebook-messenger-chatbots-skype-kik

Skov, L. (2002). Hong Kong Fashion Designers as Cultural Intermediaries: Out of Global Garment Production. *Cultural Studies, 16*(4), 553–569. doi:10.1080/09502380210139115

Srnka, K. (2004). Culture's Role in Marketers' Ethical Decision Making: An Integrated Theoretical Framework. *Academy of Marketing Science Review, 1*, 1–31.

Stokinger, E., & Ozuem, W. (2015). Social media and customer retention: Implications for the luxury beauty industry. In Bowen and Ozuem (Eds.), Computer-mediated marketing strategies: Social media and online brand communities (pp. 200- 222). Hershey, PA: IGI Global.

Strähle, J., & Grünewald, A. K. (2017). The prosumer concept in fashion retail: potentials and limitations. In *Green Fashion Retail* (pp. 95–117). Singapore: Springer. doi:10.1007/978-981-10-2440-5_6

Strauss, C., & Fuad-Luke, A. (2008). The slow design principles: A new interrogative and reflexive tool for design research and practice. In Changing the change. Torino.

Thackery, R., Neiger, B., & Keller, H. (2012). Integrating social media and social marketing: A four step process. *Health Promotion Practice, 13*(2), 165–168. doi:10.1177/1524839911432009 PMID:22382492

Thorpe, A. (2012). *Architecture and design versus consumerism: how design activism confronts growth*. London: Routledge.

Tokatli, N. (2008). Global Sourcing Insights from the Clothing Industry: The Case of Zara, a Fast Fashion Retailer. *Journal of Economic Geography, 8*(1), 21–38. doi:10.1093/jeg/lbm035

Tokatli, N., & Kizilgun, O. (2009). From Manufacturing Garments for Ready to Wear to Designing Collections: Evidence from Turkey. *Environment & Planning, 41*(1), 146–162. doi:10.1068/a4081

Turker, D., & Altuntas, C. (2014). Sustainable supply chain management in the fast fashion industry: An analysis of corporate reports. *European Management Journal, 32*(5), 837–849. doi:10.1016/j. emj.2014.02.001

Uzunoğlu, E., & Kip, S. M. (2014). Brand communication through digital influencers: Leveraging blogger engagement. *International Journal of Information Management, 34*(5), 592–602. doi:10.1016/j. ijinfomgt.2014.04.007

Vecchi, A. (Ed.). (2016). *Handbook of Research on Global Fashion Management and Merchandising.* Hershey, PA: IGI Global. doi:10.4018/978-1-5225-0110-7

Visitsweden (2011), What makes Swedish fashion so unique? Viewed 27 March 2017, http://www. visitsweden.com

Watts, G., Cope, J., & Hulme, M. (1998). Ansoffs matrix, pain and gain: Growth strategies and adaptive learning among small food producers. *International Journal of Entrepreneurial Behavior & Research, 4*(2), 101–111. doi:10.1108/13552559810224567

Wertime, K., & Fenwick, I. (2011). *DigiMarketing: The essential guide to new media and digital marketing.* New York: John Wiley & Sons.

Wigmo, J., & Wikström, E. (2010). Social media marketing: What role can social media play as a marketing tool? [Bachelor Thesis]. Linnaeus University, School of Computer Science, Sweden.

Wolny, J., & Mueller, C. (2013). Analysis of fashion consumers motives to engage in electronic word-of-mouth communication through social media platforms. *Journal of Marketing Management, 29*(5-6), 562–583. doi:10.1080/0267257X.2013.778324

Wu, J. (2014). *Consumer Response to Online Visual Merchandising Cues: A Case Study of Forever* (Doctoral dissertation, University of Minnesota).

Wu, Z., & Pagell, M. (2011). Balancing priorities: Decision-making in sustainable supply chain management. *Journal of Operations Management, 29*(6), 577–590. doi:10.1016/j.jom.2010.10.001

Youell, M. (2013). An analysis of the growth and success of H&M. How they could impact the largest Swiss watch company. Swatch Group.

Yu-Fan, C. (2011). How International fast fashion brands use Facebook as direct marketing tool.

Zarley Watson, M., & Yan, R. N. (2013). An exploratory study of the decision processes of fast versus slow fashion consumers. *Journal of Fashion Marketing and Management International Journal, 17*(2), 141–159.

Zhao, Z., & Balagué, C. (2015). Designing branded mobile apps: Fundamentals and recommendations. *Business Horizons, 58*(3), 305–315. doi:10.1016/j.bushor.2015.01.004

Zhenxiang, W., & Lijie, Z. (2011). Case study of online retailing fast fashion industry. *International Journal of e-Education, e-Business, e-. Management Learning, 1*(3), 195.

KEY TERMS AND DEFINITIONS

Digital Marketing: Is a marketing medium in which marketers utilize electronic media to introduce and promote their products in today's rapidly changing digital environment.

Fast-Fashion: Is a contemporary phenomenon in the fashion industry that mimics current luxury trends and offers the latest consumer styles at affordable prices in a short time period.

Globalization: Is the process whereby markets are rapidly evolving and businesses are expanding across the world into becoming global market leaders.

Mobile Marketing: Is a form of marketing that involves the use of mobile devices to directly communicate the value of products while offering personalized information to consumers.

Prosumer: Is an evolved customer engendered by social media, who serves as an active influencing agent in the dissemination of product information to new consumers.

Social Media Network: Is an extensive online ecosystem consisting of both traditional and digital media that connects people around the globe.

User-Generated Content: Is a communication platform where consumers share their first-hand experiences about products, either positive or negative, with a multitude of potential consumers.

This research was previously published in Digital Marketing Strategies for Fashion and Luxury Brands; pages 62-88, copyright year 2018 by Business Science Reference (an imprint of IGI Global).

Section 6
Managerial Impact

Chapter 78
Management and Marketing Practices of Social Media Firms

Abdulaziz Alshubaily
University of Liverpool, Jeddah, Saudi Arabia

ABSTRACT

This paper examines the key variances in application and strategy between different social media management strategies and its effective marketing. Social media firms have shown a great ability to control the stages in their product life cycles. These practices lead to managers in these firms overachieving on their respective KPIs and garnering industry attention. An analysis of social media management firms practice shows that high participatory decisions and intellectual and manual skills contributed to these organizations' successes. Other factors like introducing the 'Like' button and various innovations are observed to have improved consumers' attitudes towards the social media brand. Customer engagement and content enrichment are proven to be driving forces in how online consumers perceive the social media brand. Consumers are demonstrated to be the main means of continuous sustainability and growth.

INTRODUCTION

Management Theory and Practice Related to Social Media Firm

It is without a doubt that social media practices and content have taken the world by storm (Pan & Crotts, 2012). With the inception of social media, consumers are responding to its call by engaging in social network sites. Online customers are also taking part in microblogging, as well as indulging in the download of applications that can be used in their social lives by enhancement of sharing activities (Andzulis, Panagopoulos, & Rapp, 2012). The most interesting bit as presented by Divol, Edelman, and Sarrazin (2012) is that if Facebook users, a leading social networking site, constituted a country, they would, in fact, be considered to rank as the third in the number of "citizens" after the populous China and India. Application of social media in a vast number of sectors seems to be taking effect.

A majority of businesses are incorporating the social media tools in their marketing strategies among many other activities that the media is applied. Social media takes note of mobile and technology that

DOI: 10.4018/978-1-7998-9020-1.ch078

is web-based, to come up with platforms that are very interactive (Zhangand & Sarvary, 2011). Social media has generated what can be said to be a new communication landscape. The development of this communication landscape began many years back. Currently, the social media ecology constitutes a diverse pool of sites. These sites are different regarding their functionality, scope and focus (Kietzmann et al., 2011).

A recap of the functionality and focus of some of the social media sites is that some are meant for the general public, some are more of professional networking purposes, some are meant for sharing with a bias to photos and videos. For these social media firms to thrive as quite some of them have been noted to, certain theoretical models and frameworks are in place to ensure that they are properly managed (Kietzmann et al., 2011). It is critical to note that theorists have for a long time tried to identify the most suitable management tool when it comes to dealing with people. The theories in management that have been determined by the said theorists, as mentioned by Business.com (2014), are aimed at bringing out the best of the personnel in organizations. Managers may incorporate bits of the management theories that are in place; however, understanding of the application of the said theories is critical.

Social media is a very powerful tool and its management ought to be powerful as well. Management theories are aimed at enhancing the quality of the product and services that organizations offer as well as increasing the productivity of the said organizations as noted by Hawthorne (n. d.).One management theory that applies to the management of social media firms is the Y theory. This Management Theory is also referred to as the Human resources management theory. The factors that are attributed to this theory include the fact that people have the desire to work and that they have some sense of responsibilities and objectives that ought to meet. The theory further holds that these people would want to acquire success in what they do when they are aware of their place in the organizational structure (Dininni, 2011).

The theory Y is at times considered to be a motivational theory as noted by Dininni (2011). The theory views individuals as being independent and is quite the opposite from theory X which employs the rules of autocracy in the management of the organization. The application of theory Y managers, to their subjects promotes the active participation of other staff (See Figure 1 in the Appendix for the differences between theory X and Y). According to Lowe and Brown (2016), when looking at this kind of management theory, certain factors come in handy for managers to understand and which they ought to embrace in their day to day management activities. These factors include knowledge of intellectual perspectives, manual skills, and the interaction of the social aspects as well as skills in problem-solving. It is the embrace of such like factors, by the managers of social media firms that are attributed to the growth which is noted in these companies.

Social media companies that apply the above practices are bound to achieve outstanding performances not only for the company but at a personal level, as depicted by Lowe and Brown (2016). Management that is deemed to be participative is considered to be the best option for social media companies. This is critical when making participatory decisions that are aimed for the benefit of the company, especially with the incorporation of input from the competent task force who were molded by the effective leadership present in the respective company.

Identification of the components of theory Y is important, especially for the understanding of its application in the organizational setting, in this case, social media firms. According to Friesen (2014), some pointers are crucial to understanding the application of theory Y. Having a vision is critical where expectations for the future are noted. In this component, strategic planning may be applied in the bid to realize the vision of the company. Leadership that is effective is paramount where in this case; reduction in the gap between the management and the staff is advised. Thirdly, planning activities and decision-making ought to go hand in hand. Participative leadership is imperative to uphold in this sense.

Communication that is free of errors is crucial where honesty, simplicity, positivity and good listening skills are necessary. The control that is administered by the management ought to be reasonable where over-controlling instances are eliminated. Promotion of trust will facilitate the control that is administered to the employees. Recognition is the other component that is mandatory to emphasize and here, both formal and informal recognitions can be offered to the employees in the hunt to garner maximization in motivation.

After having noted the above factors that pertain to theory Y, and looking at the application of the theory in social media firms and further narrowing down to the most successful firms, it is evident that the theory is deeply rooted in these companies. For these businesses to thrive, the management practices have incorporated the components of the theory Y. The success that is noted in Facebook is attributed to the productivity of the employees who are in a position to work in a motivating environment that they are subjected. The employees have been part of the team that has churned out products and services that are gaining user popularity by the day and are as a result producing revenue for the company. Facebook, according to Wilson, Gosling and Graham (2012), is integrated with applications and websites in the range of millions a scenario that adds to the productivity of the company. The outcome of the integration is consumer traffic. These consumers are interested in the content available on the social site. The user traffic that is evident on Twitter and Facebook sites, for instance, are a clear depiction of the success of companies that are both very productive and fruitful.

METHODOLOGY

Social Media Firms in the Efficient Management of the Products Lifecycle

Using secondary sources and data, analysis was conducted to examine motivational, participational, operational and contextual factors to aid in the research.

Before looking at the management of the product's lifecycle, it is critical to note the stages that are present in any given product's lifecycle. It is notable that a product lifecycle consists of five stages which include; product development, introduction, growth, maturity and finally, the decline stage (Claessens, 2015). It is critical to note that not all stages of the product lifecycle apply to all products; the strategies that are employed in the lifecycle are what make the difference.

Social media products like applications and platforms are creating a buzz in the technology platform, a phenomenon that calls for product awareness, a critical function for the introductory phase of a lifecycle. Social media engagement is essential at this stage, and this has facilitated the effectiveness of the said social sites. YouTube, Facebook, blogs, and widgets have been noted to engage the consumers quite well. The customer traffic pointed out in these sites is a real testimony of their engagement ability.

Social media firms have been effective in the management of the growth and maturity stages of their PLC. The development of products and services that are new, by the companies dealing with social media have facilitated the amassing of a high number of users that are massive in numbers. These companies have as a result been able to grow with every developmental step that they make and by the time a product or service hits the decline stage, a new product is already introduced or modified which further increases the attention of their users. Social media companies have been able to record a high number of users because of the attitudes that they convey to the consumers. The attitudes expressed by these firms, to their customers, affect the consumer behavior. This information is covered in the section below.

Attitudes Towards the Consumer that the Social Media Companies Convey

As noted by Ioanăs, and Stoica (2014), the media has got a huge influence on the perception that its users have. The users can air their criticisms based on the information that is presented on the social media sites. Having an understanding of the consumer behavior on the online platform is critical given the statistics that is present concerning worldwide online users (Schivinski, & Dabrowski, 2016). The number of online consumers has been noted to be growing worldwide as mentioned by Schivinski, and Dabrowski, (2016), and this calls for the need for understanding consumer behavior as mentioned earlier.

Social network sites like YouTube, Facebook, and Twitter, provide avenues for promoting their brand awareness because of the products and services that they offer. These sites have visitors on a daily basis who reach to the tune of five million users, and this occurrence makes them the best shot when it comes to marketing. Social media communication has a potential effect on the consumer by the promotion of the following aspects; brand equity, brand attitude as well as the purchasing intention (Schivinski, & Dabrowski, 2016). It is essential to note at this juncture that social media communication has transformed the one-way communication that is traditional in nature. The communication that is promoted by social media is one that is said to be multidimensional and two-way (Schivinski, & Dabrowski, 2016).

Social media has been noted to influence consumer behavior by affecting the perception of the consumer. Provision of content and information that is deemed to be relevant is critical in this respect. Consumer participation in the social media is also likely to promote the perception of the customer. According to Naidoo (2011), to determine the influence that is present on a given brand, using social media, consideration must be offered to the content source, source authority, and the content.

Social media companies promote beliefs in their brands. The views that an individual may have about a product can be either positive or negative. Social media companies, attempt to influence the positive opinions of a consumer and mask the negative ones. Social media users, based on their beliefs will tend to be affected given the feelings that they hold. It is critical to note that some feelings that the consumer develops regarding a particular brand, product or service may be free from the beliefs that they hold, rather, the feelings may be attributed to other circumstances. After the customer is affected by either beliefs or other conditions, their intention to purchase will ensue from the developed brand attitude, as noted by (Schivinski, & Dabrowski, 2016).

The attitudes that social media companies convey are facilitated by factors like the promotion of consumer engagement, building of brand attitudes that are deemed to be very positive, as well as through customer relationship management enhancement as noted by Naidoo (2011). The means through which social media companies utilize the above factors distinguish the sites that are very popular. The section below will expound more on the above factors and thus explain why one social media version tends to be more popular compared to the others.

FINDINGS

The Reason Why One Version of Social Media may be More Popular or More Successful Than Others:

Research has proven that among the many social media sites that are available, Facebook tops the list. Facebook is an example of the social networking sites, which is a component of the larger social media. Other versions of social media include; microblogging sites, blogs, podcasts, forums, wikis, and content communities (Yudhokesumo, 2011). The success and popularity of social networking sites are subject to debate. Social networking sites are more popular, in as far as the number of users is concerned as well as the brand names that are present under the heading (Helmrich, 2016). This social networking site is noted to have active users that total over 1 billion, on the global platform. This platform is used to connect individuals in personal as well as in business perspectives. This site is noted to be very versatile, and it connects people in different aspects.

Multiple options are available on Facebook which facilitates its usage. Depending on the industry that an individual is noted to be part of, Facebook meets a majority of the needs. Facebook, as noted by Helmrich (2016), as compared to other social sites, tend to have low maintenance. The element of low maintenance is attributed to the difference that exists, regarding the fans of an individual, when one posts many or few updates in a day. In summary, Facebook has seen its success because the site is easy to use, has features that are very accessible and its name that is noted to be very memorable (Shah, 2016). It is also clear that Facebook's success is connoted to the fact that the site promotes both openness and honesty. The meaning of this is that people desire to be themselves and so Facebook comes in handy to offer a platform where people can, in fact, be themselves (Shah, 2016).

Facebook has grown tremendously since its inception, and is just but an example of a social networking site, a version of social media that is seen to have thrived globally. Some factors have been attributed to its growth in as far as popularity and success are concerned. These factors will be addressed in the section below.

Factors That Lead to the Success and Popularity of Social Networking Sites

As mentioned earlier, Facebook has grown over the years since it was introduced back in 2004 (Maina, 2016). The factors that have placed Facebook in its number one position in the area of the leading social media sites in the world are as follows:

Innovativeness and Smart Actions

Social networking sites are considered to be very innovative with a good example being Facebook. Facebook is one of the most innovative companies on the web which is noted to make very smart moves as far as product development is concerned. These smart moves are the ones that differentiate this site from other sites in social networking. Ever since the company's inception back in 2004, Facebook has introduced some innovative products that include the Facebook platform which boasts many apps that have gained the attention of the users in the global arena (See Figure 3 in the Appendix for review of Facebook). These Facebook apps prompted the inception of the Facebook Application store where the organization of information would be facilitated (Shah, 2016). The introduction of this display brought attention to Facebook which further brought its success.

"Like Button"

Facebook was one of the first social media sites that introduced it's famous "like button" (Shah, 2016). This button allowed users to enhance the power associated with social networking by the creation of impressions and other users enjoying the positive content that is displayed by others (Chou, & Edge, 2012). Other social networking sites followed suit with the incorporation of the "like button." Google was one of the companies that embraced the leadership of Facebook and it in fact gained in the number of people that visited the site on a daily basis. This service allowed Facebook to gain more visits by new users and within a short while, many visitors indulged in the now famous, "liking" trend.

Ability to Induce Positivity

Social networking sites have been noted to cause positive reactions among its users, and it is for this reason that they tend to be very successful (Mauri et al., 2011). Some social networking sites, like Facebook, have been noted to induce positive emotions on the users an occurrence that further promotes the discovery of creative and novel actions as well as the discovery of social bonds and ideas. The outcome of the above discoveries is the development of personal resources that are relevant to an individual for survival purposes (Mauri et al., 2011). It is this reason that prompts users to be hooked to a Social Networking site and such people will tend to be active on these sites.

DISCUSSION

The Most Valuable Resource for Social Media Firm Management

In social media firm management, the most important resource is the consumer. Some differences exist when looking at the traditional and social media spending (Weinberg & Pehlivan, 2011). The similarity, however, is that the spending places the consumer at the focal point of the activities of the firm. The management of a social media company, therefore, ought to address the issues that surround the customer. The term "social" in social media sheds light on the social aspect, and it is this component that brings in the perspective of the consumer. It is critical to understand that social media, as pointed out by Weinberg and Pehlivan (2011), is not a substitute for the traditional media, in the sense that social media can be used even with the incorporation of the traditional media perspectives.

A social approach is critical when dealing with consumers given the digital age that is currently in place. Social media can offer empowerment to consumers and thus allow them to garner influence which in turn creates a relationship that is enabling, between individuals and the respective organizations. The management of social media companies should. Therefore, address matters revolving around the consumers given that it is the consumer traffic that will ensure that these sites are successful and are popular at the end of the day. The management of these companies can promote their spending in this area by making sure that the following areas are addressed in their strategic planning procedures, engagement, conversation, human voice, sharing, collaboration and openness (Weinberg & Pehlivan, 2011) (See Figure

2 in the Appendix). In summary, control centers for social media will promote consumer evangelism which would further boost consumer traffic and which ensures success for a given social media site.

Sound management functionality in a social media firm will, therefore, look into the consumer resource in its management procedures, a phenomenon dubbed as customer relationship management. Companies ought to embrace this new form of strategy that shifts from managing customers, but instead, looks at the collaborations that can be done with the consumers. Getting closer to customers should be the priority of the management of social media firms if they are to offer to value to the consumers, which is tangible and as a result gain from the consumer's time, money, attention, information and endorsement (Heller Baird, & Parasnis, 2011).

Social Media Firms from USA and China and Their Effect on Customer Loyalty

It is critical to note that the US and China are part of the biggest consumers of social media with China topping the list of the said customers. The information presented below provides insights of the social media firms in China and the US.

According to the information presented by Olivier (2015), 91% of the people that use online facilities have active social media accounts. The amount spent on the internet on a daily basis, among the Chinese consumers is 46 minutes, and part of this time is spent navigating through eight popular brands where choices that pertain to marketing are made (Olivier, 2015). The choices are made regarding the recommendations that are placed on these social media sites. It is, therefore, imperative for marketers to increase their brand presence by being very active on the social media sites.

According to Olivier (2015), online discussions that the Chinese consumers indulge in, concerning product brands, are capable of directly affecting the businesses in question. Companies that market their brands online in China have resorted to standing out from others in the industry by being conversant with what consumers feel about products. The fast-changing consumer market in China requires the exploitations of five trends that are paramount for the success of businesses. Decision-making, social media, innovation, loyalty and setting of high expectations are part of the trends that are critical for businesses to exploit (Chan, Chen, & Ying, 2012). The patterns as mentioned earlier have the capability to enforce a marketing strategy that is deemed to be unique, promote a customer enabling environment as well as promote customer retention activities. Businesses that have the ability to see success in their endeavors are the ones that pursue the trends as presented above (Chan, Chen, & Ying, 2012).

Social media in the US on the other hand is well established and isone of the biggest markets in the Western world. According to Burkhalter, and Wood (2015), as of 2012, the number of adult online subscribers in the US was at 69%. Out of the 69%, Facebook was utilized by two-thirds of the proportion; LinkedIn was used by 20%, while 16% of the proportion self-reported to be using Twitter (Burkhalter, & Wood, 2015). Almost all age groups were noted to have used social networking sites in the US, at some points of their lives. The average age of consumers who utilize social media in the US is 40 years old (Burkhalter, & Wood, 2015). The American social media companies have gained popularity overseas, in particular with the presence of loyalty from these foreign groups (Burkhalter, & Wood, 2015).

CONSUMERS

Social media in China is influenced by word of mouth that spreads concerning brands that are marketed. Opinions from colleagues, family members and friends concerning products are treasured in China as noted by Chan, Chen, and Ying (2012). Other Chinese consumers made their marketing choices based on the information presented in social media by strangers as well. It is because of the online market in China that social media sites are noted to have multiple reviews and views on an annual basis with a good example being the Shanghai city guide referred to as the www.dianping.com. In the site as mentioned earlier, consumers rate both restaurants and merchants that are present in Chinese cities. The meaning of the above occurrence is that for companies to appeal to the Chinese markets, they ought to employ the usage of distribution channels that are aimed at delivering an experience that is consistent. With the consistency, the companies will have news concerning the compelling experiences they offer, spread by consumers in social media and this would, in turn, spark the development of the companies and in the case of poor reviews, such businesses can engage in continuous improvement techniques.

The majority of Chinese online market consumers tend to share their impressions concerning the products that they have used. Chinese consumers use social media sites as well as blogging sites for the purpose of gaining insights on products and services that are offered. SinaWeibo is an example of a microblogging site where consumer traffic is evident. The site is visited by more than half of Chinese internet users who follow brands that were referred to them by other consumers. Research has revealed that Chinese consumers believe that social media has promoted their engagement with popular brands. The users are also aware of the fact that their indulgent in social media has promoted the fact that they are aware of the providers of certain services and products which they were not aware. Their decision-making processes influence the consumers in the Chinese market, who use social media in their decision-making by the remarks indicated in the sites concerning products and services. For companies to reap full benefits from the services that they offer, in the Chinese market particularly, they ought to identify ways of engaging the Chinese consumers by social media usage. Interaction in the setting of social networks is critical in the Chinese market where consumers will view businesses that are active in social media as being favorable.

Customer experiences are essential in creating impressions. A negative customer experience is likely to undermine customer relationships. Undermining customer relations will tend to have an effect on customer loyalty. It is rather hard to maintain customer relationships, as mentioned by Chan, Chen, and Ying (2012), particularly in the Chinese market. The reason for this occurrence is because a good proportion of Chinese consumers report bad customer experiences, a good number of these clients post about the negative experiences that they have had. Chan, Chen, and Ying (2012), however, mentioned concerning the presence of customer loyalty programs that are available in China, which are aimed at combating adverse experiences that consumers face. The programs use mobile platforms as well as programs provided by both the internet service providers and the banks. Here, consumers are urged to maintain their service providers in the relevant industries.

These programs are seen to be fruitful in persuading consumers to observe their loyalty with their providers. The very presence of these programs shows that Chinese consumers are critical when it comes to impression and that a single ill experience can, in fact, go viral and thus affect the development of "culprit companies" associated with negative experiences. It was noted by Chan, Chen and Ying (2012) that customer loyalty for the Chinese consumers was more than financial incentives. Other factors played a critical role in customer loyalty and these include; CSR, communication that is both honest and truthful as well as the avenues for consumers to engage in activities that pertain to improvement in the design of products and services that are offered by companies. These factors ought to be addressed by companies that utilize social media in their business activities.

Chinese consumers expect service acquisition that is not barred by hassles. These consumers expect customer service speed, product knowledge by the provider as well as the ease in acquisition of information concerning a product or service. Companies in China, through social media, struggle to ensure that negative customer experience is avoided by providing the consumers with what they require. Businesses, as a result, become well-positioned for the provision of customer experience that is said to be holistic where an improvement in customer service is notable. Companies, therefore, distinguish themselves from competition that is available in the social media industry.

Consumers may be the source of innovation because they provide feedback on products and services that they find to be very innovative. They also portray their preferences and behavior regarding a particular product, and the outcome is that the information garnered can be used in innovation activities. Consumers in the Chinese markets are very adventurous and will, as a result, seek to identify new experiences that aid customers in the launching of new products and services. With the technology craze that has set roots in the Chinese social media market, the young, as well as the population that is connected, tends to engage in innovation programs that are technology based. The average age of the social media consumers in China are of the mean age of 28 years, and these consumers are well educated (Burkhalter, & Wood, 2015). The outcome is that innovation becomes promoted in the Chinese companies through social media.

The customers in the US that use social media do not rely on referrals like their Chinese consumers. They, in fact, are not swayed by social media to make purchases like their Chinese counterparts (Swift, 2014). The percentage of individuals who heed the opinion of their referrals in the US is at 38% compared to the Chinese counterparts who almost double the consumers in the US market, at 66% (Chiu, Ip, & Silverman, 2012). Social media in the US, among its customers, is not a large occurrence or phenomenon like it is in China (Chiu, Ip, & Silverman, 2012). On the contrary, the social media consumers in China provide feedback on innovative products, expect accessible services that are available through social media, and worry about impression creation, sharing impression by offering referrals (Chiu, Ip, & Silverman, 2012). This shows that the Chinese consumers consider social media to be a significant phenomenon in their lives (Chiu, Ip, & Silverman, 2012). Social media users in the US tend to prefer easy navigation tools showing that the social media culture in the US is less technical (Lee, 2014).

CONTENT

Social media in China is highly competitive in nature. This competitive market has sparked the inception of writers who are artificial (Chiu, Ip, & Silverman, 2012). The writers have the intention of identifying positive feedback for the companies that they work for, and at the same time, they use negative news to attack competitors and their products (Chiu, Ip, & Silverman, 2012). The development of microblogs was aimed at addressing such negative reports by competitors whose names have been at the point of being tarnished. Biased views concerning consumer behavior and preferences may be present in the cases where countermeasures aimed at addressing social media crises are not utilized very well (Chiu, Ip, & Silverman, 2012). The content that is mostly shared in China's social media is one that constitutes retweets, images, videos and jokes (Yu, Asur, & Huberman, 2011).

Social media in the US is competitive similarly to China. The content in Twitter revolves around current trends that are present in the current world as well as stories that pertain to news (Yu, Asur, & Huberman, 2011).

Social Media Platforms

Twitter, according to Burkhalter, and Wood (2015), is the leading microblogging site in the US. The other social media site that is very popular in the US is Facebook as noted by Burkhalter, and Wood (2015). These sites, in the bid to gain customer loyalty, employ the usage of the following characteristics; authenticity, accessibility, and interactivity (Burkhalter, & Wood, 2015). Social media tools in the US are less developed compared to the explosive development in China (Chiu, Ip, & Silverman, 2012). Twitter, for instance, set foot in the US eighteen months after social media content began to embed the users in China (Chiu, Ip, & Silverman, 2012).

Chinese social media does not have shared sites like Facebook, Twitter, and YouTube, instead, the sector boasts of local sites which have employed a strategy that is, in fact, winning the heart of the social media market in the country (Chan, Chen, & Ying, 2012). The social media in China is characterized by having the most active pool or rather, environment for consumers (Chiu, Ip, & Silverman, 2012). The social media scene in China began back in 1994, eighteen months before its adoption began in the US (Chiu, Ip, & Silverman, 2012). The explosive growth of sites Dianping (review site), blogging sites, Renren (site in social networking), SinaWeibo and Jiepang, over a span of almost two decades, is part of the reason why the Chinese social media market is unique.

China's social media platforms tend to be not only local, as earlier mentioned, but they are also fragmented as noted by Chiu, Ip, and Silverman, (2012). Platforms in social media and e-commerce have key players. These are as follows; in microblogging, there is the TencentWeibo and SinaWeibo (Chiu, Ip, & Silverman, 2012). In social networking, there is the Kaixin001 and Renren (Chiu, Ip, and Silverman, 2012). It is critical to note that these social media sites have differences in the areas of expertise, strengths, focus and priorities of the geographical perspectives (Chiu, Ip, & Silverman, 2012). The fragmentation present in China's social media enhances complexity in the sector which in turn requires expertise and resources for proper monitoring and development the key players and platforms in the industry (Chiu, Ip, & Silverman, 2012).

Management Practices and Theories from Social Media Firms that are Most Effective for the Industry Player

When narrowing down to the practicality of the social media companies, certain practices are adopted in the bid to garner strategies that provide winning results. The strategies that are employed have seen the success of social media companies in countries like China and the US. The management theories that are practiced in the social media companies facilitate the adoption of practices that ensure that they are successful. The adoption of theory Y has resulted in the productivity of employees who come up with creative materials that promote consumer engagement. The most successful companies in social media are known to have content that is authentic which in turn engage the customers. In their social media efforts, these firms embrace brand goals. Information regarding the management practices is as mentioned below.

Authenticity of Content as well as Flexibility

The incorporation of content authenticity in social media has set companies apart from their competitors, and as a result, seen companies enjoy success in their endeavors. In China, the launch of Clinique's drama series, Sufei's Diary, was met by success given that the product was marketed on a daily basis via a dedicated website. As part of the content of the drama was a storyline in skin care and products. The series was advertised in segments and could be viewed in monitors displayed on transport media like trains, buses, and planes. The outcome was that the product received multiple views that resulted in an increment in Clinique's online brand awareness compared to competitors who utilize traditional marketing approaches (Chiu, Ip, & Silverman, 2012).

QZone is a successful networking site in China which is noted to be attractive because of its flexibility. This site allows for content customization which allows the user to acquire new and original experiences for the consumers (Olivier, 2015).

WeChat, a social network site in China practices strategies that are involved in the provision of content that is unique, to its consumers. Customer loyalty and brand reputation of the site has seen a positive impact where tremendous growth has been promoted in the social site (Olivier, 2015).

Testing and Learning Approach

The list of examples of companies that have seen social media success is long, with an example of Dove China which employed the testing and learning approach. In this example, Dove China, in the bid to market beauty product lines among women, the company collaborated with a Chinese version of Ugly Betty dubbed as Ugly Wudi, in the effort to pass beauty messages to the target market. Blogs, initiatives, and chats (online) sparked an increment in the searches related to the product as well as blogs and usage of the Dove line of goods by the time the show was coming to an end of its first season. 44% of brand awareness was achieved among the target population with an increment in profitability from the usage of the Dove product lines (Chiu, Ip, & Silverman, 2012). The profitability was much higher as opposed to when the usage of television marketing media is applied.

CONCLUSION

Some businesses have employed this form of company approach in China. In this method, companies ensure consistency in the promotion of messages that pertain to quality, social responsibility, and community development, in the online platform as well as in the in the stores (Chiu, Ip, & Silverman, 2012). This technique has been applied by Starbucks in China as well as Durex. Durex, has, in fact, employed the usage of the services of SinaWeibo, where the marketing executives that are on standby monitoring the comments that are presented online and as a result respond by the incorporation of content which consumers will find to be funny. This approach is involved with the creation of an interactive platform which is aimed at gaining customer engagement, which further builds brand loyalty (Chiu, Ip, & Silverman, 2012).

SinaWeibo is a company that benefits from acquiring feedback from consumers. This site is concerned with customer engagement activities. From such engagement, the site has been able to grow to become one of the leading social media sites in China.

Twitter and Facebook, are the largest social media sites in the West, in particular among the young population. These social media consumers follow brands online, and they, as a result, end up spending a lot of time in the sites as mentioned earlier. Twitter is being utilized in Corporates for communication as well as for enhancing consumer engagement as noted by Burkhalter, and Wood (2015). Corporations are paying significant attention to the younger generation (Generation Y), even as they work to make sure that this generation is reached and as a result, promote brand engagement.

It would be appropriate action for a company to take on social media presences in different markets if they are multi-targeting consumers. Research has proved that the management practices of social media firms have been adopted into other industries to gain further penetration into the customer wallet by increasing brand awareness, loyalty, and spend. This indicated that the management practices of social media firms have stood their ground and should be assimilated by companies in other industries if they are to reach connect to and reach a larger audience on a more personal level.

REFERENCES

Andzulis, J. M., Panagopoulos, N. G., & Rapp, A. (2012). A review of social media and implications for the sales process. *Journal of Personal Selling & Sales Management, 32*(3), 305–316. doi:10.2753/PSS0885-3134320302

Burkhalter, J. N., & Wood, N. T. (2015). Maximizing commerce and marketing strategies through micro-blogging.

Business.com. (2014). Popular Management Theories Decoded: Learn the teachings of Max Weber, Elton Mayo, Frederick W. Taylor and more. Retrieved from http://www.business.com/management/popular-management-theories-decoded/

Chan, T. C., Chen, X., & Ying, D. (2012). Winning the hearts of the Chinese consumer Capitalizing on five trends to drive growth and high performance. *Accenture.com*. Retrieved from https://www.accenture.com/us-en/~/media/Accenture/Conversion-Assets/DotCom/Documents/Global/PDF/Strategy_3/Accenture-Winning-Hearts-Chinese-Consumer.pdf

Chiu, C., Ip, C., & Silverman, A. (2012). Understanding Social Media in China. *McKinsey.com*. Retrieved from http://www.mckinsey.com/business-functions/marketing-and-sales/our-insights/understanding-social-media-in-china

Chou, H. T. G., & Edge, N. (2012). They are happier and having better lives than I am: The impact of using Facebook on perceptions of others lives. *Cyberpsychology, Behavior, and Social Networking, 15*(2), 117–121. doi:10.1089/cyber.2011.0324 PMID:22165917

Claessens, M. (2015). Product Life Cycle Stages (PLC) – Managing the Product Life Cycle. *Marketing-Insider*. Retrieved from http://marketing-insider.eu/product-life-cycle-stages/

Dininni, J. (2011). Human Relations Management Theory: Using human relations theory to motivate employees to excellence. *Business.com*. Retrieved from http://www.business.com/management-theory/human-relations-management-theory/

Divol, R., Edelman, D., & Sarrazin, H. (2012). Demystifying Social Media. *McKinsey.com*. Retrieved from http://www.mckinsey.com/business-functions/marketing-and-sales/our-insights/demystifying-social-media

Friesen, W. (2015). Are You a Theory X or a Theory Y Leader? Retrieved from http://www.inplantgraphics.com/article/are-you-theory-x-theory-y-leader/

Hawthorne, M. (n. d.). Management Theories & Concepts at the Workplace. *Chron.com*. Retrieved from http://smallbusiness.chron.com/management-theories-concepts-workplace-17693.html

Heller Baird, C., & Parasnis, G. (2011). From social media to social customer relationship management. *Strategy and Leadership*, *39*(5), 30–37. doi:10.1108/10878571111161507

Helmrich, B. (2016). Social Media for Business: 2016 Marketer's Guide. Retrieved from http://www.businessnewsdaily.com/7832-social-media-for-business.html

Ioanăs, E., & Stoica, I. (2014). Social media and its impact on consumers' behavior. *International Journal of Economic Practices and Theories*, *4*(2), 295–303.

Kietzmann, J. H., Hermkens, K., McCarthy, I. P., & Silvestre, B. S. (2011). Social media? Get serious! Understanding the functional building blocks of social media. *Business Horizons*, *54*(3), 241–251. doi:10.1016/j.bushor.2011.01.005

Lee, I. (2014). Integrating social media into business practice, applications, management, and models.

Lowe, G. F., & Brown, C. (2016). Managing media firms and industries: What's so special about media management?

Maina, A. (2016). 20 Popular Social Media Sites Right Now. *SmallBizTrends*. Retrieved from https://smallbiztrends.com/2016/05/popular-social-media-sites.html

Mauri, M., Cipresso, P., Balgera, A., Villamira, M., & Riva, G. (2011). Why is Facebook so successful? Psychophysiological measures describe a core flow state while using Facebook. *Cyberpsychology, Behavior, and Social Networking*, *14*(12), 723–731. doi:10.1089/cyber.2010.0377 PMID:21879884

Naidoo, T. (2011). The effectiveness of advertising through the social media in Gauteng/Naidoo. [Doctoral dissertation]. North-West University.

Olivier. (2015). Chinese users are more likely to purchase products recommended by other social networks users. *MarketingtoChina*. Retrieved from http://marketingtochina.com/promote-brand-social-media-china-2/

Pan, B., & Crotts, J. (2012). Theoretical models of social media, marketing implications, and future research directions. In M. Sigala, E. Christou, & U. Gretzel (Eds.), *Social Media in Travel, Tourism, and Hospitality: Theory, Practice, and Cases* (pp. 73–86). Surrey, UK: Ashgate.

Schivinski, B., & Dabrowski, D. (2016). The effect of social media communication on consumer perceptions of brands. *Journal of Marketing Communications*, *22*(2), 189–214. doi:10.1080/13527266.2013.871323

Shah, S. (2016). The history of social networking. *DigitalTrends.com*. Retrieved from http://www.digitaltrends.com/features/the-history-of-social-networking/

Swift, A. (2014). Americans Say Social Media Have Little Sway on Purchases. *Gallup*. Retrieved from http://www.gallup.com/poll/171785/americans-say-social-media-little-effect-buying-decisions.aspx

Weinberg, B. D., & Pehlivan, E. (2011). Social spending: Managing the social media mix. *Business Horizons*, *54*(3), 275–282. doi:10.1016/j.bushor.2011.01.008

Wilson, R. E., Gosling, S. D., & Graham, L. T. (2012). A review of Facebook research in the social sciences. *Perspectives on Psychological Science*, *7*(3), 203–220. doi:10.1177/1745691612442904 PMID:26168459

Yu, L., Asur, S., & Huberman, B. A. (2011). What trends in Chinese social media. arXiv:1107.3522

Yudhokesumo, A. (2011). Social Network Advertising: Investigating what factors affect the change of consumers' attitudes. Retrieved from http://dare.uva.nl/cgi/arno/show.cgi?fid=447847

Zhang, K., & Sarvary, M. (2011). Social media competition: Differentiation with user generated content. *Marketing Science*.

This research was previously published in the International Journal of Customer Relationship Marketing and Management (IJCRMM), 8(2); pages 45-59, copyright year 2017 by IGI Publishing (an imprint of IGI Global).

APPENDIX

Figure 1. Comparison between Theory X and Theory Y

Comparison between Theory X and Theory Y

Theory X	Theory Y
1. Inhernet dislike for work.	Work is natural like rest or play.
2. Unambitious and prefer to be directed by others.	Ambitious and capable of directing their own behaviour.
3. Avoid responsibility.	Accept and seek responsibility under proper conditions.
4. Lack creativity and resist change.	Creativity widely spread.
5. Focus on lower-level (physiological and safety) needs to motivate workers.	Both lower-level and higher-order needs like social, esteem and self-actualisation are sources of motivation.
6. External control and close supervision required to achieve organisational objectives.	Self-direction and self-control.
7. Centralisation of authority and autocratic leadership.	Decentralisation and participation in decision-making. Democratic leadership.
8. People lack self-motivation.	People are self-motivated.

Source Lowe and Brown (2016)

Figure 2. Social process for media spending

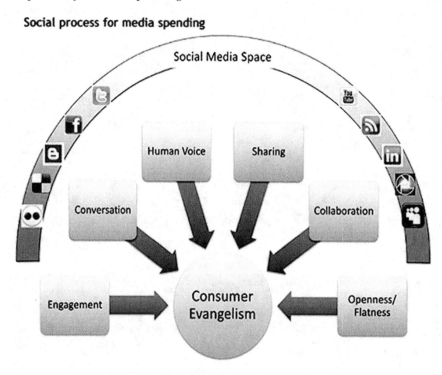

Source: Shah (2016)

Figure 3. Facebook users and articles: cumulative totals by year

A Review of Facebook

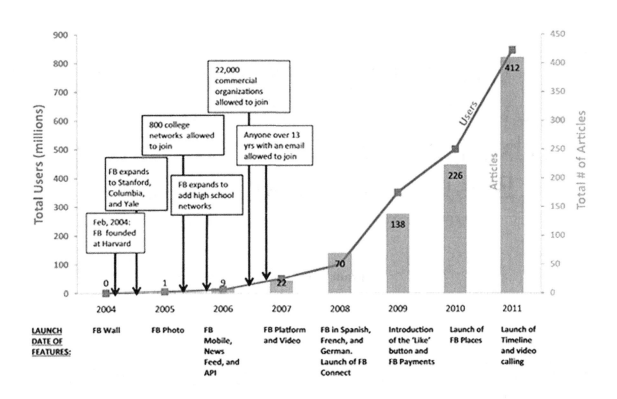

Source: Weinberg and Pehlivan, 2011

Chapter 79
Exploring Determinants of Knowledge Sharing and the Role of Social Media in Business Organizations:
Overview and New Direction

Francesca Di Virgilio
University of Molise, Italy

ABSTRACT

Knowledge sharing is one of the greatest challenges for a business organization. Organizations not only need to focus on innovation of new products and services, but also to pay specific attention to effective knowledge sharing which is of vital importance to their success. In this context, social media have become increasingly popular. They have a profound impact on personal relationships, enable individuals to contribute to a number of issues and generate new possibilities and challenges in order to facilitate knowledge sharing. However, scarce attention has been devoted so far to the theme of social media security and its effects on behavioral intention in relation to knowledge sharing. As a response to this challenge, this chapter illustrates a research roadmap of knowledge sharing which includes important collective variables. This study aims at highlighting a new direction for the evaluation of social media as a tool for knowledge sharing in business organizations. Finally, it concludes with the discussion of several open issues and cutting-edge challenges.

INTRODUCTION

The rising popularity and the recent development of knowledge management are considered to be the result of the organization's needs to obtain a competitive edge and strategic differentiation, in the face of globalization and of the explosion of media and information phenomena. Industrially developed coun-

DOI: 10.4018/978-1-7998-9020-1.ch079

tries claim that the third era of development has not been recently induced by agriculture or industry, but by information and knowledge (Gaál et al. 2015; Usman, & Oyefolahan, 2014; Yassin, et al. 2013).

This is an era of rapid change and uncertainty, characterized by both the increasing importance of knowledge and knowledge management as well as a wide use of new information technologies which can, potentially, change radically the way organizations work. As it has already been stated, the Internet has been the single most significant technological development in the last 20 years. It allows individuals to connect, collaborate and share knowledge, information, documents, photos, videos, etc. continuously with anyone in any place around the world. As several authors (Gaál et al. 2015; Usman, & Oyefolahan, 2014; Yassin, et al. 2013) have noticed, second generation web-based technologies are increasingly becoming popular in the managerial context.

This phenomenon is emphasized by the dramatic development of social media that constitute a meaningful example of users' involvement in knowledge dissemination and in collaborative content creation. In particular, new web technologies enable people to engage and to share information all over the world and across different platforms through the use of multiple modalities for interaction and contribution (Eijkman, 2011). While relying on the same knowledge framework (Dawson, 2007; Vuori & Okkonen, 2012), these technologies support and encourage collaborative writing (e.g., Wikis), content sharing (e.g., text, video, and images), social networking (e.g., Google+, LinkedIn, Facebook, Twitter), training (e.g. webinar) social bookmarking (e.g. ratings, tagging), and syndication (e.g., web feeds: RSS, Atom) (Dawson, 2008).

More recently, as organizations have recognized the power and purpose of these tools, they have begun incorporating social media into their business processes (Gaál et al., 2014). However, with increased collaboration and communication, there are cyber security risks that a company may monitor and/or face with new technologies, especially with social media (Zhang & Gupta, 2016). Given the numerous cases of data interception, information fraudulence, privacy spying, and copyright infringement from disorganized social organizational forms and non-friendly participation bodies that have been reported and discussed over the last few years, it is now even more crucial that organizations address this fundamental issue.

The first part of this chapter aims to present an overview of previous studies conducted on knowledge and knowledge sharing. In analyzing the literature it becomes evident that there is a research gap between the importance of social media tools as a source of knowledge sharing and the role of security as a level of analysis in knowledge sharing mechanisms. The second part of this chapter develops a research roadmap of knowledge sharing which includes important collective variables of organizational factors: individuals, groups, organizational culture, and technological factors as security, to determine whether they influence users in organizations or institutions to share knowledge via social media. Finally, this study discusses the role of social media tools in knowledge sharing in relation to our roadmap.

Specifically, the present study aims to introduce a new framework which may serve both as a tool for enhancing the understanding of knowledge sharing mechanisms in business organizations and also more generally as a useful guide for future research on knowledge and social media. This study could also be further elaborated, as it would be interesting to make a comparison between knowledge sharing practices and usage of social media across different countries. The content discussed herein attempts to establish the building block toward the development of a theory of knowledge sharing and usage of social media tools. Conclusive comments and managerial implications, as well as new directions for future research, are presented in the final part of this chapter.

BACKGROUND

Knowledge Background

The term "knowledge" is one which has caused confusion in knowledge management research. Within this field, it has acquired a variety of meanings that describe a particular piece or process in the scope of knowledge (Alavi & Leidner, 2001; Grant, 1996; Lehner & Maier, 2000; Stankosky & Baldanza, 2001; Weick, 1995). Drawing from prior studies, we distinguish knowledge from data and information and see it as a "fluid mix of framed experience, values, contextual information and expert insight that provide[s] a framework for evaluation and incorporating new experiences and information" (Davenport & Prusak, 1998, p. 5).

The knowledge process acts on information in order to create new information that allows for greater possibilities to fulfill old or possibly new organizational needs (Gaál et al. 2015; Usman, & Oyefolahan, 2014; Yassin, et al. 2013). Moreover, according to Grover and Davenport (2001), many cycles of generation, codification, and transfer are concurrently occurring in businesses.

To be successful, firms must not only exploit their existing knowledge but must also invest heavily in the exploration of new knowledge in order to determine future strategies and obtain competitive advantages (Sambamurthy et al., 2003).

As I have noted above, knowledge is becoming a strategically important resource and a powerful driver of organizational performance (Yesil & Dereli, 2013). Either located in the minds of the individuals (tacit knowledge) (Polányi, 1966), or embedded in organizational routines and norms, or even codified in technological devices (explicit knowledge) (Nonaka & Takeuchi, 1995), knowledge enables the development of new competencies (Choo, 1998). Successful companies are those that consistently create new knowledge, disseminate this knowledge throughout the organization, and embody it in technologies, products and services (Gottschalk, 2007; Gaál et al., 2008)..

A major concern for researchers and practitioners is to understand how knowledge flow can be facilitated to gain positive results on the organizational level in terms of performance, innovativeness and competitive advantage. For the last few years, the knowledge governance approach has been emerging to address these issues. But a further question needs to be posed: can knowledge be conceived as existing at multiple (individual, group, intra-organizational and inter-organizational relationships) levels?

Significantly, after having recognized the strategic importance of organizational knowledge at multiple levels, a wide range of firms has implemented various knowledge management initiatives. In most studies, the main attention has focused on the knowledge management system architecture, on the building process and on the mechanism for agent-based knowledge sharing. For example, Liu and colleagues (2010) presented a knowledge sharing community model and adopted an agent-based solution to perform the functions of knowledge sharing in virtual enterprises. However, overall, empirical research on knowledge management systems is still limited.

Therefore, there is growing interest of among both researchers and practitioners to understand processes, antecedents, and results of employees' knowledge sharing within organizations. In the following section, I argue for a frame to describe the content of knowledge sharing in the literature review.

MAIN FOCUS OF THE CHAPTER

Knowledge Sharing

Sharing occurs commonly among people, but knowledge sharing within an organization is a complex and complicated issue. Knowledge sharing is the process by which individuals' knowledge is converted into a form that can be understood and used by other individuals (Ipe, 2003). Knowledge sharing refers to the task of helping others through knowledge, and to collaborate with others to solve problems, develop new ideas, or implement processes (Cummings, 2004). The definition implies that knowledge sharing is seen as the willingness act whereby knowledge is capable of being used again or repeatedly in the course of its transfer from one party to another (Lee & Al-Hawamdeh, 2002). Similarly, knowledge sharing is a routine activity that entails guiding individuals or audience to adopt a specific way of thinking and reasoning. It also requires understanding and consideration of the individuals' problem situation (McDermott, 1999; Wang & Noe, 2010).

Knowledge sharing is a key asset to almost all organizations (Chen, et al., 2009; Yu, et al., 2009). It is also a multilevel phenomenon (Foss, 2007), and in order to find out how managerial practices facilitate sharing to get organizational level results, it is essential to identify what kind of knowledge sharing behaviors influence positively organizational performance, also what motivates individuals to share knowledge in a particular way, and finally, how organizations can facilitate that motivation and enable individual sharing behavior (Foss, et al., 2010). Furthermore, in several studies, the differences between various types of knowledge sharing were found (i.e. Teng & Song 2011; van den Hooff & de Ridder, 2004).

Knowledge sharing is understood nowadays as a dynamic social process (Von Krogh, 2011) through which knowledge possessed by one person is translated into a form that can be understood, absorbed and used by another (Ipe 2003). This definition shows that in the process of knowledge sharing there are two types of behavior, namely donating and receiving. Consequently, the success of knowledge sharing is achieved when the knowledge receiver internalizes a piece of knowledge (has a better understanding of the problem or the situation) and is able to use it in the future. This indicates that knowledge sharing is not just passing on some information from one person to another, but it is rather giving the information with some context or explanation. Knowledge sharing is a highly diversified process of interaction (direct and indirect) between the knowledge donor and knowledge receiver – that influences the success of the sharing process. As an example, Haas and Hansen (2007) proved that the behavior of the knowledge donator can hinder the performance of the knowledge recipient. Moreover, Foss and colleagues (2009) found that a reward system influences negatively donating knowledge and positively collecting knowledge. Durmusoglu and colleagues (2013) also identified the different influence of culture and rewards on the behavior of a person that is sharing knowledge, and of a person that is receiving knowledge.

Teng and Song (2011) distinguished two types of knowledge sharing looking from the perspective of a knowledge donator and identified diverse reasons of for sharing, for instance whether sharing is solicited by the receiver (on request) or if it is instead the voluntary decision of the donator. They found that different work unit related factors influence each type of sharing.

Cummings and Teng (2006) differentiated four characteristics of knowledge sharing that influence knowledge internalization and usage of knowledge: source, recipient, relational and environmental. While relational and environmental contexts create opportunities for knowledge sharing; the source, recipient and knowledge context are the key elements of the sharing process and they form what the process looks like.

Several previous studies have shown that both knowledge-sharing types have different antecedents, for example rewards (Hau et al. 2013; Cabrera, et al. 2006; Reychav & Weisberg 2009), and different outcomes (Haas & Hansen 2007) deriving from different theoretical perspectives (i.e. theory of planned behavior/theory of reasoned action; motivation-opportunity-ability framework; social exchange theory, economic exchange theory; social interdependence theory, agency theory), of which the results in many areas are inconsistent. The reward system could be an example, as there is no consensus whether rewards facilitate or hinder sharing (Rudawska, 2015; Witherspoon, 2013).

Bartol and Srivastava (2002) focused on the manner of sharing knowledge proposing four knowledge sharing mechanisms: contribution to databases, informal interactions, formal interactions and communities of practice. Their approach was operationalized by Yi (2009) who proposed a knowledge sharing behavior measure. In this chapter, we draw from the literature which has found several factors that influence knowledge sharing activities (Lin, 2007). Besides personal and organizational factors, researchers have identified the role of the technological factors as the influencing factor in knowledge sharing (e.g., Lin, 2007; Paroutis & Al Saleh, 2009; Wahlroos, 2010; Rehman, et al., 2011; Gaál et al. 2015; Usman, & Oyefolahan, 2014; Yassin, et al. 2013). .

Consequently, individual, group, organizational culture and technological factors are the starting point when investigating knowledge sharing using web technologies (Lin, 2007; Paroutis & Al Saleh, 2009; Wahlroos, 2010; Cabrera & Cabrera, 2002). By giving an account of individual and group characteristics, the theories outlined in this chapter serve as the foundation for developing a new research model. Figure 1 illustrates the research roadmap.

Figure 1. Knowledge Sharing Roadmap

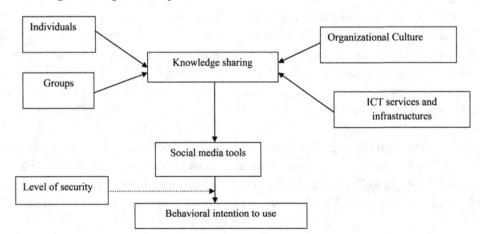

ORGANIZATIONAL FACTORS DETERMINING KNOWLEDGE SHARING

Individuals

Literature indicates that knowledge sharing depends on individual factors (Cummings & Teng 2006; Teng & Song, 2011; Berends et al., 2011; Berends et al., 2006), such as beliefs, experience, values, motivation (Lin, 2007), as well as expectations, perceptions, attitudes and mindset towards knowledge sharing (Volady, 2013). As Van den Hooff, Elving, Meeuwsen, and Dumoulin (2003) show, knowledge sharing also relies on communication skills comprising both verbal and written practices (Riege, 2005). Moreover, Volady (2013) and Wangpipatwong (2009) claim that an individual's ability to share or willingness to share positively influence the knowledge sharing process. In other words, persons who have enough confidence in their efficacy to share valuable knowledge have greater chances to achieve their goals as well as to experience a higher level of engagement in knowledge sharing (Wang & Noe, 2010). A study by Wahlroos (2010) provides relevant research findings on the role of individual factors (costs and benefits) in the use of social media as a form of organizational knowledge sharing. It was found that the knowledge sharing process is dominated by the intrinsic factors of the employees, rather than by the extrinsic factors. Although the impact of costs is not discussed in her study, the outcome of the research shows that an effective and beneficial use of social media has a significant influence on individual factors.Other studies explain that knowledge sharing takes place in different contexts. For example, Ipe (2003) differentiates purposive and relational learning channels in relation to the conceptual framework of individual knowledge sharing. The former provide an individual with a structured environment for knowledge sharing by giving relevant tools, while the knowledge is explicit in nature. The latter are based on personal contact and relationship between the sharing actors (Ipe 2003). Sometimes the personalized, direct sharing is needed in order to gain knowledge on where and how to retrieve information and knowledge from a non-human knowledge repository.

Groups

The second dimension concerns groups or units as actors engaged in knowledge sharing (Yi, 2009). The most common definition of a group is "a collection of two or more interacting individuals with a stable pattern of relationships between them who share common goals and who perceive themselves as being a group" (Davenport, 1999, p. 71-78). This definition can be applied also to group knowledge conceived as two or more persons in social interaction who share common goals and information. The literature on small groups has shown that the knowledge possessed by group members varies according to the dimensions of the type of knowledge/ability (Jones, 1974; Kennedy, 1971), as well as according to the level of knowledge/ability (Tziner & Eden, 1985), and to the distribution of knowledge (Liang, 1994). Consistent with this argument, Stasser and colleagues (1989) found that broadly distributed or shared information is more likely to be retrieved by the group than unshared information. They further found that as a piece of information was is distributed among more individuals within the group, the retrieval of this information becomes more probable and thus facilitates group decision-making; when instead information is held by multiple members, not only more people within the group possess the information, but group members who possess this information may also provide retrieval cues to one another in order to aid the introduction of the knowledge and the decision making (Okhuysen & Eisenhardt, 2002; Moreland et al., 1997; Liang et al., 1995; Larson et al. 1994; Wegner, 1986).Shared conceptualization of other group members allows to pool information more effectively and to make better group decisions(Gruenfled et al., 1996; Stasser et al., 1995). Conversely, when group members have non-overlapping information, group members have difficulty discussing or sharing that knowledge; and, as a result, the group does not reach the optimal decision (Stasser & Titus, 1987; Stasser & Stewart, 1992). This sharing is based on the direct interaction and communication between the knowledge donor and receiver (personalized sharing), but this interaction is not totally easy-going (rather formal) because it is contrived by a leader, supervisor or manager, who creates the opportunity for that interaction – time, place, subject, and participants.

When information is held by multiple members, not only more people within the group possess the information, but group members who possess the information may also provide retrieval cues to one another in order to aid the introduction of the knowledge and decision making (Bagozzi, 2000; West, Garrod & Carletta, 1997). In this scenario groups bring assets, adding knowledge and creativity, which increases the understanding and the acceptance of ideas (Tosi, et al., 2000). Numerous studies have demonstrated the benefits for groups that engage in information sharing and communication within the group (Keller & Staelin, 1987; Gruenfeld, et al.1996; Rulke & Galaskiewicz, 2000). Emphasis on workgroup to share knowledge has been brought forward in contexts where individuals come together in a particular platform and on a regular basis to share their experience and expertise in order to achieve a common goal (Schermerhorn, et al., 1994).

Though successful groups take advantage of the perspectives, talents, and ideas of different members, a well-designed group can also create a common understanding of the web 2.0 context through shared knowledge. In the next section, this study discusses the organizational culture and technology factors in business organizations that can help to explain the role of social media tools in knowledge sharing.

ORGANIZATIONAL CULTURE AND MANAGERIAL IMPLICATIONS

As observed by previous researchers, organizational factors play a significant role in knowledge sharing (Riege, 2005; Yassin, et al., 2013). According to Wahlroos (2010), in the context of knowledge sharing, knowledge culture is one of the organizational factors that have attracted the attention of some researchers due to the changes in the nature of knowledge generation, production, and distribution in business organizations.

Culture is usually defined as a social or normative "glue" that holds an organization together (Siehl & Martin, 1981; Tichy, 1982). It expresses the values or social ideals and beliefs that organization members come to share (Louis, 1980; Siehl & Martin, 1981). Culture, conceived as shared key values and beliefs, fulfills several important functions. First, it conveys a sense of identity for organization members (Deal & Kennedy, 1982; Peters and Waterman, 1982). Second, it facilitates the generation of commitment to something larger than the self (Schall, 1981; Siehl & Martin, 1981; Peters & Waterman, 1982). Third, culture enhances social system stability (Louis, 1980; Kreps, 1981). Fourth, culture serves as a sense-making device that can guide and shape behavior (Louis, 1980; Meyer, 1981; Pfeffer, 1981; Siehl & Martin, 1981). This is only a sampling of the research on the various dimensions of organizational culture. As the number of studies increases, however, there is some convergence among them the findings tend to converge.

Schein (1985, p. 9) describes organizational culture as the pattern of basic assumptions that a given group has invented, discovered, or developed in learning to cope with its problems of external adaptation and internal integration, and that have worked well enough to be considered valid, and, therefore, to be taught to new members as the correct way to perceive, think, and feel in relation to these problems. It is a perspective for understanding what is occurring in an organization and "refers to a collection of theories that attempt to explain and predict how organizations and the people in them act in different circumstances" (Ott, 1989, p. 32). This theory was developed in response to researchers feeling that the more conventional structural and systematic perspectives of organizations did not include a human factor that acknowledged life within organizations.

To implement a culture of knowledge sharing within an organization, leadership or management play an important role because the responsibility lies not only on workers, but above all on the senior managers who need to create an environment that encourages the sharing of knowledge. Organizational culture involves feedback and valuable contributions and participation from colleagues and the level of collaboration in and across business units; while managerial implications cover the responsibility of providing sufficient training, valuing contributions, giving positive feedback, allowing participation and supplying organizational guidelines for using social media tools (Wahlroos, 2010).

In this study, Information communication technologies (ICT) services and infrastructures serve as facilitators that encourage and support knowledge sharing (Riege, 2005) because they are related to the knowledge management technology used in the sharing activity (Volady, 2013; Lin, 2007).

SOCIAL MEDIA TECHNOLOGIES AND KNOWLEDGE SHARING

The term "Web 2.0" was coined by O'Reilly (2005), and it refers to technologies that allow individuals to interact and share information, allowing to build networks based on mutual personal or professional interest. Web 2.0 facilitates social networking, and therefore is also referred to as the social media.

Social media have a variety of broad definitions, such as "collaborative online applications and technologies which enable and encourage participation, conversation, openness, creation and socialization amongst a community of users" (Bowley, 2009, p.15), web-based tools and practices enabling participation and collaboration based on individuals' activities (Storey et al., 2010). Surowiecki (2005) argued that social media is to make use of the "wisdom of the crowd". Groups of people are better at problem-solving and at fostering decision-making than the individuals alone. New ways of inspiring and exploiting knowledge sharing are forcing organizations to expand their knowledge sharing technologies and practices (Mentzas et al., 2007).

These technologies – blogs (like Blogger), video sharing (like YouTube), presentation sharing (like SlideShare), social networking service (like Facebook, LinkedIn), instant messaging service (like Skype) and groupware (like Google Docs) – foster a more socially connected platform (Anderson, 2007).

Several studies (Vuori, 2011; Jalonen, 2014; Bonson &Flores, 2011) explore how and to what extent social media support communication (social media provide new tools to share, store and publish contents, discuss and express opinions and influences); enhance collaboration (social media enable collective content creation and editing without location and time constraints), aid connection (social media offer new ways of networking with other people, socializing within the community), enable completion (social media tools are used to complete content by describing, adding or filtering information, tagging contents, and showing a connection between contents or mixing and matching contents deriving from separate online environments) and provide a combination of pre-existing web services that allow a certain user within a platform to use another application, in a specific window, without the need to leave the initial website. Tab.1 includes the different purposes of social media tools.

Table 1. Five C. (Jalonen, 2014)

Five C	Technologies	Tools
Communication	Blogs	Blogger
	microblogs	Twitter
	Video sharing	YouTube
	Presentation sharing	Slide Share
	Instant messaging service	Skype
Collaboration	Wikis	Wikipedia
	Groupware/shared workspaces	Google Docs
Connecting	Social networking services	Facebook LinkedIn
Completing	Visual bookmarking tool	Pinterest
	News aggregator	Digg
Combining	Mash-ups	Google Maps

Several research studies have been conducted to investigate the use of social media and Web 2.0 for sharing knowledge in the workplace. Paroutis and Saleh (2009) identified the key determinants of knowledge sharing and collaboration using Web 2.0 technologies within a large multinational enterprise by exploring the reasons for and barriers to employees' active participation across the various platforms. Using insights from both Web 2.0 users and non-users, the following four key determinants were identified: history, outcome expectations, perceived organizational support and trust. Dumbrell and Steele (2014) presented an informal knowledge management framework based on the system capabilities of social media technologies as well as the requirements of older adult users. The system capabilities distinct from social media technologies are the following: public peer-to-peer sharing, content evaluation amongst peers, and the "push" nature of these systems. Behringer and Sassenberg (2015) studied the relation between the importance of knowledge exchange, deficits in knowledge exchange, perceived usefulness of social media for knowledge exchange, as well as social media experience on the one hand and the intention to use knowledge exchange technology on the other. The results showed that the interplay between these criteria jointly affected the intention to apply social media for knowledge exchange after their implementation.

Another study (Sigalaa & Chalkiti, 2015) investigated the relation between social media use and employee creativity by adopting a knowledge management approach in order to consider the influence of social networks and interactions on individuals' creativity. Their findings highlighted the need to shift focus from identifying and managing creative individuals (micro level) and/or organizational contexts (macro level) to creating and managing creative social networks (meso level). The use of social media for externalizing, disseminating and discussing information with others within various social networks as well as for combining and generating shared (new) knowledge can further trigger, enrich and expand the employees' individual cognitive abilities and provide them with stimuli for generating and (co)-creating more and newer ideas/knowledge.

Social Media Security and User Behavior in Business Organizations

As a form of presentation and typical application of Web 2.0 technology, (mobile) social media have been constituted by the relations between different kinds of agents (individuals, groups, organizations, institutions) with the aids of modern (mobile) Internet technology and platforms. As the Internet has evolved into a more social and communicative venue more undesirable security and privacy risk issues have emerged. In particular, the concerns related to ethical issues such as participant knowledge and consent, data privacy, security, confidentiality, integrity of data and availability of Internet platforms are persisting in social media ecosystems. Further, considering the emergence of trust and cyber risk issues coupled with the proliferation of social media users, as well as their various identifications, roles, groups and corresponding behaviors, the investigation of social media security and vulnerability has become more sophisticated and challenging than ever before. With the ever-increasing craze of mobile tools and apps over the past few years, it has become important for business organizations to have clear social media policy best practices in order to both safely maintain a credible and lasting social profile (Zhang, 2015) and mitigate cyber risks.

Summarily speaking, the available studies on social media technology mainly use traditional security techniques such as cryptography and image processing methods to address problems related to partial security, privacy protection, and copyright protection. Most studies are grounded in social media analysis, searching, exploration, assessment, and sentiment analysis on the basis of machine learning and deep learning.

In this section, an overview of the most prominent cyber attack types directly affecting the intention to engage in knowledge sharing behaviors will be briefly presented (Zhang, & Gupta, 2016; Joshi & Kuo, 2011; Cutillo et al. 2010).

Identity Theft

Identity thefts via social media takes numerous forms. Some of the more common schemes include creating a fictitious social media account. Here, the criminal defendant is able to use a victim's social media site to learn enough personal information with the intent to commit fraudulent activities or cause a reputational damage.

Spam Attack

Email spam, also known as junk email, is unsolicited bulk messages sent through email. Recipients of spam often have had their email addresses obtained by spambots, which are automated programs that crawl the internet looking for email addresses. Spammers use spambots to create email distribution lists. A spammer typically sends an email to millions of email addresses, with the expectation that only a small number will respond or interact with the message. The spam emails sent in bulk cause network congestion and the cost of sending emails falls mostly upon the service providers and sometimes on the user.

Malware Attacks

They are becoming very common among social networking sites. The attackers send malware injected scripts to the legitimate user. On clicking the malicious URL a malware might be installed on the devices or can lead to a fake website which attempts to steal personal information from the target user.

Sybil Attacks

It is an attack wherein a reputation system is subverted by forging identities in peer-to-peer networks. It can be used for the distribution of junk information or even malware over the network.

Social Phishing

Social phishing is the attempt to obtain sensitive information such as usernames, passwords, and credit card details (and, indirectly, money), often for malicious reasons, by disguising as a trustworthy entity in an electronic communication.

Impersonation

Here, the aim of the attacker is to create a fake profile in order to successfully impersonate a real-world person. This attack highly depends on the authentication techniques used for registering new accounts.

Domain Name Hijacking

Domain name hijacking is when someone changes registration data of a domain name without the original holder's permission. Usually this happens by someone pretending to be the domain name holder and convincing the registrar to modify the registration information. Once this information is altered, the hijacker can then transfer the domain to another registrar and take control of websites and emails. Weak passwords are the primary cause for most hijacked accounts. So more complex passwords and mandated password changes are a long-standing security practice.

Fake Requests

The attacker sends a fake request with his/her own profile, so as to enlarge his/her network and steal sensitive information from a victim's profile. The actual dissemination of fake requests cannot be prevented, thus, the individual should make a more responsible use of social media.

Image Retrieval and Analysis

Here, the attacker uses various face and image recognition softwares to find more information about the target and his/her linked profiles. It not only affects the target but also his/her circle. This type of cyber attack aims to steal images, videos and other sensitive information from the target.

In earlier studies, Barbara and colleagues (2011) pointed out that an enhanced access control system for social networks is the first step to address online security and privacy risks. With regard to the personal information disclosure and privacy protection of social media users, Fogues and colleagues (2015) argued that given the massive number of social media users in the last few years, the current beneficial services of Social Networking Service (SNS), such as Facebook and Twitter, while providing social users with convenient and rich experiences, are being overshadowed due to the existence of privacy hazards. Therefore, they listed all the types of privacy hazards that may potentially affect SNSs privacy settings and provided insight on the privacy mechanism enabling the restraint of threats and the protection of data in physical, virtualized and cloud-based environments. They further described and analyzed the current solutions that can be put into place to fulfill the whole range of needs and specifications. Viejo and colleagues (2016) indicated that the big data available on social media platforms contains sensitive personal information that can be collected and used for various types of profit fraud and security lapses. Moreover, current practical solutions mainly adopt strict access control systems only to protect, but not support, users in identifying what information is sensitive or confidential. However, this may not be practically feasible since the set of software programs and/or services that companies employ to prevent cyber attacks require a direct involvement of social media operators which should intervene to optimize the control mechanism.

RECOMMENDATIONS FOR BUSINESS ORGANIZATIONS: MAJOR CONCERNS AND CHALLENGES

The never-ending security breaches over social media have entitled the organizations to safeguard the information that is shared over the network. Any violation of security hinders directly with economic growth of the organization. Social media can be analyzed by studying online behavior, whether the user is an individual or a group. Internet users need to be well informed of the threats posed by the circulation of their personal and financial information. Moreover, they should have the capability to employ appropriate and reliable security measures at their disposal. However, it must be observed that online users' behavior is influenced by subjective factors and personal experience. For example, the experience of being a cyber victim will make a difference in the way that social media consumption behavior is experienced (Scott, & Weems, 2010). Business organizations are also making more efforts in protecting their consumers' private information because the consumers' trust in the service might be greatly diminished or lost. The existing social media research is still on its way towards obtaining a sufficient security analysis from both a qualitative and quantitative point of view.

With regard to the fundamental and common features of the newly developed social media applications, this chapter suggests a novel research direction for the security of the main social media platforms by defining the attacks as evidence-driven research on knowledge sharing. The aim is to encourage or to direct more attention towards the construction of "a behavioral intention, to use security-preserving social media for optimizing knowledge sharing" (Zhang & Gupta, 2016).

As of today, researchers and practitioners in the field of social media networks are still tackling various attacks from (or against) social network and social platforms (NaliniPriya & Asswini, 2015) and endeavor to cope with those challenging security (Guerar et al., 2016, Dhouioui, et al., 2016), privacy and measurement (Sarkar & Banerjee, 2016; Alduaij, et al., 2016) issues. Social media on the one hand allow us to share our information with people across the globe, but on the other it gives organizations that handle our information access control to our private information. These issues need to be addressed as user trust can only be gained by increasing perceived user control and lowering such risks.

Consequently, the current study addresses the following important scientific questions regarding the role of social media and their integration in the knowledge sharing process: are social media able to develop organizational memory classified in internal (group's skills and organizational culture) and external (formal policies, procedures, manual and computer files)? Is security-preserving social media able to optimize knowledge sharing? Is social media security able to influence the behavioral intention of the group/individual to continue to use social media tools? Is organizational culture positively influenced by knowledge sharing via web 2.0 technologies?

In considering social media, I argue that it is not if and how social media and security can play a role in our knowledge sharing system, but rather what we want social media to be capable of doing. Thus, with the rapid advancement of IT (Information Technologies), the question is not actually what social media can do for researchers and practitioners, but instead what we want social media to do for all people in business organizations.

FUTURE RESEARCH DIRECTIONS

Although the study contributes to fill a research gap due to the lack of theoretical and empirical literature on the role of social media in knowledge sharing, there are some limitations that should be taken into account. Contrasting findings on the use of IT tools were however shown in previous studies (Olivera, 2000). For example, Goodman and Darr (1998) found that, in the absence of external rewards, employees were not willing to update shared databases, while Constant et al. (1996) found that employees usually liked to answer posted questions to help each other despite the absence of external rewards. Research also found that the decision of not updating the systems was partially explained by the lack of motivation to be held accountable for posted contributions (Orlikowski, 1996).

The lack of attention on individuals' interactions was also addressed as one of the main limits of the knowledge sharing debate (Hansen, 1999). As Brown and Duguid wrote "[a] great deal of hope (and money) is thus being placed on the value of Intranets. Intranets are indeed valuable, but social knowledge suggests that there is more to consider both with regards to search and retrieval" (1998, p. 98), because as also pointed out by Gherardi and colleagues (1998) knowledge is out there somewhere, stored in places (books, databases, minds) waiting to be transferred to and acquired by another mind for future use.

Currently, another obvious drawback is that the study of knowledge sharing security across social media in business settings is still in its infancy and is very limited in scope. Nowadays it is very difficult to evaluate the role of security in this field because no one is able to learn and evaluate the dynamics of security and to understand how to support knowledge sharing. Anyway, considering that social media is a global phenomenon, cross-cultural research on the knowledge sharing effect would be a promising area for further investigation.

This chapter highlights the existing opportunities for an active involvement of social media tools in business organizations. Numerous social-based strategies can be adopted to increase the operational performance or reduce corporate costs, but the following may serve as practical examples and procedures: communication between employees can be encouraged to support problem-solving (if organization needs an expert for a specific task, a post can be placed on a blog and likely receive a response from another employee or search on LinkedIn to find the person who can help); the conversion of personal knowledge into shared knowledge (if the senior employees record videos about their work and share them with the new employees, the organization can use these videos instead of expensive training programs to explain the details); the discussion of work-related problems (with a group of people who are active practitioners in a particular area; professional communities can be useful because they are neutral and can provide a way to share best practices, to ask questions and to provide support for each other outside the organization). Reduction of time and costs through integrated tools (the digital calendar, for example, which allows to organize and share events, meetings, and expedite matters, as compared to phone calls or e-mails). Several managerial processes can also be implemented. For example, it is recommended that the introduction of new social media technologies be supported for establishing the terms and conditions of usage, communicating the benefits or providing the necessary training. Moreover, organizations should develop a reward system to encourage employees' willingness to use social media tools for knowledge sharing.

CONCLUSION

From a research perspective, this chapter sets a broad agenda for future research. Due to the fact that only limited research has examined knowledge sharing and the role of social media in business organizations, it is believed that this study can inspire subsequent scientific inquiries in this recently emerging, but promising area of research. Possible future research directions may provide some responses to my initial questions about the role of security and the way social media can be successfully applied in order to interpret the impact of determinants on knowledge sharing. Moreover, my study can be tested by a team of experts (e.g. Delphi methodology).

It also aims to contribute to the management and organizational fields in two separate but related ways. First, future studies may compare firms that use social media tools with those that do not and determine their impact on knowledge sharing. At a larger scale, a comparison could be made between a firm that uses this approach and one that does not in terms of the impact on job satisfaction, employee loyalty, and development of a new idea. The issue of how to effectively design and deploy security policies is the second recommended research direction. It has become clear that security offers many opportunities for firms to interact with their groups along the entire knowledge-sharing process. Future research could also analyze and develop a training system for employees and companies to gather security data with respect to the variables governing relations and dynamics between individuals and groups. In general, firms have only a few opportunities to gather knowledge.

Using the determinants interpretation and the knowledge sharing theory, and guided by the theoretical approaches from related research in business and management, this chapter provides an analytical approach to explore the knowledge sharing by investigating the influence of social media tools and security on knowledge sharing systems. Here some important potential applications of knowledge sharing representation in the study of social media have been discussed. In particular, an outline of the major theoretical approaches to these applications has been provided. Gaining and utilizing consistent knowledge sharing by an organizational group is not a simple or straightforward task. It is a highly involved and multidimensional process, which is seldom complete or errorless. Furthermore, companies have to clearly identify what information and knowledge are to be kept confidential and what instead can be shared and made available to others. Such practices such as crowdsourcing and open innovation practices have demonstrated the value of sharing information and knowledge that has previously been considered to be confidential. In this study, social media emerge as a new perspective. Enormous information and knowledge can be shared using powerful tools in a world in which social factors play an essential role. In our new, accelerated world, numerous technologies have been developed to support social capital connections (social networking services like Facebook, LinkedIn) and to communicate in a more effective way (instant messaging services like Skype, Viber). For organizations that ensure value to knowledge sharing, integrating social media tools into their daily business life is essential to enable employees an easy access and to offer training to inexperienced users. For example, it would be a gross mistake to underestimate the power of social media that everyone uses daily while developing documents or knowledge management systems.

As previously stated, social media can be analyzed by studying online behavior, whether the user is an individual or a group. The Internet users need to be well informed about the threats posed by the circulation of their personal and financial information. Moreover, they should have the capability to employ appropriate and reliable security measures to aid them. Building and strengthening trustworthiness will provide awareness and safeguard all users.

Practitioners can use this study not only to evaluate knowledge sharing and the role of social media in targeting better future security interventions in business settings, but also to gain a better understanding of the determinants of knowledge sharing that a company needs to be aware of and responsive to human resources' needs and expectations.

REFERENCES

Alavi, M., & Leidner, D. E. (2001). Review: Knowledge Management and Knowledge Management Systems: Conceptual Foundations and Research Issues. *Management Information Systems Quarterly*, *25*(1), 107–136. doi:10.2307/3250961

Alduaij, S., Chen, Z., & Gangopadhyay, A. (2016). Using crowd sourcing to analyze consumers response to privacy policies of online social network and financial institutions at micro level. *International Journal of Information Security and Privacy*, *10*(2), 41–63. doi:10.4018/IJISP.2016040104

Anderson, P. (2007). *What is Web 2.0? Ideas, technologies and implications for education*. JISC reports. Available: http://www.jisc.ac.uk/media/documents/techwatch/tsw0701b.p

Bagozzi, R. P. (2000). On the concept of intentional social action in consumer research. *The Journal of Consumer Research*, *27*(3), 388–396. doi:10.1086/317593

Barbara, C., Elena, F., & Raymond, H. (2011). Semantic web-based social network access control. *Computers & Security*, *30*(2), 108–115.

Bartol, K. M., & Srivastava, A. (2002). Encouraging Knowledge Sharing: The Role of Organizational Reward Systems. *Journal of Leadership & Organizational Studies*, *9*(1), 64–76. doi:10.1177/107179190200900105

Behringer, N., & Sassenberg, K. (2015). Introducing social media for knowledge management: Determinants of employees intentions to adopt new tools. *Computers in Human Behavior*, *48*, 290–296. doi:10.1016/j.chb.2015.01.069

Bonson, E., & Flores, F. (2011). Social media and corporate dialogue: The response of the global financial institutions. *Online Information Review*, *35*(1), 34–49. doi:10.1108/14684521111113579

Bowley, R. C. (2009). *A comparative case study: Examining the organizational use of social networking sites (Thesis)*. Hamilton: The University of Waikato. Available http://researchcommons.waikato.ac.nz/bitstream/handle/10289/3590/thesis.pdf?sequence=1&isAllowed=y

Brown, J. S., & Duguid, P. (1998). Organizing knowledge. *California Management Review*, *40*(3), 90–111. doi:10.2307/41165945

Cabrera, A., & Cabrera, E. F. (2002). Knowledge-Sharing Dilemmas. *Organization Studies*, *23*(5), 687–710. doi:10.1177/0170840602235001

Cabrera, Á., Collins, W. C., & Salgado, J. F. (2006). Determinants of individual engagement in knowledge sharing. *International Journal of Human Resource Management*, *17*(2), 245–264. doi:10.1080/09585190500404614

Chen, I.Y., & Chen, N.S., & Kinshuk. (2009). Examining the Factors Influencing Participants' Knowledge Sharing Behavior in Virtual Learning Communities. *Journal of Educational Technology & Society*, *12*(1), 134–148.

Choo, C. (1998). *The Knowing Organization: How Organizations Use Information for Construct Meaning, Create Knowledge and Make Decisions*. New York: Oxford Press.

Constant, D., Sproull, L. S., & Kiesler, S. B. (1996). The kindness of strangers: The usefulness of electronic weak ties for technical advice. *Organization Science*, *7*(2), 119–135. doi:10.1287/orsc.7.2.119

Cross, R., & Sproull, L. (2004). More than an answer: Information relationships for actionable knowledge. *Organization Science*, *15*(4), 446–462. doi:10.1287/orsc.1040.0075

Cummings, J. L., & Teng, B. S. (2006). The keys to successful knowledge sharing. *Journal of General Management*, *31*(4), 1–18. doi:10.1177/030630700603100401

Cummings, J. N. (2004). Work groups, structural diversity, and knowledge sharing in a global organization. *Management Science*, *50*(3), 352–364. doi:10.1287/mnsc.1030.0134

Cutillo, L. A., Manulis, M., & Strufe, T. (2010). Security and privacy in online social networks. In *Handbook of Social Network, Technologies and Applications*. Springer. doi:10.1007/978-1-4419-7142-5_23

Davenport, T. H. (1999). Groups and teams. In *Organisational behaviour*. London: Financial Times Pitman Publishing.

Davenport, T. H., & Prusak, L. (1998). *Working Knowledge: How Organizations Manage What They Know*. Boston: Harvard Business School Press.

Dawson, R. (2007). *Future of Media Report 2007*. Available at: www.rossdawsonblog.com/Future_of_Media_Report2007.pdf

Dawson, S. (2008). A study of the relationship between student social networks and sense of community. *Journal of Educational Technology & Society*, *11*(3), 224–238.

Deal, T. E., & Kennedy, A. A. (1982). *Corporate Cultures*. Reading, MA: Addison-Wesley.

Dhouioui, Z., Ali, A. A., & Akaichi, J. (2016). Social networks security policies. *Proceedings of 9th KES International Conference on Intelligent Interactive Multimedia Systems and Services*, 395–403.

Di Pietro, L., Di Virgilio, F. & Pantano, E (2013). Negative eWOM in user-generated contents: recommendations for firms and organizations. *International Journal of Digital Content Technology and its Applications, 7*(5), 1-8.

Dumbrell, D., & Steele, R. (2014). Social Media Technologies for Achieving Knowledge Management Amongst Older Adult Communities. *Procedia: Social and Behavioral Sciences, 147*, 229–236. doi:10.1016/j.sbspro.2014.07.165

Eijkman, H. (2011). Dancing with Post Modernity: Web 2.0+ as a New Epistemic Learning Space. IGI Global.

Fogues, R., Such, J. M., Espinosa, A., & Garcia-Fornes, A. (2015). Open challenges in relationship-based privacy mechanisms for social network services. *International Journal of Human-Computer Interaction, 31*(5), 350–370. doi:10.1080/10447318.2014.1001300

Foss, N. J., Husted, K., & Michailova, S. (2010). Governing Knowledge Sharing in Organizations: Levels of Analysis, Governance Mechanisms, and Research Directions. *Journal of Management Studies, 47*(3), 455–482. doi:10.1111/j.1467-6486.2009.00870.x

Foss, N. J., Minbaeva, D. B., Pedersen, T., & Reinholt, M. M. (2009). Encouraging knowledge sharing among employees: How job design matters. *Human Resource Management, 48*(6), 871–893. doi:10.1002/hrm.20320

Gaál, Z., Szabó, L., Kovács, Z., Obermayer-Kovács, N., & Csepregi, A. (2008). Knowledge Management Profile Maturity Model. *ECKM 2008 - Conference Proceedings, 9th European Conference on Knowledge Management*, 209-216.

Gaál, Z., Szabó, L., & Obermayer-Kovács, N. (2014). Personal knowledge sharing: Web 2.0 role through the lens of Generations. *ECKM 2014 – Conference Proceedings, 15th European Conference on Knowledge Management*, 362-370.

Gaál, Z., Szabó, L., Obermayer-Kovács, N., & Csepregi, A. (2015). Exploring the role of social media in knowledge sharing. *Electronic Journal of Knowledge Management, 13*(3), 185–197.

Gherardi, S., Nicolini, D., & Odella, F. (1998). Toward a social understanding of how people learn in organizations: The notion of situated curriculum. *Management Learning, 29*(3), 273–297. doi:10.1177/1350507698293002

Goodman, P. S., & Darr, E. D. (1998). Computer-aided systems and communities: Mechanisms for organizational learning in distributed environment. *Management Information Systems Quarterly, 22*(4), 417–440. doi:10.2307/249550

Gottschalk, P. (2007). *CIO and corporate strategic management: changing role of CIO to CEO*. Hershey, PA: Idea Group Publication. doi:10.4018/978-1-59904-423-1

Grant, R. M. (1996). Prospering in dynamically-competitive environments: Organizational capability as knowledge integration. *Organization Science, 7*(4), 375–387. doi:10.1287/orsc.7.4.375

Grant, R. M. (1996). Toward a Knowledge-Based Theory of the Firm. *Strategic Management Journal, 17*(2), 109–122. doi:10.1002mj.4250171110

Grover, V., & Davenport, T. (2001). General Perspectives on Knowledge Management: Fostering a Research Agenda. *Journal of Management Information Systems, 18*(1), 5–22.

Gruenfeld, D. H., Mannix, E. A., Williams, K. Y., & Neale, M. A. (1996). Group composition and decision making: How member familiarity and information distribution affects process and performance. *Organizational Behavior and Human Decision Processes, 67*(1), 1–15. doi:10.1006/obhd.1996.0061

Guerar, M., Migliardi, M., & Merlo, A. (2016). Using screen brightness to improve security in mobile social network access, IEEE Trans. *Dependable Secure Computer, 99*, 1545–5971.

Haas, M. R., & Hansen, M. T. (2007). Different knowledge, different benefits: Toward a productivity perspective on knowledge sharing in organizations. *Strategic Management Journal, 28*(11), 1133–1153. doi:10.1002mj.631

Hansen, M. T., Nohria, N. & Tierney, T. (1999, March). What is your strategy for managing knowledge. *Harvard Business Review,* 106-116.

Hau, Y. S., Kim, B., Lee, H., & Kim, Y. G. (2013). The effects of individual motivations and social capital on employees tacit and explicit knowledge sharing intentions. *International Journal of Information Management, 33*(2), 356–366. doi:10.1016/j.ijinfomgt.2012.10.009

Ipe, M. (2003). Knowledge sharing in organizations: A conceptual framework. *Human Resource Development Review, 2*(4), 337–359. doi:10.1177/1534484303257985

Jalonen, H. (2014). Social media and emotions in organisational knowledge creation. *Conference Proceedings, Federated Conference on Computer Science and Information Systems*, 1371–1379. 10.15439/2014F39

Jones, M. B. (1974). Regressing group on individual effectiveness. *Organizational Behavior and Human Performance, 11*(3), 426–451. doi:10.1016/0030-5073(74)90030-0

Joshi, P., & Kuo, C. C. (2011). Security and privacy in online social networks: A survey. *Proceedings of IEEE International Conference on Multimedia and Expo.* 10.1109/ICME.2011.6012166

Keller, K. L., & Staelin, R. (1987). Effects of Quality and Quantity of Information and Decision Effectiveness. *The Journal of Consumer Research, 14*(2), 200–213. doi:10.1086/209106

Kennedy, J. L. (1971). The system approach: A preliminary exploratory study of the relation between team composition and financial performance in business games. *The Journal of Applied Psychology, 55*(1), 46–49. doi:10.1037/h0030599

Kreps, G. (1981). *Organizational folklore: The packaging of company history at RCA.* Paper presented at the ICA/SCA Conference on interpretive approaches to organizational communication, Alta, UT.

Larson, J., Christensen, C., Foster-Fishman, P. G., & Keys, C. B. (1994). Discussion of shared and unshared information in decision-making groups. *Journal of Personality and Social Psychology, 67*(3), 446–461. doi:10.1037/0022-3514.67.3.446

Lee, C. K., & Al-Hawamdeh, S. (2002). Factors impacting knowledge sharing. *Journal of Information & Knowledge Management*, 49-56.

Lehner, F., & Maier, R. K. (2000). How can organizational memory theories contribute to organizational memory systems? *Information Systems Frontiers, 2*(3/4), 277–298. doi:10.1023/A:1026516627735

Liang, D. W., Moreland, R., & Argote, L. (1995). Group versus individual training and group performance: The mediating role of transactive memory. *Personality and Social Psychology Bulletin, 21*(4), 384–393. doi:10.1177/0146167295214009

Lin, H. F. (2007). Knowledge sharing and firm innovation capability: An empirical study. *International Journal of Manpower, 28*(3/4), 315–332. doi:10.1108/01437720710755272

Liu, K. L., Chang, C. C., & Hu, I. L. (2010). Exploring the Effects of Task Characteristics on Knowledge Sharing in Libraries. *Library Review, 59*(6), 455–468. doi:10.1108/00242531011053968

Louis, M. R. (1980). *A cultural perspective on organizations: The need for and consequences of viewing organizations as culture-bearing milieux.* Paper presented at the National Academy of Management Meetings, Detroit, MI.

McDermott, R. (1999). Why information technology inspired but cannot deliver knowledge management. *California Management Review, 41*(4), 103–117. doi:10.2307/41166012

Mentzas, G., Kafentzis, K., & Georgolios, P. (2007). Knowledge services on the Semantic Web. *Communications of the ACM, 50*(10), 53–58. doi:10.1145/1290958.1290962

Meyer, A. (1981). How ideologies supplant formal structures and shape responses to environments. *Journal of Management Studies, 19*(1), 45–61. doi:10.1111/j.1467-6486.1982.tb00059.x

Moreland, R. L., Argote, L., & Krishnan, R. (1997). Training people to work in groups. In Applications of Theory and Research on Groups to Social Issues. Plenum.

NaliniPriya, G., & Asswini, M. (2015). A survey on vulnerable attacks in online social networks. *Proceedings of 2015 International Conference on Innovation Information in Computing Technologies*, 1–6.

Nonaka, I., & Takeuchi, H. (1995). *The Knowledge-creating Company.* New York: Oxford University Press.

O'Reilly, T. (2005). *What is Web 2.0? Design patterns and business models for the next generation of software.* Available: http://www.oreilly.com/pub/a/web2/archive/what-is-web-20.html

Okhuysen, G. A., & Eisenhardt, K. M. (2002). Integrating Knowledge in Groups: How Formal Interventions Enable Flexibility. *Organization Science, 13*(4), 370–386. doi:10.1287/orsc.13.4.370.2947

Olivera, F. (2000). Memory systems in organizations: An empirical investigation of mechanisms for knowledge collection, storage and access. *Journal of Management Studies, 37*(6), 811–832. doi:10.1111/1467-6486.00205

Orlikowski, W. J. (1996). Improving organizational transformation over time: A situated change perspective. *Information Systems Research, 7*(1), 63–92. doi:10.1287/isre.7.1.63

Ott, J. S. (1989). *The organizational culture perspective*. Pacific Grove, CA: Brooks/Cole Publishing Company.

Paroutis, A., & Al Saleh, A. (2009). Determinants of knowledge sharing using Web 2.0 technologies. *Journal of Knowledge Management, 13*(4), 52–63. doi:10.1108/13673270910971824

Peters, T. J., & Waterman, R. H. Jr. (1982). *In Search of Excellence: Lessons from America's Best-Run Companies*. New York: Harper & Row.

Pfeffer, J. (1981). Management as symbolic action: The creation and maintenance of organizational paradigms. In L. L. Cummings & B. M. Staw (Eds.), Research in Organizational Behavior (vol. 3, pp. 1-52). Greenwich, CT: JAI Press.

Polányi, M. (1966). *The Tacit Dimension*. London: Routledge & Kegan Paul.

Rehman, M., Mahmood, K. B., Salleh, R., & Amin, A. (2011). Review of Factors Affecting Knowledge Sharing Behavior. *2010 International Conference on E-business, Management and Economics, 3*, 223-227.

Reychav, I., & Weisberg, J. (2009). Good for Workers, good for Companies: How Knowledge Sharing benefits Individual Employees. *Knowledge and Process Management, 16*(4), 186–197. doi:10.1002/kpm.335

Riege, A. (2005). Three dozen knowledge sharing barriers managers must consider. *Journal of Knowledge Management, 9*(3), 18–35. doi:10.1108/13673270510602746

Rudawska, A. (2015). System nagród jako mechanizm wspierający wewnątrzorganizacyjne dzielenie się wiedzą. *Studia i Prace Wydziału Nauk Ekonomicznych i Zarządzania, 34*(4), 289–301.

Rulke, D. L., & Galaskiewicz, J. (2000). Distribution of Knowledge, Group Network Structure, and Group Performance. *Management Science, 46*(5), 612–625. doi:10.1287/mnsc.46.5.612.12052

Sambamurthy, V., Bharadwaj, A., & Grover, V. (2003). Shaping Agility through Digital Options: Reconceptualizing the Role of Information Technology in Contemporary Firms. *Management Information Systems Quarterly, 27*(2).

Sarkar, M., & Banerjee, S. (2016). Exploring social network privacy measurement using fuzzy vector commitment. *Intelligent Decision Technologies, 10*(3), 285–297. doi:10.3233/IDT-160256

Schall, M. S. (1981). *An exploration into a successful corporation's saga-vision and its rhetorical community*. Paper presented at the ICAl SCA Conference on Interpretive Approaches to Organizational Communication, Alta, UT.

Schein, E. H. (1985). *Organizational Culture and Leadership*. San Francisco, CA: Jossey-Bass.

Schermerhorn, J. R., Hunt, J. G., & Osborn, R. N. (1994). *Managing organizational behavior*. New York: Wiley.

Scott, B. G., & Weems, C. F. (2010). Patterns of actual and perceived control: Are control profiles differentially related to internalizing and externalizing problems in youth? *Anxiety, Stress, and Coping, 23*(5), 515–528. doi:10.1080/10615801003611479 PMID:20155530

Serdar, D., Jacobs, M., Nayir, D. Z., Khilji, S., & Wang, X. (2013). The quasi-moderating role of organizational culture in the relationship between rewards and knowledge shared and gained. *Journal of Knowledge Management, 18*(1), 19–37.

Siehl, C., & Martin, J. (1981). *Learning organizational culture*. Working paper, Graduate School of Business. Stanford University.

Sigalaa, M., & Chalkiti, K. (2015). Knowledge management, social media and employee creativity. *International Journal of Hospitality Management, 45*, 44–58. doi:10.1016/j.ijhm.2014.11.003

Stankosky, M., & Baldanza, C. (2001). *A systems approach to engineering a KM system*. Unpublished Manuscript.

Stasser, G., & Stewart, D. (1992). Discovery of hidden profiles by decision-making groups: Solving a problem versus making a judgment. *Journal of Personality and Social Psychology, 63*(3), 426–434. doi:10.1037/0022-3514.63.3.426

Stasser, G., & Titus, W. (1987). Effects of information load and percentage of shared information on the dissemination of unshared information during group discussion. *Journal of Personality and Social Psychology, 53*(1), 81–93. doi:10.1037/0022-3514.53.1.81

Stasser, G., Titus, W., & Wittenbaum, G. M. (1995). Expert roles and information exchange during discussion: The importance of knowing who knows what. *Journal of Experimental Social Psychology, 31*(3), 244–265. doi:10.1006/jesp.1995.1012

Storey, M. A., Treude, C., Deursen, A., & Cheng, L. T. (2010). The Impact of Social Media on Software Engineering Practices and Tools. *FoSER '10 Proceedings of the FSE/SDP workshop on Future of software engineering research*, 359-364. 10.1145/1882362.1882435

Surowiecki, J. (Ed.). (2005). *The Wisdom of the Crowds*. New York: Anchor Books.

Teng, J. T. C., & Song, S. (2011). An exploratory examination of knowledge sharing behaviors: Solicited and voluntary. *Journal of Knowledge Management, 15*(1), 104–117. doi:10.1108/13673271111108729

Tichy, N. M. (1982). Managing change strategically: The technical, political, and cultural keys. *Organizational Dynamics, 11*(Autumn), 59–80. doi:10.1016/0090-2616(82)90005-5 PMID:10298937

Tosi, H. L., Mero, N. P., & Rizzo, J. R. (2000). *Managing organizational behaviour* (4th ed.). Oxford, UK: Blackwell Blackwell Business.

Tziner, A., & Eden, D. (1985). Effects of crew composition on crew performance: Does the whole equal the sum of its parts? *The Journal of Applied Psychology, 70*(1), 85–93. doi:10.1037/0021-9010.70.1.85

Usman, S., H. & Oyefolahan, O. (2014). Determinants of Knowledge Sharing Using Web Technologies among Students in Higher Education. *Journal of Knowledge Management, Economics and Information Technology, 4*(2).

Van den Hooff, B., & de Ridder, J. A. (2004). Knowledge sharing in context: The influence of organizational commitment, communication climate and CMC use on knowledge sharing. *Journal of Knowledge Management, 8*(6), 117–130. doi:10.1108/13673270410567675

Van den Hooff, B., Elving, W. J. L., Meeuwsen, J. M., & Dumoulin, C. M. (2003). *Knowledge Sharing in Knowledge Communities*. In M. H. Huysman, V. Wulf, & E. Wenger (Eds.), *Communities and Technologies*. Deventer: Kluwer Academic Publishers. doi:10.1007/978-94-017-0115-0_7

Viejo, A., & Sánchez, D. (2015). Enforcing transparent access to private content in social networks by means of automatic sanitization. *Expert Systems with Applications*, *42*(23), 9366–9378. doi:10.1016/j.eswa.2015.08.014

Volady, L. (2013). *An Investigation of Factors Influencing Knowledge Sharing Among Undergraduate Teacher Education Students*. Retrieved September 9, 2013, from http://volady0002.wordpress.com/knowledge-sharingamong-undegraduate-students/

Von Krogh, G. (2011). Knowledge Sharing in Organizations: The role of communities. In E.-S. Mark & L. Marjorie (Eds.), *Handbook of Organizational Learning and Knowledge Management* (pp. 403–432). Wiley & Sons.

Vuori, V. (2011). *Social Media Changing the Competitive Intelligence Process: Elicitation of Employees' Competitive Knowledge*. Academic Dissertation. Available: http://dspace.cc.tut.fi/dpub/bitstream/handle/123456789/20724/vuori.pdf

Vuori, V., & Okkonen, J. (2012). Refining information and knowledge by social media applications: Adding value by insight. *VINE Information and Knowledge Management*, *42*(1), 117–128.

Wahlroos, J. K. (2010). *Social Media as a Form of Organizational Knowledge Sharing. A Case Study on Employee Participation*. Unpublished thesis of the University of Helsinki. Retrieved from https://helda.helsinki.fi/bitstream/handle/10138/24624/Thesis.Johanna.Wahlroos.pdf?sequence=1

Wang, S., & Noe, R. A. (2010). Knowledge sharing: A review and directions for future research. *Human Resource Management Review*, *20*(2), 115–131. doi:10.1016/j.hrmr.2009.10.001

Wang, S., & Noe, R. A. (2010). Knowledge sharing: A review and directions for future research. *Human Resource Management Review*, *20*(2), 115–131. doi:10.1016/j.hrmr.2009.10.001

Wangpipatwong, S. (2009). Factors Influencing Knowledge Sharing Among University Students. *Proceedings of the 17th International Conference on Computers in Education*, 800-807.

Wegner, D. M. (1986). Transactive memory: A contemporary analysis of the group mind. In G. Mullen & G. Goethals (Eds.), *Theories of Group Behavior*. New York: Springer-Verlag.

Weick, K. E. (1995). *Sensemaking in Organizations*. Thousand Oaks, CA: Sage.

West, M. A., Garrod, S., & Carletta, J. (1997). Group decision-making and effectiveness: unexplored boundaries. In C. L. Cooper & S. E. Jackson (Eds.), *Creating tomorrow's organizations a handbook for future research in organizational behaviour*. New York: John Wiley & Sons.

Witherspoon, C. L., Bergner, J., Cockrell, C., & Stone, D. N. (2013). Antecedents of organizational knowledge sharing: A meta-analysis and critique. *Journal of Knowledge Management*, *17*(2), 250–277. doi:10.1108/13673271311315204

Yassin, F., Salim, J., & Sahari, N. (2013). The Influence of Organizational Factors on Knowledge Sharing Using ICT among Teachers. *Procedia Technology*, *11*, 272–280. doi:10.1016/j.protcy.2013.12.191

Yesil, S., & Dereli, S. F. (2013). An empirical investigation of organisational justice, knowledge sharing and innovation capability. *SciVerse Science Direct*, *75*, 199–208.

Yi, J. (2009). A Measure of Knowledge Sharing Behavior: Scale Development and Validation. *Knowledge Management Research & Practice*, *7*(1), 65–81. doi:10.1057/kmrp.2008.36

Yu, T., Lu, L., & Liu, T. (2009). Exploring factors that influence knowledge sharing behavior via weblogs. *Computers in Human Behavior*. doi:10.1016/j.chb.2009.08.002

Zhang, Z., & Gupta, B. B. (2016). Social media security and trustworthiness: Overview and new direction. *Future Generation Computer Systems*. doi:10.1016/j.future.2016.10.007

Zhang, Z. Y. (2015). Security, trust and risk in multimedia social networks. *The Computer Journal*, *58*(4), 515–517. doi:10.1093/comjnl/bxu151

KEY TERMS AND DEFINITIONS

Content Sharing: Is the textual, visual, or aural content that is encountered as part of the user experience on websites. It may include—among other things—text, images, sounds, videos, and animations.

Groupware: Is an application software designed to help people involved in a common task to achieve their goals. One of the earliest definitions of collaborative software is intentional group processes plus software to support them.

Mash-Ups: Is a song or composition created by blending two or more pre-recorded songs, usually by overlaying the vocal track of one song seamlessly over the instrumental track of another.

Messaging Service: Is a service that is process oriented and exchanges messages/data calls.

Social Bookmarking: Is a centralized online service which allows users to add, annotate, edit, and share bookmarks of web documents.

Social Networking: (Also social networking site, SNS or social media) Is an online platform that is used by people to build social networks or social relations with other people who share similar personal or career interests, activities, backgrounds or real-life connections.

Web Tools: Are tools used for testing the user facing interface of a website or web application.

This research was previously published in Social Media for Knowledge Management Applications in Modern Organizations; pages 1-30, copyright year 2018 by Business Science Reference (an imprint of IGI Global).

Chapter 80

Organizing, Organizations, and the Role of Social Media Conversations

Veronica R. Dawson

California State University – Stanislaus, USA

ABSTRACT

This chapter traces the concept of organizational identity in organization theory and places it in the social media context. It proposes that organizational communication theories intellectually based in the "linguistic turn" (e.g., the Montreal School Approach to how communication constitutes organizations, communicative theory of the firm) are well positioned to illuminate the constitutive capabilities of identity-bound interaction on social media. It suggest that social media is more than another organizational tool for communication with stakeholders in that it affords interactants the opportunity to negotiate foundational organizational practices: organizational identity, boundaries, and membership, in public. In this negotiative process, the organizing role of the stakeholder is emphasized and legitimized by organizational participation and engagement on social media platforms. The Montreal School Approach's conversation–text dialectic and the communicative theory of the firm's conceptualization of organizations as social, are two useful concepts when making sense of organization–stakeholder interaction in the social media context.

INTRODUCTION

This essay frames organization–stakeholder conversations on social networking platforms as organizational communication. While popular media examples of organizations and their brands failing and winning at social media conversations abound, theoretical and empirical insight into the organizational practices and processes contributing to and stemming from these failings and successes is more difficult to find. Based on the premise that social media provide organizations with a tool for communication with various stakeholders, the author interrogates notions of organizing, identity, organizational boundaries, and membership. By doing so, the author examines the boundaries of the organizational communication

DOI: 10.4018/978-1-7998-9020-1.ch080

discipline and suggests that researchers should move beyond the container metaphor and ought to look at how stakeholder interaction on social media platforms influences organizational processes.

Organizational identity as practice (Carlsen, 2006) helps explain how structural and communicative characteristics and affordances of the social media impact organizing. Specifically, external organizational stakeholders have the communicative power to constitute an organization's identity through online conversations by incenting organizational action. To some extent the effects of this communicative power might only be facilitated by social media platforms, not created completely anew. Researchers do not appear to understand or even pay attention to how social media contributes to the communicative constitution of the organization. This essay interrogates these processes and in doing so, provides suggestions for future research.

BACKGROUND

More broadly, social media platforms are defined by interactivity and participation, giving rise to a more participatory audience and eventually, a participatory culture (see, Jenkins, 2006, 2012; Jenkins, Purushotma, Weigel, Clinton, & Robison, 2009). Originally related to fandom, participation through and on social media platforms by various organizational stakeholders presents if not new, then differently contextualized challenges for organizing. Social media has a unique combination of affordances that function simultaneously (Scott & Orlikowski, 2012), and how well organizations and stakeholders understand their function determines the successful utilization of social media platforms for the various purposes of organizing.

Branding social media "blunders" have become de rigueur in popular media news – the now numerous occasions of organizations posting the wrong thing online, or alternatively, not commenting, when they perhaps should. Conversations carried out by J.P. Morgan Chase, Kmart, Home Depot, HMV, DiGiorno Pizza and the hashtags #askJPM, and #WhyIStayed present just a few examples of social media strategy gone wrong (Feloni, 2013; Griner, 2014). Then there are the organizations such as TacoBell and Oreo have become famous for their excellent conversational skills on various social networks (Abramovich, 2013; Watercutter, 2013). Organizational blunders and successes on social media platforms exist because of the various digital stakeholders, a multitude of voices, participating in interaction with said brands and communicatively *creating* failure and success.

Communication as constitutive force is prominent in the social media context, making the Montreal School of organizational communication's conceptualization of the conversation–text dialectic (Taylor & Van Every, 2000; Putnam, 2013) a useful framework. Social media discourse, involves ongoing interactivity characterized by many-to-many communication between companies and stakeholders, as well as between stakeholders themselves (Goldfarb & Tucker, 2011). Interactivity refers to the degree to which two or more communicative parties can act on each other and the degree to which such influences are synchronized (Liu & Shrum, 2002). The ongoing interaction characteristic of social networking platforms is a process of negotiation in the form of conversations. The underlying negotiation is most apparent since organizations often engage with conflicting internal and external stakeholders.

For the purposes of this essay, a stakeholder is someone who has an interest in the organization sufficient to prompt (digital) interaction where the interaction might be of supporting or conflicting nature but is no less directed at the organization. The definition is purposefully broad, because it attempts to account for a wide range of communicative processes overlooked in a more traditional understanding of the role of the stakeholder. It aims to encompass a wide variety of stakeholders, both external and internal to the organization, and sits in between Cheney's (1991) definition of a stakeholder as anyone who is affected by or can affect the actions of the organization, and Scott and Lane's (2000) more specific defintion of stakeholders as groups and individuals inclusive of employees, customers, suppliers, shareholders, and in general all those who have expectations of gain based on organizational success.

A focus on the constitutive power of online organization–stakeholder communication brings forth "the *social* side of firms," suggesting that organizations are embedded in discourse. Organizations are subject to negotiation by internal and external actors, balancing on the verge of the social and material, and organizations are generated, sustained, and continually modified through communication (Kuhn, 2008). As such, communication is the constitutive procees functioning internally and externally in organizations and includes the online interactions of various stakeholders.

All social media interactions between organizations and stakeholders are about negotiating an organization's representation online and hence, its identity. The consequences of this negotiation are not to be taken lightly (e.g., Kuhn, 2008). Without a clear vision of the whole organization, routine organizational practices and activities become meaningless. It is in this sense important to investigate how organizational members such as social media representatives perform these negotiative interactions, interpret them, and "scale them up" to identity-constituting organizational practices. Organizations are socio-material entities (Orlikowski, 2000; Orlikowksi & Scott, 2008), and while organizational identities, boundaries, and membership may all be negotiated in the social media interactions of stakeholders, organizations and their social media brands also exist as corporations, nonprofits, and so on.

CONVERSATION, TEXT, AND COORIENTATION IN SOCIAL MEDIA

Since the "linguistic turn" in the 1980s, organizational communication scholarship has shifted from a conduit model of language and communication to a constitutive model (Ashcraft, Kuhn, & Cooren, 2009). Organizational communication researchers transformed their work from the study of communication in organizations to the study of communicative politics of organizing (Mumby, 2013). We find ourselves in this state of exploration currently. It is this general framework that makes the research of organizing and social media possible and relevant. A particular theory and theoretical concepts facilitate an argument about the development of organizational communication in the age of social networks and continuous interaction.

The Montreal School Approach (MSA) to communication constituting organizations (CCO) (Taylor & Van Every, 2000) is rooted in ethnomethodology where meaning is found in everyday practices such as conversations, and speech act theory where words perform actions. This approach to the constitution of organizations is particularly useful to the present argument because of MSA's emphasis on everyday conversations and their "translation" to a more global, organizational text (Brummans, Cooren, Robichaud, & Taylor, 2013) that would include practices related to social media and even policy designed to address online interactions. The concept of translation is integral to the process of organizing according to MSA.

Translation is a sort of upgrading and downgrading. The upgrade is from everyday practices, through collective experiences, which are then transformed into organization through the processes of distanciation and textualization. Taylor, Cooren, Giroux, and Robichaud (1996), explain distanciation as the consequence of the dialectic of speaking and writing. By writing the discourse, textualizing it, discourse is objectified and it becomes part of practice. Distanciation and textualization thus allow for local interactions to "transcend themselves," establishing links with past and future events and guiding actions accordingly (Cooren, 2006). This upgrade process of translation can be downgraded going backwards to conversation based on everyday local practice.

Social media interaction such as posts, comments, and reactions, is a form of everyday conversation. Conversations and the situated activities and experiences they address make up what Brummans and colleagues (2013) call a network of practices. It is this network of practices that constitutes the organization or what the MSA calls the organizational text. This interplay between conversation and text can be described as recursive, thus effectively reframing "the age-old tensions between stability and change" and suggesting that conversations produce texts and texts mediate conversations (Putnam, 2013, p. 29). A good example to illustrate this is when ideas regularly expressed in conversation lead to organizational rules, policies, norms, and expectations derived from earlier conversations. Organizations then use these polices to coordinate organizational functions such as when organizations use polices as discussion topics and action items during meetings and as guides to how an organization responds to negative comments online.

The translation between conversation and text, or the lived experience and its narrated abstraction, is reconciled through the process of coorientation. Coorientation is a key element in MSA's theorizing about the process of organizing, particularly because it is through coorientation that the act of organizing and the organization come to exist though the interdependent activity. Coorienation refers to how two or more social actors attempt to relate attitudes to some object in the same way (Taylor & Van Every, 2000). The beginnings of coorientation can be found in Weick's (1995) explanation of action. To him, action is almost always social, and is almost never solitary, meaning that individual action is (in fact) interaction. Similarly, Taylor (2006) sees coorientation as never solitary and always interactive. Coorientation is the root of organizing because it implies action, but also collectivity, interdependence, and a common object to be oriented towards. An interesting example of coorientation is the concept of "organizing without organizations" (Shirky, 2008), often used within the social media and networking literature.

The basis of the "organizing without organizations" concept stems from what various social media platforms seem to afford in terms of collective action without formal organization leadership or management such as in social movements (e.g., the Occupy Wall Street and the Arab Spring). Unlike this essay, "organizing without organizations" explicitly negates the usefulness of formal organizations to organizing in the social media context. Similarly to this chapter, "organizing without organizations" suggests a process applied here to the study of formal organizations. That is, "organizing without organizations" involves the ability of individuals to coorient toward something that has to get done—whether that involves bringing down an Arab government or achieving a production goal. If organizational boundaries and even traditional membership are no longer a prerequisite for organizing, then Kuhn's (2008) theorizing on the communicative side of firms and the social organization become even more relevant in an argument about the constitutive role of conversation on social media platforms.

Kuhn (2008) suggests that organizational interaction with external stakeholders has a constitutive effect of the "authoritative (yet never monolithic) system of cooriented and distributed action" within and around organizations. In other words, the process of organizing, which is generally understood as one taking place between organizational members, can be "extracted" and extended to external stakeholders. This conclusion is entirely consistent with the understanding that organization is achieved through a series of textually mediated practices—such as online conversations. This view is well suited to the social media context, which even in its theoretical rejection of formal organizations (Shirky, 2008), is still governed by the idea of the organizing process and thus, coorientation of multiple stakeholders toward a common goal. Yet, this process of "extending" the organization to the external stakeholder has not been described in the field of formal organizations. Because the social media context is characterized by frequent and ongoing interaction between organizations and their stakeholders, it presents an excellent opportunity to reimagine the constitution of the organization.

Once an organization is authored through recursive conversation, the organization becomes capable of representing the collective comprising it. This is what Cooren (2006) calls, "organizational presentification," perhaps the closest link to the relationship between organizational identity and image that exists within the MSA to CCO. This representation also allows for the organization to make itself present to its stakeholders and speak on behalf of the collective as an entity beyond any one individual. Alternatively, authorized organizational agents, such as social media writers, "become" the organization in online conversations. These relationships are important because they can effectively explain how online organizational presence can act simultaneously as presentation and representation of the organization's identity and image, thereby discursively linking identity and image.

AUTHORED ORGANIZATIONAL IDENTITY

The concept of organizational identity (OI) has a long and colorful history within organizational studies. Reviewing it in its entirety is beyond the scope of this chapter. The various definitions of OI oscillate between a traditional interpretation of the concept as a relatively stable and central social characteristic of organizations (see Albert & Whetten, 2004; Dutton & Dukerich, 1991; Hatch & Schultz, 2002) and an alternative that OI is a process of flux and transformation authored practice in everyday work and conversation (see Carlsen, 2006; Czarniawska, 1997; Gioia, Schultz, & Corley, 2000). Addressing OI as authored practice in the context of social media interactions is useful because it readily substantiates claims of flexible boundaries, non-traditional membership, and stakeholder involvement in digital organizing (see Bimber, Flanagin, & Stohl, 2012). OI as a rhetorical construct is a well-established perspective in organizational communication and is the basis of the present argument because it seamlessly builds toward OI as authored practice while providing conceptual "room" for the notion of control.

Organizational rhetoric emphasizes an element of communicative cooperation since language is a symbolic means for inducing cooperation (Burke, 1969). Meisenbach and McMillan (2006) posit that this emphasis on cooperation "leads naturally to issues of organizing and organizations" (p. 102). Further, "an organizational rhetoric perspective suggests focusing on messages created within and/or on behalf of organizations that seek to create identification, solicit cooperation, and/or persuade" (p. 102).

This view of organizations as persuasive entities is taken up by the MSA in the concept of presentification where a "collective entity can be made present through a variety of entities that appear to materialize or incarnate it" (Cooren, 2006, p. 91). For MSA scholars, the idea of organization as presentification through communication is central. "In the domain of language-mediated cognition, there is no syntactic discrimination between individual and collective actors: Bill 'decides,' but so does Microsoft" (Taylor, 2006, p. 153). In this sense, communication is persuasion is practice and an antecedent to the organization.

From communication as constitutive perspective, there are also no restrictions on who may be counted as an organizational actor as long as that actor is part of the conventions of language and the process of communication (Taylor, 2006). This notion refers back to one of the central ideas of the MSA toward organizing—that communicative constitution depends on and is rooted in coorientation. This means that if two actors engage in co-oriented communication, one on behalf of the organization and one as external stakeholder, then their interaction could be constitutive of the organization itself. Similarly, organizational rhetoricians suggest that audiences can "talk back" to the organization and we ought to study this process because of its potential to "blur boundaries" between the internal and external rhetoric of organizations and their relationship (Meisenbach & McMillan, 2006). This connection between the main postulates of CCO and organizational rhetoric is essential here, because it suggests that the communicative processes surrounding organizational identity can be both persuasive (on behalf of the organization) and co-constructive (on behalf of various stakeholders).

When it comes to organizations as persuasive agents however, organizations strive to control image representation, thus evoking the more traditional conceptualization of identity as relatively stable and central. The ideas of "talking back" and cooriented digital stakeholders are significantly complicated by this organizational desire for control. If an organizational identity represents what an organization stands for, the process by which members and sometimes, arguably, non-members, take on aspects or attributes of the organization as their own is identification. The act of persuasion aims at facilitating identification through controlling perceptions, interpretations, opinions, and actions, going back to the more traditional view of OI (Cheney, 1983a, 1983b; Cheney & McMillan, 1990; Meisenbach & McMillan, 2006). Identification has long been considered a prerequisite for decision-making aligned with organizational values (Simon, 1976) and as such it is no surprise that organizations aim at fostering identification in the ranks of their members and spend great resources to accomplish it (Cheney & Christensen, 2001).

One method of organizational control that informs the notion of control in social media contexts is that of the enthymeme. The enthymeme is one of several truncated syllogisms used as rhetorical devices to persuade an audience. Enthymemes may become the premises for drawing conclusion and making decisions in organizations (Simon, 1976). However, speakers focus enthymemes on an audience as part of interaction (Tompkins & Cheney, 1985). A rhetor gives an internal or external organizational audience enthymemes as premises for forming an organization's identity. or the representation of what an organization stands for. The interaction culminates in the concept of identification (Tompkins & Cheney, 1985).

When it comes to organizations controlling identity representation, perception, and ultimately identity practices, the concept of the enthymeme is central. As a link to identity, identification, persuasion, decision-making, and attempts to control identity through interaction on social media platforms, it is also somewhat problematic. The problem resides in an affordance and signature characteristic of social media – its publicity. Publicity creates an infinite organizational audience, one difficult to conceptualize, and hence difficult to inculcate with premises. Enthymemes may not work as well as an organizational tool in a social media world of interaction.

Additionally, the structure of social media platforms is such that interactions are highly visible, creating the possibility that one "bad apple" can spur endless conversation quickly spiraling off-topic, and out of organizational control. In this sense, social media ideologically and structurally forces and challenges the management of multiple identities (Cheney, 1991). However, further complicating the situation are demands of transparency and authenticity (Cheney et al., 2013; Gilmore & Pine, 2007; McCorkindale, DiStaso, & Sisco, 2012).

But what if organizational identity and the related process of identification were "social" concepts? What does it mean to like, follow, and at least apparently associate with an organization as a digital stakeholder on social networking platforms? Organizational identification has been mostly studied as a process within the organization, one that comes with and after socialization. Yet, organizational identification largely depends on how attractive the organization's identity is to the individual and how well it resonates with personal needs (Mael & Ashforth, 1992). The process does not have to be confined within the formal boundaries of the organization. Pratt (1998) suggests that one path of organizational identification is affinity, or similarity, a path that does not require organizational membership. In fact, branding scholars have studied customer–company identification through the same definitions and theories and have shown that outsiders do identify with the brands of organizations of which they are not members (Aaker, 1996; Ahearne, Bhattacharya, & Gruen, 2005; Hughes & Ahearne, 2010; Scott & Lane, 2000).

Ahearne and colleagues (2005) suggest that customers, much like organizational members, develop deep cognitive bonds with organizations. In social media context, customers express these bonds with various organizations communicatively. Hughes and Ahearne (2010) assert that brands people choose to *like* and *associate with* have a symbolic power over the construction of people's social identity and are used to appropriate meaning for the self and to communicate this meaning to others. These scholars define brand identification as a social construction, which involves the integration of perceived brand identity and/or perceived brand image into self-identity. Brand identity then refers to the associations a person derives for functional, emotional, and self-expressive benefits. This theorizing on brand identity appears especially relevant when considering the benefits of membership itself, such as self-enhancement and belonging. Further, expressed in the context of social media, it seems that the characteristics of brand identification can be easily applied to facilitate our understanding of nonmember identification processes online.

Management and branding scholars have explored the impact of perceived organizational image by organizational members. Dutton and colleagues (1991, 1994) extensively studied how New York Port Authority organizational member identification was enhanced by the positive perceptions outsiders had of the organization's identity representation. Expanding on the role of the outsider in the construction of organizational identity, Hatch and Schultz (2002) argue that external stakeholder perceptions of the organization are *not* completely internalized by organizational members, as Dutton and colleagues suggested, but instead, traces of these perceptions "leak" into an organization's identity directly as a result of stretched organizational boundaries. As observed by management scholars, member identification is greatly influenced by how the organization's identity representation is perceived by outsiders going as far as claiming that these outsiders might have an even more direct influence on an organization's identity. As observed by branding scholars, customer–company association in part determines the customer's social identity and suggests that individuals associating with organizations online may be experiencing the same benefits (especially when stakeholder–organization relationship is visible to others). In all, these observations suggest that forces within an organization's environment might influence internal processes such as identification and likely decision-making.

In organizational communication, Kuhn (2008) has noted that organizational practices, including identity, are authored in conversation and text, and in part, this authoring process is influenced by external stakeholder input. The interactions taking place on social media platforms also suggest that organizational identity is one such element that can be explicitly co-authored by organizational members and non-members, while rising issues of control, power, decision-making, and strategy. Yet, because concepts as social networking, social media, and branding, which bring such issues to the foreground, are not what organizational communication traditionally considers as a discipline, we have been missing an obvious opportunity. Examples of opportunities for future connections are presented below.

STRETCHING BOUNDARIES – ORGANIZATIONAL AND DISCIPLINARY

While the history of OI within CCO has been a brief one, it has fed off of the extensive identity work done by organizational rhetoricians, and added a flavor of its own in exclusively focusing on the lamination and imbrication of everyday interaction to the level of organizational text. One study specifically focused on identity while presenting both traditional and novel scholarly approaches. Chaput, Brummans,and Cooren (2011) demonstrated (1) that organizations were represented but also made present or "presentified" by the individual members who spoke on their behalf and (2) that organizations were consubstantialized, especially when organizational members found themselves in situations where *"they have to restate what identifies them as an organization by negotiating who or what substantiates it"* (p. 268, *italics* in original). This organizational "substance" or identity was always "under construction" within conversation, and only made temporarily stable and present in organizational texts (i.e., written and unwritten practices).

Scholars outside of the CCO field of inquiry have also suggested the perspective's potential in the study of the organizational identity and identification. For example, some corporate communication scholars have argued toward a more constitutive approach seeking to bridge macro and micro perspectives toward organizational image and identity, and to interpret them as based in interaction (Christensen & Cornellisen, 2011; Cornelissen, Haslam, & Balmer, 2007). In these studies, corporate communication scholars argue, in respect to organizational image and organizational identity specifically, that corporate and organizational communication scholarship should "cross-fertilize" through a framework of communication as constitutive of organization and specifically using the MSA (Taylor & Van Every, 2000).

Notably, corporate communication focuses on how organizations manage and integrate communication with various stakeholders, particularly in the way of organizational image and identity. Van Riel and Fombrun (2007) propose that corporate communication encompasses "the set of activities involved in managing and orchestrating all internal and external communications aimed at creating favorable starting points with stakeholders on which the company depends (p. 25)." The goal of projecting a favorable organizational image underlined in corporate communication is echoed in the use of social media channels as the newest tool for this purpose. Stakeholders can easily challenge the successful management of organizational image (and identity) on social media, however. It is helpful that a striking similarity exists between the concepts of organizational identity and organizational image in corporate communication, an idea not readily explored in organizational communication. This is so much so that some have suggested that image and identity represent one and the same, at least as far as external stakeholders are concerned (Christensen & Askegaard, 2001; Hatch, Schultz, & Larsen, 2000). The goal of corporate communication is to project "a consistent and unambiguous image of what the organization 'is' and stands for" (Christensen & Cornellisen, 2011, p. 387). In essence then, the difference between corporate communication and organizational communication, as far as identity is concerned, can be summed up under the tension-ridden belief that a corporate identity should invoke and represent the whole organization, while organizational identity is tied to identification and thus is often also situationally dependent.

There need be no tension. Christensen and Cornellisen (2011) posit that the problematic relationship between corporate and organizational views of identity is resolved in co-construction. For example, organizational members and external stakeholders alike co-construct (and de-construct) meanings of corporate messages in ways not intended by management, suggesting that the ones communicating on behalf of the organization "are not the masters of meaning able to control reception" (p. 391). To control and minimize "messy" interpretations from leaking out into the public, many organizations implement "policies of consistency." Yet, the authors suggest, we ought to understand these interpretive processes through a communication as constitutive lens where organizing, and its elements, such as identity, are viewed as a collective process of sensemaking and coordination. By 'collective,' Christensen and Cornellisen (2011) mean "people inside and outside organizations" who "pay attention to certain things, like 'gaps' and inconsistencies in corporate messages" (p. 403) and proceed to interpret, negotiate, and co/de-construct these messages accordingly.

When the social media context is introduced to a conversation about the communicative construction and management of identity, it would be a mistake not to mention the lead public relations has taken on describing and prescribing how organizations (should) use social media. Notably, the public relations literature has promoted social media platforms like Facebook and Twitter as organizational methods for relationship building (Geyer, Dugan, Brownholtz, Millen, & DiMicco, 2009; McCorkindale et al., 2012; Waters, Burnett, Lamm, & Lucas, 2009). Most commonly, organizations employ three strategies for relationship building online: disclosure or transparency, provision of useful information or message dissemination, and interactivity or involvement with the public.

Being a signature characteristic of social media use by organizations and one central to the present argument, the notion of interactivity comes up in the public relations literature as a prescription to organizational participation online. Public relations scholars have heralded the internet's potential for dialogue and two-way communication (Kelleher, 2009). However, what public relations scholars mean under dialogue in the context of the internet is far from the Habermasian definitions of dialogue as a negotiated exchange of ideas and opinion and a process of open and negotiated discussion, rather they focus on how dialogically oriented an organization *appears* to be (Kelleher, 2009; Kent & Taylor, 1998, 2002; Kent, Taylor, & White, 2003). This preoccupation with appearance is exemplified by a case reported by Taylor, Kent, and White (2002) where organizations that aimed at facilitating a "dialogic loop through online calendars, downloadable information, and regularly updated news feed on their websites, actually spent *less* time interacting with external stakeholders via email.

Kelleher (2009) is one prominent public relations scholar to claim that organizational blogs and other participatory platforms used by organizations actually facilitate conversation. In fact, his work suggests that organizations utilizing social media have a better chance at establishing what PR professionals know as "dynamic touch" of engaging with their stakeholders with "conversational human voice." Kelleher's claim seems to be based on the affordances of social media, particularly immediacy, publicity, and visibility, allowing multiple organizational representatives to engage in conversations with dauntingly large audiences, while arguably communicating more effectively, and more adaptively. Kelleher (2009) and Kelleher and Miller (2006) go on to suggest that this type of conversational interactivity humanizes the organization, resulting in improved trust, satisfaction, control mutuality, and commitment. While all informative, the control mutuality outcome suggests a stakeholder relationship with an organization that is "dynamic and negotiable" and further exemplified by the stakeholder's perception that "the organization believes that opinions of people like me are legitimate" (Kelleher, 2009, p. 178).

These examples of disciplinary "cross-pollination" in respect to organizational identity are representative of the argument behind this essay because they stretch not only organizational boundaries, but also implicitly, disciplinary boundaries. The extension of CCO and the MSA, in particular, into corporate communication is emblematic of what organizational communication has begun to consider recently – all organizational stakeholders, internal and external. The importance of conversation, emphasized within public relations, and the complexities of organizations practicing these important yet difficult to control conversations online, is emblematic of organizing in the social media realm. Disregarding whether referring to organizational identity or organizational image, both are processes and products of stakeholder co-construction. At the same time, organizations continuously attempt to control this process, most often through some kind of governance, which in turn is also a product of interactional co-construction.

ORGANIZING, COLLECTIVE ACTION, AND ORGANIZATIONS IN SOCIAL MEDIA

The last part of this essay connects organizing to social networking and media. Social media and network theorists have interpreted digital organizing as grounded-in-action (Benkler, 2006; Fuchs, 2013; Morozov, 2009, 2012; Shirky, 2008). While some theorizing is critical of social networks, most theory development still points to the power of social interaction to produce informal, yet powerful, social organization, suggests a communicative coorientation toward a specific goal or object, and resulting in the organizing of some form of digital organization. Organizations are ultimately brought into existence by discursive processes online (i.e. "the Twitter Revolution"). The appropriateness of a general constitutive perspective is undeniable in the social media context as space where organizing occurs. However, most social networking theorists focus on the informal organization (i.e., grass roots, social movements) and steer clear of formal organizations (i.e., commercial, nonprofits) on the internet. It is in the establishment of a connection between theories of informal organizing online and the formal organizational representation online that a communication as constitutive framework is theoretically useful. And while an empirical CCO example of linking informal, digital organizing and formal organization does not yet come to mind, Bimber and colleagues (2012) assist in imagining this link through an interpretation of collective action theory.

Traditional collective action theory is flexible and easily makes individual to organization-level jumps, while balancing individual agency against structure (Bimber et al., 2012). Linking collective action theory, social media, and the organization, allows for the introduction of formal organizations in the social media space. Much of organizational communication theorizing comes down to the complex relationship between individuals and organizations and their abilities to act independently or in concert toward a common goal (i.e., coorientation). Both individual agency and organizational structure play important roles constructing organizational identity and image online. However, one problem consistently harangues formal organizations in the digital world—that of stretched, permeable boundaries.

When organizational communication researchers consider formal organizations, one of the traditional metaphors we use is that of the container (Deetz, 2001). Even though the container metaphor is one of many, the associated idea that organizations have some kind of symbolic boundary delineating them from the environment is a fairly dominant one. Organizational boundaries are constituted through and in interaction, but the structural and material attributes of the formal organization are stretched if not collapsed by contemporary digital media (Bimber et al., 2012; Stohl & Ganesh, 2013). What the complex situation suggests is that social media problematizes the very notion of formal organization or at the very least, its boundaries. Various and non-traditional stakeholders continuously negotiate an organization's identity, membership, and related organizational practices in what Kuhn (2008) calls "an infinite game". There is little empirical research about these challenges.

Two recent studies focus on the internal and public, respectively, organizational use of social media networks and platforms. Unlike scholars of social networks and media, Treem and Leonardi (2013) suggest that social media use in organizations affords new types of behaviors that were previously difficult or impossible to achieve without new technology, thus suggesting that social media do *change* organizations. The authors take on a sociomaterial approach to technology (Orlikowski, 2000) and focus on affordances. An affordance is the perception of the material features of a technology in relationship to what social actors may want the technology to do (Treem & Leonardi, 2013).

Four affordances of social media in organizational contexts are visibility, persistence, editability, and association (Treem & Leonardi, 2013). Visibility refers to the extent people may easily and effortlessly fined information about some else by using the technology. When actors perceive they may use a technology to extend visibility for long periods after the original display of data, the actors perceive persistence. Editability refers to the perception that actors may spend time altering and changing a message before it is viewed by others. When actors perceive they can readily connect to each other or that others can easily connect them to information (e.g., a posting), the actors are perceiving a technology's potential for association. Treem and Leonardi (2013) reviewed the literature on materiality and affordances as well as the published empirical literature about these affordances and social media.

Similarly, Scott and Orlikowski (2012) explored publicity, persistence, editability, and immediacy. When actors perceive they can easily manipulate, display, and share information using a technology, the actors perceive the actors perceive using the technology is more immediate. Their analysis focused on affordances on TripAdvisor.com, a public social networking site for travel reviews.

Both studies suggest that the effects of social media within and for organizations are mostly dependent on how stakeholders, be they employees or not, use social media.,. The concurrent individual and organizational realization that social media afford certain behaviors, unique to the technology's context, is the key to social media's widespread and successful use. This implies coorientation between individuals and their organizations when it comes to what and how social media is *doing*.

Scott and Orlikowski (2012) view TripAdvisor.com as organization, and they make an argument focusing on public organizational use of social media. Similarly to Treem and Leonardi (2013), the authors claim that social media is indeed a game changer. Because Scott and Orlikowski look at the effects reviewer feedback has on organizations represented on TripAdvisor's website (hotels mostly, but also other business establishments), they are able to discuss the material consequences social media interactions, such as ratings and reviews, had on businesses in the tourist industry. The eye-opening example here is of a hotel going out of business due to bad reviews. While in itself a correlation between bad reviews and losing business is not surprising, what the authors claim as interesting is the specific structure and rules of TripAdvisor.com that allow for the material consequence of going out of business to occur. Although hotels could respond to comments, the site was designed so that the rating based on the original comment could not be changed, effectively pushing a hotel's image down, when in fact all the negative issues could have been addressed in the follow-up interactions and situated organizational action.

Scott and Orlikowski (2012) suggest that organizations today are almost entirely dependent on how these affordances are interpreted by the users. The sociomateriality (Orlikowski's original terminology) of social media depends on how well employees or non-member stakeholders understand social media's characteristic affordances. In terms of the current argument, social media's affordances contribute to the stretching of organizational boundaries to possibly uncomfortable degree (e.g., the "blunders"). Conversations, originating with the organization or with the "external" stakeholders, carried out on social media platforms effectively "spill" the organization outside its boundaries and create a potential for discussion of foundational organizational matters, such as identity, previously reserved for "insiders." However society and researchers choose to think of organizations, their identities, memberships, and formality, social media interaction comes to affect how organizations think of themselves.

CONCLUSION

This chapter made an argument pertaining to foundational organizational communication concepts of organizing, identity, boundaries, stakeholders, and membership. It reviewed research, theory, and examples from organizational communication, corporate communication, public relations, and social media. The chapter argued that through cross-pollination between this diverse literature, scholars can come to understand organizations in the social media context. Organizational communication scholars can lead the way by applying a specific organizational communication framework (CCO) to a non-organizational communication context (social media). The chapter makes a case for the constitutive powers of conversation with various organizational stakeholders.

The essay focused on organizational identity as a central concept, while also suggesting that the stretching of organizational boundaries in the social media affected current conceptualizations of membership, and organizing in general. Areas of future development involve an emphasis on the inclusion of non-traditional, "external" areas to organizational communication, such as the organizational impact of digital stakeholders. Ultimately, by interrogating the boundaries of organizations, the meaning of organizational identity, and the span of organizing in social media, the paper simultaneously questioned disciplinary boundaries.

REFERENCES

Aaker, D. A. (1996). Measuring brand equity across products and markets. *California Management Review*, *38*(3), 103–123. doi:10.2307/41165845

Abramovich, G. (2013). Inside Taco Bell's social media strategy. *CMO by Adobe*. Retrieved from http://www.cmo.com/features/articles/2013/9/6/inside_taco_bell_s_s.html#gs.Crq3y8g

Ahearne, M., Bhattacharya, C. B., & Gruen, T. (2005). Antecedents and consequences of customer-company identification: Expanding the role of relationship marketing. *The Journal of Applied Psychology*, *90*(3), 574–590. doi:10.1037/0021-9010.90.3.574 PMID:15910151

Albert, S., & Whetten, D. A. (2004). Organizational identity. In M. J. Hatch & M Schultz (Eds.), Organizational identity: A reader (pp. 89–118). Oxford, England: Oxford University Press.

Ashcraft, K. L., Kuhn, T. R., & Cooren, F. (2009). Constitutional amendments: "Materializing" organizational communication. In J. P. Walsh & A. P. Brief (Eds.), *The Academy of Management Annals* (Vol. 3, pp. 1–64). New York, NY: Routledge.

Benkler, Y. (2006). *The wealth of networks: How social production transforms markets and freedom*. New Haven, CT: Yale University Press.

Bimber, B., Flanagin, A. J., & Stohl, C. (2012). *Collective action in organizations: Interaction and engagement in an era of technological change*. Cambridge: Cambridge University Press. doi:10.1017/CBO9780511978777

Brummans, B. H. J. M., Cooren, F., Robichaud, D., & Taylor, J. R. (2013). Approaches to the communicative constitution of organizations. In L. L. Putnam & D. K. Mumby (Eds.), *The SAGE handbook of organizational communication* (3rd ed., pp. 173–194). Los Angeles, CA: Sage Publications.

Burke, K. (1969). *A rhetoric of motives*. Berkley, CA: University of California Press.

Chaput, M., Brummans, B. H. J. M., & Cooren, F. (2011). The role of organizational identification in the communicative constitution of an organization: A study of consubstantialization in a young political party. *Management Communication Quarterly, 25*(2), 252–282. doi:10.1177/0893318910386719

Cheney, G. (1983). The rhetoric of identification and the study of organizational communication. *The Quarterly Journal of Speech, 69*(2), 143–158. doi:10.1080/00335638309383643

Cheney, G. (1991). *Rhetoric in an organizational society: Managing multiple identities*. Columbia, SC: University of South Carolina Press.

Cheney, G., & Christensen, L. T. (2001). Organizational identity: Linkages between internal and external communication. In F. M. Jablin & L. L. Putnam (Eds.), *New handbook of organizational communication: Advances in theory, research, and methods* (pp. 231–269). Thousand Oaks, CA: Sage Publications. doi:10.4135/9781412986243.n7

Cheney, G., & McMillan, J. J. (1990). Organizational rhetoric and the practice of criticism. *Journal of Applied Communication Research, 18*(2), 93–114. doi:10.1080/00909889009360318

Cheney, G., & Tompkins, P. K. (1987). Coming to terms with organizational identification and commitment. *Communication Studies, 38*(1), 1–15.

Christensen, L. T., & Askegaard, S. (2001). Corporate identity and corporate image revisited-A semiotic perspective. *European Journal of Marketing, 35*(3/4), 292–315. doi:10.1108/03090560110381814

Christensen, L. T., & Cornelissen, J. (2011). Bridging corporate and organizational communication: Review, development and a look to the future. *Management Communication Quarterly, 12*(3), 383–414. doi:10.1177/0893318910390194

Cooren, F. (2006). The organizational world as a plenum of agencies. In F. Cooren, J. R. Taylor, & E. J. Van Every (Eds.), *Communication as organizing: Empirical and theoretical explorations in the dynamic of text and conversation* (pp. 81–100). Mahwah, NJ: Lawrence Erlbaum Associates.

Cornelissen, J. P., Haslam, S. A., & Balmer, J. M. (2007). Social identity, organizational identity and corporate identity: Towards an integrated understanding of processes, patternings and products. *British Journal of Management, 18*(s1), S1–S16. doi:10.1111/j.1467-8551.2007.00522.x

Deetz, S. (2001). Conceptual foundations. In F. M. Jablin & L. L. Putnam (Eds.), *The new handbook of organizational communication: Advances in theory, research, and methods* (pp. 3–46). Thousand Oaks, CA: Sage Publications. doi:10.4135/9781412986243.n1

Dutton, J. E., & Dukerich, J. M. (1991). Keeping an eye on the mirror: Image and identity in organizational adaptation. *Academy of Management Journal, 34*(3), 517–554. doi:10.2307/256405

Dutton, J. E., Dukerich, J. M., & Harquail, C. V. (1994). Organizational images and member identification. *Administrative Science Quarterly*, *39*(2), 239–263. doi:10.2307/2393235

Feloni, R. (2013). 10 worst social media marketing fails of 2013. *Business Insider*. Retrieved from http://www.businessinsider.com/10-worst-social-media-marketing-fails-of-2013-2013-11?op=1/#-strip-club-chain-spearmint-rhinos-melbourne-team-thought-theyd-be-naughty-and-have-facebook-users-guess-whose-baby-picture-they-uploaded-it-didnt-take-long-for-users-to-look-at-the-vhs-sceenshots-time-stamp-and-realize-that-the-future-stripper-was-now-only-14-years-old-spearmint-rhino-liked-its-own-post-1

Fuchs, C. (2013). *Social media: A critical introduction*. Los Angeles, CA: Sage Publications.

Geyer, W., Dugan, C., Brownholtz, B., Millen, D. R., & DiMicco, J. M. (2009). People sensemaking and relationship building on an enterprise social network site. *Proceedings of the 2014 47th Hawaii International Conference on System Sciences* (pp. 1–10). IEEE.

Gilmore, J. H., & Pine, B. J. (2007). *Authenticity: What consumers really want* (Vol. 1). Boston, MA: Harvard Business School Press.

Gioia, D. A., Schultz, M., & Corley, K. G. (2000). Organizational identity, image, and adaptive instability. *Academy of Management Review*, *25*(1), 63–81.

Goldfarb, A., & Tucker, C. E. (2011). Privacy regulation and online advertising. *Management Science*, *51*(1), 57–71. doi:10.1287/mnsc.1100.1246

Griner, D. (2014). DiGiorno is really, really sorry about its tweet accidentally making light of domestic violence: Reminder to always check the context on hashtags. *Adweek*. Retrieved from http://www.adweek.com/adfreak/digiorno-really-really-sorry-about-its-tweet-accidentally-making-light-domestic-violence-159998

Hatch, M. J., & Schultz, M. (2002). The dynamics of organizational identity. *Human Relations*, *55*(8), 989–1018. doi:10.1177/0018726702055008181

Hughes, D. E., & Ahearne, M. (2010). Energizing the resellers sales force: The power of brand identification. *Journal of Marketing*, *74*(4), 81–96. doi:10.1509/jmkg.74.4.81

Jenkins, H. (2006). *Fans, bloggers, and gamers: Exploring participatory culture*. New York, NY: New York University Press.

Jenkins, H. (2012). *Textual poachers: Television fans and participatory culture*. New York, NY: Routledge.

Jenkins, H., Purushotma, R., Weigel, M., Clinton, K., & Robison, A. J. (2009). *Confronting the challenges of participatory culture: Media education for the 21st century*. Cambridge, MA: MIT Press.

Kelleher, T. (2009). Conversational voice, communicated commitment, and public relations outcomes in interactive online communication. *Journal of Communication*, *59*(1), 172–188. doi:10.1111/j.1460-2466.2008.01410.x

Kelleher, T., & Miller, B. M. (2006). Organizational blogs and the human voice: Relational strategies and relational outcomes. *Journal of Computer-Mediated Communication*, *11*(2), 395–414. doi:10.1111/j.1083-6101.2006.00019.x

Kent, M. L., & Taylor, M. (1998). Building dialogic relationships through the World Wide Web. *Public Relations Review, 24*(3), 321–334. doi:10.1016/S0363-8111(99)80143-X

Kent, M. L., & Taylor, M. (2002). Toward a dialogic theory of public relations. *Public Relations Review, 28*(1), 21–37. doi:10.1016/S0363-8111(02)00108-X

Kent, M. L., Taylor, M., & White, W. J. (2003). The relationship between Web site design and organizational responsiveness to stakeholders. *Public Relations Review, 29*(1), 63–77. doi:10.1016/S0363-8111(02)00194-7

Kuhn, T. (2008). A communicative theory of the firm: Developing an alternative perspective on intra-organizational power and stakeholder relationships. *Organization Studies, 29*(8-9), 1227–1254. doi:10.1177/0170840608094778

Liu, Y., & Shrum, L. J. (2002). What is interactivity and is it always such a good thing? Implications of definition, person, and situation for the influence of interactivity on advertising effectiveness. *Journal of Advertising, 31*(4), 53–64. doi:10.1080/00913367.2002.10673685

Mael, F., & Ashforth, B. E. (1992). Alumni and their alma mater: A partial test of the reformulated model of organizational identification. *Journal of Organizational Behavior, 13*(2), 103–123. doi:10.1002/job.4030130202

McCorkindale, T., DiStaso, M. W., & Sisco, H. F. (2012). How millenials are engaging and building relationships with organizations on Facebook. *The Journal of Social Media in Society, 2*(1), 66–87.

Meisenbach, R. J., & McMillan, J. J. (2006). Blurring the boundaries: Historical developments and future directions in organizational rhetoric. In C. S. Beck (Ed.), *Communication Yearbook* (Vol. 30, pp. 99–141). Mahweh, NY: Lawrence Erlbaum Associates.

Morozov, E. (2009). Iran: Downside to the Twitter revolution. *Dissent, 56*(4), 10–14. doi:10.1353/dss.0.0092

Morozov, E. (2012). *The net delusion: The dark side of Internet freedom*. New York, NY: Public Affairs.

Mumby, D. K. (2013). Critical theory and postmodernism. In L. L. Putnam & D. K. Mumby (Eds.), *Handbook of Organizational Communication* (pp. 101–126). Los Angeles, CA: Sage Publications.

Orlikowski, W. J. (2000). Using technology and constituting structures: A practice lens for studying technology in organizations. *Organization Science, 11*(4), 404–428. doi:10.1287/orsc.11.4.404.14600

Pratt, M. G. (1998). To be or not to be: Central questions in organizational identification. In D. A. Whetten & P. C. Godfrey (Eds.), *Identity in organizations: Building theory through conversations* (pp. 171–208). Thousand Oaks, CA: Sage Publications. doi:10.4135/9781452231495.n6

Putnam, L. L. (2013). Dialectics, contradictions, and the question of agency: A tribute to James R. Taylor. In D. Robichaud & F. Cooren (Eds.), *Organization and organizing: Materiality, agency, and discourse* (pp. 23–36). New York, NY: Routledge.

Schultz, M., Hatch, M. J., & Larsen, M. H. (Eds.). (2000). *The expressive organization: Linking identity, reputation, and the corporate brand*. Oxford, England: Oxford University Press.

Scott, S. G., & Lane, V. R. (2000). A stakeholder approach to organizational identity. *Academy of Management Review*, *25*(1), 43–62.

Scott, S. V., & Orlikowski, W. J. (2012). Great expectations: The materiality of commensurability in social media. In P. M. Leonardi, B. A. Nardi, & J. Kallinikos (Eds.), *Materiality and organizing: Social interaction in a technological world* (pp. 113–133). Oxford, England: Oxford University Press. doi:10.1093/acprof:oso/9780199664054.003.0006

Shirky, C. (2008). *Here comes everybody: The power of organizing without organizations*. New York, NY: Penguin Books.

Shirky, C. (2011). Political power of social media-Technology, the public sphere, and political change. *Foreign Affairs*, *90*, 28–30.

Simon, H. A. (1976). *Administrative behavior: A study of decision making processes in administrative organization* (3rd ed.). New York, NY: Free Press.

Stohl, C., & Ganesh, S. (2013). Generating globalization. In L. L. Putnam & D. K. Mumby (Eds.), *The SAGE Handbook of Organizational Communication* (3rd ed., pp. 717–742). Sage Publications.

Taylor, J. R. (2006). Coorientation: A conceptual framework. In F. Cooren, J. R. Taylor, & E. J. Van Emery (Eds.), *Communication as organizing: Empirical and theoretical explorations in the dynamic of text and conversation* (pp. 141–156). Mahwah, NJ: Lawrence Erlbaum Associates.

Taylor, J. R. (2011). Organization as an (imbricated) configuring of transactions. *Organization Studies*, *32*(9), 1273–1294. doi:10.1177/0170840611411396

Taylor, J. R., & Cooren, F. (2006). Making worldview sense: And paying homage, retrospectively, to Algirdas Greimas. In F. Cooren, J. R. Taylor, & E. J. Van Every (Eds.), *Communication as organizing: Empirical and theoretical explorations in the dynamic of text and conversation* (pp. 115–140). Mahwah, NJ: Lawrence Erlbaum Associates.

Taylor, J. R., Cooren, F., Giroux, N., & Robichaud, D. (1996). The communicational basis of organization: Between the conversation and the text. *Communication Theory*, *6*(1), 1–39. doi:10.1111/j.1468-2885.1996.tb00118.x

Taylor, J. R., & Van Every, E. J. (2000). The emergent organization: Communication as its site and surface. New York, NY: Psychology Press: Taylor & Francis Group.

Tompkins, P. K., & Cheney, G. (1985). Communication and unobtrusive control in contemporary organizations. In R. D. McPhee & P. K. Tompkins (Eds.), *Organizational communication: Traditional themes and new directions* (pp. 179–210). Beverly Hills, CA: Sage Publications.

Treem, J. W., & Leonardi, P. M. (2013). Social media use in organizations: Exploring the affordances of visibility, editability, persistence, and association. In C.T. Salmon (Ed.), Communication Yearbook (Vol. 36, pp, 143-189). New York, NY: Routledge.

Van Riel, C. B., & Fombrun, C. J. (2007). *Essentials of corporate communication: Implementing practices for effective reputation management*. New York, NY: Routledge. doi:10.4324/9780203390931

Watercutter, A. (2014). How Oreo won the marketing Super Bowl with a timely blackout on Twitter. *Wired.* Retrieved from https://www.wired.com/2013/02/oreo-twitter-super-bowl/

Waters, R. D., Burnett, E., Lamm, A., & Lucas, J. (2009). Engaging stakeholders through social networking: How nonprofit organizations are using Facebook. *Public Relations Review*, *35*(2), 102–106. doi:10.1016/j.pubrev.2009.01.006

Weick, K. E. (1995). *Sensemaking in organizations*. Thousand Oaks, CA: Sage Publications.

KEY TERMS AND DEFINITIONS

Conversation: The ongoing, interactive posts and comments made by organizations and their digital stakeholders in the social media space.

Coorientation: An interactive process of orientation toward a common object or goal, key to successful organizing.

Organizational Identification: The appropriation of organizational identities by internal and external stakeholders. Identification is associated with persuasion, control, and decision-making in the sense that an identifying stakeholder would act in the interest of the organization without necessarily being told to by a manager.

Organizational Identity: The somewhat stable, yet continuously negotiated organizational sense of itself, generated and given substance by various organizational stakeholders in conversation and text, action and practice, and seen in organizational representation and presentification online.

Organizational Presentification: Indicates the process of the organization becoming *it* – representative of the collective comprising it, but beyond any one individual or collective identity. An example of presentification is a reference such as: "The U.S. Government said…"

Social Media: Social media is a way of sharing information with a broad audience, where every participant has an opportunity to create and distribute, via variety of platforms. Social media often facilitates social networking, a behavior indicating an act of engagement.

Text: The semi-permanent, written or unwritten, product of conversation referring to anything from organizational practice to policy or governance. The relationship between conversation and text is recursive, meaning that conversation generates texts over time, and text spurs conversation.

This research was previously published in Transformative Practice and Research in Organizational Communication; pages 62-78, copyright year 2018 by Business Science Reference (an imprint of IGI Global).

Chapter 81
Uncertainty Avoidance and Consumer Cognitive Innovativeness in E–Commerce

Osama Sohaib

University of Technology Sydney, Sydney, Australia

Kyeong Kang

University of Technology Sydney, Sydney, Australia

Iwona Miliszewska

University of Technology Sydney, Sydney, Australia

ABSTRACT

This article describes how despite the extensive academic interest in e-commerce, an investigation of consumer cognitive innovativeness towards new product purchase intention has been neglected. Based on the stimulus–organism–response (S–O–R) model, this study investigates the consumer cognitive innovativeness and the moderating role of the individual consumer-level uncertainty avoidance cultural value towards new product purchase intention in business-to-consumer (B2C) e-commerce. Structural equation modelling, such as partial least squares (PLS) path modelling was used to test the model, using a sample of 255 participants in Australia who have had prior online shopping experience. The findings show that the online store web atmosphere influences consumers' cognitive innovativeness to purchase new products in countries with diverse degrees of uncertainty avoidance such as Australia. The results provide some guidance for a B2C website design based on how individual's uncertainty avoidance and cognitive innovativeness can aid the online consumer purchasing decision-making process.

DOI: 10.4018/978-1-7998-9020-1.ch081

INTRODUCTION

The primary way a business-to-consumer (B2C) e-commerce firm communicates with its consumers is through their website. According to the Australian Nielsen Connected Consumers Report (2016), a large number of consumers go to manufacturers' and retailers' website directly, with 65% of consumers visiting the retailer's website and 36% visiting the manufacturer's website for online purchase (Zrim, 2016). Therefore, it is necessary to evaluate the effectiveness of websites' components to understand whether online stores are providing the interaction desired by the consumers. E-retailers should provide important stimuli and ensure that their website offers unique benefits and values to encourage consumers to buy products online. If e-retailers intends to turn first-time consumers into repeat online consumers, the e-retail experience has to deliver unique value regarding the consumer's interaction with the website. In the area of B2C e-commerce, the web cognitive landscape refers to whether consumers believe that the information presented on the website makes it easy for them to purchase products. E-commerce web design is vital because businesses can lose 50% of the potential consumer due to consumer unable to find the product what they want (van der Merwe & Bekker, 2003). This means that the structural assurance of the website provided by the e-retailer should demonstrate a clear understanding of the reasons why consumers cognitively believe that they should shop at one specific website rather than at other ones (Li, Yen, Liu, & Chang, 2013).

Countries vary significantly on innovativeness as measured by consumer reluctance (Tellis, Yin, & Bell, 2009). The concept of consumer innovativeness denotes "inter-individual differences that characterize people's responses to new things" (Goldsmith & Foxall, 2003). The success of e-commerce also depends on a consumer's culture (Sohaib and Kang, 2015a) as culture influences consumer innovativeness. Often country is used as a proxy for culture at a group level; however, it is more appropriate to measure culture at the individual level because online purchasing is an individually oriented one-person action (Sohaib and Kang 2015b). The innovative consumer plays a vital role in the adoption of new products. There are at least three approaches to the conceptualisation of innovativeness: behavioural, global traits and domain-specific activity (Goldsmith & Foxall, 2003). Behavioural refers to whether consumers are innovators or non-innovators in their attitude to adopting new products, global traits are personality traits, while domain-specific activity denotes a consumer's innovativeness within specific product categories. The most significant aspect of behaviour is its connection to cognition. Behaviour results from some form of cognition (Faiola & Matei, 2006). Our concern is with the behavioural perspective of consumers' innovativeness, which identifies consumers as innovators or non-innovators depending on their purchase of a new product. A person's perceptions may change their attitudes to new products and ideas and their level of innovativeness (Rogers, 1995).

In the context of e-commerce, how consumers react to innovation, specifically whether consumers adopt new products or not, depends on their purchasing decision-making process and a variety of internal and external influences. The measurement of cognitive innovativeness is important to this process. Consumer perception of information is directly related to cognition (Ha, John, & Chung, 2016). In addition to this, cultural experiences influence cognitive processes (Faiola & Matei, 2006), for example, online transactions can provoke a high level of uncertainty (Sabiote, Frías, & Castañeda, 2012). The cultural value of uncertainty avoidance is significantly connected to innovativeness (Dobre, Dragomir, & Preda, 2009). Therefore, consumer innovativeness plays an important role in encouraging consumers to shop online.

The first objective of this study is to investigate the influencing factors of consumer cognitive innovativeness regarding new product purchase intention. This study extends the work of Sohaib and Kang (2015b) by including the role of cognitive innovativeness towards new product purchase intention and using the moderating role of individual consumer level uncertainty avoidance (UA) cultural value. The second objective of this study is to investigate whether high UA and low UA consumers have different cognitive innovativeness towards purchasing intentions. The research questions of this study are as follows:

Research Question 1: Do web design factors affect consumer cognitive innovativeness towards purchase intention of new products in B2C e-commerce?
Research Question 2 and 3: Does the consumers' level of UA play an important moderating role between factors that affect new product purchase intention in B2C e-commerce? Moreover, what are the difference between high UA and low UA consumers?

For this study, 'new product purchase' refers to any product not purchased online in the past. To the best of the authors' knowledge, this is the first research study that investigates the role of consumer cognitive innovativeness and different levels of uncertainty avoidance cultural value in e-commerce. As such, it contributes to the understanding of online vendors' perception of innovative approaches to B2C websites.

This paper is structured as follows. We first critically analyse the literature on the consumer cognitive innovativeness, web cognitive landscape, and the cultural value of uncertainty avoidance. We then discuss the theoretical background from which we developed our research model and hypotheses. Following that, we describe our research methodology and present the results of this study. Finally, we discuss the practical and theoretical implications of the study and conclude with the limitations and future direction for research.

THEORETICAL BACKGROUND

Consumer Cognitive Innovativeness

This research defines 'consumer cognitive innovativeness' as a consumer's rational thinking, problem-solving and decision-making tendencies as related to new product purchase in a B2C e-commerce website. Scholars have enriched consumer innovativeness by measuring its various dimensions. Venkatraman and Price (1990) distinguish cognitive from sensory innovativeness, with cognitive innovativeness referring to cognitive qualities that influence individuals to seek stimulation of the mind while sensory innovativeness refers to the cognitive qualities that influence individuals to seek sensory stimulation. Consumer innovativeness refers to consumers' proneness to adopt new products (Tellis et al., 2009).

Manning, Bearden and Madden (1995) characterise two aspects of consumer innovativeness: consumer independent judgment-making and consumer novelty-seeking. Consumer independent judgment-making refers to the degree to which an individual makes innovation decisions independently, while consumers' novelty-seeking denotes the desire to look for new product information. According to Blake, Neuendorf and Valdiserri (2003), innovativeness is the relative willingness of an individual to try a new product. In the context of B2C e-commerce, this means the tendency to buy new products soon after they appear online. Consumers are categorised as innovators or non-innovators depending on their purchase of a new product (Goldsmith & Foxall, 2003). According to Lim et al. (2004), the cognitive cues of a B2C website form a basis of consumer trust in an online store that does not have an established reputation. Kim (2005) notes that cognition-based trust is associated with consumers' observations and perceptions regarding the features and characteristics of an e-commerce website.

The value with the most proximate impact on an individual's cognitive interpretations is personal innovativeness (Lu, 2014). According to Venkatraman and Price (1990), individuals who have a high need for cognition are more likely to analyse information than those with a low need for cognition because they have a need to structure situations in meaningful ways. In particular, consumers with high cognitive innovativeness are more likely to adopt a technology (Venkatraman and Price, 1990). In addition to this, online consumers with high cognitive innovativeness put more emphasis on usefulness and aesthetic design (T.-L. Huang & Liao, 2014). However, "consumers with low cognitive innovativeness lack ability, knowledge, and involvement with regard to new technology; they are insensitive to the effect of the new technology in accomplishing a task" (T.-L. Huang & Liao, 2014). Considering B2C e-commerce websites, various web cognitive factors may stimulate a positive relationship with consumers with different levels of cognitive innovativeness.

Website Accessibility/Ease of Use

Website accessibility increases when a website has a high ease of use. Ease of use includes accessibility factors such as navigation, website content structure and search facilities (Lodorfos, Trosterud, & Whitworth, 2006). When a consumer visits a website for the first time, their trust is primarily based on initial perceptions of the trust-related attributes of the website, such as the cognition-based aspects which are formed from quick cognitive cues or first impressions (McKnight, Cummings, & Chervany, 1998). For example, the visual design of a website consists of graphical and structural factors from which consumers develop their first impression (Karimov, Brengman, & Hove, 2011). In the context of e-commerce, usefulness is how effective shopping on the Internet is in helping consumers to accomplish their task, and ease of use is the consumer's perception regarding how easy the Internet is to use as a shopping medium and how free the process is of effort in leading the consumer to achieve their final task (Monsuwe, Dellaert, & Ruyter, 2004). Brick-and-mortar stores are not designed to improve efficiency but to enhance persuasion opportunities. The same principle applies in the e-commerce environment, such as in designing web usability to maximise persuasion interaction (Schaffer, 2009). Website design factors such as information design and navigation design should be used in e-commerce websites to build consumer trust and subsequently enhance purchase intention (Dianne Cyr, 2013; Ganguly, Dash, & Cyr, 2010).

Therefore, the website accessibility concept adopted here considers the ease of use and usefulness aspects together with various design features that contribute to the overall website usability such as navigational design, information content and design.

Colour and Product Images

Once consumers interact with an e-commerce website, initial perceptions concerning website aesthetics often persuade the consumer to stay on the website for a longer duration (Alhammad & Gulliver, 2013). The aesthetic elements of a website such as colour and graphics usage are the most effective trust attributes of B2C websites (Tan, Tung, & Xu, 2009). The colour appeal of a B2C website is the degree to which the colours used, for example the background and font colour, are perceived as pleasing, appealing and appropriate. Product images are interactive image features, such as 3D virtual models, that consumers can operate to view product information by zooming in on product features, rotating a product to different angles and changing product colours. Visual design cues such as colour and product images can provide information about the Internet vendor as well as have an impact on consumers' emotional responses (Eroglu, Machleit, & Davis, 2003).

Social Networking Services

Social networking services are defined as a set of actors (people/organisations) and the set of connections among the actors representing some relationship (friendship/affiliation/information exchange) (Grabner-Kräuter, 2009). These include web communities and communication media. Web communities are online social networking sites, blogs, newsletters, forums and online product reviewing/ratings. Communication media include instant messaging, online help emails and chat. Social influence is a vital factor that determines user behaviours on social networking sites (Cheung, Lee, & Chan, 2015). Persuasive interaction ensures the perception of an acceptable level of social interaction via the use of social networking services (Alhammad & Gulliver, 2013). Consumers' trust is formed through permeating the mode of communication with a high social presence in a B2C e-commerce website. Gefen and Straub (2004) found a significant influence of social presence on consumer trust in B2C e-commerce, such as ability, integrity, predictability and benevolence. The opinions of others can impact consumers' purchasing intention (Lee, Shi, Cheung, Lim, & Sia, 2011). A model proposed by Brengman and Karimov (2012) investigated whether integrating social media cues (such as Facebook and blogs) as stimulus into an online store's website may provide a signal regarding the cognitive trust (organism) of an online vendor. The results show that social media cues have a significant effect on consumers' cognitive-based trust towards purchase intentions (response). In addition to this, Facebook advertising has a significant positive influence on consumer attitude towards the intention to purchase (Duffett, 2015). Guo, Wang, and Leskovec's (2011) study shows that information processing and trust positively influence consumer choice.

Uncertainty Avoidance

Geert Hofstede (1980) refers to the uncertainty avoidance cultural as having a certain degree of uncertainty. Australia is a practical society regarding uncertainty avoidance, with an index score of 51, and has a high degree of acceptance for new ideas, technology and business practices. For a B2C e-commerce to be successful, it is essential to note the cultural themes of targeted consumers. In particular, the uncertainty avoidance (UA) cultural value is closely associated with innovativeness in e-commerce (Dobre et al., 2009). Due to the high level of uncertainty of the virtual world, individual trust is affected (Al-Debei, Akroush, & Ashouri, 2015). As noted by Karahanna, Williams, Polites, Liu, and Seligman (2013), "Online purchasing is a decision-making process that involves inherent uncertainty". Uncertainty is an important moderator in online purchasing (Zhu, Chang, & Chang, 2015). Individuals with high uncertainty avoidance tend to desire outcomes by following the right direction for action (Duffett, 2015). Existing studies have applied Hofstede's (1980) cultural dimensions to examine the effect of cultural values on online purchasing decisions. However, in these studies, national cultural differences were observed at the country level. This is an issue as the assumption of homogeneity in any nation is not suitable, in particular, if the national cultural concepts are to be integrated into information systems models that reflect individual behaviour (McCoy, Galletta, & King, 2005).

Culture is a significant influence on consumers' purchasing decisions (Constantinides, 2004; Ha & Janda, 2014), producing a range of emotional effects to a given stimulus (G. Hofstede, 2001). Srite and Karahanna (2006) argue that national culture is a macro-level phenomenon, whereas online purchasing is a one-person action; therefore, measuring culture at the individual consumer level is the most appropriate way to look at the effect of technology acceptance (Sohaib & Kang, 2015a). In addition, consumers with dissimilar cultures might have different expectations of what makes an online store trustworthy (Ganguly et al., 2010; Kim, 2005; Kim & Park, 2013; Sia, Lim, Leung, Lee, & Huang, 2009), which affects the establishment of trust.

Researchers (Hwang & Lee, 2012a; McCoy et al., 2005; Srite & Karahanna, 2006; Yoon, 2009) found Hofstede's cultural scales at the individual level acceptable in information systems research (more specifically, in e-commerce research). As B2C e-commerce continues to grow across cultures, it becomes critical to understand the cognitive influences between the consumer and the Internet vendor and the nature of cultural differences at the individual consumer level (Hwang & Lee, 2012a). Furthermore, cultural experiences influence cognitive processes that influence website design and its use (Faiola & Matei, 2006).

RESEARCH MODEL AND HYPOTHESES DEVELOPMENT

The stimulus–organism–response (S–O–R) model identifies cognitive aspects to determine the cognitive innovativeness towards purchasing intention. The S-O-R paradigm was first proposed by Mehrabian and Russell (1974) in the context of environmental psychology. The paradigm suggests that stimuli from the environment influence an individual's cognitive reactions, which in turn lead to a response. This paradigm was later extended and has been extensively applied to online shopping outcomes (Sohaib & Kang, 2015b).

The stimulus (S) is defined as "the total sum of all the cues that are visible and audible to the online shopper"; for example, "cognitive states are related to a consumer's information processing, retention, and retrieval ability" (Sheng & Joginapelly, 2012). The organism (O) represents the consumer's intermediary states of cognitive innovativeness. These internal states affect the consumer's approach, such as new product purchase intention, which is the response (R). Additionally, we also suggest the uncertainty avoidance cultural orientation moderates the effects of cognitive influences and cognitive innovativeness towards new product purchase intention. Research has shown that the uncertainty avoidance cultural value is significantly connected to innovativeness (Dobre et al., 2009). Figure 1 shows the proposed research model.

Hypothesis Development

Website Accessibility/Ease of Use

The navigation, page layout consistency and ease of access to an e-commerce website have to be designed with a complete understanding of a consumer group's culture (Cyr, 2008). According to Huang and Liao (2014), the perceived ease of use means that the consumer does not need to employ excessive cognitive resources when using technology. Singh, Kumar and Baack (2005) state that online consumers from high uncertainty avoidance (UA) societies need better e-commerce website accessibility so that they do not leave the website. D. Cyr (2008) also finds that consumers who are high on the UA scale give a high value to web navigational design about to their purchasing intention. Therefore, we hypothesise:

H1: Individual level UA will moderate the relationship between website accessibility and consumer cognitive innovativeness such that the relationship is stronger for consumers in Australia.

H1a: The relationship between website accessibility and consumer cognitive innovativeness is stronger for high UA individuals than low UA individuals.

Figure 1. Research model

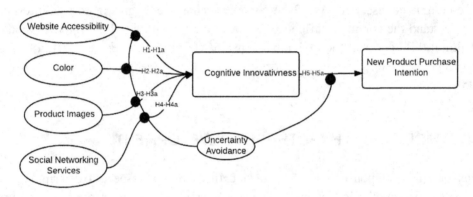

Colour and Product Images

The complexity of a B2C website, which includes the richness of factors such as colour scheme and use of product images, impacts online consumers with high cognitive innovativeness (T.-L. Huang & Liao, 2014). Additionally, S. Lee and Rao (2010) argue that in B2C e-commerce, aesthetic design produces differential responses in individuals. These visual appearances (colour and images) are more important to high UA consumers than low UA consumers (Ganguly et al., 2010). Therefore, we hypothesise:

H2: Individual level UA will moderate the relationship between colour and consumer cognitive innovativeness such that the relationship is stronger for consumers in Australia.

H2a: The relationship between colour and consumer cognitive innovativeness is stronger for high UA individuals than low UA individuals.

H3: Individual-level UA will moderate the relationship between product images and consumer high cognitive innovativeness such that the relationship is stronger for consumers in Australia.

H3a: The relationship between product images and consumer cognitive innovativeness is stronger for high UA individuals than low UA individuals.

Social Networking Services

Online consumers with high cognitive innovativeness tend to make decisions on their own (T.-L. Huang & Liao, 2014). The integration of virtual communities like social network sites has a positive influence on cognitive-based trust towards purchasing intentions (Brengman & Karimov, 2012). In addition to this, social influence can build consumer trust in online shopping more effectively in high UA cultures than in low UA cultures (M. K. O. Lee et al., 2011). For example, people in high UA cultures such as South Korea, which has a UA index score of 85, are likely to obtain opinions of a website's reputation from friend and family recommendations, whereas those from low UA cultures such as Australia are more likely to make independent decisions. This means consumers who are from low UA cultures avoid getting into groups and instead perform online purchasing on their own without asking anybody for any help. Therefore, we hypothesise:

H4: Individual level UA will moderate the relationship between social networking services and consumer cognitive innovativeness such that the relationship is stronger for consumers in Australia.

H4a: The relationship between social networking services and consumer cognitive innovativeness is stronger for high UA individuals than low UA individuals.

Cognitive Innovativeness and New Product Purchase Intention

According to Thakur and Srivastava (2014), innovativeness affects purchasing intentions. High cognitive innovative consumers not only enjoy thinking for its sake but also tend to apply a great deal of mental energy to solve problems they encounter (Huang & Liao, 2014). Additionally, as noted by Lim, Leung, Sia and Lee (2004), online shopping naturally involves more uncertainties than buying from a brick-and-mortar business. Therefore, the adoption rates of online shopping are higher for high UA cultures than for low UA cultures (Lim et al., 2004). Yoon (2009) also highlights that high UA cultures are usually more willing to rely on online purchasing than low UA cultures. Therefore, we hypothesise:

H5: Individual level UA will moderate the relationship between cognitive innovativeness and new product purchase intention such that the relationship is stronger for consumers in Australia.

H5a: The relationship between cognitive innovativeness and new product purchase intention is stronger for high UA individuals than low UA individuals.

RESEARCH METHODOLOGY

To validate the research model, we carried out an empirical survey. This study used an online survey methodology where participants were asked to choose a localised online vendor. A localised retailer website is considered to be appropriate to the culture and the most workable option for research (Dianne Cyr, 2013). The survey was announced through university webmail and social network pages. For the validation and testing of the hypotheses, data were collected from online shoppers in Australia. Criteria for selecting participants were to have a minimum of six months online shopping experience and is an Australian citizen by birth. To determine the participant's culture, it is important to ensure that each participant had lived in Australia for most of their lives and spoke the native language (English) as their primary language (Dianne Cyr, 2013).

After visiting the chosen website e-commerce website, respondents were required to fill out a closed-ended questionnaire on a seven-point Likert scale, with responses ranging from (1) strongly disagree to (7) strongly agree. Multi-scale items using at least three observable indicators measured all constructs. Previously validated survey instruments were modified to ensure the adequate reliability and validity of the measurement scales. Table 5 in the Appendix shows all items used in the study.

DATA ANALYSIS

A total of 260 responses were collected. After removing incomplete responses, a total of 255 samples were used to test the proposed model. 53% of respondents were males, and 47% were females, 95% respondents had seven or more years of Internet experience, 65% respondents had online purchasing experience of between one to three years, and 35% had more than three years.

To test the research model, a variance-based structural equation modelling (SEM) statistical technique, partial least squares (PLS) path modelling using SmartPLS version 3 (Ringle, Wende, & Becker, 2015), was used. The partial least squares (PLS-SEM) approach is a preferred analysis technique in information systems and business research because it offers several flexibilities. For example, this approach is well suited for prediction-oriented research, does not require a large sample size, does not require normality and subsequently works without distributional assumptions and with nominal, ordinal and interval-scaled variables (Haenlein & Kaplan, 2004; F. Hair, Marko, Lucas, & Volker, 2014). PLS is considered suitable as it allows investigators to evaluate measurement model parameters and structural path coefficients at the same time. It also allows both formative and reflective factors to be tested together (Chin, Marcolin, & Newsted, 2003).

In our research model, website accessibility, colour and product images, cognitive innovativeness and new product purchase intention were modelled as reflective indicators because they were viewed as effects of latent constructs (Hwang & Lee, 2012b; D. J. Kim, 2005). This is because reflective indicators are interchangeable. For example, different indicators reflect website accessibility, such as easy to learn, understandable and easy to use, to which these indicators are highly correlated. This means that an increase in website accessibility is reflected by increases in all indicators. Social networking service (SNS) is formative because it is a multidimensional factor (Sohaib & Kang, 2015b) that covers various referent groups such as social networking sites, friends and family, online help, reviews and rankings. Formative constructs are not interchangeable, which means a change in one indicator does not necessarily denote a change in other indicators. For example, an increase in influence from family would influence individuals to purchase online even if there were no influence from other sources. Additionally, the moderating effects of culture (UA) were performed using the product indicator approach. The product indicator approach by Chin (2003) refers to the products of each indicator of the independent latent variable with each indicator of the moderator variable.

To investigate the moderating influences of individuals' cultural orientation, we used the multi-group PLS analysis method to determine whether the individual uncertainty avoidance (UA) differs for high versus low uncertainty avoidance (UA) subgroups of participants, which is considered appropriate for this study (Sia et al., 2009). Multi-group PLS analysis allows for the comparisons of structural model differences between groups (Chin, 2004). The analysis was conducted by taking the standard errors of the structural models' paths by comparing equivalent paths across two groups (high UA and low UA) by performing t-tests on their path coefficients.

Although Hofstede's (1980) cultural values are significant at the societal level, his cultural dimensions also tend to differ widely over individual members within societies (Tsai & Bagozzi, 2014). Yoon (2009) found Hofstede's national cultural values at the individual level impact consumers' acceptance of e-commerce. We use a median split to separate the sample according to the participants' composite score of high versus low on two UA items: (1) "I prefer to avoid making changes while online shopping because things could get worse"; and (2) "The rules and regulations of the online stores are important to me because they inform buyers what the online store does."

Reliability and Validity Assessment

The reliability and validity of the measurement model in PLS were assessed by examining internal consistency, convergent validity and discriminant validity. Convergent and discriminant validity were assessed by applying two criteria: (1) that the square root of the average variance extracted (AVE) by a construct from its indicators was at least 0.70 and was greater than that construct's correlation with other constructs; and (2) item loadings were at least 0.70 and are more strongly on their assigned construct rather than on the other constructs. Table 5 in the Appendix shows all item loadings the social networking service (SNS) factor weights. Table 1 shows the Cronbach's reliability, composite reliability and the AVE of all constructs values exceed the recommended value of 0.70. An SNS is a formative construct that cannot be analysed in this procedure. For formative indicators (social networking services), the validity of variables using outer weights was significant (p-value < 0.05). In addition to this, to determine the reliability for formative indicators, the variance inflation factor (VIF) value was less than 5, which means there is no multi-collinearity.

Cross-sectional design surveys are susceptible to common method bias, particularly if the data collection method is only perceptually anchored (Sharma, Yetton, & Crawford, 2009). However, the PLS method requires practically no bias when estimating data from a composite model population, regardless of whether the measurement model is reflective or formative (Sarstedt, Hair, Ringle, Thiele, & Gudergan, 2016). However, according to Kock (2015), if all factor level VIFs resulting from a full collinearity test are equal to or lower than 3.3, the model can be considered free of common method bias. In our research model, all factor level VIFs are lower than 3.3, indicating no bias data.

Table 1. Cronbach's reliability, composite reliability and the AVE

	AVE	CR	C-Alpha	CInn	COL	IMG	SNS	WA	UA	NPINT
CInn	0.81	0.91	0.88	**0.90**						
COL	0.75	0.87	0.81	-0.18	**0.86**					
IMG	0.73	0.84	0.73	0.10	0.10	**0.84**				
SNS	NA	NA	NA	0.14	0.07	-0.08	**1**			
WA	0.88	0.89	0.91	0.21	0.10	0.05	0.07	**0.93**		
UA	0.84	0.88	0.82	0.09	0.05	0.13	-0.1	-0.02	**0.85**	
NPINT	0.88	0.90	0.87	0.47	0.01	-0.02	0.1	0.05	0.14	**0.93**

Notes: CR: composite reliability, C-Aplha: Cronbach's alpha, CInn: cognitive innovativeness; COL: colour; IMG, image; SNS: social networking services; WA: website accessibility; NPINT: new product purchase intention; UA: uncertainty avoidance

Concerning goodness-of-fit (GoF) indices for partial least squares path modelling, Jörg Henseler and Sarstedt (2013) show that the GoF and the relative GoF index are not appropriate for model validation. However, the model fit was assessed by examining the model fit of the PLS path models; namely, the standardised root mean square residual (SRMR). The SRMR 0.07 is lower than the recommended value of 0.08, which indicates a good fit.

Structural Model Testing

The structural models and hypotheses were tested by examining the significance of the path coefficients and the R^2 variance for the dependent variable. The significance of the paths was determined using the t-statistical test calculated with the bootstrapping technique. A 5% significance level was employed. SmartPLS 3 can perform bootstrapping (a nonparametric procedure that can be applied to test whether coefficients such as outer weights, outer loadings and path coefficients are significant by estimating standard errors for the estimates) (Ringle et al., 2015) for both the inner and outer model to specify the t-value for significance. In order to get approximate t-values for the significance test, we used a large subsample (5,000) from the original sample to draw a standard error and the number of cases were equal to the number of observations in the original sample (F. Hair et al., 2014; J. F. Hair, Ringle, & Sarstedt, 2011). We examined the coefficients of the causal relationships between constructs in our model in order to approve or disprove the hypotheses. The coefficients and their t-value on the structural model are shown in Table 2 and 3 and the coefficients of determination (R^2) for the dependent constructs are shown in Figure 2.

The Stone-Geisser criterion Q^2 is also measured using the blindfolding method to compute the construct cross-validated redundancy for assessing the predictive relevance (Jorg Henseler, Ringle, & Sinkovics, 2009). In our analysis, all Q^2 value range of the 'new product purchase intention' endogenous construct (i.e., 0.315) is above the threshold value of zero, thus indicating a strong predictive relevance.

As Table 2 shows, all hypotheses are supported except H2, which suggests there is an insignificant relationship between the individual level UA moderation between colour and consumer cognitive innovativeness. This indicates website colour perception is not shaped by the consumer's uncertainty avoidance. However, previous research (such as Cyr et al., 2010) indicated that colour is an influencing factor in e-commerce across national cultures. Variance in consumers' cognitive innovativeness ($R^2 = 0.55$) and new product purchase intention for Australia sample ($R^2 = 0.42$) is significant, which shows that the Australian sample indicates a 42% variance in consumers' new product purchase intention.

Table 2. Hypothesis testing

	Path	Path Mean	StDev	t-Value	P Value	Supported?
H1	WA * UA -> CInn	0.25	0.03	1.98	0.003*	Yes
H2	COL* UA -> CInn	0.14	0.03	1.20	0.336	No
H3	IMG * UA -> CInn	0.31	0.03	3.61	0.000***	Yes
H4	SNS * UA -> CInn	0.42	0.05	4.79	0.000****	Yes
H5	CInn* UA -> NPINT	0.24	0.03	1.99	0.002*	Yes

Notes: CInn: cognitive innovativeness; COL: colour; IMG, image; SNS: social networking services; WA: website accessibility; NPINT: new product purchase intention; UA: uncertainty avoidance; * Significant at 0.05 level; ** Significant at 0.01 level; *** Significant at 0.001 level

Furthermore, to meet the second objective of the study we compared the differences in coefficients of the corresponding structural paths of the high UA and low UA subsamples. As shown in Table 3, colour still does not affect consumers' cognitive innovativeness, so H2a is not supported. However, the paths from website accessibility, product images and social networking services to cognitive innovativeness is significant.

Table 3. Hypothesis testing

	Path	High UA (Subsample 140)		Low UA (Subsample 115)		Mean Difference	t-Value	p-Value	Supported?
		Mean	SD	Mean	SD				
H1a	WA -> CInn	0.20	0.04	0.15	0.04	0.05	1.957	0.049**	Yes
H2a	COL -> CInn	0.17	0.04	0.10	0.03	0.07	0.159	0.77	No
H3a	IMG -> CInn	0.23	0.05	0.19	0.04	0.04	1.960	0.048**	Yes
H4a	SNS -> CInn	0.33	0.05	0.24	0.03	0.10	3.247	0.001*	Yes
H5a	CInn -> NPINT	0.28	0.05	0.25	0.04	0.03	3.176	0.001*	Yes

Notes: CInn: cognitive innovativeness; COL: colour; IMG: image; SNS: social networking services; WA: website accessibility; NPINT: new product purchase intention; UA: uncertainty avoidance; * Significant at 0.05 level; ** Significant at 0.01 level; *** Significant at 0.001 level

Figure 2. Path testing

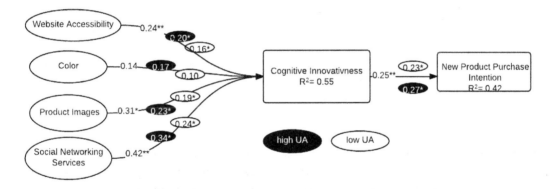

Importance-Performance Map Analysis

We also performed importance-performance map analysis (IPMA) for two groups (low UA and high UA) to produce additional findings and conclusions for managerial actions (Christian and Sarstedt, 2016). Performing an IPMA requires determining a targeting construct, such as 'new product purchase intention,' in our PLS path model.

The performance of each factor was measured on a scale from 0 to 100. The closer the value is to 100, the higher the performance of the factor. All total effects (importance) larger than 0.10 are significant at the p ≤0.05 level. Table 4 and Figure 3 show the IPMA result of the all the predecessors of the selected target construct (new product purchase intention).

Table 4. IPMA result of new product purchase intention

Criterion: New Product Purchase Intention	Low UA		High UA	
	Importance	Performance	Importance	Performance
WA	0.15	68.73	0.20	66.93
COL	0.10	49.24	0.17	47.01
IMG	0.19	56.10	0.23	58.13
SNS	0.24	65.90	0.33	66.64
CInn	0.25	62.50	0.28	63.61
NPINT	0.23	69.96	0.27	72.78

UA: Uncertainty avoidance; CInn: cognitive innovativeness; COL: colour; IMG: image;
SNS: social networking services, WA: website accessibility; NPINT: new product purchase intention

Figure 3. IPMA of the target construct (new product purchase intention)

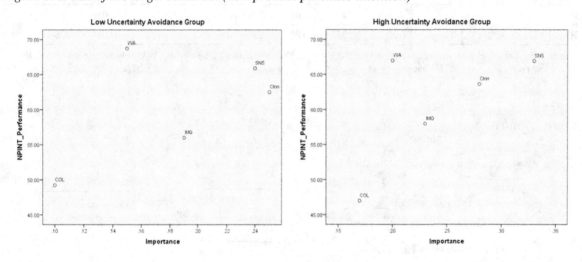

Regarding the new product purchase intention, as presented in Table 4 and Figure 3 the highest performance construct is 'web accessibility' followed by 'social networking services.' This means an increase in web accessibility performance would increase the performance of the target construct 'new product purchase intention' by the size of the total effect. However, the direct consequence of the 'cognitive innovativeness' construct is higher in the high UA group than in the low UA group. This means an increase in cognitive innovativeness performance would increase the performance of the target construct new product purchase intention by the size of the total effect 0.28 in the high UA group more than the 0.23 total effects in the low UA group.

DISCUSSION AND CONCLUSION

This study highlights the effects of web cognitive landscape on consumer cognitive innovativeness towards new product purchase intention. In addition to this, it examined how the individual consumer level uncertainty avoidance cultural value moderated the relationship between B2C web cognitive landscape and consumer cognitive innovativeness towards new product purchase intention.

The findings of this study are as follows. First, cognitive innovativeness regarding the B2C website accessibility, colour and product images, and social networking services significantly influence consumers' new product purchase intentions. This argument is consistent with the findings of T.-L. Huang and Liao (2014), who have reported that cognitive innovativeness influences consumer behaviour towards using technology. Second, consumer cognitive innovativeness has a significant positive relationship with online purchase behaviour. This is in line with Y.-A. Huang (2003). Consumers with high cognitive innovativeness are more likely to accept an innovation (Venkatraman, 1991) such as a new product purchase. Third, cognitive innovative consumers usually trust other reliable information sources to ease the uncertainties inherent in a B2C website. For example, the findings of this study indicate that website accessibility, colour and product image, and social networking services positively affect consumer cognitive innovativeness towards new product purchase intention at the individual level. This view is consistent with Tellis et al. (2009). Fourth, consumers' level of the uncertainty avoidance cultural value is significantly connected to cognition and innovativeness in e-commerce. Consumers with low uncertainty avoidance are characterised by a higher cognitive innovativeness than high uncertainty avoidance consumers, who analyse information in a meaningful way. This is consistent with Dobre et al. (2009). Fifth, in cultures with a low degree of uncertainty avoidance (such as Australia), consumers are tolerant of uncertain situations and with innovations. We found that consumers in Australia tend to be as being highly innovative overall. Additionally, consumers' intention for purchasing new products differs considerably depending on their uncertainty avoidance. This is consistent with Tellis et al. (2009).

In conclusion, the web design factors (stimulus) of a B2C website towards which a reaction is made provides a signal regarding the consumer cognitive innovativeness (organism) influence new product purchase intention (response). Therefore, B2C websites should be designed according to consumers' level of cognitive innovativeness depending on the consumer's individual cultural orientations.

Theoretical Implications

Several theoretical implications resulting from this study. Firstly, the main theoretical contribution of the study is the development of a research model that can be used in further studies. Secondly, this study extended prior research on the effects of web cognition on innovativeness towards online purchasing intentions and provided necessary results. Additionally, this research addresses the shortcomings in the existing literature by applying individual cultural values (UA) as moderators to a proposed model to uncover new and improved methods for consumer uncertainty in a B2C website. Thirdly, this study provided an understanding of the new drivers of online consumer purchase intention. Specifically, a consumer's cognitive innovativeness towards the key components on in a B2C e-commerce website, such as web design (website accessibility, visual appearance, and social networking services), which are viewed as the vital aspects of consumer trust in an online store. Fourth, this study examined how online consumer responses towards a B2C online store differ across two different cultural value systems (high uncertainty avoidance and low uncertainty avoidance). This is the first research that has investigated this phenomenon within the Australian context. Finally, the various hypotheses supported in this study all add to the literature for developing hypotheses for future studies. Additionally, this study contributes to validating the survey instrument of the various factors used in a proposed model. Researchers can now use the survey instrument with increased confidence in an e-commerce context.

Practical Implications

The findings provide some practical implications and guidelines for online vendors to include innovative approaches to B2C websites. The results of this study may help online shopping managers who could use the insights of this research to modify their web strategies, not only for considering a country's culture but also for culturally diverse countries such as Australia. Developers and website designers can use these results to increase desirable outcomes by focusing on the relationship between web cognitive evaluations and consumer innovativeness to increase the chances that an online business will succeed in countries with diverse degrees of uncertainty avoidance. The practical implications extend to business firms to make changes to their market strategies to improve their online sales across cultures; for example, e-businesses should specifically consider introducing new products first in highly innovative countries.

Limitations and Recommendations for Future Research

Like most survey research, this study has some limitations. Firstly, data were collected from Australia only. Therefore, caution is advised in making generalisations from the study findings. Secondly, a larger sample size would have been more useful for evaluating the constancy and dependability of the findings. Thirdly, although the sound judgment was used in the selection of factors for the research model, the study did not consider all possible factors that could impact cognitive influences towards purchase intention that have been used in prior studies. While the results of this study clearly indicate there are individual-based differences in online purchasing behaviour, it will be interesting to see if there is some evidence that consumer innovativeness could be a link between country level and individual level cultural analyses. More practical support at the individual consumer level cultural values using this study's research model could be included in future studies of e-commerce, such as including Hofstede's (1980) other cultural dimensions such as power distance index (PDI), masculinity versus femininity (MAS), long-term orientation versus short-term normative orientation (LTO) and indulgence versus restraint (IND). Finally, this research did not provide a complete view of all aspects of the web cognitive landscape and new product purchase intentions, such as privacy, security, brand, advertising, and price.

REFERENCES

Al-Debei, M. M., Akroush, M. N., & Ashouri, M. I. (2015). Consumer attitudes towards online shopping. *Internet Research*, *25*(5), 707–733. doi:10.1108/IntR-05-2014-0146

Alhammad, M. M., & Gulliver, S. R. (2013). Context Relevant Persuasive Interaction and Design: Consideration of Human Factors Influencing B2C Persuasive Interaction. *Paper presented at the 35th Int. Conf. on Information Technology Interfaces*, Cavtat, Croatia.

Blake, B. F., Neuendorf, K. A., & Valdiserri, C. M. (2003). Innovativeness and variety of Internet shopping. *Internet Research*, *13*(3), 156–169. doi:10.1108/10662240310478187

Brengman, M., & Karimov, F. P. (2012). The effect of web communities on consumers' initial trust in B2C e-commerce websites. *Management Research Review*, *35*(9), 791–817. doi:10.1108/01409171211256569

Casaló, L. V., Flavián, C., & Guinalíu, M. (2011). The Generation of Trust in the online service and product distribution. the case of spanish electronic commerce. *Journal of Electronic Commerce Research*, *12*(3), 199–213.

Chen, J., & Dibb, S. (2010). Consumer trust in the online retail context: Exploring the antecedents and consequences. *Psychology and Marketing*, *27*(4), 323–346. doi:10.1002/mar.20334

Chen, Y.-H., & Barnes, S. (2007). Initial trust and online buyer behaviour. *Industrial Management & Data Systems*, *107*(1), 21–36. doi:10.1108/02635570710719034

Cheung, C., Lee, Z. W. Y., & Chan, T. K. H. (2015). Self-disclosure in social networking sites. *Internet Research*, *25*(2), 279–299. doi:10.1108/IntR-09-2013-0192

Chin, W. W. (2004). Multi-Group analysis with PLS.

Chin, W. W., Marcolin, B. L., & Newsted, P. R. (2003). A Partial Least Squares Latent Variable Modeling Approach for Measuring Interaction Effects: Results from a Monte Carlo Simulation Study and an Electronic-Mail Emotion/Adoption Study. *Information Systems Research*, *14*(2), 189–217. doi:10.1287/isre.14.2.189.16018

Constantinides, E. (2004). Influencing the online consumer's behavior: The web experience. *Internet Research*, *14*(2), 111–126. doi:10.1108/10662240410530835

Cyr, D. (2008). Modeling Web Site Design Across Cultures: Relationships to Trust, Satisfaction, and E-Loyalty. *Journal of Management Information Systems*, *24*(4), 47–72. doi:10.2753/MIS0742-1222240402

Cyr, D. (2013). Website design, trust and culture: An eight country investigation. *Electronic Commerce Research and Applications*.

Cyr, D., Head, M., & Larios, H. (2010). Colour appeal in website design within and across cultures: A multi-method evaluation. *International Journal of Human-Computer Studies*, *68*(1–2), 1–21. doi:10.1016/j.ijhcs.2009.08.005

Dobre, C., Dragomir, A., & Preda, G. (2009). Consumer Innovativeness: A Marketing Approach. *Management & Marketing*, *4*(2), 19–34.

Duffett, R. G. (2015). Facebook advertising's influence on intention-to-purchase and purchase amongst Millennials. *Internet Research*, *25*(4), 498–526. doi:10.1108/IntR-01-2014-0020

Eroglu, S. A., Machleit, K. A., & Davis, L. M. (2003). Empirical Testing of a Model of Online Store Atmospherics and Shopper Responses. *Psychology and Marketing*, *20*(2), 139–150. doi:10.1002/mar.10064

Faiola, A., & Matei, S. A. (2006). Cultural Cognitive Style and Web Design: Beyond a Behavioral Inquiry into Computer-Mediated Communication. *Journal of Computer-Mediated Communication*, *11*(1), 375–394. doi:10.1111/j.1083-6101.2006.tb00318.x

Ganguly, B., Dash, S. B., Cyr, D., & Head, M. (2010). The effects of website design on purchase intention in online shopping: The mediating role of trust and the moderating role of culture. *International Journal of Electronic Business*, *8*(4/5), 302–329. doi:10.1504/IJEB.2010.035289

Gefen, D., Karahanna, E., & Straub, D. W. (2003). Trust and TAM in Online Shopping: An Integrated Model. *Management Information Systems Quarterly*, *27*(1), 51–90. doi:10.2307/30036519

Gefen, D., & Straub, D. W. (2004). Consumer trust in B2C e-Commerce and the importance of social presence: Experiments in e-Products and e-Services. *Omega*, *32*(6), 407–424. doi:10.1016/j.omega.2004.01.006

Goldsmith, R. E., & Foxall, G. R. (2003). The Measurement of Innovativeness. In L. V. Shavinina (Ed.), *The International Handbook on Innovation* (Vol. 5, pp. 321–330). Elsevier Science Ltd. doi:10.1016/B978-008044198-6/50022-X

Grabner-Kräuter, S. (2009). Web 2.0 Social Networks: The Role of Trust. *Journal of Business Ethics*, *90*(4), 505–522. doi:10.100710551-010-0603-1

Guo, S., Wang, M., & Leskovec, J. (2011). The role of social networks in online shopping: information passing, price of trust, and consumer choice. *Paper presented at the Proceedings of the 12th ACM conference on Electronic commerce*, San Jose, CA. 10.1145/1993574.1993598

Ha, H.-Y., & Janda, S. (2014). The effect of customized information on online purchase intentions. *Internet Research*, *24*(4), 496–519. doi:10.1108/IntR-06-2013-0107

Ha, H.-Y., John, J., & Chung, Y.-K. (2016). Temporal effects of information from social networks on online behavior. *Internet Research*, *26*(1), 213–235. doi:10.1108/IntR-03-2014-0084

Haenlein, M., & Kaplan, A. M. (2004). A Beginner's Guide to Partial Least Squares Analysis. *Understanding Statistics*, *3*(4), 283–297. doi:10.120715328031us0304_4

Hair, F., Marko, J. S., Lucas, H., & Volker, G. K. (2014). Partial least squares structural equation modeling (PLS-SEM) An emerging tool in business research. *European Business Review*, *26*(2), 106–121. doi:10.1108/EBR-10-2013-0128

Hair, J. F., Ringle, C. M., & Sarstedt, M. (2011). PLS-SEM: Indeed a Silver Bullet. *Journal of Marketing Theory and Practice*, *19*(2), 139–151. doi:10.2753/MTP1069-6679190202

Hasslinger, A., Hodzic, S., & Opazo, C. (2007). *Online consumer behavior in online shopping*. Kristianstad university.

Henseler, J., Ringle, C. M., & Sinkovics, R. R. (2009). The use of partial least squares path modeling in international marketing. *New Challenges to International Marketing*, *20*, 277–319.

Henseler, J., & Sarstedt, M. (2013). Goodness-of-fit indices for partial least squares path modeling. *Computational Statistics*, *28*(2), 565–580. doi:10.100700180-012-0317-1

Hofstede, G. (1980). *Culture's Consequences: International Differences in Work-related Values. CA.* Beverly Hills: Sage.

Hofstede, G. (2001). *Culture's Consequences: Comparing Values, Behaviors, Institutions, and Organizations Across Nations* (Vol. 2). CA: SAGE Publications, Inc.

Huang, T.-L., & Liao, S. (2014). A model of acceptance of augmented-reality interactive technology: The moderating role of cognitive innovativeness. *Electronic Commerce Research*. doi:10.100710660-014-9163-2

Huang, Y.-A. (2003). Consumer Innovativeness and Consumer Expectations for New IT Products: Implications for Purchase Behavior. *Asia Pacific Management Review*, 3(2), 113–134.

Huynh, P. T., & Andrade, A. D. (2012). Effects of Web 2.0 Experience on Consumers' Online Purchase Intention: The Social Networking and Interaction Orientation Factors. *Paper presented at the International Conference on Information Resources Management*.

Hwang, Y., & Lee, K. C. (2012a). Investigating the moderating role of uncertainty avoidance cultural values on multidimensional online trust. *Information & Management*, 49(3-4), 171–176. doi:10.1016/j. im.2012.02.003

Hwang, Y., & Lee, K. C. (2012b). Investigating the moderating role of uncertainty avoidance cultural values on multidimensional online trust. *Information & Management*, 49(3–4), 171–176. doi:10.1016/j. im.2012.02.003

Karahanna, E., Williams, C. K., Polites, G. L., Liu, B., & Seligman, L. (2013). Uncertainty Avoidance and Consumer Perceptions of Global e-Commerce Sites: A Multi-Level Model. *Drake Management Review*, 3(1), 12–47.

Karimov, F. P., Brengman, M., & Hove, L. V. (2011). The Effect of Website Design Dimensions on Initial Trust: A Synthesis of the Empirical Literature. *Journal of Electronic Commerce Research*, 12(4), 272–301.

Kim, D. J. (2005). Cognition-based versus affect-based trust determinants in e-commerce: A cross-cultural comparison study. *Paper presented at the Twenty-Sixth International Conference on Information Systems (ICIS)*.

Kim, J., & Forsythe, S. (2007). Hedonic usage of product virtualization technologies in online apparel shopping. *International Journal of Retail & Distribution Management*, 35(6), 502–514. doi:10.1108/09590550710750368

Kim, S., & Park, H. (2013). Effects of various characteristics of social commerce (s-commerce) on consumers' trust and trust performance. *International Journal of Information Management*, 33(2), 318–232. doi:10.1016/j.ijinfomgt.2012.11.006

Kock, N. (2015). Common Method Bias in PLS-SEM: A Full Collinearity Assessment Approach. *International Journal of e-Collaboration*, 11(4). doi:10.4018/ijec.2015100101

Lee, M. K. O., Shi, N., Cheung, C. M. K., Lim, K. H., & Sia, C. L. (2011). Consumer's decision to shop online: The moderating role of positive informational social influence. *Information & Management*, 48(6), 185–191. doi:10.1016/j.im.2010.08.005

Lee, S., & Rao, V. S. (2010). Color and store choice in electronic commerce: The explanatory role of trust. *Journal of Electronic Commerce Research*, 11(2), 110–126.

Li, E. Y., Yen, H. R., Liu, C.-C., & Chang, L. F. K. (2013). From Structural Assurances to Trusting Beliefs: Validating Persuasion Principles in the Context of Online Shopping. *Paper presented at the PACIS 2013 Proceedings.*

Lim, K., Leung, K., Sia, C. L., & Lee, M. K. (2004). Is Ecommerce Boundary-Less? Effects of Individualism–Collectivism and Uncertainty Avoidance on Internet Shopping. *Journal of International Business Studies, 35*(6), 545–559. doi:10.1057/palgrave.jibs.8400104

Lodorfos, G. N., Trosterud, T. A., & Whitworth, C. (2006). E-Consumers' attitude and behaviour in the online commodities market. *Innovative Marketing, 2*(3), 77–96.

Lu, J. (2014). Are personal innovativeness and social influence critical to continue with mobile commerce? *Internet Research, 24*(2), 134–159. doi:10.1108/IntR-05-2012-0100

Manning, K. C., & William, O. (1995). Consumer Innovativeness and the Adoption Process. *Journal of Consumer Psychology, 4*(4), 329–345. doi:10.120715327663jcp0404_02

McCoy, S., Galletta, D. F., & King, W. R. (2005). Integrating National Culture into IS Research: The Need for Current Individual Level Measures. *Communications of the Association for Information Systems, 15*, 211–223.

McKnight, D. H., Choudhury, V., & Kacmar, C. (2002). The impact of initial consumer trust on intentions to transact with a web site: A trust building model. *The Journal of Strategic Information Systems, 11*(3-4), 297–323. doi:10.1016/S0963-8687(02)00020-3

McKnight, D. H., Cummings, L. L., & Chervany, N. L. (1998). Initial trust formation in new organizational relationships. *Academy of Management Review, 23*(3), 473–490.

Mehrabian, A., & Russell, J. A. (1974). *An Approach to Environmental Psychology.* Cambridge, MA: MIT.

Monsuwe, T. P. y., Dellaert, B. G. C., & Ruyter, K. (2004). What drives consumers to shop online? A literature review. *International Journal of Service Industry Management, 15*(1), 102–121. doi:10.1108/09564230410523358

Ringle, C. M., Wende, S., & Becker, J.-M. (2015). Smartpls 3. Hamburg: SmartPLS. Retrieved from http://www.smartpls.com

Rogers, E. M. (1995). *Diffusion of Innovations.* New York: The Free Press.

Sabiote, C. M., Frías, D. M., & Castañeda, J. A. (2012). The moderating effect of uncertainty-avoidance on overall perceived value of a service purchased online. *Internet Research, 22*(2), 180–198. doi:10.1108/10662241211214557

Sarstedt, M., Hair, J. F., Ringle, C. M., Thiele, K. O., & Gudergan, S. P. (2016). Estimation issues with PLS and CBSEM: Where the bias lies! *Journal of Business Research, 69*(10), 3998–4010. doi:10.1016/j.jbusres.2016.06.007

Schaffer, E. (2009). Beyond Usability: Designing Web Sites for Persuasion, Emotion, and Trust. *UXmatters*. Retrieved from http://www.uxmatters.com/mt/archives/2009/01/beyond-usability-designing-websites-for-persuasion-emotion-and-trust.php#sthash.12RABAUa.dpuf

Sharma, R., Yetton, P., & Crawford, J. (2009). Estimating the effect of common method variance: The method--method pair technique with an illustration TAM research. *Management Information Systems Quarterly*, *33*(3), 473–A413. doi:10.2307/20650305

Sheng, H., & Joginapelly, T. (2012). Effects of Web Atmospheric Cues on Users' Emotional Responses in E-Commerce. *Transactions on Human-Computer Interaction*, *4*(1), 1–24. doi:10.17705/1thci.00036

Sia, C. L., Lim, K. H., Leung, K., Lee, M. K. O., Huang, W. W., & Benbasat. (2009). Web strategies to promote internet shopping: Is cultural customization needed? *Management Information Systems Quarterly*, *33*(3), 491–512. doi:10.2307/20650306

Singh, N., Kumar, V., & Baack, D. (2005). Adaptation of cultural content: Evidence from B2C e-commerce firms. *European Journal of Marketing*, *39*(1/2), 71–86. doi:10.1108/03090560510572025

Sohaib, O., & Kang, K. (2015a). Individual Level Culture Effects on Multi-Perspective iTrust in B2C E-commerce. *Paper presented at the 26th Australasian Conference on Information Systems*, Adeliade.

Sohaib, O., & Kang, K. (2015b). Individual level culture influence on online consumer iTrust aspects towards purchase intention across cultures: A S-O-R Model. *International Journal of Electronic Business*, *12*(2), 142–161. doi:10.1504/IJEB.2015.069104

Srite, M., & Karahanna, E. (2006). The Role of Espoused National Cultural Values in Technology Acceptance. *Management Information Systems Quarterly*, *30*(3), 679–704. doi:10.2307/25148745

Tan, F. B., Tung, L.-L., & Xu, Y. (2009). A study of web designer criteria for effective business to-consumer websites using repertory grid technique. *Journal of Electronic Commerce Research*, *10*(3), 155–177.

Tellis, G. J., Yin, E., & Bell, S. (2009). Global Consumer Innovativeness: Cross-Country Differences and Demographic Commonalities. *Journal of International Marketing*, *17*(2). doi:10.1509/jimk.17.2.1

Thakur, R., & Srivastava, M. (2014). Adoption readiness, personal innovativeness, perceived risk and usage intention across customer groups for mobile payment services in India. *Internet Research*, *24*(3), 369–392. doi:10.1108/IntR-12-2012-0244

Tsai, H.-T., & Bagozzi, R. P. (2014). Contribution behavior in virtual communities: Cognitive, emotional, and social influences. *Management Information Systems Quarterly*, *38*(1), 143–164. doi:10.25300/MISQ/2014/38.1.07

van der Merwe, R., & Bekker, J. (2003). A framework and methodology for evaluating e-commerce web sites. *Internet Research*, *13*(5), 330–341. doi:10.1108/10662240310501612

Venkatraman, M. P. (1991). The impact of innovativeness and innovation type on adoption. *Journal of Retailing*, *67*(1), 51–67.

Venkatraman, M. P., & Price, L. L. (1990). Differentiating between cognitive and sensory innovativeness: Concept, measurement, and implications. *Journal of Business Research*, *20*(4), 293–315. doi:10.1016/0148-2963(90)90008-2

Yoon, C. (2009). The effects of national culture values on consumer acceptance of e-commerce: Online shoppers in China. *Information & Management*, *46*(5), 294–301. doi:10.1016/j.im.2009.06.001

Zhu, D. H., Chang, Y. P., & Chang, A. (2015). Effects of free gifts with purchase on online purchase satisfaction. *Internet Research*, *25*(5), 690–706. doi:10.1108/IntR-12-2013-0257

Zrim, L. (2016). Information is crucial for online Australian shoppers. *Australian Nielsen Connected Consumers Report, 2016*. Retrieved from http://www.nielsen.com/au/en/insights/news/2016/information-is-crucial-for-online-australian-shoppers.html

This research was previously published in the Journal of Global Information Management (JGIM), 27(2); pages 59-77, copyright year 2019 by IGI Publishing (an imprint of IGI Global).

APPENDIX

Table 5. Questionnaire items

		Measures	Loadings	p-Value
Website Accessibility (Casaló, Flavián, & Guinalíu, 2011; Chen & Dibb, 2010; Chen & Barnes, 2007; Gefen, Karahanna, & Straub, 2003; Yoon, 2009)	WA1	The structure of this website is easy to understand.	0.89	0.00***
	WA2	Learning to operate this website is easy.	0.90	0.00***
	WA3	When I am navigating this website, I feel that I am in control of what I can do.	0.86	0.00***
	WA4	This website responds quickly.	0.93	0.00***
	WA5	This website helps me correct the errors I made.	0.87	0.00***
	WA6	My interaction with the website is understandable.	0.89	0.00***
Color (Chen & Dibb, 2010; Cyr, Head, & Larlos 2010)	COL1	The colours used on the website are emotionally appealing.	0.73	0.00***
	COL2	The colour use on this website is attractive overall.	0.70	0.01*
	COL3	The brightness of pages on this website is adequate.	0.95	0.00***
Images (Chen & Dibb, 2010; Dianne Cyr, 2013; Kim & Forsythe, 2007)	IMG1	This website has eye-catching images on the home page.	0.87	0.00***
	IMG2	Zooming and 3D images are helpful in buying what I want through this website.	0.73	0.00**
	IMG3	Overall, the screen design (i.e. images, layout etc.) is attractive.	0.87	0.00**
Social Networking Services (Hasslinger, Hodzic, & Opazo, 2007; Huynh & Andrade, 2012; McKnight, Choudhury, & Kacmar, 2002)	SNS1	This website clearly shows how I can contact the company.	0.74 (Weight)	0.00***
	SNS2	I believe using social networks services (YouTube/Facebook/twitter/Google+) would help me in decision making to purchase online.	0.17 (Weight)	0.005*
	SNS3	I believe using the other support services (such as, FAQs, ranking, online help, and contact details) would help me to buy a product I really want.	0.52 (Weight)	0.00***
	SNS4	My friends or family tell me about the new products.	0.62 (Weight)	0.00**
Cognitive Innovativeness (Manning et al., 1995; Venkatraman & Price, 1990; Manning et al., 1995; Tellis et al., 2009)	CInn1	I am usually among the first to buy a new product.	0.88	0.00***
	CInn2	I am continually seeking new product experiences online.	0.93	0.00***
	CInn3	I usually find out the meaning of words I don't know.	0.92	0.00***
	CInn4	I am among the last in my circle of friends to buy a new product when it appears online.	0.74	0.01**
	CInn5	When I go shopping online, I find myself spending very little time checking out new products.	0.82	0.002**
	CInn6	Purchasing new products online takes too much time and effort.	0.92	0.005**
New Purchase Intention (Tellis et al., 2009; Yoon, 2009)	NPINT1	I am likely to purchase the new product(s) from this retailer website.	0.87	0.00***
	NPINT2	I frequently look for new products online.	0.84	0.00***
	NPINT3	I am eager to buy new products as soon as they come out online.	0.88	0.00***
Uncertainty Avoidance (Hwang & Lee, 2012a; Srite & Karahanna, 2006; Yoon, 2009)	UA1	I prefer to avoid making changes during online shopping because things could get worse.	0.92	0.00***
	UA2	Rules and regulations of the online stores are important to me because they inform buyers what the online store does.	0.87	0.00***
	UA3	Standard operating procedures for an online store are helpful to me for the purchase decisions.	0.91	0.00***

*Significant at 0.05 level; ** Significant at 0.01 level; *** Significant at 0.001 level

Chapter 82
Understanding Generational Impact on Online Business:
The Virtual Communities and Social Collaborations Scenario

Karthikeyan Shanmugam

(iD) https://orcid.org/0000-0003-4276-2663

SASTRA University (Deemed), India

Vijayabanu C

(iD) https://orcid.org/0000-0002-0125-4534

SASTRA University (Deemed), India

ABSTRACT

In today's age of technology and exploding internet penetration, customers are rapidly moving toward continuous connectivity across every facet of their lives. Similarly, business is also changing in response to this digital boom. This chapter analyzes digital tools such as virtual communities, social collaboration, and its impact on the multiple generations in managing connected customers for organizations. The technological tools make it simple for customers to be connected at all times, which has become the major challenge for organizations to formulate strategies and be competent in the market. The major types of virtual communities that can be associated with businesses were discussed in detail. This chapter proposes a model for organization to manage their customers effectively. The above-mentioned digital tools are playing vital role in retaining customers and strategies can be formulated to manage the connected customers successfully. Thus, the chapter analyzed the major areas that are important to the organizations in order to succeed in formulating competitive strategy.

DOI: 10.4018/978-1-7998-9020-1.ch082

INTRODUCTION

Evolution of information sharing is worldwide and it is to the extent of around 10 percent of the total population. They are sharing information through informal networks frequently, for various purposes. When information sharing is intelligently accessed, it acts as an efficient method for any organization either it is public or private. Information sharing is essential to most of the businesses, aiding quickly to meet customer desires through CRM systems.

In today's age of technology and exploding Internet penetration, Indian retail customers are rapidly moving toward continuous connectivity across every facet of their lives. Today's customers are more tech-savvy and more open than ever before to try out new experiences enabled by unfettered digital access. Virtual communities are virtual in some extent. However, they are not something beyond our conventional societies. Virtual communities are genuine parts of our public and in that capacity additionally part of the progressing change and advancement of society. Regardless of whether we trust that a virtual community is just a gathering of individuals utilizing the equivalent "news" gathering, or meeting around an accumulation of homepages, or imparting through a "mailing list", it is considered as a "basic" specialized frameworks will impact the manner in which society is organized and how that structure will change (Schuler, 1996).

This digital transformation is bringing about a profound shift in how customers interact with retailers as they make their purchase decisions. Indian retailers that take note of, and act on, these changes would best placed to win customers in this connected retail environment. A number of researches have discounted that how an exchange of information and societal support are the two major facts behind why people join and then chose a virtual community.

Virtual Communities

Virtual community is web-based gathering of individuals who share similar interests, fears, and sincere beliefs. (Dennis, Pootheri, & Natarajan, 1998), a subject important to all individuals have been discussed by the groups of individuals who meet frequently (Figallo, 1998), and the shared interests or a geographic bond which brings groups of individuals together (Kilsheimer, 1997). Virtual communities are defined as "social aggregations that emerge from the Internet when enough people carry on those public discussions long enough, with sufficient human feeling, to form webs of personal relationships in cyberspace" (Rheingold, 1993).

Virtual communities and collaborations facilitate various value additions like active participation and promotion. (Pentina et al., 2008). Virtual communities are online spaces where individuals serach for peples and talk with them electronically about the similar interested topics. Being competent for enhancing attachment to online and the websites, virtual communities can possibly develop future plans of action, particularly in business to consumers. Hagel and Armstrong (1997) discussed the business viewpoint and characterize virtual communities as a gathering of individuals drawn together by a chance to impart a feeling of the network to similarly invested outsiders having normal premium. Virtual communities are fundamentally characterized as the gatherings of similarly invested outsiders who interface prevalently on the internet to frame connections, share learning, have a great time or take part in economic transactions.

Among the rapidly growing different types of websites (Peterson, 1999; Wingfield and Hanrahan, 1999), community sites places the major role. Assessments of virtual community membership have surpassed twenty-five million (Gross, 1999) and the Pew Internet and American Life Project reports that ninety million Americans have taken part in an online gathering (Horrigan, Rainie, and Fox, 2001). Along these lines, important reasons why users join specific communities and build up a web presence and for scholastics attempting to comprehend user behavior. Hence, it becomes essential for organizations to understand the virtual communities that facilitate them to take advantage of using vast information for enhancing income expanding potential. The introduction of virtual communities related to the recent trends of e-commerce (Othmani and Bouslama, 2015). Acquiring high technology security along with sociability is easy to use which helps virtual communities to collect the needs of customers and their interest.

BACKGROUND OF THE STUDY

Almost twenty-five years from now officially, digital has been transforming our society by changing the everyday life of markets and general peoples. One important dimension of this digital advancement is the expanded probability for customers to make a move in all directions.

In the mid-90s, because of sites and the advancement of web-based business (e-commerce), consumers used the capacity to influence demand and "churn". This impact keeps on developing and, towards the end of the 90s, customers started the attack by delivering information, positioning the products and brands on an expanding number through blogs and forums. The customer's impact escalated significantly due to social networks as "Facebook, Twitter and YouTube" in the 21st century: for huge sharing of information. Towards the end of the 2000s, consumer's empowerment achieved peak, in light of groups: the group and communities even helped consumers to mold up themselves as service providers.

Today the period is, described by the rise of connected devices and the expansion of the social networks of individuals through networks by both individuals and devices. This period of the Social Internet of Things addresses a huge change for market borders, focused universes and economic stakeholders. In this new universe, consumer behavior is always an unexplored field of research. The "Connected Consumers in a Digital World" inquire and disclose to the organizations how to adjust their marketing strategies and techniques to stay aggressive in markets where rivalry is expected.

In recent years, efforts to create innovations and new values accelerated by utilizing networked machines and information in the industry. We expected that not only the manufacturing industry but also the service industry are going to change with the use of Internet of Things (IoT). An effective platform creates an interdependent ecosystem in which companies collaborate independently seeking their own goals. The system that has contributed to the development of the hyper-connected society is especially depends on information and communication. Including the emergence of information exchange, the typical changes in through various equipment and systems such as smartphones, ICT convergence, media convergence, the emergence of big data, and cloud computing. In the pre-connectivity era, the customer buying behavior typically followed the 4A's framework that consists of awareness, attitude, and actions. In this straightforward process of the network era, the company's touch points have a major influence on customer decision making.

In the high connectivity era, customers tend to connect with their peers and ask their opinions. They are influenced by the netizens who are considered as one of the most active players in the consumer's forums and communities. Besides that, customers who need more information would go online and read the reviews to see what other consumers have told about the product or service. The amount of positive or negative opinions, reviews and recommendations will either strengthen or weaken the brand's initial appeal through the connectivity among the customers.

Social media platforms and live chat put organizations directly before customer; organizations could not forfeit their customer to keep up the brand position. In fact, when organizations do not react to an inquiry, it harms the brand reputation since that information is open to a huge number of individuals. The upside of these new devices is that it has a more extensive information accumulation pool; organizations can quickly track their innovative work by using this huge information. The studies show that behaviors of consumers in virtual community were influenced by the recommendations and online reviews plays a vital role (Menon et al, 2005; Bickart and Schindler, 2001).

Consumers and Digital Marketing (E-Commerce and Mobile App)

Digital marketing is a form of marketing that can be accessed either through online or offline utilization of electronic gadget, it brings completely every form of advertising via electronic gadget and inclines to view it on screen through television sets or electronic billboards, also it can be viewed through the internet via social media and through radio termed as offline.

Some of the benefits of social media are

Reduced Cost: The cost for creating a digital marketing strategy through online is comparatively lower than telecasted on televisions, radios and paper media.

Flexibility: The digital form has more flexibility with the advantage of easily moving from one channel to another with very little or no cost incurred compared to other forms.

Viral: Social media plug-ins is helpful in making viral the products and services of top app development companies on websites.

Measurable Result: Digital marketing makes it easy to know, evaluate the number of views or click of the content at the back end but it is hard to get the same evaluation on either TV, radio or billboard commercials.

Saves Time: With the use of digital marketing, the consumer can purchase the products of their need at ease with a simple click from where they reside. This saves more time for the customers.

The magnitude of digital marketing and its impact on the current business world is undoubtedly huge despite its contributing factors. Thus, E-commerce has emerged as a lifestyle for millions of people over the globe. As much as e-commerce has turned out to be instilled in everyday existence, so has the utilization of apps, those help to link our short-lived interests, benefits and specific needs in a given activity cycle.

With social media outlets being so predominant, apps that encourage the communication process between users are fundamental to everybody's shared digital encounters, by means of Facebook, Instagram, or Twitter. As everything changing into digital, that states every company getting themselves into online for marketing. Brands have to stay alive with recent trends that help them to face the challenges of digital marketing. The leading digital marketing trends that are paving the way in 2018 are Interactive Chatbots, Voice Search, Integrating AI and Blockchain Technologies, Influencer marketing.

OBJECTIVES OF THE STUDY

- To know and understand the role of virtual communities of connecting consumers.
- To identify the various types of virtual communities and their relationship to various generations.

- To identify the need of virtual communities to face future challenges for various generation of consumers.

Types of Virtual Communities

Typology of virtual communities is not conformed to the single, widely accepted classification and definitions of "virtual community". According to Preece(2000) Stanoevska – Slabeve (2002) most of the researchers, likely to classify virtual communities with a single variable which they feel the prime source of their discipline. For instance, researchers based on information system often classify by the supporting communication technology design like chat, blogs or other functional requirements. On the other side, there are researcher's looks through sociological perspective, who uses the structure of interaction network or the location of interaction like physical or virtual space as a classifying variable, Virnoche & Marx (1997).

Another major categorization by business researchers based on the purpose of communities such as revenue generation or consumer needs satisfaction based on the attributes like fantasy and interaction.

Classification Based on Information System Researchers

Virtual community is where people joining and meeting together with related interests, and connected over the Internet. Virtual communities based on usage of information systems can be distinguished, as shown in Table 1. Even though the reasons behind these virtual communities are amazing, creation and support of social networks became general among these communities.

Table 1. Types of virtual communities (e-commerce, Web 2.0)

Type	Details	Websites
Commercial communities	"To encourage business transactions and other businesses". They are related to e-commerce and centered on a commercial area.	Amazon, e-Bay
Communities of practice	Impart ideas, experiences, and opinions.	Twitter
Virtual reality communities	Imaginary environments experiences.	Second Life (Site 24)
Social communities	To set up or keep up social or expert or professional associations.	Facebook, Linkedin, MySpace

Source: (Turban et al. 2008)

Commercial Communities

The commercial communities are the type of virtual communities that are strongly associated with businesses, and e-commerce sites are the options how they directly associated with businesses. Some of them are developing normally towards such ideas, especially to encourage greater associations with their users or to give them information needed for making a better purchase. Nowadays e-commerce sites permit buyers to review the purchases they made using the e-commerce sites, which enables prospective customers to think and decide about future purchases based on these reviews (Easley and Kleinberg, 2010). Thus, e-commerce sites are advancing into virtual communities, and virtual communities supported by online social networks incorporated with the features of e-commerce.

Communities of Practice

Communities of practice also termed as a virtual community of practice and is developed and maintained by using the internet. Professionals are grouped together by shared objectives and common concerns about participation, exchange of inferred and clear knowledge to improve their professional experience and the performance of their organizations. Communities of practice are mainly characterized by self-regulations. These communities depend majorly on internet virtual space like social networks. Professionals use communities of practice as a critical resource to provide them the need of suggestions, best practices, tips and tricks, insights. Along with these facts, which makes a community of practice strong is the collection of relationships, i.e., people and information are associated to a rational set of the area which people will find helpful, interesting and potentially profitable.

CLASSIFICATIONS BASED ON BUSINESS RESEARCHERS

Content-Based Classifications

The virtual communities include two first-level categories, and they are Member-initiated and Organization-sponsored. The second level category of virtual communities' states is the kind of association or affiliation prevails between the participants of society. "Member-initiated communities promoting either social or professional relationships among members have been done by the member-initiated communities". "Organization-sponsored communities promote develop relationships both among members and between individual members and the sponsoring organization".

Member-initiated communities and member-generated content focused majorly by the maximum researchers moderate than on organizations of virtual communities sponsored. Virtual communities of these types are becoming popular with organizations (Bughin & Zeisser, 2001; Balasubramanian & Mahajan, 2001). Member-generated content communities are widely accessed by both the members and organizations, which also contributes to the content as well as participation in building relationships (Mcwilliam, 2002). Thus, the proposed classifications are helpful across many disciplines for both the researchers and organizations as well.

Figure 1. Typology of virtual communities
Source: Porter, 2004

1691

Individuals create and set up virtual communities online to offer a forum by which people can share information paying little mind to the topic. Some virtual communities developed for individuals and occupied with business-related activities. In this kind of community, individuals normally share trade secrets. Moreover, a customer based virtual community shaped by business organizations builds up a situation where customers can transparently share and spread information to different customers and company agents.

From the past researches to characterize virtual communities, we suggested the following attributes: "Purpose, Place, Platform, Population Interaction Structure, and Profit Model". It will be thoughtful to have essential attributes in conceptualizing virtual communities as it is consistent and easy to describe them while organizations and researchers planning. The distinctive mixtures of features comprises precarious success factors and relative results that help both members and organizations. The differentiating variables, establishment, and relationships differentiate each kind of virtual community from others. Hence, the attributes explained below helps in label any virtual community despite its type.

The key attributes of virtual communities can be termed as the Five Ps of virtual community. The summarized attributes as follows:

Purpose: This attribute describes the specific focus of discourse, or focal content of the communication, among community members.

Place: This attribute defines the location of the interaction, where interaction occurs either completely virtually or only partially virtually.

Platform: This attribute refers to the technical design of interaction in the virtual community where designs enable synchronous communication, asynchronous communication or both.

Population: This attribute refers to the pattern of interaction among community members as described by group structure (e.g. small group or network) and type of social ties (e.g. strong, weak, stressful).

Profit Model: This attribute refers to whether a community creates tangible economic value where value is the revenue-generation.

Table 2. Key attributes of virtual communities

Attribute	Explanation
Purpose - content of interaction	The content of information which is used for interaction, (Example., Sports or general discussions on the environment, politics, etc.,)
Place - extent of technology mediation of interaction	• Virtual "exists only in virtual space" • Hybrid "exists in both physical and virtual space"
Platform - design of interaction	• Synchronous for example chat. • Asynchronous for example email • Hybrid
Population interaction structure - pattern of interaction	• computer oriented social networks • small groups or networks • virtual public
Profit model - return on interaction	This attributes concentrates in identifying the creation of tangible economic value by virtual communities. • Income -generating (host, facilitator, owner) - host communities by the enablers of certain community's (e.g.Yahoo) • Non-revenue generating

Source: (Porter, 2004)

Revenue-Based Classifications

The revenue-based classification of virtual community focuses not only on the content but also on the profitability that relates more to the business model perspective. The revenue-based virtual communities can be classified into two main groups namely standalone or add-on according to revenue generation model (Franz and Wolkinger, 2003). The organizations concentrate more towards indirect effects of the virtual communities rather than generating revenues through the standalone basis includes revenues from e-commerce trading, subscriptions, advertising, and other relevant sources. However, an add-on basis community includes revenues from integrating various customer, analyzing research about markets, and product development.

Figure 2. Types of virtual communities (revenue based)Source: (Franz and Wolkinger 2003)

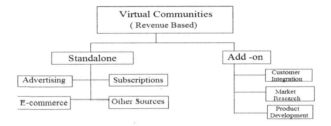

There are some additional elements frequently mentioned that provide indirect revenue for the company:

- Customer Loyalty
- Customer Feedbacks / Suggestions
- Improve products
- Consumer Stickiness
- discover new streams of revenue
- Innovation process
- Customer Information

The virtual community based on revenue by Cothrel (2000) has similar objectives of Franz and Wolkinger (2003) model. The Cothrel (2000) model aims to build a stronger relationship, innovations, increase efficiency, acquiring new customers and direct revenues. The first three elements of the model envelop add-on part and the direct earnings are comparable to standalone elements of previous model.

IMPACT OF VIRTUAL COMMUNITIES ON MULTI-GENERATIONS

Generations are a group of people who born during a particular timeframe. They have more similar life circumstances, same perspectives, and dispositions, and separated from different ages. Currently, five generations namely Maturists, Baby Boomers, Gen X, Gen Y or Millennials ad Gen Z are prevailing. Multi-Generations has a greater impact on the virtual world. Understanding these issues is indispensable for organizations: they can influence everything at various stages to connect with customers and other stakeholders. The organizations should handle the issues of the virtual world across generations. Generally, millennials spend much time on the web, and live in internet-based life for various individual reasons. More youthful millennial tend to balance life, work, daily activities, network, etc., through technology. Internet users of the Middle Ages are more inclined towards information technology than older ages to understand other people's perspectives through blogs compared to older generations. The middle ages also utilize social networking sites to make profiles on that locale. In contrast, teenagers and Gen Y utilize virtual communities to mingle and develop a relationship, business databases, and grouping. Hence, the challenge for the organization lies with the product, quality, competition and price wars that managed through effective social collaboration and with different generations.

Raymond Morin, Canada-based social media expert, speaker, author in his new book "Generation C - The Confluence Marketing at the Era of Connected Consumers" in which he examines the challenges and opportunities presented by content and influencer marketing in relation to successive generations that are increasingly less receptive to traditional communication. He explores the evolution of individuals' behavior as consumers but also workers and members of society. Raymond provides invaluable insights and advice for anyone interested in marketing in our digital age.

The new connected generation, also known as Generation C, encompasses successive generations of active users and consumers on the internet. From elders and baby boomers to digital natives, they are now all involved in the social and digital transformation of organizations. Today, as technological innovations transform society at an accelerated pace, we see micro-generations emerging, each with specific characteristics and motivations. In reality, the concept of Generation C is not new and goes back to 2004 with the appearance of social networks, and when Dutch magazine TrendWatching.com observed behavioral traits linking the different generations of connected consumers. Each of these new generations of "connected consumers" wants to be heard, and demands that companies and brands respond to their requests. Fourteen years later, they each uniquely influenced several aspects of society: from home to the workplace, to education, communication, social relations, and entertainment.

The connected consumer is empowered by the endless choices resulting from accessibility to the web and social media, which profound changes the business/customer relationship. Today, connected consumers rely more on their peers' recommendations to seek information and prioritize the quality of their experience and the brand. This forces companies and brands to adapt their message and communicate differently with their clients. In this context and thanks to new technological innovations (augmented reality, artificial intelligence, 3D printing) and the analysis of personal data accessible online, it is believed that marketing campaigns will be more personalized, more targeted towards the connected consumers, and will have the priority to satisfy the customer's experience.

SOCIAL COLLABORATION: IMPORTANCE AND BENEFITS

Sharing and interacting information with more people in a public forum to achieve a common goal, support, acceptance are about social collaboration. Social collaboration plays a vital role in improving the enhanced perception of the quality of products and services. This complex problem, by far more assorted and least consistent of all business software categories, is social collaboration. Among other business software category in social collaboration is fair and diverse in solving various diverse problems. When the collaboration tool is properly utilized it creates more positive eWOM, ends in satisfied customers.

The organization can use these satisfied customers as their brand ambassadors whose perception results in sharing positive experiences via reviews, feedbacks, and conversations with their friends, family, and colleagues. Most of the time this will be based on the what are the products and services, overall objectives, and only the tip of the iceberg. Social collaboration tools simply help to do existing business activities in a faster and easier way.

Generally, social collaboration software classified into three different types, relevant to businesses, namely people oriented, task-oriented and file oriented. Social collaboration tools aims to promote impulsive, non-mandated knowledge between customers in the form of comments, status updates, microblogs etc.

Below are some neglected advantages:

- **Time-Saving:** One of the major crux of any industry is its effective usage of its time and the way they spent it with their customers. This also include how employees of the organization spent their time in accomplishing their tasks to attain the objectives of the organization.
- **Strong Relationship Among Team Members:** Building effective working relationships among employees is vital in any organization. Collaboration tools are path development for employees of a team to work conveniently for achieving a common goal.
- **Goal-Based Performance:** The Better organization is something that each organization ought to make progress toward, regardless of whether things are as of now going great. Collaboration tools are the best medication when you are endeavoring to enhance the organization.
- **Increased Productivity:** Employees spend almost 50 percent of their time searching for information and managing communications. Social collaboration tools dramatically streamline that process, enabling people to find what and whom they need more efficiently and effectively - which means they have more time to get real work done.
- **Clear, Consistent Communication:** Social collaboration tools allow organizations to communicate meaningfully at every level. Corporate-wide and executive announcements shared and interacted. Therefore, everyone aligned with the company vision, mission, and news. Departments gain a digital meeting space to work on projects and build relationships.
- **Stronger Corporate Memory:** Corporate culture – and its longer-term counterpart, corporate memory – stem from a communal understanding of an organization's values and knowledge. Social collaboration provides the framework to connect people to each other and to the historical and real-time information that is critical to organizational success.

Online collaboration tools help in enhancing efficiency, productivity, and innovation, online collaboration aspects of social media, traditional business, and crowdsourcing to create an experience, not at all like whatever else. Collaboration tools also include a broad range of functions, from instant messaging to company intranets to document collaboration to knowledge bases, forums, and user groups. At the highest level, social collaboration tools break down silos to improve access to the people and information that help work done more quickly and accurately. Those silos may be technological, geographical, organizational, personal, or all of the above.

The advantages of social collaboration enhance profitability, knowledge management, group commitment, and competitiveness. It is useful for a group of people to work together, and ideally dealt with each sort of information - records, projects, plans, and discussions. Social collaboration enables committed workspaces for customers and partners to share information, and arrange exertion or construct customer communities. In addition to the fact that it bring customers and partners into collaboration work process, to inspire and build more strong relationships.

Future of Social Collaboration Tools

Emerging technologies like artificial intelligence (AI) and machine learning will transform social collaboration tools into smart, predictive hubs when and where you need it. Foreseeing the future of work has become a most loved pastime for most of the people. More important, it is accomplished a lot of progress – with constant revolution. Creation of a perfect flawless collaboration tool experience to all stakeholders will be the future of business collaboration. Such tools experience and their collaborative processes would save money on travel and other material costs. Important conclusions about consumer behavior attained by decision-makers with the aid of integrated systems and data collaboration. Social collaboration aids the organizations to take advantage over their businesses in everything from innovation, design, invention, marketing plans and a million other tasks easily. According to Holly Simmons, senior director of marketing for SAP's cloud collaboration and analysis products, "Social collaboration is not just about replacing email or sharing a document, it is about moving the business ahead, solving problems and making strategic decisions".

In comparing with traditional marketing method, virtual communities are promising and increase efficiency element. The new combinations of information, products and services and innovative integrations of resources and relationships between consumers and companies seemed to provide more market potential with the addition of virtual communities. It is in the preliminary stages, the studies on understanding the impact of virtual communities on marketing strategies. As a result, there are other studies in the future. Above all the literature indicates that the degree of consumer commitment towards virtual community is the major factor in deciding the success of virtual communities (Cothrel 2000). Hence, it is important to plan a reliable measuring scale for the degree of individual involvement in the community. While measuring these following aspects are need to be taken into considerations like the trust or increasing degree of commitment one have on the brand as a limitation in representing a particular community (Morgan and Hunt, 1994). Until now, online auctions and the retail markets are some of the sectors. A full assessment of the consequences of virtual communities in different sectors will also be required. However, the use of virtual communities could also address broader types of relationships.

CONNECTING CONSUMERS OF VARIOUS GENERATIONS

Organizations that will succeed in retaining new recruits and in collaborating with the Generations Y and Z are those who know how to integrate them into their change-management process and appeal to their curiosity and natural creativity, notably for content creation and duration. Some of the measures to regain trust among customers are:

- Never walk away from the commitments you make
- Make sure of quicker response to all situations
- Show integrity in approach
- Adopt an open and transparent set of guidelines
- Establish a history of positive actions with the customers

The type of influencers and the role they play in online and social media marketing strategies will always depend on the objectives and target audiences. Celebrity or social media celebrity endorsement will never generate the same impact as a corporate ambassador program or a long-term business relationship. Companies and organizations must clearly define their objectives first, and identify the type of influencers that will best fit the context of the new era. The four generations have shared the same working environments. This is a new paradigm of today's digital society, which will accelerate the social and digital transformation of organizations. At this level, Generation X, which has just taken over decision-making positions, also has a new responsibility to undertake, and handle connected generations. The digital era has led to the emergence of micro-generations with specific expectations and needs, and it is time for marketing to adapt to this new reality.

CONCLUSION

The chapter reviewed and analyzed the impact of virtual communities and social collaboration for the effective performance of an organization. It states the realistic situations in breaking down generation and age barriers to access the information shared through virtual communities. It also confirms that the primary reasons why virtual communities and social collaboration are essential in managing the global business through connected customers, e-commerce, e-tailing of new emerging economies. Businesses can gain by enriching their websites to present highly interactive sessions. This can restrained through experts and motivates sharing opinions, exchanging various thoughts and news that effects in the discussions product related decisions. Valuable information can be created with the help of these events to increase loyalty among customers and able to develop potential customers concurrently. Additionally, by creating an online space in the trading website will attract customers in socializing and in turn helps the organizations to build loyal customers.

REFERENCES

Bagozzi, R. P., & Dholakia, U. M. (2002). Intentional social action in virtual communities. *Journal of Interactive Marketing*, *16*(2), 2–21. doi:10.1002/dir.10006

Balasubramanian, S., & Mahajan, V. (2001). The Economic Leverage of the Virtual Community. *International Journal of Electronic Commerce*, *5*(3), 103–138. doi:10.1080/10864415.2001.11044212

Bughin, J., & Zeisser, M. (2001). The marketing scale effectiveness of virtual communities. *Electronic Markets*, *11*(4), 258–262. doi:10.1080/101967801753405544

Cothrel, J. P. (2000). Measuring the success of an online community. *Strategy and Leadership*, *28*(2), 7–21. doi:10.1108/10878570010341609

Dennis, A. R., Pootheri, S. K., & Natarajan, V. L. (1998). Lessons from the early adopters of Web groupware. *Journal of Management Information Systems*, *14*(4), 65–86. doi:10.1080/07421222.1998.11518186

Easley & Kleinberg. (2010). Networks, Crowds, and Markets: Reasoning about a Highly Connected World. Cambridge University Press.

Figallo, C. (1998). *Hosting Web communities: Building relationships, increasing customer loyalty and maintaining a competitive edge*. New York: John Wiley & Sons, Inc.

Franz, R., & Wolkinger, T. (2003). Customer Integration with Virtual Communities. Case study: The online community of the largest regional newspaper in Austria. *Proceedings of the Hawaii International Conference on System Sciences*.

Gross. (1999, March 22). Building global communities: How business is partnering with sites that draw together like-minded consumers. *BusinessWeek Online*. Retrieved October 17, 2004, from http://businessweek.com/datedtoc/1999/9912.htm

Hagel, J., & Armstrong, A. G. (1997). *Net Gain: Expanding Markets through Virtual Communities*. Harvard Business School Press.

Horrigan, J. B., Rainie, L., & Fox, S. (2001). *Online communities: networks that nurture long-distance relationships and local ties*. Washington, DC: Pew Internet & American Life Project. Available at: http://www.pewinternet.org

Kilsheimer, J. (1997, April 7). Virtual communities; Cyberpals keep in touch online. *The Arizona Republic*, p. E3.

McWilliam, G. (2002). Building stronger brands through online communities. *Sloan Management Review*, *41*(3), 43–54.

Morgan, R. M., & Hunt, S. D. (1994). The commitment-trust theory of relationship marketing. *Journal of Marketing*, *58*, 20–38. doi:10.1177/002224299405800302

Othmani, L., & Bouslama, P. N. (2015). Highlighting the Influence of Virtual Communities on the online shoppers trust. *Journal of Internet Social Networking & Virtual Communities*, *6*, 1–8.

Pentina, I., Prybutok, V. R., & Zhang, X. (2008). The Role of Virtual Communities as Shopping Reference Groups. *Journal of Electronic Commerce Research*, *9*(2), 114–136.

Petersen, A. (1999, January 6). Some places to go when you want to feel right at home: Communities focus on people who need people. *The Wall Street Journal*, p. B6.

Porter, C. E. (2004). A Typology of Virtual Communities: A Multi-Disciplinary Foundation for Future Research. *Journal of Computer-Mediated Communication*, *10*(1), 101–121. Retrieved from https://academic.oup.com/jcmc/article/10/1/JCMC1011/4614445

Preece, J. (2001). Sociability and usability in online communities: Determining and measuring success. *Behaviour & Information Technology*, *20*(5), 347–356. doi:10.1080/01449290110084683

Schindler, R. M. (2001). Internet Forums as Influential Sources of Consumer Information. *Journal of Interactive Marketing*, *15*(3), 31–40. doi:10.1002/dir.1014

Schuler, D. (1996). *New Community Networks – Wired for Change*. New York: Addison-Wesley.

Smith, D., Menon, K. S., & Sivakumar, K. (2005). Online Peer and Editorial Recommendations, Trust, and Choice in Virtual Markets. *Journal of Interactive Marketing*, *19*(3), 15–37. doi:10.1002/dir.20041

Stanoevska-Slabeva, K. (2002). Toward a community-oriented design of Internet platforms. *International Journal of Electronic Commerce*, 6(3), 71–95. doi:10.1080/10864415.2002.11044244

Turban, E., King, D., McKay, J., Marshall, P., Lee, J., & Viehland, D. (2008). *Electronic Commerce 2008: A Managerial Perspective*. Pearson.

Virnoche, M. E., & Marx, G. T. (1997). Only connect-E. M. Forster in an age of electronic communication: Computer-mediated association and community networks. *Sociological Inquiry*, 67(1), 85–100. doi:10.1111/j.1475-682X.1997.tb00431.x

Wingfield, N., & Hanrahan, T. (1999). Web firm salon buys 'the Well,' an online pioneer. *The Wall Street Journal*, p. B9.

KEY TERMS AND DEFINITIONS

Digital Marketing: Marketing products and services with the use of internet, mobile phones, and social media are termed as digital marketing.

E-Commerce: Buying and selling of goods and services using internet, also referred as E-commerce or Electronic Commerce.

Gen X: Gen X is referred to as Baby Boomers, who are the group of people born during 1960s to 1980.

Gen Y: Gen Y is referred to as Millennials, who are the group of people born during 1980s to 2000.

Gen Z: Gen Z is the group of people born after 2000.

Online Business: Any business activity such as advertising, selling, and buying handled through internet.

Social Collaboration: The process that aids various people or group to interact and share information to achieve common goals.

Virtual Communities: A group of people with similar interests, ideas, and feelings share their views through online networks or society.

Chapter 83

Hiring the Best Job Applicants?
The Effects of Social Media as an Innovative E-Entrepreneurship Recruitment Method

Anthony Lewis
University of South Wales, UK

Brychan Celfyn Thomas
University of South Wales, UK

ABSTRACT

Human resources (HR) management professionals have been using different methods of social media (SM) in their recruitment strategies with varying degrees of success. Through examining SM and its effect, this can support the development of a more effective HR recruitment strategy. This research investigates effects and issues associated with SM and recruitment and whether SM is effective as an innovative e-entrepreneurship method of hiring the best job applicants for enterprises. Professionals, recruiters, and employees were questioned on their views of SM from a personal and professional perspective through a variety of methods including focus groups and questionnaires. It is argued that the advantages of using SM for online recruitment include increased efficiency and convenience for both potential employees and enterprises, whereas where the systems are not designed correctly, it can create increased difficulties for the enterprises in communicating with potential employees. A framework is provided that can be used by enterprises in order to create their own SM recruitment cycle.

INTRODUCTION

Social media is a term used to describe platforms and tools including blogs, bookmarks, photosharing websites, podcasts, wikis, which are used to publish and share content online (Burrows, 2011). In recent years, social media has become a powerful recruitment method for enterprises to hire employees. Consequently, this research is a further investigation, to previous studies of e-recruitment (Lewis et al,

DOI: 10.4018/978-1-7998-9020-1.ch083

2010; Lewis et al, 2013; Lewis et al., 2018a&b), with an aim to critically explore whether social media and online recruitment are effective innovative e-entrepreneurship methods (Lewis, 2019) in hiring the best job applicants for enterprises.

Innovative e-entrepreneurship methods are an effective new approach used by enterprises involving electronic processes. Further dimensions, not covered in this study, are recruiting for new enterprises and new ventures for recruiting, which are interesting avenues for further research. Social media enables enterprises to provide a dedicated service (vehicle) to attract appropriate employees to augment their talent management strategy (Eduardo, 2006). It is used by many enterprises and individuals in order to market their corporate brands and can give the enterprise a new identity to compete in a competitive market (Doherty, 2010). Social media can be an excellent starting point for recruitment as "key metrics" such as cost and time to hire are measurable providing the ability to substantiate improvement (Doherty, 2010). It allows individuals to create an online profile with a network of friends and colleagues (Henderson & Bowley 2010). They can then upload pictures and personal details enabling users to create an online profile and a visible, virtual network (Hsu et al., 2007) of their friends (Henderson & Bowley 2010).

There has been dramatic growth in online recruitment since the mid 1990's when the economic climate created a considerable demand for employees with a strong academic background and relevant experience (Lee, 2005:175). Recruitment methods have consequently changed in enterprises, and by individuals when looking for their next opportunity, and also looking at the ways in which they are applying for roles. Online recruitment has consistently shown itself to be one of the most substantial shifts in recruitment practice in recent years (Lee, 2005:175).

In this paper, the literature review details previous research and media coverage regarding social media and online recruitment. Most of the research is focused on the importance of having a clear social media strategy and how the subsequent changes implemented by these enterprises might impact on individuals who use these sites. Although existing research indicates that recruitment websites are used, it does not comprehensively cover industry specific recruitment agencies. This paper considers social media and online recruitment tools and processes from the perspective of employers, recruitment agencies and individuals in an attempt to ascertain the relevance to enterprises and individuals.

Several areas such as intellectual property law, good Human Resources practice and how practical these methods are in recruitment are explored in the literature review and discussed throughout the paper. Social media is a relatively new area of interest and yet something which adapts quickly and could be instrumental in selecting and retaining the best people for an enterprise.

Through almost two billion internet users Worldwide in 2010, increasing from approximately 360 million at the end of 2000, and more than four billion in 2018, there has been dramatic growth in internet usage over the last two decades (www.internetworldstats.com). A growing number of enterprises are using social media in order to communicate with their staff and customers. Some social media tools (Anari et al., 2013) may be viewed as being more suited to different individuals; however, the number of users grows rapidly.

Goals of this research paper are therefore to critically explore the effects of social media as an innovative e-entrepreneurship method of recruitment; whether it is an effective method of hiring the best employees for an enterprise, and what the associated problems may be in using this method of recruitment. With regard to this, the following research questions have been formulated and are investigated:

- RQ_1: What are the advantages and disadvantage of Social Media (SM) from the perspectives of Human Resources (HR) professionals, recruitment professionals, and potential job seekers?
- RQ_2: What factors are likely to drive/reduce the effectiveness of recruitment via SM?
- RQ_3: What are the legal considerations associated with recruitment via SM?

LITERATURE REVIEW

This literature review is organized beginning with a definition of social media; the use of social media for recruitment; enterprises, social media and online recruitment; social media's impact on recruitment in enterprises and enterprises' and employees' search strategies.

Definition of Social Media

A current definition of social media is "forms of electronic communication (such as web sites) through which people create online communities to share information, ideas, personal messages, etc." (Merriam-Webster, 2016). Social networking sites include Facebook (online social networking site), Twitter (internet service enabling the posting of "tweets") and LinkedIn (networking web site for the business community) (Christensson, 2013). Various forms of social media technologies are apparent which include social networks, forums, enterprise social networks, business networks and blogs (Aichner & Jacob, 2015). The leading social networks based on active user accounts in April 2018 are listed in Table 1 (Statista, 2018).

The of Use of Social Media for Recruitment

It is suggested by Cober et al. (2000) that individuals who are most likely to benefit from online applications are those who already have jobs, but are interested to see which other opportunities may be available. Using social media may allow an individual to search for enterprises related to their industry, e.g. Accountancy, and search for information using social media, which can be targeted at specific groups, such as with KPMG's general page (http://www.facebook.com c, http://www.twitter.com b) and the graduate recruitment page (http://www.facebook.com d). It is also possible to have separate pages for specific geographic areas (http://www.twitter.com c), and alumni pages in order to keep in contact with former employees (http://www.facebook.com e).

Many recruitment pages on social media have links to the large amount of content available about corporate enterprises through the websites. There is a far greater amount than could previously be communicated through traditional methods, such as print advertisements, journals, and corporate literature, such as brochures (Cober et al., 2000; Cober et al., 2004). McKeown (2003) also explains that additional paperwork, such as application forms may also be available online.

According to Smith (1999, cited in McKeown 2003:23) one of the best features of using online recruitment is that an individual is able to ascertain what the work is, what skills they need to do it, salary expectations, and location before applying for a role. Hoffman et al. (1995) and Lee (2005) remind us that this information is available 24 hours a day. Cober et al. (2000) add that relevant information relating to a role can be found (at least in theory) speedily and easily using online recruitment methods.

Table 1. Leading social networks based on active user accounts

No	Social network name	Users (in millions)
1	Facebook	2,270
2	YouTube	1,900
3	WhatsApp	1,500
4	Facebook Messenger	1,300
5	WeChat	1,040
6	Instagram	1,000
7	QQ	806
8	QZone	563
9	Tik Tok	500
10	Sina Weibo	411
11	Twitter	336
12	Reddit	330
13	Baidu Tiba	300
14	Skype	300
15	LinkedIn	294
16	Viber	260
17	Snapchat	255
18	Line	203
19	Pinterest	200
20	Telegram	200
21	Tinder	100

Source: Statista (2018)

Further, Cober et al. (2000) warn there is a correlation between the image an applicant has of the enterprise, and the likelihood of that individual applying for a role within the enterprise. An enterprise's e-recruitment section of their website will give potential employees the opportunity to gather information about the enterprise, including its "mission, diversity, benefits, career development and corporate culture" so that they are better prepared to make decisions about any potential career with the enterprise (Lee, 2005). There had been complaints about enterprises failing to "sell themselves" and as such, giving the candidate little incentive, or desire, to work within the enterprise (Hilpern, 2001). Rebecca Baker, head of recruitment at network 3 said that the company redesigned its recruitment website to make it simpler in order to give candidates a good experience which will reflect well on the company (Chubb, 2008). A personalised service also offers consumers a positive experience when using a recruitment website; it makes it easier for consumers to find job opportunities (Marketing Week, 2006).

Moreover, Cober et al. (2000: 493) propose that additional information enables candidates to make an informed decision regarding how well they will fit within an enterprise. However, candidates should be aware that it is possible enterprises will "project only what they desire others to see" (Miller & Arnold, 2000:337).

Enterprises, Social Media and Online Recruitment

The CIPD report cited by Berry (2005:43) shows that the job pages of an enterprise make it the "fourth most popular recruitment method" (Goldberg & Allen, 2008) and suggests that websites differ from other recruitment methods; they are a more vivid and varied method of communicating, and it is here that social media allows enterprises to interact with potential candidates. In order for any enterprise to use social media and online recruitment to its best advantage, Human Resources professionals must include it as part of their recruitment strategy (King, 2004).

The accountancy firm KPMG were the leaders in moving recruitment online, this was perceived as a somewhat risky move since candidates may not have been secure in their applications for the roles (Personnel Today, 2008:8). Using social media, and online recruitment, the time taken to recruit new employees has fallen; it is a fast way to attract a large number of candidates globally, as long as they are able to access the technology (Taylor, 2001; Hall, 2004; Lee, 2005; Crail, 2007; Smethurst, 2004; People Management, 2008). Tulip (2003) reports that 44% of internet users have searched online for jobs and 28% of the working population expect to find their next role online. Generation Y candidates can juggle more than one task at a time, and are more flexible than previous generations, they are eager to move to a new role, or even a new country with very little notice (The Economist, 2009). Cober et al. (2000) recommend enterprises should design recruitment pages on the website so that the needs of the enterprise are explicitly met.

Taylor (2001) and Lee (2005) suggest benefits of using online recruitment include increased efficiency and convenience for both potential employees and enterprises, however, where systems are not designed correctly, this can create increased difficulties for the enterprise in communicating with potential employees. Berry (2005) notes that a significant problem could be the high number of candidates applying for positions through online recruitment websites, who may not have the qualifications and skills required for the position for which they are applying (HR Focus Hiring survey, 2004:S2). Sorting inappropriate, irrelevant applicants can result in increased administration costs, outweighing any potential savings in reduction of recruiting cost (Manufacturers' Monthly, 2004).

It is argued by Harvey Sinclair (Tulip, 2003) that employers have been slower to adapt to online recruitment, where potential employees have been looking for an online presence for a longer period of time. Mannion (2008) also warns that the process of filtering applications is challenging as people may seem highly qualified but can often lack the necessary practical experience. An enterprise with recruitment pages which are unable to discern appropriate candidates of the right calibre in a resourceful and time efficient manner may struggle to survive in the current economic climate (Long, 2009).

HR Focus 2004 Survey (S2) suggests that using online recruitment is only successful where an "industry specific website is used". Subsequently Spence (2009) suggested a 7 step process to successfully filter applications: develop clear job descriptions, use targeted advertising, consider the application method, consider automated selection, profile the candidate as well as the role, ensure interviewers know what they are looking for and monitor the process carefully. When using social media for recruitment, employers may have the opportunity to "fine tune" their applications appropriately to ensure that recruiting for the enterprise remains manageable.

Social Media's Impact on Recruitment

According to Pitcher (2008) many high street retailers were not focusing on the recruitment areas of their websites. In certain cases, stores received applications from only 2% of individuals who had visited the website in order to apply online. Reasons for this could be the time taken to investigate the availability of applying for appropriate positions and the time incurred in completing the form. Further, Cober et al. (2000: 481) state that "through a corporate Web page, information can be presented that highlights unique aspects of the corporate culture that may attract individuals whom would fit especially/particularly well within the enterprise".

Screening methods have been included by enterprises such as Signet throughout their recruitment process, so that candidates who do not fit the "corporate culture" of the enterprise are eliminated through use of a questionnaire (Weekes, 2004). In 2008, River Island restricted applications for temporary Christmas positions so that the process had to be completed online. Although 100,000 people applied for roles, 46,000 failed to complete the applications, effectively screening themselves out (People Management, 2008). Further, Cober et al. (2000: 481) suggest it is the enterprises' recruitment pages which provide the first impression to potential employees. Enterprises have the opportunity to strengthen their corporate identity (Hall, 2004:21; Smethurst, 2004:38). By using social media as a tool to assist in this, they may well be successful.

There is a need for enterprises to be aware of how information available on a website may influence a potential employees' perspective of them (Wilmott, 2003). Curry (2000) suggests although negative information about an enterprise may also be available online, it is not necessarily damaging, as it could serve to shape an individual's perception of the enterprise. Problems will occur where information might be construed as out-of-date. It will give a negative impression to how potential applicants may view the webpage. Cober et al. (2000) advise that the attitude of the individual towards the recruitment site will influence the intention of the person to apply for a position.

Current University graduates appear to use the internet more extensively and effectively than ever before (Curry, 2000) for all aspects of their day-to-day lives from social networking to shopping, and they expect fast response times (Weekes, 2004). In their online graduate programme, KPMG ensure they respond to applications with feedback within 24 hours. They (KPMG) feel that they are able to do this through using available technology to the best of their capabilities (Personnel Today, 2008: 1).

It has been attempted by KPMG to minimize difficulties in recruiting within its Graduate Programme by using social media sites used frequently by their target market (Personnel Today, 2008). Minton-Eversole (2007) and Schramm (2007) argue enterprises can use social media sites to uncover information about candidates not available on the application form. Indeed, Peacock (2009) warns that 12% of enterprises in the United Kingdom (UK) are looking at a potential candidate's social networking (Buettner, 2016; Lewis et al., 2018b) profile before making the decision to interview them.

Enterprises' and Employees' Search Strategies

Recruiters and Human Resources personnel are under pressure to attract suitably qualified applicants when there are lower levels of unemployment which means the enterprise's recruitment search strategies should be innovative in order to retain sustainable competitive advantage (Cober et al., 2000; Lee, 2005). Here, Cober et al. (2000:484) suggest three stages that need to be considered when a company is designing a recruitment search strategy. Initially, they must have the ability to attract potential candidates to the website, and then successfully engage with the candidates in order to pass on the information posted on the site. Finally, the enterprise needs to ensure that the candidate actually applies for the position from the web site. Figure 1 shows these steps clearly illustrating each component.

Figure 1.

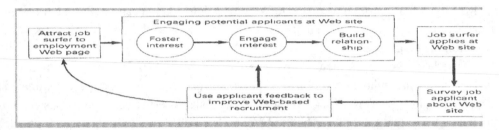

A CIPD e-recruitment fact sheet (2009:5) states there are "no fundamental philosophical differences" between using traditional methods, such as print media and using e-recruitment. It suggests a mix of old and new media to meet their target applicants in the most efficient manner.

Literature suggests problems with social media and online recruitment stem from poor information that is not kept up-to-date, and where there is no clear social media strategy implemented throughout the enterprise. Online recruitment has been used to effectively select candidates based on selection criteria, and potential candidates will have an idea what the corporate culture of an enterprise is before they apply, so effectively, the potential candidate can select whether or not they feel they would fit in with the enterprise or not. It is also more possible than ever to access wide amounts of information, including using a Smartphone to keep up-to-date with new roles enabling individuals to be first in line to apply for their desired role within an enterprise.

METHODS

There are elements of both positivist and interpretivist research methods in this investigation. A theoretical framework has been used for the questionnaires and the majority of the remainder of the study has a more emergent approach to the way the information has been gathered. Primary data was collected for this research (Zikmund, 2003) by the researchers from an "original source" (Collis & Hussey, 2009: 73). This type of research is useful from new "insights" which come to light, providing the researchers with more confidence in the validity of the data gathered (Easterby-Smith et al, 2008:11). Here, primary data may take the form of "questionnaire survey, interviews or focus groups" (Collis & Hussey, 2009:73). All three data collection methods were used in order to investigate information from different perspectives. More than one method of research is used in order to examine the same phenomenon (Collis & Hussey, 2009). Bryman & Bell (2007) describe this type of investigatory research as methodological triangulation, since the results from each type of investigation will be cross checked. These techniques can be used to provide rich data and provide the opportunity to recognize anomalies in data analysis. Webb et al. (1998) conceptualised this concept as a way of developing how information was collated and reviewed, resulting in a greater level of confidence in the findings (Bryman & Bell, 2007). Triangulation is a way of "cross-checking findings derived from both qualitative and quantitative research" (Bryman & Bell, 2007:413). In fact, triangulation was a key concept for this research and the initial personal interviews were what the questionnaires were based on, with subsequent focus groups and follow-up personal interviews. The research tools were both qualitative and quantitative. The study was therefore conducted through: (i) an employees/prospective employees' questionnaire survey, (ii) an employers' questionnaire survey, (iii) a focus group and (iv) personal interviews.

1. First, the employees/prospective employees' questionnaire survey had a sample size of 100 and the respondents were mainly from the Channel Islands and the UK, focusing more on the British employment market. The questionnaires were conducted using the online survey website http://www.surveymonkey.com. Using this method, the researchers were able to conduct the survey in a timely manner, using Facebook, Twitter, LinkedIn and e-mail to ask respondents to complete the survey online. It took less than 72 hours for the 100 responses to be received. The research population was made up of contacts of the researchers; this was limited to around 1,000 contacts giving a 10% response rate (Bryman & Bell, 2007). Respondents were represented from a variety of sectors including students, unemployed, banking/finance, IT, healthcare, beauty/fitness, factory, call centre, agriculture, tradesperson, hospitality, and other sectors. Main questions asked concerned age, location, industry, gender, how often social media was used, would social media be used when seeking their next job, their online presence, how social media is accessed, and whether they would use social media to help obtain an introduction to an employer.

2. For the employers' questionnaire survey there was a sample size of 25 and again the respondents were mainly from the Channel Islands and the UK. Employers were represented from banking/finance, trades people, hospitality, and other sectors. Major questions asked concerned location, industry, whether they would use social media when advertising their upcoming vacancies, their online presence, how social media is accessed, and whether they thought social media was effective when looking for potential employees.

3. The focus group size was 22 participants who were all Human Resources professionals working in Guernsey. They were selected through an invitation to attend the focus group and were representative of HR professionals working in the various sectors. This method was used in order to find out the key methods that HR practitioners would use to find suitable employees. Major questions asked in the focus group concerned how social media could be used in their organizations, understanding terminology, how to use groups, how to add contacts, technological understanding and timing issues. Interviewees for the focus groups were members of the researchers' CIPD group and the results were filmed so that notes could be made.

4. Personal interviews were undertaken with the selection of 2 recruitment agents who agreed to be interviewed following contact by the researchers, and were representative of recruitment agents in Guernsey. The personal interviews were carried out initially in person, and later by telephone. Major questions asked concerned users of recruitment websites, what practices were in place, competition from other recruitment agencies on the island of Guernsey, whether the agency was affected by increasing numbers of organizations having more advanced social media and online recruitment sites, the impact of global economic pressures on the organization (Cummings, 2004; Foss et al., 2010) and how the offshore economy had been affected by such measures. For the purpose of the initial interview the researchers felt it would be appropriate for this type of interview not to have a prescribed structure and to see which subjects were emergent from the subsequent conversation.

The research used cross-sectional methodologies due to financial resources and time constraints (Bryman & Bell, 2007). Furthermore, the research objectives meant existing perceptions of individual's opinions of social media were explored. Therefore, obtaining and analysing information over a short cross-sectional period of time is crucial to enhance the contextual validity of results (Saunders et al., 2007). Nonetheless, cross-sectional studies are associated with static positivistic epistemological considerations. Furthermore, the complexities in research which are associated with cross-sectional time horizons involve selecting "a large enough sample to be representative of the total population" (Collis & Hussey, 2009:346).

RESULTS, ANALYSIS AND DISCUSSION

Employee/Prospective Employee and Employer Questionnaires

Key research findings for: i) the employee/prospective employee questionnaire survey, and ii) the employer questionnaire survey are presented at iii) the aggregate level with statistical information involving percentages.

1. One hundred respondents to the employee/prospective employee questionnaire survey, was limited by using the free version of Survey Monkey. There were a further 28 respondents during the time the survey remained open, but these had to be disregarded as they were inaccessible. From the responses collected, 64% were female and 34% male with the remaining 2% not wishing to answer. Although responses were predominately from women, it is useful to see female perceptions.

More respondents were under forty than of any other age group, particularly those aged 25-35. This may be related to the fact respondents were all acquaintances of the researchers. It may also be related to theory that it is predominately "Generation Y", where the request to complete questionnaires was sent. "Generation Y" is more likely to be on social networking sites with 89% of that generation having an online presence, rather than the "baby boomers" which only 72% have an online presence (Heller-Baird & Parasnis, 2011),

Nearly half the respondents were from Guernsey, with the remainder mainly resident in the UK. The employment status of respondents was varied, with 75% being employed, 6% unemployed, and further 4% homemakers. Some 15% of the respondents were students. The researchers had thought it likely that most of the respondents would use social media, as the majority of requests to complete the questionnaire were sent using Facebook and Twitter, this was confirmed with 96% of the respondents using Facebook (the most used social media platform by the respondents).

According to Collis & Hussey (2009:194) "two major problems in using questionnaires...Questionnaire fatigue" where individuals are reluctant to respond to questionnaires as they are "inundated with requests by post, e-mail, telephone and in the street" (Collis & Hussey, 2009: 145) and "non response bias" where not all of the questionnaires are returned, which could have an impact on validity and reliability of findings (Collis & Hussey, 2009: 145).

Responses to the questionnaire were also affected by "non response" (Collis & Hussey, 2009: 204) since certain aspects of questions were left unanswered. This could be related to the questionnaire design of the questionnaire, as some respondents early in their questionnaire response stated that they did not use certain social media platforms and so could not have responded to further questions about the platforms along the survey.

2.   Again the employer questionnaire survey involved using the free version of Survey Monkey which was undertaken at about the same time as the employee/prospective employee questionnaire survey. None of the respondents from the employer's survey said that their decision regarding employing an individual would be affected by pictures of an employee or potential employee drinking. The important factor (Lauby 2010) is what a candidate is capable of, "their ability to perform the appropriate tasks in relation to the position". Employers need to look at postings to determine how they wish to proceed with applications. The respondents from the employer's survey concur, by stating that the things that would most likely affect their opinion of a candidate are photographs of the potential employee being perceived as unsocial.

There is considerable variation in the number of people who use social media and how they use it, with Twitter and LinkedIn being less used than Facebook, and even less using MySpace and YouTube, amongst the participants in the questionnaire surveys. This has an impact on the results gathered, as those platforms will likely not be considered as first choice methods of looking for work.

3.   Results for the questionnaire surveys for employees/potential employees, whether they used social media when looking for their next job, and employers when advertising upcoming vacancies, are shown in Tables 2 and 3.

Results in Table 2 show that 55% of employees/potential employees would use Facebook, 18% Twitter, 21% LinkedIn, 5% MySpace and 6% You Tube, when looking for their next job. The results show that Facebook is the platform that the highest percentage of participants would choose in order to look for work, but the results are indicative that using social media is not one of the main ways that respondents would choose to look for work.

It is shown in Table 3 that 56% of employers would use Facebook, 28% Twitter, 28% LinkedIn, 4% My Space and 8% You Tube, to advertise upcoming vacancies. The results therefore show employers appear to be more likely to advertise roles on social media, particularly on Facebook.

Table 2. Employees/Potential Employees - Would you use Social Media when looking for your next job?

Would You Use Social Media when looking for your next job?	%
Facebook	
My friend's post	22
A recruitment Agency post	17
A promoted advert from an employer	11
An organisation looking directly	5
None	12
I would not use this platform	25
No reply	8
Twitter	
My friend's post	6
A recruitment Agency post	2
A promoted advert from an employer	3
An organisation looking directly	7
None	8
I would not use this platform	54
No reply	20
Linked in	
My friend's post	2
A recruitment Agency post	9
A promoted advert from an employer	5
An organisation looking directly	5
None	9
I would not use this platform	52
No reply	18
My Space	
My friend's post	0
A recruitment Agency post	2
A promoted advert from an employer	0
An organisation looking directly	3
None	13
I would not use this platform	62
No reply	20
YouTube	
My friend's post	2
A recruitment Agency post	0
A promoted advert from an employer	2

continues in next column

Table 2. Continued

Would You Use Social Media when looking for your next job?	%
An organisation looking directly	2
None	10
I would not use this platform	64
No reply	20

n= 100

Table 3. Employers - Would you use Social Media when advertising your upcoming vacancies?

Would You Use Social Media when advertising your upcoming vacancies?	%
Facebook	
Yes	56
No	20
I would not use this platform	20
No reply	4
Twitter	
Yes	28
No	20
I would not use this platform	40
No reply	12
LinkedIn	
Yes	28
No	32
I would not use this platform	28
No reply	12
MySpace	
Yes	4
No	36
I would not use this platform	48
No reply	12
YouTube	
Yes	8
No	32
I would not use this platform	48
No reply	12

n=25

Focus Group Analysis

Key research findings from the focus groups included: i) issues relating to social media, ii) social media platforms and strategy for recruitment, iii) Twinterns, and iv) internet policy and online recruitment strategies.

1. "Consequences of social exchange relationships have received significant research attention" (Dulac et al., 2008:1082). All of the respondents were currently working in HR or Senior Management in Guernsey, they were aged between 20 and 60, and with the majority being women aged 45-60. There were 4 men present, aged between 35 and 60. The results of the findings were mainly focused on the issues relating to using social media efficiently as part of a small island community. The key trends revealed as a result of these findings were issues with advertising roles so that suitable candidates would be informed of the vacancies in a timely manner and who would be finding candidates who could meet the skills requirements of the enterprise's needs and would be able to work in part of the World with strict housing laws (Economist, 2009). There were also issues with how it could be done, the potential for time-wasting and sifting through applicants without the correct skills and qualifications for the role.

2. Considerable information is available on social media platforms, and it is important that the enterprise remains vigilant in the amount of time spent on updating social media platforms to ensure the brand stays on message. Many of the respondents struggled with the basics of social media, with two of the participants not having a Facebook account. In these cases, in order to establish an effective social media strategy for recruitment, it might be more cost effective to bring in a social media consultant. In Guernsey, one of the most well respected individuals is Jo Porrit, at Crowd Media, the team there offer training, from the most basic to higher level, and can also evolve a strategy that best fits the enterprise, and the industry in which they are working (http://www.facebook.com e). By using an external company, costs can be kept to a set level, and time taken to run the site by the enterprise can be minimized, whilst still ensuring the enterprise has an online presence, this will go some way to alleviating concerns.

3. "Twittering interns" or Twinterns are typically interns recruited by large enterprises in order to keep communication channels open on day-to-day activities, such as at Pizza Hut, who launched a campaign where potential Twinterns had to apply for a role working for the company by posting a YouTube video of themselves online (Clifford, 2009). Indvick (2011) reported on the case at Marc Jacobs where the Twittern launched a tirade against his manager, calling him a "tyrant" before leaving the enterprise. @MarcJacobsIntl's response was "All well here at MJ. Twitter is a crazy place. Protect your Passwords" (http://www.twitter.com a). This is a clear example of the importance of keeping a watchful eye on the content that is posted by employees.

4. A topic considered was internet policy "We changed our Internet Policy at work recently, so people can't use Social Media in the office" – The implementation of a new internet policy, or social media policy is crucial for the enterprise. A response was "I don't think we'll use any of them, I want to employ people like me" may stem from the idea that "generally, the adoption of a technology does not take place uniformly across the entire economy or the entire population...If a person's family, friends and broader community are users... there would be increased incentive..." (Agarwal et al., 2009:277). Though the same is true the other way round, it may be seen as a negative impact on the enterprise not to have an effective social media and online recruitment strategy in place.

Personal Interviews

The researchers discussed several issues with the agencies as the key topics became emergent through the literature. The recruitment agencies operating in Guernsey are functioning in a very competitive market, and have diversified to continue trading in the current economic climate, including developing their offshore payroll services, and providing HR consultancy to small businesses. This should not have an impact on their ability to remain specialised in their field and grow.

Key research findings from the personal interviews included: i) current legislation, ii) tools available to update social media platforms, iii) topics concerning information about a candidate, iv) candidates online, v) content uploaded to social media sites, vi) effective communication with candidates, and vii) an effective social media strategy.

1. Agencies need to be up-to-date with current legislation, as employment legislation is different from UK and European Union (EU) legislation and there are professional bodies active on LinkedIn, Facebook and Twitter, such as the CIPD who strive to keep people who are interested and up-to-date with current changes in the legislation.

2. Several tools are available to update all of the social media platforms that the agencies choose to use such as http://www.twitterfeed.com, which can convert an RSS feed of the information which has been uploaded into the content management system that keeps the website up-to-date into Tweets, and then there are several applications which allow Tweets to be "fed" into Facebook (http://www.facebook.com a) and LinkedIn (http://learn.linkedin.com/twitter). After these applications have been set-up, they need to be checked periodically to ensure that they are functioning correctly.

3. There were several issues raised as the researchers found new topics through the critical literature review, and were discussed at length with the agencies to see how they would respond and what their thoughts were on certain things. Guernsey is a very close knit community and so it is relatively simple to "Google" a candidate on Google (http://www.google.com) and see what comes up about what an individual may have done by a relatively simple search. There is also a website from the local newspaper (www.thisisguernsey.com) where it is also possible to gather information about a candidate. This is a standard policy for some recruitment agencies. Additionally, it is common for an agency to have a policy relating to Criminal Convictions which have not been "spent" under the Rehabilitation of Offenders Act (Bailiwick of Guernsey Act, 2002) and whether the agency decides to take on the individual to help them find work. Some agencies on the Island will not deal with candidates who have unspent convictions.

4. From the development of social media strategies which include checking available information about candidates online, more information can be gathered. As a recruitment agent, it can be common for candidates to "like" the agency on Facebook and to "follow" them on Twitter, so it can be very easy to access information about the candidates which they may not otherwise wish to divulge, it is then up to the agent to decide how they use the information. It is suggested (Lauby, 2010) any enterprise that is going to conduct a background check on an individual on any social media sites which are available in the public domain ought to "provide notice" before conducting searches.

5. Content uploaded by recruitment agencies to social media sites can vary from staff events, corporate events which the enterprise may have sponsored or participated in, to charity work in which the enterprise participates, and local enterprises that staff participate in. A good example of this

is Guernsey Recruitment agency "Situations Recruitment" and their Facebook page (http://www.facebook.com b).

6. To facilitate effective communication with employees of the enterprise and candidates of the agency, the personal interviews also highlighted the need for "fake" corporate accounts that can be monitored centrally. This could be as simple as employees setting up accounts for use at work. It only takes a few minutes to set-up a basic Facebook Profile, where all of the contact details and work history (Rowlands et al., 2011) can be set-up with details of the recruitment agency, corporate images can be used, so that there is continuity between images that appear on the enterprise's website, and other social media platforms. This is a different way of communicating with candidates, and another way it is possible to keep candidates updated "on the go". Information can be monitored by a central person, who would be "friends" with the individuals, and would also have access to the passwords and usernames of the employees.

7. There is a need for decisions to be made for an effective social media strategy to include information about what to do when an employee leaves. If there are "corporate" Facebook and Twitter accounts, contacts of these should remain with the company. This could be more difficult using a LinkedIn account, where individuals may have built up a rapport with clients and colleagues, and wish to retain contacts, or could easily do so again. However, it is stated that "the formation and maintenance of relationships is predicated on the reciprocation of valued resources" (Dulac et al., 2008: 1079).

CONCLUSION

Recruitment is expensive ("contracting a recruiter to find an executive who earns $150,000 annually can cost $15,000 in fees" (Koeppel, 2009)) and often a time-consuming process. By using "social media tools are mostly free and offer added value: candidates bring their own online networks...and references which speeds up the recruitment process" (Koeppel, 2009). Therefore, it is vital for the employer to ensure they get it right the first time to avoid further cost implications.

If an enterprise has chosen to implement its social media and recruitment strategy through an external enterprise the next step will be to bring the implementation of the social media strategy back "in house" over a period of time, and only if the budget allows. This Organic Development Strategy known as "knowledge and capability development" (Johnson et al., 2008:357) within a social media and recruitment strategy will continue to grow, as employee's have "greater market knowledge and therefore competitive advantage over other rivals more distant from their customers".

From the literature review and subsequent analysis of the primary data it is evident that quality of information is a key factor. Therefore it is crucial that any enterprise attempting to recruit staff ensure they provide as much information as possible in order to allow the candidate to make a more informed decision about their potential decision to apply and/or accept a position. If this information is in place, it should reduce the time taken to process the application for all parties involved. Here, it is important that all parties keep their information up-to-date at all times. For agencies and enterprises, this is perhaps more important, for the initial impression the candidate has of the enterprise may have an impact on whether or not they will choose to apply for a position (Cober et al., 2000).

Though LinkedIn profiles may seem to take longer to complete than Facebook (a few minutes) or Twitter (a couple of minutes) as an individual has to upload a certain amount of information, such as a

CV, write a summary, as well as asking people to recommend their work, it is possible to display many of the key skills above in about 30 minutes, and the information stored on the LinkedIn profile can be quickly kept up-to-date.

Interestingly, Facebook was by far the preferred social media platform for the majority of respondents from the focus group and the questionnaire respondents, as well as being firm favourites with the recruitment consultants in conjunction with other social media platforms.

From the questionnaires and focus group it was not clear whether LinkedIn, Twitter, YouTube are not well used due to lack of interest? Or was it a lack of training? From the results from all three stakeholders, however, in the case of MySpace, it is now viewed as a platform to share music on, not a social network anymore, so there would be little point building a social media strategy including MySpace, unless of course the enterprise was working in the Music, or Arts industries. It is also important to ensure that other sorts of information on roles, and what is going on within the enterprise is kept up-to-date, and information is readily available for all applicants. A member of staff can explain the recruitment process, and have that available from YouTube, with links from Facebook and Twitter.

The approximate costs to keep company x's website, and social media platforms updated throughout one calendar year in terms of time are around £5,000 per annum. This includes an hour of administrative time on the website and social media platforms per day to ensure that the information available is as comprehensive as possible. There is also two hours senior administrator monitoring time per week to ensure other sorts of data are kept up-to-date, as well as time to make videos and other items for YouTube, to keep the content fresh. This keeps the website available and relevant to as many people as possible.

With regard to cost, each individual company needs to be costed according to its needs and to fit in with the social media strategy that had been worked out. Using outside companies such as web developers and social media experts may add significant costs to the strategy. However, Ochman (2009:4) warns that "many people claim to be "social media gurus" but hype doesn't compare to experience". It is important to investigate consultants or firms, for other work they have done, and to seek testimonials before spending money on a campaign.

Participants in the focus group were not frequent users of social media, so the topics were more on "how to use" social media, rather than how they were using it as part of their social media and recruitment strategy. The focus group could be repeated with a group of individuals who were using social media more frequently in order to gain higher levels of validity for the research (Collis & Hussey, 2009:204). With the responses collected from the focus group, it would not be fair to say that the "research findings accurately represent what is happening in the situation" (Collis & Hussey, 2011:204).

With regard to the first research question concerning the advantages/disadvantages of Social Media (SM) from the perspectives of HR professionals, recruitment professionals, and potential job seekers, the research found the advantages of using SM for online recruitment include increased efficiency and convenience for both potential employees and enterprises, whereas where the systems are not designed correctly, it can create increased difficulties for the enterprises in communicating with potential employees. Moreover, it was found that the disadvantages with SM for online recruitment stem from poor information that is not kept up-to-date, and where there is no clear social media strategy implemented throughout the enterprise.

From the second research question concerning factors likely to drive/reduce the effectiveness of recruitment via SM it was found these included rapid changes in technology, recruitment management, the current global economic climate and the impact on the way in which individuals are now seeking employment.

For the third research question on legal considerations associated with recruitment via SM it was found that employers who wish their employees to use social media must guide the employees regarding what is expected from them, and outlining usage policies, as well as ensuring there is someone within the enterprise who takes responsibility for the policy, monitoring and updating the information as necessary.

In further studies the researchers would seek ways where there could be a more balanced age and race demographic so that further research could be carried out. This could then result in correlations between older users and those users from an ethnic background. Further investigation could also be carried out to find what characteristics make a web page more accessible to users with disabilities and to determine if there are changes which can be implemented by recruitment agencies with ease and in a cost-efficient manner.

REFERENCES

Agarwal, R., Animesh, A., & Prasad, K. (2009). Social interactions and the "Digital Divide": Explaining Variations in Internet Use. *Information Systems Research*, *20*(2), 277–294. doi:10.1287/isre.1080.0194

Aichner, T., & Jacob, F. (2015). Measuring the Degree of Corporate Social Media Use. *International Journal of Market Research*, *57*(2), 257–275. doi:10.2501/IJMR-2015-018

Anari, F., Asemi, A., Asemi, A., & Bakar, M. A. (2013). *Social Interactive Media Tools and Knowledge Sharing: A Case Study, Digital Libraries; Social Information Networks*. Retrieved February 11, 2019, from https://arxiv.org/abs/1309.182

Berry, M. (2005). Online recruitment grows in popularity. *Personnel Today*, May, 43.? Buettner, R. (2016). Getting a Job via Career-oriented Social Networking Sites: The Weakness of Ties. In *49th Annual Hawaii International Conference on System Sciences*. Kauai, HI: IEEE.

Bryman, A., & Bell, E. (2007). *Business Research Methods* (2nd ed.). Oxford University Press.

Burrows, T. (2011). Blogs, Wikis, Facebook and More: Everything You Want to Know About Using Today's Internet but Are Afraid to Ask (2nd ed.). London: Carlton.

Christensson, P. (2013). Social Media Definition. *Tech Terms*. Retrieved June 18, 2017, from https://techterms.com/definition/social_media

Chubb, L. (2008). Stripped-down jobsite is a good call for 3. *People Management*, *14*(2), 14.

CIPD. (2009). E-Recruitment Fact sheet. *CIPD Publication*. Retrieved March 17, 2011, from https://www.cipd.co.uk/subjects/recruitmen/onlnrcruit/onlrec.htm

Clark, D. (2013). *The Pros and Cons of SocialMedia Recruitment*. Retrieved August 1, 2013, from https://recruitmentbuzz.co.uk/the-pros-and-cons-of-social-media-recruitment/

Clifford, S. (2009). Tweeting Becomes a Summer Job Opportunity. *NY Times*. Retrieved April 27, 2011, from https://www.nytimes.com/2009/04/20/business/media/20twitter.html

Cober, R. T., Brown, D. J., Blumental, A. J., Doverspike, D., & Levy, P. E. (2000). The Quest for the qualified job surfer: It's Time the Public Sector Catches the Wave. *Public Personnel Management*, *29*(4), 479–496. doi:10.1177/009102600002900406

Cober, R. T., Brown, D. J., Keeping, L. M., & Levy, P. E. (2004). Recruitment on the Net: How Do Enterpriseal Web Site Characteristics Influence Applicant Attraction? *Journal of Management*, *30*(5), 623–646. doi:10.1016/j.jm.2004.03.001

Collis, J., & Hussey, R. (2009). *Business Research: A Practical Guide for Undergraduate and Postgraduate Students* (3rd ed.). Palgrave Macmillan.

Crail, M. (2007). Online Recruitment delivers more applicants and wins vote of most Employers. *Personnel Today*. Retrieved March 17, 2011 from http://www.personneltoday.com /articles/2007/11/20/43298/ online-recruitment-delivers-more-applicants-and-wins-vote-of-most-employers.html

Cummings, J. N. (2004). Work groups, structural diversity, and knowledge sharing in a global organizaton. *Management Science*, *50*(3), 352–364. doi:10.1287/mnsc.1030.0134

Curry, P. (2000). Log on for Recruits. *Industry Week*, *249*(17), 46.

Doherty, R. (2010). Getting social with recruitment. *Strategic HR Review*, *9*(6), 11–15. doi:10.1108/14754391011078063

Dulac, T., Coyle-Shapiro, J. A.-M., Henderson, D. J., & Wayne, S. J. (2008). Not all Responses to Breach are the Same: The Interconnection of Social Exchange and Psychological Contract Processes in Enterpriseations. *Academy of Management Journal*, *51*(6), 1079–1098. doi:10.5465/amj.2008.35732596

Easterby-Smith, M., Thorpe, R., & Jackson, P. R. (2008). *Management Research* (3rd ed.). Sage.

Economist. (2009). Generation Y goes to work. *Economist*, *390*(8612), 47-48.

Eduardo, M. (2006). E-Entrepreneurship. *Munich Personal RePEc Archive*. Retrieved April 24, 2011, from http://mpra.ub-muenchen.de/2237/

Facebook. (2010a). *Twitter App for Facebook*. Retrieved April 25, 2011, from https://www.facebook. com/apps/application.php?id=2231777543

Facebook. (2010b). *Situations Recruitment*. Retrieved April 26, 2011, from https://www.facebook.com/ situationsgnsy?ref=ts

Facebook. (2011c). *Facebook KPMG Recruitment Page*. Retrieved April 25, 2011, from http://www. facebook.com/profile.php?id=100001464093443&ref=ts#!/pages

Facebook. (2011d). *Facebook KPMG Graduate Page*. Retrieved April 25, 2011, from https://www. facebook.com/kpmg.graduates?ref=ts

Facebook. (2011e). *Facebook Crowd Media Page*. Retrieved April 27, 2011, from https://www.facebook. com/wearecrowd?sk=info

Foss, N. J., Husted, K., & Mcihailova, S. (2010). Governing knowledge sharing in Organizations: Levels of analysis, governance mechanisms and research directions. *Journal of Management Studies*, *47*(3), 455–482. doi:10.1111/j.1467-6486.2009.00870.x

Goldberg, C. B., & Allen, D. G. (2008). Black and white and read all over: Race differences in reactions to recruitment web sites. *Human Resource Management*, *47*(2), 217–236. doi:10.1002/hrm.20209

Hall, S. (2004, Feb.). See Website Recruitment through for best results. *Personnel Today*, 21.

Heller-Baird, C., & Parasnis, G. (2011). *From Social Media to Social CRM: What customers want*. IBM Institute for Business Value Study. Retrieved April 26, 2011, from http://www-935.ibm.com/services/us/gbs/thoughtleadership/ibv-social-crm-whitepaper.html? cntxt=a1005261

Henderson, A., & Bowley, R. (2010). Authentic dialogue? The role of "friendship" in a social media recruitment campaign. *Journal of Communication Management (London)*, *14*(3), 237–257. doi:10.1108/13632541011064517

Hilpern, K. (2001). Reading between the Lines. *Guardian Newspaper*. Retrieved October 10, 2008, from: http://www.guardian.co.uk/money/2001/jul/16/careers.jobsadvice5

Hoffman, D., Novak, T., & Chatterjee, P. (1995). Commercial scenarios for the web: opportunities and challenges. *Journal of Computer-Mediated Communication*, 5(1).

Hsu, M.-H., Ju, T. L., Yen, C.-H., & Chang, C.-M. (2007). Knowledge sharing behaviour in virtual communities: The relationship between trust, self-efficacy, and outcome expectations. *International Journal of Human-Computer Studies*, *65*(2), 153–169. doi:10.1016/j.ijhcs.2006.09.003

Indvick, L. (2011). *Marc Jacobs Intern Calls CEO a "Tyrant" in Twitter Meltdown"*. Retrieved March 30, 2011, from https://mashable.com/2011/03/28/marc-jacobs-twitter-intern-meltdown/

Internet World Stats. (2018). *Number of Internet users worldwide*. Retrieved February 11, 2019, from https://www.internetworldstats.com/stats.htm

Johnson, G., Scholes, K., & Whittington, R. (2008). *Exploring Corporate Strategy* (8th ed.). Pearson Education.

King, J. (2004, Jan.). The web habit is HR's manna from heaven. *Personnel Today*, 2.

Koeppel, D. (2009). HR by Twitter, *Fortune Small Business*, *19*(7), 57.

Lauby, S. (2010). *Should you Search Social Media Sites for Job Candidate Information?* Mashable. com. Retrieved September 6, 2010 from https://mashable.com/2010/09/05/social-media-job-recruiting/

Lee, I. (2005). Evaluation of Fortune 100 companies' career web sites. *Human Systems Management*, *24*(2), 175–182.

Lewis, A. (2019 in press). Human Capital Development: An Investigation of Innovative Methods. In B. Thomas & L. Murphy (Eds.), *Innovation and Social Capital in Organizational Ecosystems*. IGI Global. doi:10.4018/978-1-5225-7721-8.ch008

Lewis, A., Daunton, L., Thomas, B., & Sanders, G. (2010). A Critical Exploration into whether E-Recruitment is an Effective E-Entrepreneurship Method in Attracting Appropriate Employees for Enterprises. *International Journal of E-Entrepreneurship and Innovation, 1*(2), 30–44. doi:10.4018/jeei.2010040103

Lewis, A., Thomas, B., & James, S. (2018b). Social networking as an e-recruitment tool. *LAP LAMBERT Academic Publishing, 52,* 52.

Lewis, A., Thomas, B., & Sanders, G. (2013). Pushing the Right Buttons? A Critical Exploration into the Effects of Social Media as an Innovative E-Entrepreneurship Method of Recruitment for Enterprises. *International Journal of E-Entrepreneurship and Innovation, 4*(3), 16–37. doi:10.4018/ijeei.2013070102

Lewis, A., Thomas, B., & Sanders, G. (2018a). Attracting the Right Employees? The Effects of Social Media as an Innovative E-Entrepreneurship Recruitment a Method for Enterprises. In Entrepreneurship, Collaboration in the Modern Business Era. IGI Global. doi:10.4018/978-1-5225-5014-3.ch010

Long, D. (2009, Jan. 15). Monster invests $130m in face of falling vacancies. *New Media Age,* 4.

Management, P. (2008). *Fatface appetite for e-recruitment.* Retrieved March 17, 2009, from http://www.peoplemanagement.co.uk/pm/articles/2008/ 01/fatfaceappetiteforerecruitment.htm

Mannion, M. (2008). Consider differences in culture in Virgin territory. *People Management, 14*(5), 15.

Manufacturers' Monthly. (2004, Dec.). Internet job ads a turn off for industry. *Manufacturers' Monthly,* 16.

Marketing Week, . (2006). E-recruitment in Web 2.0 boost. *Marketing Week, 29*(43), 32.

McKeown, C. (2003). Applied Management: Nurse Internet Recruitment. *Nursing Management – UK,* 10(4), 23-27.

Merriam-Webster. (2016). *Dictionary and Thesaurus.* Retrieved June 18, 2017, from http://www.merriam-webster.com

Miller, H., & Arnold, J. (2000). Gender and home pages. *Computers & Education, 34*(3-4), 335–339. doi:10.1016/S0360-1315(99)00054-8

Miller Littlejohn Media (MLM). (2015). *7 Ways Students Should Use LinkedIn.* Retrieved June 18, 2017, from http://www.millerlittlejohnmedia.com

Minton-Eversole, T. (2007). E-Recruitment Comes of Age, Survey Says. *HRMagazine, 52*(8), 34.

Ochman, B. L. (2009, Apr.). It is no longer possible to resist social media. *Public Relations Tactics Magazine.*

Ozemir, V. E., & Hewett, K. (2010). The Effect of Collectivism on the Importance of Relationship Quality and Service Quality for Behavioural Intentions: A Cross-National and Cross-Contextual Analysis. *Journal of International Marketing, 18*(1), 41–62. doi:10.1509/jimk.18.1.41

Peacock, L. (2009). *Social networking sites used to check out job applicants.* Retrieved December 4, 2009, from: http://www.personneltoday.com/articles/2009/03/17/ 49844/social-networking-sites-used-to-check-out-job-applicants.html

Pitcher, G. (2008, Mar.). Unfriendly job websites lose retailers top talent. *Personnel Today,* 3.

Raynes-Goldie, K. (2010). Aliases, creeping, and wall cleaning: Understanding privacy in the age of Facebook. *First Monday, 15*(2). Advance online publication. doi:10.5210/fm.v15i1.2775

Rezaei, S., Wan, I., & Wan, K. (2014). Examining online channel selection behaviour among social media shoppers: PLS analysis. *International Journal of Marketing and Retailing, 6*(1), 28. doi:10.1504/IJEMR.2014.064876

Rowlands, I., Nicholas, D., Russell, B., Canty, N., & Watkinson, A. (2011). Social Media use in the research workflow. *Learned Publishing, 24*(3), 183–195. doi:10.1087/20110306

Saunders, M., Lewis, P., & Thornhill, A. (2007). *Research Methods for Business Students* (4th ed.). FT Prentice Hall.

Schramm, J. (2007). Internet Connections. *HRMagazine, 52*(9), 176.

Smethurst, S. (2004). The allure of online. *People Management, 10*(15), 38.

Spence, B. (2009). How to…filter job applications. *People Management*, 45. Retrieved March 19, 2009, from: http://www.peoplemanagement.co.uk/pm/articles/2009 /03/how-to-filter-job-applications.htm

Statista. (2018). *Leading global social networks 2018 Statistics*. Retrieved February 11, 2019, from https://www.statista.com/statistics

Taylor, C. (2001). E-recruitment is powerful weapon in war for talent. *People Management*. Retrieved December 5, 2009, from: https://www.peoplemanagement.co.uk/pm/articles/2001/05/856.htm

Personnel Today. (2008, Aug.). How I made a difference…? online recruitment burning career issues? closed-rank committee. *Personnel Today*, 8.

Tulip, S. (2003, Aug.). A flying start. *People Management Magazine*, 38. Retrieved February 5, 2010, from http://www.peoplemanagement.co.uk/pm/articles/2003/08/ 9256.htm

Twitter. (2011a). *MarcJacobsInt*. Retrieved May 26, 2011, from http://twitter.com/#!/MarcJacobsIntl

Twitter. (2011b). *Twitter KPMG Recruitment Page*. Retrieved April 25, 2011, from http://twitter.com/#!/KPMGRecruitment

Twitter. (2011c). *Twitter KPMG UK page*. Retrieved April 25, 2011, from http://twitter.com/ #!/KPMG_UK_LLP

Webb, T. J. (1998). *Researching for Business: Avoiding the 'Nice to know' Trap* (1st ed.). Aslib.

Weekes, S. (2004, June). Unearthing diamonds in a tough recruitment market. *Personnel Today*, 10.

Willmott, B. (2003). Firms tackle skills and diversity crisis online. *Personnel Today, 7*(1), 4.

Zikmund, W. G. (2003). *Business Research Methods* (7th ed.). Thomson South Western.

Chapter 84
Tweeting About Business and Society:
A Case Study of an Indian Woman CEO

Ashish Kumar Rathore
Indian Institute of Technology Delhi, India

Nikhil Tuli
Indian Institute of Technology Delhi, India

P. Vigneswara Ilavarasan
Indian Institute of Technology Delhi, India

ABSTRACT

This chapter examines the social media content posted by a woman Indian chief executive officer (CEO) on Twitter. The active involvement of CEO in communication activities influences the business effectiveness, performance, and standing of the business headed by her. Rstudio and Nvivo, two analytical tools, were used for different analysis such as tweets extraction and content analysis. The findings show the various themes in CEO communication which are categorized in different sectors in terms of her personal views (feelings and status updates), political views, and social concerns (ranging from education, women empowerment, governance, and policy support). The chapter extends the theoretical and empirical arguments for the importance of CEOs' social media communications. Finally, this research suggests that with a well-planned and strategic social media use, CEOs can create value for themselves and their businesses.

INTRODUCTION

Today people find themselves surrounded by multiple communication channels. The traditional mediums of communication like a newspaper, television are proven methods to disseminate information. There is a one-way sharing of information which lacks interpersonal capabilities ingrained in the way Internet

DOI: 10.4018/978-1-7998-9020-1.ch084

lets us communicate (Steyn, 2004). Moreover, the interaction through social media tends to be more informal. It revolutionizes the way people shop, pay bills, communicates, etc. E-mail, blogs, social networking sites like Twitter, Facebook, and LinkedIn etc. could be described as some of these interactive media which make information available on fingertips (Rybalko & Seltzer, 2010; Rathore & Ilavarasan, 2018). In this way, social media can become the source of information to businesses (Rathore et al., 2016). The trend of social communication via twitter exploded in 2008-09 when various companies around the world started to experiment with the application (BRAND fog, 2014).

Though, slowly and with a lot of suspicions, the top level executives of the organizations have adopted this unique media into the personal medium of communication. They are directly linked to their associated businesses, so the information shared with the audience on social media is bound to be, at least implicitly, associated with the brand the senior executive represents. There is a strong and positive connection between CEOs communication quality and responsiveness because of their social media presence (Men, 2015). It affects the behaviour of external and internal stakeholders as well. As CEO represents the higher level corporate spokesperson, their participation in communication programme influences the different public relation activities and the organizational standing. CEO plays an important role by managing effective communication system which shapes the culture and the character of organization (Hutton et al., 2001). This reshaped structure of organization includes the various relationships among communities based on communication hierarchies (Men, 2014b).

It is amply clear that social existence and the communication made by CEO straddles the borderline between what could be personal and professional space. Unlike their predecessors, memo, meetings, press releases, conference calls, Twitter or to say any social media offers a unique and supposedly unfiltered and participatory access well as strengthen existing relationships with various stakeholders to CEOs (Karaduman, 2013). CEO and C-suite participation in social media mean good things for the business such as the organization's values, shape its reputation, and enhance its brand image (PwC Report, 2013). Further, it also helps their leadership respond better in times of crisis. Therefore, the analysis of CEO's personal communication is an enigmatic space (Porter et al., 2015). And from an academic standpoint, CEOs interacting online or tweeting on social media needs to be further explored.

This study examined the social media content through Twitter on cognitive and attitudinal aspects, particularly focusing on the use of Twitter by a woman Indian chief executive officer. The paper extends the theoretical and empirical arguments for the importance of her social media communications. In next section, a review of literature is discussed highlighting stats of CEOs presence on Twitter and their public relations.

REVIEW OF LITERATURE

CEOs Presence on Twitter

Global CEOs have embraced social media communication through the growth seems to be lagging far behind compared to the general public (Social CEO Report, 2013). The two social networks, Twitter and LinkedIn, though stand out in terms of respectable growth rate in the number of CEOs embracing the new space. Twitter is a micro-blogging social media platform which is used to obtain breaking news; communicate with friends, celebrities, and companies; follow the latest score of sporting events; etc. Users post "tweets" or mini-posts up to 140 characters in length via mobile texting, instant messaging, third-party applications, or the web (Rybalko & Seltzer, 2010). Unlike other social networking sites, "following" users on Twitter is not mutual. Other users have an option to follow members if their profiles are public, or they can ask permission to follow private member profiles. There are currently (5.6% CEOs on Twitter, which is definitely an improvement over last year's 3.6% CEOs. The report categorizes certain CEOs as active Twitter users on the basis of tweets in the last 100 days. The survey highlights that only 3.8% of the Fortune 500 CEOs are active Twitter users (Social CEO Report, 2013). Further, while Twitter's active global users are tweeting about twice per day, Fortune 500 CEOs who are active on Twitter are tweeting an average of 0.98 tweets per day (Social CEO Report, 2013).

It is important to understand the CEO mediated relationships in the space of collaborative interactions. The online content form CEOs are referred as open dialogues contributing to trust inauthenticity because they are alleged as being sociable and genuine (Men & Tsai, 2016). In most of the cases, CEOs are more likely good listeners, and less scripted and distant (Shandwick, 2012). The role of CEOs has become more critical in information seeking, building connections, and job-related benefits considering user needs, expectations, and gratification. Social media also offers a tool to make a real-time and spontaneous response in the context of public engagement (Waters et al., 2009). With social media presence, CEOs participate in ongoing discussion applying leadership strategy on a global scale. Social media features allow CEOs to engage with their all stakeholders in very authentic and informal manner (Men, 2015).

Need for CEOs to Embrace Twitter

The reputation of CEO in terms of personal attitudes influences various corporate investment and risk-taking decisions (Ahern & Dittmar, 2012; Borghesi et al., 2014; Resick et al, 2009). Due to sensitive reputation, CEO communication is considered as a crucial component of leadership demonstrating assertive and responsive content. Quality communication can be determined by various characteristics such as compassionate, friendly, sincere, understanding, and interested (Men, 2015). It helps in building an organizational reputation in a dynamic and competitive environment (Kim & Rhee, 2011). For quality content, it is a critical condition for CEO to make communication positively associated with openness and transparency (Men and Stacks, 2013). As a significant predictor, social media provides useful information in defining dialogue and interaction (Watkins; 2017). Social media platforms have changed the corporate communication dynamics in several major ways. First, while only elite journalists could produce news on corporate mistakes or wrongdoings in the past, now any Internet user can publicly discuss his negative experience about a company (Jameson, 2014). Second, social media enable direct interactions between individual customers and high profile corporate figures such as CEOs. Customers, who could access CEOs only through TV or magazine interviews in the past, now have a direct conversation channel with CEOs through platforms like Twitter. Third, social media expanded the scope of corporate communication in general. Corporate communication used to exist only between the public relations team and journalists, but now it exists virtually between any corporate personals and customers" (Park, 2011).

The senior executive of a company during his interaction with college students argued in favor of price discrimination based on the content usage of internet services (Alghawi et al., 2014). All this happened in a semi-formal environment and the executive left, satisfied with having put his points forward to the next generation. Unaware, the comments went online and there was a whole lot of discussion regarding the company's policies. The CEOs comments were being directly ascribed to the way company plans for the future. Wary of social media, CEO had no presence on any of the social media – Facebook, Twitter etc. There was no way to mention his side of the story and the company let discussions die down without any comment from the top leadership on social media (Jameson, 2014). This is a typical example of CEOs trying to think that social media won't have any ramifications on the existing organizational setup.

Public Relations Through Twitter

Social media presence of top executives of a company can go a long way in managing crisis communication. The study follows a conceptual model and tries to analyze the influence of medium and message on the recipient's perception of reputation, recipients' secondary crisis communications (e.g., sharing information and leaving a message) and reactions (e.g., willingness to boycott) (Schultza et al., 2011). The influence of the different media types i.e. newspaper, blogs, and twitter was analyzed separately. Also, the different modes of crisis communication were tested for their efficacy to reduce the existing negative sentiment. The top leadership must lead this march towards digitization and ensure an active presence on Twitter. A company or a top-level executive can't afford to mitigate the crisis by starting to tweet at the time of crisis. The engagement has to be long-term, and authentic in nature.

In any organization being a high-profile, CEO is the more visible entity to the public. Most of the online users tend to build a conversational relationship with such high-profile personae (Kim et al., 2016). To understand the CEO online personality might be useful to enhance the social relationship. For instance, in a crisis response, CEO personality can be emphasized to provide a better direction to practitioners. Social media presence of CEOs improves the reputation of organization (Shandwick, 2012). Therefore, CEOs are shifting their image distant to approachable and personable which cultivates value connections (Vidgen et al.,2013; Men & Tsai, 2016). To achieve highly interactive communication, CEOs make social media an ideal platform for actual dialogues. For successful crisis communication, it might, therefore, be important to address twitter users (Hwang, 2012). This acts as another stimulus for the businesses to show active presence on social media.

Social media seeks to blur the existing boundaries of a traditional organization since recent years have witnessed a number of companies and their top level employees embracing this powerful medium to share information with all stakeholders (Aldoory & Toth, 2004). There have been researching studies in the past prescribing the best practices of online communication, the power of engaging online with the customers with examples of few CEOs from western countries tweeting and using the social media as an extension of their workplace. But, there is less literature on the practices followed by C-Suite employees from developing countries like India and there is a lot of scope for research on how exactly the top level executives communicate. In next section, the adopted methodologies for this study are discussed.

METHODOLOGY

For this paper, Twitter data related to Ms. Kiran Mazumdar Shaw (CEO and Founder, Biocon) were collected between March 1 and April 25, 2014. During the period, R, an open source tool, was used to extract tweets from twitter through streaming API containing search words. The study involved analysis of three datasets namely Ms. Shaw's tweets, her tweets retweeted by other users and mentions for Ms. Shaw on Twitter. Data analyses were carried in three different phases to identify her communication style and discussion topics in tweet data. For that, few particular methods were used: word frequency analysis, metadiscourse, and content analysis. For that, we use another tool called NVivo which is a qualitative data analysis (QDA) computer software package. Results are presented and discussed in next section.

RESULTS AND FINDING

Content Analysis

Word Frequency Analysis

Word Frequency analysis is a method to quantitatively present how often words, phrases, and events occur. In the literature, researchers have used frequency analysis with words to examine significant meanings and characteristics (Ghiassi et al., 2013). Word Clouds are a visual representation of text data and help us to quickly understand the most prominent terms of discussion. It takes into account frequency of occurrence of the various terms and accordingly certain terms appear bolder with respect to the other terms in word clouds. For this paper, we demonstrated word clouds for three datasets as Ms. Shaw's tweets, her tweets retweeted by other users and mentions for Ms. Shaw on twitter (Figure 1), (Figure 2), (Figure 3).

Figure 1. Word cloud tweets posted by Ms. Kiran Shaw

India	59
Bangalore	58
Good	55
Thanks	51
Govt	47
Mdpai	39
Political	36
Time	36
Women	34
Yes	34
Support	32
Aap	29
Agree	29
Bioconlimited	28
Kamataka	26
Parties	26
missionnamopm	25
Indian	24
Change	23
Great	23

Figure 2. Word cloud for retweets posts shared by other users

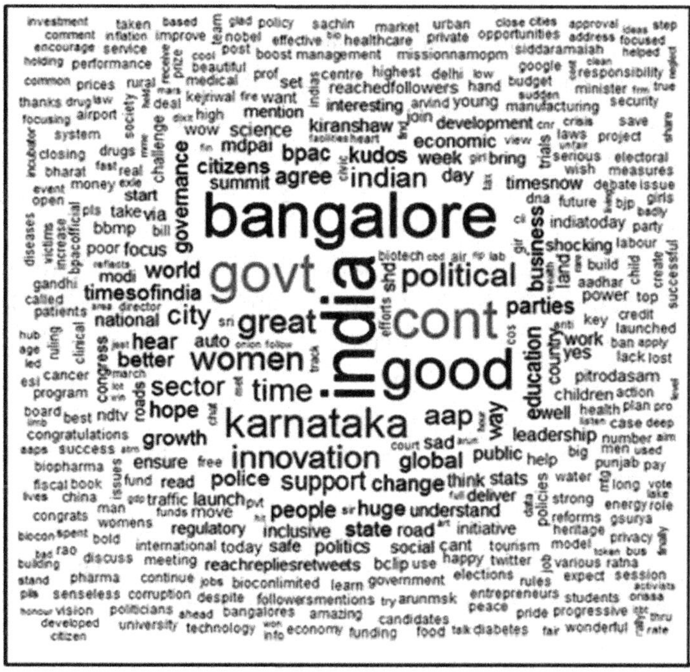

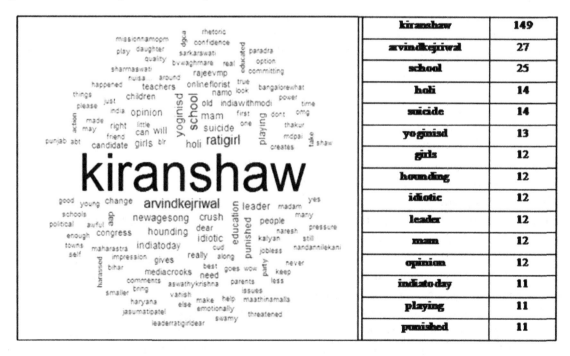

india	95
bangalore	84
good	74
cont	68
govt	67
karnataka	49
great	38
women	38
political	37
innovation	36
time	35
aap	29
city	29
indian	29
sector	26
support	25
global	23
agree	21
change	21
Kudos	21

Figure 3. Word cloud for mentions by other users

kiranshaw	149
arvindkejriwal	27
school	25
holi	14
suicide	14
yoginisd	13
girls	12
hounding	12
idiotic	12
leader	12
mam	12
opinion	12
indiatoday	11
playing	11
punished	11

These figures provide a comparison between Ms. Kiran Shaw's tweets and her tweets retweeted by other users. The prominent terms from Figure 1 indicate Ms. Kiran Shaw's social media communication is not limited to Biocon or pharma sector. Her tweets show continuous focus on emerging political landscape with aap, missionnamopm, political, parties coming out boldly in the word cloud. The individuals' mdpai, arunmsk and organizations bpac, timesofindia, bbmp are finding the equal reference. She tends to keep her discussion focused on multiple issues and tweets on length about them as we can see number of bolder terms emerging from Figure 1 compared to Figure 2. The conversation tends to be longer, probably involving two-way exchange of ideas which can be considered as the reason for the discussion themes coming out so clearly in Figure 1. Compare this with Figure 2, where there are fewer prominent themes emerging out of the word cloud, and can be broadly identified as India, Bangalore, Karnataka, Political, Women, Innovation, Support. The themes which can be easily identified in both the datasets range from Bangalore, India, Govt, Karnataka, Women.

The retweeted tweets by a user illustrate his interest or support for the messages shared by Ms. Kiran Shaw (Figure 2). With limited knowledge about the discussion topics from the word clouds, we can still assume maximum retweets are being done for issues of social concern - women, about communities – whether Bangalore, Karnataka, India. Also, the tweets addressed towards govt. are being retweeted to a large extent by her followers. At, the same time there are lesser retweets relating to her company Biocon or pharma sector by followers of Ms. Kiran Shaw. Her followers are retweeting about politics or say different political parties, which can be ascribed to the current scenario with general elections scheduled in the months of April-May'14. Also, dependent on the time frame for which analysis is being on Ms. Shaw's tweets, certain aspects would be highlighted more in the word cloud which might not be the case otherwise. To illustrate, the current period of discussion involved a lot of political activity on account of national elections and hence her communication involves reference to the same. In the subsequent portions, an effort has been put to study tweet contents manually in order to gain a better understanding of the themes of discussion. The tweets have been bifurcated on the basis of content to learn about the broader fields of her twitter communication.

Semantic Analysis

The semantic analysis provides the better understanding of the communication style of Ms. Kiran Shaw on Twitter. We divided tweets into three broad categories to understand tweet contents: Business (Table 1), Personal (Table 2), and Social (Table 3). The analysis demonstrates that she makes her case amply clear by comparing better research carried out in countries owing to the support which government offers. Findings, from a CEO's perspective, highlight that IT sector has become a model for development owing to the governmental support in terms of regulatory support offered over the last few years. So, her communication with reference to business includes the news related to company's promotion for pharmaceutical sector and views on governmental policy. The personal tweets are related to updating status, sharing photographs, increase in a number of followers, retweets, replies etc. over a period of time. The personal tweets could be categorized as personal feelings and status updates.

The findings show that for business perspective Ms. Kiran Shaw refers not to confine herself and is vocal about the economic growth of the country, the learning from the other sectors and how governmental policy could impact the growth story. In few tweets, she quotes how companies like AstraZeneca have moved their research facilities outside India owing to the poor research support which according to her thwarts innovation and has a direct bearing on the economic growth of the country. Various topics in her tweets are presented in Figure 4. The Figure shows a wide range of topics on different categories discussed above. Her major discussion is about political activities by political parties such as 'arvind kejriwal vanish along congress', 'idiotic hounding related to namo', and 'political parties' rally and agendas'. She also discussed some shocking and sad news for a specific government (e.g. Karnataka government). For more information at that point, she was looking for more stats and hoped for good news and engaging news for better governance. In general elections, a transparent electoral process is much required for the common man.

Table 1. Business category

	Promote/share company news	Promote/share news for Pharmaceutical sector	Tweets/Retweets about other sectors	Comments on Governmental Policy/ Regulations, Lobbying
Tweets	22	41	40	60
Re tweeted tweets	19	55	42	58

Table 2. Personal category

	Personal interests/feelings	Promote yourself/company	Status Update
Tweets	212	55	46
Retweeted tweets	264	38	50

Table 3. Social category

	Politics/Governance	Healthcare	Education	Women Empowerment	Other issues
Tweets	28	45	15	24	36
Re tweeted tweets	29	23	18	23	52

Apart from political agendas, she felt a need of more research for criminal cases against women. Based on her discussion, it influences the growth of socio-economic development. Ms. Shaw also shared her views on equal opportunities for women. In the business category, she talked about jobs created by real states and start-ups. In her view, these sectors are changing things tremendously. Her posted content also showed her views on e-health and agri-biotechnology. In tweets, she showed her gratitude for different foundations for their support. Her discussion also raised the current society related issues, for instance, there was a suicidal case of the young girl in Bangalore. Another case was about few students being punished by the local school for playing Holi in Bangalore. In this way, Ms. Shaw talked about the safety issue in the city as a primary concern for society. Adding to it, she also shared her views on equality rights of education, especially in private sector. In summary, the semantic analysis highlights the variety of concerns and views of a woman CEO in a public platform. In next section, sentiment analysis has been carried to get a brief view of different emotions in her content.

Figure 4. Semantic Analysis

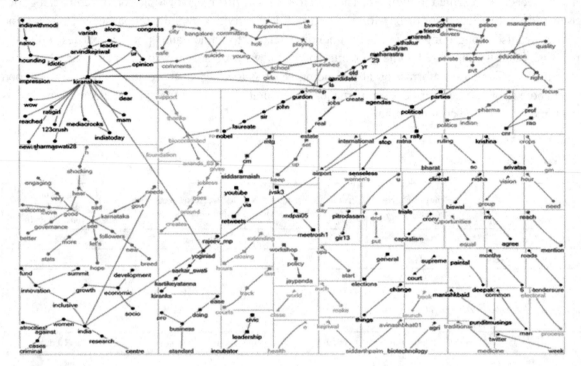

Sentiment Analysis

Sentiment analysis shows the various emotions which were classified as anger, anticipation, disgust, fear, and joy. In this analysis, there is a score associated with each emotion based on the word sentiments (Figure 5). This combined score helps in identifying the major emotion which reflects the emotional personality of the person. The Figure shows that there are more positive emotions than negative which means that Ms. Shaw shares and discusses better happening content. People have more trust on her content in terms of views and opinions. On the other hand, there are emotions such as anger, disgust and sadness indicate her negative thoughts on various social issues, political agendas, and government policies. Such negative emotions lead to fear emotion highlighting her concern for growth and development. However, she is expecting few good moves from the government for a society which is reflected by anticipation emotion. In summary, she had positive thoughts about business related discussion and negative emotions with social issues.

Metadiscourse Analysis

It is important to analyze the tweets irrespective of propositional content. Using metadiscourse, an attempt is made to understand the textual and interpersonal components by discerning the tweet contents. The approach, thereby, seeks to understand following appeals in the tweets made by Kiran Shaw: Rationality, Credibility, and Emotionality. These components together form pillars of effective communication stated by Aristotle. The textual discourse analysis of Ms. Kiran Shaw's tweets takes into account logical connectives, sequencers, frame makers and code glosses. The medium of communication reduces the scope of usage of endophoric markers (e.g. noted above, see below) and they have a minimal existence in the tweet sample. Therefore, the study disregards this category while understanding textual metadiscourse. The language of discourse on social media tends to be informal; it has been kept in mind to include all possible text tokens required for a complete analysis. The need to include (n, nd, &, and) while looking out for logical connective and in the tweet contents is on account of the informality of the communication medium.

Figure 5. Emotion classification

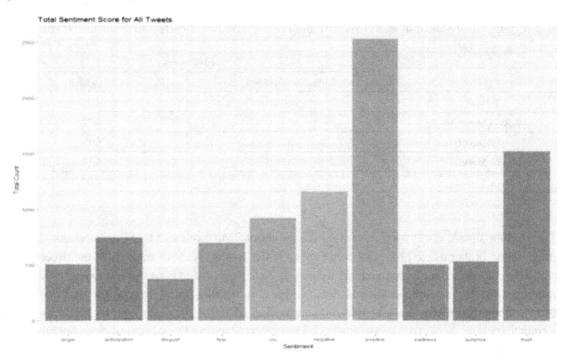

A sample of 300 tweets was analyzed for Ms. Kiran Shaw to understand her communicative appeal. The model is highly adaptive since it makes use of the elementary components of effective communication, irrespective of the communication medium. The analysis was done on 4735 words in the 300 tweets sample. The research doesn't ignore the possibility of multiple categorizations of text tokens. However, in the current study, the primary purpose of the text token has been taken into account and double counting (considering them in multiple categories) has been avoided. Various categories of textual metadiscourse and text tokens corresponding to them are (shown in Table 4): logical connectives (and, or, but, however), sequencers (first, then, next, finally, number used for listing), frame makers (well, now, as a result, conclude), and code glosses (such as, namely, example, parentheses, for instance).

There is an attempt to generate a coherent and convincing piece of information, which is done with the help of above-mentioned text tokens. The quantitative analysis of these tokens helps us to understand the rational appeal of the tweets. The use of these tokens can determine what message Kiran Shaw wants to convey to the readers, influence them and restrict other possible understanding of the tweets. We also tried to compare the same with others CEOs speeches available in the literature (Table 5).

Table 4. Textual metadiscouse categorization frequency

	n	Per 100 words	% of total
Textual	109	2.30	36.82
Logical Connectives	81	1.71	27.36
Sequencers	8	0.17	2.70
Frame Markers	5	0.11	1.69
Code Glosses	15	0.32	5.07

Table 5. Comparison of textual metadiscourse between Ms. Shaw's tweets and other CEOs speeches

	Per 100 words	
	Kiran Shaw's tweets	**CEO speeches**
Textual	2.30	1.29
Logical Connectives	1.71	0.91
Sequencers	0.17	0.19
Frame Markers	0.11	0.11
Code Glosses	0.32	0.02

The finding shows, the textual metadiscourse is about 75% more in Ms. Shaw's tweets. This can be attributed to higher usage of logical connectives in her tweets. A close analysis of the tweets would illustrate her social media communication style as discussing multiple issues in her tweets. She prefers considering various possibilities/factors even while commenting/discussing issues and contributes towards a thoughtful discussion. In addition, she focuses on citing examples and highlighting certain important text in her tweets (read code glosses). The preferred use (0.32 vs. 0.2) indicates her propensity to use citations to convey her message, which also helps readers to easily understand and relate to her message. Further, the interpersonal discourse tends to evaluate the tenor of tweets such as the degree of reader involvement, commitment to shared information, writer's attitude etc. (Table 6). The interpersonal discourse analysis helps to understand the credibility and emotional appeal of tweets.

Table 6. Interpersonal discourse

	n	Per 100 words	% of total
Interpersonal	187	3.95	63.18
Hedges	2	0.04	0.68
Emphatics	6	0.13	2.03
Attributors	80	1.69	27.03
Attitude markers	12	0.25	4.05
Relational markers	87	1.84	29.39

Ms. Kiran Shaw prefers to be considered as part of the general public, though throughout the discussion she dons the mantle of a corporate citizen, raises multiple issues of social issues in her tweets. The analysis shows that effective (or emotional) appeal tends to dominate the discourse of Ms. Kiran Shaw's communication on Twitter.

In summary, Ms. Kiran Shaw's tweets can bring the spotlight to existing evils which can have a positive effect to bring about the governmental action. Her views can bring about systematic changes in the way society as a whole shares views on certain issues of public importance. The issues can vary in terms of significance and might have limited scope. In few of the tweets, she reflects strong support for the governmental setup and individuals for their visionary leadership shown at various levels. Ms. Kiran Shaw tweets are comparatively more about personal content (sharing information/feelings) than being related to business or social issues.

CONCLUSION

This study shows the various different perspective of discussion and opinions of an Indian woman CEO in her communication on Twitter. Interestingly, CEOs are more likely to share the newspaper article than the long blog post. As findings show the presence of broad different categories in Ms. Shaw's tweets, it reflects the balanced approach to creating content and engaging with public on social media. Her content is quite vocal about the social issues affecting the local community and even at the national level. She follows the accountability of the public relations professional to connect with different stakeholders (public and media) in relationship building activities. Her views also reflect lobbying for better support in research and development. This broader interaction strategy by a CEO may work better if it accompanies a suitable and strategic social media communication way involving severe ethical issues, and moral challenges.

LIMITATION AND FUTURE SCOPE

The current study analyzes an Indian CEOs twitter communication over a small period of time and takes into account only limited data. As the datasets are very limited due to restrictions imposed by Twitter APIs, it requires few advanced techniques to extract a larger set of tweets to generate more generalize results. It is proposed that further studies should move beyond content analysis or in-depth understandings such as influencer identification through network analysis.

REFERENCES

Aldoory, L., & Toth, E. (2004). Leadership and gender in public relations: Perceived effectiveness of transformational and transactional leadership styles. *Journal of Public Relations Research, 16*(2), 157–183. doi:10.12071532754xjprr1602_2

Alghawi, I. A., Yan, J., & Wei, C. (2014). Professional or interactive: CEOs' image strategies in the microblogging context. *Computers in Human Behavior, 41*, 184–189. doi:10.1016/j.chb.2014.09.027

Borghesi, R., Houston, J. F., & Naranjo, A. (2014). Corporate socially responsible investments: CEO altruism, reputation, and shareholder interests. *Journal of Corporate Finance*, *26*, 164–181. doi:10.1016/j.jcorpfin.2014.03.008

BRANDfog Survey. (2014). *The Global, Social CEO*. Retrieved April 20, 2014, from http://brandfog.com/ CEOSocialMediaSurvey/BRANDfog_2014_CEO_Survey.pdf

Di Giuli, A., & Kostovetsky, L. (2014). Are red or blue companies more likely to go green? Politics and corporate social responsibility. *Journal of Financial Economics*, *111*(1), 158–180. doi:10.1016/j.jfineco.2013.10.002

Getting social: Social media in business. (n.d.). PwC. Retrieved March 19, 2014, from http://www.pwc.com/my/en/issues/socialmedia.html

Ghiassi, M., Skinner, J., & Zimbra, D. (2013). Twitter brand sentiment analysis: A hybrid system using n-gram analysis and dynamic artificial neural network. *Expert Systems with Applications*, *40*(16), 6266–6282. doi:10.1016/j.eswa.2013.05.057

Hutton, J. G., Goodman, M. B., Alexander, J. B., & Genest, C. M. (2001). Reputation management: The new face of corporate public relations? *Public Relations Review*, *27*(3), 247–261. doi:10.1016/S0363-8111(01)00085-6

Hwang, S. (2012). The strategic use of Twitter to manage personal public relations. *Public Relations Review*, *38*(1), 159–161. doi:10.1016/j.pubrev.2011.12.004

Hyland, K. (1998). Exploring corporate rhetoric: Metadiscourse in the CEO's letter. *Journal of Business Communication*, *35*(2), 224–244. doi:10.1177/002194369803500203

Jameson, D. A. (2014). Crossing Public-Private and Personal-Professional Boundaries How Changes in Technology May Affect CEOs' Communication. *Business and Professional Communication Quarterly*, *77*(1), 7–30. doi:10.1177/2329490613517133

Karaduman, İ. (2013). The effect of social media on personal branding efforts of top level executives. *Procedia: Social and Behavioral Sciences*, *99*, 465–473. doi:10.1016/j.sbspro.2013.10.515

Kim, J. N., & Rhee, Y. (2011). Strategic thinking about employee communication behavior (ECB) in public relations: Testing the models of megaphoning and scouting effects in Korea. *Journal of Public Relations Research*, *23*(3), 243–268. doi:10.1080/1062726X.2011.582204

Kim, S., Zhang, X. A., & Zhang, B. W. (2016). Self-mocking crisis strategy on social media: Focusing on Alibaba chairman Jack Ma in China. *Public Relations Review*, *42*(5), 903–912. doi:10.1016/j.pubrev.2016.10.004

Men, L. R. (2014). Why leadership matters to internal communication: Linking transformational leadership, symmetrical communication, and employee outcomes. *Journal of Public Relations Research*, *26*(3), 256–279. doi:10.1080/1062726X.2014.908719

Men, L. R. (2015). The internal communication role of the chief executive officer: Communication channels, style, and effectiveness. *Public Relations Review*, *41*(4), 461–471. doi:10.1016/j.pubrev.2015.06.021

Men, L. R., & Stacks, D. (2014). The effects of authentic leadership on strategic internal communication and employee-organization relationships. *Journal of Public Relations Research*, *26*(4), 301–324. doi: 10.1080/1062726X.2014.908720

Men, L. R., & Tsai, W. H. S. (2016). Public engagement with CEOs on social media: Motivations and relational outcomes. *Public Relations Review*, *42*(5), 932–942. doi:10.1016/j.pubrev.2016.08.001

Park, J., Kim, H., Cha, M., & Jeong, J. (2011). *Ceo's apology in twitter: A case study of the fake beef labeling incident by e-mart.* Springer Berlin Heidelberg.

Porter, M. C., Anderson, B., & Nhotsavang, M. (2015). Anti-social media: Executive Twitter "engagement" and attitudes about media credibility. *Journal of Communication Management*, *19*(3), 270–287. doi:10.1108/JCOM-07-2014-0041

Rathore, A. K., & Ilavarasan, P. V. (2018). Social Media and Business Practices. In Encyclopedia of Information Science and Technology, Fourth Edition (pp. 7126-7139). IGI Global. doi:10.4018/978-1-5225-2255-3.ch619

Rathore, A. K., Ilavarasan, P. V., & Dwivedi, Y. K. (2016). Social media content and product co-creation: An emerging paradigm. *Journal of Enterprise Information Management*, *29*(1), 7–18. doi:10.1108/JEIM-06-2015-0047

Report - 2013 Social CEO Report: Are America's Top CEOs Getting More Social? (n.d.). Domo. Retrieved March 3, 2014, from https://www.domo.com/learn/2013-social-ceo-report-are-americas-top-ceos-getting-more-social

Resick, C. J., Whitman, D. S., Weingarden, S. M., & Hiller, N. J. (2009). The bright-side and the dark-side of CEO personality: Examining core self-evaluations, narcissism, transformational leadership, and strategic influence. *The Journal of Applied Psychology*, *94*(6), 1365–1381. doi:10.1037/a0016238 PMID:19916649

Rybalko, S., & Seltzer, T. (2010). Dialogic communication in 140 characters or less: How Fortune 500 companies engage stakeholders using Twitter. *Public Relations Review*, *36*(4), 336–341. doi:10.1016/j.pubrev.2010.08.004

Schultz, F., Utz, S., & Göritz, A. (2011). Is the medium the message? Perceptions of and reactions to crisis communication via twitter, blogs and traditional media. *Public Relations Review*, *37*(1), 20–27. doi:10.1016/j.pubrev.2010.12.001

Steyn, B. (2004). From strategy to corporate communication strategy: A conceptualisation. *Journal of Communication Management*, *8*(2), 168–183. doi:10.1108/13632540410807637

Vidgen, R., Mark Sims, J., & Powell, P. (2013). Do CEO bloggers build community? *Journal of Communication Management*, *17*(4), 364–385. doi:10.1108/JCOM-08-2012-0068

Waters, R. D., Burnett, E., Lamm, A., & Lucas, J. (2009). Engaging stakeholders through social networking: How nonprofit organizations are using Facebook. *Public Relations Review*, *35*(2), 102–106. doi:10.1016/j.pubrev.2009.01.006

Watkins, B. A. (2017). Experimenting with dialogue on Twitter: An examination of the influence of the dialogic principles on engagement, interaction, and attitude. *Public Relations Review*, *43*(1), 163–171. doi:10.1016/j.pubrev.2016.07.002

Weber Shandwick. (2012). *The social CEO: executives tell all*. Retrieved from. http://www.webershandwick.com/uploads/news/files/Social-CEO-Study.pdf

This research was previously published in Modern Perspectives on Virtual Communications and Social Networking; pages 196-212, copyright year 2019 by Information Science Reference (an imprint of IGI Global).

Section 7
Critical Issues and Challenges

Chapter 85
E–Reputation in Web Entrepreneurship

Vincent Dutot
Paris School of Business, France

Sylvaine Castellano
 https://orcid.org/0000-0003-4487-5565
Paris School of Business, France

ABSTRACT

E-reputation is what you say, what you do and of course how others perceive all of your actions. As an entrepreneur, knowing what your customers think about you is crucial. But managing it is way more than just hiring someone to be active on some social platforms. It implies the definition of a real strategy as well as hiring specific resources to successfully manage its reputation online. By presenting what e-reputation is, what are its main components, how to measure it and what tools exist, this chapter wants to give to web-entrepreneurs the key elements in order to manage their e-reputation efficiently.

INTRODUCTION

Examining reputation is becoming increasingly important today, mainly due to factors such as word-of-mouth and online communication (Shamma, 2012). To date, few academic researches have analyzed the influence of the Internet on reputation or its role in positioning reputation and e-reputation (Castellano and Dutot, 2013). For instance, according to Fillias and Villeneuve (2010), e-reputation has not been considered as a revelation but more as a continuing process of technology adoption and usage by companies or individuals.

Along the same lines, some authors consider e-reputation as the extension of reputation on-line (Chun and Davies, 2001). Therefore, we can extend previous works (Hatch and Schultz, 1997) and consider e-reputation to be the perception that stakeholders hold towards the activities of an organization when evolving online. For Frochot and Molinaro (2008), e-reputation is the reflection of the image that Internet users have of a company or an individual based on information available online and on what others say

DOI: 10.4018/978-1-7998-9020-1.ch085

about the company or the individual. However, recent studies have shown that e-reputation is more than just reputation online (Dutot and Castellano, 2015).

Professionals have paved the way by measuring e-reputation using tools such as Social Mention, Mention or Synthesio. Although these studies present interesting insights for e-reputation, they mainly focus on content analysis, and their measurement grid may lack scientific rigor. The academic arena has started to investigate this field of research. For instance, Chun (2004) proposed an e-reputation mix composed of 3 blocs: e-character (personality of the company), e-identity (website's structure and ergonomics) and e-experience (defines the user experience online). This definition offers some interesting concepts but fails to capture social media's current influence on action. Addressing this gap, Dutot and Castellano (2015) developed the first academic measurement scale for e-reputation.

This chapter will explain why e-reputation is a crucial factor of success for web entrepreneurship. More precisely, it will position reputation and e-reputation, present the main components of e-reputation, present tools and finally give insights on how to manage the e-reputation.

WHY TALKING ABOUT E-REPUTATION?

Because like it or not, we are all concerned. Any company is present on the web, no matter if it decided to be present or because someone is talking about it. From a more traditional perspective, media such as television, radio or the press, have very long allowed them to present their creations to consumers and generate a positive word of mouth. However skids are recurrent and the impact on the organization is real.

Times have changed and the speed with which information travels today is almost impossible for a company to manage (especially as often it lacks the resources to manage it efficiently). In 60 seconds, the reality of the web is that simple (Excelacom, 2016):

- Nearly 2.5 million searches just been performed on Google: and your company is part of the research.
- 2.78 million Videos were viewed: what are your employees doing?
- 527 000 photos were shared on Snapchat, and 38 000 new posts on Instagram: do you control your corporate image?
- 700 000 individuals just log on Facebook.
- Almost 350 000 new tweets were added on Twitter.

In a very simplistic way, e-reputation can be summarized "in what you do, what you say and what others say about you." As a company, you should control "What you do and say". On the opposite side, you have little control on "What others say about you". In most cases you do not know what is told about you online, so it's even harder to control it?

POSITIONING REPUTATION AND E-REPUTATION

From Reputation to E-Reputation

Reputation contributes to the development of sustainable competitive advantage and the creation of long-term relationships with multiple stakeholder groups (Boyd et al., 2010). This concept has been widely analyzed and studied for the past two decades in the academic literature (Logsdon and Wood 2002). However, this interest has led to an abundance of definitions of reputation (Fombrun and Shanley, 1990; Gotsi and Wilson, 2001; Rindova *et al.*, 2005).

The concept of reputation is even more important in an online context (Volle *et al.*, 2013). E-reputation refers to the elements of reputation that are specifically derived from electronic contacts. E-reputation is occasionally termed 'cyber reputation', 'web reputation', 'digital reputation', and 'online reputation' (Dutot and Castellano, 2015).

The impact of the Internet may vary because the technology used is diverse. For instance, discussion groups, brand communities and anonymous consumer profiling, communication systems, file transfer, email and global information access and retrieval systems foster interactivity and allow enhanced consumer experiences and tailored and rapid responses (De Chernatony, 2001). Overall, the Internet and new technologies have altered two crucial factors that potentially impact reputation – information and interactivity.

The influence of Internet on how a company should manage its e-reputation has become crucial not only for academics as we pointed out, but also for the professionals (AFNOR, 2015). The impact of technology may vary because of two main factors. The first one is the technology used. Indeed, Internet has altered both the information and the interactivity between a firm and its customers. It is clear that Internet (and tools such as social networks, discussion groups or e-mails) helps individuals developing exchanges of information and communication. It has led to bypassing existing intermediaries (search engines) to answer directly and faster than ever to stakeholders' enquiries (Chen, 2001). At the same time, the flow of information is quicker, cheaper and richer than ever (Michell, 2001). It creates, according to Aaker and Joachimsthaler (in Uncles, 2001), the potential for a meaningful social experience, leading to enhanced consumer benefits.

The second factor is the context of the firm. Indeed entrepreneurs, such as SMEs, have specificities. SMEs have highly centralized structures and typically employ generalists rather than specialists (Thong, 1999); (2) SMEs often lack in-depth IT/IS knowledge and technical skills within the organization leading to a lower level of awareness of the benefits of IT (DeLone, 1988); (3) SMEs have limited funds to develop and maintain sophisticated IT infrastructures (Thong et al., 1996); and (4) SMEs have much less access to the necessary management and financial resources to correct situations arising from an unwise or unsuccessful IT investment (Zhang et al., 2007). Overall this could lead to the underestimation of the e-reputation and its impacts. Moreover, web-entrepreneurs may not realize how crucial it is to manage its e-reputation.

Comparing Reputation and E-Reputation Based on Their Attributes

Fombrun's (1996) proposed three key attributes of reputation that can help to position e-reputation. First, reputation is based on perceptions, which means that it is outside the control of the firm. Second, reputation represents the aggregate perception of all of a firm's constituents. Third, reputation is comparative

(Wartick, 2002), allowing rankings to be developed (i.e., Fortune or Inc's Top Internet Companies). Later on, the corporate reputation literature identified two additional attributes. Fourth, reputation can be positive or negative. Fifth, reputation is stable and enduring (Walker, 2010). If it takes time to build a reputation, the development of the web makes it more difficult for firms to control their reputation as individuals can quickly and instantaneously share information, give opinions, recommend, react or comment online.

We reproduce below a table (Table 1) that compares reputation and e-reputation based on the previous works from Dutot and Castellano (2015: 300).

Table 1. Comparison of reputation and e-reputation based on attributes

Attributes	Characteristics of Reputation	Specificities of E-Reputation
Perceptual	Out of the hand of the firm	Internet increases the difficulty to keep control
Aggregate perception	General (overall perception of stakeholders) or specific (examined from specific stakeholder perspective)	Appropriation of reputational dynamics due to interconnection of all stakeholders
Comparative	Compare the reputation of different organizations	Possible to compare offline and online reputation within each organization
Positive and negative	Whether offline or online, reputation can be positive or negative	
Stable, enduring and time dimension	Reputation is formed over time	With the Internet, information flow is faster. Building and/or destroying e-reputation is almost immediate as information spreads Instantaneously through social media

Challenges of E-Reputation for Web-Entrepreneurship

Going from reputation to e-reputation implies that we need to consider the links between firms and the Internet, especially in an entrepreneurial context. Overall, three profiles of firms have been previously identified: brick-and-mortar companies (firms that have a physical presence only), pure-players (firms that evolve only on the Internet) and clicks-and-mortar (firms that evolve both online and offline). Because the Internet can be fully or not integrated in their core business, firms will manage their e-reputation differently. These three types of firms will face different challenges when dealing with their e-reputation. It is of strategic importance for pure-player as their business model is based on the Internet. E-reputation might just represent a communication challenge for brick-and-mortar companies. In fact, their survival does not necessarily fully depend on their activities on the Internet. Still, the Internet can be further integrated in the long run as the quality of the digital communication can provide some added value to the firm such as influence and positive image, which positively impact the firm's e-reputation. Finally, the e-reputation issue is very even more challenging for bricks and clicks. These firms need to find the right balance and alignment between the strategic and communicational challenges, both off and online (see Table 2).

Table 2. Challenges of firms

	Bricks and Mortar	**Bricks and Clicks**	**Pure Player**
Main assessment mode	Reputation	Reputation e-Reputation	e-Reputation
Type of risks related to the Internet	Communicational	Coherence and alignment between strategic and communicational	Strategic and communicational
Examples of signals sent over the Internet	Manage a reputational crisis	Present a new product	Daily activities

STRATEGIES AND DIMENSIONS OF E-REPUTATION

Overall e-reputation needs to be understood depending on the firm's strategies as well as some key issues when deciding to manage its e-reputation. Three strategies can be deployed by a company: monitoring, defensive or promotional. These strategies have to be understood as orientations. They are underpinned by key elements: transparency and honesty of the message and the company, internal processes to be linked to the strategy, flexibility of the firm and employees, the delay of answer and finally the integration within the entire company of the e-reputation vision.

Strategies

As presented, three strategies can be deployed by a firm when talking about e-reputation. The first one is called 'monitoring'. Any company wishing to understand or to know what is said about it, on the web, can implement BI tools (see the next section for examples of tools). In doing so, it can be alerted whenever its name is mentioned and may take supporting or corrective actions.

Example of Monitoring Strategy: BareMinerals©

- **The Firm:** BareMinerals is a US company selling cosmetics products made of minerals. In France, the products are sold only through Sephora stores and the management of the brand online is ensured only by a very small team under the leadership of one community manager.
- **The E-Reputation Fact:** Start of 2014, in a TV show about relooking and make-up, the presenter mentioned 'mineral products' (without explicitly saying bareMinerals).
- **The Reaction:** The community manager had alerts on her smartphone indicating every time the word "mineral" was mentioned in these programs or on the web. Based on the potential of influence of the show, she decided to stock up on additional products all Sephora in France.
- **Impact on Organization and Sales:** Starting the next day, sales went up and in the following week, the firm performed as many as sales as the previous two months
- **Take Away:** Because social networks are characterized with instantaneity, the Internet requires adopting a proactive behavior in order for the firm to get the best of it.

The second strategy is 'the defensive'. In this context, the company just waits for something to happen (a rumor launched, a video on the organization) and then react. In many cases, if the organization has a crisis management team, it will be the latter that will be responsible for responding quickly and effectively to the situation.

Example of Defensive Strategy: La Redoute©

- **The Firm:** La Redoute is a French distance selling company created in 1837. Exclusively through catalogs until recently, the company operated a total shift to digital to become the first French platform for clothing and decoration purchase (7 million unique visitors per month).
- **The E-Reputation Fact:** 2012, an advertisement from the company shows four children running on the beach with a naked man in the background coming out of the water. This picture, discovered by an Internet user, quickly becomes a real buzz on the web.
- **The Reaction:** The head of communication at Red Cats (owner of La Redoute) quickly announces a "genuine mistake", and the picture is used to produce a lot of parodies. 3 Suisses (one of the main competitor) will even use the picture for their campaign. In the end the company has set up a real "hunt for mistakes" within their catalog, asking Internet users to help identifying such mistakes. The reward was to be dressed from head to foot by the brand.
- **Impact on Organization:** In one single day, 14 photos/ mistakes were identified by the crowd and the firm acknowledged a "significant increase of traffic on the website". Sales also went up as well as the brand reputation.
- **Take Away:** To change a potential bad buzz into a successful marketing strategy, the firm uses the Internet and its customers. It also admitted the mistake publicly. Based on the recovery paradox, an initial negative situation can turn out to something very positive if well-managed.

The third and final strategy is called 'promotion'. The company will use digital channels to launch or relaunch its brand and will rely on all stakeholders to support its strategy. In doing, it will seek to improve its position online or its perception among consumers.

Example of Promotional Strategy: Oasis©

- **The Firm:** Oasis is a French beverage brand, non-carbonated, established in 1966 and owned since 2006 by Orangina Schweppes Group. They are the first beverage brand in the non-carbonated segment and is second in the market of soft drinks.
- **The E-Reputation Fact:** The brand has experienced a significant slowdown in sales and an erosion of its reputation notably coinciding with the arrival of energy drinks. The willingness of the company was to reposition itself as an innovative brand for very young audiences and young parents.
- **The Reaction:** The brand has opted to rely on social media for its strategy, all with humor. By staging the fruit in different situations (the papayon effect, www.youpomme.com, parodies of Iron Man, Captain America), and accompanying its communication with dedicated media (own social networks, websites), the company used the right channels with the right online strategy.
- **Impact on Organization:** Sales doubled in the next year, reputation rose also and engagement with younger audiences was observed.
- **Take Away:** It is crucial to link strategy and channels of communication.

Components

In support of these three strategies, 6 components are to be integrated in any organization: transparency, honesty, processes, speed of response, flexibility, and integration.

By transparency, we mean the social practice guided by sincerity and total accessibility to information. The idea is to be able to report activities carried out by the organization and acknowledge mistakes. By doing so, the company establishes a relationship of trust with its consumers and different audiences online.

Honesty is understood as the conformity to morality and what is a socially recognized as standard. In the business field, honesty is the quality of being faithful to its obligations, its commitments. The idea is to meet commitments, without deceiving stakeholders. Honesty is sometimes close to the concept of trust.

These first two components are often the most difficult to implement in any organization as they are often reluctant to admit their mistakes. With the different sources of information available to customers, it would be appropriate for an organization to tell the truth from the start, otherwise they may later reconsider their actions. When it comes to communication strategies, especially in times of crisis, denying is the worst move to take, which is even more crucial in the virtual sphere as information spreads much faster.

The next component is the timing before answering. On the Web, everything goes very fast and any information left without reaction is likely to be misinterpreted by those who can read it. Silence is not bad per se, but it should be used in a proper manner. Silence is an appropriate strategy when considering small crisis. To be social, an organization has to answer in a short time (less than 2 hours on Facebook, less than 30 minutes on Twitter) to any comment from their customer online. Conversely, a firm has to identify (and monitor) potential threats and respond them.

The fourth essential component of the management of online reputation is the establishment of internal reaction process. Is there, within the organization, a crisis management team or at least one person in charge to communicate quickly when something happens? Smoldering crisis represent 75% of all crisis and can therefore be anticipated. It is often the handling of a crisis that leads to more damage than the crisis event itself. Online, the community manager is usually the fireman and must answer as quickly as possible (and unfortunately often without consultation with other members of the organization) to any questions or comments. However, a company must define upstream ways to respond such as the tone or the person in charge. Hiring external third parties might be relevant in very specific situations only such as in the case of sudden crisis. Third parties are perceived more objective and more efficient especially when the internal team is not in control any more.

The fifth component is flexibility. Does the company have a real ease to apprehend external data from a different angle? Can it imagine various solutions to a problem? What is its responsiveness to an external stimulus that it did not see coming? The company must develop ways to adapt most effectively to changes of environment or its consumers.

Finally the sixth and final component is integration. Any organization wishing to establish a real online reputation management strategy has to put together a number of activities under a common authority. In this sense, a Deloitte study in 2014 shows that 87% of executives consider the "reputational risk" as the most important strategic hazard. And if only 19% of companies say they are confident in their ability to manage these risks, more than half have already to set up crisis units to anticipate and manage any risk linked to reputation.

REPUTATION AND ITS INFLUENCERS

From Stakeholders to Influencers

Stakeholders are individuals or groups of individuals who are affected or that may affect the achievement of the objectives of an organization (McVea and Freeman, 2005). Virtually everyone can be a stakeholder as any entity can affect an organization. The first studies on stakeholders go back to the 1950s and 60s with the identification of the main stakeholders: (1) Customers, (2) Suppliers, (3) Competitors and (4) regulating groups. Internal stakeholders (employees) were added in the 1970s. As John Patterson, a senior advisor at the Reputation Institute, explains "for years, corporate leaders preached the virtues of communication and engagement with three key audiences: customers, investors and employees, but focusing exclusively on this "Holy Trinity" of stakeholders is creating diminishing returns for public and private organizations" (Patterson, 2015). Finally, opinion leaders and influencers were identified in the 1980s and 1990s respectively. Influencers are specific types of stakeholders. They represent mediating audiences. The "mediating audiences" are "third party" entities; they play a mediating role regarding the dissemination of information, knowledge, practices, information, etc. both off and online.

In an online environment characterized by complexity and uncertainty, the phenomena of power and dependency towards the firms' audiences become the rule. This is even more valid for entrepreneurs and new ventures as they face some liabilities in comparison to established firms. Liability is defined as the discount the evaluating audiences place on a particular organization in comparison to similar organizations for not matching the expectations of the evaluator. New ventures face the liability of smallness and the liability of newness. These two liabilities lead to lower level of visibility, fewer resources, less well-trained managers, and less developed relationships with creditors and other external stakeholders, etc. Therefore, they have higher chances of failure.

The Growing Role of Influencers

The role of stakeholders is very of important for newly created firms. While they were previously clearly identified with taken-for-granted rules of the game, new ventures today face a multitude of potential audiences to interact with online. Such audiences are numerous and more diverse based on their status on the Internet.

Different audiences evolve on the virtual sphere through Blogs, Twitter, Facebook, LinkedIn, Vine, Instagram, etc. It is quite easy to search on the Internet and find different and rankings about "the Top 15 Most Popular Social Networking Sites", or "Interesting Statistics for the Top 10 Social Media Sites", and even "The World's 21 Most Important Social Media Sites and Apps in 2015".

Each media saw the rise of influencers who created communities and followers. The Internet gives them the opportunity the power to exert some influence sometimes greater than influencers on traditional media. These influencers have power on different levels. They first have an impact on traditional consumer behavior such as increased brand loyalty, brand awareness, and purchasing decision. But they also become marketing objects themselves. For instance, Lele Pons from is one of the most popular Vine stars in the world.

Far from fading, this phenomenon has even further developed for three main reasons.

- First, consumers have never been so connected. Today, most opinions related to purchasing and non-purchasing decisions are made online. Such decisions are made through a Google search, or by looking at comments on a post, by checking the reviews of products on specialized blogs, or by examining the ranking of a hotel or a restaurant on a web site, and even the tweet from a satisfied user. With that many ways to communicate online, the firm and the brand are not any more in control of what is said about them, and by whom. While it appears to be a constraint, many new ventures can perceive it as a great opportunity as a positive buzz and/or the speed of information as well as the number channels used are more numerous and can be as effective at a lower cost.

- Second, consumers want to be inspired by brands. Today's environment is characterized by relationship marketing. Brands need to be inspiring, hence they need to be trusted, respected and admired by their audiences, their consumers and their customers. Love brands such as Harley Davidson and Apple adopted this strategy. As pointed out by Kevin Robert explains, brand loyalty goes beyond reason. From this perspective, the Internet represents a whole new way for brands in general, and for new ventures more specifically.

- Third, in a global environment, it becomes more difficult for firms to be differentiated through higher product quality. Hence, they need to leverage on other factors. Brands need create and share their values based on their actions and messages, but also using the right media, at the right place and at the right time. Brands need to be ubiquitous and develop U-marketing strategies. A brand will get lower reputation if they do not adopt these strategies, and lower reputation has immediate negative results.

Overall, influencers represent unlimited opportunities for businesses. According to the social media specialist Kristina Cisnero, engaging with influencers on the virtual sphere participate in increasing brand awareness, in creating brand advocates, in increasing page rank, and more importantly in developing e-reputation. Hence the challenge for brands is to collaborate with influencers to manage and to optimize their reputation off and online.

Who Are the Influencers on The Internet?

As previously stated, influencers are particular types of stakeholders. Investigating what an influencer is seems to be the first step to undertake if a firm wants to include them in its communication strategy and marketing strategy. An influencer is primarily a person who has an audience, a community that trusts him/her, which gives him/her some level of authority on a given topic, and who is likely to disseminate his/her opinions.

There are many ways to categorize influencers. Traditional typologies in marketing were based on the degree of power exerted (prescription vs. recommendation) and based on the product life cycle (pioneers, early adopters, etc.). With the development of the virtual sphere, new typologies of influencers appeared.

Based on the above-mentioned factors, Stambouli and Briones (2002) created a typology of influencers:

- Trend-setters find ideas and provoke new trends;
- Traditional leaders of opinion (i.e., celebrities, journalists);
- E-influencers who are bloggers;
- Shills spread the buzz for personal gain;
- Late-adopters follow e-influencers.

The main objective in identifying different types of influences and influencers lies in reaching different objectives. Such objectives can consist in monitoring your e-reputation by listening to what your audiences – both stakeholders and influencers – say in general about you. They can also help to defend your reputation in case of crisis, rumors, negative word-of-mouth and other factors that can affect the reputation online. Finally, proactive strategies can be adopted when launching new products, or by engaging with and empowering your customers in a co-creation process.

Identifying your influencers is the first step in this process. Consulting firms specialized in e-reputation management established their own typologies. For instance, the Ipsos MORI Reputation Centre, a global leader in the field of reputation research and management, developed the Key Influencer Tracking program which examines the attitudes and opinions of a range of elite, opinion-forming stakeholder audiences. On another note, the ReputationVIP firm developed the Forteresse Digitale™, a tool that helps to better control your reputation online based on the information that first appear on the Internet.

Example of Influencers' Typology: Klout Score

- Another example of influencers' typology is based on the Klout score. As explained by Speyer (2014) on the Business 2 Community platform, Klout calculates a score from 1 to 100 for social media users based on their online influence. The influence is measured using numerous online networks such as Twitter, Facebook, Google+, LinkedIn, Foursquare, Instagram, Flicker, Tumblr, etc. The Klout score helps to define which type of influencer the firm will want to reach. The average Klout score is 40. Users with a score higher than 50 are worth consideration, those who reach 63 are in the top 5%, and top influencers are above 70.

Based on the Klout mobile app, influence is the ability to generate actions. Influence is when people react on social media or in reality to something you shared. The higher your Klout Score, the greater your influence is. Since Klout was acquired by Lithium, the two entities can combine their respective strengths to offer better tools regarding online reputation and influencers.

In a recent study by Augure (2015), we find that media and tools to identify influencers are mainly twitter and tools developed such as specific software (42%). Then, we find bloggers, the media (39%) and google (37%). Klout is at the bottom of the list (11%). Not only do influencers have specific roles, but the media used itself is also important to identify and manage your relationship with your influencers.

Aligning a Diversity of Influencers With Your Own Objectives

Overall, each firm can develop solutions that tackle the influencers' challenge for businesses, communities and individuals. Influence is context-based as it provides solutions to specific problematics and objectives. We hereafter further analyze the typology established by Augure (Launchmetrics). Each type of influencer is positioned on a hierarchy based on their respective ranking, and each type of influencer has a specific role (see Table 3).

Table 3. Augure's influencers typology

Position in the Influencers' Hierarchy	Type of Influencer	Objectives Sought
Top	Celebrities	Build brand image and brand identity
Middle	Opinion leader	Increase brand awareness and visibility
Bottom	Empowered customers	Increase purchasing decisions

Celebrities

Celebrities are well-known by large audiences all the world. Not only do they possess a global reach, but their influence transcends their initial area of expertise. They can impact their community and fans in all areas. The power they exert represents the best promotional and influencing tool.

- When pictures of George of Cambridge appear on magazines and web sites, clothing and products identified tend to sell extremely well. Boutiques and web site greatly benefit from the aura of George and his famous parents – Kate Middleton and Prince William This trend has been called the Royal Baby Effect. A web site has even been created to that purpose: http://whatprince-georgewore.com/. The Royal Family Twitter account has 620K followers. While most pictures are retweeted 1000 times on average, pictures with the royal babies are retweeted 15K times on average.

Celebrity influencers can also be identified using the Q Scores (http://www.qscores.com), which identifies the most enthusiastic consumers of a personality, character or licensed property, program, or brand. The value of Q Scores suggests appropriate choices for personalities and celebrities to achieve specific results. The Q Scores also establishes "negative" rating, which measures unpopularity among celebrities, as with "Who Is America's Most Disliked Celebrity?" published by the Hollywood Reporter. Along the same lines, when Tiger Woods represented the accounting firm Accenture, his expertise on that particular field was not questioned. It is only when Tiger Woods faced personal issues that the formal partnership ended as it could have negatively impact the firm's reputation.

Opinion Leaders: Experts

If in the previous category, the influencers have a global reach, the present category is rather comprised of influencers who are experts on specific topics. Their power derives from their expertise. Their communities give them credibility on the topics they address, and in return, their messages are widespread, which impacts their influence. These influencers are usually experts in specific fields such as fashion, cooking, make up, IT, sport, etc. Brands can use their credibility and visibility to reinforce their own brand image and reputation, and to also appear as expert in these specific issues.

- For example, fashion bloggers such as Karen Blanchard (style blog *"Where Did U Get That"*) and Jessica Quirk (Tumblr blog *"What I Wore"*) are invited to fashion shows during the fashion weeks all over the world. Traditional influencers such as Anna Wintour, editor-in-chief of American Vogue, leverage on this new type of influencers.

Empowered Consumers

Empowered consumers represent the bottom of the pyramid in the typology developed by Augure regarding their role as influencers. Many consumers are active on social networks and possess high level of involvement regarding their favorite brands. Even they individually possess a limited level of influence, they can get organized and develop collective actions with much greater impact on the reputation of the firm. They tend to use widespread social media such as Facebook, Twitter, and country specific media. Firms and brands can use such influencers on operational levels. They need their support regarding recommendations and forums online. Mechanisms such as "peer" evaluation are important as each influencer is also influenced by other participants in the community, which ultimately increases the level of trust among members. This category of influencers is crucial to identify critical incidents. In addition, if they are not part of the problem, they are definitively part of the solution.

- For instance, TripAdvisor, eBay or Amazon very much relies on the number of reviews, the quality of the reviewer and on the credibility of each review. Hence, one reviewer alone cannot influence the reputation of a brand, but all reviews together can influence e-reputation.

TOOLS TO MANAGE AND MEASURE E-REPUTATION

Managing E-Reputation From a Professional Point of View

Follow what is being said on the web is essential. In order to help companies (and individuals), many tools exist. These tools, free or not, make it possible to put together a lot of information on which organizations rely on to adjust / modify / influence their e-reputation.

Of course, it is unthinkable to be thorough in the presentation of measuring, monitoring or performance of e-reputation. It is however important to present the key players who made of the measurement of e-reputation, influence or performance analysis, their field of action on the web.

Therefore, we present 10 tools divided into 3 groups: monitoring tools (general and specialized), the tools of influence and reputable platforms (fees). For each are detailed features and specifications.

1. **Monitoring Platforms:**
   a. **Google Alerts** (www.google.com/alerts)**:** Google Alerts is for many the reference of monitoring platforms. It is a detection tool associated to a notification service. It is developed by Google and works by sending information to the user's email address. Google takes care to identify relevant results based on the desired subject. Options available include: the frequency (once the news is identified by Google), sources (news, blogs, web, video, books or discussion), the choice of language, region (selection by country), or the number of results (only the best or all of the identified results). Delivery of results is done either by email or RSS feed.
   b. **Yahoo Alerts** (http://alerts.yahoo.com)**:** The counterpart to Google is Yahoo and its Alerts' platform. The platform proposes to receive information on a mailbox or via Yahoo Messenger.

However, it requires the creation of a Yahoo account to use. The options are more limited and are grouped around 6 alerts. Specifically we talk about fantasy-sports, horoscopes, tracking the stock market, the summary of the stock market, weather, or more comprehensive research on the Yahoo search engine.

c.   **Talkwalker Alerts** (www.talkwalker.com/alerts)**:** The tool defines itself as the best and easy alternative to Google Alerts. Talkwalker Alerts is an alert service on your mailbox the latest relevant information on the web.

  i.   **The Options:** The results can go all over the web, or only activities, blogs or forums. The choice of language is as comprehensive as Google. The frequency is once a day or once a week. Regarding the volume received: two options are available either only the best results, or all results.

  ii.   **Price:** Free to a maximum of 100 alerts created.

d.   **Giga Alert** (www.gigaalert.com)**:** The platform is a tracking and monitoring tool for professional interests online. It allows tracking all the desired topics by sending you daily results.

  i.   The tool offers many options such as searching for a word of at least one of the words entered or none of the words entered. It is also possible to select the site or remove lists of the day, choose the desired document format or even to extract results .pdf, .doc, .ppt, .txt. or .xls.

  ii.   **Price:** Fees. Different options to vary the number of desired elements, the number of daily searches, language or technical support including. Warning: do not confuse their former product (Google Alert) with Google Alerts. When registering, you are not on any Google platform.

e.   **Mention:** Mention is a monitoring tool that scans in real time the main source of net and social networks, allowing not miss any "mention". The simple interface allows you to organize 4 types of alerts: (1) your name (e-reputation) - it is possible in particular to follow the twitter account or personal website; (2) a business or an institution; (3) a brand or a product, and (4) according to your choice. For each block, you can then select the desired source from Facebook, Twitter, information sites (newspapers), blogs, video platforms, forums, social networks image (Pinterest, Instagram) or other sites that you want to add. It is possible to do research in more than 10 languages. Finally, it is possible to share the results of research and choose the notification frequency (daily, weekly, or never). Monitoring results is very nice (very comprehensive statistical tools including the number of entries, support and geographical location or sentiment analysis - the latter not always reliable). *Price:* Free for a 14 day trial.

2.   **Specialized Monitoring Platforms:**

a.   **Social Mention** (www.socialmention.com)**:** Socialmention is a real-time search engine which scrolls over a hundred social media including Facebook, Twitter, FriendFeed, YouTube, Digg or Google. Its use is very simple because you simply need to type in the search bar the desired word (quoting is however recommended in order not to receive many erroneous results). Advanced preferences are limited to the choice of language and the number of results per page. However the highlight of the platform is in the presentation and analysis of results. It proposes 4 analysis criteria. The first one is the "strength" – the number of times the term is used in the last 24 hours compared to the number of total words. The "feeling" is the ratio of positive references to the negative. "Passion" is the level of likelihood of individuals that talk about your brand (the more people in your community are talking about you; the best score will be regarding passion). Finally the "reach" is a measure of influence and represents the number of unique authors compared the number of references made on the subject. *Price:* Free.

b. **Tweetalarm** (www.tweetalarm.com): Platform dedicated to Twitter analysis that allows you to sort through the 5,000 tweets circulating on the platform every second. The tool offers to receive by e-mail information about your business without having to set up a dedicated monitoring system. The tool is very simple tool to use (registration with email, password, twitter name and keywords to follow). Then, the platform forwards you as frequently as possible (it adjusts settings for sending alerts) the desired alerts. *Price:* Free.

c. Other platforms also exist such as PinAlerts (for Pinterest), Netvibes or Infoxicate.me.

3. **Measuring the Influence:**

a. **Klout** (www.klout.com): Klout is a service that lets you analyze your presence, your business and your relationships on various social networks to derive the Klout score (a score that recognizes your influence). During registration, you must add as many social networks as possible (the idea being that is to measure - and compare the score) and the platform provides your level of influence. Possible choices include Twitter, Facebook, Foursquare, Instagram, LinkedIn, Google+, Tumlbr, Flickr or YouTube.

   i. **Big Catch:** No explanation is given on the calculation of the score (Do all interactions have the same impact?) And the predominance of a presence on Twitter in calculating the score is very clear.

   ii. **Price:** Free.

b. **Kred** (www.kred.com): The idea behind Kred is to see if your company or you as an individual have credibility through your publications within your community. The more your messages are spread and commented by your community, the better your score on Kred will be (between 0 and 1000). The platform is available for free (and based mainly on Twitter), but if you want to use the paying format, you can access many advanced options (tips to improve the game, graphics, analysis of the last 1,000 days of activities, strengths and weaknesses your publications).

c. **Augure** (www.augure.com): The first two platforms calculate the influence of a particular individual. Augure is positioned as software for public relations and marketing influence allowing companies to "boost" their press coverage and earned -media. It allows the company to increase brand awareness, manage reputation, or to improve the ROI of communications campaigns by finding key influencers in the sector with which the company can push his message. The company offers three tools (Monitor, Engage Influencers and) to better support businesses. *Price:* Fees.

Measuring Reputation and E-Reputation From an Academic Point of View

If Fombrun (1996) was among the first to mention reputation from academic perspective, and to define the measuring items through its customer-centric reputation quotient (RQ), the scale of Walsh and Beatty (2007) was one of the first to operationalize the measurement of reputation. The Customer-Based Reputation (CBR) is positioned as the RQ, using a customer-centric approach. It is based on five dimensions and 28 items in total. These dimensions are the customer orientation of the organization, being (or not) a good employer, reliability and financial strength, product quality and services and finally the CSR position.

Ponzi, Fombrun and Galdberg (2011) a few years later developed a new scale, called RepTrack™ Pulse, which allows a better understanding of the affect (easier and shorter). For them, the reputation is a general impression that is included within four major dimensions: feeling, esteem, admire and trust. It is based on factors such as the performance of the company, the products and services, innovation, quality of work, governance structures, CSR and leadership (for the complete model and more information, please refer to https://www.reputationinstitute.com/reptrak-framework.aspx).

The measurement of e-reputation is even more recent and still generates discussion as understanding the concept is difficult. However, the first works to focus on this concept are those of Chun (2004) who provides a tool to measure online reputation from a stakeholder's perspective of the organization. "The e-reputation mix" consists of 3 levels. The first level is the e-character of the company. It is similar to the personality of the brand itself. The second presents the e-identity that refers to the website structure, graphics, ergonomic and aesthetic. The third level is the e-experience. He emphasized the consistency of what is promised by the brand online and physical experience. This approach has the major advantage of positioning the e-reputation as an intensity scale.

Very recently, the authors of this chapter have proposed a barometer/grid of measurement of e-reputation which details four dimensions and 16 items (Dutot and Castellano, 2015). The measuring elements are as follows (Table 4).

Table 4. Grid of measurement

Dimension	Items	Evaluation
Brand characteristic	Perception of the brand, role of the community manager	Interviews Individual
Quality of Website	Quality of images, internet users' opinion, design	Focus group and individual Quantitative or qualitative (A/B Testing for example)
Quality of service	e-commerce experience, quality of products, CRM, and after sales services, security	NETQUAL Individual analysis CRM analysis
Social media	Activity of the community, influencers' opinion on the Web, buzz, attendance on social networks, number of fans/followers/tweets, number of views	Quantitative Automatized through social networks' API.

Source: *(adapted from Dutot and Castellano, 2015)*

MANAGING ITS E-REPUTATION

Throughout this chapter, we discussed the main issues of e-reputation: its position in relation to reputation, its components (transparency, honesty and speed of response in particular), the existing tools and how to measure it. So it's time for your organization to launch and establish the foundation for e-reputation strategy. Above all, it is important to know the level of involvement that you, or your organization, are willing to put in the e-reputation strategy. Indeed even if 58% of businesses are aware of the challenges of e-reputation, only 15% of managers really set up the online reputation management strategies.

Finally, what should entrepreneurs remember about e-reputation? 5 elements can be emphasized (Figure 1). We'll then conclude with the presentation of the community management.

Figure 1. Key components of an e-reputation strategy

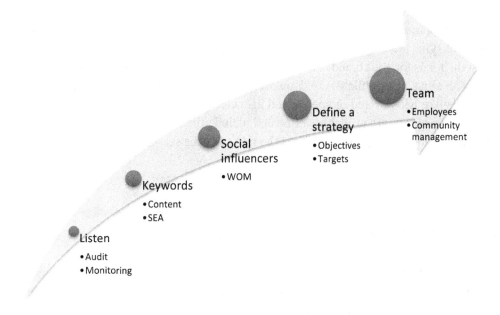

Listen

The first phase of an e-reputation strategy is the discovery and learning one. Here a company, and moreover an entrepreneur, has to be aware of what is said about it (what topics are treated, with which intensity). As we presented earlier, many tools exist to identify and monitor the elements related to your brand. However, it should be understood that all of these tools, as good as they are, will not give you a complete solutions to identified problems. They will highlight what is good or not and on what the company has to work in order to move forward.

At the same time, one must complete an audit of the main platforms on which its business or brand is present (and active) and those on which they are not. Finally, there is a real need for a company to know where the audience is acting, exchanging and creating content.

Identify the Keywords to Position the Brand

Step one allowed you to identify how you were perceived as a company; it is now crucial to position your company online in regards to this perception. Thus, SEO and SEA actions can be performed, and identifying the main keywords on which you want to be found becomes an important step. If you already have content strategy (linked to a website), the identification of keywords is something usual for you. Tools like Google Adwords allow you to know which words to position on (but also what your competitors do), such as compete.com or alexa.com do.

Find Social Influencers

The rumor quickly spreads on the web and can strongly influence the perception of each other about your brand/firm. Identifying the vectors of influence and trying to get in touch with them is a very interesting way to adjust the focus for your brand. The best promotion of your products is word-of-mouth, or in the relay made by an artist, or a public figure. However, finding these influencers remains a difficult thing, and even if tools like Klout, Kred or specialized agencies such as Augure or Vocus exist, they are not yet perfect. Many rankings are available online and include the ability to identify the top 20 influential bloggers per sector. Identifying these people is the first step, the second is to get in touch with them and make them talking about your brand.

Define a Strategy

Understand and Measure Your Actions on Social Networks

Once these the first three steps are carried out, you can now start defining your strategy on digital media (and tools for measuring the success of these actions). However, it is essential to understand that each social network has its purpose and its target (www.socialmediaexaminer.com):

- Facebook can increase the visibility of your organization;
- Twitter is the main support for a good after-sales service;
- Instagram is a strong driver for the development of awareness;
- Google+ is extremely interesting to optimize its SEO;
- Pinterest is predominantly used by and for women (fashion, recipes or weddings);
- LinkedIn has a professional orientation.

It is also crucial to understand that each network has its own standards. That is to say, for a company wishing to publish on Facebook, that they should do it based on the frequency of a post every 2 days. For Twitter, don't go over 2 tweets per hour, or the relay with your community will be almost inexistent. For a blog, 1 to 2 interventions per week are sufficient.

Likewise, the timing of publication is different depending on the social platform. In terms of number of people connected on the platform, Facebook is mainly consulted between 9am and 5pm (whether by professionals or young individuals), but in terms of engagement (a.k.a people liking, sharing or commenting your posts), 7am and 11pm are the two best periods. Twitter is privileged in the afternoon. Snapchat is a network used almost exclusively in the evening. By knowing the characteristics of each network, you can target your actions and therefore have a better control of your messages and their impact.

Finally, it is important to measure the actions on social networks. For this, the major networks offer, when you are the administrator of the page, access to a large number of statistics. For Facebook, it is called insights (www.facebook.com/insights), and it helps you tracking the number of mentions, like of the page, as well as the total scope of each post (the number of impression) or even the demographic analysis of the fans of your page.

On Twitter, each one can access to the statistics of his/her account and details for each publication (http://analytics.twitter.com). The indicators include the number of times it has been added as favorite, retweets, mentions or simply clicks on a link.

- Top 3 indicators to start with on Facebook
  - Net community growth: number of like – number of people who left the page (on a specific period)
  - Engagement ratio: (number of people engaged/ number of people reached)*100
  - Reach: (organic reach + viral reach)/audience*100
- Top 3 indicators to start with on Twitter
  - Net community growth: number of new followers – number of unfollowers (on a specific period)
  - Variation ratio: (number of new followers/ total number of followers)*100
  - Diffusion ratio: (number of retweet on a period/ number of tweet on the same period)*100

Define the Schedule of Publication

The second point is to integrate the calendar of publications. It is crucial for your organization to set up a specific content schedule to maximize your online presence. The schedule should be in line with the strategic announcements of the organization. A comprehensive approach will provide a more consistent picture and achieve better results for consumers. Finally, this communication strategy should be thinking using multiplatform formats.

Developing an E-Reputation Task Force

The fifth and final element that any company may want to put in place to manage its online reputation is a dedicated team. It must also understand that the first relay of communication/ reputation is often the employees or brand fans.

The Role of Employees and Brand Fans

The establishment of an online reputation strategy requires an understanding from all resources of the importance of corporate image. The most crucial one is your employees. CEO and owners must prepare them for the dangers associated with the use of social media. Very often the professional and personal lives are intertwined and employees may find themselves unwillingly in the heart of a controversy.

It will, of course, be the same with fans of the brand. If you are active on community platforms, they will be the first to rescue you or correct bad comments made online. By adding to your corporate message your employees and fans, your impact will be much higher.

What is the Level of Resources Needed?

Reputation management (online or offline for that matter) is far too important to be the work of one person only within your company. If, as we just mentionned, employees have a significant part to play, the fact remains that dedicated resources must be integrated. The public relations department (or press) should be closely involved in defining the e-reputation management policies (and not only for crisis management), as key departments such as marketing/ sales or partner relations. It is by combining as many resources as possible that you will have the most impact but also the strongest membership.

The Key Role of the Community Manager

With the digital channel becoming dominant for CRM, you must have in your team specialized resources that could help you in regards to the choice of platforms and content writing, but also on how to give an answer to consumers. The community manager then makes sense to support your strategy.

This resource (unfortunately very often a junior who certainly knows the tools but little about the culture of the company) will become the first relay of the company with its prospects / consumers, by ensuring the creation, animation and the management of communities. He will also be in charge of creating a content set to accompany the traditional brand communication (Table 5)

Table 5. Community management's skills

Skills	Details
Strong communication skills	As a sales representative, communication skills are essential. But we must go further: writing ability, synthesis, tone (nice, friendly or farm), have good interpersonal skills.
Good judgment	The community manager is primarily a curator. He or she must choose between the volume of information, which one to present, share and how to share it. They must also understand how to answer questions, reactions, remarks while maintaining a corporate vision.
Empathy	In any communication, it is essential to imagine yourself as the one who receives the information. What are the characteristics of the community, and how does she react? How the brand is understood by its members and thus how to generate the commitment?
Devotion	The job of a community manager will potentially never stop. From the moment the brand is present online, it needs to have a presence / availability or reach 24/7.
Organizational capabilities	The job of a community manager is divided between following the news, creation of content, responses, the implementation of strategy, information sharing etc. It must be very well organized and structured in order to properly keep a global vision of its actions.
Adaptation capabilities	The community manager is at the same time the PR, communications manager, marketing manager or the first defense of the brand. It must therefore be agile in its operation.
Step back	Some situations can quickly escalate and thus cannot be soured by the reactions or responses. The community manager must each time raise the conversation.
Analytical capabilities	Every action must be measurable and evaluated. The measurement of the commitment, the conversion rate, etc. are inextricably linked to the job of community management
Ability to develop the community	The most important for a community manager is not to sell the product or the company but to empower the community by giving it a voice. He/she must be able to generate real conversations.
Passion for the brand	The community manager is not only the eyes or ears of a company; it is also the voice and the spokesman. His passion for the business is crucial.

Insourcing or Outsourcing the Management of E-Reputation?

The question that may arise at that stage is as follows: in the end do I have enough resources to ensure that management or should I call for help? Many agencies or businesses are aware that the answer to this question is often the latest and therefore offer their business services to assist in their management of their e-reputation.

Axa© has a particular set of services that allows cleaning the online reputation of companies (and individuals). The company created the positive content and provides a big SEO work to relay bad information one pages with less visibility (pages 2 and more on Google).

Make the Case: Social CRM

The five steps presented here are only the beginning of a good e-reputation. Another component is the quality of service given to your consumers, mostly online. This is what is called Social CRM.

Social CRM in its simplest version is understood as customer relationship through social media. In its most complete application, it is a total transformation of the company based on customers' insights. That is bringing the concepts of co-creation and internal collaboration at the center of all priorities. Its scope of action is very broad and is not just to respond to Facebook posts or tweets.

Its aim is to focus on engaging with consumers through collaborative conversations that create benefits for all parties in a transparent environment.

Its scope is wider than social networks and integrates blogs, forums and all sharing or collaboration platforms (such as wikis). Social CRM should enable a company's transition to relational and conversational. It often takes the form of management of unsatisfied individuals. A study presented in "The Retail Consumer Report" during the holiday season in the United States shows the impact of an efficient processing of customer dissatisfaction on social media (Figure 2).

Figure 2. Impact of management of unsatisfied people on social media

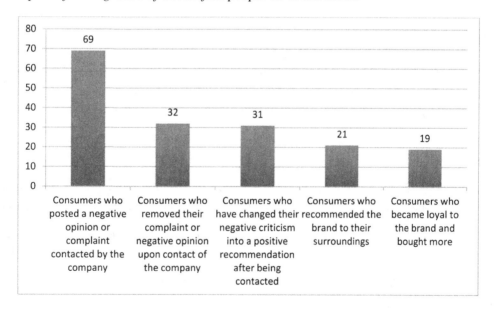

Finally, can we anticipate everything? Unfortunately the answer is no. Despite all the actions an entrepreneur can and will take, it is impossible to foresee everything and follow everything. However, by identifying the correct media, knowing the characteristics of each network and by having a dedicated internal team, you will be able to respond effectively to any bad action against your organization.

CONCLUSION

This chapter wanted to highlight the growing importance of the concept of e-reputation for firms in general and for web-entrepreneurs in particular. More importantly, it is crucial for them to incorporate the management of e-reputation in a more global strategic plan.

Indeed a good e-reputation by itself won't generate success, but ignoring what your customers or competition say about your company could drive your firm to failure. The tools and strategies presented in the chapter will give you a head start compare to your competition, but the real key is to incorporate the process of monitoring, measuring and acting on your brand image into a more global strategic orientation. Some of the key benefits of e-reputation should be presented here:

- Better knowledge of customer's perception of your brand and products;
- Better fit between the products you sell and your customers' expectations;
- Real transformation of your firm into a "customer-oriented" firm;
- Decreased stakeholder dependence through improved real-time tracking;
- On a mid-term period, increased of benefits of the company.

Finally, the management of the reputation online cannot be done in a separate way from the strategic orientation of the firm. Every action, every communication your company and you, as web-entrepreneur, do, has an impact on e-reputation. Therefore incorporating and positioning clearly the management of reputation in the business plan or the in vision and strategic definition of the firm is a "must do".

REFERENCES

AFNOR. (2015). E-reputation: présentation des premiers projets de normalisation volontaire au niveau international. Retrieved from http://www.afnor.org/liste-des-actualites/actualites/2015/janvier-2015/e-reputation-presentation-despremiers-projets-de-normalisation-volontaire-auniveau-international

Augure. (2015). Etat et Pratiques des Relations Influenceurs en 2015. Retrieved from http://www.augure.com/fr/ressources/livres-blancs

Boyd, B. K., Bergh, D. D., & Ketchen, D. J. Jr. (2010). Reconsidering the reputation-performance relationship: A resource-based view. *Journal of Management*, *36*(3), 588–609. doi:10.1177/0149206308328507

Castellano, S., & Dutot, V. (2013). Une analyse de l'e-réputation par analogie ou contraste avec la réputation: Une approche par les médias sociaux. *Revue Française du Marketing*, *243*(3/5), 35–51.

Chen, S. (2001). Assessing the impact of the internet on brands. *Journal of Brand Management*, *8*(4), 288–302. doi:10.1057/palgrave.bm.2540029

Chun, R. (2004). The E-reputation Mix: Building and protecting retailer brands online. *European Retail Digest*, *41*, 1–4.

Chun, R., & Davies, G. (2001). E-reputation: The role of mission and vision statements in positioning strategy. *The Journal of Brand Management*, *8*(4), 315–333. doi:10.1057/palgrave.bm.2540031

Cisnero, K. (2014). How To Engage And Create A Lasting Relationship With Social Media Influencers. Retrieved from https://blog.hootsuite.com/how-to-find-social-media-influencers/

De Chernatony, L. (2001). Succeeding with brands on the internet. *The journal of Brand Management*, *8*(3), 186–195.

DeLone, W. H. (1988). Determinants of success for computer usage in small business. *Management Information Systems Quarterly*, *12*(1), 51–61. doi:10.2307/248803

Dutot, V., & Castellano, S. (2014, June 4-7). From reputation to e-reputation: scale development and validation of e-reputation. *Proceedings of Track: Corporate Reputation: Antecedents effects and measures, European Academy of Management*, Valence.

Dutot, V., & Castellano, S. (2015). Designing a measurement scale for e-reputation. *Corporate Reputation Review*, *18*(4), 294–313. doi:10.1057/crr.2015.15

Fillias, E., & Villeneuve, A. (2010). *E-réputation Stratégies d'influence sur Internet*. Lonrai, Editions Ellipses.

Fombrun, C., & Shanley, M. (1990). Whats in a name? Reputation building and corporate strategy. *Academy of Management Journal*, *33*(2), 233–258. doi:10.2307/256324

Fombrun, C. J. (1996). *Reputation: realizing value from the corporate image*. Boston: Harvard Business Scholl Press.

Frochot, D., & Molinaro, F. (2008). *Livre blanc sur l'e-réputation*. Paris: Les Infostratèges.

Gotsi, M., & Wilson, A. M. (2001). Corporate reputation: Seeking a definition. *Corporate Communications*, *6*(1), 24–30. doi:10.1108/13563280110381189

Hatch, M. J., & Schultz, M. (1997). Relations between organizational culture, identity and image. *European Journal of Marketing*, *31*(5/6), 356–365. doi:10.1108/eb060636

Logsdon, J. M., & Wood, D. J. (2002). Reputation as an emerging construct in the business and society field: An introduction. *Business & Society*, *41*(4), 365–370. doi:10.1177/0007650302238773

McVea, J. F., & Freeman, R. E. (2005). A Names-and-faces approach to stakeholder management how focusing on stakeholders as individuals can bring ethics and entrepreneurial strategy together. *Journal of Management Inquiry*, *14*(1), 57–69. doi:10.1177/1056492604270799

Mitchell, A. L. A. N. (2001). The camel, the cuckoo and the reinvention of win-win marketing. *The Journal of Brand Management*, *8*(4), 255–269. doi:10.1057/palgrave.bm.2540027

Patterson, J. (2015) How the Rise of Influencers Impacts Reputation and Communications. Retrieved from http://documentmedia.com/article-1986-how-the-rise-of-influencers-impacts-reputation-and-communications.html

Ponzi, L. J., Fombrun, C. J., & Gardberg, N. A. (2011). RepTrak Pulse: Conceptualizing and Validating a Short-Form Measure of Corporate Reputation. *Corporate Reputation Review*, *14*(1), 15–35. doi:10.1057/crr.2011.5

Rindova, V. P., Williamson, I. O., Petkova, A. P., & Sever, J. M. (2005). Being good or being known: An empirical examination of the dimensions antecedents, and consequences of organizational reputation. *Academy of Management Journal*, *48*(6), 1033–1049. doi:10.5465/AMJ.2005.19573108

Shamma, H. M. (2012). Toward a Comprehensive Understanding of Corporate Reputation: Concept, Measurement and Implications. *International Journal of Business and Management*, *7*(16), 151–169. doi:10.5539/ijbm.v7n16p151

Speyer, J. (2014) What Is My Klout Score and Who Cares? Retrieved from http://www.business2com-munity.com/social-media/klout-score-cares-0816983

Stambouli, K. B., & Briones, É. (2002). *Buzz marketing: les stratégies du bouche-à-oreille*. Paris: Ed. d'Organisation.

Thong, J. Y. L. (1999). An integrated model of information systems adoption in small businesses. *Journal of Management Information Systems*, *15*(4), 187–214. doi:10.1080/07421222.1999.11518227

Thong, J. Y. L., Yap, C. S., & Raman, K. S. (1996). Top management support, external expertise and information systems implementation in small businesses. *Information Systems Research*, *7*(2), 248–267. doi:10.1287/isre.7.2.248

Uncles, M. (2001). Editorial: Interactive electronic marketing and brand management. *Journal of Brand Management*, *8*(4), 245–254. doi:10.1057/palgrave.bm.2540026

Volle, P., Isaac, H., & Charfi, A. A. (2012, September 14). Processus de visite et création de trafic en ligne: enjeux entre visibilité et e-réputation. *Colloque Marketing Digital*. Retrieved from http://www.colloquemarketingdigital.com/#!actes-2012/cb6p

Walker, K. (2010). A systematic review of the corporate reputation literature: Definition, measurement, and theory. *Corporate Reputation Review*, *12*(4), 357–387. doi:10.1057/crr.2009.26

Walsh, G., Beatty, S. E., & Shiu, E. M. K. (2009). The Customer-based corporate reputation scale: Replication and short form. *Journal of Business Research*, *62*(10), 924–930. doi:10.1016/j.jbusres.2007.11.018

Wartick, L. S. (2002). Measuring corporate reputation, definition and data. *Business & Society*, *41*(4), 371–392. doi:10.1177/0007650302238774

Zhang, M., Sarker, S., & Sarker, S. (2007). Drivers and effects of IT capability in "born-global" firms: A cross-national study. *Proceedings of the 28th international conference on information systems, Montreal*.

This research was previously published in Key Challenges and Opportunities in Web Entrepreneurship; pages 103-131, copyright year 2017 by Business Science Reference (an imprint of IGI Global).

Chapter 86
A Tale of Policies and Breaches:
Analytical Approach to Construct Social Media Policy

Neha Singh
University at Buffalo, USA

Tanya Mittal
University at Buffalo, USA

Manish Gupta
University at Buffalo, USA

ABSTRACT

While the use of social media offers great opportunities to interact with customers and business partners, there are significant risks associated with this technology if a clear strategy has not been defined to address both the risks and the benefits that come along with it. The best approach for an organization to effectively utilize the benefits of this technology is to engage all relevant stakeholders and establish a strategy that addresses the pertinent issues. The organization needs to have in place relevant policies so as to be able to achieve it. To be able to identify the most frequent risks and their source, we captured breach data from various sources. In the chapter, we analyzed that the most important source of risk that can occur due to use of social media for a company is from its own workforce and an employee might find various ways of doing so.

1. INTRODUCTION

People that have shared interests, aspirations, backgrounds have historically found a way to establish communication and share information. Use of technology for similar functions in last few decades has given rise to tremendous opportunities and efficiencies. Merriam Webster dictionary (MW, 2016) defines social media as "forms of electronic communication (such as Web sites) through which people create online communities to share information, ideas, personal messages, etc." Social Media has been

DOI: 10.4018/978-1-7998-9020-1.ch086

essentially characterized by attributes such as participation, community and connectedness (Mayfield, 2006; Marken, 2007). Social media technology consists of propagating or diffusing content through social networks over the Internet. Social media provides the power of enhanced interactivity, for example an individual might watch news on the television but cannot provide any kind of feedback over it whereas social media tools allow a person to comment, discuss and distribute information. It is one of the highly effective communication platforms that can connect n number of users virtually from any part of the world. Numerous studies have investigated different motivation behind individual's use of social media which range from relationships, connectedness, information gain, capital gain, amongst others (Bonds-Raacke and Raacke, 2010; Gangadharbatla, 2008; Nadkarni and Hofmann, 2012; Sheldon, et. al, 2011; Smith, 2011).

1.1. The Impact of Social Media & the Risks Involved

Social media is not an exception to any kind of business these days. Each and every business unit such as human resources, marketing, sales, R&D, and customer service have realized the importance of social media in order to hire employees, create & enhance brand recognition, generate revenue, drive innovation and improve customer satisfaction. A study conducted back in 2009 has found that there is high correlation between high financial performance and extensive social media engagement. However, since social media tools can be incorporated within an organization without any kind of new infrastructure, the business or marketing introduce them to the company without proper planning or risk identification/assessment, irrespective of the fact that social media introduces substantial risks to the organization. Use of social Media might lead to risks such as: information leakage, reputational damage, privacy breach, loss of intellectual property and copyright infringement. On the other hand, simply choosing not to use social media might result in opportunity cost. Therefore, every organization must be aware of all the risks & opportunities and should be able to properly manage the use of social media.

1.2. How Big is the Problem?

According to Proskauer's third annual global survey (Proskauer, 2014) about social media usage in the workplace nearly 90% of the organizations now use social media for business purposes amongst which only 60% of them have implemented social media policies. However, the misuse of social media in the organizations has increased drastically. More than 70% of the businesses had to take disciplinary action against its employees (which was initially 35% according to Proskauer's third annual global survey about social media usage).

Use of social media within an organization is not restricted to itself and therefore, risks associated with social media usage can come from both inside and out of the organization. Moreover, the organizations do not have direct control over these systems as they do not manage or own them. One of the risks that could arise is from the employee access to social media sites. According to a survey titled "Social Media & Workplace report 2012" (Hollon, 2012) 75% of the workers access social media sites from their mobile at least once a day and 60% access it multiple times a day, even though only 43% of them work in organizations that are open to the use of social media. This is a good indication of the motivation of the employees to use social media. An employee could be involved in a data breach or information leakage leading to financial and reputational damage to the company. On the other hand, any incorrect, irrelevant or inappropriate content posted on social media, whether by an employee or an external user, can steer the company into legal & compliance issues with the investors, customers or the government. Also, it would lead to financial and reputational loss for the company. Thus, to prevent the risks occurring due to the use of social media, the company requires both procedural (policies) and technical (technology) controls and these policies should not only be for the employees of the company but also for the external users (fans & followers). Also, apart from implementing policies it needs to take precautions and protect against specific risks and further assess and control the risks continuously in order to gain the benefits of social media usage.

1.3. Types of Risks due to Social Media Usage

- **Reputation Damage**

This is the greatest threat faced by an organization due to the use of social media. Anyone and everyone can post and publish on the social media. It provides a mechanism to spread a good news but also serves as a medium and acts as a host to complaints and grudges. If the reputation of a company is damaged and portrayed in a negative manner, then its customers no longer desire to conduct business with them. The loss of reputation due to breaches affects the company in many ways including weakened competitiveness, loss of trust, sometimes loss of license (Rayner, 2003). The impact is sometime felt industry-wide (Xifra and Ordeix, 2009).

- **Data/Information Leakage**

This is the second most important threat faced by an organization. The information can be owned or relate to the organization itself or can be owned by someone external to the unit for example customer details in a banking or healthcare industry. The information leakage might happen by unauthorized personnel and sometimes even done innocently with intent of no harm to the company but once the information is out there on social media, there is hardly any way to get it back. As they say "There is no delete option on social media". Any information leakage or data loss can land the company into a huge risk including legal risks and the impact leads to huge costs involved in repairing the damage and getting the lost customers back.

- **Privacy**

Privacy is not security or confidentiality. Privacy is the ability of an individual or an organization to selectively release personal/confidential information. Privacy breach may result due to data loss. The impacts of privacy loss can be something like identity theft, cyber stalking for a personnel or might lead to a financial loss to an organization.

1.4. Social Media Breaches by Employees

Social media threats to an organization might be caused by internal (employees, insiders and consultants) and external (customers, activists). However, the threats form the internal employees of the company is much more prominent as they tend to have more power and knowledge about the organization they work for. The internal employees can pose a threat to the company in a number of ways such as: misuse of confidential information, inappropriate use of business, giving false and derogatory remarks about other employees and the business etc. When viewing and examining different reports and articles regarding the misuse of social media, reputation damage and information leakage are the top two most common risks incurred by a company. These both risks are highly interrelated in the sense that data leakage can lead to reputation damage. Although someone outside the organization can cause reputation damage as well, data leakage is more related to an internal employee. Many of these incidents (as you can see in Appendix-B) can happen due to lack social media usage and policies awareness amongst the employees or due to sheer innocence. Therefore, it is highly recommended that the company organize various training session on the appropriate use of social media to its employees.

There have been recent documented and research cases where employees have been fired because of their posts to social media sites. The press has coined a phrase "Facebook Fired" in wake of growing cases of similar disciplinary actions emanating from employees' negligent and abusive posts (Hidy and McDonald, 2013). To proactively address risks from social media use by employees, employers have escalated the employee activities monitoring at workplace (Mello 2012; Kaupins and Park, 2011; Gelms, 2012; Sánchez et. al., 2012).

2. LITERATURE REVIEW

The starting point of our risk that actually got us interested into the research work was due to the ISACA White Paper on "Social media: Business benefits and Security, governance and Assurance perspective" (ISACA, 2010). It provided us with the starting point which led to further research. The paper includes the risks of a corporate media presence and employee personal use of social media along with mitigation strategies and also assurance considerations.

Employee social media policies have been widely researched over last few years. There are studies that conducted existing social media policies for their research in the legal domain (Jacobson and Tufts 2013; Vaast and Kaganer 2013). There are other studies that have provided recommendations to formulate employee social media policies based on existing legal landscape and on anticipated changes to them (Hidy and Mcdonald 2013; Mooney 2013; Younkins 2013; Jennings, Blount, and Weatherly 2014; Kirby and Raphan 2014). This research is unique because no other study has provided insights and practical recommendations based on security breaches and existing employer policies at the some of the world's leading companies across several industries.

The Proskauer came up with the work "Social media in the workplace around the world" (Proskauer, 2014) mentioning that usage of social media was still in novelty in 2011 when they first published their survey but the recent survey depicts that 90% of the business now uses social media for business purposes. However, as the usage of social media increases, the risk of blurring the fine line between usage of social media for personal use and professional uses increases. The paper also confirms through surveys that there has been a tremendous increase in the number of companies that have implemented social media policies to address the risk arising out of misuse out of social media by the employees.

The research paper "Workplace and social networking- the implications of Employment relations" (Broughton et. al., 2009) states that in recent times the use of social media by employees have received a high level of attention by Employers mainly because of the disputes between the employers and employees that gained much e media attention in recent times. Initially the focus was primarily on "work bloggers" – individuals who maintain a website discussing about content relevant to their work. But now, it's been shifted to people who have social media account like Facebook and Twitter and reference their work on such sites.

"Critical Social media issues for Retail companies" (Beringer and Southwell, 2011) identified the various risks of using social media in multiple areas of business which includes Intellectual property and Brand protection, defamation, Employment issues, Regulatory scrutiny and Reputational. It also identifies the nature and scope of social media risk are often unrolled, informal, infinite reach, fast, interconnected and blurring of professional and personal lines.

The article "Protecting your practice from social media misadventures" (PRMS, 2012) suggests the elements to be included in creating an organizational social media policy. The suggestions consists of Purpose/Objective of creating the policy, Prohibited uses, Best/Permitted Uses, Violations and Enforcements. It also covers various breaches that were in the news that demonstrates lack of knowledge among healthcare workers as to what constitutes confidential patient information which that resulted in causing reputational damage to physician practices along with board complaints, regulatory fines and litigation.

The paper "ASNE 10 Best practices for Social media - helpful guidelines for news organization" (Hohmann et. al., 2012) identifies the social media guidelines for news organizations and gives the takeaways which includes application of traditional ethic rules online, assumption that everything online is public, breaking of news on the company's website and not on Twitter, no perception, independent authentication of anything found on social networking site, transparency and admission in case of being wrong, confidentiality of internal deliberations. The paper "Sample Social media policy" (ACFE., n.d.) includes principles apply to professional use of social media on Company's behalf as well as personal use when referencing Company.

The reason why social media usage in Financial Industry lagged behind and the risk associated with its usage was identified and mentioned in the paper "Social media usage in Financial Service Industry: Toward a Business- Driven compliance approach" (Chanda and Zaorski, 2013). It also provides information about the overview of the regulatory landscape, emergence of social media in financial service industry, effective use of social media, regulatory concerns. The many risk associated with social media usage to an enterprise is discussed in "Copyright SANS Institute" (Shullich, 2011), along with ways to conduct a risk assessment and figure out which risks are applicable. The paper provides a detailed information regarding many topics like definition of Social Media, risk assessment, risk of social media use which is further classified as the impact, information leakage, data loss, piracy and infringement, corporate espionage, reconnaissance.

Another paper that efficiently put forwards the various law on social media workplace and breaches of these laws is "Blurred boundaries" (Sanchez, et. al, 2012). It consists of various information like the reasonable expectations of privacy analysis, employer evaluation of online speech and virtual identity of applicants, employer imposed limitations on Employee private life, the privacy expectation of employees, work/personal life separation. It also provides insights on the future of digital privacy of workplace. We also got some insights of recommendations for social media usage and maintaining privacy, confidentiality and professionalism for Nurse's association with the NSNA Paper (NSNA, n.d.). It gave us information regarding various examples of privacy and confidentiality breaches and suggestions to develop social media guidelines and common issues faced by its usage.

The risk involved for employers and steps taken to minimize the risk of usage of social media within organization. These questions were answered by 44 different jurisdictions in EMEA, Asia and America. The Mayer Brown publication on the "Use of social media in the workplace" (Abate et. al., 2011) helped us in collating the policies which should be mandatory to be present for successful Risk mitigation. Another key findings that we came across was from "Grant Thorton white paper"(Thompson, et al., 2011) which included the information on speed of the growth of social media, and also the finding that most companies have policies related to e-mail communication and technology but no policies that specifically address social media usage.

Another great source of information was "ace progress report" (Merrill et. al., 2011) that provides a clear understanding of reputational, legal and operational risk of social media participation and how can the company mitigate the social media risk they face. The "Accenture white paper" (Accenture, 2015) gives information regarding the shortfalls of managing social media, and a comprehensive and proactive response strategy that they came up with. They have also discussed about the evolution of social media, sources and types of social media risks and the essential components and enablers of social media risk management. Another presentation is "Learning to live with social networks: risk and rewards" (Zeltser, 2011) that explored the key risks associated with online social networking and discussed the policies and technologies that aided at mitigating these risks. It also evaluated the risk of sharing too much information online could bring value to the company or not.

3. RESEARCH METHODOLOGY

To come up with a list of critical policies that should be implemented by an organization, we started to look at and find companies that already have already implemented effective social media usage policies in their workplace. We first came up with a set of target companies from various domains (IT, financial, health, retail etc.) and then refined the list to those companies for which the policies were publically available online. The companies that we chose and the list of social media policies associated with them are appended towards the end of the paper as Appendix A.

After we were able to find the policies, we went ahead to search for articles and reports on various breaches caused by the use of social media by employees. The search terms were as follows:

Social Media AND Breaches OR Breaches by an employee OR Social media AND policy breach OR news AND social media policy AND breach OR information leakage OR data loss AND employee OR employee AND employer relations.

These were the reports that were reported by the employers and have been in the news. There would be many more breaches that were never reported. We tried to gather and analyze as many breaches as possible in this field to build our case and to come up with the most significant risks that a company could incur due to misuse of social media by its employees. The list of breaches that we found is appended towards the end of the paper as Appendix B. The list of social media policies that we analyzed is the most critical or "must have" by an employer are appended as Table 1.

4. DATA AND ANALYSIS

As mentioned in last section, we collected publicly available social media policies to represent a wide range of industries. A list of policies reviewed is shown in Table 1. As shown in Figure 1, we analyzed existing policies available publicly and also articles on best approach and best practices to construct social media policy (see Prafull, 2012; Jet, 2016; Lauby, 2009) and derived a list of policy statements that companies should include in their social media policy to avoid data breach situations.

Table 3 depicts a sample of breaches that we came across and the underlying policies that should have been helpful in preventing the breaches. It also shows whether there were policies already in place or not. In cases where the policies did exist, we analyzed and worked on finding the policies whose existence could have prevented these breaches.

Figure 1. Research methodology and contributions

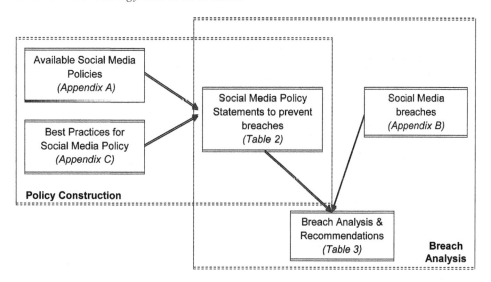

Table 1. Analyzied social media policies

Best Buy
Cisco
Dell
Intel
Coke
IBM
Los Angeles Times
GAP

Table 2. Social Media Policy statements to prevent breaches

Social Media Policy Statements
PA1: The employee should adhere to the proper copyright and reference laws set forth by the company.
PA2: Every employee should familiarize himself/herself with the Code of Conduct.
PA3: Posting any content related to race, ethnicity, religion, gender or physical disability will not be tolerated.
PA4: Maintain transparency with the things you do. Use your real name and be clear about your role at the company.
PA5: The employees should not disparage customers, suppliers, employees, and so on, using any social media sites or blogs.
PA6: The employees are not allowed to disclose any confidential information of the company. Never post anything about the financial, operational and legal information of the company.
PA6.1: Never share personal information about our clients online or offline.
PA6.2: Never share personal information about our employees online or offline.
PA6.3: Never post anything related to the company's future strategies, sales trends or promotions
PA7: Never post anything that is false, abusive, threatening or defamatory.
PA8: The employer reserves the right to monitor employees' use of email and Internet, including access to social media sites.
PA9: The Company reserves the right to review, edit or even delete any misleading or inaccurate content found on social media or blog posts.
PA10: Be conscious when mixing your business and personal lives.
PA10.1: The employees should keep company related social media accounts separate from their personal accounts.
PA11: Employees should get permission before they refer to or post images of current or former employees, members, vendors or suppliers. Additionally, employees should get appropriate permission to use a third party's copyrights, copyrighted material, trademarks, service marks or other intellectual property.
PA12: The employee should make sure that the after-hours online activities do not violate the code of conduct.
PA13: The use of social media should not cause any interference in the employee's primary job responsibilities.
B. Social Media Policies related to Healthcare
PB1: Sending, receiving, displaying, printing, or otherwise disseminating confidential information or Personal Health Information (PHI) in violation of the Health Insurance Portability and Accountability Act (HIPAA) or the Health Information Technology, Economic and Clinical Health Act of 2009 (HITECH) is not allowed.
PB2: Abide by all applicable confidentiality laws and policies.
PB3: Never disclose any individually identifiable information regarding a member, client, or patient.
C. Social Media Policies related to IT
PC1: Employees are encouraged to participate in social media and exchange ideas but remain within limits and bound by the confidentiality obligations.
PC2: Connect and have fun but always remain transparent about your identity.
PC3: Every employee should be aware of "what not to share".
PC4: Your use of social media and blog posts should add value to your users, followers and fans
D. Policies related to enforcing the Social Media Policies
PD1: Anything you post that can potentially tarnish the Company's image will ultimately be your responsibility.
PD2: You are personally responsible for the content you publish.
PD3: Violations of the social media policies and code of conduct may result in disciplinary action against the employee, including but not limited to
PD3.1: Prohibiting an employee from accessing any electronic tools or equipment
PD3.2: Possible termination of employment
PD3.3: Legal action and/or criminal liability
PD4: Attending awareness training sessions and campaigns organized by the company are mandatory for each and every employee.
PD5: Every employee needs to sign and acknowledge that he/she understands and agrees to abide by the policies set forth by the organization.
PD6: The employer has the right to obtain periodic assessment and rectification of employees' understanding of existing policies.

Table 3. Breach analysis and recommendations

BREACH (Appendix - B)	WHY IT HAPPENED?	POLICY/(IES) THAT COULD HELP AVERT THE BREACH (Table 2)
St. Mary Medical Center, Long Beach *(PRMS, 2012)*	There was no policy in place.	PA6.1 PA7 PD1
Nursing Assistant Convicted, Oregon *(PRMS, 2012)*	There was no policy in place.	PB1 PB2 PB3 PD3
Derogatory Comments on Facebook *(Scutt, 2013)*	There was no policy in place.	PA3 PA10
B&O Worker dismissed for misconduct *(Scutt, 2013)*	The social media policies in place were not communicated well to the employees and/or its compliance might not be well stated.	PD4 PD6
Gosden v Lifeline (McCay Solicitors, 2015)	Although effective policies are put in place the employers need to conduct appropriate investigations and need to be alive to the potential problem of using social media.	PA8 PA5
Preece v Wetherspoons. *(McCay Solicitors, 2015)*	The employee was well aware of the company's policy regarding the usage of social media. The policies stated that employees should not write or contribute to a blog, including Facebook, where the content lowers the reputation of the company or its customers, and the company reserved the right to take disciplinary action where this occurred.	PD5 PD3
Abusive tweets by a game retailer employee *(McDonough, n.d.)*	There was no strict policy in place.	Establish new policies including how private social media accounts should be used, especially prohibiting the making of offensive remarks & reinforce the behavior they expect from their employees.
Yath v. Fairview Clinics, N.P. *(PRMS, 2012).*	The existing policy: "Fairview gives access to personal information about consumers only to employees who require it to perform their jobs. We will take every appropriate step to keep your information secure from other employees." But the clinic failed to communicate that the violations of policies would lead to serious consequences. The compliance measures were inappropriate.	PD4 PD5 PD6
Tri-City Medical Center, California *(PRMS, 2012)*	The existing policies: "Employees who choose to use social media should be careful and avoid discussing any confidential and work information" "Always obey the law and all District policies and procedures, and act in a professional, honest, and ethical manner when acting on behalf of the District" "Complete all required training in a timely manner." The policy regarding social media usage was not detailed.	PB1 PB3 PD5 PD6
Mercy Walworth Medical Center, Wisconsin *(Lake Geneva, 2009)*	There were existing policies regarding employee acceptable behavior along with consequences in case of non-compliance. Just having existing policies provide little help as controls.	PD3 PD4 PD5 PD6

5. CONCLUSION

Social media has become one of the most widely used forms of communicating, information gathering and socializing for individuals and organizations alike. Most of the companies and organizations have a social media presence through sites such as Facebook, Twitter and Linkedin amongst others. Companies are increasingly using them to communicate with an extensive pool of current and potential customers. This has opened up new channels that can lead to data breaches, as we have seen in the chapter where several data breaches on social media were analyzed. To make the things worse from a risk standpoint, these social media platforms are constantly evolving and innovating. As far as social media is concerned, most of the breaches have had happened due to human lapses. Sometimes people share confidential information, unbeknownst to them, that they shouldn't. In response, companies are widely adopting social media policy. Most of these policies are tailored to organization-specific factors such as social media presence, propensity to risks and industry. As we saw in the chapter (Appendix A), companies take different approach on building their own social media policy. The objective of the chapter was to demonstrate how significantly different social media policies can be based on a variety of factors and how data breaches could have been prevented if only certain policy statements were in the victim company's social media policy. This chapter highlights how a well crafted and communicated social media policy can prevent data breaches and avoid companies in an adverse situation.

At the same time, companies are also turning to services that offer to monitor employees' online presence and ensure that social media policies are being enforced. This has led to serious privacy concerns and some states have enacted laws to prevent companies from checking out social media sites of their employees. Maryland and California are such states that are leading the wave and other states are considering similar legislation. Constructing a strong social media policy and increasing an awareness about the dangers of social media are one of the most effective controls that companies have. The major findings of this paper can be summarized in the below two points.

Inability of Policy Enforcement

The major finding that we came up with the paper is that most of the companies have policies related to social media usage in place but just having mere policies without any means to effectively and efficiently enforce them is an insufficient mitigation strategy. There should be policies to create awareness among employees about threats and companies' existing policies by means of training sessions and campaigns. The employees should be made aware that they themselves are the only one liable for their actions and any violations would lead to severe consequences. Regular training sessions and awareness programs can prevent breaches from occurring.

Lack of Policy

This is the age of technology where social media has become an integral part of business. The social media usage was still in it's novice stage in the year 2011 but during the recent years almost 90% of the companies use it. Although there has been tremendous increase in implementing policies addressed to social media usage. there are still some companies that have no policy in place. Absence of policies is a major threat as it does nothing in educating and guiding an employee regarding the correct usage of social media which could result in future breaches. And what that absence could lead to, has been depicted in our analysis above. Also, there are few companies that have a general policy in place but it's is equally essential to align the organizational policies to social media usage policies.

We have come up with the Master policy which states the most critical or mandatory set of policies that should exist and enforced in any organization to successfully combat the threat that technology has posed in business and hence, mitigate the risk. Many organizations are missing critical social media usage policies and their implementation strategies. At best, they are not leveraging the potential power of social media, at worst, they are exposed to social media related risks and inappropriate use by their employees.

REFERENCES

Abate, D., Hoffman, D., Robertson, N., Rogers, A., & Zeppenfeld, G. (2011, July). *The use of social media in the workplace.* Retrieved from https://www.mayerbrown.com/public_docs/ TheUseofSocial-MediainTheWorkplace.pdf

Accenture. (2015). *A Comprehensive Approach to Managing Social Media Risk and Compliance.* Retrieved from https://www.accenture.com/t20150715T045906__w__/us-en/_acnmedia/Accenture/Conversion-Assets/DotCom/Documents/Global/PDF/Dualpub_1/accenture-comprehensive-approach-managing-social-media-risk-compliance.pdf on May 1,2016.

ACFE. (n.d.). *Sample Social media policy.* Retrieved from http://www.acfe.com/uploadedfiles/acfe_website/content/documents/sample-documents/sample-social-media-policy.pdf

Barkan, T. (2011, January). *Social Strat – Special Report: How are the members of association using social media today?* Retrieved from https://www.uia.org/sites/dev.uia.be/files/misc_pdfs/roundtable/Social_Media_Use_Survey_Report_Individuals_2011.pdf on May 1, 2016.

Beringer, A., & Southwell, A. (2011, January 11). *Critical Social media issues for Retail companies.* Retrieved from http://www.gibsondunn.com/publications/Documents/WebcastSlides-CriticalSocialMediaIssuesforRetailCompanies.pdf

Bonds-Raacke, J., & Raacke, J. (2010). MySpace and Facebook: Identifying dimensions of uses and gratifications for friend networking sites. *Individual Differences Research, 8,* 27–33.

Broughton, A., Higgins, T., Hicks, B., & Cox, A. (2009). *Workplace and social networking- the implications of Employment relations.* Retrieved from http://www.acas.org.uk/media/pdf/d/6/1111_Workplaces_and_Social_Networking.pdf

Buy, B. (2016, July 21). *Best Buy Social Media Policy.* Retrieved from http://forums.bestbuy.com/t5/Welcome-News/Best-Buy-Social-Media-Policy/td-p/20492

CDM Media. (2015, April 21). *Protecting social media assets: lessons from CDM Media.* Retrieved from http://www.law360.com/articles/643290/protecting-social-media-assets-lessons-from-cdm-media

Chanda, R., & Zaorski, S. (2013, May/June). Social media usage in Financial Service Industry: Toward a Business- Driven compliance approach. *Journal of Taxation and Regulation of Financial Institution, 26*(5), 5–20.

Cisco. (2014, April). *Cisco Social Media Policy*. Retrieved from http://www.slideshare.net/Cisco/cisco-global-social-media-policy

Coke. (2016). *Social Media Principles*. Retrieved from http://www.coca-colacompany.com/stories/online-social-media-principles/

Dell. (2011, August 15). *Dell: Global Social Media Policy*. Retrieved from http://www.dell.com/learn/us/en/uscorp1/corp-comm/social-media-policy

Duara, N. (2012, March 8). *Ore. Nurse Aide Posted Facebook Photos of Patients*. Retrieved from cnsnews.com/news/article/ore-nurse-aide-posted-facebook-photos-patients-2

Editor's Choice. (2011, March 31). *Abusive Facebook comments led to pub shift manager's dismissal*. Retrieved from http://www.xperthr.co.uk/editors-choice/abusive-facebook-comments-led-to-pub-shift-managers-dismissal/108662/

Fink, J. (June 14, 2010). *Five Nurses Fired for Facebook Postings*. Retrieved from www.scrubsmag.com/five-nurses-fired-for-facebook-postings/

Gangadharbatla, H. (2008). Facebook me: Collective self-esteem, need to belong, and Internet self-efficacy as predictors of the Igenerations attitudes toward social networking sites. *Journal of Interactive Advertising*, 8(2), 5–15. doi:10.1080/15252019.2008.10722138

Gelms, J. (2012). High-tech Harassment: Employer Liability under Title VII for Employee Social Media Misconduct. *Washington Law Review (Seattle, Wash.)*, 87(1), 249–279.

Geneva, L. (2009). *Nurses fired Over Cell Photos of a patient*. Retrieved from http://www.wisn.com/Nurses-Fired-Over-Cell-Phone-Photos-Of-Patient/8076340/

Hidy, K. M., & McDonald, M. S. E. (2013). Risky business: The legal implications of social media's increasing role in employment decisions. *Journal of Legal Studies in Business*, 18, 69–88.

Hohmann, J., & The 2010-11 ASNE Ethics and Values Committee. (2011, May). *ASNE 10 Best practices for Social media - helpful guidelines for news organization*. Retrieved from http://asne.org/Files/pdf/10_Best_Practices_for_Social_Media.pdf

Hollon, J. (2012, October 3). *Survey: 75% of Workers are accessing social media while on the job*. Retrieved from: http://www.eremedia.com/tlnt/survey-75-of-workers-are-accessing-social-media-while-on-the-job/ on April 30, 2016

IBM. (2010). *IBM Social Computing Guidelines*. Retrieved from https://www.ibm.com/blogs/zz/en/guidelines.html

Intel. (n.d.). *Intel Social Media Guidelines*. Retrieved from http://www.intel.com/content/www/us/en/legal/intel-social-media-guidelines.html

ISACA. (2010). *Social media: Business benefits and Security, governance and Assurance perspective*. Retrieved from: http://www.isaca.org/groups/professional-english/security-trend/groupdocuments/social-media-wh-paper-26-may10-research.pdf

Jacobson, W. S., & Tufts, S. H. (2013). To Post or Not to Post: Employee Rights and Social Media. *Review of Public Personnel Administration, 33*(1), 84–107. doi:10.1177/0734371X12443265

Jennings, S. E., Blount, J. R., & Gail Weatherly, M. (2014). Social Media – A Virtual Pandoras Box: Prevalence, Possible Legal Liabilities, and Policies. *Business and Professional Communication Quarterly, 77*(1), 96–113. doi:10.1177/2329490613517132

Jet. (2016). *5 terrific examples of Company social media policies* [Web post log]. Retrieved from http://blog.hirerabbit.com/5-terrific-examples-of-company-social-media-policies/

Jones, L. B. (2013, Mar 28). *Best practice example: GAP Social Media Policy*. Retrieved from http://oursocialtimes.com/best-practice-example-gaps-social-media-policy/

Kaupins, G., & Park, S. (2011). Legal and Ethical Implications of Corporate Social Networks. *Employee Responsibilities and Rights Journal, 23*(2), 83–99. doi:10.100710672-010-9149-8

Kirby & Raphan. (2014). The NLRB's Continued Regulation of Social Media in the Workplace. *Journal of Internet Law, 18*(2), 13–17.

Lauby, S. (2009, June 02). *10 Must-Haves for your social media policy* [Web post log]. Retrieved from: http://mashable.com/2009/06/02/social-media-policy-musts/#225temiNmaqO

Marken, G. A. (2007). Social Media . . . The Hunted can Become the Hunter. *Public Relations Quarterly, 52*(4), 9–12.

Mayfield, A. (2006). *What is Social Media?*. Retrieved from http://www.spannerworks.com/fileadmin/uploads/eBooks/What_is_ Social_Media.pdf

McCay Solicitors. (2015). *Employees' use and misuse of social media*. Retrieved from http://www.mccaysolicitors.co.uk/employees-use-misuse-of-social-media/

Rayner, J. (2003). *Managing Reputational Risk: Curbing Threats, Leveraging Opportunities*. Chichester, UK: John Wiley & Sons.

Xifra, J., & Ordeix, E. (2009). Managing reputational risk in an economic downturn: The case of Banco Santander. *Public Relations Review, 35*(4), 353–360. doi:10.1016/j.pubrev.2009.08.004

McDonough, S. (n.d.). *How the use of social media can affect your employment*. Retrieved from http://www.md-solicitors.co.uk/how-the-use-of-social-media-can-affect-your-employment/

Merrill, T., Latham, K., Santalesa, D., & Navetta, D. (2011, April). *Social media: The business benefits may be enormous, but can the risks – reputational, legal, operational- be mitigated?* Retrieved from http://www.acegroup.com/us-en/news-room/wp-social-media-the-business-benefits-may-be-enormous-but-can-the-risks-reputational-legal-operational-be-mitigated.aspx?frmmob=tr

Mooney, J. A. (2013). Locked Out on LinkedIn: LinkedIn Account Belongs to Employee, Not Employer. *Intellectual Property & Technology Law Journal, 25*(6), 16–18.

MW. (2016). *Dictionary Definition of Social Media*. Retrieved from http://www.merriam-webster.com/dictionary/social%20media

Nadkarni, A., & Hofmann, S. G. (2012). Why do people use Facebook? *Personality and Individual Differences, 52*(3), 243–249. doi:10.1016/j.paid.2011.11.007 PMID:22544987

NSNA. (n.d.). *Recommendations For: Social Media Usage and Maintaining Privacy, Confidentiality and Professionalism*. Retrieved from: http://www.nsna.org/Portals/0/Skins/NSNA/pdf/NSNA_Social_Media_Recommendations.pdf

Prafull. (2012). *5 great corporate social media policy examples* [Web post log]. Retrieved from http://blog.hirerabbit.com/5-great-corporate-social-media-policy-examples/

PRMS. (2012). Protecting your practice from social media misadventures. *Rx for Risk, 20*(4).

Proskauer, D. (2014, July 5). *Employee access to social media in the workplace decreases*. Retrieved from http://www.danpontefract.com/employee-access-to-social-media-in-the-workplace-decreases/

Proskauer. (2014). *Social media in the workplace around the world*. Retrieved from http://www.proskauer.com/files/uploads/social-media-in-the-workplace-2014.pdf

Scutt, M. (2013, Sept). *Misuse of Social media by Employees*. Retrieved from http://www.infolaw.co.uk/newsletter/2013/09/misuse-of-social-media-by-employees/

Sheldon, K. M., Abad, N., & Hinsch, C. (2011). A two-process view of Facebook use and relatedness need-satisfaction: Disconnection drives use, and connection rewards it. *Journal of Personality and Social Psychology, 100*(4), 766–775. doi:10.1037/a0022407 PMID:21280967

Shullich, R. (2011, December 5). *Risk assessment of Social Media*. Retrieved from https://www.sans.org/reading-room/whitepapers/privacy/risk-assessment-social-media-33940

Smith, A. (2011, November 14). *Why Americans use social media*. Pew Research Center.

Thompson, T., Jr., Hertzberg, J., & Sullivan, M. (2011). *Social media and its associated risks*. Retrieved from https://www.grantthornton.ca/resources/insights/white_papers/ social%20media_whitepaper%20 CDN%20-%20FINAL.pdf

Times. (2009). *Times updates social media guidelines*. Retrieved from http://latimesblogs.latimes.com/readers/2009/11/updated-social-media-guidelines.html

Vaast, E., & Kaganer, E. (2013). Social Media Affordances and Governance in the Workplace: An Examination of Organizational Policies. *Journal of Computer-Mediated Communication, 19*(1), 78–101. doi:10.1111/jcc4.12032

Welles, K. (2008, Dec 4). *Online Comments lead to privacy complaint*. Retrieved from http://www.databreaches.net/online-comments-lead-to-privacy-complaint/

Yath v. Fairview Clinics, N. P. (2009). Retrieved from http://www.casebriefs.com /blog/law/health-law/health-law-keyed-to-furrow/the-professional-patient-relationship/yath-v-fairview-clinics-n-p/

Younkins, L. R. (2013). #IHateMyBoss: Rethinking the NLRB's Approach to Social Media Policies. *Brooklyn Journal of Corporate, Financial & Commercial Law*, 8(1), 222–252.

Zeltser, L. (2011). *Learning to live with social networks: risk and rewards*. Retrieved from: https://zeltser. com/media/docs/social-networking-risks-rewards.pdf

This research was previously published in Information Technology Risk Management and Compliance in Modern Organizations; pages 176-212, copyright year 2018 by Business Science Reference (an imprint of IGI Global).

APPENDIX A: SOCIAL MEDIA POLICIES

(Retrieved online per details in the References)

A1. Best Buy (Best Buy, 2016)

"Guidelines for functioning in an electronic world are the same as the values, ethics and confidentiality policies employees are expected to live every day, whether you're Tweeting, talking with customers or chatting over the neighbor's fence. Remember, your responsibility to Best Buy doesn't end when you are off the clock. For that reason, this policy applies to both company sponsored social media and personal use as it relates to Best Buy.

What You Should Do

- *Disclose your Affiliation: If you talk about work related matters that are within your area of job responsibility you must disclose your affiliation with Best Buy.*
- *State That It's YOUR Opinion: When commenting on the business. Unless authorized to speak on behalf of Best Buy, you must state that the views expressed are your own. Hourly employees should not speak on behalf of Best Buy when they are off the clock.*
- *Protect Yourself: Be careful about what personal information you share online.*
- *Act responsibly and ethically: When participating in online communities, do not misrepresent yourself. If you are not a vice president, don't say you are.*
- *Honor Our Differences: Live the values. Best Buy will not tolerate discrimination (including age, sex, race, color, creed, religion, ethnicity, sexual orientation, gender identity, national origin, citizenship, disability, or marital status or any other legally recognized protected basis under federal, state, or local laws, regulations or ordinances).*
- *Offers and Contests: Follow the normal legal review process. If you are in the store, offers must be approved through the retail marketing toolkit.*

What You Should Never Disclose

- *The Numbers: Non-public financial or operational information. This includes strategies, forecasts and most anything with a dollar-figure attached to it. If it's not already public information, it's not your job to make it so.*
- *Promotions: Internal communication regarding drive times, promotional activities or inventory allocations. Including: advance ads, drive time playbooks, holiday strategies and Retail Insider editions.*
- *Personal Information: Never share personal information about our customers. See the Customer Information Policies for more information.*
- *Legal Information: Anything to do with a legal issue, legal case, or attorneys without first checking with legal.*

- ***Anything that belongs to someone else:*** *Let them post their own stuff; you stick to posting your own creations. This includes illegal music sharing, copyrighted publications, and all logos or other images that are trademarked by Best Buy.*
- **Confidential Information:** *Do not publish, post, or release information that is considered confidential or top secret.*

Basically, if you find yourself wondering if you can talk about something you learned at work -- don't. Follow Best Buy's policies and live the company's values and philosophies. They're there for a reason. Just in case you are forgetful or ignore the guidelines above, here's what could happen. You could:

- *Get fired (and it's embarrassing to lose your job for something that's so easily avoided)*
- *Get Best Buy in legal trouble with customers or investors*
- *Cost us the ability to get and keep customers*

Remember: protect the brand, protect yourself.

Finally, here are some policies you should keep in mind whenever you are communicating about or on behalf of Best Buy:

- *Customer Information Policies*
- *Information Security Policy*
- *Code of Business Ethics*
- *Confidentiality Policy*
- *Policy Against Sexual Harassment*
- *Policy Against All Forms of Harassment*
- *Inappropriate Conduct Policy*
- *Securities Trading Policy*

If you still have questions please contact your leadership.

A2. Cisco (Cisco, 2014)

Policy

- *When you are participating on social networking sites using your personal social media accounts, be transparent that your thoughts are your own if discussing official Cisco business. Use your real identity— no aliases—and disclose your affiliation with Cisco. If you believe your posting might lead to any confusion with viewers about whether you are speaking on behalf of Cisco, you should clearly and specifically state as follows:*
  - ∘ *Twitter disclaimer: "These tweets are my own, not Cisco's."*
  - ∘ *Disclaimer for blogs sponsored by Cisco: "Some of the individuals posting to this site, including the moderators, work for Cisco. Opinions expressed here and in any corresponding comments are the personal opinions of the original authors, not those of Cisco."*

- ○ *Third-party blog disclaimer: "The opinions expressed in this blog are my own views and not those of Cisco."*
- *Do not commit Cisco to any action unless you have the authority to do so.*
- *Do not post any business-related confidential or internal-use – only information (marked "For Internal Use Only")that you obtain or learn about as part of your job duties with Cisco. Such information includes the following examples: information regarding the development of systems, products, processes and technology; personally identifiable information (such as telephone numbers, Social Security numbers, credit and debit card numbers or financial account numbers) of the company's employees, customers, vendors, or competitors; nonpublic financial information; marketing strategies; inventions not yet patented; or other business-related confidential or proprietary information.*
- *Respect all copyright and intellectual property laws including those protecting music, videos, text and photographs belonging to Cisco or third parties.*
- *Respect financial disclosure laws. Be very careful when making statements about Cisco's financial performance, and do not make statements that in any way could violate federal or state securities laws such as the disclosure of material, nonpublic information. For example, it is illegal to communicate or give a "tip" on inside information to others so that they may buy or sell stocks or securities. Refer any questions to a Cisco Investor Relations representative.*
- *If you are representing yourself as a Cisco employee on social networking sites like LinkedIn, you may not provide professional references for any current or former Cisco employee, contractor, vendor, or contingent worker on Cisco's behalf . However, you may provide a personal reference or recommendation r for current or former Cisco employees, contractors, vendors, and contingent workers provided a) the statements made and information provided in the reference are factually accurate; and b) you include the following disclaimer:*

"This reference is being made by me in a personal capacity. It is not intended and should not be construed as a reference from Cisco Systems, Inc. or any of its affiliated entities."

- *Respect privacy; never ask for personal social networking passwords.*
- *Do not post anything that is maliciously false, abusive, threatening or defamatory. You should not post content that is defamatory, discriminatory, harassing, or in violation of Cisco's policies against discrimination, harassment, or hostility on account of age, race, religion, sex, ethnicity, nationality, disability, or other protected class, status, or characteristic. You should not unlawfully disparage Cisco products or services, or the products or services of our vendors or competitors. Examples of such conduct include offensive posts meant to intentionally harm someone's reputation and posts that could contribute to a hostile work environment on the basis of age, race, religion, sex, ethnicity, nationality, disability or other protected class, status or characteristic.*
- *Do not engage with the news media or industry analysts (for example, Wall Street Journal, InformationWeek, Gartner, and Forrester) to discuss official Cisco strategy and/or business on Cisco's behalf without Public Relations (PR) and Analyst Relations (AR) consultation and approval. To ensure that Cisco communicates with the media in a consistent, timely, and professional manner about matters related to the company, consult your manager and your PR representative or AR representative before responding.*

- *If you see something online that alleges potentially unlawful or unethical conduct (for example, illegal, unsafe or unethical conduct by a Cisco employee, contractor or vendor), please immediately escalate this event to the internetpostings@cisco.com alias. Representatives from Legal, PR, Social Media, and HR monitor this alias. If you are uncomfortable reaching out to the internetpostings@cisco.com alias, you can contact the Ethics Resource Center, which is confidential and anonymous and is the best resource to resolve problems such as the following:*
  - *Theft, fraud or any other dishonest conduct*
  - *Discrimination or harassment*
  - *Waste or abuse of Cisco resources*
  - *Conflicts of interest*
  - *Unsafe situations*
  - *Mismanagement*
  - *Any actions that violate the COBC*

A3. DELL (Dell, 2011)

There's a lot of talk about Social Media these days both at Dell and around the world. Dell encourages all employees to use Social Media the right way and this policy should help you on that path. This policy is the first step, not the last; so if you're interested in Social Media, whether personally or professionally, you should look into our Social Media and Communities University (SMaC U) classes. Since the term Social Media is used a number of different ways, we want to make sure you understand what we mean when we say Social Media. Social Media is any tool or service that facilitates conversations over the internet. Social Media applies not only to traditional big names, such as Facebook®, Twitter and Renren, but also applies to other platforms you may use that include user conversations, which you may not think of as Social Media. Platforms such as, YouTube™, Flickr™, blogs and wikis are all part of Social Media.

Finally, even though this policy is written so it's easy to understand and conversational in tone, it's an actual policy. If you don't follow the principles laid out below when engaging in Social Media you could face serious consequences up to termination in accordance with the laws of the country where you are employed. Nobody wants that to happen though, so read over this policy and make sure you understand it. Dell has five Social Media principles that you should know before engaging in any type of online conversation that might impact Dell. You'll know these principles if you've already taken the Social Media Principles course from SMaC U.

Protect Information

Social Media encourages you to share information and connect with people. When you use Social Media, you should try and build relationships, but you should also be aware that through your relationship with Dell, you have access to confidential information that shouldn't be made public. So, you shouldn't share our confidential company information or any of our customers' personally identifiable information. Every year, you take a course on how you should protect privacy and personal information. The same thing applies on Social Media, because you mistakenly post confidential information on a Social Media platform, it will be hard to take down that information completely.

Be Transparent and Disclose

When you talk about Dell on Social Media, you should disclose that you work for Dell. Your friends may know you work for Dell, but their network of friends and colleagues may not and you don't want to accidentally mislead someone. You should know and remember the 10 magic words: "Hello, my name is [NAME], and I work for Dell." Be sure to replace [NAME] with your name because that looks odd.

Follow the Law, Follow the Code of Conduct

Social Media lets you communicate incredibly fast and have your message go viral in seconds. This makes it difficult to fix an inaccurate message once you've shared it. The best thing to do is double check all content before you share it, both for accuracy and to make sure it fits into Dell's overall Social Media strategy, our Code of Conduct and any restrictions that may apply to your content based on local law (such as the FTC Endorsement Guidelines in the US) and the platform you are using (such as terms of service for the site upon which you are sharing). One of Dell's core values is winning with integrity, and that applies to Social Media as well. Dell employees hold ourselves to high ethical standards, as our Code of Conduct spells out, and that applies to Social Media just like everything else you do as a Dell employee.

Be Responsible

Make sure you're engaging in Social Media conversations the right way. If you aren't an authority on a subject, send someone to the expert rather than responding yourself. Don't speak on behalf of Dell if you aren't giving an official Dell response, and be sure your audience knows the difference. If you see something being shared related to Dell on a Social Media platform that shouldn't be happening, immediately inform the Social Media and Communities team, your manager, Ethics and Compliance or some other appropriate contact. And always remember that anything posted in social media can go viral, no matter what your privacy settings may be, so be sure you're only posting content you would feel comfortable showing up in your boss' inbox, your coworker's Twitter feed or the front page of a major news site.

Be Nice, Have Fun and Connect

Social Media is a place to have conversations and build connections, whether you're doing it for Dell or for yourself. The connections you'll make on Social Media will be much more rewarding if you remember to have conversations rather than push agendas. Dell has always been a leader in using technology to directly connect with our customers. Social Media is another tool you can use to build our brand, just be sure you do it the right way.

Social Media Account Ownership

This section isn't a Social Media principle, but it's still important enough to be in this policy. If you participate in Social Media activities as part of your job at Dell, that account may be considered Dell property. If that account is Dell property, you don't get to take it with you if you leave the company

— meaning you will not try to change the password or the account name or create a similar sounding account or have any ownership of the contacts and connections you have gained through the account. This doesn't apply to personal accounts that you may access at work, but would certainly apply to all Dell-branded accounts created as part of your job. If you have any questions about an account you operate, please reach out to the SMaC team to discuss the account.

A4. Intel (Intel, n.d.)

- **Disclose:** *Your honesty—or dishonesty—will be quickly noticed in the social media environment. Please represent Intel ethically and with integrity.*
- **Be transparent:** *If you make an endorsement or recommendation about Intel's products/technologies, you must disclose that you work for Intel. If you do not have an "Intel" handle, then use "#iwork4intel" in your postings. Using a disclaimer in your bio or profile is not enough per the FTC.*
- **Be truthful:** *If you have a vested interest in something you are discussing, be the first to point it out and be specific about what it is.*
- **Be yourself:** *Stick to your area of expertise; only write what you know. If you publish to a website outside Intel, please use a disclaimer like this one: "The postings on this site are my own and don't necessarily represent Intel's positions, strategies, or opinions."*
- **Be up-to-date:** *If you are leaving Intel, please remember to update your employment information on social media sites.*
- **Protect:** Make sure all that transparency doesn't violate Intel's confidentiality or legal guidelines for commercial speech—or your own privacy. Remember, if you're online, you're on the record—everything on the Internet is public and searchable. And what you write is ultimately your responsibility.
- **Don't tell secrets:** *Never reveal Intel classified or confidential information. If you are posting your job description on LinkedIn, be sure not to reveal confidential product information. If you're unsure, check with Intel PR or Global Communications Group. Off-limit topics include litigation, non-published financials, and unreleased product info. Also, please respect brand, trademark, copyright, fair use, and trade secrets. If it gives you pause—pause rather than publish.*
- **Don't slam the competition (or Intel):** *Play nice. Anything you publish must be true and not misleading, and all claims must be substantiated and approved.**
- **Don't overshare:** *Be careful out there—once you hit "share," you usually can't get it back. Plus, being judicious will help make your content more crisp and audience-relevant.*
- **Use Common Sense:** Perception is reality and in online social networks, the lines between public and private, personal and professional, are blurred. Just by identifying yourself as an Intel employee, you are creating perceptions about your expertise and about Intel. Do us all proud.
- **Add value:** *There are millions of words out there—make yours helpful and thought-provoking. Remember, it's a conversation, so keep it real. Build community by posting content that invites responses—then stay engaged. You can also broaden the dialogue by citing others who are writing about the same topic and allowing your content to be shared.*

- ***Don't make claims:** *We must use FTC mandated disclaimers **in all communications** when benchmarking or comparing processors. So stay away from saying our products are smarter/ faster/ higher-performing in your social media postings. Leave that to the experts.*

- **Did you screw up?** *If you make a mistake, admit it. Be upfront and be quick with your correction. If you're posting to a blog, you may choose to modify an earlier post—just make it clear that you have done so.*

- **Contractors and Endorsements:** *As the Intel Social Media Guidelines describe, we support transparency and are committed to clear disclosure of relationships and endorsements. If you are contracted, seeded, or in any way compensated by Intel to create social media, please be sure to read and follow the Intel Sponsored, Seeded, or Incentivized Social Media Practitioner Guidelines. As part of these guidelines, you need to disclose that you have been seeded or otherwise compensated by Intel. Your blog will be monitored for compliance with our guidelines and accurate descriptions of products and claims.*

- **Moderation:** *Moderation (reviewing and approving content) applies to any social media content written on behalf of Intel by people outside the company, whether the site is on or off Intel.com. We do not endorse or take responsibility for content posted by third parties, also known as user-generated content (UGC). This includes text input and uploaded files, including video, images, audio, executables, and documents. While we strongly encourage user participation, there are some guidelines we ask third parties to follow to keep it safe for everyone.*

- **Post moderation:** *Even when a site requires the user to register before posting, simple user name and email entry doesn't really validate the person. To ensure least risk/most security, we require moderation of all UGC posts. The designated moderator scans all posts to be sure they adhere to Intel's guidelines.*

- **Community moderation (reactive moderation):** *For established, healthy communities, group moderation by regular users can work well. This will sometimes be allowed to take the place of post moderation—but it must be applied for and approved.*

- **The "house rules":** *Whether content is post moderated or community moderated, we use this rule of thumb: the Good, the Bad, but not the Ugly. If the content is positive or negative and in context to the conversation, then it can be approved, regardless of whether it's favorable or unfavorable to Intel. But if the content is ugly, offensive, denigrating, and/or completely out of context, then we ask our moderators and communities to reject the content.*

- **Intel Sponsored, Seeded, or Incentivized Social Media Practitioner Guidelines:** *Intel supports transparency. We are committed to ensuring that our social media practitioners (SMPs) clearly disclose relationships and endorsements, and that statements about Intel® products are truthful and substantiated. If you are a social media practitioner who has been seeded with product, incentivized, or otherwise has an ongoing relationship with Intel, these guidelines apply to you. If you have any questions or concerns about them, get in touch with your Intel sponsor.*

Please keep in mind that Intel monitors social media related to our business, including the activities of our sponsored, seeded, or incentivized SMPs. If we find any non-disclosed relationships or statements that are false or misleading, we will contact you for correction. If, as a sponsored SMP, you are found to repetitively make inaccurate statements about Intel, Intel® products, or Intel® services, we may discontinue our relationship with you.

Rules of Engagement for Intel Sponsored, Seeded, or Incentivized SMPs

- ***Be transparent:*** *Please clearly and conspicuously disclose your relationship to Intel, including any incentives or sponsorships. Be sure this information is readily apparent to the public and to readers of each of your posts.*
- ***Be specific:*** *Do not make general claims about Intel® products, but talk specifically about what* you *experienced.*
- ***Be yourself:*** *We encourage you to write in the first person and stick to your area of expertise as it relates to Intel® technology.*
- ***Be conscientious:*** *Keep in mind that what you write is your responsibility, and failure to abide by these guidelines could put your Intel sponsorship or incentive at risk. Also, please always follow the terms and conditions for any third-party sites in which you participate.*

A5. Coca Cola (Coke, 2016)

*"There's a big difference in speaking "on behalf of the Company" and speaking "about" the Company. This set of **5 principles** refers to those **personal or unofficial online activities** where you might refer to Coca-Cola.*

- ***Adhere to the Code of Business Conduct and other applicable policies.*** *All Company associates, from the Chairman to every intern, are subject to the Company's Code of Business Conduct in every public setting. In addition, other policies, including the Information Protection Policy and the Insider Trading Policy, govern associates' behavior with respect to the disclosure of information; these policies are applicable to your personal activities online.*
- ***You are responsible for your actions.*** *Anything you post that can potentially tarnish the Company's image will ultimately be your responsibility. We do encourage you to participate in the online social media space, but urge you to do so properly, exercising sound judgment and common sense.*
- ***Be a "scout" for compliments and criticism.*** *Even if you are not an official online spokesperson for the Company, you are one of our most vital assets for monitoring the social media landscape. If you come across positive or negative remarks about the*
- ***Let the subject matter experts respond to negative posts.*** *You may come across negative or disparaging posts about the Company or its brands, or see third parties trying to spark negative conversations. Unless you are a certified online spokesperson, avoid the temptation to react yourself.*
- ***Be conscious when mixing your business and personal lives.*** *Online, your personal and business personas are likely to intersect. The Company respects the free speech rights of all of its associates, but you must remember that customers, colleagues and supervisors often have access to the online content you post. Keep this in mind when publishing information online that can be seen by more than friends and family, and know that information originally intended just for friends and family can be forwarded on. Remember NEVER to disclose non-public information of the Company (including confidential information), and be aware that taking public positions online that are counter to the Company's interests might cause conflict.*

A6. IBM (IBM, 2010)

- *"Know and follow IBM's* Business Conduct Guidelines.
- *IBMers are personally responsible for the content they publish on-line, whether in a blog, social computing site or any other form of user-generated media. Be mindful that what you publish will be public for a long time-protect your privacy and take care to understand a site's terms of service.*
- *Identify yourself-name and, when relevant, role at IBM-when you discuss IBM-related matters such as IBM products or services. You must make it clear that you are speaking for yourself and not on behalf of IBM.*
- *If you publish content online relevant to IBM in your personal capacity it is best to use a disclaimer such as this: "The postings on this site are my own and don't necessarily represent IBM's positions, strategies or opinions."*
- *Respect copyright, fair use and financial disclosure laws.*
- *Don't provide IBM's or a client's, partner's or suppliers' confidential or other proprietary information and never discuss IBM business performance or other sensitive matters about business results or plans publicly.*
- *Don't cite or reference clients, partners or suppliers on business-related matters without their approval. When you do make a reference, link back to the source and do not publish content that might allow inferences to be drawn which could damage a client relationship with IBM.*
- *Respect your audience. Don't use ethnic slurs, discriminatory remarks, personal insults, obscenity, or engage in any similar conduct that would not be appropriate or acceptable in IBM's workplace. You should also show proper consideration for others' privacy.*
- *Be aware of your association with IBM in online social networks. If you identify yourself as an IBMer, ensure your profile and related content is consistent with how you wish to present yourself with colleagues and clients.*
- *Spirited and passionate discussions and debates are fine, but you should be respectful of others and their opinions. Be the first to correct your own mistakes.*
- *Try to add value. Provide worthwhile information and perspective. IBM's brand is best represented by its people and what you publish may reflect on IBM's brand.*
- *Don't misuse IBM logos or trademarks and only use them if you have the authority to do so. For example, you shouldn't use IBM in your screen name or other social media ID.*

A7. Los Angeles Times (Times, 2009)

"Social media networks – Facebook, MySpace, Twitter and others – provide useful reporting and promotional tools for Los Angeles Times journalists. The Times' Ethics Guidelines will largely cover issues that arise when using social media, but this brief document should provide additional guidance on specific questions.

Basic Principles

- *Integrity is our most important commodity: Avoid writing or posting anything that would embarrass The Times or compromise your ability to do your job.*

- *Assume that your professional life and your personal life will merge online regardless of your care in separating them.*
- *Even if you use privacy tools (determining who can view your page or profile, for instance), assume that everything you write, exchange or receive on a social media site is public.*
- *Just as political bumper stickers and lawn signs are to be avoided in the offline world, so too are partisan expressions online.*
- *Be aware of perceptions. If you "friend" a source or join a group on one side of a debate, do so with the other side as well. Also understand that readers may view your participation in a group as your acceptance of its views; be clear that you're looking for story ideas or simply collecting information. Consider that you may be an observer of online content without actively participating.*

Guidelines for Reporting

- *Be aware of inadvertent disclosures or the perception of disclosures. For example, consider that "friending" a professional contact may publicly identify that person as one of your sources.*
- *You should identify yourself as a Times employee online if you would do so in a similar situation offline.*
- *Authentication is essential: Verify sourcing after collecting information online. When transmitting information online – as in re-Tweeting material from other sources – apply the same standards and level of caution you would in more formal publication.*

Additional Notes

- *Using social media sites means that you (and the content you exchange) are subject to their terms of service. This can have legal implications, including the possibility that your interactions could be subject to a third-party subpoena. The social media network has access to and control over everything you have disclosed to or on that site. For instance, any information might be turned over to law enforcement without your consent or even your knowledge.*
- *These passages from the "Outside affiliations and community work" section of the Ethics Guidelines may be helpful as you navigate social media sites. For the complete guidelines, please see The Times' library's intranet site or, if you are outside the company network, see the* Readers' Representative Journal.

Editorial employees may not use their positions at the paper to promote personal agendas or causes. Nor should they allow their outside activities to undermine the impartiality of Times coverage, in fact or appearance.

Staff members may not engage in political advocacy – as members of a campaign or an organization specifically concerned with political change. Nor may they contribute money to a partisan campaign or candidate. No staff member may run for or accept appointment to any public office. Staff members should avoid public expressions or demonstrations of their political views – bumper stickers, lawn signs and the like.

Although The Times does not seek to restrict staff members' participation in civic life or journalistic organizations, they should be aware that outside affiliations and memberships may create real or appar-

ent ethical conflicts. When those affiliations have even the slightest potential to damage the newspaper's credibility, staff members should proceed with caution and take care to advise supervisors.

Some types of civic participation may be deemed inappropriate. An environmental writer, for instance, would be prohibited from affiliating with environmental organizations, a health writer from joining medical groups, a business editor from membership in certain trade or financial associations.

A8. Gap (Jones, 2013)

These guidelines are important—because if you don't follow them a few things could happen: your posts can get deleted, we could lose customers and investors, we could get in trouble, or, worst of all, you could even lose your job … So do the right thing, stick to the guidelines.

Keep in mind…

There's really no such thing as "delete" on the Internet, so please—think before you post.

Some subjects can invite a flame war. Be careful discussing things where emotions run high (e.g. politics and religion) and show respect for others' opinions.

It's a small world and we're a global company. Remember that what you say can be seen by customers and employees all over the world and something you say in one country might be inaccurate or offensive in another.

Respect other people's stuff. Just because something's online doesn't mean it's OK to copy it.

Your job comes first. Unless you are an authorized Social Media Manager, don't let social media affect your job performance.

How to be the best …

Play nice. Be respectful and considerate, no trolling, troll baiting, or flaming anybody, even our competitors.

Be yourself. Be the first to out that you are a Gap Inc. employee—and make it clear that you are not a company spokesperson.

If you #!%#@# up? Correct it immediately and be clear about what you've done to fix it. Contact the social media team if it's a real doozy.

Add value. Make sure your posts really add to the conversation. If it promotes Gap Inc.'s goals and values, supports our customers, improves or helps us sell products, or helps us do our jobs better, then you are adding value.

Don't even think about it…

Talking about financial information, sales trends, strategies, forecasts, legal issues, future promotional activities.

Giving out personal information about customers or employees.

Posting confidential or non-public information.

Responding to an offensive or negative post by a customer. There's no winner in that game.

APPENDIX B: SOCIAL MEDIA BREACHES

B.1. Yath v. Fairview Clinics, N.P.

In a 2009 Minnesota case, Yath v. Fairview Clinics, (Yath v. Fairview Clinics, 2009) a patient attempted to impose liability upon the clinic and its employee through the theory of vicarious liability due to an employee's unauthorized access and dissemination of her medical record.[1] The employee, wondering why an acquaintance was at the clinic, improperly accessed and read the patient's medical file learning that she had a sexually transmitted disease and a new sex partner other than her husband. The employee shared this information with another employee, who then disclosed it to others, and eventually the information reached the patient's estranged husband. During this time, someone created a MySpace webpage posting the information on the Internet. The patient sued the clinic and the individuals allegedly involved in the disclosure. The district court granted summary judgment to the clinic on the invasion-of-privacy and vicarious liability claims and the patient appealed. The court of appeals overturned the trial court on the invasion-of-privacy argument, stating that the "number of actual viewers [of the site] was irrelevant." Rather, the determination depends on "whether the content is conveyed through a medium that delivers the information directly to the public." Since the MySpace webpage was not password protected, and it was available to the public for at least 24 hours, the publicity element of the invasion-of-privacy claim was satisfied.

In this case, the court found that the clinic could not be held liable for the employee's wrongful access and dissemination of patient information because the patient did not present any evidence that the employee's actions were foreseeable. Notably, the clinic did have a policy against such behavior by employees, which the court acknowledged in its opinion. Without such a policy in place, the court may have found that an employee's wrongful access and dissemination of private information would be foreseeable, and thereby hold the employer responsible. (PRMS, 2012).

B.2. Mercy Walworth Medical Center, Wisconsin

Two nurses were fired from Mercy Walworth Medical Center in Lake Geneva, Wisconsin, after an anonymous call from another employee led police to investigate a story that the two had taken photos of a patient and posted them on the Internet. Each was found to have taken photos of x-rays of a patient who was admitted to the emergency room with an object lodged in his body. Although investigators were unable to find anyone who had actually seen the photos posted online, discussion of the incident was posted to one of the nurse's Facebook pages. (PRMS, 2012).

"There were two nurses that independently took a picture each of an X-ray of a patient," Walworth County Undersheriff Kurt Picknell said. (Lake Geneva, 2009)

B.3. Tri-City Medical Center, California

In June 2010, five California nurses were fired from Tri-City Medical Center in Oceanside for discussing patients on Facebook.[5] Notably, no patient names, photos, or other identifying information was included in the posts. Just a short month later, Tri-City implemented a new policy, requiring employees to sign a new social media agreement concerning such sites as MySpace, Zoho, and Eventful, specifically stat-

ing, *"Even if the patient is not identified by name or by the medical record number the information you disclose may identify that patient,"* in an effort to educate employees about what constitutes private medical information. (PRMS, 2012)

B.4. St. Mary Medical Center, Long Beach

In a particularly gruesome and cruel case, an elderly man who was stabbed more than a dozen times by a fellow nursing home resident and almost decapitated, became a source of entertainment for the nurses assigned to treat him at St. Mary Medical Center in Long Beach. At least seven staff members and two nurses snapped pictures of the dying man, instead of focusing on saving his life, and posted them on Facebook. The incident brought the hospital under intense scrutiny from the California Department of Health, who along with investigating the particular incident, also opened investigation on eight other potential breaches of patient information reported at the hospital in the same year. (PRMS, 2012)

B.5. Nursing Assistant Convicted, Oregon

A nursing assistant in Oregon was convicted by a jury for invasion of privacy for posting graphic photos of patients using bed pans.[6] Not only did she spend several days in jail for her conduct, she was forced to surrender her nursing certificate and fired by her employer, Regency Pacific Nursing and Rehab Center in the Portland suburb of Gresham. The Nursing Center was subjected to a thorough investigation by the Oregon Department of Human Services in order to determine whether the Center, along with the nursing assistant, was responsible for the invasion of privacy. According to a statement released by the Center, the employee's actions were immediately reported to the local police department, the Oregon State Department of Human Services, and the Oregon State Board of Nursing to ensure their immediate involvement in the investigation, and all appropriate notifications were made to the family members involved. (PRMS, 2012)

B.6. Derogatory Comments on Facebook

Derogatory comments on Facebook as was held in Whitham v Club 24 Ltd t/a Ventura ET/1810462/10. Mrs Whitham, a team leader employed by the Respondent, engaged in an exchange of messages with colleagues on Facebook after a difficult day: "I think I work in a nursery and I do not mean working with plants" and "Don't worry it takes a lot for the bastard to grind me down". She also sent a message saying "2 true xx" to the suggestion that she worked with a "lot of planks". Her messages were only visible to her 50 Facebook friends.

The employer took the view that these comments could damage its relationship with its main client and suspended her and issued disciplinary proceedings. (Scutt, 2013)

B.7. B&O Worker Dismissed for Misconduct

*In another example, a B&Q worker was dismissed for gross misconduct for posting on Facebook that his "place of work is beyond a ******* joke". He also posted he would do some "busting", which the employer took to be a breach of its social media policy and was threatening in tone. (Scutt, 2013)*

B.8. Gosden v Lifeline

In Gosden v Lifeline, the tribunal held that the Claimant had been dismissed fairly for sending an offensive email from his personal computer to a former colleague's personal computer on the grounds that he acted in a way which could damage the employer's reputation. (McCay Solicitors, 2015)

B.9. Preece v Wetherspoons

In Preece v Wetherspoons, a pub manager posted derogatory comments about two abusive customers on Facebook whilst at work. The employee thought her privacy settings were private but her comments could in fact be viewed much more widely, including by family members of the customers in question. Wetherspoons had a clearly worded IT policy which reserves the right to take disciplinary action should the contents of any Facebook page "be found to lower the reputation of the organisation, staff or customers and/or contravene the company's equal opportunity policy". (McCay Solicitors, 2015)

Miss Preece was employed by JD Wetherspoons plc as a shift manager, working at the company's Ferry Boat Pub in Runcorn, Cheshire. She was aware of the company's policies regarding "blogging", which expressly referred to sites such as MySpace and Facebook. The policies stated that employees should not write or contribute to a blog, including Facebook, where the content lowers the reputation of the company or its customers, and the company reserved the right to take disciplinary action where this occurred. (Editor's choice, 2011)

B.10. Abusive Tweets by a Game Retailer Employee

A recent case involved offensive and abusive tweets posted by an employee of a games retailer resulting in him being summarily dismissed for gross misconduct. The employee brought an unfair dismissal claim against his employer which was originally upheld by the Employment Tribunal on the basis that the tweets were posted for 'private use'. However, this decision has since been overturned as the Employment Appeal Tribunal found the employee's failure to use privacy settings coupled with the fact that his tweets could have been seen by both staff and potential customers sufficient to justify his dismissal. (McDonough, n.d.)

Chapter 87
Exploring the Effects of Social Media Use on Employee Performance:
Role of Commitment and Satisfaction

Asbah Shujaat
University of Central Punjab, Lahore, Pakistan

Ammar Rashid
Ajman University, Ajman, United Arab Emirates

Asif Muzaffar
Sur College of Applied Sciences, Ministry of Higher Education, Sur, Oman

ABSTRACT

This study provides some clarification and extends literature by investigating the effects of the use of social networking sites by organizational employees on job satisfaction, organizational commitment and employee job performance. A survey was conducted to empirically test the proposed research model consisting of latent constructs: social networking site use, organizational commitment, job satisfaction, and employee job performance. Data of this confirmatory study was collected from 279 employees of various organizations operating in Pakistan. The model was analyzed employing variance-based structure equation modeling. Statistical software was used to assess both measurement and structural models. Results indicate that social networking sites use is not directly associated with employee job performance but with the mediating effects of job satisfaction that is also nested with the mediating effect of organizational commitment. This study is expected to both substantiate existing theories of management, and provide some extensions to social support theory.

DOI: 10.4018/978-1-7998-9020-1.ch087

INTRODUCTION

Social networking sites have become important part of daily activities of many individuals around the world (Ferreira, 2010; Rauniar, Rawski, Yang, & Johnson, 2014). There is dramatic increase of social media users due to the ubiquity of internet and development of mobile technology. Every country of the world reported about an increase of 1 million new users each day in 2017. Annually, social media sites are observing an increase of 13% in their user base globally (Kemp, 2018). Social Network Sites (SNSs) have become the fastest emerging tool for networking and has been attracting mounted attention of practitioners as well as research scholars (Charoensukmongkol, 2014). People use social media sites for different purposes including entertainment, communication, sharing information and spending leisure time. Various aspects associated to social media use have been the focus of academic investigation for the past few years (D. Wills & Reeves, 2009). Social networking sites use on societal and psychological outcomes is one of the focal areas in research (Trepte & Reinecke, 2013).

Conflicting views have been reported by the scholars regarding the outcomes of social media use during work. Some studies reported positive effects of social media use at workplace such as high morale, improved productivity, low turnover intentions, increased innovative behaviors, high organizational commitment (Bennett, Owers, Pitt, & Tucker, 2010; Bernoff & Li, 2008; D. Leidner, Koch, & Gonzalez, 2010; Patel & Jasani, 2010). On the other hand, other researchers concluded that use of social network sites may lead to negative outcomes including loss in employee productivity, interpersonal aggression, sexual harassment and identity theft (Computing, 2009; North, 2010; O'Murchu, Breslin, & Decker, 2004; Shepherd, 2011).

Majority of the research studies that have examined use of social media and its outcomes were conducted in educational institutions and selected students as sample (Chang & Heo, 2014; Clark & Roberts, 2010; Dwyer, Hiltz, & Passerini, 2007; Ellison, Steinfield, & Lampe, 2007; Mainier & O'Brien, 2010; Claybaugh, Haried, & Yu, 2015). Additionally, studies that have investigated the use of social media sites by employed population are few in number and majority are US and UK focused (Ali-Hassan, Nevo, & Wade, 2015; El Ouirdi, El Ouirdi, Segers, & Henderickx, 2015). Literature suggests that such studies are inconsistent in findings and lack rigor as they have not comprehensively examined the effects of social networking sites usage on work outcomes (Charoensukmongkol, 2014; Parveen, Jaafar, & Ainin, 2015; Kock, Moqbel, Barton, & Bartelt, 2018; Moqbel & Kock, 2018). Considering all these factors and lack of research in Asian countries motivated this study to verify whether findings of previous studies would be consistent under different culture.

This study is conducted to acknowledge the call for research by North (2010) to investigate the relationship between social networking sites use and employee performance. This study would fill this research void by empirically testing the effects of social networking sites' use on work outcomes through the perspective of social support theory (SST) in order to solve the inconsistency of opinions regarding this relationship. Data was collected from the samples of Pakistan. Pakistan is a country where usage of social networking sites is experiencing an exponential increase (Google Insight). Users of social media have crossed 44 million in 2016-2017 and expected to increase with every passing year (Ibrahim, 2017). The increase trend of adoption and usage of social media among population makes this country relevant for social media research.

The objective of the current study is twofold. First objective is to extend the understanding of the relationship between social networking sites use and work outcomes. Second objective of this research investigation is to extend the existing understanding of social networking sites use by the theoretical lens that affect employee job performance. There is one research question that this current study is intended to address: Whether using social networking sites at workplace by employees can lead to improved work outcomes?

In the subsequent section, brief literature review is presented and concluded with proposed hypotheses to be evaluated. Next, the research methodology opted for this paper is described, and the results of the study are presented after the analysis. The paper is ended up with discussion of the results, limitations of the study, implications for both academia and industry, and conclusion.

THEORETICAL BACKGROUND

Social Networking Sites

Social Networking sites are defined as "web-based services that allow individuals to (1) construct a public or semi-public profile within a bounded system, (2) articulate a list of other users with whom they share a connection, and (3) view and traverse their list of connections and those made by others within the system" (Boyd & Ellison, 2007, p. 211). Social network sites facilitate users' interaction by allowing them to sign up their personal accounts for connecting with friends and work mates.

Mainly social networking sites are segregated into two strata: internal social network sites and public social network sites. Public social network sites refer to such sites that are supported by commercial sponsors and available free to its users such as Twitter, Facebook and LinkedIn. Internal Social networking sites are those sites that are owned by the organization and designed according to its requirements such as Beehive of IBM, Town Square used at Microsoft, etc., that facilitate internal interaction and communication of the organization. The internal social network sites are also known as enterprise social networking. Social network sites can be used for personal as well as organizational purposes. In this paper, we would be focusing on use of public social networking sites by employees at workplace (Boyd & Ellison, 2007).

Social Support via Social Networking Use

Social support refers as "...the perception or experience that one is loved and cared for by others, esteemed and valued, and part of a social network of mutual assistance and obligations..." (Wills, 1991). There are different sources from which a person can get social support such as relatives, friends, colleagues, social community and even pets (Allen, Blascovich, & Mendes, 2002). Socioemotional aid refers to the emotional support that is provided in the form of attention and nurturance by others. Instrumental aid is the help that is tangible as giving some one financial assistance and assisting someone in doing work to sharing the burden. There are two sources of getting social support work and non-work (Adams, King, & King, 1996; Beehr & McGrath, 1992).

The origin of social support literature can be found in the nineteenth century. Durkheim (1897) conducted the first study of social support that examined the impact of decreasing social connection or ties in the rural areas and how this alienation directed high number of suicide cases in the industralized communities. Advent of new technological instruments or devices providing people the option of working from their homes instead of going to workplaces which also minimize the face to face interaction between people and leads to weak social ties. People now used to interact with each other through technology rather than face to face, social networking sites has turned out to be useful platform of sharing the work and personal life happenings with friends, family members, colleagues and peers. Consequently, this study hypothized that social networking sites acts as a proxy of social support.

Social networking sites may act as social resource hub through which social ties emerge. Research found that there is a direct impact of social support on work outcomes. For example, research found a significant relationship between social support and organizational commitment. Job satisfaction is influenced by this social resource because it provides social support to the employees while working (Lin, Ensel, & Vaughn, 1981). In case of employee performance, there are scarce studies that examined the relationship of social support and employee performance. The study regarding social support has been growing for the last few decades. Most of the studies have used these terms such as "social network," "social relationships," "social support," "social ties," and "social activity" interchangeably for referring the same concept that is the existence and frequency of social ties (House, Umberson, & Landis, 1988). Resultantly, social networks facilitate the provision of social support by providing opportunities for social engagement and help in accessing tangible resources (Colabianchi, 2004; Naim & Lenka, 2017).

HYPOTHESES DEVELOPMENT

Relationship of Social Networking Sites Use: Employee Job Performance, Job Satisfaction and Organizational Commitment

Employee job performance can be described as "behaviors or actions that are relevant to the goals of the organization in question" (McCloy, Campbell, & Cudeck, 1994, p. 493). Research suggests that allowing the use of social networking sites at workplace is likely to increase the productivity of employees, because it lifts up their morale (Bennett et al., 2010; Patel & Jasani, 2010). A European study reported that more than 60% of employees from sample organization accepted that use of social networking sites assists them in increasing their productivity (AT&T, 2008). In addition to this, findings of some studies revealed that permitting the use of Facebook at workplace may help to retain new employees, because social media is a source through which they can be stay in touch with their family, peers and friends. Provisions of coworker support through social networking sites at workplace makes employees feel associated with each other and promote the use of social media more (Fay & Kline, 2011). Such ties built up among individuals through social networking sites acts as a valuable resource which aids employees to perform their jobs efficiently. Using social networking sites at workplace also enhances knowledge sharing among employees that results in improved job performance (Rothkrantz, 2015; Kwahk & Park, 2016). On the other hand, using social networking sites is regarded as one of the causes of loss in employee productivity (O'Murchu et al., 2004; Rooksby et al., 2009; Shepherd, 2011). This stance is also supported by Nuclear Research that use of Facebook in the workplace leads to nearly 2 percent loss in employee productivity.

This research study hypothesized that social networking sites use during working hours may help the employees connected with their family, friends and peers which is aligned with the concept of mass communication theory (McQuail, 2010). Social interaction that is established through social networking sites at workplace provide informal work-related support to employees in the form of peer advice, valuable information and knowledge sharing practices (Burton, Wu, & Prybutok, 2010; Rothkrantz,

2015). Research found a direct positive link between social interaction and job outcomes. This directs the hypothesis given below:

H1: Social Networking site use is positively related to employee job performance.

Similarly, social networking sites use may increase satisfaction of employees toward their job. Social support acts as a social resource in the form of social ties that provides assistance, psychological support, motivation and feedback to employees. Research suggests that use of social networking sites tends to increase employee engagement because such sites facilitate employee interaction with their colleagues within workplace, lead to increase in employee job satisfaction (Lin et al., 1981; Seers, McGee, Serey & Graen, 1983; Hanna, Kee & Robertson, 2017; Barnett, Martin & Garza, 2018). Having good relations with colleagues is associated with decreased job stress and increased job satisfaction (Lambert & Hogan, 2010). Coworker support is found to be significant predictor of increased job involvement and job satisfaction of employees (Lambert, Minor, Wells, & Hogan, 2016). Additionally, having social support from friends and family at workplace through social network sites may allow the workers to strengthen bond with organization and job (Kwok, Cheng & Wong, 2015).

A study conducted by Zyl (2009) reveals that social networks developed through social networking sites help in boosting morale and job satisfaction of employees. Moreover, the study conducted by Yang et al. (2009) delineated that "social networks serve as a social resource which affects job satisfaction through the provision of supportiveness" (p. 698). This literature helps us to deduce the following hypothesis:

H2: Social networking site use is positively related to job satisfaction.

Relationship of Job Satisfaction: Employee Job Performance and Organizational Commitment

Job satisfaction can be defined as "the attitude of workers toward the company, their job, their fellow workers and other psychological objects in the work, environment" (Beer, 1964, p. 34). Direction of relationship between job satisfaction and employee performance is still debatable and under further inquiry. Research found that job satisfaction and employee job performance are moderately correlated (Judge, Thoresen, Bono, & Patton, 2001). Human relation movement supported the notion that job satisfaction tends to improve job performance (Judge et al., 2001). Strauss (1968) asserted "Early human relationists viewed the morale–productivity relationship quite simply: higher morale would lead to improved productivity". On account of commonly believed relationship between job satisfaction and employee job performance proposed by human proponents, the study took the same view that attitude directs behavior and more satisfied employees are likely to be good performers in the organization. Research indicated a positive relationship between job satisfaction and employee job performance (Ahmad, Ahmad & Shah, 2010). Workers who are satisfied with their job are more efficient in attaining the goals of the organization (Scott & Stephens, 2009). In other words, job satisfaction can bring positive advantages for the workplace.

This lead to posit the following hypothesis:

H3: Job satisfaction is positively related to employee job performance.

Job satisfaction is also associated with organizational commitment (Burton, et al., 2010). Research suggests a positive link between job satisfaction and organizational commitment, but the direction of the relationship is still indecisive (Bluedorn, 1982). But one of the studies found that job satisfaction leads to organizational commitment, the causal relationship starts from job satisfaction to organizational commitment (Lincoln & Kalleberg, 1992). The results of the study reported statistically strong link between job satisfaction and organizational commitment as compare to the relationship in which the organizational commitment predicts job satisfaction. Consequently, on the basis of literature it has been found that satisfaction with job itself had significant and positive influence on organizational commitment of employees (Yousef, 2017; Malik, Nawab, Naeem, & Danish, 2010). The present study draws the hypothesis that job satisfaction predicts organizational commitment. The above discussion leads to draw the hypothesis given below:

H4: Job satisfaction is positively related to organizational commitment.

Relationship of Organizational Commitment with Employee Job Performance and Social Networking Sites Use

Organizational commitment can be defined as "the relative strength of an individual's identification with and involvement in a particular organization" (Allen & Meyer, 1990). Commitment can be divided in to three main categories: "affective," "normative" and "continuance." The present study has taken affective commitment that would be termed as organizational commitment in this study's context because research suggests that affective commitment has been preferably incorporated as primary and sole indicator of organizational commitment in most of the studies. Affective commitment can be described as "employee's emotional attachment to, identification with, and involvement in the organization" (Payne & Huffman, 2005). Research also supported the view point that committed employees who identify with the organization goals and mission tends to be more productive (Mathieu & Zajac, 1990; Price & Mueller, 1981). There is unanimity among scholars regarding the relationship of commitment and employee performance (Riketta, 2002). Job performance is considered as consequent of affective commitment (Allen & Meyer, 1990; Hellman & McMillan, 1994; Mathieu & Zajac, 1990; Meyer et al., 2002). With reference to the previous literature, this study draws a hypothesis that there is a relationship between affective organizational commitment and employee job performance. The hypothesis is given below:

H5: Organizational commitment is positively related to employee job performance.

Commitment is also associated with use of social networking sites. Research suggests that there are two purposes of using social networking sites at workplace i.e. work related and non-work related. Non-work-related activities on social media sites (Micro blogging) can be termed as informal and voluntary self-expression, self-revelation and interaction behaviors in corporate environment (Huang, Singh, & Ghose, 2015). Research suggests that non-work-related content sharing among employees can help them develop and maintain common topics with each other. Such practices of sharing common topics facilitate shared understanding and interest among workers, which in turn additionally assist in fostering trust and emotional attachment among them at workplace (Lu, Guo, Luo, & Chen, 2015). Social interaction (non- work related) developed and maintained through social networking sites provide employees' social support and positive emotional experience that in turn enhance organizational commitment. Because activities on such networking sites are more informal and social which make the employees more affectively committed towards their organization (Lu, et al., 2015). Research argues that non-work-related content sharing and knowledge gaining have profound positive influence on affective commitment of workers (Luo, Guo, Lu, & Chen, 2018).

Using social networking sites at workplace give employees sense of belongingness and create social bonding with each other. This social bonding and interaction act as a social resource that help employees to be more affectively committed to their workplace (Moqbel, 2012). Furthermore, research asserts that social support is positively related to organizational commitment (Rai, 2011). Figure 1 displays the proposed model. On the basis of the literature mentioned above, the following hypothesis is drawn:

H6: Social networking site use is positively related to organizational commitment.

Figure 1. Proposed model

METHODOLOGY

In this section, sampling procedure and process of data collection employed for this study are discussed.

Data Collection Procedure

Survey questionnaire is used to collect data from employed population. Sample is selected through convenience sampling. Convenience sampling was employed due to financial and time constraints and non-availability of the sampling frame of social network sites users in Lahore. Personal contacts were used to approach respondents belonging to various sectors including education, manufacturing, health, bank and telecommunication. 30% of the questionnaires were distributed by personally visiting the organizations and rest seventy percent were sent to the organizations through courier services. Eligibility criteria of respondents: well versed with Information Technology and users of social networking sites, access to internet and able to understand English.

Cover letter was attached with each questionnaire containing purpose and other details of the study. The anonymity of the participants had been assured, as participants only asked to fill the general demographics. Individual was the unit of analysis of this study. The sample comprised of various occupations including education, banking, telecommunication, health care. Almost 550 questionnaires were distributed from which 330 (60%) were received and 51 were rejected due to incomplete information. After rejecting the incomplete questionnaires, total sample size was 279 with valid 50.7% response rate.

Those questionnaires were not included in the sample in which items missing are equivalent to or greater than 10% of the overall items of variable (Malhotra, Kim, & Patil, 2006).

Facebook was the most popular social network site among respondents as approximately 93% of the respondents reported that they are the users of Facebook. Almost 22% of the respondents stated that they are the users of LinkedIn. Twitter is used by approximately 11% of respondents, 4.62% share is taken by other social network sites and Myspace gained the 0.45% share of respondents.

279 respondents participated in this study. The average age of the respondents ranged from 21-30 because almost 202 out 279 respondents fall under this category. Most of the respondents were males with the percentage of 72.8 and 27.2 percent of the respondents were females. As far as the education level is concerned, 2.86 percent of respondents were only completed intermediate, 32.6 percent had bachelor's degree, 54.8 percent participants had reached Masters' level and rest 9.67 percent of the respondents had doctoral degree. With reference to employment status, 96.4 percent of employees are full time working incumbents whereas 3.6 percent worked on part time basis. Social networking use policy had been implemented by 58.4 percent organizations in which respondents were employed, while rest 34.5 percent of the organizations had no formal policy which restricts and regulates the use of social media in organizations.

Measurement Instrument

A multifaceted scale of social networking site use given by (Ellison, Steinfield, & Lampe, 2007) was used to investigate the impact of social networking sites use at workplace after slight changes in the wordings. Scale of Social Networking Sites Use is encompassed of six measures for gauging social networking site use of employees at workplace. The measurement scale for affective organizational commitment is taken from Mowday, Porter and Steers (1982). The measurement scale of job satisfaction has been taken from Rehman (2011) and indicators of job performance were taken from (Kuvaas, 2006).

All the indicators were gauged on seven-point Likert scale except the indicators of perceived employee job performance that were measured on five point Likert scale. Social Networking Sites Use and job performance were gauged using five indicators; affective organizational commitment was measured through seven indicators; and perceived employee job performance was gauged using six indicators. Gender, education, age organizational tenure, organizational level and the policy of using social networking sites were taken in to account as control variables for this study.

ANALYSIS

Partial Least Square (PLS) was employed to evaluate the data in order to check the proposed model accuracy and its parameters (Fornell & Bookstein, 1982). PLS was chosen as analysis technique for this study due to the flexibility it offers as compare to covariance-based (SEM) techniques. Particularly in case of PLS, there is no need of normally distributed data and large sample size (Gefen, Straub, & Boudreau, 2000). In addition to this, PLS is suitable for complex models comprising of multiple latent constructs as in the case of this study. WarpPLS 5 was used to perform PLS analysis.

Measurement Model Assessment

Prior to analyzing the structural model, it is important to examine the validity and reliability of the measurement model. Measurement model was evaluated through confirmatory factor analysis (Astrachan, Patel, & Wanzenried, 2014; Hair, Sarstedt, Hopkins & Kuppelwieser, 2014).

Firstly, convergent validity is assessed through factor loadings. Results indicated that all factor loadings were greater than 0.5 having significance level of less than 0.001as shown in Table 1. These factor loadings showed that the measurement instrument of this study has good convergent validity (Hair Jr, Black, Babin, Anderson, & Tatham, 2010). Collinearity was tested with the help of cross loadings. As it can be seen from the Table 1, all the cross loadings were less than the threshold of .5 which showed that there is no problem of collinearity among latent variables (Kock, 2012). Secondly, discriminant validity was tested through matching up the correlations of constructs with their relevant AVEs. As shown in Table 2, square root of average variances extracted of each latent construct used in this study was higher than the correlation values of all latent constructs as suggested by Fornell and Lacker (1981). Square root of (AVEs) average variances extracted for every latent construct was presented diagonally under parentheses in Table 2.

In the next step, reliability of the constructs was evaluated through composite reliability coefficients and cronbach's alpha. Results as shown in table 3 indicated that value of Cronbach's alpha and composite reliability of all the latent constructs were greater than 0.7 consistent with the guidelines given by Nunnally and Bernstein (1994).

Table 1. Cross loadings

	SNSU	EJP	JS	AOC	SE	P value
SNSU1	(0.748)	0.108	0.184	-0.022	0.053	<0.001
SNSU2	(0.799)	0.061	-0.185	0.147	0.052	<0.001
SNSU3	(0.911)	-0.066	0.046	-0.076	0.051	<0.001
SNSU4	(0.829)	-0.059	-0.067	0.026	0.052	<0.001
SNSU5	(0.88)	-0.023	0.027	-0.061	0.052	<0.001
EPJ1	-0.009	(0.743)	0.123	-0.132	0.053	<0.001
EPJ2	-0.136	(0.733)	0.223	-0.201	0.053	<0.001
EPJ3	-0.031	(0.616)	-0.165	0.106	0.054	<0.001
EPJ4	0.032	(0.772)	-0.105	0.063	0.053	<0.001
EPJ5	-0.011	(0.703)	-0.145	0.22	0.053	<0.001
EPJ6	0.143	(0.755)	0.04	-0.03	0.053	<0.001
JS1	0.005	0.057	(0.911)	-0.007	0.051	<0.001
JS2	-0.05	0.039	(0.924)	0.016	0.051	<0.001
JS3	0.035	0.007	(0.867)	-0.026	0.052	<0.001
JS4	-0.053	-0.01	(0.919)	0.02	0.051	<0.001
JS5	0.083	-0.115	(0.737)	-0.004	0.053	<0.001
AOC1	0.002	-0.076	0.136	(0.776)	0.053	<0.001
AOC2	0.011	-0.032	-0.049	(0.74)	0.053	<0.001
AOC3	0.023	0.021	-0.176	(0.727)	0.053	<0.001
AOC4	-0.07	-0.097	-0.145	(0.727)	0.053	<0.001
AOC5	-0.072	0.098	0.055	(0.743)	0.053	<0.001
AOC6	0.102	0.093	-0.093	(0.621)	0.054	<0.001
AOC7	0.021	0.011	0.262	(0.691)	0.053	<0.001

-Loadings are shown within parentheses; the loadings are from a structure matrix (un-rotated), and the cross-loadings from a pattern matrix (i.e., rotated); all loadings are significant at the P<0.001

Table 2. Square root of average variances extracted of each latent constructs

	SNSU	EJP	JS	AOC
SNSU	(0.835)	0.038	0.031	0.104
EJP	0.038	(0.722)	0.232	0.286
JS	0.031	0.232	(0.874)	0.695
AOC	0.104	0.286	0.695	(0.719)

- AVE = average variance extracted.
- Square roots of AVEs are shown on diagonal within parentheses.

Table 3. Value of Cronbach's alpha and composite reliability of all the latent constructs were greater than 0.7 consistent with the guidelines given by Nunnally and Bernstein (1994)

Constructs	Composite Reliability (CR)	Cronbach's Alpha (CA)	Average Variance Extracted (AVE)
SNSU	0.92	0.89	0.698
EJP	0.867	0.815	0.522
JS	0.942	0.921	0.765
AOC	0.882	0.844	0.518

EJP = employee job performance; SNSUI = social networking site use intensity; JS = job satisfaction; AOC = affective organizational commitment.

Structural Model Assessment

Structural model of this study was estimated by employing jacknifying resampling technique. Using resampling technique eliminates biasness in data and produces stable coefficients (Kock, 2012). Model fit was assessed through the following indices, which is presented in Table 4: "Average Path Coefficient (APC), Average R-squared (ARS), and Average Variance Inflation Factor (AVIF), Tenenhaus goodness of fit (GoF)". As reported in Table 4, p- values of APC and ARC were less than 0.05, although AVIF was less than 3.3 (threshold) as suggested by Kock (2012). Tenehuas goodness of fit (GoF) index of the proposed structural model was 0.435 that is greater than the threshold (0.36) as suggested by (Wetzels, Odekerken-Schröder, & Van Oppen, 2009) there is a good fit between model and data (Rosenthal & Rosnow, 1991).

Table 4. Average Path Coefficient (APC), Average R-squared (ARS), and Average Variance Inflation Factor (AVIF), Tenenhaus goodness of fit (GoF)

GOF	APC	ARS	AVIF
0.435	0.224***	0.217***	1.333

Results

SEM analysis was carried out to test the statistical significance and strength of the proposed relationships between variables (direct effects). Gender, education, age organizational tenure, organizational level and the policy of using social networking sites were included as control variables in the model to reduce the chances of extraneous effects on the model (Figure 2). On the basis of path coefficients and significance level (p value), it is found that 4 out of 6 hypotheses are accepted as shown in Table 5 (Results Summary).

Table 5. Hypothesis

Hypothesis	Path Coefficients (β)	Supported
H1. Social Networking site use is positively related to employee job performance	0.11	No
H2. Social networking site use is positively related to job satisfaction.	0.13*	Yes
H3. Job satisfaction is positively related to employee job performance.	0.17**	Yes
H4. Job satisfaction is positively related to organizational commitment	0.71**	Yes
H5. Organizational commitment is positively related to employee job performance	0.16**	Yes
H6. Social networking site use is positively related to organizational commitment.	0.06^NS	No

Figure 2. Model

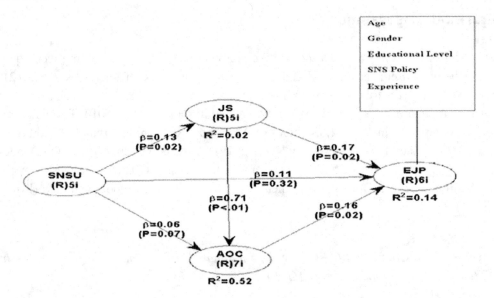

As per the results, there are no direct links between social networking site use and employee job performance ($\beta = 0.11$, P > 0.05); between social networking site use and affective organizational commitment ($\beta = 0.06$, P > 0.05). Due to which Hypothesis 1 and 6 are not supported by data.

There are significant and positive relationships between social network site use and job satisfaction ($\beta= 0.13$, p<0.05); job satisfaction and employee job performance ($\beta = 0.17$, p < 0.05); job satisfaction and affective organizational commitment ($\beta = 0.71$, p < 0.01); and between affective organizational commitment and employee job performance ($\beta = 0.16$, P > 0.05). These results indicate the acceptance of H2, H3, H4 and H5.

Mediating Effects

Besides direct effects, SEM analysis (Partial Least Square) also calculates the indirect effects (mediation) (Ned Kock, 2014). Firstly, magnitude and statistical significance of indirect effects was estimated through automatically generated indirect effects (path coefficients) and associated P values by WarpPLS. Results of the indirect effects (path with two segments) in Table 6 indicate that job satisfaction mediates the relationship between social networking site use and employee job performance (P- 0.02 < 0.05). Job satisfaction is also found to be a significant mediator between social networking site use and affective organizational commitment (P- 0.01 < 0.05). Affective organizational commitment is mediating between social networking site use and employee job performance (P-0.01 < 0.05).

Table 6. Job satisfaction mediates the relationship between social networking site use and employee job performance

	Indirect Effects	P Value
SNSU → JS → EJP	0.038	0.024
SNSU → AOC → EJP	0.045	0.01
SNSU → JS → AOC	0.094	0.016

Mediation was also tested through employing approach suggested by Hayes & Preacher (2010) that is appropriate for both linear and non-linear relationships. According to this approach, Sobel's standard error tests were used to test the statistical significance of mediating relationships. Sobel's standard error method was implemented by using a spreadsheet (available in resources of WarpPLS) that takes inputs including standard errors and path coefficients generated through WarpPLS (Kock, 2015) to calculate product path coefficients, standard errors, and P values for mediating effects. Results of Sobel test show that job satisfaction mediates the effect of social networking site use on employee job performance indicating significance level (P-0.06 marginally acceptable) (Pab') as shown in Table 7. Affective organizational commitment mediates the relationship of social networking sites use and employee job performance reporting p value (Pab' = 0.01 < 0.05) as exhibited in Table 8. P value of the indirect effects of social networking site use on affective organizational commitment through job satisfaction is significant (P-0.03 < 0.05) shown in Table 9.

Table 7. Results of Sobel test

Sample size	279
Path coefficient (a)	0.1320
Path coefficient (b)	0.2860
Standard error (Sa)	0.0620
Standard error (Sb)	0.0660
Product path coefficient for mediating effect (ab)	0.0378
P-Value for mediating effect (two-tailed) (Pab')	0.06

Table 8. Relationship of social networking sites use and employee job performance reporting p value

Sample size	279
Path coefficient (a)	0.1640
Path coefficient (b)	0.2760
Standard error (Sa)	0.0640
Standard error (Sb)	0.0590
Product path coefficient for mediating effect (ab)	0.0453
P-Value for mediating effect (two-tailed) (Pab')	0.02

Table 9. Indirect effects of social networking site use on affective organizational commitment through job satisfaction is significant

Sample size	279
Path coefficient (a)	0.1320
Path coefficient (b)	0.7100
Standard error (Sa)	0.0620
Standard error (Sb)	0.0340
Product path coefficient for mediating effect (ab)	0.0937
P-Value for mediating effect (two-tailed) (Pab')	0.03

DISCUSSION

Testing or confirming a research model was the purpose of this study explaining the proposed connections between social network site use and work outcomes. Model proposed in the present study indicated good fit with the empirically collected data. The three independent variables such as social networking sites use, organizational commitment and job satisfaction caused 14 percent variance inemployee job performance which is the main dependent variable.

Findings of this study are consistent with previous research in validating the positive influence of social networking site use on job satisfaction, the positive influence of job satisfaction on organizational commitment and employee job performance, and the positive impact of organizational commitment on employee job performance (Charoensukmongkol, 2014; Moqbel et al., 2013). In addition to this, as per the findings, there is no significant influence of social networking sites use on employee job performance and organizational commitment that is also in line with the research conducted by Moqbel et al. (2013).

Results of the indirect (mediating) effects show that job satisfaction and organizational commitment act as significant mediators between social networking sites use and employee job performance. As per findings of this study, no direct link has been found between social networking sites use and employee job performance that is in line with previous literature which suggests using social media sites at workplace may not be a sole factor that directly influences employee job performance (Smayling & Miller, 2012). It is possible that the link between these two factors would be mediated by job satisfaction which employees experience due to using social networking sites at workplace.

As employees spend most of their time at workplace, away from their family and friends, using social networking sites act as a way to approach and maintain social connections that can help in balancing work and job demands (Lin et al., 1981, Hurlbert, 1991). Thus, use of social networking sites at workplace can act as mechanism that facilitates in acquiring social support to balance work and family domains. Improved work family balance in turn leads to increase job satisfaction of employees (Charoensukmongkol, 2014; Moqbel et al., 2013; Malik, Gomez, Ahmad, & Saif, 2010). Research indicated that employees who are more satisfied with their jobs would perform better (Ahmad, Ahmad & Shah, 2010). This finding is also consistent with this study conducted by Moqbel et al. (2013) that job satisfcation proves to be a significant mediator for the relationship of social networking sites use and employee job performance.

Organizational commitment also found to have indirect (mediating) effects between social networking sites use and employee job performance. Using social networking sites gives a sense of belongingness to employees while working that resultantly keep them affectively attached to the organization. This is in line with the literature that shows organizational commitment is a significant predictor of employee job performance (Meyer et al., 2002).

As per the findings, social networking use is not significantly related to affective organizational commitment which is aligned with the results of Williams and Hazer's (1986) who proclaim commitment is a time taking process as compare to job satisfaction. The relationship between social networking sites use intensity and organizational commitment will be significant if the employees would use social networking sites for longer period of time.

Implications for Academics and Practitioners

This study contributes in the nascent discipline that focuses on the influence of social network site use on employee job performance. This study also adds to various broader disciplines such as management information systems, human resource management particularly international business. This study also offers various implications for industry. Managers' specifically human resource professionals would get advantage after understanding the proposed relationship. They will be able to understand that technology is not responsible for decreasing productivity of employees, the use of social media matters and human professionals can guide employees how they can take advantage of social media technologies in a better way.

This study would also assist organizations in making policies regarding use of social networking sites. Managers can understand the rationale of whether to allow or not to allow social networking sites' use in the organization. As posited in the study, use of social network sites keep the employees in contact with their family members, friends and peers that make them happy and satisfied in their workplace which can be positive effect on job satisfaction and employee job performance. This study will provide a new perspective to look at the use of social network site use in the workplace. Most of the prior studies in the domain of social network literature investigated the negative impact of social network sites use on the organizations.

There are some limitations of this study. First, data collection is done through self-reported questionnaires that may lead to self-reporting bias. Second, this is a cross sectional study, causality between variables cannot be easily determined (Maxwell & Cole, 2007). Lastly, all the constructs of this study are subjective in nature that can only gauge employee's present state of mind.

CONCLUSION

In conclusion, this study increases our understanding of the relationship between social networking sites use and work outcomes including job satisfaction, organizational commitment and specifically employee job performance.

Findings of this study validate the stance that use of social networking sites are one of the acceptable means for sharing experiences related to work and non -work related activities with friends, family, peers and colleagues. Findings of the study recommended that use of mechanism that provides human support is important for the organizations that facilitates the provision of both formal and informal support needed to improve employees' overall job performance.

As a whole, this study assesses social networking use from employees' perspective at workplace. Although many studies have been carried out on social networking use addressing multiple issues such as ethical, security and privacy ones (Dinh, 2011; Dwyer, 2007) but very few have examined the impact of social networking sites' use on work outcomes. The present study has been conducted to fill this void in the social network literature as well as to validate results of previous studies conducted in other countries on the tested relationships. Generally, this study has given support for several complex links and in turn significantly adds to the body of knowledge.

The findings of the present study strengthen the stance happy employees do better work. Using social networking sites facilitates employees to get socialize with their friends, family, peers and colleagues and enable them to be updated regarding the activities on social networking sites that ultimately makes them satisfied and more productive.

REFERENCES

Adams, G. A., King, L. A., & King, D. W. (1996). Relationships of job and family involvement, family social support, and work–family conflict with job and life satisfaction. *The Journal of Applied Psychology*, *81*(4), 411–420. doi:10.1037/0021-9010.81.4.411

Ahmad, H., Ahmad, K., & Shah, I. A. (2010). Relationship between job satisfaction, job performance attitude towards work and organizational commitment. *European Journal of Soil Science*, *18*(2), 257–267.

Ali-Hassan, H., Nevo, D., & Wade, M. (2015). Linking dimensions of social media use to job performance: The role of social capital. *The Journal of Strategic Information Systems*, *24*(2), 65–89. doi:10.1016/j.jsis.2015.03.001

Allen, K., Blascovich, J., & Mendes, W. B. (2002). Cardiovascular reactivity and the presence of pets, friends, and spouses: The truth about cats and dogs. *Psychosomatic Medicine*, *64*(5), 727–739. PMID:12271103

Allen, N. J., & Meyer, J. P. (1990). The measurement and antecedents of affective, continuance and normative commitment to the organization. *Journal of Occupational Psychology*, *63*(1), 1–18. doi:10.1111/j.2044-8325.1990.tb00506.x

Astrachan, C. B., Patel, V. K., & Wanzenried, G. (2014). A comparative study of CB-SEM and PLS-SEM for theory development in family firm research. *Journal of Family Business Strategy, 5*(1), 116–128. doi:10.1016/j.jfbs.2013.12.002

AT&T. (2008). *Social Networking in the Workplace Increases Efficiency*. London: Dynamic Markets Limited.

Barnett, M. D., Martin, K. J., & Garza, C. J. (2018). Satisfaction With Work–Family Balance Mediates the Relationship Between Workplace Social Support and Depression Among Hospice Nurses. *Journal of Nursing Scholarship*. doi:10.1111/jnu.12451 PMID:30570211

Beehr, T. A., & McGrath, J. E. (1992). Social support, occupational stress and anxiety. *Anxiety, Stress, and Coping, 5*(1), 7–19. doi:10.1080/10615809208250484

Beer, M. (1964). Organizational size and job satisfaction. *Academy of Management Journal, 7*(1), 34–44.

Bennett, J., Owers, M., Pitt, M., & Tucker, M. (2010). Workplace impact of social networking. *Property Management, 28*(3), 138–148. doi:10.1108/02637471011051282

Bernoff, J., & Li, C. (2008). Harnessing the power of the oh-so-social web. *MIT Sloan Management Review, 49*(3), 36.

Bhuian, S. N., & Abdul-Muhmin, A. G. (1997). Job satisfaction and organizational commitment among "guest-worker" salesforces: The case of Saudi Arabia. *Journal of Global Marketing, 10*(3), 27–44. doi:10.1300/J042v10n03_03

Bluedorn, A. C. (1982). A unified model of turnover from organizations. *Human Relations, 35*(2), 135–153. doi:10.1177/001872678203500204

Boyd, D. M., & Ellison, N. B. (2007). Social network sites: Definition, history, and scholarship. *Journal of Computer-Mediated Communication, 13*(1), 210–230. doi:10.1111/j.1083-6101.2007.00393.x

Burton, P., Wu, Y., & Prybutok, V. (2010). Social network position and its relationship to performance of IT professionals. *Informing Science: The International Journal of an Emerging Transdiscipline, 13*(1), 121–137. doi:10.28945/1180

Chang, C. W., & Heo, J. (2014). Visiting theories that predict college students' self-disclosure on Facebook. *Computers in Human Behavior, 30*, 79–86. doi:10.1016/j.chb.2013.07.059

Charoensukmongkol, P. (2014). Effects of support and job demands on social media use and work outcomes. *Computers in Human Behavior, 36*, 340–349. doi:10.1016/j.chb.2014.03.061

Chu, K.-M., & Chan, H.-C. (2009). Community based innovation: Its antecedents and its impact on innovation success. *Internet Research, 19*(5), 496–516.

Clark, L. A., & Roberts, S. J. (2010). Employer's use of social networking sites: A socially irresponsible practice. *Journal of Business Ethics, 95*(4), 507–525. doi:10.100710551-010-0436-y

Claybaugh, C. C., Haried, P., & Yu, W.-B. (2015). Diffusion of a professional social network: Business school graduates in focus. *International Journal of Human Capital and Information Technology Professionals, 6*(4), 80–96. doi:10.4018/IJHCITP.2015100105

Colabianchi, N. (2004). *Social support. In Encyclopedia of Women's Health* (pp. 1231–1233). Springer. doi:10.1007/978-0-306-48113-0_411

Computing, W. (2009). Social Networking Or Social Not-working?

Dinh, A. K. (2011). Privacy and security of social media in health care. *Journal of Health Care Compliance, 13*(1), 45–46.

Doma, S., Elaref, N., & Elnaga, M. A. Research Article Factors Affecting Electronic Word-of-Mouth on Social Networking Websites in Egypt–An Application of the Technology Acceptance Model.

Dwyer, C., Hiltz, S., & Passerini, K. (2007). Trust and privacy concern within social networking sites: A comparison of Facebook and MySpace. In *AMCIS 2007 Proceedings*.

El Ouirdi, A., El Ouirdi, M., Segers, J., & Henderickx, E. (2015). Employees' use of social media technologies: A methodological and thematic review. *Behaviour & Information Technology, 34*(5), 454–464. doi:10.1080/0144929X.2015.1004647

Ellison, N. B., Steinfield, C., & Lampe, C. (2007). The benefits of Facebook "friends:" Social capital and college students' use of online social network sites. *Journal of Computer-Mediated Communication, 12*(4), 1143–1168. doi:10.1111/j.1083-6101.2007.00367.x

Fay, M. J., & Kline, S. L. (2011). Coworker relationships and informal communication in high-intensity telecommuting. *Journal of Applied Communication Research, 39*(2), 144–163. doi:10.1080/00909882.2011.556136

Ferreira, N. (2010). Social networks and young people: A case study. *International Journal of Human Capital and Information Technology Professionals, 1*(4), 31–54. doi:10.4018/jhcitp.2010100103

Fornell, C., & Bookstein, F. L. (1982). Two structural equation models: LISREL and PLS applied to consumer exit-voice theory. *JMR, Journal of Marketing Research, 19*(4), 440–452. doi:10.1177/002224378201900406

Fornell, C., & Larcker, D. F. (1981). Evaluating structural equation models with unobservable variables and measurement error. *JMR, Journal of Marketing Research, 18*(1), 39–50. doi:10.1177/002224378101800104

Freeman, P., & Rees, T. (2009). How does perceived support lead to better performance? An examination of potential mechanisms. *Journal of Applied Sport Psychology, 21*(4), 429–441. doi:10.1080/10413200903222913

Gefen, D., Straub, D., & Boudreau, M.-C. (2000). Structural equation modeling and regression: Guidelines for research practice. *Communications of the Association for Information Systems, 4*(1), 7.

Hair, J.F. Jr., Sarstedt, M., Hopkins, L., & G. Kuppelwieser, V. (2014). Partial least squares structural equation modeling (PLS-SEM) An emerging tool in business research. *European Business Review, 26*(2), 106–121. doi:10.1108/EBR-10-2013-0128

Hair Jr, J., Black, W., Babin, B., Anderson, R., & Tatham, R. (2010). SEM: An introduction. In *Multivariate data analysis: A global perspective* (pp. 629-686). Pearson.

Hanna, B., Kee, K. F., & Robertson, B. W. (2017). Positive Impacts of Social Media at Work: Job Satisfaction, Job Calling, and Facebook Use among Co-Workers. *Paper presented at the SHS Web of Conferences.* 10.1051hsconf/20173300012

Hasgall, A., & Shoham, S. (2007). Digital social network technology and the complex organizational systems. *Vine, 37*(2), 180–191. doi:10.1108/03055720710759955

Hayes, A. F., & Preacher, K. J. (2010). Quantifying and testing indirect effects in simple mediation models when the constituent paths are nonlinear. *Multivariate Behavioral Research, 45*(4), 627–660. doi:10.1080/00273171.2010.498290 PMID:26735713

Hellman, C. M., & McMillin, W. L. (1994). Newcomer socialization and affective commitment. *The Journal of Social Psychology, 134*(2), 261–262. doi:10.1080/00224545.1994.9711393

House, J. S., Umberson, D., & Landis, K. R. (1988). Structures and processes of social support. *Annual Review of Sociology, 14*(1), 293–318. doi:10.1146/annurev.so.14.080188.001453

Hsia, T. L., Lin, L. M., Wu, J. H., & Tsai, H. T. (2006). A framework for designing nursing knowledge management systems. *Interdisciplinary Journal of Information, Knowledge, and Management, 1*(1), 13–22. doi:10.28945/110

Huang, Y., Singh, P. V., & Ghose, A. (2015). A structural model of employee behavioral dynamics in enterprise social media. *Management Science, 61*(12), 2825–2844.

Ibrahim, S. (2017, February 17) Pakistan Social Media Users Crossed 44 million in 2016-2017 [Blog post]. *Phoneworld.* Retrieved from https://www.phoneworld.com.pk/pakistan-social-media-users-crossed-44-million/

Judge, T. A., Thoresen, C. J., Bono, J. E., & Patton, G. K. (2001). The job satisfaction–job performance relationship: A qualitative and quantitative review. *Psychological Bulletin, 127*(3), 376–407. doi:10.1037/0033-2909.127.3.376 PMID:11393302

Kemp, S. (2018, January 30). Digital In 2018: World's Internet Users pass the 4 Billion Mark [Blog post]. Retrieved from https://wearesocial.com/blog/2018/01/global-digital-report-2018

Kock, N. (2012). WarpPLS 5.0 User Manual.

Kock, N. (2014). Advanced mediating effects tests, multi-group analyses, and measurement model assessments in PLS-based SEM. [IJeC]. *International Journal of e-Collaboration, 10*(1), 1–13. doi:10.4018/ijec.2014010101

Kock, N. (2015). *WarpPLS 5.0 User Manual.* Laredo, TX: ScriptWarp Systems.

Kock, N., Moqbel, M., Barton, K., & Bartelt, V. (2018). *Intended Continued Use Social Networking Sites: Effects on Job Satisfaction and Performance Social Issues in the Workplace: Breakthroughs in Research and Practice* (pp. 472–493). IGI Global.

Kuvaas, B. (2006). Work performance, affective commitment, and work motivation: The roles of pay administration and pay level. *Journal of Organizational Behavior: The International Journal of Industrial, Occupational and Organizational Psychology and Behavior, 27*(3), 365–385. doi:10.1002/job.377

Kwahk, K. Y., & Park, D. H. (2016). The effects of network sharing on knowledge-sharing activities and job performance in enterprise social media environments. *Computers in Human Behavior, 55*, 826–839. doi:10.1016/j.chb.2015.09.044

Kwok, S. Y., Cheng, L., & Wong, D. F. (2015). Family emotional support, positive psychological capital and job satisfaction among Chinese white-collar workers. *Journal of Happiness Studies, 16*(3), 561–582. doi:10.100710902-014-9522-7

Lambert, E. G., & Hogan, N. L. (2010). Wanting change: The relationship of perceptions of organizational innovation with correctional staff job stress, job satisfaction, and organizational commitment. *Criminal Justice Policy Review, 21*(2), 160–184. doi:10.1177/0887403409353166

Lambert, E. G., Minor, K. I., Wells, J. B., & Hogan, N. L. (2016). Social support's relationship to correctional staff job stress, job involvement, job satisfaction, and organizational commitment. *The Social Science Journal, 53*(1), 22–32. doi:10.1016/j.soscij.2015.10.001

Leader-Chivee, L., Hamilton, B. A., & Cowan, E. (2008). Networking the way to success: Online social networks for workplace and competitive advantage. *People and Strategy, 31*(4), 40.

Leidner, D., Koch, H., & Gonzalez, E. (2010). Assimilating generation Y IT new hires into USAA's workforce: The role of an enterprise 2.0 system. *MIS Quarterly Executive, 9*(4), 229–242.

Leidner, D. E. (2010). Globalization, culture, and information: Towards global knowledge transparency. *The Journal of Strategic Information Systems, 19*(2), 69–77. doi:10.1016/j.jsis.2010.02.006

Lin, N., Ensel, W. M., & Vaughn, J. C. (1981). Social resources and strength of ties: Structural factors in occupational status attainment. *American Sociological Review, 46*(4), 393–405. doi:10.2307/2095260

Lincoln, J. R., & Kalleberg, A. L. (1992). *Culture, control and commitment: A study of work organization and work attitudes in the United States and Japan.* CUP Archive.

Lu, B., Guo, X., Luo, N., & Chen, G. (2015). Corporate blogging and job performance: Effects of work-related and nonwork-related participation. *Journal of Management Information Systems, 32*(4), 285–314. doi:10.1080/07421222.2015.1138573

Luo, N., Guo, X., Lu, B., & Chen, G. (2018). Can non-work-related social media use benefit the company? A study on corporate blogging and affective organizational commitment. *Computers in Human Behavior, 81*, 84–92. doi:10.1016/j.chb.2017.12.004

Mainier, M. J., & O'Brien, M. (2010). Online social networks and the privacy paradox: A research framework. *Issues in Information Systems, XI, 1*, 513–517.

Malhotra, N. K., Kim, S. S., & Patil, A. (2006). Common method variance in IS research: A comparison of alternative approaches and a reanalysis of past research. *Management Science, 52*(12), 1865–1883. doi:10.1287/mnsc.1060.0597

Malik, M. E., Nawab, S., Naeem, B., & Danish, R. Q. (2010). Job satisfaction and organizational commitment of university teachers in public sector of Pakistan. *International Journal of Business and Management, 5*(6), 17. doi:10.5539/ijbm.v5n6p17

Malik, M. I., Gomez, S. F., Ahmad, M., & Saif, M. I. (2010). Examining the relationship of work life balance, job satisfaction and turnover in Pakistan.

Mathieu, J. E., & Zajac, D. M. (1990). A review and meta-analysis of the antecedents, correlates, and consequences of organizational commitment. *Psychological Bulletin*, *108*(2), 171–194. doi:10.1037/0033-2909.108.2.171

Maxwell, S. E., & Cole, D. A. (2007). Bias in cross-sectional analyses of longitudinal mediation. *Psychological Methods*, *12*(1), 23–44. doi:10.1037/1082-989X.12.1.23 PMID:17402810

McCloy, R. A., Campbell, J. P., & Cudeck, R. (1994). A confirmatory test of a model of performance determinants. *The Journal of Applied Psychology*, *79*(4), 493–505. doi:10.1037/0021-9010.79.4.493

McQuail, D. (2010). *McQuail's mass communication theory*. Sage publications.

Moqbel, M., & Kock, N. (2018). Unveiling the dark side of social networking sites: Personal and work-related consequences of social networking site addiction. *Information & Management*, *55*(1), 109–119. doi:10.1016/j.im.2017.05.001

Moqbel, M., Nevo, S., & Kock, N. (2013). Organizational members' use of social networking sites and job performance: An exploratory study. *Information Technology & People*, *26*(3), 240–264. doi:10.1108/ITP-10-2012 0110

Mowday, R. T., Porter, L. W., & Steers, R. (1982). Organizational linkage: The psychology of commitment, absenteeism and turnover. *Organizational and Occupational Psychology*, *10*(3), 2008.

Naim, M. F., & Lenka, U. (2017). Investigating the Impact of Social Media on Gen Y Employees' Engagement: An Indian Perspective. *International Journal of Human Capital and Information Technology Professionals*, *8*(3), 29–48. doi:10.4018/IJHCITP.2017070103

North, M. (2010). An evaluation of employees' attitudes toward social networking in the workplace. *Issues in Information Systems*, *11*(1), 192–197.

Nunnally, J. C., & Bernstein, I. (1994). *Psychometric Theory (McGraw-Hill Series in Psychology)* (Vol. 3). McGraw-Hill New York.

O'Murchu, I., Breslin, J. G., & Decker, S. (2004). Online Social and Business Networking Communities. *Paper presented at the ECAI Workshop on Application of Semantic Web Technologies to Web Communities*.

O'Reilly, C. A., & Chatman, J. (1986). Organizational commitment and psychological attachment: The effects of compliance, identification, and internalization on prosocial behavior. *The Journal of Applied Psychology*, *71*(3), 492–499. doi:10.1037/0021-9010.71.3.492

Parveen, F., Jaafar, N. I., & Ainin, S. (2015). Social media usage and organizational performance: Reflections of Malaysian social media managers. *Telematics and Informatics*, *32*(1), 67–78. doi:10.1016/j.tele.2014.03.001

Patel, N., & Jasani, H. (2010). Social Media Security Policies: Guidelines for Organizations. *Issues in Information Systems*, *11*(1), 628–634.

Payne, S. C., & Huffman, A. H. (2005). A longitudinal examination of the influence of mentoring on organizational commitment and turnover. *Academy of Management Journal, 48*(1), 158–168. doi:10.5465/amj.2005.15993166

Price, J. L., & Mueller, C. W. (1981). A causal model of turnover for nurses. *Academy of Management Journal, 24*(3), 543–565. PMID:10252608

Rauniar, R., Rawski, G., Yang, J., & Johnson, B. (2014). Technology acceptance model (TAM) and social media usage: An empirical study on Facebook. *Journal of Enterprise Information Management, 27*(1), 6–30. doi:10.1108/JEIM-04-2012-0011

Rees, T., & Freeman, P. (2009). Social support moderates the relationship between stressors and task performance through self-efficacy. *Journal of Social and Clinical Psychology, 28*(2), 244–263. doi:10.1521/jscp.2009.28.2.244

Rehman, M. S. (2011). Exploring the impact of human resources management on organizational performance: A study of public sector organizations. *Journal of Business Studies Quarterly, 2*(4), 1.

Rosenthal, R., & Rosnow, R. L. (1991). *Essentials of behavioral research: Methods and data analysis.* McGraw-Hill Humanities Social.

Rothkrantz, L. (2015). How social media facilitate learning communities and peer groups around MOOCS. *International Journal of Human Capital and Information Technology Professionals, 6*(1), 1–13. doi:10.4018/ijhcitp.2015010101

Schneckenberg, D. (2009). Web 2.0 and the empowerment of the knowledge worker. *Journal of Knowledge Management, 13*(6), 509–520. doi:10.1108/13673270910997150

Scott, C. R., & Stephens, K. K. (2009). It depends on who you're talking to…: Predictors and outcomes of situated measures of organizational identification. *Western Journal of Communication, 73*(4), 370–394. doi:10.1080/10570310903279075

Seers, A., McGee, G. W., Serey, T. T., & Graen, G. B. (1983). The interaction of job stress and social support: A strong inference investigation. *Academy of Management Journal, 26*(2), 273–284.

Shepherd, C. (2011). Does social media have a place in workplace learning? *Strategic Direction, 27*(2), 3–4. doi:10.1108/02580541111103882

Siegel, S. C., & Castellan, J. N. J. (1988). *Nonparametric statistics for the behavioural sciences.* New York: McGraw-Hill.

Smayling, M., & Miller, H. (2012). Job satisfaction and job performance at the internship level. *Journal of Leadership, Accountability and Ethics, 9*(1), 27.

Smith, M. A., & Kollock, P. (1999). *Communities in cyberspace.* Psychology Press. doi:10.5117/9789056290818

Sophia van Zyl, A. (2009). The impact of Social Networking 2.0 on organisations. *The Electronic Library, 27*(6), 906–918. doi:10.1108/02640470911004020

Stanton, J. M. (2002). Company profile of the frequent internet user. *Communications of the ACM*, *45*(1), 55–59. doi:10.1145/502269.502297

Steininger, K., Ruckel, D., Dannerer, E., & Roithmayr, F. (2010). Healthcare knowledge transfer through a web 2.0 portal: An Austrian approach. *International Journal of Healthcare Technology and Management*, *11*(1-2), 13–30. doi:10.1504/IJHTM.2010.033272

Strauss, G. (1968). Human relations—1968 style. *Industrial Relations*, *7*(3), 262–276. doi:10.1111/j.1468-232X.1968.tb01080.x

Thoits, P. A. (1982). Conceptual, methodological, and theoretical problems in studying social support as a buffer against life stress. *Journal of Health and Social Behavior*, *23*(2), 145–159. doi:10.2307/2136511 PMID:7108180

Trepte, S., & Reinecke, L. (2013). The reciprocal effects of social network site use and the disposition for self-disclosure: A longitudinal study. *Computers in Human Behavior*, *29*(3), 1102–1112. doi:10.1016/j.chb.2012.10.002

Wetzels, M., Odekerken-Schröder, G., & Van Oppen, C. (2009). Using PLS path modeling for assessing hierarchical construct models: Guidelines and empirical illustration. *Management Information Systems Quarterly*, *33*(1), 177–195. doi:10.2307/20650284

Wills, D., & Reeves, S. (2009). Facebook as a political weapon: Information in social networks. *British Politics*, *4*(2), 265–281. doi:10.1057/bp.2009.3

Wills, T. A. (1991). Social support and interpersonal relationships.

Yousef, D. A. (2017). Organizational commitment, job satisfaction and attitudes toward organizational change: A study in the local government. *International Journal of Public Administration*, *40*(1), 77–88. doi:10.1080/01900692.2015.1072217

Zhang, J., & Zheng, W. (2009). How does satisfaction translate into performance? An examination of commitment and cultural values. *Human Resource Development Quarterly*, *20*(3), 331–351. doi:10.1002/hrdq.20022

This research was previously published in the International Journal of Human Capital and Information Technology Professionals (IJHCITP), 10(3); pages 1-19, copyright year 2019 by IGI Publishing (an imprint of IGI Global).

Chapter 88
Running with the Pack:
The Impact of Middle–Status Conformity on the Post–Adoption Organizational Use of Twitter

Thomas Mattson
University of Richmond, Richmond, VA, USA

Salvatore Aurigemma
Collins College of Business, University of Tulsa, Tulsa, OK, USA

ABSTRACT

Prior literature has utilized many theories to explain an organization's post-adoption technology use of social media platforms, but none of the common models include status as either a primary or a moderating variable. This is a significant gap in the literature because status is a structural enabler and inhibitor that determines acceptable and unacceptable behavior in a given setting. In an empirical study of Twitter and the cultural norm of retweeting for a sample of US colleges and universities, the authors demonstrate the following: (1) middle-status institutions had a higher likelihood of following the retweeting cultural norm relative to their high- and low-status counterparts, (2) middle- and low-status institutions who followed the retweeting cultural norm in a manner consistent with their status experienced greater post-adoption success relative to those institutions who did not, but the reverse was evident for high-status institutions (who appear to be rewarded for deviation from this cultural norm), and (3) the negative effect of deviating from retweeting cultural norms on post-adoption success is more pronounced with decreasing status.

INTRODUCTION

Popular external social media platforms give organizations the ability to disseminate information, to collaborate with others, to enhance worker productivity, and to build relationships with stakeholders who may have previously been unreachable (Aggarwal, Gopal, Sankaranarayanan, & Vir Singh, 2012;

DOI: 10.4018/978-1-7998-9020-1.ch088

Aral, Dellarocas, & Godes, 2013; Hemsley & Mason, 2013; Kane, Alavi, Labianca, & Borgatti, 2014). Consequently, it is now common practice for organizations in all types of industries to have a social media presence on external social media platforms (Kiron, Palmer, Phillips, & Kruschwitz, 2012; Qualman, 2013). However, many organizations have yet to tap the full potential of these platforms even though they have been widely adopted (Kane et al., 2014). This may be the case because simply choosing to adopt a social media platform is only a small step toward extracting value from the platform. The larger value for the organization is determined post-adoption whereby value is co-created through the continuous engagement by the organization and its followers (Culnan, McHugh, & Zubillaga, 2010; Prahalad & Krishnan, 2008; Stieglitz, Dang-Xuan, Burns, & Neuberger, 2014).

Similar to other technologies, each social media platform may have different cultural norms that form around features embedded in and the people using the technology (DeSanctis & Poole, 1994; Germonprez & Hovorka, 2013). Cultural norms are explicit or implicit guidelines that designate acceptable conduct within the framework of a particular group of people (Triandis, 1994). In the context of social media platforms, for instance, the following are all cultural norms: (1) how often to retweet content posted by others on Twitter, (2) when to re-pin pictures and videos on Pinterest, and (3) how frequently and when to like content on Facebook (Al-Debei, Al-Lozi, & Papazafeiropoulou, 2013; boyd, Golder, & Lotan, 2010; Hall & Zarro, 2013). Although cultural norms may form around a technical feature, the explicit and implicit guidelines for how and when the feature is used (i.e., the cultural norm) are determined by the users who are appropriating the feature (Germonprez & Hovorka, 2013).

Social media platforms are used in the public, which means that how one organization chooses to use the social media platform is influenced by how others are using the platform (boyd et al., 2010). For example, how often an organization conforms to the cultural norm of re-pinning content on Pinterest is, in part, determined based on how frequently similar organizations are conforming to the cultural norm of re-pinning. Yet, some companies knowingly or unknowingly do not follow the platform's cultural norms and following the cultural norms is not always indicative of an organization's successful or unsuccessful post-adoption use of a given social media platform. Anecdotally, it is easy to find examples of organizations across multiple industries where following the social media platform's cultural norms leads to a successful adoption of the platform and an unsuccessful adoption for others. The purpose of our paper is to theoretically and empirically investigate whether and how often organizations follow the cultural norms associated with a social media platform and whether following those cultural norms leads to greater post-adoption success.

We argue that an organization's status (i.e., hierarchical ranking of similar organizations) impacts how frequently it will follow the social media platform's cultural norms, because an organization's status helps determine what acceptable and unacceptable behavior is in a given context (Phillips & Zuckerman, 2001). We specifically hypothesize that middle-status organizations will have a higher likelihood of following the social media platform's cultural norms, because middle-status organizations have equal amounts of upside potential and downside risk and following the norms is the safest course of action (Durand & Kremp, 2016; Phillips & Zuckerman, 2001). We finally assert that organizations following the cultural norms in line with normative expectations will be more successful (ceteris paribus) relative to those who do not, because conforming to norms minimizes negative sanctions and maximizes positive rewards (Axelrod, 1986). However, we further theorize that the negative impact of deviating from the cultural norms will be greatest for low-status organizations, because it is more socially acceptable for higher status organizations to deviate from social and cultural norms (Phillips & Zuckerman, 2001;

Podolny, 2005). We provide empirical evidence supporting these theorized relationships using the Twitter platform for a sample of US colleges and universities.

SOCIAL MEDIA PLATFORMS

Consistent with prior literature (Ellison & boyd, 2013; Kane et al., 2014), we define a social media platform as having four defining characteristics: (1) the ability for users to create a unique profile, (2) the ability of users to search for digital content within the platform, (3) the ability to create relationships with others on the platform, and (4) the ability to view their connections and the connections made by others. Based on these defining characteristics, Twitter, Facebook, Weibo, and LinkedIn are all social media platforms (boyd & Ellison, 2007).

Twitter, which is the empirical context of our study, is a micro-blogging social media platform where members post short 140 character tweets (messages), reply to tweets posted by other members, reply to other members more generally, retweet (repost) content previously posted by other Twitter users, and/ or follow other members. Nodes (Twitter account holders) on the Twitter platform are both information producers and information consumers (Jansen, Zhang, Sobel, & Chowdury, 2009; Shi, Rui, & Whinston, 2014). Organizations typically use the Twitter platform to advertise their products and services (information production) and to listen to (metaphorically speaking) conversations that are happening on the platform related to their product or service offerings (information consumption) (Shi et al., 2014).[1]

The retweet has been referred to as the lifeblood of Twitter and it represents the core cultural norm associated with the platform (boyd et al., 2010; Murthy, 2013). In 2007, retweeting informally emerged without a technical feature as a cultural norm through social interactions between early Twitter adopters who were looking for unique ways to share and communicate on the Twitter platform (Helmond, 2013; Stone, 2009). A feature to support this cultural norm wasn't implemented until 2009. Retweeting is a normative expectation for Twitter users, which means users are expected to regularly find content to retweet to its followers (boyd et al., 2010; Murthy, 2013).

POST ADOPTION USE OF TECHNOLOGY AND SOCIAL MEDIA PLATFORMS

Previous research on social media platforms has primarily investigated adoption patterns (who adopted, when was it adopted, and why was it adopted) associated with these technologies at both the individual and the organizational levels (Aggarwal et al., 2012; Chau & Xu, 2012; Kane & Fichman, 2009; Koch, Gonzalez, & Leidner, 2012; Majchrzak, Wagner, & Yates, 2013; Parameswaran & Whinston, 2007; Wamba & Carter, 2014). Much has been learned from this adoption research but just adopting a social media platform is a very small component of the value proposition for organizations. It is not enough for an organization to simply have a Twitter or Facebook account. In fact, having an account on these platforms may even be detrimental for the organization if the account is not maintained and used appropriately, because value on these platforms is co-created through the continuous engagement by the organization and its followers (Culnan et al., 2010; Prahalad & Krishnan, 2008; Stieglitz et al., 2014).

Post-adoption use refers to the use practices after a technology has been adopted and implemented (Fichman & Kemerer, 1999; Zhu & Kraemer, 2005). Many theories have been used to explain the post-adoption use of a specific technology by organizations such as structuration theory (Orlikowski, 2000), adaptive structuration theory (DeSanctis & Poole, 1994), technology acceptance model (Venkatesh & Davis, 2000), expectation-confirmation theory (Bhattacherjee, 2001), institutional theory (King et al., 1994), and the resource-based view of the firm (Wade & Hulland, 2004). Across all of these theories, however, one factor that has received minimal attention is an organization's status (i.e., hierarchical ranking of similar organizations), which is an important omission because status is an organizational resource that may be leveraged to generate future returns (DiPrete & Eirich, 2006; Gould, 2002). Interestingly, in one of the original studies on adoption patterns, Rogers (1995) argued that organizational laggards or non-adopters may lose status and economic viability, which creates a contextual pressure to adopt a specific technology in order to protect its status and legitimacy. However, the post-adoption literature has largely not investigated status as a structural enabler or inhibitor in terms of how a technology (social media platforms in this case) is used post-adoption. Yet, an organization's status helps determine what acceptable and unacceptable behavior is in a given context (Phillips & Zuckerman, 2001), which may impact post-adoption use particularly on public social media platforms.

STATUS AND THE THEORY OF MIDDLE-STATUS CONFORMITY

Status is generally defined in one of two ways in the literature: (1) a social rank ordering of actors or (2) economic class distinctions between different groups (Berger, Fisek, Norman, & Zelditch Jr., 1977; Washington & Zajac, 2005). In our paper, we follow the former by defining status as the "prominence of an actor's relative position within a population of actors" (Wejnert, 2002, p. 304). In this manner, status refers to a hierarchical relationship among actors within a particular social setting (Piazza & Castellucci, 2014; Skvoretz & Fararo, 1996). Furthermore, those actors in high-status positions are awarded benefits and behavioral liberties not typically available to those actors in low-status positions (DiPrete & Eirich, 2006; Gould, 2002).

Hierarchies may be formally defined (i.e., authoritative or official rankings of law firms, colleges and universities, and hospitals) or informally defined (i.e., networks or clusters of firms with informal linkages) (Washington & Zajac, 2005; Wejnert, 2002). In this paper, we are theoretically interested in status within formal hierarchies, because these hierarchies are published by authoritative sources within an industry and are widely known by a variety of institutional stakeholders across industries (Washington & Zajac, 2005). It is important to note, however, that an organization's formal status may or may not be determined based on prior performance or the quality of the institution (George, Dahlander, Graffin, & Sim, 2016; Jensen & Roy, 2008; Washington & Zajac, 2005). In the field of academia, for instance, a college may have a reputation as being a diploma mill but have a relatively high formal status.

The theory of middle-status conformity postulates that there is an inverted U-shaped relationship between status and the likelihood of following social, cultural, and societal norms (Blau, 1960; Dittes & Kelley, 1956; Phillips & Zuckerman, 2001). This means that middle-status actors are expected to follow norms more than their high- and low-status counterparts, because middle-status actors have a degree of uncertainty in terms of possibly moving up or down within the social order, which makes following the norms the safest course of action (Blau, 1960). Contrarily, low-status and high-status actors have less pressure to conform to norms due to their structural position within the social hierarchy (Dittes & Kelley, 1956). Low-status actors have less at stake to conform to norms because actors in this status group are typically excluded regardless of whether they conform to or deviate from behavioral expectations (Durand & Kremp, 2016; Phillips & Zuckerman, 2001). High-status actors are typically comfortable in their position in the social hierarchy, so they feel more at ease deviating from the norms (Hollander, 1958). We assert that the theory of middle-status conformity is applicable to the post-adoption use of social media platforms, because the social penalties for non-conformity in terms of creating negative viral messages or simply being ignored can be particularly severe on large social media platforms such as Twitter and Facebook (boyd & Ellison, 2007). Moreover, the theory of middle-status conformity offers a parsimonious and effective explanation for when and why certain organizations conform to or deviate from norms in a variety of settings based on the presumed risk tolerance of firms in relation to status reduction (Durand & Kremp, 2016).

RESEARCH HYPOTHESES

There is a tension between attempting to establish distinctiveness by acting differently versus conforming to the practices of others (Durand & Kremp, 2016; Navis & Glynn, 2011). On the one hand, organizations have a desire to act similarly in order to establish legitimacy with peers and competitors, which protects them from being negatively perceived in the marketplace (Durand & Kremp, 2016; Phillips & Zuckerman, 2001; Scott, 2008). On the other hand, however, differentiation (or legitimate distinctiveness among peers and competitors) is one potentially important source of competitive advantage that cannot come from conforming to the practices of others (Durand & Kremp, 2016; Navis & Glynn, 2011). We propose that this tension coupled with an organization's status in the marketplace is an important factor in determining whether an organization will conform to the norms on a social media platform, because low-, middle-, and high-status organizations have different presumed risk profiles associated with non-conformity.

We argue that high-status organizations have less of a need to follow the cultural norms associated with the social media platform (i.e., retweeting on Twitter, liking on Facebook, re-pinning on Pinterest, and so on), because high-status organizations can withstand external criticism if they are perceived to be appropriating the platform in a non-normative manner (Hollander, 1958). For example, in the field of academia, a high-status institution such as Harvard or Yale bears minimal risk of losing status as a result of being criticized for not abiding by the cultural norms associated with the social media platform. New York University (NYU), for instance, received criticism for being a late adopter of social media and for not following the cultural norms associated with the social media platforms that they did adopt (Taylor, 2008). Yet, NYU did not have any noticeable reduction in their status.

We also expect low-status organizations to have a reduced likelihood of following the cultural norms associated with the social media platform but for different reasons. Low-status organizations have minimal downside risk because they are already at the bottom of the social hierarchy (Phillips & Zuckerman, 2001). In the field of academia, for example, for-profit schools are generally ranked at the bottom or excluded by many ranking institutions. Yet, it is important for these institutions to establish legitimacy within the field of academia, because employers are seeking graduates from legitimate academic institutions (Wellen, 2006) and being considered illegitimate for an extended period of time will hurt their chances of survival (Durand & Kremp, 2016). One way for a low-status institution to establish legitimacy within the field of academia is by being distinct and the reduced downside risk enables low-status firms to engage in distinctive actions. On Twitter, for example, it is not uncommon for these institutions to not engage in or to minimally engage in the typical interactive norms of mentioning and retweeting content posted by others.

Middle-status organizations, however, are unique in the sense that they are mired in the middle. Therefore, we argue that these organizations will have a higher likelihood of following the cultural norms associated with the social media platform, because these organizations have to balance the risk of losing status with potentially gaining status (Blau, 1960; Dittes & Kelley, 1956; Phillips & Zuckerman, 2001). In researching this potential relationship, we informally spoke to the social media staff at a middle-status bank and a middle-status US university. Both of these organizations were very concerned about using Twitter and Facebook in a manner that could potentially exclude them from possibly becoming grouped with higher status peers.[2] The downside risk due to non-conformity was more important to both of these organizations than attempting to use the platform in a distinctive manner. Therefore, we hypothesize the following curvilinear relationship:

H1: Middle-status organizations will follow the cultural norms associated with the social media platform more than their high- and low-status counterparts (see Figure 1).

Figure 1. Hypothesis 1

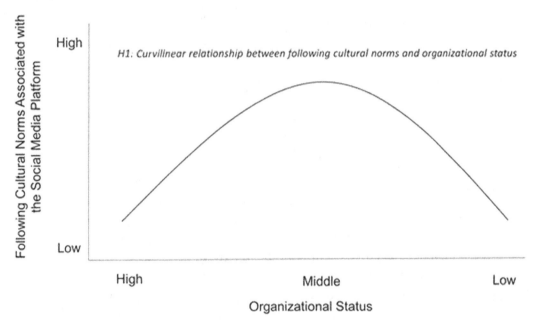

Whether following the cultural norms is a more or less productive strategy depends, in part, on whether the enforcement of the cultural norms by the community leads to better or worse outcomes. For example, if the Facebook community rewards organizations who adhere to the normative use of the "Like" cultural norm with greater attention and punishes organizations that do not conform to the normative use of the 'Like' cultural norm with less attention, then organizations will have a higher likelihood of adhering to the "Like" cultural norm. This is consistent with rational choice theory, which suggests compliance with social and cultural norms is a utility maximizing strategy because organizations will not knowingly engage in behaviors that attract punishments (Rommetveit, 1968; Thibaut & Kelley, 1986). In this manner, conforming to social and cultural norms minimizes negative sanctions and maximizes positive rewards (Axelrod, 1986). On Twitter, for instance, if an organization is not retweeting content in line with normative expectations, then one sanction is that the community will not retweet the organization's tweets or mention the organization in future posts (i.e., it will be less successful at having its content 'trend'). As such, we hypothesize the following:

H2: Ceteris paribus, organizations who follow the social media platform's cultural norms in line with normative expectations will have greater post-adoption success relative to those organizations who do not.

However, this effect may not be consistent for high-, middle-, and low-status organizations. Status hierarchies tend to be stable at the higher end of the social structure, which means that high-status organizations have more freedom to deviate from behavioral norms without fear of decreasing in status (Dittes & Kelley, 1956; Phillips & Zuckerman, 2001). In many industries, high-status firms maintain their place in the hierarchy by being distinct and are typically rewarded by exhibiting this type of legitimate distinctiveness, but this is often not the case for middle- and low-status institutions (Durand & Kremp, 2016; Navis & Glynn, 2011; Podolny, 1993). Additionally, communities may be looking for reasons to criticize lower status institutions (Phillips & Zuckerman, 2001). For example, in the field of academia higher status not-for-profit institutions rarely pass up an opportunity to criticize their lower status for-profit counterparts. As such, we hypothesize the following moderating relationship:

H3: Ceteris paribus, the negative impact of deviations from the social media platform's cultural norms on post-adoption success will be more pronounced with decreasing status.

RESEARCH DESIGN AND METHODS

We empirically tested our hypotheses using a sample of tweets and re-tweets on the Twitter platform in calendar year 2012 for a sample of US colleges and universities. We investigated US colleges and universities and the Twitter platform for several reasons. First, retweeting as a cultural norm has been well established within the Twitter platform prior to 2012 (boyd et al., 2010; Murthy, 2013). Second, irrespective of the status of the institution, US colleges and universities are both information consumers as well as information producers on the Twitter platform. Third, US colleges and universities regularly retweet content posted by other Twitter users on a variety of topics and their tweets are regularly retweeted by others, so these institutions and their followers are active participants related to the cultural norm of retweeting. Finally, using a single context in a single country allows us to control for differences in audience preferences between institutions. The followers of different US colleges and universities on Twitter are similar in the sense that they are typically students, employees, alumni, or other institutional stakeholders. Although differences may exist between institutions, we have no reason to believe the followers of, for instance, Michigan State University are significantly different from the followers of the University of North Carolina.

In order to determine our sample and the 'formal' status of US colleges and universities, we used the 2012 US News and World Report rankings. Although many different published rankings exist, the US News and World Report publication is considered the authoritative source, the one that most typically appears in general marketing materials, is relatively stable from year to year, and has been referred to as the "granddaddy of college rankings" (Chisolm, 2010, p. para 1). However, many US colleges and universities vehemently complain that the rankings are biased. Notwithstanding these complaints, whether this ranking is based on prior performance, institutional quality, institutional age, enrollments, or endowment size is not relevant to our study, because we are not theoretically interested in the source of an institution's formal status. This list provides an authoritative source in terms of the hierarchal ranking of one college relative to another college using a consistent methodology (irrespective of any systematic biases). Furthermore, institutions are acutely aware of their standing on this list.

The US News and World Report publishes many different categories of rankings. In our study, we used the general national ranking category, which lists US colleges and universities who offer a full collection of undergraduate majors, master's degrees, and Ph.D. programs. We used one category within the US News and World Report's list in order to get a ranking of schools using the same ratings criteria for each institution. Of the 281 schools in the published rankings in the general national ranking category in 2012, 8 were removed because they did not adopt Twitter in calendar year 2012. For the remaining 273 schools, we went to each institution's home webpage and found their primary Twitter account.

We have two dependent variables in our study: (1) how frequently an institution retweets content posted by other Twitter users (H1) and (2) how frequently an institution's tweets are retweeted by others plus how frequently an institution is mentioned by others (H2 and H3). Prior literature has established the retweet as a core cultural norm (since 2007) associated with Twitter whereby there is a normative expectation that Twitter users will retweet previously posted content (boyd et al., 2010; Murthy, 2013). Using the Twitter API, we counted the number of tweets that were retweets that each US college or university had in calendar year 2012. Given that some institutions adopted the platform during 2012, we standardized these counts by the number of months that an institution was active in order to facilitate comparisons.

The second dependent variable is a proxy for post-adoption success. Success on Twitter is determined by active engagement of its followers (Culnan et al., 2010; Hemsley & Mason, 2013; Prahalad & Krishnan, 2008), which is determined based on how many times a user's tweets get retweeted and how many times a user is mentioned by others (Bruns & Stieglitz, 2013). Together, these two measures determine how much buzz an organization is creating on the platform. Mentions capture how frequently the community is discussing the account (the organization) and retweets capture the spread of a specific tweet (the content). These two are inter-related and success or buzz on the platform is a function of both metrics. Using the Twitter API, we counted the number of times that a tweet posted by a US college or university was retweeted by another Twitter user and how many times each institution was mentioned by another Twitter user in calendar year 2012. We then standardized these values based on institutional followership due to significant follower differences between institutions.

Hypothesized Independent Variables

The status of each institution was determined using the aforementioned published 2012 rankings. We then grouped institutions into status clusters of 25. US News and World Report only publishes the continuous rankings of the top 200 institutions in the general national ranking category. The remaining institutions are clustered into either a "ranked not published" or "unranked" cluster of schools, making the use of continuous scale not feasible. Clustering in groups of 25 was chosen as opposed to, say, groups of 20 or 30, because of the significance and prevalence of the 'top 25' marketing tactic used in admission's advertising in the field of academia. Using this approach, the relative ranking of the 'ranked not published' group is number 9 and the unranked cluster of schools is status group 10.[3] Using these ten status groups, status groups 4 (75-100), 5 (101-125), and 6 (126-150) are mathematically and conceptually in the middle relative to the other institutions in our sample. We then mean centered the ten status groups in order to reduce the variance inflation factors associated with testing the squared term.

To measure how far an institution deviated from the retweeting cultural norm based on the status of the institution, we first estimated the number of times an institution in each status group was expected to retweet content posted by other Twitter users. To do this, we used the model that was used to estimate the frequency of retweeting (see Model 3 in Table 4 in the results section) using the group means for each control variable and the reference posting platform for each status group. We then did a simple subtraction between each institution's actual number of retweets per month active and the calculated baseline for each status group.[4] This difference may be negative (retweeting less than expectations for their status group), positive (retweeting more than expectations for their status group), or zero (retweeting in line with expectations for their status group). We, however, are only hypothesizing about how far an institution deviates from normative expectations. Whether the institution is over- or under-following cultural norms is not relevant to our hypotheses, so we took the absolute value of the difference. Table 1 displays the descriptive statistics for all hypothesized independent and dependent variables.

Context Specific Control Variables

We control for the following possible alternative explanations: (1) number of tweets per day, (2) average number of hashtags used per tweet[5], (3) number of followers[6], (4) number of Twitter users an institution is following, (5) the primary platform each institution used to post its tweets, (6) the size of the institution, (7) reciprocity, and (8) tweet content. The first five control variables were determined using data elements from the Twitter API. Firm size was determined by the published 2012 enrollment figures. For reciprocity, we conservatively assume that all retweeting activity is the result of reciprocal behavior, because we do not have the Twitter handles for all of the retweets in our sample. To do this, we calculated a ratio of the number of retweets and the number of tweets that were retweeted by others. For example, if an institution retweeted 50 posts and had 100 of its tweets retweeted by others, then we assume that 50% of all retweeting behaviors is the result of reciprocity, which is obviously an overstatement.

Determining tweet content involved two steps. We first identified tweet topics and then counted the frequency of tweets in each topic. In order to identify tweet topics, we sampled the most popular tweets from 30 schools (three from each status group) and conducted an iterative content analysis involving multiple researchers grouping logically related tweets. The result was five topical categories (see Table 2).

We then coded the top 5 tweets that were retweeted by other Twitter users for each institution against these five topical categories.[7] We coded 50 of these tweets together to refine the process and then independently coded a sample of the same 100 tweets to assess inter-rater reliability, which resulted in a simple Cohen's Kappa value of 0.85. The remaining tweets were divided between two coders. After the coding was completed, we counted the number of tweets in each category for each institution. Table 2 displays the category counts and Table 3 displays the descriptive statistics for all other control variables.

Table 1. Descriptive Statistics for Hypothesized Independent Variables & Dependent Variables

Status Group[1]	US News & World Report Rank		Sample Size	Expected Number of Retweets (Per Active Month)			Absolute Value Deviation From Cultural Norm[5]		Tweets that were Retweets		Months Active		Tweets that were retweets / Months Active		Tweets Retweeted by Other Twitter Users		Mentions		Number of Followers		Post-Adoption Success	
				Estimated Avg[2]	Alt Estimated Avg[3]	Simple Avg[4]	Avg	S.D.	Avg	S.D.	Avg	S.D.	Avg	S.D.	Avg	S.D.	Avg	S.D.	Avg	S.D.	Avg	S.D.
-4.8	1	25	26	13.5	16.0	17.6	15.4	15.7	187.8	227.1	10.8	2.3	18.5	21.2	5,316	6,046	880	607	35,858	46,444	21.2	12.8
-3.8	26	50	22	16.2	20.6	21.2	18.9	17.0	281.8	264.7	11.2	2.3	25.0	23.9	3,743	4,783	832	509	17,170	14,757	29.1	18.0
-2.8	51	75	25	18.7	24.5	21.4	15.2	13.1	167.1	189.7	11.1	2.7	16.9	19.8	5,713	13,035	569	527	20,321	16,546	24.5	18.5
-1.8	76	100	22	20.7	26.9	18.4	27.5	36.0	179.6	351.7	10.3	3.2	24.5	45.2	2,638	3,200	524	462	14,194	15,871	24.3	16.4
-0.8	101	125	29	22.0	27.3	20.4	24.3	32.4	245.2	258.2	9.7	3.5	30.9	39.8	2,633	3,117	688	620	12,993	11,511	29.1	18.1
0.2	126	150	18	22.5	25.5	21.5	30.1	33.4	252.8	212.3	8.9	3.9	37.7	42.4	3,173	5,608	738	574	12,778	12,531	30.6	22.5
1.2	151	175	27	22.1	22.1	19.5	19.2	17.2	166.6	195.4	10.9	1.8	18.0	25.3	1,987	2,418	557	559	8,980	8,558	27.6	21.7
2.2	176	200	26	20.8	17.6	18.6	15.1	6.6	149.1	173.6	11.4	1.8	12.8	14.3	1,090	1,056	297	323	5,858	3,883	25.8	21.3
3.2	Ranked Not Published		66	18.9	13.0	23.3	15.1	21.2	142.1	140.1	10.6	3.0	16.0	25.7	1,345	1,581	342	401	5,003	3,684	31.3	20.5
4.2	Unranked		12	16.4	8.8	8.6	12.2	4.3	53.6	73.6	9.7	3.0	5.7	6.4	455	840	440	554	3,702	4,952	26.4	24.6

[1]The status group was grand mean centered for the status groupings (1 to 10) of all 273 institutions in the sample. That is why the status group variable is not a simple count from 1 (high-status) to 10 (low-status).

[2]We used the results from Model 3 in Table 4 using the group means for all control variables and the reference group platform in order to estimate the expected average.

[3]This alternative estimate was calculated using the status only model (Model 2 in Table 4).

[4]For each status group, we took the average of each institution's actual retweets per month active instead of using the results from Models 2 or 3.

[5]This column is based on the first estimated average values column in this table.

Table 2. Frequency of Content Category by Status Group

	Mean Centered Status										
	-4.8	**-3.8**	**-2.8**	**-1.8**	**-0.8**	**0.2**	**1.2**	**2.2**	**3.2**	**4.2**	**Total**
Sports	25	33	32	31	51	16	40	43	80	1	352
Community Activities	10	20	22	16	16	14	18	16	59	25	216
Campus Life	39	26	24	19	37	28	42	42	103	10	370
Administrative	11	6	23	19	17	17	18	14	56	9	190
Academia & Scholarship	45	25	24	25	24	15	17	15	23	11	224

Table 3. Descriptive Statistics for the Control Variables by Status Group

Mean Centered Status	Followers[v]		Following[v]		Tweets Per Day		Hashtag Use Per Tweet		Enrollment[v]		Reciprocity		# of Institutions whose Primary Posting Platform is		
	Avg	S.D.	Avg	S.D.	Avg	S.D.	Avg	S.D.	Avg	S.D.	Avg	S.D.	Twitter	Prof Mgt Apps	Other
-4.8	35,858	46,444	1,128	1,505	3.79	1.72	0.44	0.39	17,213	9,593	0.07	0.09	9	17	0
-3.8	17,170	14,757	2,093	2,463	3.49	1.61	0.49	0.26	22,190	15,186	0.15	0.15	16	6	0
-2.8	20,321	16,546	1,946	2,993	2.93	1.56	0.46	0.45	29,213	15,214	0.06	0.09	12	12	1
-1.8	14,194	15,871	1,008	2,375	2.40	2.28	0.76	1.33	18,637	12,085	0.13	0.19	15	5	2
-0.8	12,993	11,511	1,105	1,539	2.87	1.59	0.66	0.44	18,997	10,476	0.16	0.16	15	12	2
0.2	12,778	12,531	1,861	3,330	3.11	1.49	0.43	0.32	23,352	15,228	0.17	0.16	8	8	2
1.2	8,980	8,558	2,290	4,402	2.94	2.00	0.37	0.28	18,973	12,498	0.15	0.19	13	13	1
2.2	5,858	3,883	1,016	2,363	2.38	1.53	0.48	0.39	16,662	8,709	0.18	0.22	12	10	4
3.2	5,003	3,684	870	1,374	2.24	1.55	0.39	0.30	16,659	9,901	0.20	0.23	32	26	8
4.2	3,702	4,952	671	644	1.75	1.74	0.53	0.40	41,643	82,927	0.35	0.33	5	4	3

[v]In the data models, we took the natural log of these values due to excessive deviations from normality.

RESULTS

We used negative binomial regression models to analyze our non-negative count dependent variables, because a negative binomial is particularly appropriate when count data are over- or under-dispersed and do not contain an excessive number of zeroes (Cameron & Trivedi, 2013), which is the case with both of our dependent variables. In each reported model, the negative binomial dispersion parameter was estimated by maximum likelihood using a log link function. For the hypothesized independent variables, all variance inflation factors (VIFs) were below 2. The content type control variables had VIFs between 10.0 and 20.4, but all other control variables were below 3.5. Therefore, we ran all models with and without the content type control variables and the results were not materially different, so these variables were included in the final analyses. An outlier analysis revealed no data points had undue influence on the results.

Following Cultural Norm of Retweeting Models

The model used to test Hypothesis 1 is the following:

$$Y = \exp\left(\beta_0 + \beta_1(\text{Mean Centered Status}) + \beta_2(\text{Mean Centered Status})*(\text{Mean Centered Status}) + \beta_c\mathbf{X}_c\right)$$

where Y is the standardized count of the number of tweets that were retweets and $\mathbf{X}_c$ is the vector of control variables. The results for these models are reported in Table 4.

Model 1 tests a linear relationship between the status of the institution and the frequency that an institution retweeted content previously posted by other users of the platform. In this model, the linear status coefficient is significant and negative, which suggests that higher-status institutions have a higher likelihood of retweeting content relative to their middle- and low-status counterparts. However, Model 2 tests a curvilinear relationship between the status of the institution and the frequency that an institution retweeted content previously posted by other users of the platform. Model 2 is a better fit than the linear model (Model 1) and the mean centered status squared term is highly significant. As shown in Table 5, the inverted-U in Model 2 peaks at institutions rated 101 to 125 and in Model 3 peaks at institutions rated 126 to 150 (assuming average values for all control variables), which are the middle-status institutions in our sample. Therefore, the proposed H1 curvilinear relationship is supported.

Control Variables (for H1)

The statistical significance of the control variables reveals some interesting effects. First, institutions posting tweets directly on the Twitter platform instead of via other social media platforms such as Facebook or professional social media management applications such as Sprout Social or Hoot Suite have an increased likelihood of following the cultural norm of retweeting. The use of professional social media management applications may distance organizations from directly interacting with participants on the social media platform, which may impede understanding and appropriately following of the platform's cultural norms. Second, the more hashtags that an institution uses per tweet decreases the likelihood that an institution will follow the cultural norm of retweeting. This may be the case because an institution may be focused on finding and re-using hashtags instead of finding previously posted content to retweet. Third, the more followers an institution had and the more times an institution's tweets were retweeted by others (reciprocity), the more likely that the institution was to follow the norm of retweeting.

Robustness Check on H1 Conclusions

We ran all negative binomial models testing H1 clustering the US colleges and universities in groups of 20 (Models 7-9) and groups of 30 (Models 4-6) in order to ensure that our results were not due to our decision to group the institutions in status groups of 25. In all instances, the curvilinear models were the best fit using the AIC measure of model fit, the apex of each curve peaked between institutions ranked from 101 to 125 or from 126 to 150, and the direction (sign) and statistical significance of all coefficients were the same. Therefore, the curvilinear relationship is not due to how we clustered the institutions in our sample.

Table 4. Models Testing the Following Cultural Norms Hypothesis

	Status Groups of 25			Status Groups of 30[v]			Status Groups of 20[v]		
	Model 1	Model 2	Model 3	Model 4	Model 5	Model 6	Model 7	Model 8	Model 9
Intercept	2.99***	3.26***	0.61	2.99***	3.26***	0.58	2.99***	3.26***	0.69
Status[1]	-0.06**	-0.09***	0.02	-0.07**	-0.09***	0.02	-0.05**	-0.07***	0.01
Status*Status[2]		-0.04***	-0.03***		-0.05***	-0.03***		-0.02***	-0.02***
Platform (Twitter Reference Group)									
Other			-1.15***			-1.13***			-1.15***
Professional			-0.35***			-0.35***			-0.36***
Tweets Per Day			0.26***			0.26***			0.27***
Avg. Hashtags Per Tweet			-0.36**			-0.35**			-0.36**
ln(Followers)			0.28***			0.28***			0.28***
ln(Following)			0.06			0.06			0.06
ln(Enrollment)			0.04			0.04			0.03
Reciprocity			3.07***			3.08***			3.08***
Number of Tweets about:									
Sports			-0.34*			-0.34*			-0.34*
Community Activities			-0.28			-0.28			-0.28
Campus Life			-0.44**			-0.44**			-0.44**
Administrative			-0.34*			-0.35*			-0.35*
Academia & Scholarship			-0.26			-0.27			-0.26
Dispersion[3]	1.40	1.35	0.83	1.40	1.35	0.83	1.40	1.35	0.83
Model Details[4]									
Scaled Deviance	311.73	310.34	290.30	311.68	310.30	290.35	311.77	310.36	290.34
Degrees of Freedom (DFs)	271	270	257	271	270	257	271	270	257
(Scale Deviance) / (DFs)	1.15	1.15	1.13	1.15	1.15	1.13	1.15	1.15	1.13
AIC	2180	2172	2046	2180	2171	2047	2180	2172	2047

* Significant at 0.1, ** Significant at 0.05, ***Significant at 0.01; [v]Clustering in status groups of 5, 10, and 15 yield the same pattern of results as the three status groups reported in this table.

[1]We mean centered the status variable in all models. That is why the status group variable is not a count from 1 (high-status) to 10 (low-status)...[2]The squared term is the mean centered status variable squared...[3]The negative binomial dispersion parameter was estimated by maximum likelihood for each model...[4]All models were specified using a negative binomial distribution and a log link function.

Table 5. Expected Retweeting Frequency By Firm Status (Models 2 and 3)

	Mean Centered Status									
	1 to 25	26 to 50	51 to 75	76 to 100	101 to 125	126 to 150	151 to 175	176 to 200	Ranked not published	Unranked
	-4.8	-3.8	-2.8	-1.8	-0.8	0.2	1.2	2.2	3.2	4.2
Expected Retweeting Frequency Model 2	16.0	20.6	24.5	26.9	27.3	25.5	22.1	17.6	13.0	8.8
Expected Retweeting Frequency Model 3[v]										
Twitter Platform	13.5	16.2	18.7	20.7	22.0	22.5	22.1	20.8	18.9	16.4
Other Platform	4.4	5.8	7.2	8.4	9.3	9.6	9.4	8.7	7.5	6.2
Professional Management Applications	9.7	12.8	16.0	18.7	20.6	21.4	21.0	19.3	16.8	13.7

[v]These values were derived using the averages across the entire sample for each control variable.

Deviations from Cultural Norms and Successful Post-Adoption Models

The model used to test H2 and H3 is the following:

$$Y = \exp(\beta_0 + \beta_1(\text{Deviation From Cultural Norm}) + \beta_2(\text{Mean Centered Status}) + \beta_3(\text{Deviation From Cultural Norm})*(\text{Mean Centered Status}) + \beta_c X_c)$$

where Y is the standardized count of the number of tweets retweeted by other Twitter users plus the number of mentions by other Twitter users and X_c is a vector of control variables. The results for these models are reported in Table 6.

The main effects model (Model 10) shows evidence supporting the conjecture that greater deviations from normative expectations leads to decreased post-adoption success. However, Model 11 reveals that the effect is qualified by organizational status (see Table 7). The effect of greater deviations from following the cultural norm of retweeting is positive for institutions ranked 1 to 25, 26 to 50, and 51 to 75, which means that high-status institutions are rewarded with greater follower engagement by not retweeting content in line with normative expectations. This effect is reversed for institutions ranked greater than 75 whereby greater deviations from following the cultural norm of retweeting results in less follower engagement. Therefore, the main effect proposed in H2 is only supported for middle- and low-status institutions.

The effect of deviations from following the cultural norm of retweeting is greater for low-status firms relative to high- and middle-status firms (see 'difference row' in Table 7). The community is punishing low-status institutions with fewer retweets and mentions for not following the cultural norm of retweeting in line with expectations more than the community is punishing high- and middle-status firms. The effect of status is greater for larger deviations from following the cultural norm of retweeting relative to smaller deviations (see 'difference column' in Table 7). Along with the statistically significant interaction effect in Model 11, Model 11 is a better fit than Model 10, which supports H3.

Control Variables (for H2 & H3)

Institutions posting more tweets about sports, campus life, and general administrative topics were more likely to have those tweets retweeted by others. Interestingly, institutions posting tweets via professional social media management applications had no effect on the likelihood of having its tweets retweeted on the platform. This is interesting because many of these platforms have proprietary algorithms that are supposed to increase the likelihood of those tweets being retweeted by others, but this does not appear to be the case with our data. The more hashtags that an institution uses per tweet on average results in an increased likelihood of having its tweets retweeted by others. This makes logical sense because the use of hashtags makes the tweets more findable by others on the platform.

Table 6. Models Testing Post-Adoption Success Hypotheses

	Status Groups of 25						Status Groups of 30[v]			Status Groups of 20[v]		
	Model 10	Model 11	Model 12	Model 13	Model 14	Model 15	Model 16	Model 17	Model 18	Model 19	Model 20	Model 21
Intercept	1.72**	1.74**	1.71**	1.69**	1.71**	1.65**	1.73**	1.69**	1.76**	1.71**	1.68**	1.73**
Deviation From Cultural Norm:												
Estimated from Full Models[1]	-0.005***	-0.007***					-0.007***			-0.008***		
Estimated from Status Only Models[2]			-0.005***	-0.007***				-0.007***			-0.007***	
Average[3]					-0.005**	-0.006***			-0.008***			-0.008***
Status[4]	0.02	0.06***	0.02	0.05**	0.02	0.05**	0.07***	0.05**	0.09***	0.06***	0.05**	0.07***
(Deviation From Cultural Norm)*(Status)		-0.003***		-0.002*		-0.002*	-0.003**	-0.002	-0.004***	-0.002**	-0.002**	-0.003***
Tweets Per Day	0.02	0.02	0.02	0.02	0.02	0.02	0.02	0.02	0.02	0.02	0.02	0.02
Average Hashtags Per Tweet	0.28**	0.30***	0.28**	0.29***	0.29**	0.30***	0.30***	0.29***	0.30***	0.30***	0.29***	0.31***
ln(Following)	0.03	0.02	0.02	0.02	0.03	0.02	0.02	0.02	0.01	0.02	0.02	0.009
ln(Enrollment)	0.03	0.02	0.02	0.02	0.02	0.02	0.03	0.02	0.03	0.04	0.02	0.03
Reciprocity	0.54**	0.46**	0.54**	0.50**	0.53**	0.49**	0.47**	0.49**	0.31	0.47**	0.47**	0.30
Platform (Twitter Reference Group)												
Other	-0.38***	-0.37**	-0.39**	-0.40**	-0.39**	-0.40**	-0.37**	-0.40**	-0.35**	-0.36**	-0.40**	-0.35**
Professional	0.11	0.12	0.11	0.10	0.10	0.10	0.11	0.10	0.12	0.11	0.11	0.12
Number of Tweets About:												
Sports	0.23**	0.23**	0.23**	0.24**	0.23**	0.25**	0.22*	0.25**	0.24**	0.21**	0.25**	0.23**
Community Activities	0.09	0.10	0.10	0.11	0.10	0.12	0.09	0.11	0.10	0.08	0.11	0.11
Campus Life	0.24**	0.26**	0.25**	0.27**	0.24**	0.27**	0.24**	0.27**	0.27**	0.23**	0.27**	0.28**
Administrative	0.23**	0.24**	0.23**	0.25**	0.23**	0.25**	0.23**	0.25**	0.25**	0.22**	0.25**	0.25**
Academia & Scholarship	0.12	0.14	0.13	0.14	0.13	0.14	0.13	0.15	0.15	0.12	0.15	0.15
Dispersion[5]	0.40	0.39	0.40	0.40	0.40	0.40	0.39	0.40	0.39	0.39	0.39	0.38
Model Details[6]												
Scaled Deviance	297.60	296.21	297.56	296.54	297.62	296.59	296.45	296.68	296.13	296.23	296.29	295.97
Degrees of Freedom (DFs)	258	257	258	257	258	257	257	257	257	257	257	257
(Scaled Deviance) / (DFs)	1.15	1.15	1.15	1.15	1.15	1.15	1.15	1.15	1.15	1.15	1.15	1.15
AIC	2289	2284	2290	2288	2291	2289	2286	2288	2279	2283	2285	2277

* Significant at 0.1, ** Significant at 0.05, ***Significant at 0.01; [v]Clustering in status groups of 5, 10, and 15 yielded the same pattern of results as the three status groups reported in this table (with the interaction effect significant at least at the 0.1 level). The main effects only models for status groups 20 and 30 are not reported in this table due to space limitations, but the interaction effect models all had better model fit statistics than the main effect only models.

[1]The baseline for each status group was calculated using the full models (Model 3 for status groups of 25, Model 6 for status groups of 30, and Model 9 for status groups of 20) using the group means for each control variable and the reference group platform...[2]The baseline for these deviation from norm values were calculated using the status only models (Model 2 for status groups of 25, Model 5 for status groups of 30, and Model 8 for status groups of 20) instead of the full models with all of the control variables...[3]The baseline for these deviation from norm values were calculated using a simple average of the actual retweets per month active for each institution in each status group...[4]The status variable was mean centered in all models. That is why the status group variable is not a simple count from 1 (high-status) to 10 (low-status)...[5]The negative binomial dispersion parameter was estimated by maximum likelihood for each model...[6]All models were specified using a negative binomial distribution and a log link function.

Table 7. Interaction Between Status & Deviation From Cultural Norm of Retweeting (Model 11)

Deviation From Norm	Mean Centered Status										Difference Column
	1 to 25	26 to 50	51 to 75	76 to 100	101 to 125	126 to 150	151 to 175	176 to 200	Ranked not published	Unranked	
	-4.8	-3.8	-2.8	-1.8	-0.8	0.2	1.2	2.2	3.2	4.2	
0	21.7	23.1	24.5	26.0	27.6	29.3	31.2	33.1	35.1	37.3	-15.6
10	23.4	24.1	24.9	25.6	26.4	27.2	28.0	28.9	29.8	30.7	-7.3
20	25.2	25.2	25.2	25.2	25.2	25.2	25.2	25.2	25.2	25.2	0.0
30	27.1	26.3	25.6	24.8	24.1	23.4	22.7	22.0	21.4	20.7	6.4
40	29.2	27.5	25.9	24.4	23.0	21.7	20.4	19.2	18.1	17.0	12.2
50	31.5	28.8	26.3	24.0	22.0	20.1	18.3	16.8	15.3	14.0	17.5
Difference Row	-9.8	-5.7	-1.8	2.0	5.6	9.2	12.9	16.3	19.8	23.3	

These estimates assume average values for all control variables and the reference platform as the primary posting platform.

Robustness Checks on H2 & H3 Conclusions

We made two study design decisions that may impact the results: (1) clustering institutions in status groups of 25 and (2) using the full models from the first set of negative binomials to determine normative expectations for retweeting content for each status group. As such, to test the robustness of our findings, we ran models using different methods for measuring deviations from the cultural norm of retweeting and different clusters of institutions. We calculated normative expectations using two alternative methods: (1) using the status only models (Model 2 in Table 4) instead of the full model (Model 3 in Table 4) and (2) using a simple average of the actual retweets per month active for each institution in each status group. Models using these two alternative definitions and clustering institutions in groups of 25 are reported as Models 12-15 in Table 6. All models yield the same pattern of results, but the interaction effect is only significant at the 0.1 level.

We then clustered institutions in groups of 20 and 30 and ran models using all three operational definitions of the deviations from following the cultural norm of retweeting variable for each clustering. These results are report as Models 16-21 in Table 6. In all cases, the primary operational definition yielded a highly significant interaction effect with the same sign as reported in clusters of 25. The results for the alternative operational definitions were the same in all models except in Model 17 (status clusters of 30 and using status only models to determine normative expectations) where the interaction effect dropped out of significance. Therefore, with the exception of one model, our results are robust to alternative operational definitions and different status clusters.

DISCUSSION AND CONCLUSION

Our data analysis yielded several important and interesting insights. First, middle-status institutions have a higher likelihood of following the cultural norm of retweeting content previously posted by others on Twitter relative to their high- and low-status counterparts. Second, following the cultural norms is a more productive strategy for middle- and low-status institutions but not for high-status institutions. The Twitter community is rewarding high-status institutions for deviating from the cultural norms rather than following the cultural norms. Finally, low-status institutions are punished by the Twitter community for not following the cultural norm of retweeting in line with expectations more than high- and middle-status institutions.

The main practical ramification of our study is that organizations should know their place in the formal hierarchy and act accordingly when using public social media platforms. Doing so may encourage an environment where its followers will be more likely to spread information (retweet content previously posted by the US college or university and/or mention the organization) throughout the network. As such, managers should understand the social positioning of their organization and the cultural norms associated with the specific social media platforms when interacting on these platforms. Acting appropriately based on the organization's formal status increases the chances of successful post-adoption usage. Knowing one's place in the formal social hierarchy is often easier said than done for organizations, because organizations are often delusional or in denial of their actual status in the formal hierarchy. For example, administrators of US colleges and universities consistently try to group themselves with higher ranked institutions instead of accepting their actual position and behaving accordingly. Our study suggests that managers need to recognize their actual placement in the formal hierarchy and not their idealized placement in the formal status hierarchy.

Additionally, we found that organizations who mostly used professional social media management applications (such as Hoot Suite and Sprout Social) were less likely to follow the cultural norm of retweeting (across all status groups) relative to organizations who posted their content directly on Twitter. In our Twitter dataset, US colleges and universities who used these professional social media management applications had no statistically significant impact on their post-adoption success, which was operationalized as having the organization's tweets retweeted by other Twitter users and an organization being mentioned by other Twitter users. Based on a sampling of marketing materials, professional social media management platforms proffer to increase the likelihood that a tweet will be retweeted based on their proprietary algorithms. In our sample, however, we do not find any statistically significant effect of using one of these platforms. This is contrary to the findings reported by Risius and Beck (2015) who demonstrate the positive effects of social media management tools. From a practical perspective, this means organizations should be cautious in terms of not over relying on these algorithms to manage each platform. While these services may provide other benefits besides getting messages to trend and spread throughout the social media platform, our data do not show any correlation between post-adoption success and the use of professional social media management applications. The use of professional social media management applications does, however, distance organizations from directly interacting with participants on the social media platform, which may impede understanding and appropriately following of the platform's cultural norms.

Our primary theoretical contribution is to demonstrate the importance of status to the post-adoption use of public social media platforms, specifically the applicability of the theory of middle-status conformity. Status is an important variable to include in the post-adoption literature for the following reasons: (1) status is a structural enabler and inhibitor (Phillips & Zuckerman, 2001; Podolny, 1993; Washington & Zajac, 2005), (2) status is an organizational resource that may be leveraged to generate future returns (DiPrete & Eirich, 2006; Gould, 2002), and (3) status helps determine acceptable and unacceptable behavior in a given social setting (Phillips & Zuckerman, 2001). Therefore, future research investigating the post-adoption of public social media platforms should, at a minimum, control for the effect of status.

Like all research, our research has its limitations. First, we only investigated a single industry within a single country, but previous research might suggest cultural differences in the use of social media platforms (specifically Twitter) (Pentina, Zhang, & Basmanova, 2013; Yin, Feng, & Wang, 2015). It might be possible that the cultural context of the institution mediates or moderates the relationships we reported in this paper. Several context extensions are necessary and provide interesting future lines of research in order to maximize (and to test) the generalizability of our findings. Second, our empirical investigation used the Twitter social media platform. Social media platforms have unique users, cultural norms, and different success metrics (Hughes, Rowe, Batey, & Lee, 2012), so future empirical work is necessary. We, however, are generalizing to theory not to a population (Lee & Baskerville, 2003) in our paper. Third, institutions may go through many different stages of post-adoption use of a social media platform and our study assumes all institutions are at more or less the same stage of use. Success, however, may be defined differently depending on the stage of post-adoption use. For example, initial post-adoption success on Twitter may be accumulating followers whereas a later measure of post-adoption success may be mentions and retweets. In our study, we control for this by standardizing mentions and retweets per followers, but an interesting future study may be to conduct a longitudinal analysis of tweeting based on different post-adoption stages with different metrics at each stage.

Fourth, we theoretically and empirically investigated formal status and not informal status. It is possible that informal status among colleges and universities has a complementary impact on following the cultural norms and post-adoption success. Therefore, an interesting future research project may add informal status to our research model or substitute formal status with informal status to investigate those effects. Finally, Shi and colleagues (2014) demonstrate that network ties impact the likelihood of retweeting content on the Twitter platform, but we did not have the data to test these effects in our models. Future research can investigate the network level effects in conjunction with the status effects on the likelihood of following cultural norms and post-adoption success.

REFERENCES

Aggarwal, R., Gopal, R., Sankaranarayanan, R., & Vir Singh, P. (2012). Blog, Blogger, and the Firm: Can Negative Employee Posts Lead to Positive Outcomes. *Information Systems Research*, 23(2), 306–322. doi:10.1287/isre.1110.0360

Al-Debei, M. M., Al-Lozi, E., & Papazafeiropoulou, A. (2013). Why People Keep Coming Back to Facebook: Explaining and Predicting Continuance Participation from an Extended Theory of Planned Behaviour Perspective. *Decision Support Systems*, 55(1), 43–54. doi:10.1016/j.dss.2012.12.032

Aral, S., Dellarocas, C., & Godes, D. (2013). Social Media and Business Transformation: A Framework for Research. *Information Systems Research*, 24(1), 3–13. doi:10.1287/isre.1120.0470

Axelrod, R. (1986). An Evolutionary Approach to Norms. *The American Political Science Review*, 80(4), 1095–1111. doi:10.2307/1960858

Berger, J., Fisek, M. H., Norman, R. Z., & Zelditch, M. Jr. (1977). *Status Characteristics and Social Interaction*. New York: Elsevier.

Bhattacherjee, A. (2001). Understanding Information Systems Continuance: An Expectation-Confirmation Model. *Management Information Systems Quarterly*, *25*(3), 351–370. doi:10.2307/3250921

Blau, P. M. (1960). Patterns of Deviation in Work Groups. *Sociometry*, *23*(3), 245–261. doi:10.2307/2785889

boyd, d. m., & Ellison, N. B. (2007). Social Network Sites: Definition, History, and Scholarship. *Journal of Computer-Mediated Communication, 13*(1), 210-230.

boyd, d. m., Golder, S., & Lotan, G. (2010). Tweet, Tweet, Retweet: Conversational Aspects of Retweeting on Twitter. *Paper presented at the HICSS-43*, Kauai, HI.

Bruns, A., & Stieglitz, S. (2013). Towards More Systematic Twitter Analysis: Metrics for Tweeting Activities. *International Journal of Social Research Methodology*, *16*(2), 91–108. doi:10.1080/13645 579.2012.756095

Cameron, A. C., & Trivedi, P. K. (2013). *Regression Analysis of Count Data* (2nd ed.). New York, NY: Cambridge University Press. doi:10.1017/CBO9781139013567

Chau, M., & Xu, J. (2012). Business Intelligence in Blogs: Understanding Consumer Interactions and Communities. *Management Information Systems Quarterly*, *36*(4), 1189–1216.

Chisolm, A. C. (2010). US News Best Colleges Rankings 2011: Changes in Methodology Make Them Less Helpful!

Culnan, M. J., McHugh, P. J., & Zubillaga, J. I. (2010). How Large U.S. Companies Can Use Twitter and Other Social Media to Gain Business Value. *MIS Quarterly Executive*, *9*(4), 243–259.

DeSanctis, G., & Poole, M. S. (1994). Capturing the Complexity in Advanced Technology Use: Adaptive Structuration Theory. *Organization Science*, *5*(2), 121–147. doi:10.1287/orsc.5.2.121

DiPrete, T. A., & Eirich, G. M. (2006). Cumulative Advantage as a Mechanism for Inequality: A Review of Theoretical and Empirical Developments. *Annual Review of Sociology*, *32*(1), 271–297. doi:10.1146/ annurev.soc.32.061604.123127

Dittes, J. E., & Kelley, H. H. (1956). Effects of Different Conditions of Acceptance Upon Conformity to Group Norms. *Journal of Abnormal and Social Psychology*, *53*(1), 100–107. doi:10.1037/h0047855 PMID:13345577

Durand, R., & Kremp, P.-A. (2016). Classical Deviation: Organizational and Individual Status as Antecedents of Conformity. *Academy of Management Journal*, *59*(1), 65–89. doi:10.5465/amj.2013.0767

Ellison, N. B., & boyd, d. m. (2013). Sociality through Social Network Sites. In W. H. Dutton (Ed.), *The Oxford Handbook of Internet Studies* (pp. 151-172). Oxford, United Kingdom: Oxford University Press.

Fichman, R. G., & Kemerer, C. F. (1999). The Illusory Diffusion of Innovations: An Examination of Assimilation Gaps. *Information Systems Research*, *10*(3), 255–275. doi:10.1287/isre.10.3.255

George, G., Dahlander, L., Graffin, S. D., & Sim, S. (2016). Reputation and Status: Expanding the Role of Social Evaluations in Management Research. *Academy of Management Journal*, *59*(1), 1–13. doi:10.5465/amj.2016.4001

Germonprez, M., & Hovorka, D. S. (2013). Member Engagement within Digitally Enabled Social Network Communities: New Methodological Considerations. *Information Systems Journal, 23*(6), 525–549. doi:10.1111/isj.12021

Gould, R. V. (2002). The Origins of Status Hierarchies: A Formal Theory and Empirical Test. *American Journal of Sociology, 107*(5), 1143–1178. doi:10.1086/341744

Hall, C., & Zarro, M. (2013). Social Curation on the Website Pinterest.com. In *Proceedings of the American Society for Information Science and Technology, 49*(1), 1–9.

Helmond, A. (2013). On Retweet Analysis and a Short History of Retweets.

Hemsley, J., & Mason, R. M. (2013). Knowledge and Knowledge Management in the Social Media Age. *Journal of Organizational Computing and Electronic Commerce, 23*(1-2), 138–167. doi:10.1080/109 19392.2013.748614

Hollander, E. P. (1958). Conformity, Status, and Idiosyncrasy Credit. *Psychological Review, 65*(2), 117–127. doi:10.1037/h0042501 PMID:13542706

Hughes, D. J., Rowe, M., Batey, M., & Lee, A. (2012). A Tale of Two Sites: Twitter vs. Facebook and the Personality Predictors of Social Media Usage. *Computers in Human Behavior, 28*(2), 561–569. doi:10.1016/j.chb.2011.11.001

Jansen, B. J., Zhang, M., Sobel, K., & Chowdury, A. (2009). Twitter Power: Tweets as Electronic Word of Mouth. *Journal of the American Society for Information Science and Technology, 60*(11), 2169–2188. doi:10.1002/asi.21149

Jensen, M., & Roy, A. (2008). Staging Exchange Partner Choices: When Do Status and Reputation Matter. *Academy of Management Journal, 51*(3), 495–516. doi:10.5465/AMJ.2008.32625985

Kane, G. C., Alavi, M., Labianca, G. J., & Borgatti, S. P. (2014). What's Different About Social Media Networks? A Framework and Research Agenda. *Management Information Systems Quarterly, 38*(1), 275–304. doi:10.25300/MISQ/2014/38.1.13

Kane, G. C., & Fichman, R. G. (2009). The Shoemaker's Children: Using Wikis for Information Systems Teaching, Research, and Publication. *Management Information Systems Quarterly, 33*(1), 1–17.

King, J. L., Gurbaxani, V., Kraemer, K. L., McFarlan, F. W., Raman, K. S., & Yap, C. S. (1994). Institutional Factors in Information Technology Innovation. *Information Systems Research, 5*(2), 139–169. doi:10.1287/isre.5.2.139

Kiron, D., Palmer, D., Phillips, A. N., & Kruschwitz, N. (2012). Social Business: What Are Companies Really Doing? *MIT Sloan Management Review.*

Koch, H., Gonzalez, E., & Leidner, D. (2012). Bridging the work/social Divide: The Emotional Response to Organizational Social Networking Sites. *European Journal of Information Systems, 21*(6), 699–717. doi:10.1057/ejis.2012.18

Lee, A. S., & Baskerville, R. L. (2003). Generalizing Generalizability in Information Systems Research. *Information Systems Research, 14*(3), 221–243. doi:10.1287/isre.14.3.221.16560

Majchrzak, A., Wagner, C., & Yates, D. (2013). The Impact of Shaping on Knowledge Reuse for Organizational Improvement with Wikis. *Management Information Systems Quarterly*, *37*(2), 455–469.

Murthy, D. (2013). *Twitter: Social Communication in the Digital Age*. Cambridge: Polity Press.

Navis, C., & Glynn, M. A. (2011). Legitimate Distinctiveness and the Entrepreneurial Identity: Influence on Investor Judgments of New Venture Plausibility. *Academy of Management Review*, *36*(3), 479–499.

Orlikowski, W. J. (2000). Using Technology and Constituting Structures: A Practice Lens for Studying Technology in Organizations. *Organization Science*, *11*(4), 404–428. doi:10.1287/orsc.11.4.404.14600

Parameswaran, M., & Whinston, A. B. (2007). Research Issues in Social Computing. *Journal of the Association for Information Systems, 8*(6), 336-350.

Pentina, I., Zhang, L., & Basmanova, O. (2013). Antecedents and Consequences of Trust in a Social Media Brand: A Cross-Cultural Study of Twitter. *Computers in Human Behavior*, *29*(4), 1546–1555. doi:10.1016/j.chb.2013.01.045

Phillips, D. J., & Zuckerman, E. W. (2001). Middle-Status Conformity: Theoretical Restatement and Empirical Demonstration in Two Markets. *American Journal of Sociology*, *107*(2), 379–429. doi:10.1086/324072

Piazza, A., & Castellucci, F. (2014). Status in Organization and Management Theory. *Journal of Management*, *40*(1), 287–315. doi:10.1177/0149206313498904

Podolny, J. M. (1993). A Status-Based Model of Market Competition. *American Journal of Sociology*, *98*(4), 829–872. doi:10.1086/230091

Podolny, J. M. (2005). *Status Signals: A Sociological Study of Market Conditions*. Princeton: Princeton University Press.

Prahalad, C. K., & Krishnan, M. S. (2008). *The New Age of Innovation: Driving Co-Created Value Through Global Networks*. New York: McGraw Hill.

Qualman, E. (2013). *Socialnomics: How Social Media Transforms the Way We Live and Do Business* (2nd ed.). Hoboken, NJ: John Wiley & Sons, Inc.

Risius, M., & Beck, R. (2015). Effectiveness of corporate social media activities in increasing relational outcomes. *Information & Management*, *52*(7), 824–839. doi:10.1016/j.im.2015.06.004

Rogers, E. M. (1995). *Diffusion of Innovation*. New York: Free Press.

Rommetveit, R. (1968). *Social Norms and Roles*. Oslo: Universitetsforlaget.

Scott, W. R. (2008). *Institutions and Organizations: Ideas and Interests*. Los Angeles: Sage.

Shi, Z., Rui, H., & Whinston, A. B. (2014). Content Sharing in a Social Broadcasting Environment: Evidence from Twitter. *Management Information Systems Quarterly*, *38*(1), 123–142. doi:10.25300/MISQ/2014/38.1.06

Skvoretz, J., & Fararo, T. J. (1996). Status and Participation in Task Groups: A Dynamic Network Model. *American Journal of Sociology*, *101*(5), 1366–1414. doi:10.1086/230826

Stieglitz, S., Dang-Xuan, L., Burns, A., & Neuberger, C. (2014). Social Media Analytics. *Business & Information Systems Engineering*, 6(2), 89–96. doi:10.100712599-014-0315-7

Stone, B. (2009). Project Retweet: Phase One.

Taylor, A. (2008). *Old Thinking Permeates Major Journalism School.*

Thibaut, J. W., & Kelley, H. H. (1986). *The Social Psychology of Groups*. New York: Wiley.

Triandis, H. C. (1994). *Culture and Social Behavior*. New York: McGraw-Hill, Inc.

Venkatesh, V., & Davis, F. D. (2000). A Theoretical Extension of the Technology Acceptance Model: Four Longitudinal Field Studies. *Management Science*, 46(2), 186–204. doi:10.1287/mnsc.46.2.186.11926

Wade, M., & Hulland, J. (2004). The Resource-Based View and Information Systems Research: Review, Extension, and Suggestions for Future Research. *Management Information Systems Quarterly*, 28(1), 107–142.

Wamba, S. F., & Carter, L. (2014). Social Media Tools Adoption and Use by SMES: An Empirical Study. *Journal of Organizational and End User Computing*, 26(2), 1–17. doi:10.4018/joeuc.2014040101

Washington, M., & Zajac, E. J. (2005). Status Evolution and Competition: Theory and Evidence. *Academy of Management Journal*, 48(2), 282–296. doi:10.5465/AMJ.2005.16928408

Wejnert, B. (2002). Integrating Models of Diffusion of Innovations: A Conceptual Framework. *Annual Review of Sociology*, 28(1), 297–326. doi:10.1146/annurev.soc.28.110601.141051

Wellen, A. (2006, July 30). Degrees of Acceptance. *The New York Times*.

Yin, J., Feng, J., & Wang, Y. (2015). Social Media and Multinational Corporations' Corporate Social Responsibility in China: The Case of ConocoPhillips Oil Spill Incident. *IEEE Transactions on Professional Communication*, 58(2), 135–153. doi:10.1109/TPC.2015.2433071

Zhu, K., & Kraemer, K. L. (2005). Post-Adoption Variations in Usage and Value of E-Business by Organizations: Cross-Country Evidence from the Retail Industry. *Information Systems Research*, 16(1), 61–84. doi:10.1287/isre.1050.0045

ENDNOTES

[1] Individuals may use these platforms for different purposes, but our focus is on how organizations use Twitter and other social media platforms.

[2] A cursory investigation of the tweets and Facebook activity of both institutions revealed a very similar pattern of re-tweeting and Facebook liking with several of their middle-status peer institutions.

[3] Each status group may not have an equal number of schools in it due to ties in the rankings and how US News & World Report lumps schools into the last two status groups. Therefore, the 'middle' in our sample is not simply 273/2. The middle is determined based on the relative ranking of the

status groups. We ran several robustness checks to ensure that our results were not due to how we were clustering the schools (see robustness checks sub sections in the results section).

[4]   We considered other options for measuring deviation from norms such as using the grand mean across all 10 status groups, but using the grand mean loses the fact that the normative expectations are different for each status group. We also considered further clustering the institutions into three groups (high-, medium-, and low-status groups), but we have no solid justification to group the institutions different for each part of the study and the three categorical groupings would be quite arbitrary.

[5]   A hashtag is a metadata tag prefixed with a "#" in order to group related tweets.

[6]   The number of followers is a component of the second dependent variable so this control is only used in the H1 models.

[7]   These represented 107,878 out of the 120,397 total tweets that were retweeted in our sample.

This research was previously published in the Journal of Organizational and End User Computing (JOEUC), 30(1); pages 23-43, copyright year 2018 by IGI Publishing (an imprint of IGI Global).

Chapter 89
Ethical Dilemmas Associated With Social Network Advertisements

Alan D. Smith
Robert Morris University, USA

Onyebuchi Felix Offodile
Kent State University, USA

ABSTRACT

A significant amount information can be relayed on Facebook, MySpace, and Twitter, but the question remains whether or not organizations are using this to their advantage, especially in the era of big data. The present study used a sample of working professionals that were knowledgeable in the various options of social networking to test these assumptions. The three hypotheses dealt with the interplay of online social networking, advertising effectiveness, gender and age trends, and remaining the interplay with positive comments of the use of the "like" function and its impacts on consumer behavior, as derived from the review of relevant operations literature and from applying the basic tenants of uses and gratification theory. All three specific research hypotheses were accepted in the null form.

INTRODUCTION

Popularity of Social Media, Branding, and Consumer Tribalism

Social networking systems are relatively new to our society and clarification on certain aspects of the system can be obtained through further research. There are many positive aspects of social networks, such as Facebook, that organizations could benefit from including stronger CRM-embedded techniques. On the-other-hand, questions are raised as to whether or not an organization who advertises on social networking systems experiences an increase in sales as a result. It is unclear whether or not these advertisements actually deter individuals from further using these types of social networking systems. If

DOI: 10.4018/978-1-7998-9020-1.ch089

individuals who spend a large amount of time on social networking sites are deterred from further usage due to these advertisements, are there any benefits to them? An increasing number of individuals are utilizing social networking sites, such as Facebook on a daily basis. As Taylor, Lewin, and Strutton (2011) pointed out, both Facebook and Twitter reported an increase in users in the triple digits in 2009. Founded in 2004 by Mark Zuckerberg, Facebook's mission is to "give people the power to share and make the world more open and connected" (Facebook). Facebook began by being exclusive to college students only, but through the years has opened memberships up to everyone over the age of 13 with an email address. Facebook helps people stay connected with friends and family, learn what is happening around them, as well as share moments. Fernandez (2009) noted that a recent study found that 35% of all adults, 75% of adults in the range of 18-24 years old, and 65% of teenagers utilize a social networking site. It has been noted that individuals have increased their time spent on these sites. Social networking sites can be categorized as web-enabled services that engage users to create and maintain openly or partially open profiles, create and update preferred list of users that they want to personalize connections with, and view and interact their list of preferred connections with other lists within the networking system (Greenhow, 2011). Under the recent congressional hearings that concluded April 11, 2018 concerning Mark Zuckerberg's testimony on privacy violations of Facebook data, renewed scrutiny on the public value of social media platforms have surfaced. Much of the publicity surrounding Cambridge Analytica, a political data mining enterprise hired by President Trump's 2016 election campaign, illegally gained access to private information on more than 50 million Facebook users via offering tools that could identify the personalities of American voters and influence their voting behavior (Granville, 2018). That number of affected Facebook users was updated to over 80 million. Recent trend involving fake news and questionable ads have rekindled a debate if social platforms are really a force for good, but can be used to undermine democratic societies.

Social network sites allow consumer to interact and enhance self-expression and self-presentation. One tool to achieve enhancement is self-expression via brands. Hence, consumer with greater social network influence may be more likely to express themselves via brands. Brands are an extension of the consumer's self-concept, allowing consumers to express and define them. Brands enable consumers to become a part of a group membership. Tribes facilitated collective social actions within members of the group. Brands offer more than the product itself, they offering value through self-expression and linking value. This paper aims to examine brand loyalty and word-of-mouth (WOM) as an outcome of self-expression tribal consumption.

Existing literature suggest that self-expressing brands positively affect WOM and brand loyalty and improve brand success. Yet, little is known about the relationship between the role of the brand for the self and consumers' purchase motivation. In addition, little is also known about consumer tribes and their influence on consumer behavior. Brand-supporting consumer tribes reflect a strategic resource for brand managers. A tribe refers to a loose network of heterogeneous persons who share passion and emotions for a product. Such groups of empowered consumers boost brand loyalty through creating exit barriers. Additionally, WOM is also considered to be an outcome of tribal membership. Brand passion enhances relationships within the tribe and increases information sharing. Tribe members tend to evangelize the brand to others. However, due to the loose connection, consumer tribes are short-living. This paper explores the influence of tribal membership on WOM and brand loyalty. This study analyzed the influence of reference groups on self-expressive brands because the role of reference groups on tribal behavior towards brands is not fully understood. Further, the research focuses on the influence of online social networks on the susceptibility to interpersonal influence (SUSCEP). Finally, the paper examines the impact of SUSCEP and SNI on consumers' self-expressive brand consumption and brand tribalism.

Brands act as an enabler for consumers to express themselves through creating meaningful association and help them to reinforce their self-concept. The motivation of expressing oneself is often the stimulus that influences the purchase decision. "Self-expressive brands reward consumers with certain social benefits that allow them to enhance their self-concept, make a social impression and display the group they belong to" (Ruane & Wallace, 2015, p. 334). Consumer tribalism refers to the connectedness of consumers to brands. Brand tribalism are networks of social micro-groups with shared emotional links, a common sub-culture and a vision of life. This paper considers the influence of consumer tribes and examines their influence on brand choices of their members.

The results show that SUSCEP and SNI had a positive effect on self-expressive brands as well as brand tribalism. Hence, there was a positive impact of self-expressive brands on brand tribalism, brand loyalty and WOM. In contrast, there was a negative relationship between brand tribalism and both brand loyalty and WOM. Ruane and Wallace (2015) provided evidence that consumers who are more influenced by others brand choices are more likely to choose more self-expressive brands. Hence, SUSCEP drives tribal membership as consumers who seek self-expression engage on social network sites are more likely to consume self-expressive brand as well as are part of consumer tribes. In contrast to previous research, it was demonstrated that consumers express greater brand tribalism when they have a high motivation for self-expression and engagement on social network sites. Further, they discovered that tribe members were less loyal and practiced less WOM. In contrast, self-expressive brand users who are not part of a consumer tribe were the loyalist and have offered the most WOM. Consumer tribes may not be loyal to a specific brand. It is more likely that the members are loyal to the group.

Such research efforts illustrate to manager of self-expressive brand how important other consumers are on an individual's consumer decision and that social media campaigns have an effect on consumption. Managers should also be aware of the fact that consumers may not be loyal to the brand rather to the tribe they are a part of. To increase brand loyalty and WOM, they should consider brand endorsers. Lastly, managers should be aware of the different types of consumers and should be able to separate them according to their needs. There are two main types of consumers, those who use a brand for differentiation and those who use their brand to belong to a group.

Corporate Social Responsibility

Essentially, the goal of every firm is to maintain viability through long-run profitability. Until all costs and benefits are accounted for, however, profits may not be claimed. In the case of Corporate Social Responsibility (CSR), costs and benefits are both economic and social. While economic costs and benefits are easily quantifiable, social costs and benefits are not. Managers therefore risk subordinating social consequences to other performance results that can be more straightforwardly measured. The dynamic between CSR and success (as measured in profits) is complex. While one concept is clearly not mutually exclusive of the other, it is also clear that neither is a prerequisite of the other. Rather than viewing these two concepts as competing, it may be better to view CSR as a component in the decision-making process of business that must determine, among other objectives, how to maximize profits.

Social responsibility is a broad and encompassing term that can be broken down in to a number of responsibilities. Economic responsibilities are the duty of managers, as agents of the company owners, to maximize stockholder wealth. Legal responsibilities are the firm's obligations to comply with the laws that regulate business activities. Ethical responsibilities are the strategic managers' notion of right and proper business behavior. Discretionary responsibilities are the responsibilities voluntarily assumed by a business, such as public relations, good citizenship, and full corporate responsibility.

In addition to a commonsense belief that companies should be able to "do well by doing good," at least three broad trends are driving businesses to adopt CSR frameworks: the resurgence of environmentalism, increasing buying power, and the globalization of business. The most prevalent forms of environmentalism are efforts to preserve natural resources and eliminating pollution, often referred to as the concern for "greening". Consumers are becoming more interested in buying products from socially responsible companies. There has also been a dramatic increase in the number of people interested in supporting socially responsible companies through their investments. It is difficult enough to come to a consensus on what constitutes socially responsible behavior within one culture, let alone determine common ethical value across cultures.

The rise of the consumer movement has meant that buyers – consumers and investors – are increasingly flexing their economic muscle. Consumers are becoming more interested in buying products from socially responsible companies. Organizations such as the Council on Economic Priorities (CEP) help consumers make more informed buying decisions through such publications as *Shopping for a Better World*, which provides social performance information on 191 companies making more than 2,000 consumer products. CEP also sponsors the annual Corporate Conscience Awards, which recognize social responsible companies. One example of consumer power at work is the effective outcry over the deaths of dolphins in tuna fisherman's nets.

Investors represent a second type of influential consumer. There has been a dramatic increase in the number of people interested in supporting socially responsible companies through their investments. Membership in the Social Investment Forum, a trade association serving social investing professionals, has been growing as a rate of about 50 percent annually. As baby boomers achieve their own financial success, the social investing movement has continued its rapid growth. For example, firms such as ice cream maker Ben & Jerry's have successfully argued that CSR and profits do not clash; their stance was that doing good lead to making good money, too. Managed properly, CSR programs can confer significant benefits to participants to participation in terms of corporate reputation; in terms of hiring, motivation, and retention; and as a means of building and cementing valuable partnerships. The benefits extend well beyond the boundaries of the participating organizations, enriching the lives of many disadvantages communities and individuals and pushing back on problems that threaten future generations, other species, and precious natural resources.

Research suggests that such single-minded devotion to CSR may be unrealistic for larger, more established corporations. Companies need to view their commitments to corporate responsibility as one important part of their overall strategy but not let the commitment obscure their broad strategic business goals. A balance has to be reached however, because if the broad strategic goals of a business do not follow what is expected of a corporation's social responsibility, the response can be very negative. While some corporations may have gotten away with past discrepancies, advances in technology have changed not only the competitive landscape but the landscape in which companies are looked at from under a microscope. CSR strategies can also run afoul of the skeptics, and the speed with which information can be disseminated via the web – and accumulated in web logs – makes this an issue with serious ramifications for reputation management.

Implementing CSR-embedded programs have some promotional barriers to overcome as for all their resources and capabilities, corporations will face growing demands for social responsibility contributions far beyond simple cash or in-kind donations. Aggressive protesters will keep the issues hot, employees will continue to have their say, and shareholders will pass judgment with their investments – and their votes.

Perhaps, many of the recent mergers and acquisitions by Internet and mobile technology industry leaders are at least partially geared to control these corporate images and reputations. Figure 1 highlights some of these features that social networking providers are concentrating on promoting in order to attract and retain customers (e.g., advertising promotions, market segmentation and targeting, open and semi-secured communications, promoting newer forms of communication technologies and mobile applications) through a more ethical viewpoint.

Figure 1. Conceptual framework for present study dealing with social networking

Purpose of Study

The purpose of this study is to determine whether or not social networking advertisements should continue to be utilized by organizations. Social networking systems are relatively new to our society and clarification on certain aspects of the system can be obtained through further research. Questions are raised as to whether or not an organization who advertises on social networking systems experiences an increase in sales as a result. This paper will explore the following three issues surrounding social networking advertisements: Do advertisements used on social networking systems deter individuals from using these sites? Do consumer purchases increase as a result of social networking advertisements? Is the "like" function on organizations' Facebook pages being utilized to the full extent and influential in consumer behavior?

BACKGROUND

Advertising Promotion

Companies are realizing that social network advertisements are an easy way to reach their target market and get promotional information to consumers quickly. In general, online advertisements are a cost-effective way for organizations to get information about their products or services to the community. "Online advertising reduces costs, increases efficiency, provides more flexibility and as a global medium, the Internet enables buyers and sellers to interact and manage business transactions" (Alijani et al, 2010, p.1). Todor (2016) examined the current strategies of marketing that are being used to target consumers in the current market by comparing traditional print marketing such as magazines, newspapers, and billboards in comparison to the more modern use of digital marketing. What is the best way to reach consumers and create a campaign that create new customers, as well as maintaining loyal customers? What is right combination of both digital and traditional marketing?

Digital marketing, commonly known as online marketing, Internet marketing, and/or Web marketing, is considered to be the targeted, measurable, and interactive marketing methods used to reach customers through a type of digital technology in order to create and maintain customers for either a good or service (Todor, 2016). Inbound marketing, while similar to digital marketing, is a more embedded marketing tool. Inbound marketing is when a company promotes it products or services through a blog, eBook, video, social media campaign, and podcasts. Digital and inbound marketing have many advantages in terms how and when they reach the consumer. Digital marketing comes with many advantages as well as some disadvantages. One large advantage to digital marketing is that it is more cost efficient. When digital marketing campaigns are deployed on websites that generate traffic on their own, the cost to market on this website is much lower than it would be to use a marketing strategy that requires the campaign to drive its own traffic. The cost advantage also closely ties into the advantage that web can reach an unlimited number of consumers, whether the campaign be driven worldwide or locally.

An advantage to digital marketing is that the online user is generally in control of their exposure to the ad. This allows the user to turn off the ad if they are not interested, which reduces the chance that the ad will become associated with annoyance rather than a positive opinion. User-controlled exposure is also great because it allows the consumer to immediately pursue the product being marketed to them. A significant advantage over traditional marketing is that digital marketing has is that it is easily changed. Digital marketing can be adaptable almost immediately and either displayed or taken down with a matter of minutes. This is great for situations such as marketing sports championship apparel. Companies like Dick's Sporting Goods immediately switched their marketing from saying they had Pittsburgh Penguins Eastern Conference Championship memorabilia to Pittsburgh Penguins Stanley Cup Champion memorabilia. Lastly, digital marketing can be made personal, or be directly at very distinct groups of people. This way the marketing budget is spent on those consumers who are the most likely to become or remain loyal customers. With advantages, come disadvantages and digital marketing has a few significant ones to control. A large disadvantage to digital marketing is the risk of copyright infringement. Marketing campaigns can easily be copied or be falsely created in order to defraud customers.

Digital marketing is not always as successful, is with products that consumers are still interested in seeing in person, touching, experiencing prior to making the actual purchase. This is a great disadvantage because there is no way for digital marketing to recreate the physical sensations require to eliminate this part of the purchasing process. There may be significant distrust in the conduction business over the Internet by many consumers. Distrust effects the success of digital marketing because many people, particularly those who have had negative experiences previously and those from older generations are still not willing to purchase online. Many people are skeptical of anything online that is too "personal" and may be deterred by marketing strategies that are to tailored to them or that require them to make a purchase online using electronic payment. As digital marketing evolves the advantages will become greater, as the disadvantages are mended through new technological advances.

The underlying assumption brand loyalty goes beyond the name of a particular brand and the type of media that serves to promote it. A general definition of brand as being a frame of mind towards a particular perceived notion of loyalty in general. As suggested by Yee and Sidek (2008), although their research was related to brand loyalty among sports apparel manufacturers, brand loyalty can come in the form of loyalty towards the notion of the product or what the product symbolizes. This can include a lifestyle, such as the subculture of those who identify with a particular brand, as well as what implications the brand has on the subculture. Identifying with a brand based on the attributes the brand is merely a preference for that type of product and the values that the product instill upon the user. Loyalty towards the specific brand carry over into the lifestyle of the user and the identity that the user can establish with the brand as it relates to the subculture of the users of that brand.

Amine (1998) suggests that brand loyalty has two main approaches: the behavioral approach is that repeat purchases over time expresses their loyalty to the brand, and; the attitude assumes that it must be complimented with a positive attitude towards the brand to ensure that the behavior will be further pursued. This suggests that behavior and attitude are both functions of brand loyalty. Image is a key determinant in the lifestyle selection among a subculture group. Displaying the correct image to your peers relies on the brand selected in a continuous pattern, as a form of social acceptance. Prestigious brand names and their associated images promote repeat purchases if the subculture feels that these brands and images portray the desired attitude towards the lifestyle of the group, linking the emotional and self-expressive benefits for differentiation Cadogan and Foster (2000) suggested that differentiation, as it relates to those outside the group, are key factors of inclusion by the group. This creates an image of the consumer that can relate to the consumer tribe who views the brand as a symbol of the subculture; hence differentiating the consumer from those outside the subculture as evident from the divisiveness of social media platforms that emphasizes people identify with their unique characteristics and not overall inclusiveness.

Other attributes include quality, price, store environment, promotion, and service quality, usually do not apply when the brand loyalty is generated from lifestyle choices of the subculture. If these attributes were more of a key factor of social acceptance within the subculture, the subculture lifestyle would reflect a more consumer conscious attitude, thus defeating the rebellious nature of the group. It is important to acknowledge that image is an important aspect of choice in brand loyalty, especially when choice of selection relates to subcultures. Many typical attributes that the general consumer feels are vital are less important when peer pressure is involved. Quality is a key determinant to brand loyalty and should be an important factor when making a choice, whereas image may not be as important as other attributes. However, many consumers feel that image is vital when brand loyalty is selected, making the consumer appear to be one of the followers instead of having value-seeking qualities, especially on many social media platforms. If the attributes suggested for the factors that influence consumers' brand loyalty towards a specific brand created positive relationships that encourage brand loyalty, marketers would have a better understanding of what creates brand loyalty. This seems to be not quite the revelation that one would expect based on the notion that hedonic principles suggest that more pleasure is desirable as opposed to less pleasure.

Todor (2016) explored the value in the advantages of traditional marketing, as well as the disadvantages that are holding it back from being a superior choice for brands. Traditional marketing is categorized as marketing delivered through tangible items such as print ads from newspapers or magazines, business cards, commercials delivered through radio or television, billboards, posters, and brochures. Traditional marketing however is not limited to these examples as it includes anything that is not considered to be digital marketing. Traditional marketing is its ability to produce fast results. Traditional marketing ads that are placed well for their targeted audience often have the ability to reach the audience faster than digital marketing which could take a few weeks to reach the audience. An example of this is with sales flyers. A store that displays its sales flyers in the entrance is more likely to reach the audience than they would if they only posted their flyer digital online. The other main advantage listed is trust. With so much mistrust and misuse online, traditional marketing is generally more widely accepted by those who are skeptical of digital marketing. Traditional marketing reduces many opportunities for fraud to occur making it a safer option for consumers.

The ultimate recommendation is to find a balance between the use of traditional marketing and digital marketing. While consumers are increasingly becoming more involved with the internet and often exposed to digital marketing, traditional marketing still has much to offer in order to balance the advantages and disadvantages of both strategies. Todor (2016) suggested that many believe that digital marketing is overtaking traditional marketing, however others believe that the balance is essential and currently very much in place.

Target Market Segmentation

In addition to being cost effective, Schroeder (2004) explains that companies have found that online advertisements were able to reach a large audience when no other form of advertisement does; during work hours. Individuals who work in an office setting during the day spend the majority of their day in front of the computer rather than watching television. Online advertisements are a way for organizations to reach a larger percentage of their target market. Ankeny (2011) explores how organizations including movie theaters, restaurants and photographers do this. It is not just about putting advertisements on their own Facebook page; it is about reaching out to the individuals that they consider part of their target market. Advertising within these social networking systems is unique due to the fact that the majority of the information used to qualify an organization's target market is often times readily available on their consumers' personal webpages. For example, Ankeny (2011) pointed out that a photographer targeted females who were 24-30 years old with their profiles indicated as being engaged. Ankeny (2011) indicated that this individual became one of the busiest photographers in their local area as their target market was successfully reached through the use of social networking sites.

Open Communication and Technologies

In order to clarify what affect social networking advertisements have, we must first explore the reasons why these sites, such as Facebook and Twitter, are so popular. Ankeny (2011) explains that one reason for the sites' popularity is because they allow open communication between individuals as well as with organizations. Ankeny (2011) outlined that today's society is more geared towards open communication between consumers and businesses rather than the latter guessing what their consumers want. Social networks allow companies to not only compete with other companies that are located down the road from them, but also with ones that are located across the country. "Users desire social interaction and connectivity and disclosing information plays an essential role; yet users may not wish to have their information publicly accessible to unknown parties" (Bateman, Pike, & Butler, 2010, p. 79).

Operational and Big Data Applications

The emergence of networked businesses through social media and the associated analytics has dramatically enhanced the volume, variety, and velocity of information available to management. This relatively recent trend is often referred to the emergence of big data. Big data analytics (BDA), if properly organized, can result in many positive (Mateen & More, 2013; Nobari, Khierkhah, & Hajipour, 2018; Park & Min, (2013) as negative outcomes. Positive outcomes can influence business productivity and growth, which are the key drivers of organization usage of BDA. In terms of operational and supply chain management (SCM) that has recently received much attention is the collection of digitally enabled interfirm processes. The basic issue at hand is how the emergence of BDA can positively affect the productivity and enhanced customer benefits from tapping into this wealth of transactional and personal information through data mining activities. In general, performance impacts of BDA may not produce the transactional and relational information that can be drawn from other SCM systems (Rajapakshe, Dawande, & Sriskandarajah, 2013; Rajeev, Rajagopal, & Mercado, 2013; Senthilmurugan, Jegadheesan, & Devadasan, 2018). Since the operational, tactical and strategic information are generally shared across all of the supply chain there is a greater need for business to rationalize the transactional and relational information that can be collected.

The types of operational that are readily available from BDA are typically classified as asset productivity, business growth, and environmental dynamism (Chen, Preston, & Swink, 2015). The functionality of dynamic capabilities is likely to be common and similar BDA technologies that can be obtained in the open market. Based on the logic of opportunity, dynamic capabilities are frequently used to build new resource configurations in the pursuit of a continual series of temporary advantages. The potential the long-term competitive advantage through the use of BDA lies in the dynamic capabilities than the need to create a resource configuration that have that advantage (Chen, et al., 2015; Sharma & Sharma, 2018; Verma, Sharma, & Kumar, 2018; Xu, Tiwari, Chen, & Turner, 2018; Yazdi & Esfeden, 2018). Asset productivity is the primary measure used to assess supply chain performance, describing the extent to which business productivity uses their current assets as well as their fixed assets. It is important to establish indictors of asset productivity.

In general, there are number of insights developed through BDA usage that create opportunities for organizations to reconfigure their resources in ways that are in greater alignment with trends and shifts in both demand and supply markets. As opposed to the traditional operational models of data collection tied to continuous improvement of specific processes. Many chaos and complexity theorists commonly believe that collecting information and taking measurements may blind us to the world of larger possibilities. These theorists believe that instead of attempting to impose structure, leaders should relinquish control. By accepting that SCM is dynamic and all-encompassing with many players and agents, no one metric is sufficient. This situation may well be the case in SCM. Therefore, we need a cluster of metrics, certainly more than just cost. If we cannot adequately measure customer satisfaction and utility, we need to have more subjective ways to measure it. Unfortunately, it is unlikely that there is a one-size-fits-all solution. Typically, in times of crisis, many managers are more prone to try something that's worked elsewhere. This is particularly true if they are afforded a budget to spend without any personal consequences (relative to their take-home pay). Operational and SCM applications requires a more comprehensive approach and with the availability BDA, 3PL (third-party logics providers), and 4PL (fourth-party logistics providers) applications, an organization does not have to do it all.

Environmental dynamism is another key situational parameter in dynamic capabilities theory, which suggests that the variance of competitive advantage created by organizational capability is contingent upon environmental dynamism (Chen, et al., 2015). An environment will provide greater opportunity for companies to capitalize on BDA. It is very likely that the influence of BDA use on operational and supply chain performance will be amplified in high velocity markets. Hence, there is little doubt that the influence of BDA on organizational outcomes, as well as the key factors that facilitate BDA use are well entrenched in many global service and manufacturing firm.

Examining the Roles of Advertising on Social Media Websites

McCormick (2006) indicates that not only do people feel this type of advertising is a violation to their privacy, the advertisements were sometimes misdirected. It was found that MySpace was allowing gambling advertisements to be seen by children that were younger than sixteen years old. Morimoto and Chang (2009) further look into the intrusiveness of advertisements. Their research explores consumers' attitudes on unsolicited advertisements in emails, which could also be felt regarding unsolicited advertisements on social networking systems. Morimoto et al (2009) indicated that approximately 86% of consumers felt that these unsolicited advertisements were seen as being a big problem or annoying. In order to determine how consumers will react to advertising, the level of intrusiveness must be addressed. The research completed by Morimoto et al. (2009) indicated that individuals not only felt that unsolicited advertisements were a big problem when there was intrusion into their personal affairs, but also when their thought process was interrupted as it would be with pop up advertisements or banners.

Further research is needed in order to determine how social network advertisements affect the acceptance of these sites. Although social network advertisements have a lot of positive outcomes for the companies who are utilizing them, excessive advertisements may deter individuals from using the sites. According to Taylor et al (2011), it is widely believed that MySpace usage deteriorated due to the increased commercialization in the form of advertisements, specifically pop-up advertisements. "The Federal Trade Commission found that more than 40% of consumers who experienced pop-up ads believe the Web site they were on – not the pop-up advertiser – had permitted the ad to appear" (Zaney, 2004, p.42). In this same study completed by the Federal Trade Commission, one-third of the consumers that participated in the research indicated that the pop-up advertisements caused them to view the Website they were on unfavorably.

In order to understand whether or not advertisements will deter individuals from utilizing social networking sites, we must first look into what motivated them to go online in the first place. A study referenced in the article written by Taylor et al (2011) indicates that the motives for going online include filling up one's time, entertainment or informational value, and to connect with others. Social networking systems are designed to help individuals to connect with others. "They are online forums in which users with common interests or connections 'can gather to share thoughts, comments, and opinions. There are other aspects of social networking systems such as Facebook that meet the consumers' criteria of educational or informational value as well as simply to help them pass the time. Due to the fact that Facebook and Twitter have a majority of the aspects described above, they are widely accepted in today's society. As social network advertisements increase, the question remains whether or not these sites will remain accepted and this paper will research this question further. Taylor et al (2011) indicates that Facebook will remain accepted by today's society as it has TOCAS, which stands for Targeted Opt-in Customer Ads. The advertisements are only shown to individuals who have 'liked' the organization's Facebook page, therefore the general public is not bombarded with unwanted advertisements in their newsfeeds. This seems to be the big difference regarding the success of Facebook and MySpace and my research will look into this aspect further.

Relationships Between Purchases and Social Networking Advertisements

The research second question that will be explored in the present study is whether social networking advertisements actually increase an organization's sales. There are a lot of articles and research completed that takes the point of view of the organization doing the advertising. As indicated in the article written by Goldie (2007), social networks now have strategies in place to generate high levels of advertising revenues from their sites. Jaffe (2009) explored ways that organizations can maximize their advertising budgets such as obtaining a computer program to track consumers' purchases, email advertising and the use of social networking advertisements. When it comes to social networks, the article indicates that organizations are not likely to obtain new customers. In spite of this, the author recommended organizations obtain social networking sites due to the fact that marketers continue to research how these sites could be used to acquire new customers. Booth and Matic (2011) indicated that companies that do not currently participate in social networking sites, such as Facebook, feel the need to establish a presence. "Establishing a presence on Twitter or Facebook without the due diligence required to make the effort worthwhile will produce few worthwhile results" (Booth et al, 2011, p.185). Another aspect of social media advertising that affects consumers' purchases is the idea of group sales such as Groupon and Living Social. Ham (2011) explores how Jump on it Deal, which is similar to the two sites previously mentioned, enables bigger discounts for the consumer. Organizations have found that these programs have added to their sales and have brought customers through their doors that were not familiar with their product or service prior to participating in these programs.

Is the "like" function on organizations' Facebook pages being utilized to the full extent? Engagement of consumers on the computer has been difficult to measure. Howell (2009) references a report that indicates less than 5% of social network users have ever clicked on a banner site. Even if the banner is clicked on, it does not mean that the customer was engaged with the brand or was motivated to make a purchase. Shields (2009) explores the fact that Facebook users are less likely to click on an advertisement that takes them away from the site they were originally on. Therefore, Facebook advertisements encourage users to actually interact with the brand by posting comments near a video advertisement or reading what their friends had posted. As Shields (2009, p. 8) indicates, "the idea is to build ad products that users can interact with in the same way they do with other things on the site." Ang (2011) explains that when a social media user 'likes' an organization on Facebook, this information is saved in their profile where other people can see this information. The research indicated by Ang (2011) found that an ad will achieve 30% higher recall if the social media user sees that their friends have either 'liked' it or commented on it. The question remains whether or not this increases the consumers' purchases. Ang (2011) references a time when Honda Japan decided to launch a new car. The organization created a social networking site and also ran a competition. If users of the social networking site added CRZ on the end of their username, their names were entered for a chance to win a new car. Research indicated that this helped increase brand awareness prior to the launch and orders reached 4500 units during the prelaunch period.

The "like" function on Facebook is an easy way for an organization to focus on which aspect of their corporate strategy they need to focus on. It is a basic assumption of the present study that by businesses being able to keep an open means of communication with their consumers, they will be able to quickly react and switch their focus according to their consumers' needs.

METHOD

Specific Research Hypotheses

Large portions of society use social networking systems regularly, creating potential for both consumers and businesses to benefit from social networking advertisements. This paper will further explore three specific issues previously outlined to more fully understand the effects of social networking advertisements on both consumers' acceptance of the systems as well as the effect on their purchases. The three hypotheses presented in this paper dealing with the interplay of online social networking, advertising effectiveness, gender and age trends, and remaining the interplay with positive comments of the use of the 'like' function and its impacts on consumer behavior, as derived from the review of relevant operations literature and from applying the basic tenants of Uses and Gratification Theory (Papacharissi & Mendelson, 2011; Smock, Ellison, Lampe, & Wohn, 2011) are as follows:

H1: There should be no statistical relationship between the use of social networking advertisements on Facebook and related social networking sites and users' feelings toward the site.

H2: Social networking advertisements will not have an effect on consumers' purchases.

H3: Users of social networks primarily utilize such systems to stay connected with their personal connection. The "like" function is used, but it is not a major reason that individuals utilize social networking sites.

A combination of statistical techniques that were deemed appropriate to analysis the survey data included Chi-square, multiple linear regression, and independent t-test among means.

Derivation of H1

There will be no relationship between the use of social networking advertisements on Facebook and individuals' feelings or personal attachment toward the site, since it is a mutual business transaction. The reason being is that the only advertisements that appear in a user's newsfeed are from organizations that this individual has shown an interest in. People are not bombarded with unwanted advertisements. In fact, individuals may 'like' an organization so that they will be kept up-to-date on any sale items or services that this organization may offer.

Derivation of H2

Social networking advertisements will not have an effect on consumers' purchases. The main reason is that Facebook seems to be utilized primarily to spread brand awareness and word of mouth advertising rather than to increase consumers' purchases. Some individuals may choose to 'like' an organization's page because they see that their friends are interested in the company. This is a way for organizations to spread the awareness for their products or services and reach individuals who would normally not follow their organizations. It is unlikely that consumers' purchases will increase based on receiving these advertisements on Facebook.

Derivation of H3

The "like" function on organizational Facebook pages is not a major function used by individuals. Organizations have yet to master all of the benefits that social networks have to offer. Users of social networks, such as Facebook, primarily utilize the systems to stay connected with their friends and family. The "like" function is used, but it is not a major reason that individuals utilize Facebook.

Sample Selection and Instrument

In order to test the hypotheses listed above, individuals were questioned from various age groups who currently utilize Facebook by sending them a questionnaire on the site as well as questioning co-workers. The research concentrates on Facebook/LinkedIn as this is the most widely used social networking system that most working business professionals (as well as the general public) are familiar with and, hence, should be able to reach a larger sample of individuals to complete the research. The collected variables of the present research effort include the demographics of the participants involved in the research such as their age and gender. The variables that are randomized deal with whether or not the participants utilize the 'like' function on Facebook regularly, and whether or not they actually have advertisements appear in their newsfeeds as a result. The questionnaire was electronically distributed to individuals within a business professional setting as well as users of the Facebook and LinkedIn that one of the authors of the present study has developed over the past two years.

The individuals chosen to be included in the research are from a comprehensive selection of users from the friends list of the present study's authors who currently use Facebook and/or LinkedIn, comprising of individuals within associated professional work groups. In regards to the individuals that participated, they ranged in age from 20 to 63. There is a mix of individuals from every age group as well as both males and females. Not only did this sample enable the researchers to have a relatively large portion of individuals participate in the research, but it may also help to clarify whether there are certain trends within the age groups or whether males and females are affected differently by social networking advertisements.

In order to question the participants, they were a link to the questionnaire to individuals from the friends list on Facebook/LinkedIn who were preselected based on business professional status. Although there were a few who did not wish to participate in the study, the response rate was over 86% and it was felt that there were enough collected responses from this sample of individuals to obtain the statistical power data needed to formally test the specific research hypotheses. The survey has questions to clarify the participant's demographic information as well as questions dealing with their thoughts on social networking advertisements. The answers are in a multiple choice format and a majority utilized the Likert scale. The Likert scale has been the preferred format with public surveys that typically deals with the measurement of opinions or attitudes (Ridinger & Funk, 2006; Robinson & Trail, 2005; Seguin, Richelieu, & O'Reilly, 2008; Smock, Ellison, Lampe, & Wohn, (2011). Since a majority of individuals who utilize social media tend to be in the younger age groups, it is important to understand the participant's age. By using this information, it was a simple task to group the participants' answers according to their age in order to clarify whether trends exist within the certain age groups.

Another demographic that is important to clarify is the gender of the participant involved. By determining whether an individual is male or female aids in determining whether they are affected by advertisements utilized on Facebook. Are females more likely to purchase a product or service after viewing an advertisement in their newsfeed? Are males less likely to 'like' a business? By asking how many organizations a participant has 'liked' on Facebook, it was possible to determine the extent to which this function is utilized on average, among the participants.

The questionnaire was sent to the participants via links embedded in common social media platforms, such as Facebook and LinkedIn, to business professional within the Pittsburgh area workplaces. As the participants responded to the survey, the data collected was entered into a spreadsheet to enable me to keep track of the various answers. Within two weeks of sending the survey out to a representative group of potential participants on Facebook/I\LinkedIn, it was reassessed whether additional surveys should be sent in order to receive a proper sample size.

RESULTS

Descriptive Analysis

The data collected were then categorized according to the controlling variables. The men's answers were separated from the females' answers to determine if there any statistically significant gender biases present in the present study. The same procedure was applied to the different age ranges, since the majority of the participants lie into two separate age groups. Accordingly, there are two subgroups under the men's category and two subgroups under the women's category. A total of 102 participants answered the survey that was sent via the message function on Facebook/LinkedIn. As evident in Table 1 and Figure 1, a majority of the participants, 81.4% (n = 83), were in the 31-40 years of age range. Clemmitt (2006) outlined that most individuals who utilize social networking sites are between the ages of 12 and 25 years. Given the results of this study are not consistent with this demographic, it is a possibility that the numbers were skewed due to the participants that were targeted for this study. On-the-other-hand, the study did reach a significant number of business professionals who were 41 years of age or older, 15.7% (n = 16). Of the 102 participants, an overwhelming 72.5% were female.

Table 1. Basic frequencies of selected variables used in the present study

A. Age (years).				
Variable Coding Scheme	Frequency	Percent	Valid Percent	Cumulative Percent
20 or younger	3	2.9	2.9	2.9
21-30	40	39.2	39.2	42.2
31-40	43	42.2	42.2	84.3
41-50	8	7.8	7.8	92.2
51-60	7	6.9	6.9	99.0
Older than 60	1	1.0	1.0	100.0
Total	102	100.0	100.0	
B. Gender Status.				
Variable Coding Scheme	Frequency	Percent	Valid Percent	Cumulative Percent
Female	75	73.5	73.5	73.5
Male	27	26.5	26.5	100.0
Total	102	100.0	100.0	
C. Frequency of Facebook use.				
Variable Coding Scheme	Frequency	Percent	Valid Percent	Cumulative Percent
Daily	84	82.4	82.4	82.4
Weekly	11	10.8	10.8	93.1
Bi-weekly	3	2.9	2.9	96.1
Monthly	4	3.9	3.9	100.0
Total	102	100.0	100.0	
D. Average social networking hours per week.				
Variable Coding Scheme	Frequency	Percent	Valid Percent	Cumulative Percent
1-2	54	52.9	52.9	52.9
2-6	33	32.4	32.4	85.3
6-8	8	7.8	7.8	93.1
8+	7	6.9	6.9	100.0
Total	102	100.0	100.0	
E. Major purpose to stay connected with friends, family, co-worker.				
Variable Coding Scheme	Frequency	Percent	Valid Percent	Cumulative Percent
Strongly Agree	52	51.0	51.0	51.0
Agree	36	35.3	35.3	86.3
Neutral	13	12.7	12.7	99.0
Disagree	1	1.0	1.0	100.0
Total	102	100.0	100.0	
F. Number of organizations liked on Facebook.				
Variable Coding Scheme	Frequency	Percent	Valid Percent	Cumulative Percent
1-5	47	46.1	46.1	46.1
5-10	35	34.3	34.3	80.4

continues on following page

Table 1. Continued

10-15	10	9.8	9.8	90.2
15+	10	9.8	9.8	100.0
Total	102	100.0	100.0	

G. Major use to obtain information on savings on potential purchases.

Variable Coding Scheme	Frequency	Percent	Valid Percent	Cumulative Percent
Strongly Agree	2	2.0	2.0	2.0
Agree	10	9.8	9.8	11.8
Neutral	21	20.6	20.6	32.4
Disagree	32	31.4	31.4	63.7
Strongly Disagree	37	36.3	36.3	100.0
Total	102	100.0	100.0	

H. Would continue using social media if banners and pop-ups common.

Variable Coding Scheme	Frequency	Percent	Valid Percent	Cumulative Percent
Strongly Agree	3	2.9	2.9	2.9
Agree	21	20.6	20.6	23.5
Neutral	32	31.4	31.4	54.9
Disagree	29	28.4	28.4	83.3
Strongly Disagree	17	16.7	16.7	100.0
Total	102	100.0	100.0	

I. Advertisements newsfeed are distractive and annoying.

Variable Coding Scheme	Frequency	Percent	Valid Percent	Cumulative Percent
Strongly Agree	22	21.6	21.6	21.6
Agree	38	37.3	37.3	58.8
Neutral	32	31.4	31.4	90.2
Disagree	9	8.8	8.8	99.0
Strongly Disagree	1	1.0	1.0	100.0
Total	102	100.0	100.0	

J. Major reason to like company is due to their products/services.

Variable Coding Scheme	Frequency	Percent	Valid Percent	Cumulative Percent
Strongly Agree	4	3.9	3.9	3.9
Agree	26	25.5	25.5	29.4
Neutral	35	34.3	34.3	63.7
Disagree	25	24.5	24.5	88.2
Strongly Disagree	12	11.8	11.8	100.0
Total	102	100.0	100.0	

K. Formally searched a company before following on social network.

Variable Coding Scheme	Frequency	Percent	Valid Percent	Cumulative Percent
Strongly Agree	8	7.8	7.8	7.8
Agree	24	23.5	23.5	31.4

continues on following page

Table 1. Continued

Neutral	26	25.5	25.5	56.9
Disagree	31	30.4	30.4	87.3
Strongly Disagree	13	12.7	12.7	100.0
Total	102	100.0	100.0	
L. Made purchases after seeing advertisements in newsfeed.				
Variable Coding Scheme	Frequency	Percent	Valid Percent	Cumulative Percent
Yes	12	11.8	11.8	11.8
No	90	88.2	88.2	100.0
Total	102	100.0	100.0	
M. Purchases per month based on advertisements on social media.				
Variable Coding Scheme	Frequency	Percent	Valid Percent	Cumulative Percent
0-2	101	99.0	99.0	99.0
2-4	1	1.0	1.0	100.0
Total	102	100.0	100.0	

Figure 2. Age range of respondents

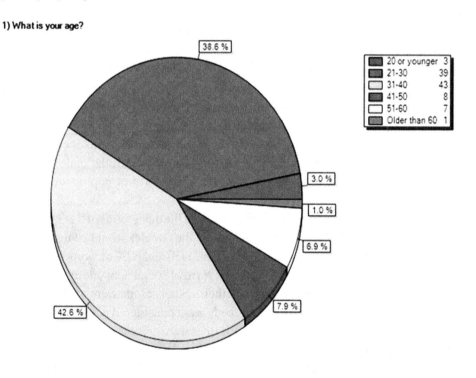

H1 Results

The findings seem to support H1, which stated that there will be no relationship between the use of social networking advertisements on Facebook and individuals' feelings toward the site. A majority of the questions relating to H1 were answered with a split decision. As indicated earlier in this paper, there is evidence that the usage of MySpace dropped primarily due to the use of excessive advertising. In order to determine if individuals would continue to utilize Facebook if pop up advertisements were to begin to be used, participants were asked to rate the degree to which they agree with that statement. Slightly more of the individuals agreed they would continue using Facebook regardless of whether or not pop up advertisements were to begin to be used; 51% of the participants were either neutral on the subject or agreed that they would continue using Facebook, while 46% either strongly disagreed or disagreed. Again, this result indicates that users are unsure whether or not pop up advertisements would deter them from further utilizing the site. Slightly more than half of participants did not seem to like the current form of advertisements on Facebook wherein the advertisements appear in their newsfeed. When asked whether these types of advertisements annoy the participants, 59.4% either strongly agreed or agreed. This was an unexpected result due to the fact that the advertisements only appear in their newsfeeds if the individual 'likes' the organization. Random advertisements do not appear unless the user shows an interest in the organization. This result may be further explained in the discussion that follows later in this paper regarding the other hypotheses.

In order to further explain the results regarding H1, an analysis was completed by separating the participants further into the variables of gender and age groups. When inspecting the male participants (27.5% or sample), 39% were 31-40 years of age, while 35.7% were 21-30 years of age. Overall, there did not seem to be a difference in these two age groups regarding males. The variable of age in the male participants did not seem to affect their answers when asked if they would continue to utilize the site if pop up advertisements were to begin to appear. 60% of males 21-30 years of age either strongly disagreed or disagreed that they would continue to use Facebook, while 72.4% of males 31-40 years of age answered the same. The advertisements appearing in the participants' newsfeed seem to annoy approximately 80% of males ranging in age from 21-40 years. Overall, the males seem to not care for the social networking advertisements, whether they are in the form of pop up advertisements or ones that appear in their newsfeed.

The results are similar when dealing with females within the age groups of 21-30 and 31-40 than with males of the same age groups. When asked whether or not the females would continue using Facebook if pop up advertisements began, 68.9% of the women ages 21-30 and 62% of women ages 31-40 either are neutral or disagree. In order to determine if the current form of social networking advertisement troubles the women participants, it was decided to analysis their responses answers to the question of whether or not the advertisements appearing in their newsfeeds were considered a distraction. It was found that 72.4% of females, aged 21-30 and 63.7% aged 31-40 either were neutral or disagreed with this statement. This result is similar to that of the male participants within the same age groups.

Due to the small amount of participants that were outside of the age groups previously discussed in this study, it was decided to focus on an analysis of respondents that were 41-50 years of age to determine if there trends in their answers. This group represents only 7.9% of the total participants, but it was thought it would give an insight as to whether there are trends within the older age group. Interestingly, the 41-50 age group had exactly 50% male and 50% female responses, therefore, the gender variable should not be a factor in a sample of a majority of female respondents. The participants in this age group reported similar results as compared to the previously discussed groups when asked whether they use Facebook primarily to connect to friends and family; 50% of these participants strongly agreed with this statement. This group also indicated that 25% of them disagreed with the fact that Facebook is utilized to obtain information on products or services that organizations were offering. Where the results differ is when these participants were asked whether or not they would continue to use Facebook if pop up advertisements began on the site; 37.5% stated they agreed. This differs from the other groups previously analyzed as a large percentage of the other groups, which included males and females who were 40 years old or younger, indicated they would actually stop using Facebook if the pop up advertisements were to start appearing. Participants in the 41-50 age groups also did not seem to care about advertisements appearing in their newsfeed; 62.5% of these individuals were either neutral or disagreed with the current form of advertising on Facebook.

In in an effort to formally test H1, a series of statistical tests were performed. Tables «tbc2»2 and «tbc3»3 displays the relevant independent test for differences among means for traditional and non-traditional aged groups for variables associated with consumer behavioral and social networking and advertising preference characteristics as a function of gender status (i.e., as shown in Table 3, the mean differences were completed as female's mean less male's mean). As evident from an inspection of Tables 2 through Table 3, there were no significant differences among the various factors due to differences between equal or not equal variance assumptions. The same was true that there were on statistically significant difference among the various factors as a function of gender. Hence, even though there were more females represented in the same than females, there was no evidence of a gender bias in the sample.

A multiple linear regression analysis was conducted, with number of organizations liked on Facebook used as the dependent variable. As shown in Table 4, a relatively moderate portion [24.7% (15.5% adjusted)] of the total variance in number of organizations liked as the dependent variable was explained by the independent variables used in the analysis. The overall relationship was found to be highly significant, as expected (F = 2.684, p = 0.005).

Not surprisingly, if assuming H1 to be true, the independent variables of average social networking hours per week (t = 4.275, p < 0.001), and advertisements newsfeed are distractive and annoying (t = 2.114, p = 0.037) were found to be statistically significant. As hypothesized, critical consumer behavior-related success factors of major purpose to stay connected with friends, family, co-workers (t = 1.110, p = 0.270), major use to obtain information on savings on potential purchases (t = 1.441, p = 0.661), would continue using social media if banners and pop-ups common (t = 0.828, p = 0.410), major reason to like company is due to their products/services (t = -0.856, p = 0.394), formally searched a company before following on social network (t = -0.139, p = 0.890), majority of companies on social network page obtained from friends' pages (t = -0.351, p = 0.726), purchases per month based on advertisements on social media (t = 0.146, p = 0.885), as well as others studied. As these professionals have undoubtedly experienced, there will be no relationship between the use of social networking advertisements on Facebook and individuals' feelings or personal attachment toward the site, since it is a mutual business transaction. Based on the statistical analysis associated with the formal testing of H1; hence, it was accepted in the null form. The overall results show that individuals who currently utilize Facebook do not seem to be affected by the use of social networking advertisements in terms of liking or being personally attached to the companies providing the advertisements.

Table 2. Group statistics in terms of selected variables and gender (H1)

Variable Description	Gender Status	N	Mean	Std. Deviation	Std. Error Mean
Age (years)	Female	75	2.85	.954	.110
	Male	27	2.63	.967	.186
Frequency of Facebook use	Female	75	1.23	.649	.075
	Male	27	1.44	.847	.163
Average social networking hours per week	Female	75	1.77	.924	.107
	Male	27	1.44	.751	.145
Number of organizations liked on Facebook	Female	75	1.88	.999	.115
	Male	27	1.70	.869	.167
Major use to obtain information on savings on potential purchases	Female	75	3.85	1.099	.127
	Male	27	4.04	.980	.189
Would continue using social media if banners and pop-ups common	Female	75	3.35	1.033	.119
	Male	27	3.37	1.214	.234
Advertisements newsfeed are distractive and annoying	Female	75	2.31	.885	.102
	Male	27	2.30	1.103	.212
Major reason to like company is due to their products/services	Female	75	3.12	1.052	.121
	Male	27	3.22	1.086	.209
Formally searched a company before following on social network	Female	75	3.12	1.196	.138
	Male	27	3.30	1.068	.205
Majority of companies on social network page obtained from friends' pages	Female	75	2.71	.897	.104
	Male	27	2.67	.961	.185
Purchases per month based on advertisements on social media	Female	75	1.01	.115	.013
	Male	27	1.00	.000	.000

Table 3. Equality of means tests results compared variables as a function of gender (H1) (note mean differences were completed as female's mean less male's mean)

Independent Variables and Variance Assumptions		t-test	df	Sig. (2-tailed)	Mean Difference	Std. Error Difference
Age (years)	Equal variances	1.041	100	.300 (NS)	.224	.215
	Not equal variances	1.035	45.476	.306 (NS)	.224	.216
Frequency of Facebook use	Equal variances	-1.375	100	.172 (NS)	-.218	.158
	Not equal variances	-1.214	37.545	.232 (NS)	-.218	.179
Average social networking hours per week	Equal variances	1.661	100	.100 (NS)	.329	.198
	Not equal variances	1.831	56.176	.072 (NS)	.329	.180
Number of organizations liked on Facebook	Equal variances	.812	100	.419 (NS)	.176	.217
	Not equal variances	.868	52.484	.390 (NS)	.176	.203
Major use to obtain information on savings on potential purchases	Equal variances	-.765	100	.446 (NS)	-.184	.240
	Not equal variances	-.808	51.195	.423 (NS)	-.184	.227

continues on following page

Table 3. Continued

Independent Variables and Variance Assumptions		t-test	df	Sig. (2-tailed)	Mean Difference	Std. Error Difference
Would continue using social media if banners and pop-ups common	Equal variances	-.098	100	.923 (NS)	-.024	.243
	Not equal variances	-.090	40.370	.928 (NS)	-.024	.262
Advertisements newsfeed are distractive and annoying	Equal variances	.049	100	.961 (NS)	.010	.212
	Not equal variances	.044	38.716	.965 (NS)	.010	.236
Major reason to like company is due to their products/services	Equal variances	-.429	100	.669 (NS)	-.102	.238
	Not equal variances	-.423	44.744	.674 (NS)	-.102	.242
Formally searched a company before following on social network	Equal variances	-.675	100	.501 (NS)	-.176	.261
	Not equal variances	-.712	51.154	.480 (NS)	-.176	.248
Majority of companies on social network page obtained from friends' pages	Equal variances	.195	100	.846 (NS)	.040	.205
	Not equal variances	.189	43.379	.851 (NS)	.040	.212
Purchases per month based on advertisements on social media	Equal variances	.598	100	.551 (NS)	.013	.022
	Not equal variances	1.000	74.000	.321 (NS)	.013	.013

NS denotes not statistically significant at the .05 level for a two-tailed test; S denotes statistically significant at the .05 level for a two-tailed test; HS denotes significant at the .01 level for a two-tailed test.

Table 4. Relevant statistics associated with specific hypothesis-testing results (H1). Part A displays the model summary, Part B the overall results, and Part C inspects specific contributions of each component in the hypothesis (Dependent variable: Number of organizations liked on Facebook).

Part A. Model summary.				
R	R Square	Adjusted R Square	Std. Error of the Estimate	
.497	.247	.155	.888	
Part B. ANOVA results.				
Source of Variation		Sum of Squares	df	Mean Square	F-ratio	Significance
	Regression	23.263	11	2.115	2.684	.005 (HS)
	Residual	70.903	90	.788		
	Total	94.167	101			
Dependent Variable: Number of organizations liked on Facebook.						
Predictors: (Constant), Purchases per month based on advertisements on social media, Frequency of Facebook use, Age (years), Majority of companies on social network page obtained from friends' pages, Advertisements newsfeed are distractive and annoying, Major purpose to stay connected with friends, family, co-workers, Formally searched a company before following on social network, Would continue using social media if banners and pop-ups common, Major use to obtain information on savings on potential purchases, Average social networking hours per week, Major reason to like company is due to their products/services. HS denotes significant at the .01 level for a two-tailed test.						

continues on following page

Table 4. Continued

Part C. Coefficients-testing results.					
Independent Variables	Unstandardized Coefficients		Standardized Coefficients	t-test	Significance
	B	Std. Error	Beta		
(Constant)	.269	1.358		.198	.843
Age (years)	-.077	.098	-.076	-.782	.436 (NS)
Frequency of Facebook use	-.012	.144	-.009	-.085	.932 (NS)
Average social networking hours per week	.520	.122	.479	4.275	>.001 (HS)
Major purpose to stay connected with friends, family, co-workers	.141	.127	.108	1.110	.270 (NS)
Major use to obtain information on savings on potential purchases	.049	.110	.054	.441	.661 (NS)
Would continue using social media if banners and pop-ups common	.077	.093	.086	.828	.410 (NS)
Advertisements newsfeed are distractive and annoying	.234	.111	.228	2.114	.037 (S)
Major reason to like company is due to their products/services	-.098	.114	-.107	-.856	.394 (NS)
Formally searched a company before following on social network	-.013	.092	-.015	-.139	.890 (NS)
Majority of companies on social network page obtained from friends' pages	-.037	.104	-.034	-.351	.726 (NS)
Purchases per month based on advertisements on social media	.146	1.000	.015	.146	.885 (NS)

Dependent Variable: Number of organizations liked on Facebook. NS denotes not statistically significant at the 0.05 level for a two-tailed test; S denotes statistically significant at the 0.05 level for a two-tailed test; HS denotes significant at the 0.01 level for a two-tailed test.

H2 Results

The results of the survey emphatically support H2, which stated that social networking advertisements will not have an effect on consumers' purchases. If one inspects the results of all the participants, essential the same amount of individuals, 25.5%, both agreed and disagreed that the reason they 'like' an organization is to purchase the organization's products or services, with 40.4% liked an organization merely because they saw that their friends had done the same, whereas 23.5% searched for organizations to like. This result seems to indicate that the 'like' function on Facebook is used primarily because people are curious about what their friends are interested in. This result also brings us back to a point made in the analysis of the results as they pertain to H1. It was surprising that participants reported being bothered by the advertisements that appear in their newsfeed when these advertisements only show up when the individual shows an interest in the organization by liking the organization's page. The analysis of the results as they pertain to both H1 and H2 seems to indicate that individuals 'like' an organization for reasons other than to purchase their products. Therefore, individuals are somewhat bothered by any advertisements that appear in their newsfeeds, regardless of whether or not they show an interest in the organization. H2 is further confirmed by the fact that an overwhelming 88% of individuals never made a purchase as a result of seeing an advertisement in their newsfeed. For the small percent of participants that actually did make a purchase, 99% of the individuals purchased only two products or less.

Female participants' answers were inspected in the same age groups, 21-30 and 31-40, as they related to H 2. It was found that 31% of the female respondents who were 21-30 years of age 'liked' an organization in order to purchase the product or service offered by that organization. Similarly, 25% of the female participants who were 31-40 years of age also agreed with this statement. Females of both age groups consistently answered with both the overall results and the male participants when asked if they searched for organizations to 'like'. On-the-other-hand, the female participants seemed more concerned with what their friends were interested in than the male participants were; 55.2% of females who were 21-30 years of age agreed that they typically 'liked' an organization due to the fact that they saw their friends had done the same and 43.8% of females in the 31-40 age group also agreed with this statement. As in the other groups analyzed, females did not typically make purchases based on seeing advertisements in their newsfeeds. 86.2% of the females ages 21-30 and 83.9% of the females ages 31-40 never made a purchase as a result of seeing a social networking advertisement. Out of the small percentage that did make a purchase, 96.6% of the participants purchased two products or less.

As with H1, the answers of the participants were also analyzed, male and female, who were 41-50 years of age. The results were consistent with the overall results as well as with the results of the age groups analyzed that were 40 years of age and younger. Specifically regarding the amount of purchases made as a result of social networking advertisements, 87.5% of the participants 41-50 years of age indicated that they never made a purchase. Similarly, out of the small percent of participants that did make a purchase, 100% of them purchased two or less products.

To further test these research assumptions associated with H2, Chi-square analyses were conducted, with cross-tabulation statistics associated with made purchases after seeing advertisements in newsfeed and major reason to like company is due to their products/services (Table «tbc5»5), and gender added to the same mix of variables (Table «tbc6»6). As shown in Table «tbc5»5, the vast majority of respondents felt that liking and organization based on its products/services had little to do with completing purchases after seeing advertisements in newsfeed (Chi-square = 11.802, p = 0.019). The same overall relationship has found to be statistically true for females (Chi-square = 14.338, p = 0.006), but not true for males (Chi-square = 3.536, p = 0.472). Males were apparently more indifferent to the concept of madding of purchases after seeing advertisements in newsfeed and it acting as the major reason to like a company. Hence, as stated earlier, the results of this study suggest that H2 is accepted as the statistical evidence supports that fact that social networking advertisements do not have a significant positive impact or effect on consumers' purchases. If fact, it might well be the complete opposite.

Table 5. Cross-tabulation statistics associated with Made purchases after seeing advertisements in newsfeed and Major reason to like company is due to their products/services (H2)

Part A. Actual count.							
Variable Descriptions		Major reason to like company is due to their products/services					Total
		Strongly Agree	Agree	Neutral	Disagree	Strongly Disagree	
Made purchases after seeing advertisements in newsfeed	Yes	1	8	1	2	0	12
	No	3	18	34	23	12	90
Total		4	26	35	25	12	102

Part B. Chi-square test results.			
Statistics	Value	df	Asymptotic Significance (2-sided)
Pearson Chi-Square	14.338	4	.006 (HS)
Likelihood Ratio	14.275	4	.006 (HS)
Linear-by-Linear Association	8.064	1	.005 (HS)
N of Valid Cases	102		

Note, 6 cells (60.0%) have expected count less than 5. The minimum expected count is 0.47. HS denotes significant at the 0.01 level for a two-tailed test.

Part C. Symmetric measures.			
Statistics		Value	Approx. Sig.
Nominal by Nominal	Contingency Coefficient	.351	.006 (HS)
N of Valid Cases		102	

HS denotes significant at the .01 level for a two-tailed test.

Table 6. Cross-tabulation statistics associated with Made purchases after seeing advertisements in newsfeed and Major reason to like company is due to their products/services and Gender Status (H2)

Part A. Actual count.								
Gender Status			Major reason to like company is due to their products/services					Total
			Strongly Agree	Agree	Neutral	Disagree	Strongly Disagree	
Female	Made purchases after seeing advertisements in newsfeed	Yes	1	6	1	1	0	9
		No	2	13	27	15	9	66
	Total		3	19	28	16	9	75
Male	Made purchases after seeing advertisements in newsfeed	Yes	0	2	0	1	0	3
		No	1	5	7	8	3	24
	Total		1	7	7	9	3	27
Total	Made purchases after seeing advertisements in newsfeed	Yes	1	8	1	2	0	12
		No	3	18	34	23	12	90
	Total		4	26	35	25	12	102

continues on following page

Table 6. Continued

Part B. Chi-square test results.				
Gender Status		Value	df	Asymptotic Significance (2-sided)
Female	Pearson Chi-Square	11.802[b]	4	.019 (S)
	Likelihood Ratio	11.411	4	.022 (S)
	Linear-by-Linear Association	7.446	1	.006 (HS)
	N of Valid Cases	75		
Male	Pearson Chi-Square	3.536[c]	4	.472 (NS)
	Likelihood Ratio	4.182	4	.382 (NS)
	Linear-by-Linear Association	.883	1	.347 (NS)
	N of Valid Cases	27		
Total	Pearson Chi-Square	14.338[a]	4	.006 (HS)
	Likelihood Ratio	14.275	4	.006 (HS)
	Linear-by-Linear Association	8.064	1	.005 (HS)
	N of Valid Cases	102		

a. 6 cells (60.0%) have expected count less than 5. The minimum expected count is 0.47; b. 6 cells (60.0%) have expected count less than 5. The minimum expected count is .36; c. 7 cells (70.0%) have expected count less than 5. The minimum expected count is 0.11.
NS denotes not statistically significant at the .05 level for a two-tailed test; S denotes statistically significant at the .05 level for a two-tailed test; HS denotes significant at the .01 level for a two-tailed test.

Part C. Symmetric measures.				
Gender Status			Value	Approx. Sig.
Female	Nominal by Nominal	Contingency Coefficient	.369	.019 (S)
	N of Valid Cases		75	
Male	Nominal by Nominal	Contingency Coefficient	.340	.472 (NS)
	N of Valid Cases		27	
Total	Nominal by Nominal	Contingency Coefficient	.351	.006 (HS)
	N of Valid Cases		102	

NS denotes not statistically significant at the .05 level for a two-tailed test; S denotes statistically significant at the .05 level for a two-tailed test; HS denotes significant at the .01 level for a two-tailed test.

H3 Results

Finally, the results of the formal testing of H3 suggested that there is evidence to support the claim that the "like" function on organizational Facebook pages is not a major function used by individuals. As previously suggested, the format of all the specific research hypotheses were stated in the null form. The reasons that many individuals use social networking sites, like Facebook and LinkedIn, are less about commercial and consuming motivations, and more about maintaining personal connections. Krivak (2008) suggested that Facebook started in 2004 as a way for individuals to stay connected with friends and family, even if they were considerable distances apart. The results of this study indicate that this very basic fact remains to be true, even though commercialism seems to drive the profits of the social networking industry. Of the 102 participants, 86.3% either strongly agreed or agreed with the fact that

that they participated in Facebook mainly to stay connected to friends and family. When asked whether or not they utilized Facebook primarily to obtain information on deals available through different organizations, 58.6% of the participants either strongly disagreed or disagreed. Regarding the 'like' function, 46.1% indicated that they have only 'liked' five organizations or less. This finding further confirms that Facebook is primarily used to stay connected with friends and family, rather than to benefit from the social networking advertisements. The amount of time the participants spent on Facebook was important to measure. The longer an individual is on Facebook, the more likely they would take advantage of all of the site's features, such us 'liking' an organization. A majority of the participants, 82.4%, included Facebook and other social networking sites as part of their daily routine. Not only do individuals utilize such sites on a daily basis, they spend multiple hours per day on Facebook, as 85.3% spent six hours or less on the site, which is close to what many working adults may spend working daily for a full-time position.

As with H1 and H2, a further breakdown of the respondents was performed in terms of gender status and age groups, using the same age groups, 21-30 and 31-40, when analyzing whether the 'like' feature was a major function used on Facebook. It was found that 100% of the males that were 21-30 years of age indicated that they either strongly agreed or agreed that they utilize Facebook primarily to stay connected with friends and family while 81.8% of males that were 31-40 years of age either strongly agreed or agreed with this statement. When the males were asked whether they primarily utilize Facebook to obtain information pertaining to deals from different organizations, 90% of the male participants in the 21-30 age group either strongly disagreed or disagreed while 63.7% in the age group of 31-40 did the same. Of the 72.5% female participants, 39.7% were 21-30 years of age while 43.8% were 31-40 years of age. When asked if Facebook is used primarily to stay connected with friends and family, 75.9% of females ages 21-30 either strongly agree or agree while 80.7% of females ages 31-40 answered the same. Accordingly, the same percentage, 34.5%, in both age groups of females disagree that they use Facebook primarily to obtain information on products or services that are for same.

To formally test H3, Table 7 illustrates the cross-tabulation statistics associated with major purpose to stay connected with friends, family, co-workers and age (years) and gender status. As presented in the table, all relationships with staying connected with friends, family, co-workers and age did not statistically differ as a function of gender [male (Chi-square = 5.848, p = 0.664), female (Chi-square = 8.292, p = 0.912)], with the vast majority of respondents accepting, regardless of gender status and age. Once again, the testing of H3 supports the fact that Facebook is primarily utilized to stay connected with friends and family, although the males in the 31-40 age groups showed some interest in what the organizations had to offer through the 'liking' feature. Therefore, H3 is formally accepted in the null form.

MANAGERIAL RECOMMENDATIONS

The general findings of the present study provide some insight to the understanding of communication and analytical power of social platforms and BDA usage in modern societies. It also provides guidance regarding what managers should expect from using this technology. It describes that the organizational level BDA use has significant impacts on type types of supply chain value creation; asset productivity and business growth. Also, technological factors have a direct influence on organizational BDA use. It is extremely useful with the proper environmental factors and can have an influence on organizational BDA through the use of top management support.

Table 7. Cross-tabulation statistics associated with Major purpose to stay connected with friends, family, co-workers and Age (years) and Gender Status. (H3)

Part A. Actual count.									
Gender Status			Age (years)						Total
			20 or younger	21-30	31-40	41-50	51-60	Older than 60	
Female	Major purpose to stay connected with friends, family, co-workers	Strongly Agree	1	15	16	2	4	1	39
		Agree	0	7	15	1	2	0	25
		Neutral	0	6	3	1	0	0	10
		Disagree	0	0	1	0	0	0	1
	Total		1	28	35	4	6	1	75
Male	Major purpose to stay connected with friends, family, co-workers	Strongly Agree	1	4	4	3	1	0	13
		Agree	1	7	3	0	0	0	11
		Neutral	0	1	1	1	0	0	3
	Total		2	12	8	4	1	0	27
Total	Major purpose to stay connected with friends, family, co-workers	Strongly Agree	2	19	20	5	5	1	52
		Agree	1	14	18	1	2	0	36
		Neutral	0	7	4	2	0	0	13
		Disagree	0	0	1	0	0	0	1
	Total		3	40	43	8	7	1	102

Part B. Chi-square test results.				
Gender Status		Value	df	Asymptotic Significance (2-sided)
Female	Pearson Chi-Square	8.292[b]	15	.912 (NS)
	Likelihood Ratio	9.978	15	.821 (NS)
	Linear-by-Linear Association	.624	1	.429 (NS)
	N of Valid Cases	75		
Male	Pearson Chi-Square	5.848[c]	8	.664 (NS)
	Likelihood Ratio	7.776	8	.456 (NS)
	Linear-by-Linear Association	.636	1	.425 (NS)
	N of Valid Cases	27		
Total	Pearson Chi-Square	8.638[a]	15	.896 (NS)
	Likelihood Ratio	10.689	15	.774 (NS)
	Linear-by-Linear Association	1.138	1	.286 (NS)
	N of Valid Cases	102		

a. 18 cells (75.0%) have expected count less than 5. The minimum expected count is 0.01.
b. b. 20 cells (83.3%) have expected count less than 5. The minimum expected count is 0.01.

c. 14 cells (93.3%) have expected count less than 5. The minimum expected count is 0.11.
NS denotes not statistically significant at the .05 level for a two-tailed test.

continues on following page

Table 7. Continued

Part C. Symmetric measures.			Value	Approx. Sig.
Gender Status			Value	Approx. Sig.
Female	Nominal by Nominal	Contingency Coefficient	.316	.912 (NS)
	N of Valid Cases		75	
Male	Nominal by Nominal	Contingency Coefficient	.422	.664 (NS)
	N of Valid Cases		27	
Total	Nominal by Nominal	Contingency Coefficient	.279	.896 (NS)
	N of Valid Cases		102	

NS denotes not statistically significant at the .05 level for a two-tailed test.

Although there is overwhelming evidence based on the statistical testing of the three specific research hypotheses that consumers' purchases do not increase as a result of seeing advertisements in their newsfeeds on social networking sites (e.g., Facebook/LinkedIn), there is still some inherent benefits to organizations who do utilize social networking advertisements. The results of this study indicate that 48.5% of all participants indicated that the primary reason that they 'liked' an organization was because they saw that their friends had done the same. This is a great form of free advertisement for an organization known as positive word-of-mouth (WOM) advertisements. There is considerable evident that positive WOM influences consumers to more likely to purchase a product if they see that their friends or relatives have also shown an interest in the organization (Brown, Broderick, & Lee, (2007; Cafferky, 1995; Chang, Hsieh, & Tseng, 2013). WOM advertising can me defined as "a personal referral from someone whose opinions are trusted by others" (Arya, 2010, p. 3). Mulvihill (2011) further outlined the importance of advertising on social networking systems by commenting on the value of an individual 'liking' an organization on Facebook or having a Facebook fan. It is not only about whether or not the individual purchases the organization's product or service, it is about spreading brand awareness. Perhaps, "Facebook's potential for building brand-to-customer relationships is priceless" (Mulvihill, 2011, p. 8). It was further discussed that organizations need to learn how to use these social networking systems to have more meaningful interactions with their consumers or target market. Facebook and other social networking sites should be utilized by businesses of essentially all categories as a way to communicate with their consumers openly and freely. These organizations can obtain immediate feedback from their target consumers and react more swiftly to their concerns. Managers can locate their target market through the information provided by their consumers on such networking sites. This is an easy way for managers to analyze trends within their target market.

GENERAL CONCLUSION AND IMPLICATIONS

The transformation power of the Internet has greatly impacted and revised theoretical frameworks for research, especially concerning media coverage and content of social media-related activities. As web-based technological innovations increase, so have empirically-based methodologies to measure their impacts on consumers of such social media. Mass communication, coupled with technical innovations that promote ease-of-use and greater accessibility, has significantly changed the commercial landscape of social media-related information and marketing gathering by its consumers. The results, in general, indicate that there is no relationship between the use of social networking advertisements and individuals' feelings toward the site.

Although there is indication that individuals do not care to see the advertisements appear in their newsfeeds, it does not bother them enough to discontinue utilizing the site. Interestingly, the majority of working professionals indicated they would discontinue using Facebook/LinkedIn if pop-up advertisements were to begin to be used. Organizations must be mindful of this as social networking sites continue to evolve and grow to meet the expectations of its user base. The information and form of communication found on social networking sites are priceless to an organization and can help these businesses increase their market share. By establishing strong IT systems, responsive systems that are CRM (customer relationship management)-embedded, etc., there is still a need to reduce waste and become more lean. There is a general changing view of management theory from one of a Newtonian view (i.e., linear systems or trade-offs) to possibly one involving complexity theory (not mutually exclusive, but mutually benefiting) with companies as treating organizations as complex adaptive systems. Social media and BDA are becoming for mainstream and an excepted part of the business landscape.

Directions for Future Research

There are many opportunities in SCM, customer relationships, that social network advertisements can have a major impact. In particular, sport-related advertisement is especially promising for future research. According to Pedersen (2013), has an enviable position in that it has a universal significance, ubiquitous presence, and overall importance to its growth and viability in society. Unfortunately, this popularity greatly influences what is considered relevant themes or research threads, especially among doctorial students. Both Frisby (2005) and Pederson (2013) have commented that much research in sport management has been done at the micro-level, catering to new and emerging issues that have caught the attention of the public. Although some attempt to explain the results of the study have been made at the macro-level (e.g., Stakeholder theoretical and ethical orientation/belief systems), micro-level theoretical considerations still dominate as the major factor in explaining participants' views on sport-related gambling and office pooling within the workplace environment. Future studies need to be aware of such issues.

Various theories at the marketing segment or individual level, such as Uses and Gratifications Theory (i.e., used in the present dissertation effort) and Social Learning theories, have been employed with various methodologies, such as experimental design studies, content analyses, and case studies) to investigate sport-related scientific inquiries. Pederson (2013) went a step further to suggest that, based on his experience working with the next generations of doctorial students, because of the limited publication outlets for sport communication research, their work is often published in sport management instead of communication journals.

Both Frisby (2005) and Pederson (2013) have written their essays after the advent of the Internet and social networking and advertising have become main stream avenues for research in studying the impact of social media platforms for increasing involvement in sport management activities. Pederson, for example, suggested that even contemporary studies in sport communication have used primarily content analysis to take mere snapshots of social media and its impact on sport. He suggested doing further research by examining the audience consumption and effects, framed by a strategic communication perspective. Morgan (1983), on-the-other-hand, framed sport research in historical terms at the macro level via Neo-Marxist and Utilitarian Theories of the continuous struggle of the masses on economic and/or political dominance. Both Morgan and Frisby have implied that consumerism and capitalism are at least partially responsible for sport research to be framed in a materialistic lifestyle that related self-esteem to consumption of goods, resulting in exploitation, pollution, and increased poverty. Sport research should be based on understanding the wider and more fundamental questions of utility at the society level. Perhaps commercialization and influence of big business are the greatest limitations associated with this dissertation, as money and self-esteem are important factors that were not investigated. Again, future studies can more effectivity deals with such pressing considerations in social media advertising.

ACKNOWLEDGMENT

The authors wish to thank most heartedly for the valuable contributions by the reviewers for their input into the final paper. Peer reviewing and editing are often tedious and thankless tasks.

REFERENCES

Alijani, G. S., Mancuso, L. C., Kwun, O., & Omar, A. (2010). Effectiveness of online advertisement factors in recalling a product. *Academy of Marketing Studies Journal*, *14*(1), 1–11.

Amine, A. (1998). Consumers' true brand loyalty: The central role of commitment. *Journal of Strategic Marketing*, *6*(4), 305–319. doi:10.1080/096525498346577

Ang, L. (2010). Community Relationship Management and Social Media. *Database Marketing & Customer Strategy Management*, *18*(1), 31–38. doi:10.1057/dbm.2011.3

Ankeny, J. (2011). Face lift. *Entrepreneur*, *39*(1), 56–59.

Arya, D. P. (2010). Advertisement effectiveness: Role of 'word-of mouth' in success of educational institutes in non-metro cities. *IUP Journal of Management Research*, *9*(1), 1–20.

Bateman, P. J., Pike, J. C., & Butler, B. S. (2010). To disclose or not: Publicness in social networking sites. *Information Technology & People*, *24*(1), 78–100. doi:10.1108/09593841111109431

Bennett, S. (2014). Pinterest, Twitter, Facebook, Instagram, Google+, LinkedIn – Social Media Stats 2014 [INFOGRAPHIC]. *AllTwitter*. Retrieved July 8, 2017 from http://www.mediabistro.com/alltwitter/social-media-stats-2014_b5424.3

Bonson, E., & Flores, F. (2010). Social media and corporate dialogue: The Response of global financial institutions. *Online Information Review*, *35*(1), 34–49. doi:10.1108/14684521111113579

Booth, N., & Matic, J. A. (2011). Mapping and leveraging influences in social media to shape corporate brand perceptions. *Corporate Communications*, *16*(3), 184–191. doi:10.1108/13563281111156853

Brown, J., Broderick, A., & Lee, N. J. (2007). Word of mouth communication within online communities: Conceptualizing the online social network. *Interactive Marketing*, *21*(3), 2–20. doi:10.1002/dir.20082

Cadogan, J. W., & Foster, B. D. (2000). Relationship Selling and Customer Loyalty: An Empirical Investigation. *Marketing Intelligence & Planning*, *18*(4), 185–199. doi:10.1108/02634500010333316

Cafferky, M. E. (1995). *Let your customers do the talking: 301 + WOM Marketing Tactics Guaranteed to Boost Profits*. Chicago, IL: Upstart Publishing Co.

Chan, C. (2010). Using online advertising to increase the impact of a library Facebook page. *Library Management, 32*(4/5), 361–370. doi:10.1108/01435121111132347

Chang, A., Hsieh, S., & Tseng, T. H. (2013). Online brand community response to negative brand events: The role of group eWOM. *Internet Research, 23*(4), 486–506. doi:10.1108/IntR-06-2012-0107

Chen, D. Q., Preston, D. S., & Swink, M. (2015). How the use of big data analytics affects value creation in supply chain management. *Journal of Management Information Systems, 32*(4), 4–39. doi:10.1080/07421222.2015.1138364

Clemmitt, M. (2006). Cyber socializing. *CQ Researcher, 16*(27), 625–648.

Clemmitt, M. (2010). Social networking. *CQ Researcher, 20*(32), 749–772.

Fernandez, P. (2009). Balancing outreach and privacy in Facebook: Five guiding decisions points. *Library Hi Tech News, 26*(3/4), 10–12. doi:10.1108/07419050910979946

Finn, G. (2014). Still the One: Facebook gains ground as the leader in social logins. *Marketing Land*. Retrieved July 9, 2017 from http://marketingland.com/still-one-facebook-gains-ground-leader-social-logins-81115

Frisby, W. (2005). The good, the bad, and the ugly: Critical sport management research. *Journal of Sport Management, 19*(1), 1–12. doi:10.1123/jsm.19.1.1

Gans, H. (2009). Public ethnography: Ethnography as public sociology. *Qualitative Sociology, 33*(2010), 97-104. Retrieved August 4, 2017 from http://herbertgans.org/wp-content/uploads/2013/11/Public-Ethnography.pdf

Goldie, L. (2007). Social networks build up brand opportunities. *News Analysis,* 16.

Granville, K. (2018). Facebook and Cambridge Analytica: What you need to know as fallout widens. *The New York Times*. Retrieved April 12, 2018 from https://www.nytimes.com/2018/03/19/technology/facebook-cambridge-analytica-explained.html

Greenhow, C. (2011). Online social networks and learning. *On the Horizon, 19*(1), 4–12. doi:10.1108/10748121111107663

Ham, L. (2011). Chasing a bargain: Who pays? *Media Watch,* 7-8.

Howell, N. (2009). If click-through isn't a measure, what's engagement? *New Media Age,* 2.

Jaffie, B. (2009). Getting more bang for your marketing buck – leveraging technology to help your effectiveness. *Proofs,* 62-63.

Krivak, T. (2008). Facebook 101: Ten things you need to know about Facebook. *Information Today, 25*(3), 42-44.

Mateen, A., & More, D. (2013). Applying TOC thinking process tools in managing challenges of supply chain finance: A case study. *International Journal of Services and Operations Management*, *15*(4), 389–410. doi:10.1504/IJSOM.2013.054882

McCormick, A. (2006). Everyone needs to keep an eye on the ball. *News Analysis,* 16.

Morgan, W. J. (Ed.). (1979). *Sport and the humanities: A collection of original essays*. Knoxville, TN: University of Tennessee.

Morimoto, M., & Chang, S. (2009). Psychological factors affecting perceptions of unsolicited commercial email. *Journal of Current Issues and Research in Advertising*, *31*(1), 63–73. doi:10.1080/106 41734.2009.10505257

Mulvihill, A. (2011). Measuring the value of a 'like.'. *EContent (Wilton, Conn.)*, *34*(6), 8–12.

Nobari, A., Khierkhah, A. S., & Hajipour, V. (2018). A Pareto-based approach to optimise aggregate production planning problem considering reliable supplier selection. *International Journal of Services and Operations Management*, *29*(1), 59–84. doi:10.1504/IJSOM.2018.088473

Park, B.-N., & Min, H. (2013). Global supply chain barriers of foreign subsidiaries: The case of Korean expatriate manufacturers in China. *International Journal of Services and Operations Management*, *15*(1), 67–78. doi:10.1504/IJSOM.2013.050562

Pedersen, P. M. (2013). Reflections on communication and sport: On strategic communication and management. *Communication and Sport*, *1*(1/2), 55–67. doi:10.1177/2167479512466655

Pookulangara, S., & Koesler, K. (2011). Cultural influence on consumers' usage of social networks and its impact on online purchase intentions. *Journal of Retailing and Consumer Services*, *18*(4), 348–354. doi:10.1016/j.jretconser.2011.03.003

Raice, S., & Ante, S. (2012). Insta-Rich: $1 Billion for Instagram. *The Wall Street Journal*. Retrieved July 9, 2017 from http://online.wsj.com/news/articles/SB10001424052702303381540

Rajapakshe, T., Dawande, M., & Sriskandarajah, C. (2013). On the trade-off between remanufacturing and recycling. *International Journal of Services and Operations Management*, *15*(1), 1–53. doi:10.1504/ IJSOM.2013.050560

Rajeev, V. (2013). Impact of service co-creation on performance of firms: The mediating role of market oriented strategies. *International Journal of Services and Operations Management*, *15*(4), 449–466. doi:10.1504/IJSOM.2013.054885

Ridinger, L. L., & Funk, D. C. (2006). Looking at gender differences through the lens of sport spectators. *Sport Marketing Quarterly*, *5*(3), 155–166.

Robinson, M. J., & Trail, G. T. (2005). Relationships among spectator gender, motives, points of attachment, and sport preference. *Journal of Sport Management*, *19*(1), 58–80. doi:10.1123/jsm.19.1.58

Ruane, L., & Wallace, E. (2015). Brand tribalism and self-expressive brands: Social influences and brand outcomes. *Journal of Product and Brand Management*, *24*(4), 333–348. doi:10.1108/JPBM-07-2014-0656

Schroeder, C. (2004). Online ads. *Campaigns and Elections*, *25*(1), 38–39.

Seguin, B., Richelieu, A., & O'Reilly, N. (2008). Leveraging the Olympic brand through the reconciliation of corporate and consumers' brand perceptions. *International Journal of Sport Management and Marketing*, *3*(1/2), 3–22. doi:10.1504/IJSMM.2008.015958

Senthilmurugan, P. R., Jegadheesan, C., & Devadasan, S. R. (2018). Improving the quality and yield in the casting of compressor pulley through the application of total failure mode and effects analysis. *International Journal of Services and Operations Management*, *29*(1), 42–58. doi:10.1504/IJSOM.2018.088472

Sharma, A., & Sharma, R. K. (2018). Modelling and analysis of enablers for successful implementation of cellular manufacturing system. *International Journal of Process Management and Benchmarking*, *8*(1), 103–123. doi:10.1504/IJPMB.2018.088659

Shields, M. (2009). Facebook friends' brands. *Media Week*, *18*(30), 8.

Smock, A. D., Ellison, N. B., Lampe, C., & Wohn, D. Y. (2011). Facebook as a toolkit: A uses and gratification approach to unbundling feature use. *Computers in Human Behavior*, *27*(6), 2322–2329. doi:10.1016/j.chb.2011.07.011

Taylor, D. G., Lewin, J. E., & Strutton, D. (2011). Friends, fans, and followers: Do ads work on social networks? *Journal of Advertising Research*, *51*(1), 258–275. doi:10.2501/JAR-51-1-258-275

Todor, R. D. (2016). Blending traditional and digital marketing. *Bulletin of the Transilvania University of Brasov. Series V, Economic Sciences*, *9*(1), 51–56.

Verma, P., Sharma, R. R. K., & Kumar, V. (2018). The sustainability issues of diversified firms in emerging economies context: A theoretical model and propositions. *International Journal of Process Management and Benchmarking*, *7*(2), 224–248. doi:10.1504/IJPMB.2017.083107

Xu, Y., Tiwari, A., Chen, H. C., & Turner, C. J. (2018). Development of a validation and qualification process for the manufacturing of medical devices: A case study based on cross-sector benchmarking. *International Journal of Process Management and Benchmarking*, *8*(1), 79–102. doi:10.1504/IJPMB.2018.088658

Yazdi, A. K., & Esfeden, G. A. (2018). Designing robust model of Six Sigma implementation based on critical successful factors and MACBETH. *International Journal of Process Management and Benchmarking*, *7*(2), 158–171. doi:10.1504/IJPMB.2017.083103

Yee, W. F., & Sidek, Y. (2008). Influence of brand loyalty on consumer sportswear. *International Journal of Economics and Management*, *2*(2), 221–236.

Zaney, K. (2004). Down with pop-ups. *Education Week*, *21*(1), 41–42.

Zimmerman, M. H., Clavio, G. E., & Lim, C. H. (2011). Set the agenda like Beckham: A professional sports league's use of YouTube to disseminate messages to its users. *International Journal of Sport Management and Marketing*, *10*(3/4), 180–195. doi:10.1504/IJSMM.2011.044789

This research was previously published in the Handbook of Research on the Evolution of IT and the Rise of E-Society; pages 337-369, copyright year 2019 by Information Science Reference (an imprint of IGI Global).

Index

A

Absorptive Capacity Theory 202, 204, 207-208, 212, 215-216, 219, 221, 225-226

Academic Library 1001-1003, 1460-1461, 1466, 1473, 1475-1477, 1479

Accessibility 20, 111, 152, 169, 194, 224, 237, 307, 338, 340, 342, 349-350, 360, 691, 729, 817, 854, 860, 865, 951, 1103, 1182, 1186, 1230, 1304, 1313, 1578, 1585, 1617, 1667, 1669-1670, 1672-1677, 1694, 1742, 1860

Ad Audience 1027

ad optimization 607

ad placement 599, 605, 623-624, 672, 686-687

Ad Targeting 599, 624

Advertising Effectiveness 195, 582, 601-602, 610, 620-621, 642, 649, 665, 683, 685, 1318-1319, 1661, 1833, 1844

Advertising Media 134, 138, 149, 604, 626, 1005

advertising value model (AVM) 647-648, 651, 653, 661

affective components of destination image 284, 286, 289-290, 303

affective-based 357, 359, 364

Analytic Tools 406

Apis 41, 408, 417-419, 518, 551, 1277, 1521, 1731

Artificial Intelligence 143, 152-153, 315, 374, 379, 382, 403, 417, 539-540, 555-556, 585, 595-596, 598, 705, 707, 710, 720, 722, 725, 736, 763, 790, 859, 867, 1080, 1082-1083, 1694, 1696

Automatic Personalization 582

Avatar 707, 709, 725

B

Ban 400, 807, 1169-1175

bandwagon effect 1014, 1027

Beauty Industry 952, 1084, 1086-1087, 1090, 1094-1096, 1105-1106, 1604

Big Data 27, 34-41, 43, 110, 115, 127, 160, 229, 233, 243, 245-246, 248-251, 253, 255-256, 260, 263, 289-290, 293-294, 296, 298, 415-416, 418-419, 538-539, 541-542, 551, 553, 555, 644-645, 736, 767, 788-789, 792-794, 796, 798, 802-805, 808, 850-851, 855-856, 858-859, 865, 868, 870-872, 1003, 1027, 1079, 1165-1166, 1168-1169, 1175-1179, 1273, 1281-1282, 1287-1288, 1292, 1298, 1300, 1517-1518, 1521, 1536-1537, 1635, 1688, 1833, 1841, 1863

Big Data Analysis 249, 294, 415, 767, 793, 796, 798, 802-805, 858, 1165, 1517

Blogging 22, 34, 47, 51, 56, 59, 143, 194-195, 206, 408, 411, 752, 810, 815, 821, 823, 827, 830, 936, 1084, 1097, 1106, 1413, 1417, 1588, 1615, 1617, 1787, 1793, 1806

Blogs 3, 33, 46, 53, 64, 78, 87-88, 114, 143, 145, 159, 164, 173-175, 185, 190, 198, 206, 224, 271, 279-280, 287, 289, 299, 301, 379, 385, 418-419, 422, 425, 429, 431, 442, 455, 544, 603, 646, 693, 740, 808, 815, 821, 851-852, 855, 868, 875, 880, 895, 920-921, 936-938, 941, 945, 1028, 1049, 1053-1054, 1084-1085, 1087-1088, 1090-1092, 1096-1097, 1145, 1155, 1161, 1175, 1177, 1181, 1186, 1201, 1205-1206, 1237, 1261, 1294, 1321, 1335, 1348, 1352, 1364, 1375, 1394, 1440, 1452, 1462, 1485, 1487, 1521, 1573, 1587-1589, 1600, 1610, 1612, 1618, 1631, 1655, 1660, 1668, 1688, 1690, 1694, 1700, 1702, 1715, 1721, 1723, 1733, 1743-1744, 1747-1748, 1755, 1770, 1775, 1777, 1828

Bollywood 1497-1498, 1501, 1508-1510, 1512

Boycott 53, 795, 1165, 1169, 1171-1175, 1723

Brand Ambassador 56, 1270, 1587

Brand Associations 68, 80, 161, 177-178, 183, 200, 1240-1241, 1243-1244, 1258-1259, 1365

Brand Attitude 184, 199, 606, 640, 665-666, 1053, 1234, 1237, 1240-1241, 1245-1247, 1253, 1351, 1358-1359, 1362, 1367, 1543, 1611

Brand Awareness 49, 51-52, 83, 91-93, 95, 98, 100, 167, 176-177, 189, 326-327, 457, 483, 498, 588, 594,

G

U

V

W

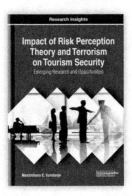

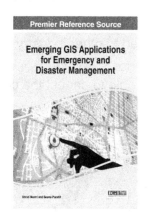
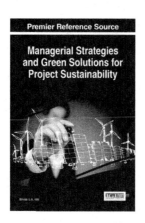

Printed in the United States
by Baker & Taylor Publisher Services